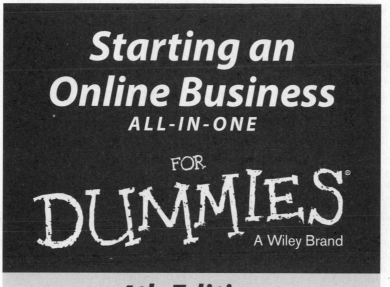

Starting an
Online Business
ALL-IN-ONE

FOR
DUMMIES

A Wiley Brand

4th Edition

WITHDRAWN

by Shannon Belew and Joel Elad

FOR
DUMMIES
A Wiley Brand

Starting an Online Business All-in-One For Dummies®, 4th Edition

Published by: **John Wiley & Sons, Inc.,** 111 River Street, Hoboken, NJ 07030-5774, www.wiley.com

Copyright © 2014 by John Wiley & Sons, Inc., Hoboken, New Jersey

Published simultaneously in Canada

Library of Congress Control Number: 2014936391

ISBN 978-1-118-92670-3 (pbk); 978-1-118-92666-6 (ebk); ISBN 978-1-118-92667-3 (ebk)

Manufactured in the United States of America

10 9 8 7 6 5 4 3 2 1

Contents at a Glance

Table of Contents

Introduction

Online businesses have finally found a permanent foothold in today's marketplace, leaving little doubt that the Internet is a viable and often necessary tool for building, managing, and growing a business. Even traditional retailers are consistently seeing their e-commerce sales eclipse in-store sales during major shopping holidays, such as Black Friday.

We are excited about the potential that an online business holds and the fact that e-commerce is now thought of as a necessary component of almost any business. Since beginning our own online endeavors, we have had the privilege of meeting and working with a variety of entrepreneurs — people who, much like you, share a dream of finding economic independence by running their own businesses. As you might have guessed, many of them found success on the Internet.

The Internet provides not only a legitimate resource for starting a business that will offer a steady source of income for your family but also a nearly endless source of ideas and opportunities to market and grow your company. It can even give you the flexibility to work from home, the freedom to work part-time, or the ability to earn an additional source of income to help make your life more enjoyable. And maybe your online business could be the next Amazon, eBay, or Facebook! Almost anything is possible with the Internet, but the pursuit of success starts with a good idea, a solid business foundation, and an endless amount of determination and hard work.

In this book, we help get you started by sharing with you the knowledge and tools we've picked up along the way and by providing you with a few short-cuts to help further your own online endeavors.

About This Book

Much has changed since we wrote the first edition of this book in 2006, but much has stayed the same. Our goal — to cover the many ways you can start or expand a business by using the Internet — is still the same. Likewise, many of the basic principles for starting your online business are still tried-and-true methods. For this fourth edition, we took great care to update all the key information that has remained valid in the past few years. We also searched out many of the new opportunities that have evolved since then. One of the more important changes is the increased use of mobile devices, including smartphones and tablets. Not only has the number of mobile users grown exponentially worldwide (the total number of mobile devices is expected to outnumber the total world population by 2016!), but also dependency upon mobility has affected almost every area of online businesses, from site design principles and shopping cart features to downloading mobile applications and making mobile payments. Another change that continues to gain momentum in almost all areas of starting and growing an online business is the use of social media. Social networking sites, such as Twitter, Facebook, LinkedIn, Pinterest, and Instagram, are now staples for both promoting your business and making money. Industry giants such as Amazon are pioneering the way in which online shoppers can make purchases directly through Twitter by using special hashtags, and more companies are sure to follow this trend toward social commerce. Even nonprofit organizations are realizing significant boosts in fundraising dollars thanks to the power of donations through social media. In addition to the fervor over social commerce and mobility, apps (applications) and videos are proving to be important influences in online marketing and legitimate revenue makers. All these changes are captured in this newest edition of our book.

The book also provides you with details regarding specific online business strategies and moneymaking opportunities but also covers basic offline information. It's the stuff that every small-business owner needs to understand, such as how to apply standard accounting principles and keep up with the legal side of running a business.

Of course, using this book doesn't guarantee that you will make a lot of money — or any money, for that matter. We provide you with just enough knowledge and inspiration to keep your online business dreams on track. Running a business is hard work and requires persistence, dedication, and perhaps an equal mix of patience and luck.

Foolish Assumptions

While we wrote this book, we assumed a few things about you:

✦ You're a smart, inquisitive person who is seeking information about running a business on the Internet.

✦ You have an entrepreneurial spirit and are a bit of a risk taker — at least in the area of starting a business.

✦ You may be looking for ways to use the Internet to build an existing bricks-and-mortar business or to increase online donations for a nonprofit organization.

✦ You're comfortable using computers and browsing the Internet.

✦ You use e-mail regularly.

✦ You're willing to find out about new technologies.

✦ You want to use websites and online technologies to build a brand.

✦ You're open to the idea of reaching out to others on the Internet using social media, such as Facebook, LinkedIn, and Twitter.

✦ You want to use the Internet to make money.

✦ You've bought items online and maybe even sold a few things.

Icons Used in This Book

Throughout the book, icons call attention to important details.

This friendly reminder serves up important information. Whenever you see this icon, know that this information is something worthwhile to keep in mind as you move forward.

You can usually understand an idea without having to know its behind-the-scenes details. Even when we point them out with this icon, feel free to skip them and move on.

Check out this helpful hint. We picked up this information somewhere along the way.

Pay special attention when this icon appears. It could save you from making a fatal error — at least in your online business!

Beyond the Book

We've written additional content that you won't find in this book. Go online to find the following:

✦ **Online articles covering additional topics at**

`www.dummies.com/extras/startinganonlinebusinessaio`

Here you'll find out how to use Twitter for customer service, enhance your online security, use the right mix for your content marketing strategy, add a mobile credit card reader to your business, create a Google+ business profile, and more.

✦ **The Cheat Sheet for this book is at**

`www.dummies.com/cheatsheet/`
`    startinganonlinebusinessaio`

The cheat sheet shows you how to build a loyal online customer base and promote your business through social media. Also check out our list of web resources for online businesses as well as our handy checklist when launching your online business.

✦ **Updates to this book, if we have any, are at**

www.dummies.com/extras/startinganonlinebusinessaio

Where to Go from Here

You can start reading any section of the book that most interests you or that you think is helpful to you and your business. For example, if you're starting a business for the first time, you might want to begin with Book I. For those needing a boost in marketing or expanding an existing business, you probably want to go directly to the books that discuss those specific topics.

However, you should at least browse through *every* section of this book. Even if your e-commerce skills are more advanced, it never hurts to have a refresher course on some business basics. Considering that the Internet touches many different aspects of people's lives, you never know what unexpected tidbits of information you might discover.

If you have questions or comments, you are welcome to share them with us on Twitter (http://www.twitter.com/ShannonBelew and www.twitter.com/JoelElad) or connect with us on LinkedIn.

Book I
Online Business Basics

getting started with an Online Business

Contents at a Glance

Chapter 1: Starting from Scratch

In This Chapter

⤙ **Recognizing when the time is right**

⤙ **Understanding the different types of online businesses**

⤙ **Gathering your thoughts and getting started**

*O*nce upon a time, start-up businesses that operated over the Internet were considered risky ventures with uncertain futures. No longer is that the case! Consider how many ways you interact with businesses over the Internet every day: You probably buy gifts for friends and family members, look up health-related information, make vacation travel arrangements, buy products for work, stream movies and music, and even pay bills online. You buy online using everything from a desktop computer or laptop, to a tablet or a Web-enabled mobile phone (smartphone). And individuals like you are not the only ones spending more on online transactions. Increasingly, businesses of all sizes are also buying products and services. Those same companies are also spending money to advertise on the Internet and reach their customers through traditional websites and social media sites. All these interactions represent a business opportunity by which people earn a living on the Internet.

Online revenues continue to grow — for all types of products and services in almost every industry. Even during challenging economic conditions, when traditional retail stores have struggled with growth, online retail sales continue to surge. In 2013, online retailers in the United States generated $231 billion in sales; and with continued double-digit growth, sales are projected to hit $370 billion by 2017, according to industry analysts Forrester. U.S. companies selling services online to other businesses (B2B) are also seeing impressive growth. Companies adopting an online software as a service (SaaS) business model are experiencing two times the revenue growth and three times the customer growth, according to research from McKinsey and Company.

Consider that North America represents only a small portion of potential online consumers. The international market is growing, with Europe accounting for more than 22 percent of Internet users and Asia accounting for nearly 45 percent, according to Internet World Stats. Some European countries continue to have double-digit growth in online sales, according to Forrester. These statistics represent a substantial number of potential online shoppers. Why shouldn't you be the next person to take advantage of these rapidly growing markets and start an online business? In this chapter, we answer that question, describe the kinds of businesses that exist online, and motivate you to get started.

What Are You Waiting For? Start Your Business Now!

You might have dreamed for years about starting an online business. Or perhaps you woke up just yesterday with a brilliant idea. What are you waiting for? The truth is that the most difficult part of beginning a new endeavor is making the decision to do it. You can easily get bogged down with excuses for why your business won't happen. To keep you motivated and on track, here's a list of the top reasons to start an online business *now:*

✦ **You can gain financial freedom.** One major incentive for owning any business is the potential for a better income. The Internet offers the opportunity to create your own wealth.

✦ **You have unlimited customer reach.** No geographical boundaries exist when you run a business over the Internet. You can choose to sell your products or services in your community, in your own country, or to the entire world.

✦ **It's affordable.** You can now create a website inexpensively and sometimes for free. The cost to maintain your site, secure products, and cover related expenses is often relatively low. This low start-up cost is especially evident when you compare the start-up costs of an online business and a traditional *bricks-and-mortar business* (a physical building from which to sell retail merchandise).

✦ **Your schedule is flexible.** Part time, full time, year round, or seasonal: Your schedule is up to you when you operate your virtual business. You can work in the wee hours of the night or in the middle of the day. An online business affords you the luxury of creating a work schedule that works for you.

✦ **Novices are welcome.** As the Internet has grown, *e-commerce* (a type of business activity conducted over the Internet, such as sales or advertising) applications have become increasingly simple to use. Although you benefit by having experience with your products or services, the process of offering those items for sale online is easy to understand. You can set up shop with little or no experience under your belt!

✦ **You can start quickly.** From online auctions such as eBay to storefronts powered by Amazon.com, the tools that can help get you started are readily available, essentially overnight. Many of these sites (such as Amazon) handle all the details for you — they set up the website infrastructure, manage the payment and shopping cart system, and even provide easy access to merchandise.

✦ **You can expand an existing business.** If you already own a business, the Internet provides you with the most economical and most efficient way to expose your business to a huge new group of customers and increase sales.

✦ **No age barriers exist.** You might be retired and itching for extra income, or perhaps you're a teenager who's only beginning to consider career opportunities. Online businesses provide economic opportunities for entrepreneurs of all ages.

✦ **A variety of ideas qualify.** As proven time and again, the Internet supports a broad range of business concepts. Although some ideas are better suited to long-term success, almost all your ideas have potential.

✦ **Niche products hold unlimited potential.** Thanks to the reach of the Internet, unique or custom products have a potentially lucrative home in e-commerce. These products may not generate a large enough demand in a local market to sustain an offline business but can find a significant customer base through the broad reach of an online audience.

✦ **Everyone else is doing it.** Okay, maybe your parents wouldn't approve of using this logic. It's certainly true, though: People around the world are finding success and more financial freedom by starting businesses online. It's one leap you should be proud to take!

If you're still hesitant, consider this bonus reason: The information you need to take your business online is *right at your fingertips* — literally. This book gives you most of what you need to get started. Whatever else you require, such as information about conducting business in your specific state or regulations for your specific industry, is on the Internet (put there by some other enterprising entrepreneur, no doubt). You have no more excuses!

Choosing Just the Right Business

After you decide to start your own online business, you should look at the different categories of online businesses from which you can choose. In this section, we conveniently provide those categories.

Not all online businesses will explode like Amazon, eBay, or Facebook. But even if your business never grows into a megabrand, you need to plan for the long haul. You want your business to succeed and survive. Also, selecting the right type of online business is just as important. Losing interest or lacking an understanding of your chosen business area can hinder the growth of your new online business. Putting some thought into the type of online business you want to pursue pays off.

Creating online businesses for today and tomorrow

The secret to e-commerce success is to create a business that will stand the test of time. Sure, some people take advantage of relatively short-lived trends and make a mint (from Beanie Babies and Hacky Sacks to Napster and MySpace, for example). The odds that you could create the same magnitude of buying hysteria with a product or service, however, are small. Instead, hundreds of thousands of entrepreneurs are quietly and steadily making a respectable living by using the Internet, and their ideas will find a market for many years. They're not making millions of dollars a month, but they're paying their bills and making a profit.

The widely used term *online business* can be used in different ways. It sometimes refers to a company that operates only over the Internet and has no other physical location from which to sell goods or services. It can refer to a traditional bricks-and-mortar business that also sells over the Internet. And we sometimes use it to reference a segment of revenues generated from the web for traditional businesses or organizations. In this book, an online business is any entity (or person) using the Internet, in whole or part, as a source of income for itself, its business, or its organization (such as a club or a nonprofit agency).

Finding a business that's your type

You can pursue a variety of businesses to earn money online. Almost all types of income-generating opportunities fall into one of two categories:

- ✦ **Business to consumer (B2C):** Customers are typically the individual consumers who make up the general public. They buy products or services designed for personal use.

- ✦ **Business to business (B2B):** Customers are most likely other businesses. They might buy steel by the ton, employee uniforms, or anything that would be used primarily by a company.

Crossover between the two categories can occur. Sometimes, either type of customer can use the products or services you offer, as is the case with office supplies. And with more businesses now shopping online, this crossover occurs frequently.

Knowing whether your primary customers are individuals or businesses helps you to create more effective marketing campaigns. Typically, these two groups buy from you for very different reasons. By marketing to each individual group, you can better target your advertising messages for increased sales. You may find that your primary customers require (or respond better to) one type of marketing and that your secondary customers require another type.

Within the two primary categories, you find the different types of businesses you can operate. Here are a few examples of the ways in which you can generate revenue online:

- ✦ **Online retail:** When you have a bricks-and-mortar store and offer your retail products for sale online as well, you enter the world of online retailing. You're responsible for hiring the resources and purchasing the tools needed to sell your wares over the Internet. One example of an online retailer is the Barnes & Noble bookstore — you can buy your books online or visit the bricks-and-mortar store. As mentioned, most traditional businesses now have some component of revenue that comes from online sales.

✦ **E-commerce storefront:** E-commerce is a broad term used to describe the transaction of business via the Internet. E-commerce can also refer to any website where you sell merchandise but lack a physical location for customers to visit in person (bricks-and-mortar store). The term commonly used for this type of online business is an e-commerce *storefront.* (Offline, the retail industry uses this term to describe the outside of a building, which includes its signage, front door, and over-all image.) In this book, a *storefront* is a one-stop shop for setting up an online presence to sell products. Etsy.com and CafePress.com are examples of storefronts. Both storefront sites provide you with a custom page that displays all your wares. Etsy.com allows you to customize the page from which you sell your handcrafted or vintage wares. Your page on CafePress.com has a structure that matches the overall CafePress.com site. Think of it as a flea market or one of those small kiosks you see in the mall — you get your very own little shopping area that you can customize, and visitors to your page see your merchandise and can learn a little about you if you choose to include personal information about yourself or your business.

We discuss storefronts in more detail in Book VIII, "Storefront Selling." For now, you need to know that good storefront providers offer the following:

- *Templates for your website:* You don't need to build a site from scratch. Many storefront providers provide you with wizards or HTML files that you can customize for your storefront.

- *Hosting options:* Many storefront providers have a variety of options for you, some free and some for a fee. These options might include shopping cart systems, phone support for your storefront, and discounts on fees if you pay rent by the year rather than monthly.

- *A shopping cart solution:* The method that customers use to purchase products from you.

- *Payment options (possibly):* The capability to accept online payment (credit card or debit card) is an absolute must. But other options allow payment to be deferred or even allow financing of purchases.

- *Products (in some cases):* Your preferred storefront solution may offer you everything but the kitchen sink, as the saying goes. Increasingly, you have the option to use a provider that also supplies the product. Your contribution is providing unique artwork or con-tent (as with CafePress), or simply providing traffic, or customers (as with an Amazon storefront).

- *An auction:* The way your customers buy products is somewhat different when you auction items. Your customers can bid on the final purchase price, as opposed to buying at a price you set. (eBay, the daddy of all online auction sites, has become so popular, however, that it has blurred the lines among auction, storefront, and online retail. We discuss eBay in Book VIII, Chapter 4.)

✦ **Service business:** You don't have to sell products to have an online business. From doing taxes to writing brochures, most professional services can be sold online, just like physical products. Web-based services or applications, also called software as a service (SaaS), is another type of service business and is often sold business to business (B2B).

✦ **Content site:** Charging a fee for all types of content and information products has become an accepted business model, especially in the last few years. And as a content site becomes more popular with visitors, options such as paid advertisements on the site can also generate income. The growing use of electronic readers (such as the Kindle and Nook) as well as Apple's iPad are helping create more acceptance and demand for paid content in the form of *e-books* (electronic formats of books or manuals). Similarly, the popularity of YouTube and other social media sites is driving interest in video. When you consider types of content to offer for sale, include video as an option for your paid content offerings.

✦ **Social commerce:** A growing online moneymaking opportunity is found in a category labeled *social commerce.* People are discovering ways to earn revenue from Facebook, Twitter, Pinterest, Instagram, LinkedIn, and other *social sites* (online venues that connect and engage consumers). Whether it's selling games and apps through social media sites or boosting online sales through engagement in social networks, one thing is certain: Social commerce is a real opportunity for a viable online business.

✦ **E-commerce applications:** If anything lends itself for sale over the Internet, it's technology. *E-commerce* (or electronic commerce) applications continue to provide lucrative growth for innovators. Think of e-commerce as any type of technology product that makes doing business online (and offline) easier. Inventory programs, shopping cart solutions, and payroll management software are all examples of innovations that fit nicely in this category.

In Book IV, we explain how to create a revenue model for your business; you can apply this model to any of the types of businesses in the preceding list.

As you can see, you have no shortage of opportunities to satisfy your urge to start a business. After you officially decide to take the plunge, you can narrow the field and get started.

Getting Started

Even after reading this entire chapter, you might still consider having an online business to be a dream — a vision for your future. You might want to take small steps, testing the water to see whether an online business is right for you, just as you dip your toe into a pool before diving in. At some point, though, you have to decide to go for it. To that end, this checklist describes what you need to do to begin wading into your own online business:

✦ **Make the decision to commit.** Although you don't have to quit your day job, you need to acknowledge that you're ready to pursue your goal. Say aloud, "I want to start an online business!"

✦ **Set clear goals.** Write down *why* you want this business and what you expect to gain from it. These goals can be related to financial objectives, lifestyle goals, or both. If you know what you're looking for, you can also more easily choose the right business to meet your needs.

✦ **Talk with your family.** After you commit to your idea and establish your goals, share your plan. If you're married or living with a partner, talk about your vision for the future. After all, your dream for an online business affects that person's life too. Discussing your plans with family is also a helpful step in making your business a reality.

✦ **Create an action timeline.** Unlike the broad goals you set in the first item in this list, writing down specific action steps can help you realize tangible results. From researching business ideas to obtaining a business license, assign a targeted date of completion to further ensure that you make each step happen. (Figure 1-1 shows an example of an action timeline for use with your business.)

✦ **Identify a business.** As we show you in the preceding section, you can choose from different types of businesses to operate online. Before going any further, however, you have to decide which business to pursue. Narrow your choices by thinking about what you enjoy doing or which specific qualifications you already possess. Consider your professional experience and your personal desires. You might even have a hobby that can be developed into a moneymaking business.

✦ **Develop your business idea.** Define your idea and determine how you will turn it into a profitable online business. (Read Book I, Chapter 2 when you're ready to evaluate whether your idea is feasible.)

After you make it through this checklist, you're ready to go to work and transform your dream into a legitimate business.

(Sample) Start-Up Action Timeline for Your Online Business

Start date: January 15
Estimated start-up date: June 30

Action	Completion Date	Status/Comments
Finalize/validate business idea	1/30	
Write formal business plan	2/15	
Select business name	1/30	
Register business name	2/15	
Choose domain name	1/30	
(if different from corporate name)		
Register domain name	1/31	
Identify business location	2/01	
Check zoning laws (if home-based)	2/05	
Set up office (computer, telephone, and so on)	2/15	
Decide organization status of company	1/30	
(sole proprietor, corporation)		
Legalize business structure	2/28	
(file incorporation papers)		
Obtain business license	2/05	
(and other necessary permits)		
Set up business bank account	2/05	
Meet with accountant to review tax requirements	2/10	
Obtain Employer Identification Number (EIN)	2/15	
Secure business insurance/health insurance/other	2/28	
Secure funding (if using outside sources)	3/31	
Apply for sales tax certificate (if applicable)	3/01	
Select:		
Hosting service	3/02	
Web developer	3/02	
Distributor or drop shipper (if applicable)	3/30	
Create content for website	4/29	
Select products, or finalize services, or both	5/20	
Develop website	6/10	
Add shopping cart or other e-commerce applications	6/15	
Obtain merchant account	6/15	
File trademarks and/or copyrights	6/16	
Submit site to major search engines	6/17	
Initiate marketing plan	6/20	
Test (and correct) all site functions	6/28	
Launch site to public!	6/30	

Figure 1-1:
A timeline for starting your online business.

Chapter 2: Turning Internet Dreams into Reality

In This Chapter

✔ Training yourself to think like an online entrepreneur

✔ Evaluating your business idea's chances for success

✔ Scrutinizing your future customers

✔ Picking apart your competitors

Congratulations! After you make the emotional commitment to get started, you have to shift gears and concentrate on the next set of actions that will make your Internet business a reality. From evaluating the potential success of your idea to identifying who will buy your products, in this chapter you gain the tools to help get your idea off the ground. In the process, you begin thinking like an online entrepreneur and find out how to start your business on the right track.

Thinking Like an Online Entrepreneur

Using the Internet to conduct business is similar in many ways to operating a traditional company. In fact, many traditional offline businesses now conduct part of their business online. Today, consumers research products and services online and expect to be able to buy products or services online, even from bricks-and-mortar stores. For those reasons, the lines between online and offline businesses are increasingly blurred.

Profitability (or how much money you make after subtracting your expenses), taxes, marketing, advertising, and customer feedback are other examples of factors that affect your business whether it's online or offline. However, some exceptions set apart an online business, particularly with regards to how you deliver products and service your customers. Even the most experienced entrepreneur can get caught in the trap of forgetting those differences. Your attitude and how you approach the business as an online entrepreneur can make a huge difference in how successful you are online.

Adjusting your attitude slightly and viewing business from behind the lens of an online entrepreneur isn't difficult. Doing so is simply a matter of recognizing that the Internet changes the way you can and should operate your online business.

When you think like an online entrepreneur, you

✦ **See the invisible storefront.** Although the doors, walls, and even the salesclerk for your online business might be invisible, they definitely exist. In fact, every part of your web business leaves a distinct impression. Yet rarely do you hear or see the response to your storefront directly from customers. Consequently, and contrary to popular belief, a website demands your continual care and attention — adding products, fixing bugs, replying to e-mail, and more.

✦ **Understand who your customers are.** Even if you don't personally greet your online visitors, don't be fooled: The Internet offers the unique opportunity to learn and understand almost everything about your customers. You can learn where else they shop, how much time they spend on your site, what products they're interested in, where they live and work, how much they earn annually, whether they are parents, and which magazines they read. Online entrepreneurs collect and use this information regularly in an effort to increase sales and better serve their customers. (When you're ready to meet your customer, turn to Book VI, where we explain how to get and use this wealth of customer information.)

✦ **Respond to fast and furious changes.** The way people use the Internet to buy, sell, or search for products and services changes rapidly. Also, the rules for operating an online business as imposed by both the government and the business world in general are modified almost daily. Sustaining success online means that you must take the initiative to keep up with new trends; laws and regulations; safety and security concerns; technology; and even marketing and social media tools.

✦ **Speak the language.** Communicating to your customers through a website can be challenging. Your buyers want and expect quick and easy access to information. Because attention spans are limited, content should always be relevant, easy to find, and to the point.

✦ **Communicate visually.** Equally important to the words you choose are the images you incorporate into your site. Whether you use purchased stock photos or pictures that you take yourself, you want images to be crisp, clear, and relevant to the message you are communicating. In addition, product images should be the best quality possible.

As an entrepreneur, you must choose both your words and images carefully. Your site's content, including the words and pictures you use on your web, will

- Help sell your products or services to visitors.

- Serve as interesting and useful content to share on social media, which is an important method of marketing your online business.

- Play a big role in *search engine optimization (SEO),* or the way you can increase visits to your site by placing higher on the list of rankings by Internet search engines. (Yes, images, like words, are searchable and can help increase your rankings in search engines!)

✦ **Know when (or whether) to innovate.** You might be able to develop a new or different method for doing business online, although it's probably not necessary. Innovative tools already exist, and you can often find them on the Internet quickly and cheaply. You don't need to reinvent the wheel — you just have to know how to find and apply the tools that are already out there.

✦ **Reap repeated rewards.** Establishing multiple streams of revenue or maximizing a single source of revenue is a common practice online. For instance, you might have an outstanding information product for sale on your site. The same product can just as easily be sold on other websites in exchange for a small percentage of earnings. Or you can choose to add a product from another website to your site and pay that site a percentage of earnings. (To begin increasing your earnings, read about affiliate programs in Book IV.) Similarly, you may decide to sell cloud-based or web-based services to other businesses on a monthly basis. This software as a service (SaaS) online business model provides recurring revenue for your online business.

Putting Your Business Idea under the Microscope

Every successful business begins with that first idea. From fast-food restaurants to selling cosmetics from home, Ray Kroc first dreamed of hamburgers at McDonald's and Mary Kay visualized selling makeup door to door. When the Internet first provided similar opportunities, Jeff Bezos visualized a way for consumers to buy everything from books to clothing and have it delivered straight to their doorsteps through Amazon. Your dream for an innovative new business is no exception — and the Internet has continued to make it easier than ever to launch a successful business. Maybe you have several unique concepts to choose from or are firmly set on a single one. Either way, how do you decide whether you should quit your day job and focus on your brilliant idea? You have to pick apart the idea, observe closely, and determine whether it merits a full-time (or part-time) business.

One question often asked is whether or not the idea has to be original. Innovative, never-before-broached ideas for an online business certainly exist. But being the first to have and implement an original idea is not a guarantee for success. Ultimately, your concept for the business, whether it's a new idea or a twist on an existing idea, must be well thought out to increase your probability for success. This section describes the three methods you can use to decide whether your idea has potential.

Using informal research to verify your idea

The best place to begin gathering information is from sources closest to you. Be prepared to receive varying opinions — both positive and negative. Use this input as a general gauge of whether to continue reaching out to the next source of information. You and your idea are in the center, surrounded by three rings from which to collect input, as shown in Figure 2-1. If the ring closest to you provides mostly positive input, proceed to the next ring.

Three Rings of Decision

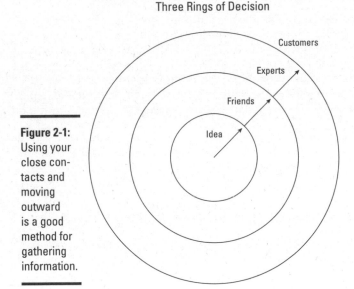

Figure 2-1:
Using your close contacts and moving outward is a good method for gathering information.

Ring 1 consists of your friends, family, and coworkers. Ask them these questions:

✦ Have you ever heard of this type of product or service?

✦ Would you buy this product or service?

✦ Do you think it's a good idea?

✦ What challenges do you think I will encounter?

✦ What are the benefits?

✦ Can you envision me selling this product or service? Why or why not?

In Ring 2, seek input from industry professionals, investors, other entre-preneurs, and organizations that offer support to small businesses. Ask questions similar to those listed for Ring 1. Because of the experience of the people in Ring 2, you should give more weight to their responses. Small-business support resources include

✦ **Small Business Administration (SBA) at** `www.sba.gov`: The SBA, a government-sponsored organization, helps small-business owners with loans, paperwork navigation, free seminars, and other services.

✦ **Small Business Development Center (SBDC) at** `www.sba.gov/sbdc`: The SBDC is a partnership between the SBA and universities. Together, they provide support, mentoring, training, and educational services to both new and established small businesses. SBDCs are available through local branches, often located in a partnering university or Chamber of Commerce.

✦ **Chamber of Commerce at** `www.uschamber.com`: From small towns to large cities, all local chambers help owners develop their small businesses.

✦ **SCORE at** `www.score.org`: This network of retired executives matches small-business owners with business-exec retirees who volunteer their time to help small businesses develop and prosper.

In Ring 3 are your potential customers. Ask them these questions:

✦ Would you use this product or service?

✦ Have you used something similar?

✦ How much would you be willing to pay?

✦ How often would you use it?

✦ Where would you normally go to buy this product or service?

✦ Would you order it over the Internet?

If you find that you're receiving a majority of positive feedback from sources in all three rings, you can consider your idea worthwhile. Or at least you have enough validation to continue to the next phase of your evaluation process.

Applying a SWOT analysis to your idea

Another popular method for determining the pros and cons of an idea is referred to as *SWOT analysis.* (SWOT is short for strengths, weaknesses, opportunities, and threats.) Companies use it for several reasons, including as a decision-making tool for product development. The simple process also lends itself to a more thorough investigation of your business idea. This section covers how you can put your idea to the SWOT test!

Create your own SWOT chart by following these steps:

1. **On paper, draw a cross (or a box divided in half both horizontally and vertically) to create four quadrants, and label them as shown in Figure 2-2.**

   After you draw and label the chart, you can begin to fill in the details.

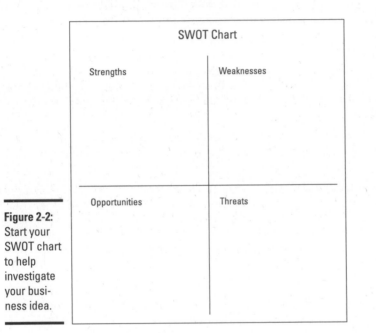

SWOT Chart

Strengths | Weaknesses

Opportunities | Threats

Figure 2-2: Start your SWOT chart to help investigate your business idea.

2. **In each quadrant, write down the factors that influence or contribute to each of your four SWOT categories.**

   Strengths and weaknesses are considered *internal* factors that control or specifically contribute (good or bad) to the business concept. Opportunities and threats are *external* factors that are influenced to some extent by the environment or are otherwise outside of your control.

3. **Analyze the information you filled in. Ask yourself the following questions to start developing your SWOT analysis:**

   Strengths

   - What advantages does the product or service offer?

   - Do I have expertise in this business or industry?

   - Can I get a patent to protect the idea?

Weaknesses

- How much does developing the product cost?
- Is getting suppliers difficult?
- Am I learning a new industry from the ground up?

Opportunities

- Does my idea take advantage of a new technology?
- Is my product or service in demand?
- Have changes in policies or regulations made my idea necessary?

Threats

- Does my product or service have established competitors?
- Do my competitors sell the product or service for less than I can?
- Will changes in technology make my product obsolete?

Use the feedback you receive from your informal research (during the Three Rings exercise) as factors in your SWOT quadrants. Combining other people's opinions with your own provides a more comprehensive — and useful — SWOT analysis.

4. **After you fill in the categories of your first SWOT analysis, take a look at which quadrants contain the most factors or the most significant factors.**

   The listed strengths and opportunities indicate the advantage you might have in the marketplace. If you're lucky, they outweigh your weaknesses and challenges. Perhaps you can now see what you must do to offset those disadvantages if you really want your idea to work.

Whatever the outcome of your analysis, you should have a better feel for the value of your business idea after viewing the completed SWOT analysis.

Creating a feasibility study to validate an idea

After your idea gains a nod of approval from friends and family and the SWOT analysis indicates that your product has merit, your idea must jump through one more hoop for complete validation. A *feasibility study* is a somewhat formal, written process that helps you determine whether your idea is realistic. The goal of the study is to provide you with final proof that your business concept is viable.

A feasibility study answers these basic questions:

+ Will the product or service work?

+ How much will it cost to start?

+ Can your idea make you money?

+ Is the business concept *really* worth your time and energy?

A feasibility study kicks your analysis up a notch. It relies on in-depth research to provide more detailed answers to questions in five primary areas, as shown in Figure 2-3.

Now you know how much information you have to gather in your feasibility study. As you answer all these questions, make sure that you back up those answers with detailed research. Then write your results in a one-page summary that discusses what you discovered. Your summary should answer the five basic questions in each category and provide proof of whether you have a viable idea. After the validation process is complete, you can turn your attention to the next piece of the business success puzzle: potential customers.

Choosing the best idea for *you*

Perhaps you have no trouble dreaming up new ideas for a business. Instead, your challenge is deciding which one to pursue. Unlike the SWOT analysis or feasibility study, no established test determines which of your many pursuits is best suited for you. This decision is much more subjective and personal. When deciding which idea is best for you, consider the following questions. Use your answers to help gauge such things as how passionate you are about a particular idea or which ideas may be better suited for your current skills or lifestyle.

✔ Does this idea interest you?

✔ Does this product or service *excite* you?

✔ Do you have experience with this product or service?

✔ Does it require a large investment?

✔ Do you have money readily available to fund the concept?

✔ Will starting this business require you to alter your lifestyle?

✔ Are you willing to change your lifestyle for this idea?

✔ Does this business reflect your personal goals?

✔ Does this idea reflect your professional goals?

✔ Can you imagine owning this same business in ten years?

* **Your product and service**
    * What is the product or service?
    * How will my customers use it?
    * Where or how will my customers buy it?
    * How is it designed, and how is it delivered to my customers?
    * Am I testing to ensure that my product works correctly? (Describe these tests in detail.)
* **Your experience (including your management team's experience)**
    * Who is my management team?
    * What experience do I (and my employees) have?
    * What are my specific skills and credentials?
    * Which skills am I missing, or in which areas am I weak?
    * How much time can I devote to my business?
* **The market in which you're competing**
    * What is the demand for my product?
    * Who are my customers? (What is the target market?)
    * How big is the market I'm selling to?
    * What is the status of the market? Is it growing or stagnant?
    * Where and how can I reach those customers?
* **Your competition**
    * Who are my primary and secondary competitors? (Describe each of your competitors in detail.)
    * How do my competitors market their products or services?
    * What makes me different or better than my competitors?
    * Is my product easy to copy? How can I prevent copycats?
* **Your costs**
    * How much does it cost to make my product or produce my service?
    * What other business costs do I have?
    * What amount of money do I need to start?
    * Do I have access to funding?
    * When will I make a profit?

Figure 2-3:
Answer these questions for your feasibility study.

Identifying Your Market and Target Customer

The terms *target market* and *target customer* are defined as the entities that buy your product or service. Although these phrases are sometimes used interchangeably, *market* is often used to describe a collection of individual target customers. The term *buyer persona* is also used as a way of providing a detailed description (or persona) of your typical customers. You most likely have several types of customers, each with a unique persona — and you mostly likely have several buyer personas that make up your target customers.

Classifying your customer

Knowing your target customer is an important advantage when you begin marketing. As we explain in earlier sections in this chapter, recognizing your primary customers lends credibility to your business concept. The more you know about your target customers, the more easily and cost-efficiently you can build your business and market to these folks.

How do you decide who this person is or who the groups of people are? You can create buyer personas by describing or segmenting your customers based on different traits or classifications. The two most common classifications are

✦ **Demographics:** Age, income, gender, and occupation are examples of common factors used to describe your customers.

✦ **Psychographics:** Music choices, hobbies, and other preferences make up this category. Usually, psychographics reflect lifestyle choices.

You can describe your customers in other terms as well, such as these categories:

✦ **Benefits:** Describe why customers use your product or service. For example, customers might need it for medical purposes. Or they might receive a luxury benefit, where they don't *need* the product or service but choose to invest in it for perceived benefits.

✦ **Geographic preferences:** Point out where people live. The location can include a specific neighborhood, city, state, region, or even country. Customers can also be segmented according to home (or residential) locations versus business locations.

Technology has made it easy to target your customers by location. Knowing where your customers are in terms of geography can be a critical competitive advantage.

✦ **Use-based preferences:** Specify how frequently customers want or need your product.

Typically, your target market includes customers described by a mixture of the terms and categories in this list, which you use to develop your buyer persona. For instance, if you sell trendy men's clothing at discounted prices, one buyer persona for your target market might be described this way:

Male

Age 25 to 30

Professional

Owns home or rents high-end apartment, with a total annual household income of $50,000 or more

Lives in urban area or major metropolitan city

Buys clothing at least monthly and updates style seasonally to enhance appearance

Depending on what type of product you sell, your target market most likely includes a wider mix of customer types — not just one.

Going to the source

In the preceding section, we talk about the components of a market description. Where do you get the information to build this type of description, though? You can use any or all of the following methods to gather information for your customer profile:

✦ **Survey potential (or existing) customers.** Conduct a focus group in which you interview a small group of likely customers. Or distribute a survey or registration form online to gather the data.

✦ **Observe competitors' customers.** Stake out your competitors by visiting them online. You can often discover exactly what competitors think about their own customers by reading through their sites. (This information is often readily available on competitors' websites in sections labeled About Us or Company Information.) For competitors with retail locations, visit their stores and observe the customers and their habits in person.

✦ **Use published market research.** To identify the types of customers most likely to buy your products, read about trends in reputable market reports. You can find much of the research for free online. Larger research firms charge a fee (which can range from several hundred dollars to several thousand dollars per report) for detailed reports. If this type of research interests you, start with companies such as Gartner (www.gartner.com), Forrester (www.forrester.com), or IDC (www.idc.com).

Use this information to pinpoint who your customer is.

Competing to Win: Analyzing Your Competition

If you're serious about developing a successful online business, you need every advantage possible. That means getting to know not only who your customers are but also who else is after their business. Start by writing down a list of your top three to five competitors.

Keep this list on hand, and document basic information, such as

✦ Website address

✦ Physical address (if they have one) and number of locations

- ✦ Annual sales
- ✦ Number of employees
- ✦ Types of products or services offered (with full description)
- ✦ Strengths and weaknesses
- ✦ Copies of ads, flyers, and brochures
- ✦ Special promotions (especially online offers)
- ✦ Pricing information for products or services similar to yours

As a quick and easy way to keep up with your competition, visit their websites and sign up for their newsletters and other promotional offers by e-mail. You can also follow them on social media sites such as Facebook and Twitter.

Be sure to maintain a list of your secondary competitors, too. These companies don't sell your exact products or services but come close enough to compete for your customers' dollars.

Hooray! You completed your due diligence and have a fat file of information about your stiffest competition. What now? This kind of data does you no good when it just takes up space in a filing cabinet. Use it to your advantage.

Sift through your collected information again to refresh your memory (because you probably have lots of information), and then follow these steps:

- ✦ **Compare apples to oranges.** Using the information you collect, compare both your strengths and weaknesses to that of the competition. (You can even do a complete SWOT analysis on each of your competitors!) This comparison identifies where you fit in the marketplace relative to other players in your area of interest.

- ✦ **Plan your marketing strategy.** You have access to your competitor's marketing material, so use it to define your own marketing strategy. Play up your company's strengths in ads; advertise in markets that your competitors missed; and plan to educate your customers on the benefits that separate you from your competition.

- ✦ **Create a competitive pricing model.** Maybe you discovered that you could beat a competitor's price. Or perhaps your research shows that you *must* price lower to survive. Use a competitor's pricing data to map out the best pricing model for your product or service.

- ✦ **Determine growth models and financial requirements.** Suppose that a major competitor is ready to partner with a big distributor. Although you might not be able to compete immediately, this information helps you plan for growth. Use this knowledge to better understand your competitor's growth and financial strategies, and then adjust yours accordingly.

The old cliché is still accurate: Knowledge is power. Don't let good information go to waste. Use what you learn to differentiate yourself and win points with your customers.

Chapter 3: Getting Real: Creating a Usable Business Plan

In This Chapter

✔ Understanding the purpose of a business plan

✔ Organizing the pieces of your dreams into tangible goals

✔ Determining when you need help and what to expect

✔ Getting long-term value from the plan you make today

*O*ne big complaint from entrepreneurs, especially those running small companies, is "Why do I have to write a business plan?" Quite honestly, you don't. Some entrepreneurs who choose to forgo a business plan do just fine, but others struggle.

In this chapter, we tell you why having a business plan is a good idea and show you the benefits you can reap from not only having one but also reviewing and updating it regularly.

We can't possibly cover everything about writing and using a business plan in this chapter. After all, entire books are devoted to business plans. In fact, a good one to look into is *Business Plans Kit For Dummies,* 4th Edition, by Steven D. Peterson, Peter E. Jaret, and Barbara Findlay Schenck.

Understanding the Value of a Plan

Starting and managing a business without a business plan is, like it or not, the same as searching for a buried treasure without a map: Although you know that the gold is in the ground somewhere, you're wasting an awful lot of time by randomly digging holes in the hope of eventually hitting the jackpot. Without a plan, the odds of success aren't in your favor.

Why, then, do people resist using this tool? They resist it for two reasons:

✦ **Having a plan involves a great deal of work.** Don't despair: You can minimize the amount of work involved, which we get to momentarily.

✦ **They don't understand the importance of having a plan.**

To help you overcome your business plan angst, we provide these reasons for having a plan — you can decide whether to take another step without one:

✦ **You can more easily secure money.** This goal is probably the most common reason for the creation of a business plan. If you decide to ask strangers to lend you money, whether those strangers are bankers or private investors, they want to see a plan. Lenders have a better chance of protecting (and recouping) their investments when a formal strategy documents your projected income and profits. Even if you're counting on family members for a loan or are using your own funds, having a business plan confirms that you have thought about how to use the money wisely.

✦ **A plan creates a vision that gives you a well-defined goal.** Coming up with a great idea and transitioning it into a viable business opportunity can be challenging. Having a written plan forces you to fully develop the long-term vision for your product or service. With those clearly defined goals in place, you stand a much better chance of accomplishing your vision.

✦ **A plan can provide timeless guidance.** Done correctly, this document provides a concrete plan of operation for your business — not only during your start-up phase but also for three to five years down the road. Keep in mind that the plan might need occasional tweaking (as discussed at the end of this chapter). However, investing the time now to create a strong foundation ensures that you have a barometer to help you make decisions for managing your company.

Chances are that at least two of the three reasons on this list are valuable to you. Even if you don't plan to attract investors, you're already forming a picture about what your company looks like, and you're setting goals to make sure that you get there. The only remaining step is to make your thoughts more permanent by writing them down in a business plan.

Recognizing That the Parts of the Plan Make a Whole

A traditional business plan is sectioned into seven or eight major parts. At first, that number of parts might seem a bit overwhelming. Consider, however, that most experts recommend keeping a finished business plan to fewer than 20 pages. (You can usually get by with many fewer pages.) When you break down that recommendation, each section becomes only 2 or 3 pages long, which translates to 5 or 6 paragraphs per page. It's not so much after all.

Each part plays a critical role in your overall plan. Although each section can almost stand alone, the sections work together to present a complete picture, or vision, of your business. Don't even think about omitting one of them.

Depending on your main purpose for having a business plan, you can develop sections with more diligence. For example, if you're seeking outside funding, make sure that the financials section is as thorough and accurate as possible.

Before you start writing, get a sense of the scope of your plan by reading these brief descriptions of the basic parts you need to cover:

✦ **Executive summary:** Although this part comes first in your plan, you typically write it last. This brief page does just what it says: It highlights the major points from each of the other parts of the plan. This page is usually the first one that investors and other advisors read, and how well it's written can determine whether they turn the page or show you the door.

✦ **Business or product description:** This section provides a detailed description of your overall business and your product or service. You should include a *vision statement* (or *mission statement*), which summarizes your goals for the business. When you describe your product or service, don't forget to pinpoint what makes it a unique and viable contender in the marketplace.

✦ **Market analysis:** Provide a thorough description of your target market. In this case, discuss both the overall industry in which you're competing and the specific customers to whom you're marketing. Don't forget to include a description of any market research you conducted.

✦ **Competitive analysis:** In much the same way as you describe your target market in the market analysis, in this section you provide an in-depth view of your competitors in that market. The more detail you can provide, the better, to show exactly how well you understand (and are prepared for dealing with) your competition. Address your competitors' weaknesses and also state how you can counter their strengths.

Don't double up on your work. Use information you gather during your SWOT analysis and feasibility study (see Chapter 2 of this minibook). Adapt the research and results of both to include in the market analysis and competitive analysis sections of your business plan.

✦ **Management team:** Whether you're flying solo on this operation or working with a team, highlight the expertise that you and your executives bring to the table. Include summaries of your key professional experience, educational and military background, additional certifications and completed training programs, and all other relevant accomplishments. Remember to include a copy of your full resume.

✦ **Operations:** Here's where the "rubber meets the road." Use this section to describe your marketing and operations strategies. Then detail *how* you plan to implement these strategies in your business. Think of the operations section as your chance to prove that you know how to convert innovative ideas into a successful business.

✦ **Financials:** Start talking money. In this section, you include projections (or estimates) of how much money the business will earn and your expenses, or costs of doing business. This combination is typically referred to as a *profit-and-loss statement.* For the first year, break down this information for each month. (This listing demonstrates how far you must proceed into your first year before you start making money and indicates where seasonal slow points might occur, with smaller amounts of income coming in.) After the first year, show your projections annually. (See Book II for complete descriptions of legal and accounting requirements.)

When you're pursuing outside funding, try to be optimistic about your financial projections. Don't be unrealistic, but don't be too conservative, either. If you're using the plan only internally, you can play it safe and estimate your future profits toward the lower end.

✦ **Appendix:** Consider this area a catchall for important documents that support portions of your business plan. Place copies of your loan terms, patent or copyright documentation, employee agreements, and any other contracts or legal documents pertaining to your business.

You might wonder whether you can use an easier, or shorter, business plan format with an online business instead of the traditional format. No, not really. As you can see from the descriptions in the preceding list, each part or section of the plan is generic. You can use almost any business plan template, tailor it slightly to your specific type of business, and achieve the same results.

Having a sample plan written for an organization similar to your online business is helpful. Check out one of the business-planning resource centers on the web, such as Bplans (www.bplans.com), to locate a sample plan specifically for online businesses to use as a guide. (See Figure 3-1.) Free resources and tips are available to help create your plan, or you can pay for additional tools and software.

Figure 3-1: Find sample business plans for e-commerce sites by visiting Bplans.com.

Getting Help to Write the Plan

Even though you will probably feel better about writing a business plan after you read the rest of this chapter, more options can help make writing one easier. When creating a plan feels like more than you can handle alone, the solution is to hire a professional to write it for you or purchase business plan software that walks you through the process.

Don't think that a business plan template or other software package is cheating. Your goal is to get your business off the ground — don't close any doors or turn away any help. The money you spend on your business plan is an investment that has the potential to pay back many times. The time you spend on your business plan can likewise shorten the time you must spend later in preparing your business for success.

Several good options for business plan software exist, including buying an off-the-shelf version, such as Business PlanMaker Professional or BusinessPlan Pro (from Palo Alto Software). You can also use LivePlan (www.liveplan.com), an online version of Palo Alto Software's business plan software. If you need limited guidance on developing a plan, check out the free templates from Microsoft Office (www.office.microsoft.com/en-us/templates/).

Determining when to hire a professional

Not everyone needs outside help to construct a solid business plan. If you're starting the business part-time or you plan to be a one-person company for a while, the plan doesn't necessarily have to be lengthy and complicated.

As a *sole proprietor* (one-person company), part-time operator, or home-based business owner, you might write a condensed version of the business plan, with the same sections but less detail. Rather than use a 20-page document, you might be able to achieve the same objective in only 8 pages.

Alternatively, if you need to secure a large amount of money for your online business start-up, it just might pay (literally) to get help — especially if you plan to *pitch* (sell) your business idea to savvy investors, such as venture capitalists. Bringing in a seasoned business plan writer helps you

✦ Add polish to your plan

✦ Remember to include pertinent information

✦ Phrase the wording of your business plan in the best possible way so that you speak the language of investors

If you're pressed for time, getting assistance might also speed the process for you. Additionally, if you commit to using the business plan to its full potential (as a long-term operational guide), hiring an experienced consultant almost guarantees that your plan is a top-notch piece of work.

Knowing what to expect from a business plan consultant

After you decide to seek assistance with your plan, you might be surprised to find that you're still expected to contribute information. Business plan writers are often referred to as consultants, and for good reason: You consult these folks to get advice and guidance on how to make the most of your plan.

A consultant translates your thoughts into the final written document. Consultants aren't mind readers, though: You're still responsible for providing all the initial information, often in written form.

You might be wondering how much this service costs. After you realize that you're still doing a good bit of the work, your expectations on price might change. Regardless of the amount of work you must contribute, however, writing the plan still takes a great deal of time, and you're paying for the consultant's expertise. Expect to pay the minimum national average of $1,500 to $5,000 for a business plan written by a professional.

Keep in mind that wide variations might still exist, on both ends of the price scale, for this service. Much of the final price depends on

✦ Your requirements for the plan

✦ What you can contribute (to save the consultant time)

✦ The consultant's experience level

✦ The complexity of the business concept

✦ The amount of research required to substantiate the plan

Although more knowledgeable consultants might charge a higher hourly fee, they could complete the project much sooner because of their experience. A consultant who lowballs the price of the project might not fully understand the amount of time involved and might try to increase the quoted price later.

When you're working with a professional, the length of time to complete your plan depends on several factors. Here are some examples:

✦ How much information you can provide

✦ How quickly you can provide the information

✦ How extensive a plan you need

✦ The availability and accessibility of the facts about your business

If you decide to hire a professional, check first with experienced advisors who offer free assistance. Your local Chamber of Commerce or SCORE, an organization that offers guidance to new and established businesses, might provide enough to support writing the plan yourself. In addition, the Small Business Administration (SBA) offers an online tutorial for writing a business plan at www.sba.gov, as shown in Figure 3-2.

Figure 3-2:
The Small
Business
Admin-
istration
website
offers
business
plan
reference
material.

When you're ready to hire a professional, keep these points in mind:

✦ Look for someone with experience in your product or service industry.

✦ Find a consultant who's comfortable with, and knowledgeable of, online businesses.

✦ Review samples of other business plans the consultant has written.

✦ Ask for written testimonials and references you can contact.

✦ Get a firm price quote.

✦ Agree on a reasonable timeline for completing the plan.

✦ Put your final terms into a written contract, including specifics of what you're responsible for providing.

Using a Business Plan Today, Tomorrow, and Always

Ignoring your business plan or forgetting to maintain it is the same as failing to plan. To ensure that your business plan passes the test of time, consider these suggestions for ways to use it:

✦ **As reference material:** Refer to your plan often. Rereading your original plan is a good way to make sure that you're staying on track.

✦ **As a decision-making tool:** When major operational issues occur or expansion opportunities arise, turn to your business plan. Decide whether the issue at hand fits your original goals and timeline before taking action.

✦ **As a troubleshooter:** When problems surface, minimize your frustrations. Use your own words of wisdom to resolve your problems. Take a look at your plan to see where the hiccup is. More than likely, you addressed potential problems in the operations section of your business plan.

✦ **As a vision guide:** After your business is running, you can easily lose sight of the big picture. Concentrating on daily tasks and problems can derail your overall progress. Check your plan frequently and refocus your vision.

Every January, schedule at least two business plan preview sessions for the coming year. If necessary, pencil in a date and time on your calendar. (Block out three or four hours.) Do this task semiannually or quarterly, depending on whether you made, or will make, significant changes to your business.

Chapter 4: Finding Money to Fund Your Online Start-Up

In This Chapter

⮑ **Getting started with little or no money**

⮑ **Selling others on your idea**

⮑ **Searching for alternative money sources**

⮑ **Avoiding start-up costs with an upfront investment in an existing business**

*O*ne of the most important choices you make when you're creating a company is how to fund your brave new endeavor. The amount of money you have available and where it comes from truly helps you begin defining the rules by which you must operate the business.

If you borrow $25,000 from a bank, for example, right away you know what's at stake. Each month you *have* to come up with at least enough money to cover that loan payment or else you risk jeopardizing your personal credit record (if you're a sole proprietorship and aren't incorporated). On the other hand, if you borrow $5,000 from your in-laws, you're potentially inviting additional decision-makers into your business because there's no such thing as "silent" in-laws.

Whether you need $500 or $500,000 to get your business going, this chapter shows you various financing options and describes what each one means to the future of your business.

Bootstrapping the Low-Cost, No-Cost Site

We won't lie to you: Just like starting a political campaign, starting a business is easier if plenty of money is available. Fortunately, having a lot of money isn't a requirement to start an Internet business. If you don't have access to megabucks, you can always *bootstrap* your new business. (The term comes from the idea of pulling yourself up by your own bootstraps, or making your own way.) In the case of financing your entrepreneurial dream, bootstrapping is a matter of making a little money go a long way.

Making the leap to the bootstrapping lifestyle

One of the first rules of bootstrapping is to hang on to other sources of income for as long as possible. In other words, keep your day job! You might have to design your website during lunch breaks or work past midnight to prepare customer orders for shipping. Although keeping a regular job while starting a business can mean a grueling schedule, it provides you with much-needed financial security in the early stages of building your company.

Try something between maintaining a full-time job and starting a business. Many entrepreneurs worked part-time jobs at night so that they could dedicate themselves to their new businesses during the day.

If you're the all-or-nothing type, perhaps you want to throw yourself completely into the business. Or maybe you're confident enough in your idea that you just *know* success (cash!) will materialize. However, you should still plan for alternative sources of income. Look for freelance work, short-term consulting jobs, or whatever else it takes to keep money coming in while building your business.

Saving money to make money

Making sure that cash is coming into your business is only your first step. Learning to conserve your cash is the second rule of bootstrapping. Controlling the *outflow* of money, or how that money is used, is quite important.

Here are some ways that any good bootstrapper can conserve cash:

✦ **Become frugal.** Spend only when absolutely necessary, and then buy on the cheap. Rather than buy brand-new office furniture, for example, find what you need by shopping garage sales, thrift stores, and eBay.

✦ **Budget wisely.** Create a financial plan that helps you track income, expenses, and projected sales. By monitoring the money you have coming in and going out every day, you're less likely to get into trouble. Book II shows you how to establish this type of budget and set up your accounting procedures.

✦ **Use other people's money.** Rather than borrow money from banks or investors, "borrow" money from your suppliers and customers. You can negotiate terms with vendors that allow you to pay for supplies 30, 60, or 90 days out (in other words, after you receive them). Then ask customers to pay for your product or services up front or in net 15 days. This strategy lets you use your customer's money, rather than cash out of your pocket, to pay your expenses.

✦ **Sacrifice for the business.** The cash coming into your business should be just that — money for your business. If you're using revenues to support your personal lifestyle, the business doesn't stand a chance.

Bootstrappers commonly forfeit luxuries and even downgrade their living circumstances while growing a company. Could you live in a smaller house for a while or drive a less expensive car?

✦ **Inspire, don't hire.** The early stages of building your company can be overwhelming, with lots of hats for you to wear. Rather than hire full-time employees, inspire others to work with you *gratis* (for free). Not everyone wants or needs immediate compensation, so sell people on your skills as a leader and get them excited about where your company is headed. College interns are a good source of free or inexpensive labor for your business. When the economy is weak and jobs are scarce, even out-of-work professionals are willing to accept internships in an effort to improve or expand their marketable skills. The promise of a job (after you're on more stable financial ground) may be enough to get some-one working five or six hours a week right now. Some individuals are also willing to work for free, in return for a recommendation from your company. For example, a lot of people design complementary websites in exchange for using those websites as client referrals. By seeking out this type of synergistic swap, you can avoid hiring employees in the beginning.

✦ **Find a mentor.** Hiring a consultant can break the bank before you even open your doors for business. Mentoring is an alternative way to get advice from established professionals that costs you absolutely nothing. These experts probably won't do the work for you, but they can advise you on critical decisions, introduce you to other professionals and sup-pliers, and sometimes even help you find your first customers. People are generous with their time, especially when you ask them to share their personal expertise with you.

Getting resourceful

In addition to locating experts or finding cash, you need to identify other means of getting what you need. Check out these resourceful alternatives to help you jump-start your online business:

✦ **Barter and trade:** One way to keep a lid on your spending and still acquire supplies and services is to trade with other companies. Rather than pay a professional to write copy for your web pages, for example, barter with a writer for her service. *Barter,* or trade, is a method of paying for products or services without using cash. When you barter, you exchange your services or products for those of another person (or company). This method of conducting business has become so popular that you can now join formal barter-exchange organizations, such as Southern Barter Exchange (see Figure 4-1). Membership is usually free. You can find barter organizations online that serve your specific state or region or find one that has a national reach.

Figure 4-1:
Online communities let you barter goods and services.

The Internal Revenue Service (IRS) doesn't mind bartering, as long as you record on your taxes whatever you receive as income. Any transaction involving the exchange of a product or service that doesn't involve cash changing hands is considered "barter" by the IRS. The IRS has guidelines and reporting requirements for individuals and formal barter exchanges. For example, barter amounts should appear as income for both parties when you complete Form 1099. You can read the complete guidelines for how to report bartering as income on the IRS website (www.irs.gov).

✦ **Try out trial versions before you buy.** When you stock up on necessary software for your online business, don't rush to buy expensive off-the-shelf products, which can cost several hundred dollars. Instead, use free demonstration (demo) versions that are good for a specified period. Eventually these free trials run out of time, so budget accordingly if you anticipate needing to make a more permanent software purchase.

✦ **Use free tools.** Lots of free business-related software (called *freeware*) and free or almost-free applications are accessible over the Internet. Independent software developers and small companies typically offer software applications, graphics, games, and developer tools at no cost to you, and with no strings attached. Other apps cost just a few dollars. And even if you don't find a recognizable brand-name product, you might find one that has similar features. Be aware that freeware and free business apps almost never have technical support.

The following websites provide lists of freeware and apps:

- Google Play business apps (`https://play.google.com/store/apps/category/business`)

- MajorGeeks (`www.majorgeeks.com`)

- Tucows (`www.tucows.com`), shown in Figure 4-2

Figure 4-2:
Search
for free
software
at Tucows.
com.

Looking at the pros and cons of bootstrapping

Bootstrapping may sound like you're flying by the seat of your pants (or your boots), but it's quite the opposite. It requires adopting a rigorous thought process that includes detailed and innovative planning.

Although bootstrapping may seem painful, consider the alternative of bringing in other investors or borrowing money. Is it worth the sacrifice? Take a look at how a bootstrapping approach can affect your business now and down the road, and then decide for yourself:

✦ **You retain ownership.** Keeping full ownership or controlling interest of the business is one of the most important benefits of bootstrapping. You get to make all the decisions, without having to run them by investors or shareholders or even lenders first. You also choose how and when the company grows. And if you need to bring in capital (money) down the road by selling shares of your company, you don't jeopardize your control. You can sell off a minority interest and maintain controlling interest.

✦ **You can make quick decisions.** Typically, you don't have layers of departments or managers in a bootstrapper organization. You can make decisions without getting bogged down by bureaucratic red tape. The ability to make agile decisions is an important advantage over competitors, especially when you're heavily into the research-and-development (R&D) process. Your organization can offer new products or make other changes much faster than many of your competitors can.

✦ **You assume minimal risk.** Without putting much money on the line, your risk (or what you can afford to lose) is greatly reduced. You also have the most to gain because your investment and your risk factor are small. This motivating aspect can spur you to success.

✦ **You maintain a cash-is-king mindset:** Being frugal pays off now and later. Initially, your conservative decisions will assist you in building a positive cash flow for your business. As a bootstrapper, you'll tend to hold on to those same decision-making philosophies in an effort to maintain your cash reserves as the company expands. This mindset may help to keep your online business debt free.

Finding the Perfect Investor

Not everyone has what it takes to grow a successful company from nothing or while operating on a shoestring. Or maybe your business concept requires a significant injection of capital right from the start. If so, you have other alternatives to bootstrapping. The most popular approach is to find an investor.

Investors, either individuals or a group of individuals, buy into your idea and provide the money you need in exchange for stock (or a percentage of ownership) in your business. You can choose from several types of investors; each type comes with its own pros and cons, of course. The trick is to find the best type of investor for your needs.

Turning to your friends and family

You're probably familiar with the idea of turning to your friends and family (*F&F*) network for start-up funds. A major advantage of this strategy is that you have a lot of flexibility in how you structure the terms of the agreement.

The simplest method is to simply ask for a loan. You need a certain amount of cash, and your mom or best friend is happy to oblige. As a bonus, the interest amount on the loan is usually minimal or nonexistent, and the time for repaying the money is often more flexible — not a bad deal.

An alternative is to take on your friends and family as investors. In other words, you give up a percentage of shares or stock in the business for the amount of money they agree to provide. On the upside, you don't repay that money. However, if you no longer want those people to own a piece of your business, you have to buy back their stock to get rid of them.

Here are some advantages of acquiring investors from your F&F network:

✦ **You can easily obtain the money.** You have an established circle of friends and family members who already know and trust you. Sometimes, you don't even have to sell them on your business idea — let alone show them your business plan. They just want to help you.

✦ **You can get cash quickly.** Unlike going to a bank or venture capitalist, you don't have to jump through any lending hoops or participate in a series of drawn-out meetings. Friends and family may be able to get their hands on cash quickly and hand it over to you sooner.

✦ **You have a potentially large pool of investors.** You can easily find small amounts of money from lots of different sources. If you need $50,000, you can get ten friends to contribute $10,000 each rather than try to find one person who can contribute the entire amount.

This method has a few disadvantages too, of course:

✦ **You can have problems with unstructured terms.** Because you know each other, you tend to keep things informal. That opens the door to uncertainty and inconsistency and big misunderstandings. Be wary of taking on friends and family members as investors without structured, written agreements that clearly define the terms of their investments in your company or the payback terms of your loan.

✦ **You may give up too much stock.** You want to gratefully reward those who take a chance on you, especially when you're close to them. For that same reason, however, you can end up giving away too much interest in your company. Or if you turn to a large group of friends to invest, you may have to ante up a large block of stock for a small amount of cash. This uneven exchange can put you in a precarious position as the company grows.

✦ **The business can interfere with relationships.** Taking on your most trusted circle of friends or family as investors can lead to heated disagreements, hurt feelings, and your fair share of misunderstandings. Damage to these friendships or to relationships with family members isn't easy to repair.

Finding angels

If the uncertainty and lack of structure of the friends and family (F&F) network bothers you, turning to an angel may be more appealing. An *angel* investor can be an individual investor or a group of investors who are willing to put money into start-up or young companies.

Several important differences separate angels from other types of investors. Angels usually bridge the funding gap. Raising more than $100,000 or $200,000 from friends and family is tough, yet a venture capitalist usually isn't interested in investing less than a million dollars, especially in a company without a track record. An angel meets midlevel funding needs.

Another important difference is that an angel investor typically doesn't take an active role in a company. An angel wants to provide capital, not run the business, although that person sometimes becomes a member of an advisory board or board of directors. (We discuss the board of directors as part of your formal business structure in Book II.) In addition to taking this hands-off approach toward your business, an angel is less likely to demand an immediate return on an investment. Whereas your father-in-law may expect to recoup his money in a couple of years, an angel's target return may be five years.

This network of investors has become more careful, performing due diligence and examining every aspect of proposed businesses. Following a weak economy and the many lessons learned from the 1990s dot-com bust, investors aren't simply throwing money at every Internet business opportunity that appears. Fluctuations also occur in the types of businesses or industries that are most appealing to angel investors at any given time. Examples include the healthcare industry and biotechnology companies, which have been popular for the last decade; social media or social networking sites, boosted in popularity by successful social media platforms such as Twitter, LinkedIn, and Facebook; and businesses that have developed online games and apps, which are sometimes lucrative acquisition targets for the larger social media sites. Regardless what types of businesses are popular investment targets, generally angels are more willing to take risks on new, unproven businesses. But keep in mind that the overall requirements for investing are increasingly the same as those used by venture capitalists (as outlined in the next section).

A hands-off approach to long-term lending sounds great, right? It's not all roses, though. Among the negative factors in seeking money from angels is that they often require a larger stake in a business. Having a higher percentage of ownership in a company offsets their risk. When the return on investment comes, it equates to a significant amount of money for your angels. Also, acquiring money from angel networks is getting tougher. Increasingly, angels are using the same or similar funding guidelines as those of venture capitalists. Angels expect you to have a polished business plan, an experienced management team, and an *exit strategy* (a way for the angel to recoup their initial investment and then some).

If the negative side of working with an angel doesn't bother you, how do you locate one? Examine your own network of colleagues, friends, and family — ask if they have any contacts that might be interested. If that strategy doesn't provide any leads, search for angels at the regional or national level. Here are some places to begin your search:

+ Chamber of Commerce or other local business-support organizations
+ Professional associations (local and statewide) focused on technology
+ Your accountant, banker, or attorney (who often works with or knows angels)
+ Investment clubs

Online resources for angel networks and entrepreneurs include

✦ Go4Funding: www.go4funding.com

✦ Investors Circle: www.investorscircle.net

✦ National Network of Angels Investors: www.nationalnetworkofangel
investors.com

✦ KillerStartUps: www.killerstartups.com

Venturing into the world of venture capital

Venture capital (VC) funding isn't the easiest route for securing money for your business. Maybe you remember the stories of the dot-com era when millions of dollars were thrown haphazardly into Internet start-ups. Well, in spite of that bursting bubble, venture capitalists are still out in force; getting their money, however, is much more difficult now.

To be honest, we don't recommend even considering venture capital as a resource for a brand-new company. This type of funding is designed for businesses that need an aggressive (or very large) amount of money to support the next level of business growth. Venture capitalists are institutional investors (professionally managed funds) that invest anywhere from $500,000 to $10 million or more in a company. Most often, this investment is made in preparation for an initial public offering (IPO) on the stock market, a sale, or a merger with another company.

Suppose that you're thinking big and are intrigued by venture capital as a funding source. How do you know whether your company is ready to pursue VC money? Although the funding criteria vary among venture capitalists, most of them generally expect the following from your company (and you):

✦ **The company has already used seed money.** Your company is long past the point of obtaining money from friends and family as part of its start-up stage. Seeking money from a venture capitalist means that you have already received additional rounds of financing from angel investors and are now ready for a more substantial investment boost.

✦ **The company has a proven track record.** Establishing a history of success is a necessity for venture funding. Investors expect your company to have experience under its belt and proof of the underlying business concept. Having an offline (bricks-and-mortar) business that has verifiable financial records greatly increases your success of finding funding.

✦ **An experienced management team is in place.** Being the sole employee of a company isn't a good thing when you're seeking venture capital. Instead, you *must* have a seasoned team of executives with the experience to take your company to the next level.

✦ **The company is in a hot industry.** Venture capitalists invest in more than a company — they invest in an industry. And some industries or markets are hotter than others at any given time. Your business doesn't have to be in the top three industries of interest, although it certainly improves your chances for funding.

✦ **The company is in a high-growth stage.** Securing venture capital means that your company is no longer in an early growth stage. It's now positioned for significant earnings. Although the amount can vary, a good rule is that your company can achieve annual revenues of $25 million within a five-year time frame.

✦ **You're willing to relinquish control.** If you don't have in place a top-notch team of heavy hitters (including yourself), relinquishing executive control may become a condition of funding. If you previously held the title of CEO and president, you can expect to be replaced by an outsider of the venture capitalist's choosing.

If you're serious about pursuing venture capital, you should do a few things first:

1. Start making connections early.

   Go to seminars on venture capital funding (usually sponsored by professional organizations in your community) and meet the venture capitalists involved in giving the presentations.

2. Contact other companies that have recently secured funding.

   Seek out other small businesses and ask for referrals to VC firms. In addition, ask questions and get a general understanding of what the process may be like for a company similar to yours.

3. As you're building these networks, start your own form of recordkeeping.

   Securing venture capital is a tedious, time-intensive process. The sooner you begin to understand the process, the more likely you are to be successful.

4. Begin making a list of potential venture capital firms.

   Keep track of the companies in which they invest, how much they invest, and in which industries they most actively invest.

When you're ready, two established resources can assist you in locating and learning about venture capital firms that might be a good match for your business:

✦ ***The Directory of Venture Capital & Private Equity Firms, 2014 Edition*:** This extensive guide, at `www.greyhouse.com/venture.htm`, offers direct access to more than 3,000 venture capital and private equity firms worldwide. In addition to presenting basic overview information about each firm, the guide also lists extensive contact information, including phone numbers and e-mail addresses. Grey House Publishing, the publisher, offers a hardbound copy and an online database by paid subscription.

✦ ***The Money Tree Report:*** This quarterly report lists detailed information about venture capital funding in the United States. It's a collaborative effort between PricewaterhouseCoopers and the National Venture Capital Association with data from Thomson Reuters. For information, and to review the quarterly reports, visit the website at www. pwcmoneytree.com.

Check your local library and used books sold through Amazon for a copy of either resource on this list. Although you may get a slightly older edition of the book, you can save the out-of-pocket cost of several hundred dollars that you would spend for a more current edition, and many of these resources stick around for a while.

During economic downturns or when the economy is generally weakened, both venture capitalists and angel investors become increasingly selective about where and how they invest. Having a solid business plan with a strong road map to a return on investment becomes even more important.

Checking Out Alternative Financing

When all else fails, a diligent online entrepreneur still has a few alternative financing options, although they are not necessarily your best choice. These options can help you open your doors for business, so to speak. Many times, you end up combining a variety of these sources to fund your great idea:

✦ **Credit card:** For better or worse, a credit card is a popular choice for funding a business. More than 80 percent of small businesses have used personal and business credit cards as a source of money, according to the Small Business Administration (SBA). Especially during economic periods when lending tightens from banks and other traditional resources, credit cards can sometimes provide the only source of fast cash for a new or growing business. Although credit cards may be a quick and easy alternative, they can also be expensive. Some credit card companies charge interest at 20 percent or more. In addition, they can slap you with hefty fees for late payments or for exceeding your credit limit. Financial advisors also caution that fully paying down the balance of your credit cards can take decades when you're making only the minimum monthly payments.

Consider moving balances with high interest terms to another card. Credit card companies often offer limited introductory low- or no-interest rates for transferring your balances from other cards. If these offers don't come in the mail, don't be afraid to call credit card companies (including your existing one) to negotiate for a better rate.

✦ **Retirement cash:** A personal savings plan, such as a 401(k), has long been a source of money for someone opening a start-up business. Before draining your account, consider the penalties for early withdrawal and seek advice from your accountant on the pros and cons of this source of funding.

✦ **Crowdfunding:** A few years ago, a new and amazingly successful fund-raising source hit the Internet. *Crowdfunding* works as its name indicates and allows almost anyone to invest in a creative project or business. Establish how much funding you want to raise and a period of time in which the project must be funded. You can allow people to fund anywhere from a few dollars to a few thousand dollars. Funding investments are paid out only if the project is fully funded in the specified time period. You also provide a return on the investment based on the funding level, such as a product prototype, early access or beta access to a solution, or even a small number of shares in the company.

Several crowdfunding sites make it easy to set up funding projects. Some popular sites are Kickstarter, Indiegogo, and Peerbackers. Typically, the site takes a small percentage of your total funds raised if the project is successfully funded. Although these sites expose you to a much wider audience of potential investors, often the investments still come largely from people you know. Still, crowdfunding is a terrific alternative source of funding for your online business.

✦ **Home equity loan:** Depending on the state of the housing market and interest rates on various types of home loans, you may be able to use your home as a funding source for your business. As a homeowner, you can cash out the equity in your house, use it for other purposes, and pay it back at a fixed interest rate over 5, 10, 15 or more years. Similarly, you can refinance your home and use the additional funds for starting the business. Another option is to open a home equity line of credit, which gives you a fixed amount of money that you're approved to borrow. You take out the money only as you need it, rather than in one lump sum. However, all these options have become increasingly difficult to obtain after the banking and housing meltdown of 2008. Now you must have fantastic credit scores, among other things, to qualify for a loan. In addition, housing values in some areas are still climbing back up after bottoming out, leaving folks with little wiggle room for financing options.

Borrowing money against your house is always risky! Many business experts hesitate to recommend this method as an option because you could lose your home. Consult with your accountant, or other financial advisors, before making this decision.

✦ **High-interest loan:** Some specialized lenders finance loans (even high-risk ones if you have poor credit) at high interest rates. These rates are usually similar to, or higher than, credit card rates. When all other options fail, this method may be a possibility; be cautious, though, about taking this route.

✦ **Microloan:** If you're looking for a smaller amount of capital, the SBA has a microloan program for amounts up to $50,000. The average loan size is approximately $13,000. The loans are backed by the SBA but are distributed and managed by local, approved community lenders. As with any loan, there are collateral requirements, but funds can be used for working capital, equipment, inventory, and supplies. To find out who offers loans in your area, contact your state or regional SBA office or visit `www.sba.gov`.

✦ **Grant or award:** If your business concept is innovative, you may want to search out grant opportunities or contests offering financial rewards. *Grants* are monetary awards that you don't have to repay. Some organizations — such as business magazines, office-supply chains, and other large retailers — sponsor business-plan-writing contests with financial payoffs or award cash and prizes as part of their general business contests. No all-in-one resource tracks all sources of grants and awards, but Biz Plan Competitions (at `www.bizplancompetitions.com`) provides a list of business plan competitions based in the United States. Otherwise, you have to do your homework by diligently searching the Internet and thumbing through business publications for opportunities. However, the shot at free money may be well worth your time.

Be wary of websites that charge for a list of "free money" resources from government grants. Although legitimate grants are available, you don't have to pay for them: You can obtain a list for free from the Catalog of Federal Government Assistance at the U.S. government's grant site (`www.grants.gov`), shown in Figure 4-3.

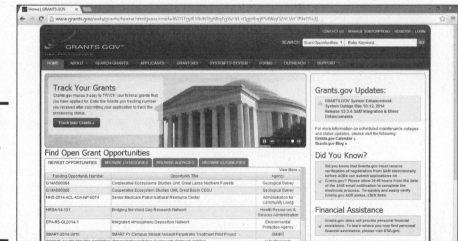

Figure 4-3: Check out Grants.gov for any potential grants for which you can apply.

✦ **Incubator:** This type of entity or organization, established to support entrepreneurial development, usually provides shared resources for businesses. Sometimes, a *shared resource* refers to a physical location (such as an office building) or access to volunteer or hired professionals who are shared by the organization's entrepreneurs. Although incubators don't traditionally provide start-up money, they're still considered an alternative funding source because they provide your business with a range of tools, resources, and services. Many types of incubators with different levels of services are available. Examples range from offering free support (such as educational workshops and training for entrepreneurs) to providing shared workspaces or office space for a reduced fee. Depending on the arrangement, incubators may require a small percentage of ownership in your business, ask for stock options, or charge a small fee for services. In most cases, this situation results in a nominal expense to you compared to other funding options. The amount of savings and the invaluable assistance (which can accelerate the growth of your business) translates into a wise investment of your start-up dollars.

Locate technology and small-business incubators in your area by contacting the National Business Incubation Association at `www.nbia.org`.

Taking a Shortcut: Purchasing an Existing Site

Securing financing for an online business takes time and persistence — no doubt about it. If you're interested in a completely different path, you can take a shortcut. Have you considered purchasing an existing website? Don't get excited — you don't have to march up the virtual steps of Amazon or eBay and put an offer on the table. (To be realistic, you'd be laughed right out the door.) Somewhere between the people dreaming of starting a business and the giants dominating the Internet, hundreds of thousands of other mom-and-pop businesses have already established a small presence online. Many of them are doing quite well, others are struggling, and some just don't have any sense of direction. Those latter categories provide you with the largest opportunity to jump-start your online dreams. Check out the following sites, which provide lists of online businesses for sale:

✦ **Shopify E-Commerce Sites for Sale (`https://ecommerce.shopify.com/c/ecommerce-job-board`):** This site is an extension of the e-commerce storefront solution, Shopify (`www.shopify.com`). In addition to providing the tools needed to start an e-commerce site, Shopify also provides a forum for buyers and sellers. It's a place to advertise existing storefronts that are for sale or to post a message indicated your interest in buying an existing site.

✦ **BizQuest (`www.bizquest.com`):** Claiming to be one of the original business-for-sale websites, BizQuest has a healthy number of business listing in all categories. To get the most relevant list of available online businesses, use their search tool to search for the term *Internet*. Last time we checked, this search term returned nearly 20 pages of results for available Internet businesses for sale.

✦ **Website Properties** (`www.websiteproperties.com`): Unlike traditional business brokers, Website Properties specializes in just that — websites. You can search a list of available sites directly from their site, and you can easily and immediately view a great deal of information about available sites, without having to request access to the details from a broker.

What makes an existing site a smart purchase?

Buying an existing online business is basically the same as purchasing any other type of business: You have to do your homework and determine whether the purchase is a wise one. Find answers to these questions about a business before you sign on the dotted line:

✔ Is the online business a viable business model?

✔ Does the purchase include existing inventory or customer contracts?

✔ Even though the site is established, does its concept pass your feasibility test?

✔ Is the site generating revenue? How much? (Ask for financial statements verified by a certified public accountant.)

✔ What expenses does it incur?

✔ Can you reduce the amount of overhead by making different management decisions?

✔ Can you increase the percentage of profit by making different management decisions? If so, how long would it take to implement these changes?

✔ When was the site established?

✔ What is the annual percentage of revenue growth? (How much more money does it make over the previous year?)

✔ How many people visit the site each day? (Ask for verification.)

✔ Does the owner maintain any logs or records verifying the number of visitors and other stats?

✔ What are the site's popularity rankings in all the major search engines?

✔ What, if anything, has the owner previously done to increase rankings?

✔ Has the site been featured in any magazines or other websites?

✔ How many other websites link to this site, and vice versa?

✔ If a product is being sold, does the site use a dedicated supplier? Are other supplier sources available?

✔ If the site sells an information product or is a service business, do you have the skills and staff to duplicate it?

✔ Does the site have a poor reputation or many unhappy customers?

✔ Is the site in good standing with the Better Business Bureau and other organizations?

✔ Does it have a current business license?

✔ Are its taxes current?

✔ Has its URL expired, or is it about to?

✔ Does it have a valid Secure Sockets Layer (SSL) certificate to allow protected, properly encrypted transactions over the Internet?

✔ Which hardware and software, if any, are included with the sale?

✔ Do you gain any proprietary software in purchasing the site?

✔ Why is the current owner willing to sell?

✔ Can you create your own site and generate similar results in a short time for less than the selling price?

Stop dreaming, and take a look at the benefits of scooping up an existing site to launch your business. You can

✦ **Override start-up costs:** Finding an existing online business means that you don't have to worry about all the initial costs and hassles of getting the site started. Maintaining or building an existing site is usually cheaper than starting from scratch.

✦ **Eliminate time to market:** Although you may have a business up and running in just a few weeks, establishing yourself in the market and gaining a presence in the search engines takes much longer. Buying a ready-made site (even a fledgling one) removes at least some of this concern.

✦ **Gain established customer base:** The "build it and they will come" theory has repeatedly been disproved when applied to websites. Purchasing an online business with existing customers is a definite perk.

To make sure that the site you're considering buying has real value when it comes to customers, ask to see proof of a current e-mail list or database of customers or members (not just a log of daily visitors).

✦ **Get a site for a steal:** Do your homework and you can purchase a site for little money. Look for businesses in which the owners

• Are tired or bored of the site

• Have no time to maintain it

• Ran out of money after putting the basics in place

• Are in a cash crunch

These factors don't necessarily mean that the business is bad — just that it was under poor management.

✦ **Negotiate payment terms, with no out-of-pocket costs:** Even if you end up with a large (but reasonable) price tag, you still have a money-saving alternative. For instance, offer to make a small down payment on the site. Then let the owner know that you will make monthly payments until the balance of the sale price is paid in full. (If the site is producing revenue, you can use a portion of that income to cover the payments, so only the deposit comes out of your pocket.)

✦ **Lease to own:** In this strategy, the seller retains ownership of the site and you manage it. You pay the owner a set monthly fee, plus a percentage of the profits, until the sale price is paid.

Chapter 5: Creating Policies to Protect Your Website and Your Customers

In This Chapter

✔ Establishing a customer service pledge

✔ Developing policies for operating your business

✔ Delivering the goods as promised

C ustomers are the reason you're in business. All too often, though, their role in your success is an afterthought. Even though you spend a great deal of time thinking about what they can do for you, sometimes you forget about what they expect of you, until a problem surfaces.

In this chapter, we show you how to invest the proper time into the "care and feeding" of your most important business asset — your customer.

Taking Care of Customers

Consider the process of starting your business. You think about your future customers, right? You anticipate who will buy your product. You research their needs and painstakingly detail how to meet those needs in your business plan. You develop a marketing plan that explains how to reach your customers, and you calculate, dollar for dollar, how their spending translates into profit for you. Something is missing, though: Where in all that research and planning is your pledge to your customers — your vow of how you will treat them? Most business plans don't include this type of pledge, unless one of your company's competitive advantages is defined as an unprecedented level of customer service.

I pledge to you

What is a customer pledge, and how do you develop one? A *pledge* to your customers is a *written* guideline of what they can expect when doing business with you. The pledge should be the basis of your overall customer service philosophy.

Start your customer service pledge internally, and make it something used only by you. From there, you can create an external (public) customer service pledge.

Put it in writing

How do you create a customer pledge? Here are a few simple steps you can follow to get going:

1. Answer a few general questions about how you really feel about customers (be honest!):

    • How do you view your customers? Do you know them personally or speak with them on the phone, or are they anonymous?

    • How important are customers to you and your business?

    • How important is repeat business?

    • What are you willing to do for customers every single day?

    • What are you *not* willing to do for your customers?

2. Define realistic parameters of how you plan to communicate with your customers every day, as shown in these two examples:

    How can customers contact you? Can they

    • Send e-mail 24 hours a day?

    • Call a toll-free phone number and leave a message 24 hours a day, or call a long-distance number during set business hours?

    • Send or post a message on social media 24/7?

    • Write a letter and send it by snail mail (through the U.S. Postal Service)?

    When and how will you respond to customers?

    • Immediately when you respond only by e-mail?

    • Within 24 hours (or less) when you respond by phone, e-mail, or social media?

3. Identify what, if anything, is special about the way you treat customers. For example, do you call customers personally to make sure that they received their orders? Or do you invite them to regular online sessions to discuss how your products or services could improve?

4. Draft a written document detailing your customer service pledge for your internal use. The document can consist of a short list of bullets or several paragraphs based on your previous answers. This guideline is your personal reminder of how you incorporate customers into your business every day.

5. Write a pledge to your customer. The pledge, which can be as general or specific as you choose, should reflect your internal customer service philosophy but be a written document that can be read and judged by the customer about how your business responds.

Putting Policies in Place

As you might expect, creating your customer service pledge is only the beginning of the customer care policy. To manage your online business successfully and legitimately, you have to put several policies in place. The government mandates some policies, and others are the result of common sense to minimize confusion for yourself, your employees, and the people with whom you do business. For example, when working with franchise organizations, one of the most critical components of doing business is the *policy manual,* a small booklet filled with written policies establishing an unwavering set of guidelines and procedures for operating. The policy manual serves as an easy reference tool when you have questions about how to operate.

Policies are equally important to customers, employees, and vendors. Although you don't have to create a formal manual filled with your policies, you must write them down somewhere. In many cases, you should also publish them on your website, to protect yourself from misunderstandings and reassure your customers about how you do business.

Privacy policy

A *privacy policy* details how you collect, treat, and use the information you receive from customers and from other people who visit your website. This policy not only covers information that customers knowingly provide but also applies to the use of *cookies,* or the information files that web servers create to track data about people and the online sites they visit. Your privacy policy should clearly state your commitment to customer privacy and data security. The Better Business Bureau offers tips for writing an effective privacy policy; go to www.bbb.org/Global/Minneapolis_MN_147/documents/BBB_Privacy Policy2013.pdf.

A privacy policy is a requirement for your online business if you're based in the United States. The U.S. government's Federal Trade Commission (FTC) mandates this policy. The policy must be properly labeled on your website and easily accessible within your site.

Your privacy policy should include these elements as well:

✦ A description of *how* you collect information from your site visitors and customers

✦ Details of *what* information you collect

✦ An explanation of what you do with the information and how and where you store it

✦ A disclosure of with whom you might share customer information

✦ Instructions for how visitors or customers can change their information or remove it from your records

Your policy on how you handle a customer's credit card data should be in line with the requirements of the Payment Card Industry Data Security Standard (PCI DSS). As an online retailer, you're required to comply with certain regulations for handling and storing sensitive customer data under the PCI DSS, or else you could face a steep financial penalty. The PCI Security Standards Council provides up-to-date information for online retailers. To find out more, visit www.pcisecuritystandards.org.

User agreement or terms and conditions

Increasingly, sites are implementing user agreements. Just like a written contract, this agreement specifies terms or conditions by which you allow visitors or customers to use your site. You might choose to post on your site a static (unchanging) page that simply lists these points. A more legally binding version of this agreement, however, requires visitors to acknowledge that they have read the terms and agree to abide by them. Usually, before visitors are allowed to go to certain areas of your site or make a purchase, they're forced to click a button verifying that they agree to the terms.

When you're creating your site's terms and conditions, you should include this information:

✦ **How visitors or customers can or cannot use your site:** Rules that apply to not only your customers but also your employees, such as posting personal information (phone numbers or physical addresses, for example) on a discussion forum

✦ **Who is allowed to view your site:** Whether visitors meet age or U.S. citizenship requirements, for example

✦ **Which other policies are in place:** Shipping, returns, or complaint procedures, for example

✦ **Legal and liability issues:** For example, details of responsibility by you and third parties for providing information and taking actions, and for specifying geographic location where legal disputes will be settled

Shipping policy

Your shipping policy should clearly explain the details of how and when customer orders are handled and shipped. Although you can determine some conditions of this policy, you must also comply with the FTC's mail or telephone-order merchandise rule.

According to the FTC, your online site must

✦ Ship an order within the timeframe you promised at the time of ordering or as stated in your advertising or on your website.

✦ Ship a product within 30 days after it's received, unless you specify an earlier timeframe.

Most online retailers ship products within seven business days at the longest. The exception is when a product is on back order, out of stock, or available for pre-order (in which case, an approximate shipping date is given). The FTC rule sets the maximum limits of what's acceptable for shipping products.

✦ Give notice to a consumer as fast as possible whenever you cannot ship that person's product when promised.

✦ Include a revised shipping date in the delay notice you send to a customer.

✦ Allow a customer to agree to a delay or to cancel an order and provide a description of the time required for a refund.

Return policy

Include in your return policy the conditions under which you allow customers to return a product or decline a service. Will the customer receive a full or partial refund from you? A good policy should protect both you and your customers. Be specific about your return policy so that customers clearly understand (and aren't surprised by) your rules. Your policy should include these elements:

✦ **Time limit:** Set the maximum number of days within which a return will be accepted.

✦ **Conditions of use:** Maintain the right to reject a return if an item shows obvious signs of use, for example.

✦ **Restock fee:** Explain any fees incurred by restocking a returned item.

✦ **Exceptions:** Specify any items that cannot be returned.

✦ **Shipping responsibility:** Determine who pays for the cost of shipping when a product is returned.

✦ **Refunds issued as cash or credit:** Decide whether to issue store credit rather than give cash back.

✦ **Third-party rules:** Direct customers to consult the return policies of third-party vendors if you sell their items.

As e-commerce grows, so does the problem of customers taking advantage of online retailers. Let your return policy protect you by limiting the number of days you agree to accept returns. Customers must have enough time to evaluate products (three to five days is a reasonable length of time) but not use it indefinitely before demanding their money back.

When you're selling products through a third-party vendor, such as a storefront or an auction site (for example, Etsy or eBay), be sure to check whether the company has a mandated return policy. The vendor site's policy can override your internal return policy.

Safety for young users

Whether or not you plan to sell to children, establish a policy about minors. If your site is targeted to children under 13 years old, has a separate section for kids, or is a general site but you know kids access it, your website must comply with the FTC's Children's Online Privacy Protection Act, or COPPA. The policy was updated in 2013 to expand the definition of the types of sites and businesses that must comply. COPPA also specifies additional permissions that must be obtained from parents, especially involving the use of video, social media, and online games or apps. See compliance details at `www.business.ftc.gov/documents/bus84-childrens-online-privacy-protection-rule-six-step-compliance-plan-your-business`. Generally speaking, the COPPA rule requires you to

✦ Post a clear and comprehensive privacy policy on your website.

✦ Notify parents about how you collect information.

✦ Get parental consent before collecting information.

✦ Allow parents to see the information you collect about their children and let the parents change or delete details.

✦ Maintain the confidentiality, security, and integrity of the information you collect.

Other online policies

Following are other polices you may want to include on your website:

✦ **Forum or chat room policies:** In these areas of your site, visitors and customers can share their opinions, ideas, and concerns. If your site offers these communication options, set up some basic guidelines for how you operate each one. Your policy should specify such items as who can participate and whether someone must register (or sign in as a member) first. Also, indicate who is monitoring these activities and in what manner. The policy should clearly specify which type of material is inappropriate for posting, and how and when you might remove it.

✦ **Social media:** When you ask customers to engage with you through social media sites, such as Facebook and Twitter, or even on your blog, these external sites should be considered an extension of your business presence. After all, on these sites you might obtain information about your customers, such as contact information upon registration for contests and polls. We recommend that you develop a social media policy that explains how your customers' personal information will or will not be used after it is collected.

✦ **Exporting:** If your site sells to customers outside the United States, you might be subject to special government regulations by the Commerce Department and Defense Department and possibly other departments. What you sell (or export) and to which countries you sell might be tightly regulated. If you believe that this is the case with your business, seek advice from your attorney about developing an exporting policy.

✦ **Spam:** Depending on your type of business, you can include a spam policy in your privacy policy. This policy states whether or not your site distributes marketing e-mail and how you respond to it.

✦ **Endorsement and linking to other sites' policies:** Whether you sell products or services from other sites, provide links to sites not owned by you, or allow other sites to link to yours, you're smart to notify customers about it. Your linking policy should simply state how external links are used and whether you endorse the information found on these linked sites. Provide customers with a way to notify you of problems with external sites or violations to your policy.

Delivering On Your Promises

After you establish your basic principles of operation, you have to deliver on them. *Executing,* or following through, on the policies you create isn't easy, but it's essential for several reasons. These policies represent promises to your customers and determine what customers come to expect from you. Failing to meet these expectations compromises your reputation and, ultimately, eats away at your sales.

Equally important are the consequences when you fail to deliver and then incur a legal liability. The government mandates and monitors several policies. Even a small oversight can land you in hot water with both your customers and federal laws.

Nobody's perfect, and you might fail to deliver on a promise now and then. If you fail, be sure to follow these steps:

1. Notify your customer immediately.

2. Apologize for your mistake.

3. Correct the problem.

4. Offer a partial or full refund, a free gift, or a discount on future purchases.

Chapter 6: Setting Up Shop: Everything You Need for Online Efficiency

In This Chapter

✔ **Organizing your workspace**

✔ **Stocking your office with necessary equipment**

✔ **Maximizing the power of your computer**

✔ **Selecting applications to enhance desktop performance**

✔ **Choosing software to increase productivity**

✔ **Identifying the best method for accessing Internet service**

For some of us, setting up a new office is part of the fun and excitement of starting a new business. It makes it "real," so to speak. But you should plan your office space also for the practical reasons of budgeting start-up costs, gaining a more efficient and functional work area, and ensuring that you have the adequate tools to build your online business and service your customers. From the chair you sit in to your filing system, you need to spend a little time setting up your office with the correct equipment and software, as well as Internet access. (That last one is obvious, eh?) Spending time up front on your workspace options and business requirements can save you plenty of time — and money — later.

A Floor Plan for Success

You might work from a cramped bedroom in your modest home or in a spacious high-rise office complex. Either way, maximizing your workspace can be an important step toward obtaining true efficiency in your business.

Follow these steps to create a floor plan for your office space:

1. **Make a list of how you will use your space.**

   Ask yourself these questions:

   - Do I need a desk? If so, how much desk space do I need?

   - Will I store paperwork and files in a central filing system or use some other method?

- Do I need storage space for inventory? Do I have a dedicated space for packing and shipping products?

- Will customers visit my office?

- Do I need working space for employees?

2. **Make a list of all your office furniture, equipment, and accessories (including office supplies and other items that should be stored but remain accessible).**

If you're sharing the space with others, make sure that you account for their belongings too. Or, if your office performs double duty as a bedroom or dining room, include on your list the non-work-related furniture that will remain in the room while you work.

3. **On a sheet of paper, sketch out the dimensions of the room with lines that represent your walls, and then draw all your furniture and large office equipment in position within those walls.**

Rather than literally draw your furniture, you can draw different shapes and label them to help plan the placement of furniture, equipment, and designated work areas.

4. **Arrange the furniture and office equipment in a way that best meets your needs, based on the list you created in Step 1.**

This arrangement should be based on function.

After your room has been put on paper, based on how you want it to function, you can put the measurements to the test to confirm your furniture and equipment fit (see Figure 6-1). This level of detail may seem like overkill, but it's particularly important if you plan to lease office space (in which case, the less you need, the lower your overhead).

When you arrange your furniture, address storage needs for your office supplies. If you don't have designated architectural space (such as a closet or built-in bookshelves), you'll have to bring in storage (for example, file cabinets, baskets, and removable shelving).

5. **Measure all pieces of furniture and major equipment.**

Using the room dimensions listed on your paper, compare measurements to see whether everything fits. If you run out of room, keep trying different arrangements until you find a floor plan that fits both your needs and your measurements.

Instead of working from a cramped home office all the time or leasing expensive office space, consider a shared coworking space. Often found in larger cities, coworking spaces have open office areas designed for technology start-ups and other small businesses. These low-cost alternatives include standard needs, such as meeting spaces and Internet connectivity, and also boasts extras, such as access to networking events with peers and investors.

**Book I
Chapter 6**

Setting Up Shop:
Everything You
Need for Online
Efficiency

Figure 6-1:
Precise measure-ments ensure that everything fits in your space.

Must-Have Equipment

You no longer have to invest several thousand dollars in big, clunky pieces of equipment because both the size and the price of these items have dropped tremendously. For example, an all-in-one item such as a fax, copier, printer, and scanner combination costs less and takes less space than separate pieces of equipment. Also available are cloud-based offerings, which provide access to web-based products and services at low monthly (or annual) rates. Typically, you don't sign a contract, so you have the flexibility to drop or change ser-vices. In addition, free and low-cost applications (apps) for mobile devices such as smartphones and tablets can replace some standard office equipment or services. All this serves as further testament to the power of the Internet, and how easy and affordable it is to start an online business.

Make form follow function

Rather than think about your office equipment in terms of a collection of cartridges and cords, think of each piece in terms of the function it provides. You need access to some key functions (equipment) to run a business.

This list describes the functions most businesses need access to most often:

✦ **Printing:** Although most of your correspondence can be conducted online, you still need to print invoices, offline marketing materials, and hard copies (printouts) of items for your files. You can choose from different types of free-standing or desktop printers with various capabilities. Printers can range from $20 to $250.

Rather than compare only printer functions, be sure to also compare ink cartridge requirements before you buy a printer. An ink cartridge is often almost as expensive as the printer itself; a $50 printer can require a $30 ink cartridge, for example. Be sure to find out whether the printer requires a particular brand of cartridge and how much the cartridges for that printer cost.

✦ **Faxing:** Sending a fax, or facsimile, may seem less like a necessity, in part due to the use of e-mail and mobile applications to send documents. The use and legal acceptance of electronic signatures has also decreased dependency on faxes. But some industries and businesses still require a fax. Rather than purchase a separate fax machine, consider buying fax software (so that your computer acts as the fax) or sign up for a web-based fax service and receive faxes as attachments to your e-mail. Services such as eFax (www.efax.com) and MyFax (www.myfax.com) offer complete fax solutions for as little as $10–$15 a month.

When comparing online fax services, make sure that you can send and receive faxes from your iPhone, BlackBerry, Android, or other smartphone. Also be aware of fees charged for overages of incoming and outgoing pages, fees for additional users, and limits on storage timeframes and volume for faxes sent or received.

✦ **Copying:** Having access to a small copier can be a good investment for your office. When you shop for a copier, decide which features you need:

  • Do you want color printing, or is black-and-white print suitable?

  • Will you use a *duplexing* feature, which prints both the front and back of the page?

  • Is *collating* (automatically stacking and binding papers as they print) a big deal?

Also look for copiers that

  • Add large amounts of paper to trays at one time so that you're not continually refilling them

  • Have a quick warm-up time (the time it takes the equipment to prepare to print) so that you can start copying quickly

  • Are suitable for small to mid-size print job volumes

✦ **Scanning:** A scanner enables you to scan images or documents into your computer for manipulation or storage or to send as files or faxes to others. This piece of equipment is particularly useful when you

**Book I
Chapter 6**

Setting Up Shop:
Everything You
Need for Online
Efficiency

frequently work with photos and other images. Most scanners come with custom software you must install. (Or try the Windows Scanner and Camera Wizard, in the Windows Control Panel.) You can choose from several types of scanners, each with different capabilities and resolutions. Some are designed for use with color; and some may have mobile options.

If you need a scanner for only documents (not images), consider downloading a scanner app for your mobile phone. Apps are available for both iPhone and Android and provide the capability to scan documents and then e-mail, fax, or print directly from your phone. You can also share scanned files to DropBox, Google Drive, or Evernote. (Use this method to track business receipts, too.) Try Scanner Pro, ShareScan Pro, or TinyScan Pro. The apps range in price from $2 to $8. Or you can get a less robust scanner app for free.

✦ **Mobile communications:** Cell phones have gone from being nice-to-have to being a must-have. Specifically, you need a smartphone that's capable of accessing various applications for maximum efficiency, whether or not you're in your office. You might even require a tablet (such as an iPad), too. These devices are important tools to help you manage your online business. Moreover, online consumers are researching and purchasing products and services directly from mobile devices, so you need to be able to test functionality and accessibility of your website from those devices.

✦ **Business communications:** Today, you have several options for using a phone in your business. For example, some business owners opt to go without a landline (traditional phone line) and use only a cellular (or mobile) phone. Others save money by sharing a residential line with both their home and business. (This option can be tricky and can come across as unprofessional.) You may consider opting for VoIP (Voice over Internet Protocol), an IP-based option that allows you to share data and voice over a single line. Web-based options, such as Google Voice and WebRTC applications, also allow you to make calls over your computer. Most cable companies are offering to bundle your Internet service and voice service. (We discuss Internet connectivity options in more detail at the end of this chapter.) Going this route is often much less expensive than using traditional phone lines and can provide a wider range of functionality. At the end of the day, know that you have lots of options when it comes to how you communicate with your customers.

✦ **Digital photography:** You might not be used to including a camera in the category of business tools. Yet, in building and maintaining an online business, a digital camera and a video camera might be a requirement, especially if you have an eBay store or any other online retail type of store. Cameras are increasingly important with the growing use of social media as a marketing tool. Sharing pictures on social networks such as Pinterest or Instagram or uploading YouTube, for example, is almost a necessity. At the very least, you need a camera to take product pictures that you can upload to your site. (Some smartphones may be suitable for taking video or pictures to share on social media, but a better quality camera is preferable for high-resolution product pictures for use on your website.)

✦ **Shredding:** Considering the rise in identity theft (we discuss this in Book V, Chapter 1), disposing of documents that contain sensitive information — such as billing statements with account numbers or credit card numbers — is more important than ever. Shredding these documents is an easy way to protect your business — and cuts down on storage. A small, portable shredder can be purchased for less than $50; a shredder designed to handle large volumes of paper may cost several hundred dollars or more. It may be worth the extra expense to get a shredder that's hefty enough to dispose of credit cards and DVDs (which you may use to store sensitive data). Data thieves consider both items to be valuable finds.

Before destroying all your documents, be mindful of any business records that the IRS requires you to keep for tax purposes. In Book II, Chapter 4, we review which type of documents must be kept and for how long. Consult a tax advisor if you're not certain about how long you should keep some business records.

If you can't afford to purchase all your equipment right away, locate a small-business service center close to your office. These centers offer fax, printing, binding, and other services at competitive prices. You can find these service centers in copy stores, such as FedEx Office, or in retail office-supply stores, such as Staples. If you rent a shared office space, or coworking space, these business tools and services are often included as part of the monthly rent.

Revving up with a powerful computer

One important piece of equipment for your new online business is a computer. It's the heart and soul of your office because all your valuable data resides on it and you use it to communicate with folks in all kinds of ways. How do you know whether your existing computer makes the grade now that you're an online entrepreneur? Should you upgrade or buy new? If you buy a new one, how can you be sure that you're investing your dollars wisely? And most importantly, should you buy a PC or a Mac? Although those questions are tricky, they have simple answers.

Jumping into the upgrade-versus-purchase debate

Overall, the cost of purchasing a basic PC computer is outrageously low. You probably receive promotions advertising new desktop computers for $299 — or less. By the time you calculate your time or pay somebody else's labor fee and buy parts, can you truly upgrade an existing computer for that price?

Book I
Chapter 6

Setting Up Shop:
Everything You
Need for Online
Efficiency

Not so fast. You have to compare apples to apples by looking at more than just the price tag. Compare capabilities. That off-the-shelf computer for $299 may be a bare-bones, stripped-down model — probably no more powerful than that old machine you used for the past couple of years. Sure, the new one might work a bit faster; to get comparable features, though, you most likely have to add memory, hardware, and other applications to truly address your needs. By the time you upgrade your new computer, you may have sufficiently passed its original $300 off-the-shelf price threshold to make you reconsider buying new. Whether or not it's truly a bargain depends on the functionality and power you need.

If you have the skills and the comfort level to take apart your computer, add components, and then put Humpty Dumpty together again, upgrading can be a cheap and relatively easy solution.

Taking the plunge: Buying new

You might be more comfortable buying a computer with all its parts already assembled. You can still design a custom computer by choosing the options you want and letting a computer retailer customize it for you. Or you can purchase an off-the-shelf machine that's already loaded and ready to go.

Desktop or laptop: Deciding on a computer

Even if you're sold on the sleek, compact size of a laptop, consider the following four Cs before you make a final purchase:

✔ **Cost:** Although desktop computers can be bulky, they're packed with options at rock-bottom prices. Comparatively, you pay for the convenience and size that a laptop offers. It's usually double the price of a desktop with similar capabilities.

✔ **Capability:** You can run the same applications on both a desktop and a laptop. If you work with a lot of graphics, though, the laptop screen might not do them justice. When you're working in one location, you can connect your laptop to a larger monitor, of course — just remember that the monitor costs extra!

✔ **Convenience:** Putting a price tag on convenience is difficult. Whether you need to tote your computer from room to room or from city to city, a laptop is your best portable solution.

✔ **Comfort:** Adjusting to a smaller screen size, a button-size mouse, and a more compact keyboard isn't always easy. Although you can attach a USB mouse or keyboard to a laptop to overcome this problem, you might be more comfortable with the larger components offered on a desktop.

Some laptops are just as powerful and full-featured as desktops. They're slightly larger and heavier, with wider screens and full-size keyboards. Although they can be considered portable, the size and weight put them closer to desktops than laptops.

How do you decide which computer is right for you? The simplest way to approach this decision is by backing into it. Follow these general guidelines:

1. **Decide how you will use the computer.**

   You're running a business with it, of course. Be specific about which type of activities you're using it for, such as accounting, word processing, keeping a database of customer records, or storing digital photos of your products.

2. **Identify the specific software applications you're using for each of those activities, such as Peachtree, Microsoft Word, Microsoft Access, or Photoshop.**

   Each of these applications recommends system requirements, including available memory and processor speed.

3. **Match and compare the requirements in Step 2 to the computer you're considering purchasing.**

   Look closely at not only the computer's processor but also the hardware and features that come with the computer, including these items:

   - Hard drive space
   - Operating system (Windows, Mac, Linux/Unix)
   - Memory capacity (RAM)
   - CD-ROM or DVD (+/- RW readable/writeable)
   - CD-ROM RW or DVD-RW (allows you to save data to a disc)
   - Modem
   - Networking card (preferably wireless-ready)
   - USB (2.0 or 3.0 compatibility)
   - Monitor (with the option for a flat screen)
   - Keyboard and mouse (wireless, to avoid clutter on your desktop)
   - External speakers
   - Installed software

4. **Compare the support service and warranties.**

   Does the manufacturer or retailer offer customer support? Be sure to find out whether this service is included in the cost of your purchase, and whether it limits the amount of support you can receive before a fee kicks in. Find out exactly what is covered under the warranty and for how long. You might have to purchase an extended warranty to cover some computer parts. Keep in mind that some manufacturers require you to ship back your hardware versus sending a repairperson to your location. Before making a purchase, determine whether on-site support is important to you.

Book I
Chapter 6

Setting Up Shop:
Everything You
Need for Online
Efficiency

Do you happen to have a computer with a small amount of memory? USB *memory sticks* are portable (and cheap) storage components that use external USB flash drives that plug in directly to your computer. You can then use them to transfer or store files. It's like having an extra hard drive, except this one can literally fit in your pocket — with room to spare! Memory sticks get smaller every day, and you can even attached to your keychain for easy portability. If you need to transfer data between computers, this tool is invaluable for your office. You can get a 16GB stick for less than $10.

Don't hesitate to minimize your learning curve before making your first computer purchase. Whether you are considering upgrading, buying new, or just sticking with what you have, learn more about your options by delving into *Troubleshooting and Maintaining Your PC All-in-One For Dummies*, 2nd Edition by Dan Gookin.

What about a Mac?

Computer users are always debating which personal computer is better for business owners: a PC or a Mac (Macintosh). The PC is usually associated with an operating system (OS) that runs Microsoft Windows; the Mac OS was created by Apple. For a long time, PCs seemed to be the preferred appliance for businesses, and Macs were favored by graphic artists. Today, either is acceptable for business use. With software compatibility for the Mac expanding, and Apple's explosive growth from the popularity of the iPhone and the iPad, business folks seem less reticent to use a Mac.

We don't want to get into a debate of which is better — that's for you to decide. But we do want to make you aware that you have options when purchasing a desktop computer.

If you are considering switching to a Mac or are ready to upgrade an existing Mac, you have lots to consider regarding which Mac is right for you and what programs to add. To help you navigate the world of Macs, dive into *Macs All-in-One For Dummies,* 4th Edition, by Joe Hutsko and Barbara Boyd.

Tools for Your Desktop

Your computer is unpacked. You're ready to explore a world of business opportunity. Before you dive in, make sure that you have these basic — but necessary — applications on your desktop, ready to run.

Inventory the built-in (supplied) programs to determine which ones work for you and which ones don't. Using the built-in software can save you money, but don't sacrifice your need for functionality by using an inferior product. Buy what you need to get your jobs done.

Searching for a web browser

Your *web browser* is the software that lets you travel from site to site across the Internet. You enter a site's address, or *URL (Uniform Resource Locator),* and the browser displays the site or page on your computer screen. For an online business, having a good web browser is an absolute requirement.

Statistics vary, but it's estimated that roughly 40 to 45 percent of computer users now choose Google's Chrome browser over the once popular Microsoft Internet Explorer. Mozilla's Firefox web browser, with its increased security features, is another consistent favorite.

Keep in mind that a browser is typically already included when you purchase a computer, although which browser varies based on your operating system. You can always download a different browser to your computer or update an older version of your existing browser. Get started downloading the browser of your choice by going to these websites:

✦ **Google Chrome:** www.google.com/chrome

✦ **Microsoft Internet Explorer:** www.microsoft.com

✦ **Mozilla Firefox:** www.mozilla.org

✦ **Opera:** www.opera.com

✦ **Safari:** www.apple.com/safari

Put access to all the major browsers on your desktop, especially as you begin creating and maintaining your business website. Then you can check for consistency among page views displayed with different browsers. For example, Internet Explorer might display your web page in a slightly different way than Mozilla. The difference might be subtle, or it might cause the loss of pertinent product information or graphics. (We talk about these and other web design details in Book III.)

Sending and receiving messages with e-mail

E-mail is a painless way to communicate with customers, vendors, and employees. Unfortunately, the popularity of this communication tool has led to a bigger problem: How do you keep up with, sort, store, and reply to all these messages? And what's the best way to combat spam, viruses, and other harmful or annoying applications to your inbox?

You can resolve these issues by finding a good e-mail program. In addition to acting as an organizer and a system for filtering junk mail, your e-mail system should be simple to use and pack a few added features.

One of these e-mail programs might meet your communication objectives:

Book I
Chapter 6

Setting Up Shop:
Everything You
Need for Online
Efficiency

✦ **Thunderbird:** The e-mail program designed by Mozilla automatically detects and sorts junk mail. Packed with features, it also offers an enhanced three-column view of your e-mail. Download Thunderbird for free at Mozilla.org (www.mozilla.org/products/thunderbird).

✦ **Gmail:** Google Gmail is a popular, free, web-based e-mail option. Gmail boasts one of the highest storage capacities (which means you don't have to delete old mail to make room for new mail) as well as offers some other cool features. In addition to one of the best spam-blocking capabilities, it can automatically sort messages based on conversations and uses tabs to further sort and categorize messages. Gmail also includes built-in chat. You can access your Gmail from your mobile phone by redirecting your phone's web browser to a Google app. Take a look for yourself at www.google.com/mail.

For only $50 per year (per user), Gmail offers businesses 30GB of storage per user to host their e-mail. The offer includes spam filtering and is compatible with iPhone, Android, and BlackBerry. Plus, you can keep your business domain for your e-mail. The business service also includes video chat, calendar functionality, and document-editing capabilities.

✦ **Outlook or Outlook Express:** Microsoft created two versions of its e-mail messaging system:

  • *Outlook Express:* The simpler version often comes free with your PC computer. The program's limited functions are suitable for your use at home or in your small business.

  • *Outlook:* If you need more capabilities accessible by more users, this version might be a better choice. Outlook comes with Microsoft Office.

The Outlook family of products has had security flaws that left people's computers vulnerable to viruses and other risks. You can obtain different security patches (problem fixes) for older versions of the e-mail program. To compare features and download the most recent version, go to the Microsoft site (www.microsoft.com).

Using document-viewing software and other useful applications

As you begin using the Internet and your computer to communicate, you might find that several programs come in handy. Frequently, you receive a document as an attachment to an e-mail message. Depending on the program the sender used to create the document, it can be in any of a number of formats: a Word file, a PDF (Portable Document Format) file, or an image saved in one of a slew of formats, such as a TIF, GIF, BPM, or JPEG. Even if you don't have exactly the same program as the sender of the file, you can still open and view these files if you have the right software.

We suggest installing the following programs on your desktop so that you're prepared to receive and view information in a variety of formats:

✦ **Adobe Acrobat (Reader):** *PDF files* are electronic documents that you might receive in e-mail or download from a website. To view, print, or search PDF files, you must have the free Adobe reader software loaded on your computer. Depending on your needs, you may benefit from other services offered as part of the Adobe solution, including Creative Cloud and Marketing Cloud (each available on a paid monthly plan). To get the free reader software, download it at the Adobe Acrobat website (www.adobe.com).

✦ **File compression:** When you send or receive large files, you should have the capability to compress the files so that you can more efficiently send them by e-mail. You can purchase a tool such as WinZip, which allows you to zip (compress) and unzip files and complete folders and is available for $29. But both Windows and Mac OS X come with a compatible compression program built-in.

✦ **File storage and sharing programs:** You'll want to back up your important files as well as access files from remote locations. In addition, you may need an easy way to share files between employees or with clients and vendors.. For cloud-based storage, check out Apple iCloud, Google Drive, or Microsoft OneDrive. One of the most popular solutions is Dropbox (www.dropbox.com), which has a basic free service and a for-fee service (100GB for $100 per year, which can be paid monthly) that has more storage, additional features, and increased security.

✦ **Movie and audio player:** If you ever visit news sites, such as CNN, you probably come across video or audio clips in news stories that you can view or listen to online. More websites are offering audio and video clips, whether as part of an online small-business training course or a preview of a newly released Hollywood movie. To hear and see these clips, you must have a viewer or player installed on your computer. Microsoft includes Windows Media Player as a built-in player for the Windows operating system.

Apple makes the easy-to-install player QuickTime Player, which works on either a PC or a Mac. To install the player, follow the download instructions at the Apple website (www.apple.com/quicktime/download). Or try RealPlayer, which also works on multiple platforms. It's available at www.real.com. Adobe Flash Player is another browser plug-in that you may need, if it's not already installed (for example, Google Chrome has Flash Player built in and will automatically update new versions). To install it, visit www.get.adobe.com/flashplayer.

Your Essential Software Toolkit

Most businesses require some robust software programs to handle their core business activities, such as generating printed letters and invoices, juggling finances, designing marketing pieces, and making sales presentations. As you might expect, your choice of business software is almost endless. Some essential programs, however, are important to add to your computer now.

Book I
Chapter 6

Setting Up Shop:
Everything You
Need for Online
Efficiency

When you buy a new computer, be aware that some basic software packages, such as Microsoft Works, are often included with the system. If the included software isn't your first choice, negotiate with the salesperson to trade for different software. Or if you order online, look for deals that let you add software programs at the time of purchase for less than the full retail price. If you're currently enrolled as a student or an educator, you may also qualify for a discounted version of some software packages.

This list describes some core software packages you should consider:

✦ **Word processing software:** Working with documents, either creating or reading them, is standard procedure in business. A few word processing software solutions are available. For instance, your computer might come with WordPad, a simple, easy-to-use program. For extended features, however, try a more advanced program, such as Microsoft Word (www.office.microsoft.com) or Microsoft Office 365 for business, which is available as a cloud-based solution for as little as $5 per month, per user. WordPerfect (www.corel.com/wordperfect) is another affordable option, as is the popular Google Docs (www.google.com/drive/apps.html). For Mac users, consider Pages (www.apple.com/mac/pages), available for a one-time fee of $20. If you're looking for a good, free alternative, try the leading open-source word processing option, OpenOffice (www.openoffice.org).

✦ **Graphics or imaging software:** Any time you work with images, graphics software becomes a necessity. You can use this software for everything from creating logos to editing digital photo images. Your computer might come with a paint program that allows you to draw images and do basic photo editing. Depending on your needs, though, you can also explore more advanced graphics software, such as Paint Shop Pro (www.paintshoppro.com) or Adobe Creative Cloud (www.adobe.com/creativecloud). Free alternatives are available, including GIMP (www.gimp.org) and Inkscape (www.inkscape.com), which are both available for the PC and the Mac.

✦ **Presentation software:** This type of software allows you to create a professional presentation by using text and graphics and applying special effects to the content. PowerPoint (www.office.microsoft.com/powerpoint), part of Microsoft Office, is one of the most recognized presentation software products. Its ease of use makes it a good match for use in your businesses. You can create information on individual slides that can be viewed one by one or run in sequence in a slide show. Good alternatives to PowerPoint are Keynote for Mac (www.apple.com/mac/keynote), Kingsoft (www.kingsosoft.com), and Prezi (www.prezi.com), which is easy to use and includes animation and sound.

Many of these software programs can be expensive. Before investing, look for trial versions, which allow you to use the full program for free for a limited time, or a cloud-based option, which provides an inexpensive, monthly pay-as-you-go plan. In this way, you can find out if you really need the program before spending a lot of money on it.

Connectivity: Today's Internet Options and More

Considering the variety of Internet service choices you have and the number of providers in business, now is certainly a great time to start an online business. You can select a plan that truly meets your needs and doesn't break the bank. One area that you should *not* skimp on for your online business is your Internet service. After all, it (along with hosting for your site) is the backbone of your business.

An Internet broadband connection works by carrying many different channels of data over a single wire, or source. The continued growth in e-commerce is credited to the ever-expanding number of consumers who have access to a broadband connection in their homes, which makes shopping online faster and easier.

Two types of broadband are commonly available:

✦ **DSL:** Digital Subscriber Service gives you a high-speed connection by using a normal phone line and digital modem capabilities. Don't worry about your phone line being constantly busy, though: After special equipment is installed on your end, your phone line can be used simultaneously for accessing the Internet and for regular voice communication. Because phone companies providing the service were slow to establish access to all areas, you might live in a neighborhood that simply cannot support the DSL option.

✦ **Cable modem:** Much like DSL, cable provides a very high-speed connection. Typically considered faster than DSL, it's chosen by many users for its outlandish speed. However, cable modems use *shared* bandwidth, whereas DSL uses *dedicated* bandwidth. The shared cable network is associated with a higher security risk. We discuss these and other security issues in Book V. (Ethernet also offers a very high-speed, dedicated bandwidth that, like DSL, is a more secure option.)

Although pricing plans for cable and DSL fluctuate, plan to spend at least $40–60 per month. With the increasing demand for faster service, companies are charging more, but bundled services (that combine connectivity for the web and voice service) may offer a break in pricing. Shop around for the best deal before you settle on a service provider.

Book II
Legal and Accounting

Contents at a Glance

Chapter 1: Minding the Law

In This Chapter

✔ Keeping your business within the law

✔ Determining whether you can legally work from home

✔ Obtaining the necessary licenses to operate your business

*O*ne of the first things you discover in owning a business is that you cannot avoid certain specific legal requirements. An Internet business is subject to not only traditional laws imposed on any company but also further regulation. As with the rest of the Net, these rules change quickly, and the burden to keep up is on you.

In this chapter, we review the basic laws so that you can start setting up shop.

We're not lawyers, and laws differ from state to state. So if you're the least bit concerned, consult a local attorney to answer any of your questions.

Keeping Your Business Legal

Whether you have an online business or an offline business, you must do certain things to set yourself up and operate legally. If you already have a business that you're taking online, this advice is probably old news. But if you're starting your online business from scratch, read on.

Admittedly, quite a few business-related laws exist. As an online business, you must comply with any government regulations specific to e-commerce, as determined by the Federal Trade Commission (FTC). In addition to all federally imposed regulations, you're also subject to any applicable state, county, and city laws. If you're selling to companies or individuals outside the United States, you must also comply with International Trade Law. On its website, the SBA provides good information about business law and regulations, as shown in Figure 1-1. You can find this information under the resource page titled "Starting and Managing a Business," when you visit www.sba.gov.

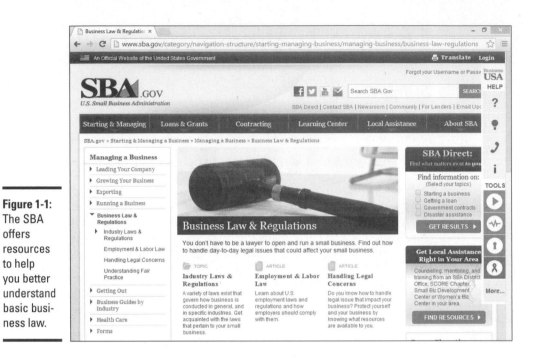

Figure 1-1:
The SBA offers resources to help you better understand basic business law.

At first pass, these legal obligations can be a bit overwhelming. Like everything else in business, though, you take one step at a time and, before you know it, you have a handle on the situation. The same is true with the legalities of operating an online business. Start out on the right foot by getting up to speed with these basic requirements.

Depending on the type of business you're conducting over the Internet, additional laws or regulations might apply to you. Several good sources to help you research this information include

✦ A trade association in your industry

✦ Your local Chamber of Commerce

✦ State and local government websites

Federal tax identification number

If you have employees or your business is a corporation or partnership, you need a federal tax ID. Officially known as an employer identification number (EIN), this 9-digit number is used to identify a company whenever its owner files certain forms and tax returns.

You can apply for a federal tax ID via the online EIN application at the IRS website at www.irs.gov/Businesses/Small-Businesses-&-Self-Employed/Employer-ID-Numbers-EINs. Or if you prefer, you can download the required Form SS-4 and submit the application by fax or regular U.S. mail.

Health department permit

If you manufacture, package, or distribute food-related products as part of your online business, you need a permit from the health department. The permit (along with any necessary on-site inspections) is handled by your city or county health department. You might also be subject to certain regulations of the Food and Drug Administration (FDA). For instance, if you're making homemade jelly and selling it over the Internet, you might be required to meet certain labeling standards that detail ingredients and nutritional information. You can obtain a complete food-labeling guide, along with other details of starting and operating an online food business, at the FDA website: www.fda.gov/food.

You can get a small-business food-labeling exemption if you don't exceed certain annual sales levels or if you don't make nutritional claims in your advertising.

The EIN is requested on many different types of business documents, from bank accounts to loan applications. If you don't have a federal tax ID number, you can use your Social Security number instead.

Resale certificate

If you sell any type of product, your state might require that you collect and pay a sales tax on every sale. If so, you need to apply for a resale certificate (often associated with buying wholesale). Be aware that the amount of sales tax to collect, the dates the tax is due, and the rules of collection vary by state. For that reason, you should check the regulations for the state in which your business is physically located. Because exceptions to the rules often exist or other details can be difficult to understand, also consider talking with a certified public accountant.

Business bank account

When you first begin to operate a business, you might be tempted to run all your money through an existing personal account. Trust us: This technique happens quite often and is rarely a good idea. Why do people do it? If you're just testing out your business idea, opening a separate account might seem unnecessary. Or perhaps you view it as a way to save some money on bank fees. Unless you plan to maintain your idea strictly as a hobby, however, you need to open a business bank account immediately. Otherwise, it becomes too easy to commingle personal and business expenses. How can you possibly separate them if they share a bank account?

When you open a business account, the bank needs specific information, such as a copy of your business license, your federal tax ID number or Social Security number, and, possibly, proof of incorporation if you want your legally incorporated business name on the account.

The $500,000 question: How do you protect customer data?

The Payment Card Industry Data Security Standard (PCI DSS) is a set of guidelines for all merchants who accept credit cards, including e-commerce merchants. PCI DSS helps ensure that merchants keep customer data secure when they're collecting, processing, and storing personal and financial information.

The release and continued maintenance of this standard is in response to the ongoing increase in identity theft and stolen credit card numbers obtained from Internet sites. Credit card companies, under pressure to tighten security measures, collaborated to issue this worldwide security standard.

Failure to comply with the standard can result in some outrageous penalties, including fines of up to $500,000 per incident or possible cancellation of your merchant account. Overall, the measure to increase the protection of your customers' data is a good one. Unfortunately, it's one more regulation that even very small companies must comply with to avoid penalties. Among the requirements of the standard, companies must

- Install and maintain a firewall configuration to protect data

- Not use vendor-supplied defaults for system passwords and other security passwords

- Protect stored data

- Encrypt the transmission of cardholder data and sensitive information across public networks

- Use and regularly update antivirus software

- Develop and maintain secure systems and applications

- Restrict business access to data based on job description and needs

- Assign a unique ID to each person who accesses the computer used for financial data

- Track and monitor all access to network resources and cardholder data

- Regularly test security systems and processes

- Maintain a policy that addresses information security

The PCI Security Standards Council (www.pcisecuritystandards.org) manages and publishes the most current guidelines for compliance with the standards, including guidelines for small merchants and for accepting mobile payments with smartphones and tablets. Payment card companies, however, are responsible for enforcing compliance with the standards.

As a merchant, and as part of the validation process, you might have to complete a PCI DSS Self-Assessment Questionnaire (SAQ). You can access the questionnaire by visiting www.pcisecuritystandards.org/merchants/self_assessment_form.php. For specific information about compliance, including information on specific payment card company requirements, go to www.pcisecuritystandards.org/merchants/how_to_be_compliant.php.

Consider opening two bank accounts: one for all your daily transactions and the other for dealing with sales tax, employee withholding, and other regular tax payments. Keeping these items separate and using simple money transfers from one account to another can help you keep your payroll and employee finances separate and easier to manage. Meet with your bank's manager to find out what perks may be available when opening one or more business accounts.

Employee forms

When you hire others to work for your company (even if you are your only employee), the IRS wants to be in the know, and that involves forms, of course. You should be familiar with several forms required by the IRS:

+ **Form W-9:** When you hire independent contractors (nonemployees), consultants, or self-employed individuals to perform work, have them complete IRS Form W-9. This form provides you with the information you need to report earnings to the IRS and generate a Form 1099 (see the next bullet point) that reports their earnings at the end of the year.

When you're hiring independent contractors, be sure to check the IRS definition of what constitutes a contractor (versus an employee). For instance, if you have workspace available at your office for the contractor or require the person to work a set schedule, you could cause an independent contractor to be considered an employee. If that's the case, you're responsible for withholding taxes. You can even be fined (with interest) if you don't withhold wages and the mistake is discovered later.

+ **Form 1099:** If you hire someone (other than an employee or a corporation) to do work for your company, you need to send that person a Form 1099 at the end of the year. You're required to complete this form only if you paid the individual $600 or more. If you're not incorporated and provide a service for another company, you receive a Form 1099.

If you barter or trade services or products with another company, the IRS expects you to report, on Form 1099, the value of that trade as income.

+ **Form W-4:** If you have employees, they must fill out Form W-4s so that you can withhold, report, and deposit their correct amount of employment-related taxes. You're responsible for *withholding,* or taking out, money for income tax, Social Security, Medicare, and federal unemployment taxes (FUTA).

+ **Form W-2:** By the last day of January following the end of each calendar year, you're responsible for sending this form to your employees. A W-2 reports the total income an employee earned from you during the preceding calendar year, along with the amount of money you withheld for various taxes during the year.

Zoning for Business (at Home)

Your home is the ideal place to start an online business. Working out of your house makes business set-up quick and easy, and it equates to low overhead. Before you convert that spare bedroom into an office, however, you need to determine whether you're allowed to operate a business from your home.

The answer typically comes down to a single word: *zoning*. Most cities and towns have zoning ordinances that define how a particular piece of land or group of properties can be used. They further specify which types of activities can occur there. For example, some neighborhoods are zoned for residential, which means that only single-family homes can be built in that area. Other areas might allow multifamily (apartments) residential. In the area of commercial or business use, the zoning becomes more complicated because businesses are often separated by types of industry. An area might also be labeled *mixed use,* which allows both residential and some types of limited commercial activity.

How do you decide whether your residential neighborhood is zoned for business? Check with your city's licensing or planning department. When you provide your address, the city clerk can tell you whether your neighborhood has any restrictions that would prevent you from opening your business.

Some cities and counties make zoning maps, along with a detailed list of city ordinances, available online. If your city has a website, start there first.

Assuming that all goes well and you find no restrictive ordinances, you'll be in business quickly. But sometimes this isn't the case and your home-based business isn't allowed. Then you have to ask for a *variance,* or an exception to the zoning ordinance. Fortunately, because millions of people are working from home now, many cities have already established criteria for such exceptions. Even if your neighborhood isn't specifically zoned for business, therefore, your city might allow small home-based businesses if they meet certain conditions.

To grant a variance, cities and counties want assurance that your business doesn't have

- ✦ High-volume street traffic
- ✦ Increased activity (by customers) in and out of the home
- ✦ Large trucks on-site (delivery trucks or company vehicles)
- ✦ Required additional parking
- ✦ Exterior signage
- ✦ The use or storage of harmful chemicals
- ✦ Warehousing of a large number of products

✦ The on-site sale of products to the public (such as what takes place at retail locations)

✦ Employees (usually more than three or four) working on-site

These conditions are in place primarily to ensure that your business activities do not adversely affect your neighbors nor have an effect on residential property values. Luckily, most Internet-based endeavors don't create such nuisances. Be sure to reiterate this point with city planners when you're pursuing a variance request for your business.

If your business involves storing and shipping large numbers of products, you might want to lease an off-site storage facility or arrange to have your products shipped from a distribution facility. It not only eases concerns from city officials initially but is also a good preventive measure to keep your neighbors happy.

Increasingly, zoning isn't the only concern when you're starting a home-based business. Many cities are now requiring home occupational permits. If you want to operate from your home, you're required to have this permit — no matter what your business. The good news is that certain occupations or business types are often automatically granted permits (and computer or Internet-related businesses are almost always included). However, you might have to qualify for a permit based on a long list of conditions that are similar to the criteria used in seeking a zoning variance (noise, traffic, on-site sales, and employees, for example). When you apply for a home occupational permit, you might also be asked to provide a list of all your neighbors and their addresses. The city then sends notice of your intent to operate a business from your home and gives your neighbors an opportunity to object. Even with this caveat, obtaining a home occupational permit can be much easier (and faster) than having to get a zoning variance granted. When you apply for the permit, expect to pay a small fee, ranging from $1 to $75.

A home occupational permit doesn't take the place of a business license. To operate legally, you must have both. See the next section to find out how to obtain the all-important business license.

Is that all you have to do? Not quite. Even if your home clears municipal zoning ordinances and home occupational permits, other obstacles can stop you from operating a home-based business:

✦ **Your homeowners' association:** Residents of subdivisions, condominiums, and some neighborhood communities often have homeowners' associations. If you're in this group, some restrictive covenants (or rules) probably govern your home and what you do to it, with it, and in it. The rules might also cover operating a business from your house. Read your covenants or bylaws carefully because even if your city doesn't restrict your business use of your home, these covenants might. If a problem exists, you can always go to the board of directors that manages your homeowners' association and try to obtain an exception.

✦ **Landlords:** If you lease an apartment or house, the rental agreement might prohibit you from conducting any business activity on the property. Review your lease thoroughly for clauses that specify how you can use the property.

If you choose to ignore legal restrictions concerning how your property can be used, you're taking a considerable risk. If your business activity is discovered, city officials could shut down your business, your homeowner's association could impose steep fines (and even put a lien on your home), or your landlord could evict you.

Obtaining Business Licenses

Regardless of where your business is located, you need a license to operate it. A *business license* is a piece of paper granting you the right to do business within a city, county, or state. Licenses are typically valid for a one- or two-year period and are nontransferable. (If you sell the business, the license is void.) You have to pay a fee when you apply for your license. The amount is often based on the type of business you operate and can range from $25 to several thousand dollars.

You (and not a city clerk) should specify which business category you fall under when you apply for your license, because a category specifically for an Internet-based, or *e-commerce,* business might not exist. Instead, you have to select a broad category based on the specific activity conducted through your site. Some categories can require steep licensing fees and might not, in fact, apply to you. Scour the entire list and the accompanying fees. Then choose the one most related to your business and with the lowest fee.

In addition to obtaining a city-issued license, you might be required to have a license for the county in which you're operating your business. This license is similar to a city license but is often less restrictive and less expensive. Be aware that some occupations (building contractors, realtors, and other professional service providers, for example) might further require that you obtain a state license. Although you probably don't need a state license to operate your online business, you can double-check by visiting your state's website.

To help you find out where to go for your city and county licenses, the SBA offers an online list for all 51 states, plus Puerto Rico, Guam, and the U.S. Virgin Islands. You can find the Where to Obtain Business Licenses list at the SBA.gov site: www.sba.gov/content/search-business-licenses-and-permits. You can search by city or zip code.

Chapter 2: Choosing the Right Foundation — from Partnerships to Corporations

In This Chapter

✔ Deciding which business form is best suited to you

✔ Establishing yourself as a sole proprietorship

✔ Evaluating alternative legal structures

✔ Operating by the rules of incorporation

✔ Modifying your ownership structure

At the top of every start-up checklist is a line item that reads "Establish the formal structure of your business." This line means that you start by deciding how you want your company legally organized. You can be the sole owner or have 2 partners or 50 shareholders. Each form of business has definite advantages and disadvantages, depending on your goals for the business.

Read the information we provide in this chapter about all these options before making your final decision.

Strategizing for the Best Organization

Choosing how to set up your business is easier than you might think. Considering that you have only four primary choices, the odds of narrowing the selection quickly are in your favor. Yet one of the most frequently asked questions when someone is starting a business is "Which structure is best for me?" To get started, you need to resolve four key issues:

✦ **Ownership:** Deciding who ultimately owns or controls your company is a primary influence on your choice of legal structure. A second factor is the number of people who control the business. Some forms of business are limited by both the number of owners and the type of owner (individual or corporation) it can have.

✦ **Liability:** You must choose where you want the legal responsibility for the business to reside. Deciding whether you're comfortable accepting full liability for the actions of the company or whether you need the protection (or veil) of a corporation is an important choice.

✦ **Taxes:** Each of the business structures is subject to various forms of taxation. For instance, you might pay a self-employment tax based on your earnings. Or you could be taxed on the dividends paid out to all owners from the business. In the case of one type of incorporation, you might even experience *double taxation* — paying tax as the business and again as an individual stockholder.

Because the tax issues are so complex, talk with a tax attorney or certified public accountant to determine which option best fits your specific circumstances.

✦ **Funding:** The way in which you finance the growth of your company can play a significant role in determining its structure. If you're *bootstrapping* (self-financing) the company, any of the structures might work for you. However, if you seek outside financing from angel investors or venture capitalists, you need the option of having stock available for distribution. If another business entity plans to own stock in your company, your choice of business structure is severely limited. See Book I, Chapter 4 for more info on how to fund your business.

Now that you understand these four primary areas of concern, you should have a better idea of where your specific requirements fit in. To make your final decision, read the detailed descriptions in the following sections for each business entity.

Operating Alone as a Sole Proprietor

If you're interested in simplicity, look no further. A *sole proprietorship* is recognized as the quickest, easiest, and least expensive method of forming a business. The main caveat is that only one person can operate as a sole proprietor. You and the business are literally the same entity. The upside of that arrangement is the ease of getting up and running. With the mere act of conducting business (and obtaining a license), you're considered a sole proprietor.

The downside of being a sole proprietor is the potential legal ramifications. Because you and the company are one, you're fully accountable for the losses of the business along with any legal matters. Whether the business is involved with lawsuits or problems with creditors, you're personally liable. No corporate protection is available — your personal assets (such as your home) can be sold and your personal bank accounts used to pay off creditors.

As a sole proprietor, you're also responsible for all taxes. The profits and losses of the business are listed on Schedule C on your personal tax return. And you pay self-employment tax (Schedule SE), which is a combined Social Security and Medicare tax. The self-employment tax is calculated as a percentage of your earnings; as of the 2013 tax year, the percentage is 15.3 percent (12.4 percent for Social Security and 2.9 percent for Medicare).

In addition to obtaining a business license and paying taxes, you must address two other topics if you're considering operating as a sole proprietor — how to

✦ Registering your company name

✦ Forming a sole proprietorship with your spouse

We discuss these topics in the next two sections.

Fictitious name registration

Unless you choose to operate your company under your exact legal name (or use your last name), you need to register a *fictitious* name with the state. The name of your company is different from that of its legal owner (you). Suppose that your name is John Smith and you decide to name your company Online Information Services. By registering that fictitious name, you become John Smith *dba* (doing business as) Online Information Services. Your business name should then appear on your checking account, business license, and any other legal documents.

Check with your city and state governments to determine how you should register your fictitious name. Some states require only that you submit an application and pay a small filing fee. Others mandate that you publish in a newspaper your intent to use the fictitious name before you begin to use it.

Husband and wife sole proprietorship

Togetherness is a wonderful thing, as you and your spouse might have found out when you got married. You and your spouse might even want to operate a business together. Does this mean that you no longer qualify for the simplified structure of a sole proprietorship? That depends.

The IRS legally recognizes a sole proprietor as having only one owner. If a spouse is working for the company, the IRS expects you to treat that person as an employee (which means that you have to pay payroll taxes). Alternatively, if your spouse has an active ownership role in the company, the IRS treats the business as a partnership (which means that both of you are taxed separately on the income). However, some tax advisors suggest that you can still file as a sole proprietor even if your spouse participates in the company. When you file a Schedule C on your joint tax return, all business income is viewed as one sum for both of you, although the IRS still views your business as belonging to a single owner.

To avoid paying payroll taxes, you may choose to classify your spouse as a *volunteer.* Your spouse is then only occasionally active in the business and doesn't get credit toward Social Security.

If the IRS determines that your spouse works regular, consistent hours, it could mean instant classification as an employee. At that point, you might be responsible for paying a hefty sum of back taxes and penalties. Always consult a professional tax advisor to ensure that you're operating within the allowable classifications designated by the IRS.

Sharing the Load with a Partnership

In some ways, a *general partnership* is similar to a sole proprietorship: It's relatively simple and inexpensive to form. Issues of liability and taxes reside fully with its owners. The primary difference with a partnership is that it allows you to have multiple owners.

Although the terms of this type of partnership can be based on a verbal agreement, you should spell out the conditions in writing, for two reasons:

✦ **Dispute resolution:** Having the specific details of your original agreement in writing is handy if a dispute arises between you and your partner (or partners).

✦ **Proof of partnership:** If something happens and a written document cannot be produced, you and your partners are assumed to share equally in all aspects of the business. Proving otherwise in a court of law, or to the IRS, could prove difficult.

When you define your partnership, the basic agreement should address these areas:

✦ **Structure:** Shows what percentage of the company is owned by each partner

✦ **Control:** Defines which partner is responsible for which part of the daily management of the company

✦ **Profits:** Details the division of profits and losses and the timeframe for distributing profits to the partners

A partnership arrangement brings up certain questions that you must consider at the beginning of a partnership:

✦ How much money and time will each partner contribute, and how will decisions for the company be made?

✦ What happens if one partner stops contributing, can no longer be actively involved, or wants out of the partnership?

✦ Can you buy out the interest of another partner, or will the partnership be dissolved automatically when a dispute cannot be settled?

✦ How will ownership be transferred if one partner dies or is involved in a divorce (especially if the partners are married to each other)?

✦ How will an owner's share in the company be redistributed?

These questions are tough to answer. You probably don't want to believe that anything will go wrong between you and your partners. Unfortunately, for one reason or another, partnerships go sour all the time.

The most successful partnerships are those in which issues such as these were openly discussed and agreed on up front. Likewise, individual owners who have survived a failed partnership have done so because a written agreement was in place. Considering that you and your partners are personally liable for the actions of your company, a formal partnership agreement is your best chance for avoiding problems.

Book II
Chapter 2

Choosing the Right
Foundation — from
Partnerships to
Corporations

Limited Liability Company (LLC)

If you prefer entering into a business using an entity that offers a bit more legal protection to you and your partners than a partnership, a *limited liability company (LLC)* might interest you. (Although some states also recognize a limited liability partnership, or LLP, the LLC is more common.)

The LLC combines the flexibility of a partnership with the formal structure and legal protection provided by a corporation. As in a general partnership, income is passed through to the individual partners, and profits can be distributed according to your agreement. (Note that profit doesn't have to be split equally among partners.) An LLC allows you to have an unlimited number of partners, and permits you to raise money for the business by taking on investors (including other corporations) as members. Additionally, members or partners of the LLC aren't personally liable for the actions of the corporation.

If you choose to form an LLC, you have to file with the state, although the requirements typically aren't as stringent as they are in a corporation. (You're not required to maintain bylaws or keep minutes of annual board meetings, for example.) However, the requirements for forming an LLC vary by state, so you have to research those requirements for the state in which you file.

Making It Official with Incorporation

One option to consider when you're establishing a business is whether to incorporate. A *corporation* is a legal entity that's separate from the individuals who create or work for it. Stock in a corporation is issued to individuals or to other business entities that form the ownership of the company.

Different flavors of corporations

Depending on your situation, you can choose one of two types of corporation:

✦ **C corporation (or C corp):** This traditional form of a corporation typically offers the most flexibility when you're seeking investors. A C corp is allowed to have unlimited shareholders, usually with no restrictions on who they are. The downside is the way in which this status of corporation is taxed. In a concept commonly referred to as *double taxation*, the business is taxed first on its income and then its individual shareholders must also pay tax.

✦ **S corporation (or S corp):** Electing to have Subchapter S status, or to become an S corp, is an option for your company if you have a limited number of shareholders (as few as just you and usually no more than 35). The shareholders must all be individuals (they cannot be corporations or other business entities), and they must be legal U.S. residents. You also have to agree to operate the business on a calendar year for tax purposes. The advantage of becoming an S corp is that you avoid double taxation. (Profits and losses are passed through to shareholders.)

The choice to incorporate

The biggest advantage to incorporating is that it offers legal protection to its owners. As an individual shareholder, you're not personally liable, as you are with a sole proprietorship or general partnership. You might find that a corporation offers significant tax advantages, too. If you're seeking investment capital or plan to take the company public with an initial public offering (IPO), a corporation gives you the most flexibility to do so. Even if you have no plans to go public, being incorporated provides the opportunity to build your personal wealth in the form of an individual or one-participant 401(k) plan, which is also referred to as a solo 401(k) plan. Saving for retirement using a traditional 401k plan can be a big advantage of incorporating as an S corp.

Incorporating has a few disadvantages, too. For starters, you must file or register your corporation with your state. This process involves a large amount of paperwork, which takes some time. To file, you have to submit articles of incorporation that state (among other information)

✦ The purpose of your business

✦ The name of the company

✦ The name of the owner

✦ The company's location

You also have to submit bylaws, which describe how the company is run, and a list of officers, or the people who direct the company in its daily decisions, such as a president, secretary, and treasurer.

After your corporation is approved by the state, your responsibilities don't end there. To maintain the corporation's status, you're required to issue stock, hold annual board meetings (with its officers), and record minutes of these meetings. These formal requirements of a corporation can be cumbersome for you, especially when you're starting a new business. In addition, a corporation has to file separate tax forms, which are typically more complicated than an individual return. You could be doubling your efforts — and your expense — while trying to comply with taxes.

WARNING!

If the corporate veil is pierced, you can be held personally responsible for the debts and legal concerns of your corporation. This situation happens when you don't properly uphold the requirements of your corporation. Any protection offered by the corporation is therefore forfeited.

Forming a corporation isn't the cheapest method of starting a business, either. If you hire an attorney to file the necessary paperwork with the state, expect to spend close to $1,000 or more in legal expenses and filing fees. Even if you elect to incorporate yourself or do it through an online service, it can still cost several hundred dollars. You pay, at the least, an initial filing fee with the state and then an annual fee to maintain your status.

**Book II
Chapter 2**

**Choosing the Right
Foundation — from
Partnerships to
Corporations**

Changing Your Organization As It Grows

Just because you select one form of structure when you're starting your business doesn't mean that you're stuck with it forever. As with other decisions you make along the way, you might find that your growing company warrants a different legal structure at some point. The ideal situation is to select a structure that gives you the most flexibility at the time you start up. Sometimes, though, that's not reasonable. The next-best plan of action is to understand when and how you should change your organization.

Perhaps the best indicators are those related to money and ownership. As a small-business owner, if you use your money better through different tax strategies, waste no time making the transition. Many businesses start out as sole proprietorships because that option is simple. When the owner hits a certain level of income, however, it makes sense to incorporate based on the amount of self-employment taxes being paid. The advantage of saving several thousand dollars outweighs the compliance burden of incorporation. As they say, it's a no-brainer!

Then there's the matter of owner status. As a sole proprietor, if you take on an additional owner, you have to convert to a partnership or some form of corporation. Similarly, if you're operating a general partnership and then decide to seek out other owners for investment purposes, forming a corporation and offering stock might make sense.

You can much more easily switch from a sole proprietorship or partnership to a corporation than vice versa. After you incorporate a business, you're expected to meet payroll and wage-related tax requirements as defined by the IRS, and you're expected to hold shareholder meetings. If you decide that you cannot maintain a formal corporation or that it's no longer the best structure for your company, you cannot simply stop meeting these requirements. Instead, you must follow certain procedures to legally dissolve the business before you can change its official ownership status. The Small Business Administration (SBA) offers detailed instructions for this process at www.sba.gov/smallbusinessplanner/exit.

Before changing the status of your business, *always* consult with your certified public accountant, attorney, or other trusted business advisor. Consider your options carefully!

Chapter 3: The Trademark-and-Copyright Two-Step

In This Chapter

✔ **Understanding trademarks and the law**

✔ **Establishing copyrights and your right to be covered**

✔ **Registering your work**

✔ **Hiring lawyers instead**

Your business is important to you, and protecting your hard work and assets is probably high on your list of concerns. From your company logo to your business documentation to your website, making certain that your intellectual property (IP) is protected from improper use, plagiarism, and defamation is a never-ending process.

In this chapter, we show you how to protect your investment by registering for trademarks and filing your copyright.

Understanding Why Trademarks and Copyrights Matter

Creating a distinctive name, symbol, or phrase for use in your business can involve a lot of work. After all, branding companies are paid tens (or hundreds) of thousands of dollars to come up with the right names for new products or services. The same hard work and amount of time invested applies to a written work of art, a clever body of text used on your website, or an original piece of artwork: If you go to the trouble of developing unique content, it's probably worth protecting it as your own.

To understand how to protect yourself, you have to enter the Land of Legalization. Start by wrapping your brain cells around some extremely important words, as defined by the U.S. government:

✦ **Copyright:** A form of intellectual property law that protects original works of authorship, including literary, dramatic, musical, and artistic works, such as poetry, novels, movies, songs, computer software, and architecture. The Library of Congress registers copyrights, which last for the life of the author plus 70 years.

✦ **Patent:** A property right granted by the government of the United States to an inventor that excludes others from making, using, offering for sale, or selling the invention throughout the United States or importing the invention into the United States, in exchange for public disclosure of the invention when the patent is granted.

✦ **Trademark:** Protects words, names, symbols, sounds, or colors that distinguish goods and services from those manufactured or sold by others and that indicate the source of the goods. Trademarks can be renewed forever, or as long as they're being used in commerce.

Obtaining one of these legal stamps to claim something as your own is a fairly painless process. Taking this precaution can eventually translate into dollars gained. Not having a product or logo protected makes it easier for someone to copy or steal your idea. That's money out of your pocket. Although having a trademark or copyright might not prevent others from infringing on your work, it certainly makes it easier to go after them in court if they do.

Although the rules for these protective marks are the same whether you're conducting business online or off, the Internet has increased the stakes in some instances. Having your information readily accessible by millions of people around the globe makes it much easier for others to "borrow" from your hard work. That's all the more reason to make the effort to officially protect your information.

Making Your (Trade)Mark

Do you have to register your work to be protected? No. You might be surprised by this answer, but a federal trademark isn't a necessity. Suppose that you design a symbol to be used as the logo for your online business. By placing that logo on your site, and using it there and on any other business materials, you have established rights to it. So, why bother to officially register it? Obtaining federal registration acts as a notice to the public that you own the mark. It can also assist you if you decide to take action in a federal court to stop someone else from using your work. Also, if you want to register your logo outside the United States, the official registration provides the basis for you to do so.

Even if you choose not to formally register your work, you can use the trademark symbol anyway. After you establish that brilliant tagline or artistic logo, go ahead and place the trademark symbol (™) near your work. However, you cannot use the symbol showing that the work is officially registered until you apply for registration and receive final notification that your mark is registered. At that time, you can use the registered symbol (®).

Having a registered trademark doesn't prevent others from infringing on its use. After your work is registered, it's up to you to enforce it.

Protecting Your Investment with Copyrights

As with trademarks, you don't have to file for copyright protection to claim your written work as your own. Copyright protection is in place at the time you create your work. However, if you choose to file a lawsuit against someone for using your information, the U.S. Copyright Office advises that you need the formal certificate of registration as proof of ownership.

The good news is that copyrighting your information isn't expensive. Filing fees, at this time, are $45 per work if filed online and $65 per work if filed by other means; a group of material typically costs a minimum of $65.

If you choose to register, certain rules pertain specifically to websites and other material (such as documents you offer for download) distributed online. For instance, you can copyright any original information you include on your site.

Here are some other variables:

✦ You can protect computer programs you have written.

✦ You can protect entire databases.

✦ You *cannot* copyright your domain name for your site (such as www. mysiteisgreat.com).

✦ If you decide to send out an electronic newsletter to your customers each week, it's protected under copyright laws, as long as the information is original.

The Digital Millennium Copyright Act

The Digital Millennium Copyright Act (DMCA) became law in 1998. This legislation is part of the World Intellectual Property Organization (WIPO) Copyright Treaty, which countries around the world had previously agreed to adopt. Its intent is to provide enhanced copyright protection, specifically within electronic media (the Internet). Generally, the DMCA makes illegal the use of technology to copy or pirate digital material, such as software, music, and video. The DMCA further prohibits you from selling or distributing technology that could permit this type of activity.

How does the DMCA affect you? The answer depends on your type of business. If your website distributes music in any way, this law requires that you, as a webcaster, pay appropriate licensing fees for that right. If you're a nonprofit organization, a library, or an Internet service provider (ISP), you gain some added protection if someone uses your system to distribute copyrighted material. If you're the owner of copyrighted material and discover an infringement, you can report it to the ISP that's transmitting the information and request that the material be removed. Other than in these situations, the DMCA might not be a concern for you. You should be aware of it, though, because this piece of legislation has been controversial. As court cases evolve, you might discover that you're more affected than you thought.

The rules become more complicated when you discuss the period over which a work is protected or the amount of work that can be copyrighted. For instance, the original words on your website pages are protected. However, if you make updates to any of your pages and change that information, it isn't protected. In other words, you aren't given an unlimited copyright to your site's content. If you change the information (which you should do to keep your site fresh and current), you must file another application and pay another filing fee.

Here's an exception to this rule: An online computer program may be treated separately. Online work that's continuously updated can be classified as an automated database, which can have a single registration that covers updates over a three-month period (in the same calendar year). Or if you have material, such as an e-newsletter, that's updated daily or weekly, you might qualify for a group registration (or a single registration that covers multiple issues).

For more flexibility when allowing others to use and share your online content, such as blogs, website copy, and images, consider a Creative Commons license. Creative Commons is a nonprofit organization that provides different types of licenses for digital content that extend the way your copyrighted content is used while remaining within the legal boundaries of copyright law. You can, for example, grant users the right to share, edit, remix, or build upon your content based on certain conditions. You choose to extend licenses based on the types of attribution and whether it is for commercial or noncommercial use. A Creative Commons license works alongside a legal copyright and is not a replacement or an alternative to copyrighting your work. Copyright laws can be inflexible, but a Creative Commons license allows widespread digital sharing while enabling you to retain ownership of your work. You can learn more at `www.creativecommons.org`.

For complete details about copyrighting your online work, check out the official site for the U.S. Copyright Office and its section about electronic content, "Copyright Information for Online Works," at `www.copyright.gov/circs/circ66.pdf`. As with all advice in this book, when it comes to legalities, we highly advise you to consult an attorney if you have any questions or concerns about any actions you need to take.

Establishing Registration Yourself

As we point out in the preceding section, establishing your work as your own is as simple as creating it and using it. When you're ready to take the extra step to obtain proof of ownership, you can easily file for a trademark or copyright yourself.

Getting your trademark

You can apply for a federal trademark all on your own. Follow these steps to work through the registration process:

1. **Go to the website of the U.S. Patent and Trademark Office:** `www.uspto.gov`.

   The main page of the site lists current news and information about trademarks and patents. In the middle of the page is a list of topics from which you can choose more information.

2. **Under the Trademarks category, click the TEAS File Forms Online link.**

   This step takes you to the Trademarks Electronic Application System (TEAS) page. The left side of the page contains links to detailed information about enhancements to the system and important notices. The center of the page contains important warnings, along with links to the application forms.

   In the Forms section in the center of the page, the Trademark Basics link, next to the headline Before Filing (General Information), provides complete filing information for first-time filers. You can also access a link that shows you each page in the registration process so that you know exactly which information you need to file. You should visit these links before you start the registration process.

3. **In the center of the page, under the word *Forms*, click the Initial Application Form link.**

   A new page opens with information about form options and filing fees. It also has links to begin the filing procedure.

4. **Click the Trademark/Servicemark Application, Principal Register link to start the application process.**

5. **Complete all steps.**

   After you complete the application tutorial, your mark is officially submitted for approval.

Have your credit card ready when you file online. A filing fee, ranging from $275 to $325 per item, must accompany your online application.

Filing for a trademark can be tricky. You must be precise in the information you provide, follow instructions to the letter, and complete the process within a specified time frame. The USPTO prefers that you get professional help and issues a warning from the start, encouraging you to hire an attorney. If you are uncertain about the filing process, it may be worth paying for a few hours of time for a trademark attorney.

When the online registration is processed, you'll receive a serial number for your application. Use this serial number to check the status of your application by calling 800-786-9199 of by using the Trademark Status and Document Retrieval (TSDR) system at `http://tsdr.uspto.gov`.

Filing for copyright

To file an application for obtaining a federal copyright of your work, follow these steps:

1. **Go to the website of the U.S. Copyright Office, at `www.copyright.gov`.**

The home page shows you a list of choices to get information, as shown in Figure 3-1.

2. **Click the How to Register a Work link.**

You can skip Step 2 and go directly to the Electronic Copyright Office login by clicking the eCO link under the How to Register a Work link. However, you'll miss lots of helpful information about the registration process and fees, so we suggest foregoing the shortcut this time.

3. **Click the Electronic Copyright Office (eCO) icon and then click the Continue to eCO button.**

4. **Register with the Electronic Copyright Office.**

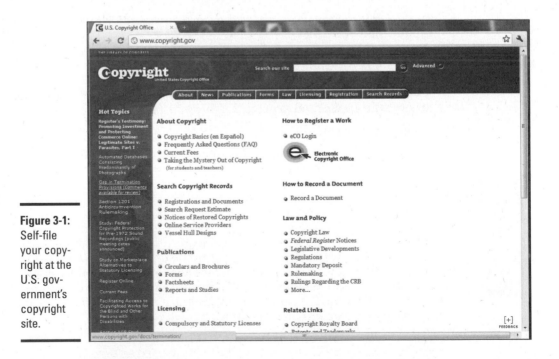

Figure 3-1: Self-file your copyright at the U.S. government's copyright site.

5. **Select the Register a New Claim link under the Copyright Services menu tab on the right side of the page.**

   The resulting page provides a list of specific steps of how to register a copyright.

6. **Follow the three steps as outlined on the site.**

   These steps include completing an online application, paying the filing fees, and uploading your work using an accepted file format. Tutorials for each stage help you complete the filing process successfully.

If you have trouble filing electronically, you can instead send the completed application and copies of your work, along with the designated filing fee, to this address:

Library of Congress Copyright Office

101 Independence Avenue, S.E.

Washington, D.C. 20559-6000

After your registration is approved, you receive a certificate of registration (usually in four or five months).

**Book II
Chapter 3**

**The Trademark-and-
Copyright Two-Step**

Retaining Professional Assistance

Hiring an attorney who specializes in trademarks, patents, or copyrights can be a good idea if your situation is complex or you're not comfortable handling the applications on your own. If you're pursuing registration in foreign countries, hiring an attorney who's familiar with international laws is invaluable. Because U.S. copyright and trademark laws are recognized in some, but not all, countries, using an attorney can ensure that you're fully protected.

You can expect to pay big bucks for the expertise of a professional. An experienced attorney might charge anywhere from $125 to $250 (or more) per hour for his or her service. This money is in addition to any filing or application fees you might have to pay. For this fee, you can expect a trademark attorney to conduct a thorough search of existing and pending marks that might conflict with yours. The attorney should also complete all forms on your behalf and act as the primary point of contact with the U.S. Patent and Trademark Office or the U.S. Copyright Office.

To protect your investment, follow these tips when you're hiring a professional:

✦ Look for an attorney who specializes in intellectual property or trademarks, copyrights, and patents.

✦ Get referrals from others you know who have used attorneys to register their businesses.

✦ Clarify which portion of the work is conducted by the attorney and which part is handled by legal aides (or junior partners).

✦ Discuss the attorney's rate and whether you're billed up front.

✦ Ask for a written statement or estimate of how much you can expect the process to cost.

✦ Confirm that the attorney is licensed.

You can search for an attorney in your area by using the referral guides on these website:

✦ **American Bar Association (ABA):** Visit www.abanet.org to locate attorneys in your area that can help you with your specific legal needs.

✦ **FindLaw:** FindLaw, at www.findlaw.com, can also help you locate local attorneys that specialize in various legal subjects, including trademark policies.

Chapter 4: Accounting for Taxes (and Then Some)

In This Chapter

✔ Keeping up with IRS expectations

✔ Tracking your profits and losses

✔ Finding software to make accounting a snap (or as close as it gets)

✔ Choosing a professional to ease your mind and protect your pocketbook

✔ Deciding what paperwork stays and what goes — and when

Unless you have a penchant for numbers, along with a love of crunching them, accounting is probably the least fun part of owning a business. Even so, we also recognize that it's one of the most necessary business functions. Why? It boils down to these two issues:

✦ **Taxes:** The Internal Revenue Service (IRS) demands that you keep accurate records of the monetary side of your business. That way, you're sure to contribute your fair share of taxes to Uncle Sam.

✦ **Profitability:** IRS aside, *you* need to understand how well (or not so well) your business is doing financially. Then you can make good strategic decisions for its future — and yours!

Dread it as you may, you have to embrace accounting. Okay, perhaps not embrace it, but you can at least learn to appreciate its value and commit to keeping up with it. To help prepare you for that financial road ahead, we start by introducing you to some basics of accounting. Before long, you may even look forward to balancing your checkbook. (Hey, anything is possible.) If you find that you just can't hack the accounting life, check out our advice on how and when to choose a professional to help you out.

The Tax Man Cometh — Again and Again

You've probably heard the saying that nothing in life is certain except death and taxes. Suffice it to say that the latter is at least predictable. As a business owner, you can count on the tax man regularly showing up on your doorstep. Rain or shine, without fail, taxes come due at certain times of the year whether you like it or not.

In Book II, Chapter 1, we give you a glimpse of what to expect of the tax man when we discuss the pros and cons of various ownership structures for your business and how each form is taxed. Regardless of which type of business structure you choose, you face many tax-related requirements when you run an online business.

For starters, several types of federal and state taxes are likely to apply to you, as we describe in the next few sections.

Income tax

You pay income tax on the money your business earns. Almost every type of company has to file an annual income tax return. (The exception is the partnership, which files only an information return.)

The important thing to know is that federal income tax is a pay-as-you-go system — the IRS doesn't want to wait until the end of the year to receive its cut of your money. Instead, you must pay the amount of taxes that are due every quarter. Because you don't always know the exact amount to pay in time to file by the IRS deadline (maybe an overdue invoice comes in at the last minute or a refund has to be issued), you can *estimate* the tax amount for each quarter and then submit that dollar amount. Table 4-1 lists the appropriate IRS form to submit when you're estimating taxes, along with many other forms that the IRS says you need, according to the type of organization you create.

Table 4-1	IRS Tax Forms Based on Business Type	
Organization Type	*Potentially Liable For This Type of Tax*	*Form or Forms Required*
Sole proprietor	Income tax	1040 and Schedule C1 or C–EZ (Schedule F1 for farm business)
	Self-employment tax	1040 and Schedule SE
	Estimated tax	1040–ES
	Employment taxes: Social Security and Medicare taxes and income tax withholding	941 (943 for farm employees)
	Federal unemployment (FUTA) tax	940
Partnership	Annual return of income	1065
	Employment taxes	Same as sole proprietor

Organization Type	Potentially Liable For This Type of Tax	Form or Forms Required
Partner in a partnership (individual)	Income tax	1040 and Schedule E
	Self-employment tax	1040 and Schedule SE
	Estimated tax	1040–ES
Corporation or S corporation	Income tax	1120 (corporation) 1120S (S corporation)
	Estimated tax	1120–W (corporation only)
	Employment taxes	940, 941, or 943
S corporation shareholder	Income tax	1040 and Schedule E
	Estimated tax	1040–ES

Employment tax

Your tax responsibilities don't end, of course, with reporting your income. Employees play a role, too. Whether you have one person (even if that's you!) or a hundred people working for your company, if you hire employees to work in your online business, you're responsible for paying certain taxes on behalf of those employees. Even if they work only part-time, you still have to keep up with the paperwork and pay up.

These obligations are commonly referred to as payroll taxes. You must file *withholding forms* (along with the accompanying payment) to both the IRS and your state treasury department. The types of taxes you pay on behalf of your employees include

✦ Medicare and Social Security taxes (as part of the Federal Insurance Contributions Act, or FICA)

✦ Federal income tax withholding

✦ Federal unemployment tax (FUTA)

Calculating the withholding amount can be complicated. You start with the information submitted by your employee on a Form W-9 and then use the tables in IRS Publication 15, *Employer's Tax Guide* (Section 16), which is available at www.irs.gov/publications/p15/index.html. Withholding guidelines are updated sometimes, so it is important to review the tax guide. The most recent changes occurred in 2014. If you are still not sure how to calculate this amount or are uncertain of changes to requirements and how they might apply to you, your financial advisor (bookkeeper or accountant) can easily make the calculations for you.

With calculated withholding amounts in hand, you need to fork over payroll taxes every quarter. You must file Form 941, *Employer's Quarterly Tax Return,* by the last day of the month that follows the end of the quarter. Table 4-2 shows the payroll due dates for both paper filing and electronic filing.

Table 4-2	Due Dates for Payroll Taxes	
Quarter Ends	*Normal Due Date*	*Extended Due Date*
March 31	April 30	May 10
June 30	July 31	August 10
September 30	October 31	November 10
December 31	January 31	February 10

In addition to providing payroll dates, the IRS website for small businesses offers easy access to almost every other type of tax form you need to submit. The site even contains an online learning center so that you can further educate yourself about all tax and business start-up issues. You can see instructional videos online at www.irsvideos.gov/smallbusinesstaxpayer.

The rule of filing quarterly has some exceptions. Always check with your accountant or CPA to confirm that you're filing properly. Otherwise, the IRS can slap you with hefty penalties and interest (never a good thing).

If you believe that your employment taxes are $1,000 or less (and your liability for Social Security, Medicare, and withheld federal income taxes is less than $2,500 for the year), you may be eligible to submit payroll taxes annually. To do so, request Form 944.

You might want to file electronically. (Come on — if you're running an online business, you ought to be set up for filing online, right?) Although the process is fairly easy, some paperwork is involved. In other words, don't assume that you can wait until the day before your taxes are due to sign up.

To start making online payments, go to the official Electronic Federal Tax Payment System (EFTPS) website at www.eftps.gov/eftps. EFTPS is a free service to business and individual taxpayers. Before you can file your taxes electronically, however, you must enroll online. Click the Enroll button at the top of the page and then follow the instructions to submit your information. Getting set up to make electronic payments generally takes five to seven days.

Before you can complete the online application, you must have an employer identification number (EIN) and provide your bank account number and bank routing number.

Sales tax

Another tax responsibility is that of tracking and collecting sales tax from your customers and then submitting it to the appropriate state and local agencies. If you sell (or manufacture) products, you probably have to deal with this issue.

You may be wondering whether you can avoid sales tax because you're selling products online and not in a particular state. Although federal legislators are debating this issue, for now it comes down to this guideline:

> If you sell to people in any state where you have a physical presence (and sometimes that can be the tiniest remote office), you must collect tax from customers originating from that same state.

The flip side of this issue is that individual states are becoming more aggressive about collecting sales tax from Internet-based companies. Yet a lot of uncertainty remains about how this obligation will play out in each state. Rest assured that this issue will get passed around legislatures like a hot potato. Our advice is to stay on top of the most current information at both the state and federal levels and to have your accountant continually keep you updated.

You're also liable for filing and paying other state-related taxes (not just sales tax). Because the amount varies greatly across states, check with your accountant to find out which taxes apply to your online business. Or you can contact your state's revenue department to learn more.

The Federation of Tax Administrators (FTA) website has a direct link to the appropriate agency websites for each state. Find the link at www.taxadmin. org/fta/link/default.html.

By the Numbers: Accounting Basics

Although we freely admit that accounting isn't our favorite activity, some elements of it are enjoyable. For example, at the end of every month, you have the opportunity to look at the profit-and-loss (P&L) statement to see how well your business is doing — on paper. It's like getting a checkup (for better or worse) and viewing a summary of every activity you performed during the month, as it relates to the bottom line of your business. If all is well, yippee! If you encounter problems, a profit-and-loss statement is bound to expose your points of weakness.

If you're still not sure what a P&L is, let alone what it means to your business, don't worry. You'll soak up the idea of a P&L in no time, along with several other important pieces of financial information in the following sections.

Determining periods and methods

Before you can walk, you have to crawl. When you're starting a business, one of the first things you have to do is select your *tax year,* or the defined period that you use to provide an annual snapshot of the financial state of your business.

You can choose from several types of tax year:

✦ **Calendar year:** This method is defined by the wall calendar you buy at the beginning of every year. The 12 months start January 1 and end December 31. Your calendar-year accounting system follows the same pattern: Move from month to month and then start all over again on the next January 1.

✦ **Fiscal year:** Although this type of tax year also has a fixed 12-month period, it never ends on the last day of December — any other month, but not that one. For example, you could choose to run from October 1 to September 30 of the following year. Why bother? If you have a seasonal business, this method provides an opportunity to adapt your operational schedule to an accounting and tax schedule. If your peak season is at the end of the year, having to worry about reporting or paying taxes can be cumbersome.

✦ **52 or 53 weeks:** In this variation of the fiscal year, you operate on a 52- or 53-week period rather than on a 12-month schedule. The catch is that your tax year must always land on the same day of the week (close to the end of a calendar month), thus requiring that an extra week be added to the period to end on the same calendar date each time.

A calendar year is probably the easiest reporting method for you to adopt. Depending on which type of business you form (an LLC or S corporation, for example), you may have difficulty getting the IRS to approve anything other than a calendar year. The IRS refers to it as a *required tax year.*

If you have good reason to think that the calendar year is a problem for your business, you must file a request with the IRS to change your tax year. For this request, you want to use the Application to Adopt, Change, or Retain a Tax Year. Unless an IRS code provides for automatic approval, be prepared to pay a filing fee for the change request.

Your next decision is to choose an *accounting method* for your business. You use this method to arrive at your income and expenses. Just as you choose your tax year, you select your preferred accounting method when you start your business. You're then expected to stick with it, unless the IRS approves a change.

Here are the two most common accounting methods for a business:

✦ **Cash basis:** Simply put, you report earnings when they're received and report expenses when they're incurred. The IRS says that you *cannot* use the cash method if any of these conditions applies:

- You're a corporation (other than an S corporation) with average annual gross receipts of more than $5 million.

- You're a partnership that has a corporation (other than an S corporation) as a partner, and the partnership has average annual gross receipts of more than $5 million.

- You're a tax shelter.

- You have inventory.

Special circumstances and exceptions to the rules always exist. Be sure to check with your CPA regarding which basis is best for your business.

✦ **Accrual basis:** In this method, your revenues can be reported when you earn them rather than when you receive the money (cash). Likewise, your expenses can be reported on the date they're owed, as opposed to the date on which you pay them. If you produce items or have inventory, accrual is considered the best way to provide an accurate picture of your financial status from year to year. Of course, that rule has some exceptions! You can use another method, even if you deal with inventory, if you are

- A qualifying taxpayer who passes the gross receipt test (with less than $1 million in gross sales for each year of the test period)

- A qualifying small-business taxpayer who passes the gross receipt test (with less than $10 million in average annual gross receipts for each year of the test period)

- An eligible business as determined by the IRS

Also, you must *not* be

- A tax shelter

- Prohibited from using the cash method

And now, your balance sheet

No matter which accounting method you choose, you need to know how to make sense of your company's financial statements. A *balance sheet,* which is one of those statements, is a detailed summary of your business's financial status.

To understand your balance sheet, here are some terms you need to know:

+ **Assets:** Everything of value that your business owns. Assets typically include

  - *Cash:* Available money in your bank accounts

  - *Accounts receivable (A/R):* The money that your customers owe you

  - *Inventory:* The monetary worth of whatever merchandise you have on hand

  - *Fixed assets:* Land, buildings, furniture, and equipment

  - *Miscellaneous:* A catchall term for anything that doesn't fit into any other category

+ **Liabilities:** All the debts of the business. Liabilities can include

  - *Accounts payable (A/P):* The money that you owe suppliers, vendors, or credit card companies

  - *Accrued expenses:* Wages, payroll taxes, and sales tax, for example, that have been collected but not yet paid

  - *Noncurrent:* Notes payable to shareholders and the portion of long-term debt that isn't yet due, for example

+ **Net worth or capital:** The amount of your ownership or equity or the amount you invested in your company

+ **Revenue or sales:** All the income your business has earned, usually recorded over a specific period

+ **Expenses:** Everything spent by your business, typically recorded (or totaled) for a specified period

Now you know all the essential terms that relate to a balance sheet. The next important point is that when a balance sheet is put together correctly, the bottom line must "balance" by using the following equation:

Assets = liabilities + net worth

That's it. See? It's not that confusing! To help you grasp how a balance sheet should look, check out the sample shown in Figure 4-1.

A quick glimpse: The P&L

Unlike a balance sheet, an *income statement* (commonly referred to as a profit-and-loss statement, or P&L) provides a quick snapshot of your revenues and expenses. It's made up of *line items,* a sequence of items providing a monetary total for every category of revenues or expenses. When you compile the statement, you can see how much money your business earned (or lost) for that specific period.

Balance Sheet
Ending December 31, 2014

	2014
ASSETS	
Current Assets	
Cash	$2,500
Accounts receivable	2,800
Inventory	5,500
Total Current Assets	**$10,800**
Fixed Assets	
Buildings	$ 0
Land	0
Furnitures and fixtures	1,200
Equipment	7,000
Accum. depreciation	(200)
Miscellaneous	0
Total Fixed Assets	**$8,000**
TOTAL ASSETS	**$18,800**
LIABILITIES AND SHAREHOLDERS' EQUITY	
Liabilities	
Accounts payable	$3,300
Taxes payable	500
TOTAL LIABILITIES	**$3,800**
Net Worth	15,000
TOTAL LIABILITIES & NET WORTH	**$18,800**

Figure 4-1:
A sample balance sheet.

Book II
Chapter 4

Accounting for
Taxes (and Then
Some)

You can create P&Ls on a quarterly basis. Looking at P&Ls monthly is more useful, however, because you can more easily spot any unusual fluctuations in your sales or expenses.

Suppose that you earn $750 in a month, which is deposited in your checking account. Then you withdraw (or spend) $800 that month. The bank also charges you $40 in overdraft fees for two bounced checks that were paid from your account. You have lost $90 for the month (you were short $50, plus $40 in overdraft fees).

Your P&L shows you the same type of information as your bank statement. If you pull up a record of your bank account online, you can see a list showing where your money went that month. By looking at your initial balance, and the checks you wrote against your deposits, you see whether you ended up with a positive balance (a profit) or a negative balance (a loss) over that period.

Check out Figure 4-2 to see what a P&L statement looks like.

Income Statement (P&L)		
For month ended July 31, 2014		
		07/31/14
Income:		
Gross Sales:		$9,115.00
Less Returns		(0.00)
Less Other Discounts		(0.00)
		$9,115.00
NET Sales		
Cost of Goods Sold:		
Beginning Inventory	$500.00	
Add: Purchases	250.00	
Freight	50.00	
		800.00
Cost of Goods Available		
Less: Ending Inventory	(400.00)	
		-400.00
Cost of Goods Sold		
		$8,715.00
Gross Profit (Less)		
Expenses:		
Advertising	150.00	
Amortization		
Bad Debts		
Bank Charges	50.00	
Commissions		
Credit Card Fees	55.00	
Depreciation		
Dues, Subscriptions (Books)	15.00	
Insurance	145.00	
Interest		
Loans		
Maintenance		
Miscellaneous	40.00	
Office Expenses – General	137.28	
Operating Supplies	124.56	
Payroll (Wages & Taxes)	2,800.00	
Permits and Licenses		
Postage	95.00	
Professional Fees	275.00	
Property Taxes		
Rent	650.00	
Telephone		
Landline	289.00	
Cell	150.00	
Training/Workshops	20.00	
Travel		
Utilities	280.00	
Vehicle Expense		
Gas/Mileage	42.14	
Maintenance		
Web Site Fees	355.00	
Total Expenses		5,672.98
Net Operating Income:		3,042.02
Other Income:	0	
*NET INCOME (LOSS):		**$3,042.02**
*This is pre-tax income.		

Figure 4-2: A sample income (P&L) statement.

In the example shown in Figure 4-2, notice two important characteristics of a P&L:

✦ **The dollar value for each line item is shown as a percentage of your gross revenues (total earnings before anything is deducted).** Using percentages gives you a clearer picture of how much (or little) you're spending from your total earnings. For example, if you find that you're spending 32 percent for banner advertising and only 5 percent on keywords, consider whether that's how you intended to spend your advertising budget.

Regularly review your P&L statement to track whether you're staying within your budget for the year.

✦ **The total dollar amount and percentages from the preceding month and for the year to-date are included.** It's all on the same page. If the line item shows that your company's water fee jumped 50 percent in one month, you might want to investigate. It could indicate a leak or other problem. Or the reason might be as simple as you having accidentally made a double payment. Don't laugh: You might be surprised at how easily events like these can slip past you.

Think of a P&L as a tool for keeping track of your business. Like the balance sheet, it provides an important glimpse of your business, over a specific period. If you review your financial statements regularly, you can catch mistakes and identify positive trends and then use that information to make critical decisions about the financial well-being of your online endeavor.

Choosing Software to Make Your Tasks Easy

Accounting software allows you to enter your daily financial activities, press a few keys at the end of the month, and — voila! — print your balance sheet and P&Ls. It's just a matter of picking the right software.

QuickBooks, the accounting software from Intuit (www.intuit.com), is a favorite among many small-business owners because it simplifies the recordkeeping process for your business and is *extremely* easy to learn and use. Many people are already familiar with it, simply because they use it for personal accounting, too. Popular brands such as QuickBooks and Sage 50 (www.sage.com) offer many versions of accounting software based on size, industry, and specific features.

Our purpose isn't to sell you on a particular brand of software. Instead, we want to help you understand which benefits and features to look for so that you can choose the best accounting software for your online business.

Going online?

The first consideration for choosing software is whether you want to use a web, or cloud-based, service provider. Many vendors provide online accounting services. FreshBooks, Zoho Books and Xero are some of the popular cloud-based options available today. Traditional accounting software providers also offer online versions of their products, such as QuickBooks Online and Sage One.

One big advantage of a cloud-based product is that the data is stored off-site and is easily accessible from any computer. Why does this matter? Well, if something happens to your office (such as a fire or a flood), you can still access your data from another location. Or if you travel, you can manage your accounting details while you're on the road.

Another perceived advantage is pricing. Rather than pay several hundred dollars out of your pocket in one whack, you pay it out every month (sometimes as little as $12 a month). After a full year or two, of course, you've paid almost the full price of a box of software. But that monthly fee can also include support and other benefits that over-the-counter accounting software might not offer. Additionally, you have a pay-as-you-grow option. In other words, you can easily upgrade to the next level of service as your business grows or choose certain add-on services, as your needs change — instead of investing upfront for services that you may not need yet.

What size are you?

Speaking of a growing business, when you're shopping for accounting software, one size doesn't fit all. The amount of revenue your business pulls in, along with the number of employees you hire, has a lot to do with which accounting program you should choose. For that matter, solo entrepreneurs may not have any employees! If you run a small business, you'll want to find entry-level software that is designed for very small businesses. If you have a larger company, you may need an enterprise edition that has more robust features.

How much do you want to pay?

Ah, it's everyone's favorite question: How much do you want (or are you willing) to invest in your accounting program? You probably prefer leaning toward the lower side of the price scale. Luckily, most over-the-counter software packages suited to truly small businesses range from $40 to $400 for single users. The price fluctuation largely depends on these factors:

✦ **Brand:** As with most business products, you usually pay more when you're using a more widely recognized brand of software. Our experience is that QuickBooks and Sage 50 are a little pricier than the Bookkeeper brand of software (by Avanquest Software), for example.

✦ **Features:** Price is affected by not only the number of features offered with various accounting software programs but also the complexity of those features. Keep these questions in mind:

- Do you want software that easily integrates with your online banking system, even if it costs more?

- Must the software communicate with your offline point-of-sale system, your online inventory system, or your payroll service? Or do you just want to track your invoices and expenses and spit out occasional reports to pass along to your CPA?

The more you expect from your accounting software, the more you can expect to pay for it!

✦ **Industry:** Similar to the issue of the type of features that are offered, some accounting software is designed for your particular type of *industry*. Consultants, manufacturers, retailers, and construction businesses are examples of some of the most common industries that use specific software. If you want accounting software designed for your kind of business, you can probably expect to pay closer to $400 (or higher).

Do you need support?

Another important part of your purchasing decision is the issue of support. One advantage of choosing software that has been around for a while is that the company is usually capable of providing decent support, both online and by phone. Access to support is also an advantage of using a cloud-based solution. Not all versions of a particular product or solution include the same level or type of support, so it is important to understand what is included with your monthly fee.

Before purchasing your software, find out the terms for receiving ongoing support and compare the product across brands. Some software comes with unlimited online support, and others offer only 30-day support and then charge a fee after that.

In addition to being able to turn to your software vendor for support, you should know that your accountant and other financial advisors are better prepared to help you when you use software that they know how to use. For that reason, don't hesitate to ask for their advice before making your final purchase.

Hiring a Professional

Regardless of the type of accounting software you install or your own ability to number-crunch, at some point you might need or want to hire outside help. An array of tax and accounting professionals are available. In the following sections, we tell you how to determine which one is right for you.

Recognizing that it takes all types

Start by reviewing the types of professionals who can help you. They include

✦ **CPA:** These initials after a person's name, which stand for certified public accountant, indicate that the person has passed a state-regulated exam and is recognized by the IRS as a paid preparer for submitting your tax returns. Typically, a CPA fully understands accounting methods and is well versed in tax regulations. Because tax laws are cumbersome and continually changing, a CPA might even specialize in a particular area. Examples of industry-based specialization are government, retail, and small business. Specialization can also be classified according to function, such as a CPA who specializes in mergers and acquisitions. Additionally, a CPA can legally conduct audits, whereas other accounting professionals cannot.

✦ **Accountant:** Except for the lack of a state-issued license or certificate, an accountant has the same basic skills as a CPA. Even so, an accountant can assist in preparing your taxes and file them, too. And like a CPA, a reputable accountant can advise you about financial decisions and should be up to date on changing tax laws.

✦ **Bookkeeper:** Someone in this category can manage the basic record-keeping activities for your small business, including these tasks:

  • Make deposits

  • Log in accounts receivables

  • Handle account payables

  • Manage payroll

  • Send out appropriate forms, such as W2s and 1099s, to employees and contractors

In addition to being able to keep the books, this person should be comfortable with creating an income statement and a balance sheet each month. Of course, bookkeepers come with all levels of experience and education. (Some are professionally certified with a college degree, and others aren't.) A basic bookkeeper is usually the most affordable outside help.

✦ **Tax consultant:** This catchall term includes both independent advisors (who can range from accountant to CPA) and tax preparers, such as the folks at your neighborhood H&R Block office at tax time. Similar to a bookkeeper, this person's range of experience, knowledge, education, and certification varies.

✦ **Enrolled agent:** This type of federally licensed professional understands both state and federal tax laws. In addition to completing an exam issued by the U.S. Department of Treasury, an enrolled agent has also passed a federal background check. He or she can also gain licensure after having worked for the IRS for at least five years. An enrolled agent is certified in the eyes of the IRS to

- Prepare your taxes

- Assist you in long-term financial planning

- Represent you in dealing with the IRS

✦ **Tax attorney:** Most tax attorneys don't handle general accounting functions. Instead, you hire an attorney specifically to deal with issues pertaining to the tax law — for example, to handle an audit requested by the IRS or to file corporate bankruptcy (which we hope you never do). Larger corporations might also keep a tax attorney on retainer or hire one in-house, if the company continually deals with complex tax issues. Your small business is less likely to need the services of a tax attorney regularly.

Attorneys, enrolled agents, and CPAs are the only professionals authorized to represent you with the IRS.

As a general rule, you need a full or part-time bookkeeper. If you're up to the task (and many small-business owners like it this way), you can wear that hat, too. If you aren't adept at follow-through or if numbers just plain scare you, consider hiring someone.

Depending on the experience (or inexperience) of the professional and the market rate in your community, you can hire a basic entry-level bookkeeper (often referred to as a *bookkeeper clerk*), for a fairly low hourly rate. (The rate can start in the range of $10–$20 an hour, depending on experience.) A more experienced person, such as a professional full-time bookkeeper or a professionally certified bookkeeper, charges a much higher hourly rate — or a mid-to-upper-end management-level salary if you hire the person full time.

When you interview bookkeeper candidates, use the free Bookkeeper's Hiring Test, available from the American Institute of Professional Bookkeepers, to qualify them. You can find and print the test at www.aipb.org/testrequest.php.

Knowing what to expect from your tax professional

In addition to having someone handle your daily financial recordkeeping, you should establish a relationship with a CPA, an accountant, or an enrolled agent. This type of professional should be available to assist you with these tasks:

✦ Prepare and file your taxes

✦ Set up your accounting system

✦ Advise you on the legal organization of your company (and other start-up issues)

✦ Compile (or review) financial statements

✦ Assist you in long-term financial planning for your business

✦ Address specific tax-law questions and concerns as they arise

✦ Ensure that the proper amounts and types of taxes are being filed

✦ Guide you in the completion of (or submit on your behalf) all quarterly tax documentation and other forms that might be required annually

✦ Answer questions and advise you about other general tax- and finance-related concerns

These professionals typically charge a high hourly rate. (A CPA's rate can start at $125 an hour.) Make sure that you clarify how you're charged for time. (Some professionals don't charge for questions asked by way of e-mail, and others do, for example.)

Before you consult with your outside professional advisor, make a list of the specific questions or issues you want addressed. This list keeps you on track and ensures that you maximize the time spent with your advisor while avoiding running up steep bills.

Finding likely candidates

After you decide which type of professional you want to hire, your next step is finding one. Fortunately, you have lots of places to turn to for a head start on this task:

✦ **Referrals:** Ask business peers and family members whom they use or recommend. Ask for specific information, such as

  • What do you like about the way this person does business?

  • What expertise does the professional have?

  • How long have you known this person or used his or her services?

  • How much does this person typically charge?

✦ **Local organizations:** Area Chamber of Commerce chapters and other local business associations often make their membership databases available to the public. Although the organizations typically don't endorse one member over another, they can suggest which professionals might be best suited for your specific requirements and tell you whether any complaints have been registered against them.

✦ **Professional associations:** Industry or professional groups are a terrific place to start your search for a CPA or other accounting professional. You can check out this list of organizations to get started:

  • American Institute of Certified Public Accountants: www.aicpa.org

  • National Association for Enrolled Agents: www.naea.org

  • American Association of Attorney-Certified Public Accountants: www.attorney-cpa.com

- CPA Associates International: www.cpaai.com
- American Institute of Professional Bookkeepers: www.aipb.org
- AGN North America (a worldwide association of separate and independent accounting and consulting firms): www.agn-na.org

✦ **Classifieds:** When you're hiring a bookkeeper or an accountant, feel free to place an ad in local newspapers, online career or job sites, or on social media sites, such as LinkedIn. These are all good resources for finding the best candidate.

When you place a help-wanted ad, you'll hear from better-qualified candidates if you're specific about the required job functions. We also recommend requesting that job candidates forward their salary requirements or salary history, along with their résumés.

✦ **Phone book and search engines:** If all else fails, the Yellow Pages usually has a substantial listing of potential financial advisors. And a quick search on Google or Yahoo! will also return a healthy list of local options.

**Book II
Chapter 4**

Accounting for Taxes (and Then Some)

Narrow the field of reputable contenders by skimming advertisements for professionals who list specific certifications, licensures, and memberships in professional associations.

Choosing the best person for you

After you create a short list of possible candidates, how do you decide which one is best suited for your business? In addition to checking for proper accreditations and confirming hourly rates, you have to consider a few other issues when you're choosing a CPA, an accountant, an enrolled agent, or even a tax attorney:

✦ **Experience:** You want to know whether the person specializes in particular areas of accounting or tax law. You should also find out, however, what type of work now takes up the majority of the professional's time and also the type of work performed in the past. Two critical questions to ask are

- What areas do you most enjoy handling?
- In which areas do you have the most up-to-date knowledge?

Because definitive rules of taxation and the Internet are still somewhat up in the air, you're not as likely to find a professional who specializes in this area. Instead, look for someone who's eager and willing to stay informed on new issues and changes to the tax law. Preferably, choose someone who's committed to tracking down the answers to difficult or lesser-known tax questions.

Ask your CPA about changes in the tax law to determine whether you're affected. The IRS provides a quick summary of those yearly changes on its website at www.irs.gov.

✦ **Availability:** A highly qualified independent professional often has a waiting list of clients. Although that's a helpful situation for the accountant, it doesn't help you. You need a professional who can work with you now. No matter what, it doesn't hurt to ask what the person's client schedule is like. For example, some professionals work part-time or have a four-day workweek. Others are eagerly growing their businesses and are available to answer your questions seven days a week. Nothing is wrong with either schedule; just find the one that you can live with as a client.

✦ **Firm size:** Size does matter, and sometimes a smaller firm is the better option. Even though some folks think that a large, recognizable accounting firm is the way to go, that's not always the case. If you have a small company, you might find yourself at the bottom of the totem pole when the firm prioritizes its clients. Your company's needs might get passed off to a junior accountant or other staff person. Unless your business is large enough to support individual departments (HR and marketing, for example), working with a large firm may mean less attention and higher rates. A smaller firm or an independent professional may give you more dedicated attention and be available immediately to answer your questions.

✦ **Philosophy:** Your financial advisors are ultimately your partners in business. Their professional views *must* complement yours. We're referring to not only ethics but also strategic philosophies. For example, if you're an aggressive risk taker in business, you may think that a conservative accountant will hold you back. Alternatively, you may prefer a conservative outlook as a means to provide a system of checks and balances to your liberal financial outlook.

✦ **Work style:** This term refers to how professionals interact with you and service your needs. For example, does the CPA insist that his firm file all required paperwork with the IRS, at a steep hourly rate? Or does he prefer to help you get started and then encourage you to take care of everything yourself to keep your expenses in check? What are his preferred methods of communication? If your tax professional isn't a fan of e-mail, he might respond to your questions only by phone. Or an assistant might serve as a middleman, so the tax professional is rarely available to talk with you unless you schedule a formal appointment. Again, none of these issues has a right or wrong answer. Find a style that best meshes with your preferences.

Spending the time to determine these concerns means a lot to the future of your online business. After all, this professional plays an integral part in your business as a trusted financial advisor. That's why we suggest taking your time to select the best match for you and your new business.

Following the Rules of Recordkeeping

After you find a CPA or another financial professional, that person no doubt instructs you on the rules of good recordkeeping. In the meantime, take our crash course to help you get started doing things right!

Dealing with all the paper

When we refer to *records* in the remainder of this chapter, we don't mean your account logs. Instead, we're talking about the physical records (the dreaded *paper trail*) that the IRS expects you to maintain. The thought of accidentally throwing out the wrong receipt or losing a copy of a questionable invoice can send chills up the spine of any well-meaning entrepreneur if the IRS comes calling. At the same time, your office space probably doesn't come with unlimited storage space.

How do you balance the need to hang on to important receipts with the need not to be overrun by the growing mounds of paper? The good news is that the IRS now recognizes electronic versions of financial records. You can therefore scan copies of receipts, invoices, logbooks, and other proof of financial transactions and save them as files on your computer or, better, back up these files online (in the cloud) or to a DVD. Then you get to throw out the hard copies! That's the easiest way to avoid the clutter that builds up with months and years of business transactions.

If you lose the electronic file and are audited, the IRS isn't sympathetic. The loss could cost you thousands of dollars — and possible jail time (in the worst-case scenario). We highly encourage you to make multiple copies and store one or more sets at another location or in a fireproof safe, or have a backup copy saved online but off-site.

You can avoid the time it takes to scan and save critical documentation by hiring a company to do it for you. In addition to making electronic copies of your paper trail, these digital documentation specialists store the electronic files for you. You can also purchase digital documentation software that makes scanning records yourself easy.

Storing records: How long is long enough?

Whether or not you "go digital" with your recordkeeping, one critical question remains: How long should you keep records? We should have a straightforward answer for you, but we haven't found one yet. That's because the IRS states (in Publication 583):

> You must keep your records as long as they may be needed for the administration of any provision of the Internal Revenue Code. Generally, this means you must keep records that support an item of income or deduction on a return until the period of limitations for that return runs out. The period of limitations is the period of time in which you can amend your return to claim a credit or refund, or the IRS can assess additional tax.

Huh? Well, the IRS says that you should keep records for as long as there's a possibility that it might audit you. We always heard that seven years is a safe bet. However, the true issue isn't the type of *documentation;* rather, it's the type of *situation* you encounter with the IRS.

For example, if you have employees, the IRS says that those tax records must be kept for at least four years from the period the tax becomes due or is paid, whichever is later. On the other hand, records about assets, such as property, should be kept until the period of limitations expires for the year in which you dispose of the property. Even tangible guidelines such as those, however, could be null and void if you're audited for a fraudulent tax return. In that case, all bets are off and you had better have ready access to *all* your records, from the beginning of time!

All these situations make up what the IRS refers to as a *period of limitations.* Table 4-3 gives you an overview of the rules for these time restrictions, as defined by the IRS.

Keep these employee records safely filed away

The IRS advises that you retain any information related to employee taxes. Even if a record relates to someone who no longer works for you, keep the following documents for at least four years:

- Amounts and dates of all wage payments (including annuity and pension)

- Amounts of tips reported by your employees and records of allocated tips

- Fair market value of in-kind wages paid to your employees

- Employee information, including name, address, Social Security number, job title, and dates of employment

- Copies of Forms W-2 and W-2c that were returned to you (undeliverable, if mailed)

- Records of sick pay or other pay due to injury or absence (including the amount and weekly rate of payments that you or a third-party payer made)

- Copies of employees' income tax withholding allowance certificates — Forms W-4, W-4P, W-4(SP), W-4S, and W-4V

- Dates and amounts of tax deposits you made, along with confirmation numbers for deposits made by Electronic Funds Transfer Protocol (EFTP)

- Copies of filed returns, including 941 TeleFile tax records and confirmation numbers

- Records of any fringe benefits provided to employees, including expense reimbursements paid

Table 4-3	IRS Periods of Limitations
If You Do This	*The Period Is This Long*
Owe additional tax and the other situations in this table don't apply	Three years
Fail to report legitimate income that's more than 25 percent of the gross amount on your return	Six years
File a fraudulent return	Unlimited
Fail to file a tax return	Unlimited
File a claim for credit or a refund after filing your return	Two to three years after tax is paid
File a claim for a loss from bad debt or worthless securities	Seven years

To play it safe, embrace the philosophy "When in doubt, hang on to it." This technique is especially manageable if you have limitless storage capacity for electronic documentation.

Businesses of all sizes may be eligible for certain deductions or tax breaks, specifically those designed to provide monetary incentive to help stimulate the economy through job growth and expansion. Tax incentives may be available for a limited time period or have exclusions and other stipulations. Take the time to discuss available deductions or incentives with your accountant or tax advisor. After all, these types of tax breaks could mean additional money in your business bank account!

We hope that you never have to worry about an audit from Uncle Sam (the U.S. government). The thought that it's always a possibility, though, is certainly incentive enough to keep all your records in order!

Book III
Website Design

Contents at a Glance

Chapter 1: What's in a (Domain) Name?

*I*n the offline world, the mantra of success for business is "Location, location, location!" It's not much different for your online business: Rather than use a numerical address on a building, though, you now use a virtual address or domain name. Usually, your online address includes your company's name or initials or some other derivation. A traditional business address is listed in the Yellow Pages, and your online address is listed with search engines.

As you might guess, securing the best possible domain name is an important piece of your overall online strategy because the name you select can influence how easily customers can find you.

How do you get the perfect name to drive customers to your online place of business? Not to worry: After using the information in this chapter, you'll find that choosing and registering your address is only a few clicks away.

Choosing Your Online Identity

Let's start with the basics. A *URL*, or *Uniform Resource Locator*, represents the unique address for each page on a website or document posted online. Your website might be made up of several web pages, each with a unique URL.

Before you start creating web pages, your first order of business is to determine your domain name, or the part of the URL that specifically identifies the name of your website. We break down a typical URL in Figure 1-1.

Figure 1-1: A URL, deconstructed.

World Wide Web · Top-level domain · Specific document

http://www.bizoffice.com/resources/new_biz/finance.html

HyperText Transfer Protocol · Registered domain · Directory

You no longer have to enter the entire URL (as shown in Figure 1-1) to get to a website. You can omit both the `http://` and `www.` when entering the site URL in your browser.

Although your website normally has only one domain name, it has more than one URL. The URL for the *home* page, or *entrance* page, of your site often looks the same as your domain name. Every page of your site, however, has a unique URL, such as

✦ `www.myveryfirstwebsite.com`: The home page

✦ `www.myveryfirstwebsite.com/index.html`: The home page (the same as omitting the `index.html` portion of the URL)

✦ `www.myveryfirstwebsite.com/services.html`: The web page that contains information about the services you offer

Approaching your domain name carefully

You can take one of two opposing approaches when you select your domain name:

✦ **You have an existing business or have already named your start-up.** If that's the case, you usually should match (as closely as possible) your company's name to the domain name. Using your existing business name is simple, straightforward, and often quite effective. It's possible that your exact name is not available, in which case you have to use some form of the name or add descriptors to the name.

✦ **The success of your online company hinges on the domain name itself.** Maybe you're starting an Internet company that sells *e-books* (electronic, downloadable information) telling readers how to start a business. In that case, your legal company name might be irrelevant. A more important consideration is to find a domain that clearly indicates your type of business or the customers you're targeting. In this scenario, your company name might be John Smith dba JS Enterprises. A more effective domain name for your business, however, might be `www.bizstartuptips411.com` because it says what you do.

Understanding what a domain name should be

No matter what approach you take to choosing your online business name, consider the following list of common denominators in determining the best possible domain for you. A good domain name should have these characteristics:

✦ **Easy to spell:** As anyone who depends on a computer's spell checker can testify, the average person doesn't do well in a spelling bee. That's why we're firm believers in avoiding hard-to-spell words in your domain name. Although www.BriansBodaciousRibs.com seems harmless enough, it's fairly easy to flub. Why not try www.briansgoodribs.com or www.goodeating.com? The easier your domain name is to spell, the more likely customers are to find you without a hassle. (And, when they do find you, the more likely they'll be in the mood to buy some of your bodacious eats!)

✦ **Simple to remember:** Your domain name doesn't have to be catchy or trendy to work. Simplicity goes a long way in our crowded, overhyped world.

✦ **Relatively short:** A shorter name is easier for customers to remember than a longer one. Consider the (fictitious) law firm Brewer, Mackey, Youngstein, Yale, and Associates. Its URL might be

    www.BrewerMackeyYoungsteinYaleandAssociates.com

Wow! That name takes a while to type, not to mention that you have to spell everybody's name correctly. Instead, consider the name www.BrewerandAssociates.com. See the difference?

✦ **Contains important keywords:** This characteristic is important for two reasons:

  • Using descriptive words in the domain clearly says what you do.

  • Using relevant words that frequently show up in search engines is potentially beneficial to your site's rankings. (We explain search engine optimization further in Book VI, Chapter 6.)

The law firm used in the preceding example can easily use *keywords,* or words that might be easily associated with the type of business, to create one of these domain combinations:

  • www.legalfirmforhire.com

  • www.breweryounglawyers.com

  • www.attorneysbmyy.com

✦ **Intuitive to customers:** You want a domain name to provide, ideally, a sense of who you are and an indication of the type of products or services you're selling. You don't need a *literal* translation, such as www.isellbooks.com — depending on your business, that approach could be detrimental to sales. What if you're selling to a highly targeted or specialized market (such as teenagers or radical sports fans)? A straightforward domain name is labeled as boring and undermines the image of your company, whereas an edgy or more creative name can win customers. For example, a bookseller specializing in romance novels might use a domain name such as www.romancingthepages.com or www.steamyreads.com. The point is that your customer base, whoever it consists of, should be responsive to your domain name.

Registering the Perfect Name

Congratulations: You chose your domain name, and you're ready to make it official. The next step is to register the name with a domain registrar. You can sign up using any company that specializes in domain registration. The registrar takes care of all the paperwork that's required to activate your new domain name, including these tasks:

✦ Submitting contact information

✦ Determining the duration of the registration period

✦ Listing your domain in the official Internet list of domains maintained by the Internet Corporation for Assigned Names and Numbers (ICANN) at www.icann.org

 If you're launching an e-commerce store, the storefront solution you use may include free domain registration, in which case it's best to register through that solution provider. We discuss getting started with storefronts in Book VIII, Chapter 3.

Who you gonna call?

Who registers domains? Your ISP (Internet service provider) might do it because many now provide this service along with hosting options. Or you can use any other company or website that acts as a third-party affiliate for registrars. If you're creating a website or blog in WordPress, you can register your domain there. In other words, now you can register a domain name with almost anyone!

Although finding a place to sign up is a piece of cake, the annual price for a domain registration varies from a few dollars to more than $30. Several factors influence pricing, including the number of years for which you're registering the domain, the provider, and the type of extension (such as .com, .net, .biz, or .tv). If you add features such as private registration (which restricts the registration details available to the public), the prices goes up. Or you can wind up paying nothing for domain registration if you buy several services at one time. (Most domain registrars also offer services such as hosting, e-mail, websites, and blogs.)

Most domain registration sites regularly offer discount domain pricing. Shop around for the best deal.

Let's make it official

After you make a decision about where to register, it's time to get down to business. The registration process is similar regardless of the service you use. To show you how painlessly you can reserve your domain name, we walk you through the process using the GoDaddy service. Note, though, that we aren't recommending GoDaddy over other services.

Follow these steps to quickly register your domain name:

1. **Go to the Go Daddy website at** `www.godaddy.com`.

2. **Enter the name you want to register in the domain search box on the home page of the site.**

   Type only the name you want, and don't preface it with www. The registrar adds that part automatically. (Some registrars' domain search boxes place the www. in front of the search box to remind you that typing that part isn't necessary.)

3. **To the right of the search box, click the Search Domain button.**

   A page appears listing the results of a search for the default extension, .com.

4. **If your domain name isn't available, start over at Step 2.**

   Read the rest of the chapter first for tips on finding a domain name.

5. **If you want to register an additional name, select its check box.**

   You can have multiple working domains even when you have only a single website. Simply *forward,* or redirect, the domain by pointing all other extensions to the designated domain of your choice.

6. **If you want to register an extension other than .com, select it from the list.**

   When you're registering a .com extension, register the matching .net version if it's available. These extensions are still the two most common. If your site is successful, a savvy competitor is more likely to snatch up the .net version over any other. This statement is especially true if the domain name is descriptive with a wide appeal (such as `partygoods.com`) or falls in a popular search category (such as `starwarsfans.com`). If the .com version of your domain isn't available and you're registering another extension, one domain is plenty for starters. After your site grows, you can determine the value of registering other names.

7. **Scroll to the bottom of the page and click the Continue to Cart button. Or click the +Submit button for each domain name you want to register and then click the Continue to Cart button.**

   You see a list of add-on products, including private registration, hosting and e-mail. At any point, you can skip these add-on suggestions and go to the bottom of the page and choose the Continue to Cart button to continue with the registration process.

   During the process of registering your domain, GoDaddy tries to get you to buy other services, from privacy protection to web hosting. If you do not want any of these additional services, you can skip the offers by scrolling down to the bottom of each page and clicking the Continue to Cart button.

8. **Select the term, or number of years for which you want to register the domain.**

   Your order's total appears.

9. **Click the Continue to Checkout button.**

10. **Log in to an existing account (as a returning customer), or set up an account as a new customer.**

    If you're a new customer, you provide basic information (your name, address, and e-mail address) to set up your account.

    To set up your account, the information you provided in the initial domain registration process is automatically used by GoDaddy to fill in your technical, administrative, and billing contact information, unless you specify otherwise. Use these default settings for now. You can always change this information later.

11. **Click the Continue button.**

    You see a page summarizing your order information.

12. **Review your information and place your order.**

    A thank-you page appears. Congratulations — you now have a domain name that's all yours!

Finding Out What to Do When Somebody Gets There First

We hope that the domain you want is the one you get when you register. Sometimes, though, your first choice for a domain isn't available. Nothing bursts a bubble faster than having this sort of event happen. Don't let it frustrate you, though. You still have several options.

Exploring your domain name options

When you initially search for your domain (as described in the preceding section), the registrar might tell you that it isn't available. Below that notification is typically a box containing a list of suggested alternative domains that the registrar has available. Don't be surprised if the automated system returns a few decent alternatives. At this point, you can choose one of the suggested runners-up generated by the registrar.

If you don't find a perfect match on the suggested list, the next-less-appealing choice takes you right back to the drawing board. Yep, you can start a brand-new search for an entirely different name.

Getting what you want — at a price

Starting from scratch again usually isn't your preference. After all, you might have fallen head over heels for a domain name and no substitute will work. In that case, you should know that you can pursue that domain name, even though it's already taken.

Here are the ways you can go in hot pursuit of your dream domain name:

✦ **Put the name on back order.** Think of this strategy as the official waiting list of domain names. A registrar keeps your name on file and notifies you when the domain you want expires and becomes available. The back-ordered domains go to auction, and you can bid for the opportunity to buy (or register) it.

✦ **Make an offer.** You might be too impatient to wait and see whether a domain expires. The owner can decide to renew it, and then it's gone for at least another year. That's why several registrars will contact the owner on your behalf and try to negotiate the purchase of the domain name. For this service, you pay a flat fee plus commission. Using this technique makes sense for a couple of reasons:

 • *You can find out quickly whether an owner is willing to give up a domain name.* The seller must respond within a specified time.

 • *Your name and personal information are kept private.* If the offer is accepted, you pay the registrar by credit card and the money is transferred to the seller. The registrar handles the entire process, including the transfer of the domain name.

✦ **Contact the owner.** If you prefer to negotiate directly, contacting the domain owner in person is another option, provided their registration information is open to the public. Even though you lose your anonymity in this process, you avoid paying service fees. Better yet, direct contact provides the opportunity to plead your case and use personal charm to try to get a good price for the name. (Okay, that's not always enough to sway a seller, but it might help.) Many companies have negotiated directly with sellers with much success. One domain owner, who no longer had an active site for the URL, gave away the domain. The moral of this story: It never hurts to ask.

TIP

If a domain owner has chosen a private registration, you may still be able to locate him or her. If the website for the domain is active (you can view it), search the pages for contact information (a phone number or an e-mail address). If you find a name, you may also be able to find the person on social media, such as LinkedIn, and make contact that way.

REMEMBER

Finding the owner of a domain name is easy to do when you use the WHOIS feature offered by registrars. The option to use WHOIS is typically provided to you automatically if your domain search shows that the name is already taken. You can also find a direct link for the WHOIS feature at the top or bottom of the registrar's home page. (Figure 1-2 shows you the information you can find about a domain order when you're using WHOIS.)

Figure 1-2: WHOIS reveals domain owners.

All the Good Ones Are (Not) Taken

Approximately 265 million top-level domain names are actively registered as of the third quarter of 2013, according to Verisign's Domain Name Industry Brief (www.verisigninc.com/en_US/innovation/dnib/index.xhtml). Moreover, the report states a year-over-year increase of approximately 8 percent. You might think that all the good domain names have been taken (or are being held hostage for a huge ransom). Not true! Plenty of great domain names are available. The continued popularity of the Internet has prompted lots of acceptable and creative alternatives for domain registration.

Varying the extension

One of the easiest ways to find a good domain name is to use an alternative extension, although we can't deny that the old favorites .com, .net, .info, and .org remain the most recognizable. Dozens of extensions, including specific country codes, are now in use, and using these alternatives is no longer considered a stigma.

Table 1-1 lists the most common U.S. extensions. We also list some additional extensions by country, but note that more are available, including the popular .Asia, for example. Don't shy away from any of these. Looking through the list is a simple way to find the domain name of your choice.

Table 1-1	Sampling of Extensions Used in Domain Registration
Extension	*Generally Used For*
.com	General business (.com stands for *commercial*)
.net	Internet business (.net stands for *network*)
.org	Nonprofit and trade association (.org stands for *organization*)
.info	Resource
.biz	Small business
.tv	Entertainment, media
.name	Personal use
.mobi	Mobile business sites
.travel	Travel industry use
.ws	Web (former country code)
.bz	Business (former country code)
.cc	Miscellaneous (former country code)
.us	United States
.vg	British Virgin Islands
.co.uk	General business in United Kingdom
.org.uk	Nonprofit and trade association, United Kingdom
.me.uk	Personal, United Kingdom
.de	Germany
.jp	Japan
.be	Belgium
.at	Austria
.com.mx	General business, Mexico
.com.nz	General business, New Zealand

(continued)

Table 1-1 *(continued)*

Extension	Generally Used For
.net.nz	Usually Internet provider, New Zealand
.org.nz	Nonprofit and trade association, New Zealand
.gs	South Georgia, South Sandwich Islands
.tc	Turks, Caicos Islands
.ms	Montserrat

Getting creative

Acquiring the domain name you view as most suitable for your business may involve a little creativity on your part. As you have probably seen, most general names (applying to wide or popular categories) were scooped up during the first Internet craze of the 1990s. All the gems — `Business.com`, `Politics.com`, `SportsFan.net` — are long gone.

Don't let this information stop you. Keep in mind that plenty of domain names are as effective as those first category-busters. Here are four creative ways to find an outstanding domain name:

✦ **Make the domain name specific.** One recent trend is that of niche (or specific) sites. You can find out more about growing a niche on the Net in Book X. For now, we want you to know that the same trend applies to domain names. Creating a more specific and telling name, rather than one that's broad, serves you well in search engine rankings and with your customer base. For example, `www.ilovecheese.com` is specific about its subject and audience.

✦ **Make the domain name creatively telling.** Ever hear that saying about thinking outside the box? Even though it's a cliché, it holds true with domain names: Sometimes, you're trapped into seeing only one way to describe something, and that usually means being literal. If you sell food and toys for cats, you're tempted to find a domain that says exactly that: `cattoys.com`. Rather than continuously circle around the same type of name, think about other ways that your products, services, or target audience are viewed. Make a list of terms and phrases that people use when they talk about these items. You can still be specific but with a more creative tone. That cat site may do extremely well using a domain name like `mouseloversonly.com` or `thescratchingpost.com`.

✦ **Make the domain name perfectly meaningless.** Have you ever stumbled across a website with an outrageously different but perfectly applicable name (like Google and Yahoo!)? Websites with extremely odd, fun, or funky domain names can grow a following like any other site. This advice is best if you're in a business that lends itself to a less conservative approach.

✦ **Use add-ins.** If your domain name uses common words, finding an exact match available isn't all that easy. Not to worry: Just mix it up a bit. Abbreviate your words or use a few initials rather than spell out the whole thing. Or break up the name with a hyphen or two (`Pearl-Earrings-For-You.com`, for example). You can also add *inc* or *corp* to the end of your company name (only if you're incorporated, of course) or add another word that indicates the industry you're in — for example, `SmithJewelersInc.com` or `SmithPearlsandDiamonds.com`. Another trick is to include words such as *official, favorite, original,* or *popular* to the domain name (`FavoritePearlEarrings.com`, for example).

Chapter 2: Designing Customer-Friendly Sites

In This Chapter

✔ Preparing for profitability

✔ Considering timeless design options

✔ Doing away with fluff

✔ Winning raves with function

You might have put most of your efforts into dreaming about and planning for your business. As you begin designing your website, though, you see your ideas come to life for the first time. Creating that first site is exhilarating! You have to stay focused, though. Otherwise, you risk becoming distracted by bells and whistles that can waste your time and money.

Experience has taught us that you can easily avoid certain common mistakes. The key is to develop a plan, keep it simple, and stick to it. If you follow these ground rules, you're rewarded with a website that's functional, timeless, and customer friendly.

Maximizing Performance for Profitability

You're in business to make a profit, so how does your website fit into that goal? Although the answer to this question might seem obvious, you can easily forget that your website is both a marketing tool and a vehicle for obtaining profits. The common denominator between those two points is a site that's functional for customers. When you maximize your customer's ease of use and experience with your site, everyone wins.

To get the most from your site, we recommend creating a *profitability plan,* which is all about efficiency. You start by strategically identifying the features, technologies, and products for sale that enhance profitability — and getting rid of those that don't.

Ideally, you want to develop this plan before your first site goes up. Then you can address profitability in every page of the site as it's built. Not to worry, though: You can apply the same methodology to an existing site. The process just might take a little more time if you need to restructure the flow of your site, or the pathway you want visitors to take to meet your goals. Either way, maximizing your profit is worth the effort.

When you're ready to create a plan that maximizes your potential for profitability, follow these steps:

1. **Define the purpose of your site.**

   The purpose should reflect your site's role in your overall business. Voice that purpose in only one or two sentences. If you have trouble getting started, try answering these questions:

   - My website exists because _____.

   - I am creating (or planning) a website because _____.

   - When my site is complete, I want it to _____.

2. **Evaluate your revenue streams by listing all the ways in which you earn, or plan to earn, revenue from your site.**

   Be specific when you list the ways in which your site contributes to your revenues. For example, divide the list into two categories: direct revenue and indirect revenue.

3. **After you list your profit sources, assign a numeric value to them.**

   The numeric value is based on both sales volume and profitability. Of course, if your site isn't developed, you don't have a sales history. Instead, you rank items according to expected profitability. (You can go back later and cross-reference them by both profitability and bestsellers.)

4. **Determine which applications or functions on your site contribute most to your revenue sources and which indirectly support revenue growth.**

   This step helps you not only understand the purpose of each site element but also prioritize where to spend your time and resources. Some components are essential to building sales, but others are just nice to have. For instance, a shopping cart or payment-processing method directly affects sales because customers use it to purchase products. Similarly, call-to-action buttons or links are important because they prompt for a desired transaction. Social media sharing buttons and a registration box to sign up for a newsletter are examples of indirect contributors. (Although social sharing and the newsletter don't lead to immediate purchases, they help future sales by creating continued awareness.)

5. **Compare your remaining list of products, services, and features with your site's purpose (as defined in Step 1) and omit the ones that don't directly contribute to it.**

   Items that don't directly reflect your site's original intent can cannibalize it down the road and eat away at your profits. By streamlining your revenue sources, you keep the site tightly focused on its target customer.

   You should understand now what adds value to your site (and to what degree).

6. **Strategically place features and revenue sources on your site map, which becomes your profitability plan.**

Usually, a site map represents all the pages that make up your website. The layout indicates the placement of the pages. In this step, you're simply creating a site map, or visitor pathway, based on profitability. In other words, specify where you want those "opportunities to purchase" to be placed on pages in the site. Is your largest revenue generator promoted or clearly visible from the top of your home page, or do customers have to click through five pages to see it? Which of your pages are top *landing pages* (pages other than your home page where visitors are likely to enter your site)? Do these landing page contain the right information or calls to action to lead to a purchase? If you receive indirect revenue when customers agree to submit a form page for more information, can they access the form from your home page or those top landing pages?

Now you have a plan! With your profitability plan in hand, you have a guide during the technical stage of building your site. (We address the technical aspect of site development in Chapter 3 of this minibook.) First, you have to tackle the style issue. No matter how much you plan for profitability, if your site isn't attractive, customers won't hang around long enough to make a purchase.

Looking Your Best

First impressions are lasting ones, or so the old saying implies. In the first few seconds of viewing your site, visitors first decide what they think about it. Often, a favorable impression is based entirely on the design elements you use. From classic to vintage or from plain Jane to modern, establishing that look sets the tone for your entire site.

Following basic design principles

When you're thinking about site design, consider the following major elements that contribute to a winning look:

✦ **Structure:** The foundation of your site's design is its structure, or *layout.* Determining the layout of your site requires that you make decisions about these elements:

- *Number of pages:* Consider the depth of the site (the number of pages that are necessary).

- *Placement of the navigational toolbar:* The series of buttons or links that people use to visit different areas of your site — referred to as a toolbar, navigation bar, or menu bar — is commonly placed along the left (or right) side of the site, along the top, or in in both places. Making your site *responsive,* or adaptive to viewing on mobile devices, is a critical part of site design today. Simple, fixed menu bars or drop-down menu bars are popular style choices when building a responsive website. Figures 2-1 and 2-2 shows one of the ways to use a simple navigational bar that expands to reveal multiple levels of navigation.

- *Buttons, tabs, and links:* Buttons you can use on the navigation bar come in unlimited designs, shapes, and colors (depending on the software you use). Additionally, you can use text, rather than a button, as a link. TravelOregon, shown in Figure 2-3, uses a different style approach to a navigation bar. You might also want to repeat a navigational bar in the form of links at the bottom of the page.

Figure 2-1:
This website starts with a simple navigation bar.

Figure 2-2:
The simple navigation bar expands to reveal more detailed options.

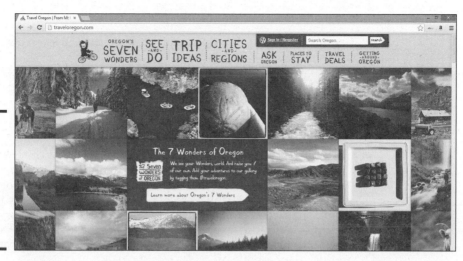

Figure 2-3:
This site takes a whimsical approach to the style of their menu bar.

✦ **Color:** An influential design element is the color scheme for your site. Do you go bold and bright or soft and understated, or do you stick to plain white or neutral colors? Another consideration is how to incorporate those colors (or lack thereof) into the site. You can use a color as a background for your entire site, to highlight sections of text, or to separate segments within your site.

✦ **Font:** The font type and size you use throughout your site makes a statement. And with thousands of font styles to select from, you can send a variety of messages to your customers in the blink of an eye. Additionally, the text size you use contributes to not only the look of the site but also its readability. For example, text that's too small might not be easy to read. *Serif* fonts, which have hooks and loops on the letters, are also difficult to view when used online. Sans serif fonts remove the extra detail and can be more easily viewed online.

Font type is an element of web design that changes often, based on current design trends. For example, using creative, artistic, or graphical fonts became popular in 2014. In previous years, a simpler font style was preferred by most designers. In either case, it's important to find a design that works for your brand. To stick to the basics, see the following table for a list of some basic web fonts.

Font	*Message It Sends*
Arial	I'm common and nondescript.
Comic Sans	I'm choosing whimsy over seriousness.
Courier New	I'm old-fashioned, from the era of newsroom typewriters.

Font	Message It Sends
Georgia	I'm classic and professional and layered with style.
Times New Roman	I'm quite traditional.
Trebuchet	I'm professional yet relaxed (similar to casual Friday in the workplace).
Verdana	I emit a friendly, modern vibe.

✦ **Images:** The use of photos and graphics (animated or otherwise) can complement your site if they're used correctly. Images draw readers' eyes to specific areas of your site and can help illustrate information and ideas. High-quality images have always been a necessity if you're selling products. But now images are must-have elements for *all* types of sites — not just e-commerce. When you're designing your site, think about how many images you'll use, their size, and which location will produce the best effect.

✦ **Social media:** Unless you've been in a cave for the past few years, you know that social media sites such as Facebook, Twitter, Pinterest, Instagram, and LinkedIn continue to increase in popularity and that businesses of all types are expected to embrace them. (You discover more about social media and how to use it in your online business in Book VI.) Social media gets your customers more involved with your brand by encouraging them to comment and share information, which in turn could lead to more customers and more sales. To promote this type of activity, a decent amount of space throughout the website is used to persuade customers to "like" you on Facebook or "follow" you on Twitter. Other common social media tactics include offering customers the ability to *pin,* or share, images and product pictures from your website on social media sites such as Pinterest or Instagram. You need to consider where and how you place these opportunities on your site.

✦ **Media:** Video has become a common element that you should consider in the design of your website. The soaring popularity of YouTube, its influence in search engine rankings, and the amount of times it is shared through social media have contributed to the widespread acceptance and use of online video for all sorts of purposes. For some sites, this capability becomes an intricate design element. For others, it may be considered only as a marketing tool. Research supports the idea that video increases customer engagement (how the customer interacts with your site and brand) and can increase product sales (when using video for product reviews or testimonials, for example). You must weigh the pros and cons of video and decide where and when it will be used across your site, along with how to use it in a way that supports, rather than detracts, from your site's usability.

Does your site design work?

Before finalizing your site's design, ask yourself these questions to determine whether your site makes a winning first impression:

✔ Does the design reflect your defined purpose for the site?

✔ Will the look of the site appeal to your customers and encourage them to buy from you?

✔ Does the site's design (especially colors and fonts) allow information and products to be easily seen? Or do your eyes strain to look at text and images?

✔ Does the choice of layout, specifically the navigational bars, make it easy to locate information and move between pages?

✔ Is the site consistent with all other marketing and promotional tools you use?

✔ When customers first view the site, will it promote the image you want them to have of your company?

Making design choices

You must make a number of decisions when you develop the look and feel of your site. How do you choose which options make the most sense for you? Generally, one or more of these characteristics dictate a site's look:

✦ **Your industry or line of business:** If you're in a conservative industry, such as accounting or financial services, consider that subdued colors with a simple layout might appear to be more professional. Alternatively, if a potential customer is searching for a graphic designer, the customer might expect to see a bright, funky design with lots of colorful images. Figures 2-4 and 2-5 show two different types of businesses and the designs they chose to reflect their particular image.

Figure 2-4: This company chose a website design that reflects a more conservative business approach.

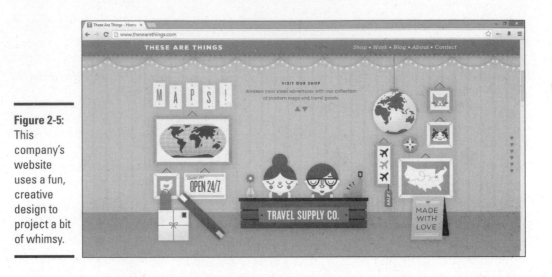

Figure 2-5:
This company's website uses a fun, creative design to project a bit of whimsy.

✦ **The types of products or services you offer:** Selling products or services that have a serious message (such as medical equipment) begs for a low-key design approach. And the information your site contains might require many layers of pages to provide research or product information. On the other hand, products that are fun or made for recreational purposes might sell better if the site is light and whimsical and filled with product images rather than with product data.

✦ **An existing brand:** Particularly if you have an established business, your site's style or look might be predetermined by your company's store or product base. You want your site's image to be consistent with your established brand. In that case, you should pull design elements for your website from a logo, marketing materials, or the design of the existing bricks-and-mortar location.

✦ **Your customers' demographics and psychographics:** Age, gender, education, and geographic location are examples of *demographics*. Attitudes, opinions, and values are considered *psychographics*. In general, the more you know about your customers, the more likely you are to create the appropriate feel for your site. Consider designing your site to fit the image of your target customer, especially with niche (or highly specialized) markets.

✦ **Your personal preferences:** Sometimes, your choice of design elements depends on which ones most appeal to your taste. (You get a say in this process, after all.) Okay, you shouldn't design a site based entirely on personal preference, but nothing is wrong with throwing in a few elements that make your heart sing.

The final consideration in designing your website is to create a timeless look — but we don't mean that you design a site once and never touch it again. A common pet peeve is a site on the Internet that's outdated and looks like an early-generation "brochure" site. We instantly feel as though the company doesn't care about its business or its customers. The company probably has a website only because someone told the company's owner that one was needed, so he or she turned a sales brochures into a basic three-page site, launched it on the World Wide Web, and never thought about it again.

If you want to create a website that's considered timeless, keep these three suggestions in mind:

✦ **Keep it simple.** Whether a site was developed in 2001 or 2014, trends change. Trust us when we say that trying to keep up with every new web design feature becomes expensive and time consuming. By keeping your design elements simple and by using only one or two trendy features, however, you increase the design lifespan of your site.

✦ **Keep the information updated and relevant.** This advice includes everything from text and photos to hypertext links and copyright dates. Keeping the substance of your site current offers value. Also, you can easily overlook a graphical design that might make a site seem dated, but having incorrect or outdated content is an e-commerce sin.

✦ **Avoid images or graphics that visually date the site.** For instance, if you use seasonal or current event photos, your site can quickly become dated. (However, these types of images are suitable in a blog or an area of the site that you plan on updating frequently.) Similarly, photos of people can be telltale signs of an outdated site because of clothing and hair. The exception is if you intentionally use graphics or photos that evoke a retro feel or provide relevant historical information.

Before designing your site, do your homework. Search the Internet for competitors' sites, and evaluate which design elements work and which don't. You can even gather a small group of prospective customers and ask them which sites they respond to most.

Choosing Substance Over Style

In case your head is filled with hot design ideas, we should mention that a good site doesn't function by design alone. In fact, sometimes you can make your site even better by sacrificing trendy design elements. The good news is that if you agree to forego a few of those high-end elements, your budget will breathe easier. The bad news is that some folks are just flashy, and breaking old habits isn't easy.

Okay, if you haven't guessed yet, we're talking about the use of Macromedia Flash, the intense graphics-animation program that some people swear is a website must-have. You've probably seen the images of fast cars that pulse across auto dealers' websites. Or maybe you noticed dancing fruit and animated paint splatters that mesmerize you while they move and twist seamlessly throughout a site — that's Flash animation. To be honest, its value is a point of contention among professional designers. Half agree that it's a beautiful, and perhaps even useful, tool. The other half think that the web would be better off without it. Confusing the matter further is that these views on the use of Flash continue to change.

Flash that's done well can be entertaining — and in some cases warranted. If you're looking for information quickly, though, or want to buy a product, having to continually trudge through Flash programs becomes annoying. For many reasons, the use of Flash has been on a steady decline; research indicates that less than 15 percent of websites now use Flash. Our professional opinion is that the majority of business websites can do without Flash. Thanks to HTML5 and its capabilities as an advanced programming language, especially when programming for mobile devices, experts agree that Flash is definitely on its way to being extinct. Here is a list of other reasons why Flash is not your friend when designing a website:

✦ **Flash is costly.** The added expense for developing Flash animation wreaks havoc on most design budgets. Also, if you need to update content frequently, the bills add up fast. Frankly, a better use of time and budget resources is to use video on your site.

✦ **Flash lacks purpose.** In most cases, high-tech Flash animations are unnecessary and don't serve a legitimate function.

✦ **Flash is a time burden.** The time it takes to load, or the need for special software to play an animation, is often frustrating to non-broadband customers.

✦ **Flash is ego driven.** A desire to develop Flash often revolves around web designers who want to flaunt their skill set, or site owners who want a jazzed-up site, as opposed to using a tool that suits the needs of the site.

✦ **Flash causes time delays.** Because the use of Flash can easily add to the development time of creating your site, using Flash adds not only cost but also time.

With so many reasons not to use Flash, you might be wondering whether you have any reasons *to* use it. Proponents of the development tool are quick to defend it (even though HTML5 is making these pro-Flash arguments increasingly difficult to defend). Here are what some people still view as positive aspects of Flash:

✦ **What you see is what everyone sees.** Flash ensures that your page appears the same way no matter which browser displays it.

✦ **Flash shows off your products.** In some cases, Flash can quickly and efficiently transfer information and dynamic images from a database and take up less bandwidth. Flash can also enhance product demonstrations.

✦ **Flash is creative.** The tool can be an interesting way to entertain, get attention, or encourage interactivity with your website.

✦ **Flash looks good when it's done well.** Flash, done well, can lend a professional, high-tech look to your site.

You don't have to completely shy away from using Flash, but be thoughtful in whether it will enhance your site's design and usability.

Whether you're pro or con about the use of Flash, the decision to incorporate it on your site ought to hinge on two questions:

✦ Does Flash enhance your customer's experience when they're visiting your site?

✦ Will your sales increase as a result of incorporating Flash into your site design?

Counting on Function to Win Customers

When discussing function and your website, it's good to take into account how function might influence a customer's overall experience, as well as the potential effect on revenue. Whether you're talking about a shopping cart application or a registration box that lets customers sign up for your newsletters, function is what drives a customer's experience. If a particular function adds value for the customer, it's likely to increase your revenues, either directly or indirectly.

Understanding the customer experience

Think back to one of your recent visits to a website. Maybe the site is one of your favorites or one you visited for the first time. How would you rate your experience? Did you find what you wanted quickly and easily? Did you glean the information you needed? Did your browsing lead to a purchase? Or were you frustrated by the whole thing and chose instead to move on to another site? Well, guess what? Your customers think about the same issues every time they visit your site.

Ultimately, customer experience leads them to make two important decisions:

✦ Whether to make a purchase from you

✦ Whether to return to your site

Throughout the rest of this chapter, we point out several examples of these functions (such as quick-loading pages, a site search function, and live customer service).

Building function into your site

When you consider what's at stake with your business when you design your own site, you have to figure out how to use function to influence customer decisions. We suggest attacking function at three levels.

At the first level are *basic functions*. Customers expect this lowest, or base, level of functionality. Basic functions include these features:

✦ **Quick-loading pages:** Customers don't have the patience to wait for pages to load. Even if they're still using slower dial-up connections, you're expected to ease that problem for them. If you don't anticipate customers having varying speeds of Internet access and account for that difference in your web design, you just missed a potential sale.

To decrease the need to load new pages in the site, consider using overlays or pop-up content boxes. These elements display additional information without the need to leave the page.

✦ **Ease of navigation:** When customers go from page to page in your site, the navigation tools you provide should allow customers to

- Readily find and identify navigational buttons and links.

- Immediately return to the home page, regardless of what page they're on.

- Return to the preceding or last-visited page by clicking a link.

- See pages and sections they have visited on the site by using a link history, usually at the top of the page.

✦ **Working links:** All internal and external links to pages on your site should be valid and working. In other words, customers don't want to click a link only to find a *Page Not Found* message. Broken links that go nowhere also diminish the credibility of your site and indicate that you don't update or maintain it.

✦ **Viewable images:** When you include photos and graphics on your site, be sure that the images — especially product images — load correctly and quickly. Additionally, avoid using grainy pictures or tiny images that are difficult for customers to see. (We provide more detail about working with images at the end of this chapter.)

✦ **Shopping carts:** Yes, this is a category unto itself (and we discuss it in detail in Book IV, Chapter 5). We list it as an interactive function because all too often small websites continue to make the mistake of not even using shopping carts on their sites. Instead, customers are asked to call the company to place orders, or to print, fill out, and fax order forms to the website owner. That's a fatal mistake! You *must* provide a method for shopping and paying for items over the Internet.

✦ **Mobile-ready:** Throughout this book we discuss the rising use of mobile devices and their effect on online businesses. Customers are using mobile devices to research, compare, and buy products. Mobile is also an increasingly important in search results. A result of this changing consumer behavior is an undeniable expectation that your website look good and function well on all types of mobile devices, including tablets and smartphones.

At the second level of site functionality are *interactive functions,* which actively engage customers with your site. Although this type of function isn't necessary to place an order, it can increase value and sales for your site. Samples of interactive functions include

✦ **Site search:** Give customers a tool that allows them to quickly search for information on your site. This function might not be as useful if your site is small. However, if you have a site filled with products or layers of data, customers appreciate having search capability.

✦ **Reviews:** Consider offering your visitors the option to review or rate the products and services you offer. This feature is particularly helpful, and almost expected, if you have an e-commerce site. Research shows that customers' buying decisions are heavily influenced by online reviews.

✦ **Community forums:** *Forums* (or types of discussion areas) provide options that let visitors interact with you and with one another. Many people consider forums a free form of technical support; if your community area or forum boards stay active and updated, this added function might keep customers coming back to your site.

✦ **Blogs:** These extremely popular online journals provide another opportunity for customers to interact with you and others. In Book X, Chapter 3, we show you how blogs not only provide enhanced functionality for your site but also serve as proven marketing tools — and can even be used as your primary site.

✦ **Member registration:** You can make registration free or make it a condition of accessing certain sections of your site. In return for signing up as members, visitors can receive newsletters, site updates, or e-mail messages announcing new products. Registration provides members with benefits and provides you with customer contact information — a win-win situation for both parties.

The third level is reserved for tools and features that offer customers an *enhanced* experience on your site. Items of enhanced functionality often include

✦ **Online demonstrations and tutorials:** Depending on the complexity of the products or services you sell, online demos and web-based tutorials can be useful. Customers receive the value of trying out the product or discovering how it's used, which often increases the likelihood of a purchase. Offering online learning options is easy and affordable by using videos (especially through YouTube).

**Book III
Chapter 2**

**Designing
Customer-Friendly
Sites**

Google Hangouts and Google Hangouts on Air are easy ways to create online tutorials or demos that you can share with your visitors. Hangouts enables you to do video calls and chats from your computer, and Hangouts on Air lets you broadcast to a wider audience and record directly to your YouTube account. Use both as quick methods for providing helpful, interactive components to your site.

✦ **Live or 24/7 customer support:** The Internet never sleeps, and neither do some of your customers. Your customer service is greatly enhanced if you can offer unlimited support. Although it isn't necessarily *technical* support, your customer might need to ask a question before making a decision to buy your service or product. Some research indicates that offering live support can increase online sales by as much as 20 percent.

You don't have to set up a full customer call center to offer live or 24/7 support. Several companies have developed the service for even the smallest online retailers. Try LiveEngage from LivePerson (`www.liveperson.com/liveengage`) to instantly add live customer support to your website. This tool offers various pricing plans based on the features you choose and the size of your business, including a pricing plan that charges only when someone uses the chat function on your site.

✦ **Geographic locators:** Okay, if you have physical locations in addition to your web presence, geography-related tools are a plus. Your customers appreciate access to maps and driving directions, store locators using interactive maps of the United States (or other countries), and even product-locator searches based on zip codes.

Customizing a map for your site is easy using Google Maps API; visit `https://developers.google.com/maps/tutorials/customizing/` to get started. This free tool lets you create maps and driving routes that you can add to your site immediately. Another free Google resource, Google Places (`www.google.com/business/placesforbusiness`), allows your offline store to be found more readily by customers searching on Google. Of course, this is useful only if you also have a physical location.

✦ **Second-language viewing options:** Not all your customers speak fluent English. Savvy website owners offer customers the option to view sites in other languages. (For example, Spanish is one of the most popular alternatives in the United States.)

✦ **Podcasts:** Giving access to information by using several different forms of media is much more common than ever before, yet is still considered an unexpected bonus. Try adding *podcasts* (self-published broadcasts over the Internet). Similar to video or Hangouts, podcasts are helpful ways to share more information about your products or services. You can also podcasts use to conduct short interviews with authors, designers, trend watchers, analysts, or anyone else your site visitors might find interesting (as they relate to your site). Because podcasts are available through Apple iTunes, you have a chance to reach visitors who might not otherwise know about your website.

As you see, understanding the value of functionality and the subsequent choices you make regarding function are major parts of developing a customer-friendly site. Building off functionality is also an opportunity to set yourself apart from your competition, by simply taking the time to plan.

You can build your site in lots of different ways: You or someone you hire might build a site from scratch, or you might buy a ready-made template or e-commerce-enabled storefront, or you could use blogging software (such as Wordpress or Drupal). Regardless of which method you use to build your site, you'll still have plenty of decisions to make when it comes to style and functionality options.

Book III
Chapter 2

Designing
Customer-Friendly
Sites

Chapter 3: Building a Site without Spending a Fortune

In This Chapter

✔ Planning a well-structured business website

✔ Finding out how to build your own website

✔ Using HTML commands effectively

✔ Building web pages with specific software tools

✔ Hiring the right professional to help you design your site

✔ Working with your professional designer

✔ Providing the right information at the right time

*I*n the early days of the Internet, simply having a website was a way to differentiate your business from the competition. As interest in the web developed and grew, companies of all shapes and sizes focused their efforts on capturing people's attention with websites. Because of this growth in online competition, planning a site and building a distinctive design and proposition became increasingly important. After all, an outstanding site encourages current customers to stay with your business and promotes your site's presence to the new shoppers who come online every day.

The same basic principles of website design apply as much now as they did when the web took off in the mid-1990s. Technologies used on the web might come and go, but you don't have to include the latest and greatest technology on your site. Customers are drawn to sites that are simple, focused, easy to use, well organized, and *useful.* Everything else is just sound and fury.

In this chapter, we present the steps for creating a website that serves your business and your customers. We direct you to spend some time defining exactly what you want on your site, and then we show you ways to implement your ideas, either by yourself or with the help of a professional. In either case, we specify the issues you need to consider and the traps you need to avoid so that you can focus on designing your website and then move on to the next phase of your business.

Mapping Your Route to a Successful Site

When people opt to build a new house or commercial building, they don't just hire a contractor, bring over the concrete and tools, and say "Go for it." Before construction even begins, they craft a carefully detailed plan that they review, edit, and approve. Your website should be treated the same way. The best sites aren't dreamed up by eccentric designers and thrown together quickly. Good sites require a clear road map from the people who run the business to ensure that the focus of the business is never lost.

Thinking about your website before you start its design is important. Start by making a list of all the functions you want to provide on your site. If you're tempted to believe that your site has just one function — to *sell stuff* — we encourage you to break down that function into subfunctions, by answering these questions:

✦ **What kinds of products do you want to sell?** The number and organization of pages you have on your site depends on the makeup and complexity of your products or services. For example, you should have at least one page for each type of service that you offer.

✦ **How many distinct categories of products will you sell?** You might need a separate page for each product category. Think about splitting up categories such as consumer electronics and computer products, for example.

✦ **Will customers be able to create an account on your site?** If so, you need to provide a page where customers can log in, update their personal information, view their orders, and enter payment information.

✦ **Will you provide customers with additional content, original or not?** Some websites make money by offering a subscription for their customers to read premium content such as special articles, interviews, and video, audio, and photo excerpts.

✦ **How will customers pay for their orders?** You need to be able to take credit card orders, and provide a mailing address if you accept personal checks or money orders.

✦ **Will you tell people about you and your business mission?** Some companies think that having a web page about their mission statement isn't important, whereas others use this page as a way to connect with customers.

✦ **Will you provide instructions for using your website?** It has been a common practice for websites to create a page for frequently asked questions (FAQs) to help their customers use the site properly and find everything that's available.

After you come up with your list of site functions, the next step is to draw a map showing the web pages you need to accomplish those functions and showing how the pages relate to one another. At this point, don't even think

Site-builder checklist

Most e-commerce websites have a basic list of pages that they provide to their customers. As you're designing your own site, take a look at the functions that most sites provide and decide which types of pages are right for your business:

✔ Home

✔ Catalog

✔ Customer account

✔ Order information

✔ Privacy policy

✔ Frequently asked questions

✔ Website and social media content

✔ Map and direction (if you have a retail site)

✔ Checkout

✔ Payment processing (PayPal or a merchant account)

✔ About Us or Company History (describes mission, purpose, or employees, for example)

about how the website or the individual pages will look; just identify the different pages that need to exist on your site. Assign each page to a box on your map, and check off the function that the page will handle. When you're done, you should have a map of your site that looks like a flowchart.

At the top of your map is the *home page,* which is your launch pad to the rest of the website (see Figure 3-1). This page answers all the basic questions that customers have about your business, just like the friendly receptionist in the lobby of a 50-story building. Whether this visit is the first — or the fiftieth — for your customers, the home page has to answer their questions in a clear, concise, organized way or be able to point them in the right direction quickly.

**Book III
Chapter 3**

Building a Site
without Spending a
Fortune

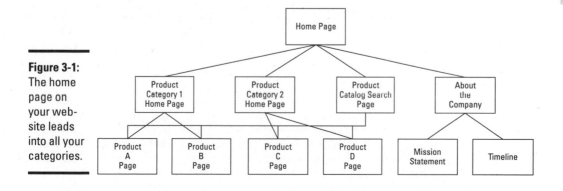

Figure 3-1:
The home page on your website leads into all your categories.

You can build a web page that holds a text version of the map you created and make it available to your customers. Just like a road atlas helps drivers follow their route, this *site map* helps your online customers find anything available on your site without taking a wrong turn — or, in this case, a wrong click.

Below the home page are your main category pages. Although your first draft might look like the one shown in Figure 3-1, the beauty of such a simple map is that your site plan can expand and grow from that basic model. As you design more complex and function-intensive websites, you can add more levels to your website map. When you build your site map this way, you can visualize how your entire site operates, because you capture how your pages support each other.

Setting reasonable expectations

When your website is in the paper-and-pen phase of design, you might find that you're adding a bunch of boxes (pages) and dreaming up the ultimate website. After all, you haven't designed or written the pages yet, so creating a gigantic, robust, fully functional site for any customer is easy — *on paper*.

Although we don't want to take the wind out of your sails (or is that *sales?*), we definitely advise you to keep these expectations and guidelines in mind as you begin to turn your road map into your virtual store:

✦ **Don't put too much stuff on one page.** Avoid tying together several product lines. If a page become bloated — too filled with information and graphics, for example — it becomes too long for customers to read and takes too long to load and display on their screens.

✦ **Position key information at the top.** Keep your pages short, and put key information at or near the top of the page. Newspapers place key articles *above the fold* (the top half of the newspaper page) because not all readers take the time to flip over the paper to read the bottom half. On the Internet, if you're asking your customers to scroll down the page to see something important, you're taking the risk that they won't do it and might leave your site without seeing your business's main functions.

✦ **Keep the number of steps to a minimum.** One reason why customers come back to a site such as Amazon is that they can find an item, click once, and have the item shipped to them. Customers turn to online shopping for convenience, so offer them a quick or smooth process to navigate the critical areas of your site. Even though some customers stay to look around, take advantage of your content, or use other functions, your site needs to appeal to the customers who want to get in, get what they want, and get out.

One way to check the complexity of your website is to look at your road map. If you have too many levels between the home page and a finishing point for placing an order, consider revamping your plan to provide a smoother path.

✦ **Remember that good design takes time.** Don't expect to have your site up in a day. Although the broad strokes of creating a website (such as creating the navigation bar and home page layout) can happen quickly, the refinement and fine-tuning of the site (such as defining button colors or the number of columns) can take much longer. Then again, fine-tuning can separate you from the competition in your customers' eyes. Give your designer enough time to do good work but not free reign to create a masterpiece.

Avoiding common holdups in developing a site

The last part of any website design process involves looking at the site map and page count and then estimating how much time you need to create the site. Expert designers typically estimate a number (of hours, days, or weeks, for example), and then pad that number by adding extra time to complete the project. You might ask, "Why pad the estimate?" After all, if someone is just implementing your well-structured plan, what can go wrong?

Developing your site can take longer than you expected for a variety of reasons. As you move from website design to implementation, beware of these traps:

✦ **Trying to design and build the site at the same time:** People like to dive in with only a few pages on their maps (*before* the design is complete) and then add pages as they build out their sites. The constant starting, stopping, and thinking about which extra pages are needed can slow you down when you're trying to build the site.

✦ **Not having the right capabilities for your site:** Some people envision having a graphics-rich, interactive, advanced website and then find out in the design process that their Internet service provider (ISP) can't support certain programs or supply bandwidth to display video properly. Careful planning helps you create specifications, which you can verify with your site provider to make sure that your site capabilities are what you want — before you buy.

✦ **Not updating the entire site when you make a change:** Even the most carefully laid website plans can require some modification when you implement them. Remember that good sites link back and forth between different sections. The last thing you want is to update one section without updating the links in the rest of your site. If this happens, your customers can get lost while surfing around — and might leave for good.

✦ **Forgetting about the message:** As your website grows and expands, you can easily lose focus on what the site should accomplish. At any time, you must be able to go back to your home page — or any other page — and determine the site focus by viewing the page for a few seconds. If you spend longer than 10 or 15 seconds interpreting the message, you're off track.

No matter how many changes you make, never let the message of your site get lost or obscured.

✦ **Not having the content ready:** You can have the plan built and promise to deliver your data or content to your website developer by a certain date. If you miss this date for some reason, you throw the developer's plans — not to mention the project's workflow — into chaos.

✦ **Not having a reliable developer:** The best-laid plans are just *plans* until someone turns them into a website. If you're depending on someone with specialized skills, make sure that he or she has the time available to deliver your site when you need it.

You Can Do It! Making a Build-It-Yourself Site

The thought of turning site maps, content lists, and other plans into a full-blown website can intimidate almost anyone — especially someone who has never created a web page. To create web pages in the early days of the Internet, you had to know the specialized computer code *HyperText Markup Language (HTML)* and be able to write that code by using a program such as Notepad. Nowadays, you can find many tools to help you design your own site without having an extensive knowledge of HTML, but you can also benefit from knowing how to implement some of the helpful features in the current HTML5 version of markup language.

Therefore, knowing how to use some HTML (specifically, HTML5) is still a good idea because this knowledge gives you more control over the site-building process. Although website tools can create a lot of HTML code and help you build functions quickly, you might have to edit the work those tools do to make your site faster, smoother, and easier for customers to use. You have to direct these efforts to make sure that your site is an effective communications tool for your customers to do business with you. These website tools can help you get something done, but *you* have to provide the "why's" of the web page: Why is it being built, and why should customers use it?

A good first step is checking with your web-hosting company to find out which site development tools it provides. Most hosting companies have site design tools and templates that work with their servers, and can get you up and running with basic web page designs. You can update those basic designs with your own content, labels, and products.

If your web host doesn't provide any site-building tools or you're not happy with its offerings, don't worry — you have more options, as outlined in this list:

✦ **Free tools online:** You can find a number of free or inexpensive site builder tools on the Internet. Table 3-1 lists some of these tools.

Table 3-1	Companies with Site-Building Tools
Company Name	*URL*
CoffeeCup	www.coffeecup.com
Creating Online	www.creatingonline.com
First Page	www.evrsoft.com
Trellian WebPage	www.trellian.com/webpage/
Web Starts	www.webstarts.com

You might also find free web tools from your Internet service provider. Companies such as your cable or Internet provider offer free web-hosting space and some basic tools for building your personal website. You can use these same tools to help create your e-commerce site. As your site grows, you should consider transitioning it to a paid account because free hosting accounts usually come with a lot of restrictions.

✦ **Your word processor:** You can even use your word processor to build a website. Microsoft Word can save any document you create as an HTML file so that you can type your site map and create web pages without much stress.

✦ **Advanced site builder software:** Later in this chapter, the section "Going modern with Adobe Dreamweaver and more" introduces some advanced, superfunctional programs that can help you build a rich, complex site for your business.

Using HTML: The old-fashioned way to build a page

Regardless of the web design tool you use to build your website, you need a basic understanding of how HTML works. This understanding helps you edit your pages and figure out what your tools are creating.

Unlike software code that has to be translated, compiled, and otherwise prepared before a consumer can use it, HTML code is written, saved as a file, and then interpreted by the program that reads the file. Usually, the software program that reads the HTML file is a web browser, such as Microsoft Internet Explorer. The web browser opens the HTML file and finds these two elements:

✦ **Text** represents the titles, headings, paragraphs, links, and other elements that you want customers to see when they visit your website.

✦ **Commands, or *HTML markup tags,*** tell the web browser how to *mark up*, or format, the text that's in the file and, therefore, control how the text looks to customers.

The browser reads all the instructions that you place in these markup tags and draws the web page on the computer screen according to your specifications. Because this language is uniform and structured, most web browsers interpret the commands in the same way. Your customers see the same design regardless of the computer or operating system they're using.

Commands are marked in the HTML file by command-start and -stop symbols: the < and > signs. They look like this:

<command>

Typically, HTML commands are implemented by indicating, in this order:

✦ The start of the command

✦ The text that will be affected by the command

✦ The end of the command

For example, if you want a word to appear bolded on your web page, you write

<B>*word*</B>

The <B> command indicates that you're turning on (starting) the Bold command. Adding a slash (/) to the ending command tag indicates that you're turning off the command. Your web browser looks at this code and creates an effect as though you're holding down the Bold key, typing a word, and then releasing that key and moving on to the next section.

If you don't provide the command tag to end a particular command, the web browser continues to format the rest of the file by using that command. If you put a <B> (the Bold command) in your file and then forget to end the command, the rest of the text in your web page appears as bold text.

Every HTML file has certain essential commands that should always be present. The following listing shows a skeleton HTML file:

```
<HTML>
  <HEAD>
  <TITLE>Basic webpage title</title
  </HEAD>
  <BODY>
  The content of your web page would go here.
  </BODY>
</HTML>
```

Always put the <HTML> tag on the first line of your HTML file. This tag tells the web browser that it can find HTML code inside your file. Next, your web page contains two sections: the *header* (marked by <HEAD>) and the *body* (marked by <BODY>).

Your header section should contain all the information that defines your web page, which includes — but isn't limited to — these elements:

✦ **Title:** Your website title appears on the browser's title bar and should instantly tell customers the purpose of the web page.

✦ **Function definitions:** For example, if you're creating a web page for customers to search your catalog, make sure to define the function as a search page.

✦ **Author information:** Fill in the author's information, whether it's you, your business name, or your web designer. That way, customers know whom to thank for a well-planned website, interesting content, and a creative design.

✦ **<META> tags:** This type of tag tells your web browser the definition and keywords of your web page. See Book VI, Chapter 6 for more information on these tags.

The body section contains everything else related to the web page, especially anything visible to your customers, such as

✦ **Your content:** For example, a description and photographs of your products or services, and any information you're displaying for your customers, might appear in this section.

✦ **Navigation information:** Usually, every web page has a consistent set of links that can take your customers to every main section of your website with one click.

✦ **Links to other parts of your website:** If your web page needs to reference another part of your website, make sure the link is present in the page.

✦ **Links to other websites:** Many times, a website offers links to other websites that are complementary to theirs or partners with them for co-promotion efforts.

✦ **Forms asking customers to fill in information:** For example, you need the name and shipping address of any customers who decide to order something or join your mailing list.

Sometimes, designers put all the information in the body and very little in the header section. Although your web page still loads and presents itself to your customers, the lack of a divider between header and body information makes it harder to update your web pages properly (for example, when you need to change some functions on your website) and maximize your outreach to the Internet community. Similarly, putting main content inside the header section can distort the display of your web page because some web browsers try to condense the header to the top of the screen.

Qualifying your HTML commands

Some HTML tags require markup instructions other than the caret signs (< and >) and the command name. These needy tags require specific information, known as *attributes*, which your web browser uses to implement the command. Like the commands, these attributes are written inside the caret signs to separate the markup instruction from the regular text of the file.

Suppose that you want to provide a web link so that when customers click the words *Order Here* from your home page, their web browsers open your catalog page. Although the command for building a web link is <A>, you have to assign the attribute of the destination page, which is known as *Hypertext REFerence,* or HREF. You would write the following HTML code:

```
<A HREF="catalog.html">Order here!</A>
```

You turn on the web link command with <A, assign the destination catalog. html as your web link (HREF), add the words Order here! as the text your customers see, and end the command with </A>. Notice that you do *not* have to close out the attribute separately; just define it within the carets surrounding the opening tag.

Table 3-2 shows some common HTML commands that have important attributes to define.

Table 3-2	HTML Commands That Require Attributes	
Command	*Attribute*	*Element That It Assigns*
<BODY>	BGCOLOR	Background color
	TEXT	Color of text in the body
	LINK	Color of web links
	VLINK	Color of visited web links
<FONT>	COLOR	Color of the font
	SIZE	Size of the text using this font
<IMG>	SRC	Source of the image file

If you don't assign attributes such as background color or size, your web browser uses the default attributes that the customer set up on his or her computer or that was supplied with the web browser software. Typically, the link color is set to blue, visited links are set to purple, and the background color is set to white.

Using tables to organize your page

After you understand the basics on how to set up a web page, you want to find ways to organize all the text, graphics, and data that you present on your web page. Specifically, if you want to show an array of products on your website, you organize the product photo, description, Buy Now button, and other specifics in a smooth, centered format. One popular way that website designers ensure a smooth presentation is to use HTML tables.

Originally designed to show numbers and data in a spreadsheet-style format, tables are now becoming the building blocks for aligning every element in a web page. Many navigation toolbars, whether they run across the top or left side of a web page, are in fact HTML tables that space the navigation commands evenly, no matter which web browser or computer screen is being used.

The easiest way to build a table is to use an automated website builder (such as the ones we discuss in the next section). However, understanding how tables are created in HTML helps you make any necessary edits, in case the builder tools don't properly create all aspects of the table.

Follow these steps to define a table in HTML:

1. **Type the** <TABLE> **command wherever you want to start building a table in your HTML file.**

2. **For every horizontal row you want to build in your table, type the** <TR> **command to start the row and the** </TR> **command to end the row.**

   You can assign as many rows to a particular HTML table as you want. Although there's no minimum number, you should try to put at least one row in each table you create.

3. **For each column cell you want within a row, type the** <TD> **command to start the cell and the** </TD> **command to end the cell.**

   Although you define the number of rows in the table, your web browser interprets the number of columns in your table by counting the number of cells created with <TD> and </TD>.

   If you create different numbers of cells within your rows of a table, your web browser tries to compensate by evenly spacing out the cells. This compensation, however, can result in an uneven display. When necessary, create cells with no content by simply putting <TD></TD> in the necessary rows.

4. **When you're finished building the table, type the** </TABLE> **command.**

Be careful if you build tables to place inside other tables. Every table on your page uses a <TABLE> command, and if you start building tables within tables, you might mix up the matching commands. If you don't provide the correct number of </TABLE> commands to end your tables, your web browser tries to format the rest of your web page into the tables you created, which can cause a disjointed appearance on your page.

Book III
Chapter 3

Building a Site without Spending a Fortune

To give you an idea of what a complete table definition looks like in HTML, we show you a basic three-row, three-column table that contains four different prices for a product:

```
<TABLE BORDER=1>
<TR>
<TD>JOEL'S SNOWBOARDS</TD>
<TD><B>UNPAINTED</B></TD>
<TD><B>PAINTED</B></TD>
</TR>
<TR>
<TD><B>MODEL 1000</B></TD>
<TD>$79.99</TD>
<TD>$129.99</TD>
</TR>
<TR>
<TD><B>MODEL 2000</B></TD>
<TD>$99.99</TD>
<TD>$179.99</TD>
</TR>
</TABLE>
```

Using this code sample results in something like the table shown in Figure 3-2.

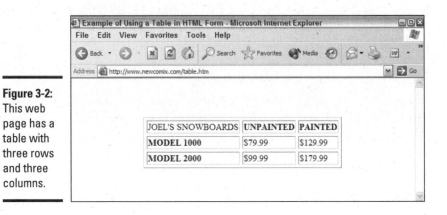

Figure 3-2:
This web page has a table with three rows and three columns.

Notice how the `<TABLE>` command has an attribute named BORDER. If you set the BORDER to 0, no lines are drawn between rows or columns. This way, your website visitors see only the contents of your table, not any defining lines.

By default, your table takes the entire width of your web page. You can assign the WIDTH attribute to your `<TABLE>`, `<TR>`, or `<TD>` commands to manually space a particular cell, row, or table to appear on the web page.

Using the preceding example, suppose that you want the cell containing the painted price to occupy just 20 percent of your table width. To accomplish this task, you can use this line of code:

```
<TD WIDTH="20%">$129.99</TD>
```

You need to assign the WIDTH attribute for all cells in the table for that same column. Otherwise, you risk throwing off the spacing for the entire table.

Your tables can contain much more than just text. You can assign pictures, buttons, text fields, or whatever elements you want to your table cells. Just make sure that you're assigning an equal amount of content to each cell and keeping track of how much is in each one. You don't want to throw off the alignment of your table by putting three pictures in one cell and only one picture in the next cell.

Going modern with WordPress, Adobe Dreamweaver, and more

Web pages have many elements you can specify, and keeping track of them all is hard when you design pages using only HTML. The growing number of commands available in HTML fueled the need for software programs to help organize all these elements. These programs create the HTML commands automatically so that you can focus on the layout, design, and content of your web page rather than worry about whether you defined all your table cells properly.

One of the most popular software applications for web page design is WordPress, which was developed by a core set of volunteer programmers. Preprogrammed templates and plug-in applications that work with WordPress enable those with little coding skill to quickly develop a dynamic website. The other program that some people use is Adobe Dreamweaver. This program provides many buttons and menus to help you place HTML commands as though you're writing a paper in Microsoft Word. The software prompts you for specific information and then displays a sample of what your web page will look like, as you're building the page. This way, you can try a command to see how it will look and then change it right there, if necessary, before continuing with your development.

The pros and cons of using automated site builders

You can use a website builder tool or application, such as WordPress, to create sophisticated web pages without having much specific knowledge, which is why millions of people buy these tools every year. However, using automated site builders isn't without a downside, and you can fall into certain traps if you rely solely on these tools.

Here are some reasons to use a site builder tool:

✦ **Ease of use:** A builder tool is designed to make the process of creating web pages as easy as possible. It looks like any other software program you're familiar with using and offers either templates or buttons, menus, and wizards to help you construct the building blocks of your web page.

✦ **Wide array of options:** A builder tool is programmed with every available HTML command as well as with functions that combine these commands. This combination gives you many options for creating your web pages, and the tool's ease of use ensures that you don't have to search through documentation to figure out a specific name and definition for a function.

✦ **Total control:** You can rely on the code that a builder tool generates (or can be purchased) or insert your own code whenever it's needed. Site builder tools help you easily validate your work by color-coding the commands in your file for easy visibility, for example.

Despite the attraction of these features, you should also see the drawbacks of relying on a builder tool:

✦ **Unneeded code:** These programs have a particular way of inserting code into your HTML files, and sometimes they insert too much code or unnecessary code that web browsers can interpret incorrectly. You should optimize your code after a builder tool creates it so that your pages load faster and cleanly. You can use a tool such as HTML Optimizer from iWebtool (`www.iwebtool.com/html_optimizer`) or the W3C Markup Validation Service (`validator.w3.org`) to help you go through your HTML files.

✦ **Exclusive functions:** Some builder tools, especially Dreamweaver, offer powerful functions that you can insert into your web pages. These functions are sometimes written with special commands that can be interpreted by only specific web server programs. Web servers advertise this capability as including *extensions*, and whoever is hosting your website has to have the right extensions file for your web pages to work properly.

✦ **Cost:** A full version of Adobe Dreamweaver software can cost hundreds of dollars. Although the software offers a huge array of options, sometimes the cost isn't justified for the website you truly need for your business.

Creating Your Site with the Pros

One way that entrepreneurs get ahead is by understanding their strengths and weaknesses: They focus on their strengths and have other people handle their weaknesses. Many people who want to operate their own online businesses aren't necessarily skilled website designers, and nothing is wrong with that. In the earlier section "You Can Do It! Making a Build-It-Yourself Site," we outline tools and technologies that can help you create your own site. You can choose another approach, however: Make the investment to have a professional website designer create your business website. The right interactions and communications with a professional designer can fuel an excellent site, and can even improve your overall business model so that increased orders and higher visibility help you recover the time and money you spent.

Some people consult with professional designers to create their sites and then give the business owners the tools to maintain their sites without any additional help. Other business owners contract with professionals to create and maintain their sites so that the designers can introduce new styles and functions as their businesses progress. Either approach can be beneficial for your business. You should decide how much help you want, as either a one-time investment or an ongoing expense.

Seeking experience: Choosing the right website designer

Half the battle of finding a website designer is deciding that you need to hire one in the first place. The other half of the battle involves knowing where to look and talking to potential candidates until you find the right fit. Finding the right designer is similar to finding other specialists you need to solve specific problems. Whether you're looking for an auto mechanic, a plumber, a dentist, or in this case, a web designer, consider these methods for finding a qualified professional:

+ **Listen to word-of-mouth advice.** Talk to your friends, business associates, partners, or anybody you do business with online or in person. Find out which website designers they have used and solicit their opinions of these professionals.

+ **See the designer's work.** Look at websites that you like or enjoy. Most of the time, a small link or reference at the bottom of the home page or About Us page mentions whether a professional designer created the site. Follow the link back to the designer's site for more information.

+ **Evaluate the designer's portfolios.** Use search engines, read relevant magazines in your area, or look around to find a few companies. Then evaluate the samples or references they provide, to see whether their work for other people is good enough or fits the style you want for your own business.

Hooking up with a web design firm

From the early days of the Internet, some web design companies have focused on providing quality work for their clients. Going to a design firm gives you specific benefits for completing your project:

✦ **Reliability:** If a particular designer is having a bad day, week, month, or even year, a design firm can shift the workload away from that person and find backup or additional resources to cover the job. Design firms typically have contacts with freelance designers who come into the firm when needed to help tackle a big problem.

✦ **Coordination:** If several designers are working on your project, a design firm can coordinate the work and give you a single point of contact who communicates your ideas and tasks to the design team.

✦ **Experience:** Design firms have a portfolio of past projects and experience that lends itself to your project. They can bring their know-how and expertise to your project without having to navigate a large learning curve.

Going with a freelancer

When you ask around to find the right website design professional, you might be pointed toward talented individuals who work on a freelance basis and take on specific clients and projects that fit into their schedules. Some freelance professionals take assignments outside their full-time jobs, as a way to make some extra money. Others have enough clients to make their freelance jobs become their full-time careers.

Choosing a freelance designer over a design firm has several benefits. A freelancer

✦ **Costs less to hire:** When you hire a design firm, part of the cost goes toward maintaining the overhead costs of the company. Although that overhead is beneficial to ensure the reliability of your project, a freelance designer typically charges less per hour or per project than the average design firm.

✦ **Works more nimbly:** You might find that a design firm you choose requires decisions and work to be done in various committees, with approval required at all stages by the firm's managers. This system can slow the progress of a website's development, and if speed is a top concern, a freelance designer who can focus on your project can produce a quicker result because the only approval that's needed is yours.

✦ **Provides a unique style:** Although designing a website is definitely a mixture of art and science, the creativity you want might not come from a firm that has developed procedures and processes for cranking out their various clients' websites. An individual freelance designer can bring his or her own quirky, creative, unique style to your project, which is what might draw you to this designer in the first place.

You can use a website such as Elance to find the right freelance designer for your project. Simply go to `www.elance.com` and choose from qualified professionals. After you create an account with Elance, you can click the Post Your Job Today button (see Figure 3-3) to post your time and cost requirements and then receive bids from freelancers.

Figure 3-3:
Post your require-
ments on
Elance so
that free-
lancers
come to
you.

Comparing apples to apples

While you're deciding whom to hire as your website designer, comparing quoted prices is a natural consideration for making up your mind. If you don't consider certain factors, however, they can skew the math and thereby make your comparison invalid.

For example, a price for designing a website is normally determined in one of two ways:

- ✦ **Flat fee:** One price covers the complete site development.
- ✦ **Per-hour pricing:** You're billed a rate per hour of development time.

Knowing a few key items from your designer or firm can help you compare prices more evenly. In this section, follow the advice that applies to your situation to find out the specific details.

If a designer or firm charges a flat fee for the entire project:

- ✦ **Ask for a specific list of what's provided for that fee.** You might assume that the price you're quoted is the only fee you have to pay but find out at the end of the project that the flat fee excludes extras that you assumed were included.

✦ **Ask what happens if someone has to spend overtime hours to complete the project.** One benefit of having a flat fee is knowing that you don't have to worry about the number of hours your designer is spending to build your website. This way, someone can't dawdle on a function to run up the bill, for example. Some design professionals offer a flat fee on the assumption that the project will take a maximum number of hours to complete. In this case, the contract stipulates that if the project exceeds that maximum number, the client pays more.

If a designer or firm charges by the hour:

✦ **Ask for time estimates on the various pieces of the project, function by function.** Website design professionals might give you different numbers for the total number of hours needed. Rather than compare total numbers, you can compare detailed quotes to know whether one firm is spending more time on specific functions or one person is forgetting to factor in pieces that other designers know are essential.

✦ **Ask for limits to be put into place.** A website designer can easily quote a specific number of hours and then exceed that number and keep the bill running while you pay for his or her excesses. That's why you must establish limits for various pages, especially less complicated pages. The designer should be forced, at the least, to call you if he or she needs to spend more time than quoted so that you can hear an explanation and make the decision.

Regardless of how you're charged, find out who pays if you find a bug or an error in the work after the fact.

Sometimes, web designers can offer a lower quote because they refuse to cover the cost of fixing the work when the project is complete. Although the initial price is low, you could pay more if a lot of reworking or correction is needed, and then you don't save anything. Request assurances that the designer will spend the time necessary at the end, and specify that no one will be fully paid until the project is completed to your satisfaction.

Your best bet is to ask your designer to provide a full checklist of every action that's necessary to build your website and then to review that checklist as your site is being designed. To ensure that the review takes place, many people tie their designer's payments to the completion of the checklist. For example, when the designer can show that 50 percent of the items were completed, he or she receives 50 percent of the payment. This strategy helps prevent someone from receiving a full payment upfront and then quitting before completing all the agreed-on tasks.

Speeding up the process

Regardless of whom you choose to be your website designer, take the time to get the following "ducks in a row" to ensure that your designer is working as efficiently as possible — and costing you less in the end:

✦ **Prepare site specifications upfront.** First and foremost, you should have a clear idea of what your site should contain before your first meeting with the designer. Prepare a written road map of your site (as discussed in the section "Mapping Your Route to a Successful Site," earlier in this chapter) and notes on the various web pages that you feel are essential. You can brainstorm with your web designer about your website, but starting with your road map and making small changes is quicker and easier than starting with a clean sheet of paper and spending hours writing down the basics.

✦ **Have your content ready.** Make sure that the content you want for your site is typed and available in electronic format. You're paying the designer by the hour, most likely, and you don't want to pay a skilled professional to type reams of data for you.

If necessary, hire a copywriter separately from your web designer, and give that copywriter the sole responsibility of creating electronic text or Word document files with your information.

✦ **Establish firm milestones.** When you meet with your web designer, work to establish rough dates for checking the progress or various milestones, which can be the end dates for specific portions of your site. Although some web designers don't like specific hard-and-fast dates, you can reasonably expect to see portions of the project completed by certain dates. This way, you can see the progress of your site, make changes (if necessary) before everything is done, and ensure that the project is progressing.

✦ **Be readily available to assist the designer.** Make sure that you're available to answer questions and feed information to your website designer. The designer shouldn't be stuck waiting days (or weeks.) to receive specific and necessary information from you. Even if you're incredibly detail oriented and spell out everything in advance, your designer might need to ask you a question, get approval for a change, or find out more information about your business before proceeding.

Keeping an eye on your business interests

When you hire a website design professional, the expectation is that you don't need to know how to use HTML or have any design skills. That is, after all, why you're hiring the professional. However, your design professional will have expectations about how you participate in the project, how your business operations are reflected in the site, and who owns the rights to the resulting site and its content. You must know your role in this process so that you can contribute to a successful site that contributes in turn to your business success.

Keep in mind the concept of scope when you're hiring someone to develop your site. *Scope,* in this case, refers to the amount of information and areas of concern that affect your website developer. She should operate within her role as specified in the contract or agreement between you and her. Don't involve your developer in other aspects of your business or create expectations that she will contribute to your business plan. Keep the developer's activities focused on the job at hand so that she can deliver your site as specified.

Drawing up your contract or agreement with a website developer provides a learning exercise for both parties. Spell out exactly what you need, and specify whether other people, yourself included, are providing pieces of the puzzle (such as product databases) that interact with their work. This way, you both know the extent of the site developer's responsibilities.

Staying true to your business and customers

As the business owner, you determine how your site fulfills your business goals. Although an eager website developer might want to build something to highlight his specialties, they can conflict with your business purpose. If you're focusing on a pure e-commerce site with little extra content, you need to communicate that fact so that your designer doesn't hand back a content-rich, bloated site.

Know your customers and the audience you want your site to attract. Talented designers can build your site in different ways to appeal to different audiences, and you must point them in the right direction to "hook" the right people. Without any specific targets, your designer might produce something that speaks to every group but says nothing of value to any of them.

Supplying the designer with the right stuff

You can't just drive your car into a service station, toss the guy the keys, say "Fix it," and then walk away and expect to get a fully repaired car hours later. The same situation applies to designing your website: You must provide the right information to your designer, and at the right time during the process, so that your site is built correctly from the start. Here are some tips:

✦ **Outline your business practices.** Your website designer isn't necessarily a businessperson and can't be expected to understand the intricacies of your business. You need to explain how your site should operate and why. If you have certain rules or exclusions for how you sell your goods and services, spell them out before development begins. For example, if you need to enforce a minimum order or disallow certain product combinations in the same order, those business rules must be a part of the proposal. Don't expect your designer to implicitly know how your business operates or understand its specific requirements.

✦ **Supply all relevant content.** At some point, you need to provide the content that will fill your website. This content consists of not only the names and descriptions of products but also any product databases, pictures, pricing information, or other data that has to interact with your site. Unless your designer is creating your company logo, you have to provide your logo, mission statement, contact information, and anything else that needs to appear on your site. Some of this information is spelled out in your agreement; other pieces, such as a customer database, can be handed in down the road or even at the end of the process.

✦ **Make your systems available when needed.** Your developer also counts on having you and your computer systems available while building your site. This statement is especially true for more complex sites that operate on a web server and communicate with programs such as a database, a supplier's inventory system, and a third-party payment solution. The quicker you can provide access, and the more documentation and notes you can provide about these interlocking programs, the quicker the designer can turn around and build you the correct website.

Clarifying who owns what

When you're hiring someone to design and build your website for you, establish the ownership of this work after it's complete. You might assume — because you're paying a professional to do the work — that this constitutes a work-for-hire agreement where you automatically own full rights to the resulting site and its content.

Never assume that you have a work-for-hire situation, and — as part of your contract — spell out the ownership rights of everything the web developer provides to you. In addition, make sure that items such as photos, graphical images, and functions don't carry any unexpected royalties or licenses that you have to pay to use.

After the job is done, ask the web designer for a copy of your website, either available online as a backup copy or on a DVD or USB drive. This way, if something happens to your web server or you have a falling-out with your designer, you still have a full copy that you can use to keep your site running. Make sure that all the images, icons, logos, buttons, and other types of graphics — not just the HTML files — are included in your copy. If your web designer also designed your company logo, ask for the logo in different file formats and sizes.

Chapter 4: Finding the Host with the Most

In This Chapter

✓ Scoping out the difference between an ISP and a host

✓ Understanding the different types of hosting

✓ Breaking down the pros and cons of various hosts

✓ Reading the legal fine print

✓ Deciding whether you're ready to be your own host

*O*ne of the many decisions you make when you're starting a website is where to host it. You might be wondering what a host does and why you even need one. A *host* site provides a place (a *server*) for your website and all the files that make up your site to reside. That host provides an address so that others can access it by using the Internet.

In this chapter, you discover the differences between a host and an Internet service provider, the different types of hosts and what they have to offer, legal agreements, and the decisions you make about becoming your own host.

Differentiating between an ISP and a Host

Try not to confuse a host with an Internet service provider. You need both! Allow us to explain the difference by using a car analogy.

Think of your website as a car. The color, interior materials, CD player, and sunroof are all parts of a car that are visible — and those visible elements are comparable to your website. Although the car's engine might be hidden away under the hood, it gives the car its power. You can rev it up with lots of horsepower to provide that extra oomph, even though the only folks likely to see this part of the car are you and your mechanic! Those under-the-hood works are the same as your hosting service. You can choose more disk space and other extras that give your site more power. If the engine isn't running, your car doesn't work; similarly, if your host's server is down, so is your website.

Where does your access to the Internet enter this picture? That's your driving lane, of course. You can stay in the breakdown lane (the equivalent of dial-up access) or hit the left lane for speed (broadband service). A tollbooth is the equivalent of the service provider that sells you access to the Net. As a benefit, most ISPs provide both Internet access and web hosting — but you must can consider lots of other options.

Determining What Makes the Difference for High-Performance Hosting

When you're gearing up for a high-performance website, you must decide how much horsepower — 'er, *hosting* power — you really need for the site. Horsepower translates into fast loading speeds, video and sounds playing without interruption, and images loading quickly. Consider these hosting options:

✦ **Disk space:** The size of your website files dictates how much disk space, or storage, you need from a host. If you use Flash, or plan to have a lot of pictures, self-hosted videos, or graphics, count on needing more storage space. Typically, disk space is measured in megabytes (MB), and 500MB is enough for a basic commerce site.

✦ **Bandwidth:** This capability controls how much data, or information, a server can send and receive at any given moment. The higher the amount of bandwidth your host's server has, the more traffic (visitors) your site can support at one time.

To give you an idea of how important bandwidth can be, consider this real-life example. When pop artist Lady Gaga launched one of her singles from her third album, she made the MP3 version available for sale on Amazon.com at the special limited price of 99 cents. Her fans rushed to take advantage of the midnight offering. The result? The site's available bandwidth was exceeded, and Amazon's server crashed — an almost unheard of occurrence for an Internet heavyweight like Amazon. And many disappointed customers were instantly unhappy Amazon customers.

Web hosting is an extremely competitive business. Now, many top hosting providers offer unlimited disk (or storage) space and unlimited bandwidth. These services often throw in free domain name registration, too. Take the time to shop around for the most benefits at the lowest monthly price — the time you invest will be worthwhile.

✦ **Data transfers:** Every time someone views information from your site (including text, images, and video), that's considered to be a transfer of data. Think of it as traffic (or data) leaving your site. Hosting plans used to allow for a specified number of transfers per month and then charged additional fees if you consistently exceeded the limit. Now, most plans no longer mention data transfers in their service description because it is unlimited. To be on the safe side, confirm that data transfers are unlimited.

✦ **Allowable languages:** Depending on which scripting language you use to create your site, you might have to find a host that supports that specific type. For instance, support of HTML5 (HyperText Markup Language 5), is standard for all hosting services these days, as is the PHP: Hypertext Preprocessor scripting language. However, if you use Ruby on Rails or Python, you might want to confirm that they are supported without hassle.

If you hire an outside developer to create your website, be sure to ask which scripting language is being used to design the site. Or ask whether you can specify which language is used. Then confirm that your hosting solution supports that language. Some add-ons for shopping cart applications, for example, require a specific programming code or OS (operating system) to customize the application. Although an entire site is rarely built in a scripting language not supported by your hosting provider, we have seen it happen. Better safe than sorry.

✦ **Database access:** If you plan to incorporate a database on your site (for inventory management, for example), the server must allow for it. Typically, you should ensure that SQL (Standard Query Language) or MySQL is available, which means that the server is set up to use this language to access and transfer information from your database. Don't be surprised if you're asked to pay extra for this feature or if it's free only to a certain extent.

✦ **E-commerce enabled:** Save yourself a headache later and confirm that your hosting plan supports e-commerce software, such as a shopping cart program, and that it supports the one you want to use. Many companies bundle hosting with a specific e-commerce solution (because they get a cut of the fees from those merchant programs). Either way, you're likely to pay more in hosting fees when you add an e-commerce feature to your site.

In addition to obtaining e-commerce software, you need a Secure Sockets Layer (SSL) certificate. It ensures that you can safely transmit data over your website when customers make purchases. Check to see whether your hosting plan offers a *shared* SSL certificate, which covers all websites located on its server — in which case, it's probably free. Otherwise, expect to shell out more bucks to purchase an individual SSL for your site. If the hosting company doesn't offer the option, you can check www.symantec.com for more information on purchasing your own SSL. Several kinds of SSL certificates are available, so weigh all your options before making a final decision.

✦ **Operating system:** Similar to your desktop computer, a server has an operating system, too. Deciding which one is right for you depends on what operating system you're using for your website. Two server options are available:

  • *Windows:* When you're using Microsoft Access, Active Server Pages (ASP), or any Microsoft-specific scripts, a Windows-based server is more suitable.

  • *Linux:* This server software supports almost any type of scripting language. It's definitely a better match for your website if you use MySQL, PHP, or Perl.

The type of operating system you have on your own computer doesn't influence which server is best suited to host your website.

✦ **Redundancy and backups:** Let's get straight to the point — if your server crashes, you're up a creek without a paddle. You must back up your website, which means that your data is copied and saved to another location so that if one server goes down, your data is still available from the second source. Your hosting plan should include frequent, and preferably daily, backups to derail any impending crisis. To prevent backups from becoming necessary in the first place, you need a reliable server — not to mention a responsible host. When you're purchasing a hosting plan, determine which type of precautions a provider has in place to prevent its server from going down. Don't forget that the problem isn't always a matter of equipment failure. Power outages, maintenance checks, and other manmade or environmental conditions (such as severe weather incidents) can cause a server — along with your website — to go out of commission. Redundancy is the best contingency plan because it means that your host has dual systems in place that allow information to remain accessible from a secondary source, even if the primary source goes out.

✦ **Web analysis:** To understand who your customers are and how they're using your site, chances are good that you need to know how many people visit your site each day, which parts of the site they frequent, and maybe even which other sites these visitors came from (based on IP addresses). To find out, you need some type of web analysis software. If this feature isn't included with your hosting plan, ask whether any restrictions exist on the type of software you can use with the site, and whether you pay an additional charge for using it.

You can embed a small bit of HTML code into your home page (and other pages) and use Google Analytics for free. Google also has a terrific resource center, including online tutorials, for using analytics. Visit the center at www.google.com/analytics.

✦ **Support:** No matter who you are, there comes a time when you need a little help. Although it's not easy to determine the quality of a host's support until you experience it, you can compare some basic features. Is support offered 24/7 (24 hours a day and 7 days a week)? If not, what are the hours of the host's customer service center? Are both online support and phone support available? If online support is offered, make sure that it offers access to answers in real time, as opposed to waiting as long as 24 to 48 hours for a response to e-mail. Always confirm whether you're charged for live tech support and whether the charge is based on use by the minute, hour, or month. Those bills can rack up fast, even for a seemingly simple question.

✦ **Other:** A host can choose to make *beaucoup* (*lots* of) extra features available with your plan. If all other factors are equal, don't hesitate to compare this assortment of small prizes to find the host with the most. For example, mailboxes (for your e-mail) are always included, although the number of mailboxes offered varies greatly. However, mailboxes might not be a big deal to you. Some competitive hosting plans offer free tools that allow you to set up a blog; easy content-management programs; polling or voting features that allow you to take surveys of your customers; calendars; access to free stock photos, and more — lots more!

Sorting Out Your Website Host Options

Although choosing a hosting plan can be overwhelming, after you begin researching all the options, you find that most hosts make comparing apples to apples easy. To ensure competitiveness, hosts often break down their plans into several categories. With a quick glance, you can determine whether a plan has all the elements you want.

Basic, or *starter,* hosting packages offer bare-bones necessities — enough to get, and keep, a simple site with minimal images up and running. When this level is all you need, you end up making your decision strictly on price. (We see it happen all the time.) What we consider to be the other *forced* option is when you require e-commerce capabilities. No matter what, you have to choose the plan that provides for this need. (Typically, no more than one e-commerce hosting plan is available from one source — so you need to shop around to get the best deal.) Again, when you're selecting among providers, your decision comes down to price and which e-commerce program is partnered with (or offered by) each host.

Midlevel plans usually leave the most room for uncertainty. These hosting options vary the most by both price and available features. To overcome indecision, make a list that prioritizes which items you need and which you're most likely to set up and use in the first three months of your site going live. Then again, budgetary decisions might rule in the end.

Another type of hosting option to consider is the turnkey version. Companies, such as Homestead (www.homestead.com), provide a complete hosting solution that includes lots of functionality and features for only a few dollars per month. However, you must build your website using their site builder software or templates. We discuss these options in more detail in Chapter 3 of this minibook.

Overall, most hosting plans now come loaded with options and all cost just a few dollars a month for a basic account. Telling one hosting service apart from another can be difficult. Your best bet is to look for providers that distinguish themselves based on reliability, support, and security. Those that offer extra features or buying incentives (such as free advertising credits on Google AdWords or Facebook) are nice, but you really want a hosting provider that will help keep your business up and running — and secure.

Putting the Long-Term Contract in the Past

An important factor in choosing a host is the nature of your contractual obligations. Long-term contracts are a distant memory when it comes to hosting a website. If a host that you're considering requires this type of contract, consider other options first. You're likely to find an equally good deal with another host that requires nothing more than a monthly or one-year commitment.

The monthly pay-as-you-go plan for services such as web hosting is now standard, and you can usually get a price break for paying a full year ahead or for signing a multi-year contract. We don't advise the latter, because the price break isn't usually large enough to warrant staying with a service provider for two or three years. It's more important to have flexibility and be free to switch providers should something go wrong. However, paying upfront for 12 months of service is a great compromise.

Don't get excited yet: Whether you pay ahead or stay on a month-to-month payment plan, you're not free and clear of all rules and obligations. You still must abide by certain terms of agreement. You might have to pay a small setup fee, along with the first few months of service in advance, none of which is refundable. Or you might be required to provide 30 days' notice before terminating service. More often than not, you pay monthly fees in advance of using the service.

Because you always sign a binding legal agreement, whether it's on paper or by clicking to accept an electronic document, a *contract* is still in place. Although it might not bind you to a block of payments over a specified period, it specifies the terms of your relationship with the host.

Always read the fine print of any contract, terms of agreement, or other legally binding document. You may find that some contracts limit what you can and cannot do on a website.

Serving Yourself: Don't Overlook Other Server Options

One decision you eventually have to make when you're selecting a host is whether you want to skip a hosting plan and rent your own dedicated server. In that case, your partnership with a particular hosting plan might require you to sign a contract — or two. To help you better understand what you might be getting into, we explain the different types of server options:

✦ **Shared server:** The hosting plans we explain earlier in this chapter are examples of how you use a shared server. In essence, you're using the same computer (or server) along with many other websites. Although that arrangement translates into lower costs, you have less flexibility in the types of applications you can run, because the server is configured with the same settings and applications for all who use it.

✦ **Dedicated server:** Gaining complete control over the type of server you use and the programs you install on it requires that you have a dedicated server. As its name implies, the bandwidth, memory, and storage space on this computer are dedicated entirely to *you.* You also typically gain root access, which means that you can configure the server to your specifications. This more expensive option is often used when you need to run special programs or when you have multiple sites or extremely high-traffic sites. The downside of using a dedicated server (in addition to the expense) is that you're usually responsible for installing software, handling regular maintenance, and fixing any unexpected problems or system failures that occur. We recommend tackling this server arrangement only if you're an experienced web master or computer technician.

✦ **Colocation:** You might like the idea of owning a server but aren't in a position to manage or repair any problems that arise. If that's the case, colocation might be the answer. You provide the hardware (or the computer) and lease space *(rack space)* for it with a host company. The host company then installs the server and ensures that you have consistent access to the Internet, which is a big advantage of colocation. Depending on your physical office space, this situation is ideal for another reason: A server requires certain environmental conditions, such as being kept in a dry, cool (or temperature controlled) room, and colocation providers maintain data centers that meet or exceed these conditions. Because you own the equipment and are responsible for all other aspects of maintaining it, this option also requires that you have advanced skills.

✦ **Managed server:** Sometimes referred to as a *virtual server,* this option is a compromise to a dedicated server. Unlike with colocation, with a managed server you lease the equipment and the hosting company takes care of most server functions, including installing software and updates; handling security and maintenance; and acting as a troubleshooter for problems. If you have specific needs for your site and aren't proficient in maintaining a server, managed servers work well.

✦ **Virtual dedicated server:** Another take on limited maintenance but increased flexibility is what some hosts refer to as *virtually dedicated.* As with shared hosting, others use the server with you, but access is limited to a small number of customers. You gain dedicated space and control because the host uses walls or partitions on the computer to separate it into several virtual dedicated servers. Although your site is on a shared server, it has been configured to appear as a standalone, dedicated server with no other users.

 As with hosting, the price and services offered with each server package vary. You're usually required to sign a long-term lease agreement, so make sure that you understand what the price covers and the responsibilities for both you and the host company. Also, make sure that cancellation terms are clearly spelled out so that you can get out of the agreement if you're unhappy with the provider.

Chapter 5: Writing Content that Search Engines Want to See

In This Chapter

✔ Recognizing the value of words

✔ Preparing web-ready content

✔ Turning words into gold — 'er, cash

✔ Mastering the words that get searched

Content is king! This mantra is popular when discussing what it takes to shine the spotlight on your website. The words you choose, and how and where you use them, are critical to the online sales process. Now, thanks to Google, the value of content is at an all-time high for helping your website rank well in search engines, too.

Content was officially promoted to royalty when search engines (specifically, Google) began placing significantly increased importance on it as part of *search engine optimization*, or SEO. In short, Google decreed a site's search results ranking is affected by the quality of the site's content and its relevance to website visitors.

To achieve that goal of a good ranking, businesses often depend on someone else to find the right words for their websites. Don't worry: When you're creating content for your own site, you don't have to hire a professional writer. You do have to understand what turns ordinary words into good web copy, which is why we devote this chapter to choosing the right words. In addition, knowing how to write good web content helps you perform well in searches — and get more sales.

Words Are Words — Right? Wrong!

How do you know what works when it comes to describing your products, welcoming your customers, and engaging in any other communication that requires the written word? Effective web copy helps you accomplish these five objectives:

✦ Help search engines notice your site

✦ Convince customers to visit your site

✦ Educate customers about your products and services

✦ Elicit in your customers a desire to act (to buy stuff!)

✦ Entice customers to come back and do it all over again (buy more stuff!)

When discussing content for the web, you often hear another term, *content marketing*. This popular term encompasses all five of the preceding objectives as well as the development of lots of different types of content (from website copy to white papers) and the way you promote and distribute that content to attract customers to your site. In this chapter, we focus on a segment of content marketing, specifically the words or copy used on your website pages. In Book VI, we discuss in more detail how to create various types of content and how to use content as part of a marketing strategy.

Now that you understand the five objectives that help earn the official stamp of approval on your web copy, it's time to start writing. You should know that not all words are created equal. Some words pack a wallop when they're delivered. Others hang in the air unnoticed.

With millions of words in the English language, choosing the *right* ones for your website might seem daunting. Not so. Writing for the web is easy if you use words, phrases, and sentences that are

✦ **Attention-getters:** *You're fired!* Real estate tycoon and on-air personality Donald Trump gave new meaning to this phrase when he used it to oust participants on his reality television show. He certainly knows how to keep a viewer's attention as he delivers the now infamous line. You have to do the same online. Visitors to your website are unforgiving. If you don't catch their attention quickly (and keep it), they desert you in a heartbeat. Choose words, especially in headlines, that command attention and pique interest — all in a blink of the eye.

The average person looks at a web page for less than a minute (as little as 10–20 seconds, according to some research) before deciding to move on. The decision your customer makes to stay or leave depends on the information you provide. Make that information

- *Meaningful:* Don't waste words. Be brief and choose words that matter and that reflect the customer's needs.

- *Easy to read:* Use short sentences. Don't bog down readers with too much detail.

Give customers a choice in seeking more in-depth information. If someone wants *all* the details, you can provide either a hypertext link to another page or an expanded viewing window. There, visitors can find complete product descriptions, case studies, or other background research.

✦ **Self-explanatory:** It's best to avoid using abbreviations, catchy product names, and industry lingo. If you can't avoid using jargon, keep in mind that customers may not understand what you mean on the first read-through. When you use these types of words, define them in parentheses or offer an expanded view that contains the complete information. Be *clear.*

✦ **Simple:** Say what you mean. Don't make your customers read between the lines or try to guess what you intended.

Getting Ready to Write for the Web

Words are catalysts that move people to action. With that in mind, what do you want your customers to do when they visit your website? If you said "Buy stuff," think again. That's a given. You need to be more specific: On each page of your website, determine which *action* or series of actions you want customers to take to lead to the decision to make a purchase. If you can answer that question, you can write words that sell.

Understanding who and why

To start writing for the web, you have to determine these factors:

✦ **Your audience:** Before you write a single word of copy, take a moment to understand whom you're writing for. Who are your potential customers? Why are they visiting your site? What are they searching for — information or products? Specifically, what problem are they trying to solve, and how can you help them solve it?

✦ **Your customers' motivation:** In addition to knowing about your customers, you need to understand what motivates them to take action. Do they want to be entertained? Educated? Are their purchases based on emotional decisions? Or do they simply want enough facts to validate their buying decisions? To some degree, their motivation might be dictated by what type of product you're offering, the age of your target customer, or the standard offering in your industry. Even so, understanding motivation helps dictate your writing style and the words you use. It also guides the tone of your writing. Your tone can be serious, whimsical, or no-nonsense. Your tone itself can motivate people to action.

✦ **Your customers' solution:** When you understand your customer's desires, needs, and motivations, you can provide a solution. Simply naming your product or showing a picture of it doesn't do the trick. You need to explain *how* your specific product solves your customer's problem and tell why your product provides the best solution. If it's the most efficient, cost-effective, or reliable one on the market, let the customer know. These benefits are all part of the solution you offer to influence a customer's final decision to buy.

Okay, so you're convinced that your product answers the needs of your customer, and you're pretty sure that you know which features move customers to action. The next part of the equation is packaging the information in a way that customers can easily accept.

Understanding that packaging is everything

The first part of what we refer to as content packaging is *specifying the outcome* you want. Consider that every single page of your website serves a specific purpose. For example, a home page might convince a visitor to stay long enough to click a specific product link. Or a source of information might encourage your customer to register as a member of your site. After you define the expected outcome for a page, it becomes easier to determine whether your content serves that purpose.

Another key to packaging your website information is making the content skimmable. Designing *skimmable* text simply means that you allow a customer to look over chunks of data rather than have to read every single word to get your message. People have short attention spans when surfing the web. The growth of social media sites, such as Facebook and Twitter, have only shortened the already-short attention span. Consider that Twitter requires that you use no more than 140 characters. The increasing use of mobile devices for viewing websites makes short copy even more important. Customers reading your content on mobile phones want to get to the specific details, quickly. In short, folks are now used to super-abbreviated communications.

Reading content on a computer screen can strain your eyesight, which is why scanning content becomes the preferred method for online reading. By using a few simple tricks, you can still draw a customer's eye to details, even if they're speed reading.

Follow these suggestions to make your text scannable:

✦ Use short paragraphs.

✦ Highlight, or **boldface,** important words and phrases.

✦ Use bullets (like the ones in this list) to call out details.

✦ Include hypertext links to draw attention to a source of more information.

✦ Increase the font size of text to put emphasis on certain words.

✦ Incorporate graphics or images that complement the text and call attention to it.

Because space is limited on your home page, you can rotate different messages at the top of your page, similar to running a banner advertisement, every 10–15 seconds, for example. Your customers will be quickly exposed to multiple offers or messages, and you won't be cluttering your home page with static content.

Getting organized

After you create killer copy that's skimmable, you might think that you're ready to transfer your final thoughts onto your web page. Wait! You must complete one more step: Organize the information on the page in a way that makes sense. Your message should be simple, concise, and easy to understand. The most important factor is the order in which the information appears on a page. The text should lead visitors to take action (the specific outcome you identified earlier).

Alexa (now owned by Amazon) tracks the popularity of websites. We used this online tool to find high-ranking examples of sites that use effective content strategies to drive traffic. Figure 5-1 illustrates how one site, Constant Contact, incorporates some of these content strategies. The desired outcome on the page shown in the figure is to have customers create a free trial account to access the promotional toolkit. The bottom of the page provides links to explore specific product features. The content is organized in a way that leads customers to that final action — clicking to create a free account or move to the next page for more information.

Book III
Chapter 5

Figure 5-1:
This site organizes its content to lead viewers to create a free account.

The home page uses a large hero banner that clearly explains the benefit of the product — *Successful Marketing* — and provides links to other pages on the site to learn more. Note how the home page uses commands, or action-oriented words and terms — such as *starts*, *try,* and *buy now* — to entice customers to take action.

Figure 5-2 shows the next page a customer might click to dig deeper for information. In this example, we clicked the Features link, followed by the View All Campaigns and Features link at the bottom of the Features page. The first features page uses a similar strategy as the home page, by first encouraging visitors to get started with the free trial.

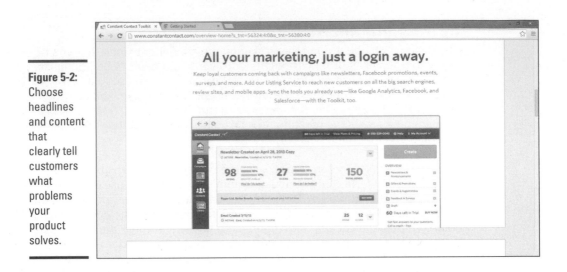

Figure 5-2:
Choose
headlines
and content
that
clearly tell
customers
what
problems
your
product
solves.

As you scroll down the page (see Figure 5-3), the site provides segments of small content blocks (paired with images) detailing how a particular feature answers the customers' needs and helps build business.

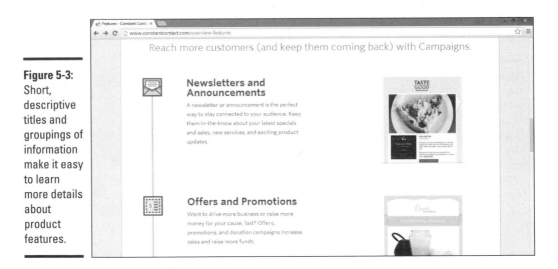

Figure 5-3:
Short,
descriptive
titles and
groupings of
information
make it easy
to learn
more details
about
product
features.

The bottom of the page has an option to learn specific details on the All Campaigns page. This page, shown in Figure 5-4, groups information related to each feature. It uses lists and short descriptions to make it easy to read the more detailed product information.

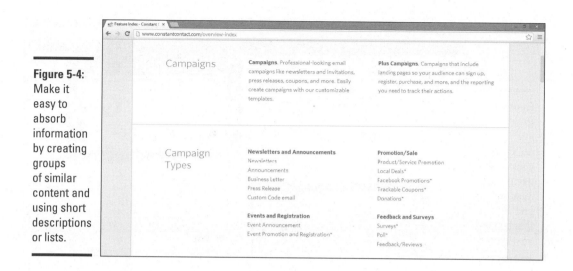

**Book III
Chapter 5**

**Writing Content
that Search Engines
Want to See**

Figure 5-4:
Make it
easy to
absorb
information
by creating
groups
of similar
content and
using short
descriptions
or lists.

Making a list and checking it twice

A single web page can have an unlimited amount of information and choices — filled with lots of links, buttons, and page sections. Your visitors can then choose from several possible actions on that one page. What do you do then?

You have to make a choice: Decide which actions take priority. You can do so by following these simple steps:

1. **Make a list of all possible decisions visitors can make when they're viewing your web page.**

2. **Prioritize the different choices or actions, from most to least desired.**

   For example, it might be more important for visitors to click a page filled with products than to click a link to sign up for a newsletter.

3. **Place the content on the page in such a way that customers view the information in your preferred order (according to your prioritized ranking).**

Our next example, shown in Figure 5-5, is from a high-ranking business solutions site, which organizes its content in one of two ways, depending on the page and desired outcome. The first goal of the Products page is to encourage visitors to view a demo of the solution and get product pricing. To support this goal, the free demo offer is clearly showcased at the top of the page, along with an option to click a button and view pricing. The other goal of the page is to educate site visitors (who aren't ready for a demo or pricing) about product features. To support this goal, visitors can scroll down the page and see short descriptive content blocks with more information about the product's features, as well as link to learn more about each particular feature. Although the site doesn't have a lot of content, the information is easy to understand and site visitors can readily see their options.

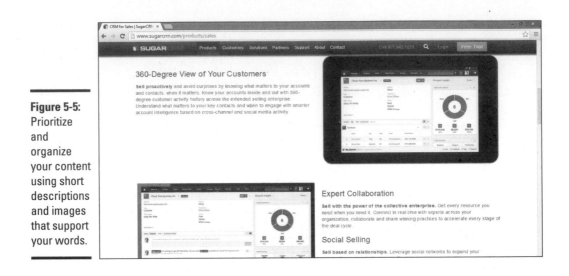

Figure 5-5:
Prioritize
and
organize
your content
using short
descriptions
and images
that support
your words.

Figure 5-6 illustrates how the site provides more detailed information targeted to a specific type of customer — in this case, real estate professionals. This content strategy enables visitors to see information on how to use the product based on their specific needs. In addition to using more content, the page provides many links to customer case studies and white papers that address that specific customer type. The page also includes links to product demos, product trials, and other company information, such as articles and press releases. The goal of this content-filled page is to educate a particular customer segment, giving visitors enough detailed information to make them comfortable with taking a *buying* action (request a demo or contact sales, for example). This type of page also lends itself to the type of content that appeals to search engines.

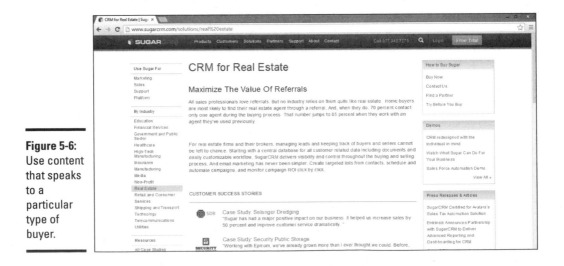

Figure 5-6:
Use content
that speaks
to a
particular
type of
buyer.

Visitors to a website read information by starting at the top of the page and moving downward. As they do with printed offline text, they also read from left to right. Therefore, content you place at the top and to the left of your pages often is noticed first, unless images or large calls to action are used to draw attention elsewhere on the page.

Moved to Purchase: Turning Words into Action

After you identify the actions you want customers to take, it's time to choose the words that elicit those responses. Choose words and phrases that accomplish these tasks:

✦ **Evoke a feeling:** Decisions to make a purchase are often influenced by emotions. Words that help conjure those emotions and feelings are more likely to get a response. Keep in mind, however, that someone shopping for plain paper napkins isn't emotionally connected to the purchase. In this case, a straightforward explanation of the product or its primary benefit (inexpensive cost, for example) probably works best.

✦ **Grab attention:** Some words naturally cause people to momentarily pause when they read them. *STOP! Don't go further until you read the next sentence,* for example, is an effective way to get your customer's attention long enough to introduce the next level of information. And don't forget *FREE!* — one of the most popular attention-grabbers.

✦ **Identify a problem:** Customers are looking for products and services that answer a need. They're drawn to words that describe the problems they're trying to solve.

✦ **Contain buzzwords.** Every industry and consumer market has keywords or keyphrases that are part of that market's lingo, such as *cross-platform* or *solution-driven.* When you talk the language, your customer is more likely to hear what you're saying and respond. However, be sure to use common, helpful phrases, not confusing abbreviations or acronyms.

✦ **Offer assurance:** Customers want to feel good about their decision to buy your products or use your services. When you use words that offer comfort or reinforce the buying decision, customers are often encouraged to make a purchase.

✦ **Request a purchase or action:** If you don't ask customers to make a purchase, your chances of them doing so are greatly diminished. The same goes for any type of action you want the customer to take, such as requesting a product demo, downloading a guide, or watching a video. The type of wording used to get a customer to do something is often referred to as a *call to action* or *CTA.* The words or phrases ask the customer to make a decision at that point. A call to action is particularly effective when it immediately follows words that offer assurance.

Eye-catching words

Use the following list of words and phrases to grab a customer's attention, provide assurance, or ask a customer to take action.

Grab Attention	Provide Assurance	Take Action
Stop	Guaranteed	Buy now
Listen	Trial version	Order here
Urgent	Risk free	Click to order
Sale	No risk	Get more information
Half off	Free sample	Request information
Clearance	No obligation	Contact us
Reduced	Money-back guarantee	E-mail us
While supplies last	Success stories	Join today
Almost sold out	Testimonials	Subscribe
Secret	Loyal customers	Buy now, pay later
Confidential	Quality	Act now
Hot	Validated or tested	Request a demo
Limited time only	Approved	Get a quote
Connect	Referrals	Like us on Facebook or follow us on Twitter

Making unsubstantiated or false earnings claims or false promises about products or services can subject you to fines and prosecution. For more information and legal guidelines, visit the Federal Trade Commission at www.ftc.gov.

Instead of using commands such as *Click here* or *Next* to get folks to click your links, use descriptive terms that are also useful in search engine rankings. For example, use *Learn how to incorporate your business now* or *Get started planning your own water garden* as the link text.

Choosing Words that Search Engines Notice

Just as we suggest that you use industry buzzwords to talk to your customers, you can use these same types of words to "talk" to search engines.

Think about how search engines work to help promote your site. A search engine starts by classifying your site, or putting it into a group of similar sites. Then it ranks your site depending on how relevant it is for that particular category of sites. As mentioned, search engines also want to see that you're providing content that is meaningful and highly relevant to the type of searches your prospective customers are conducting. Note that customers rarely search using on one or two words. Instead, they type complete questions or more lengthy descriptions (called *longtail searches*) to find specific results. For example, instead of searching for *water gardens,* customers are more likely to search for *how to install a low-cost water garden in a shady yard.* The closer your content matches this search, the more likely the search engine will rank it higher, indicating its relevancy to the search query. When you're ready to gain a thorough understanding of how to master search engines, check out Book VI, Chapter 6. For now, we simply want to make you aware of the importance of thinking about search engine rankings while you're writing the initial content for your site.

When you're writing content that's search engine friendly, remember these two brief rules:

✦ **Think like a customer:** Include content that provides answers to the type of questions your customers are asking. If your customers search for tips about removing poison ivy from yards, for example, create content that addresses this concern. You might want to include this information in the product description so your site is more likely to show up in search results.

✦ **Avoid saturation:** Keywords should be a natural part of your content, not overly obvious. For instance, if you were to write three relevant phrases repeatedly, search engines would flag that as *keyword stuffing,* or trying to trick them into having your site rank well. Your site could be penalized and lose its rankings for using this strategy.

Before writing your content, do your own search using a popular search term for your product or service. Then visit the top five sites in the returned rankings. Note which words or phrases your competitors use, and consider finding a logical place for them in your content.

Chapter 6: Lights, Camera, Action! Taking Your Site Live

In This Chapter

✓ **Figuring out what you must know before publishing your website**

✓ **Testing your site for form and function**

✓ **Trying before flying**

✓ **Launching the site**

After taking the trouble to design a site, fill it with quality content, and find the perfect place to host it, you would think that that's the end of the story. We don't want to disappoint you, but you have to deal with another major phase before you launch.

In this chapter, we break this final stage into smaller segments to make it easy to follow. For one moment, let us summarize what all those segments mean in layman's terms: Test, test, and test again. Then, and only then, blast off!

Some Things to Know Before You Start Uploading

Both *launching* and *uploading* your site are terms used to represent the point when you finally make a site viewable by the public over the Internet. Before you upload your site for the world to see, though, it should be fully functional. Your site design and content should be complete, your navigational tools should work properly, and all parts of your website, even the smallest parts and pieces, must be in place and working.

Okay, you can throw caution to the wind and launch an incomplete site. We don't advise it, though. Why not? Doing so isn't professional, and your customers will become easily frustrated when form falls short of function.

An incomplete site diminishes your business's credibility.

A haphazardly constructed and prematurely launched website can cause you to lose customers. If a section or feature of your site isn't fully developed or functional, frustrated customers may never bother coming back again.

If you take away anything from this chapter, remember these two points:

+ Fully complete your site before launching it.

+ Make darn sure that every element works.

You should know about a few other helpful concepts before launching:

+ **Little details count.** Bring out the magnifying glass when you're reviewing your site for mistakes before launching. Check for misspellings, broken links, malfunctioning applications and widgets, and other problem points.

+ **Some functions are limited until after the launch.** A few features might function fully only after your site is live. For instance, forms frequently can be activated only after the site is up for good. Remember to check all forms after the site goes live and correct problems immediately.

+ **Third-party data takes time.** If your site must integrate with any third-party applications or widgets, or you use a newsfeed or syndicated content or another type of data from outside sources, the application might not be instantly available when the site launches. Your site might have to wait several hours or even a full day before it is entered into a customer database, the switch is flipped, and the site goes live. If the information isn't accessible after two business days, contact the service provider to report the problem.

+ **Rankings aren't immediate (or guaranteed).** After your site goes live, you can submit it to be reviewed and possibly included in various search engines. (We go into the art of optimization in detail in Book VI, Chapter 6.) Right now, all we ask is that you remember that it takes a while for a search engine to scan and rank your site after it's up, so don't expect it to show up in the search engines right away. Even after your site is *spidered,* or reviewed, by the search engines, it may not appear anywhere near the top 100 listings. Initially, only people who type your URL in the address field or your company name in a search engine may be able to find your site.

+ **Automated web builders are different from designers.** If you launch (or your web designer launches) your site, it's immediate. In other words, all the files are uploaded to the server at one time. Within minutes, you're finished and the site is online. With some automated web builders or template programs, you might be required to publish your site page by page to the Internet rather than upload a complete file. You can remove a page later if you see a mistake. Be careful, though: Correcting problems to buttons or to the site's menu bar is sometimes difficult after the site is published. Be sure to account for different timelines for publishing a site or pages in a site.

Here's one last thing you should know: Sites look different to different people. We're not talking about personal style preferences. Instead, realize that the code or language used to design your site appears differently when it's viewed with various browsers. Your job is to test your content with every browser you can get your hands on and minimize the differences so that the site looks its best in any browser. In the next section, we suggest ways you can test for optimal conditions before launching your site.

Taking the Compatibility Test: Testing Screen Resolutions, Browsers, and Platforms

Compatibility testing is the fun part of launching a site — if the process doesn't require code changes to improve the way your site is displayed on various devices. Otherwise, this testing might be tedious because any slight variation between code and the way each browser interprets the code can make a noticeable difference on the screen. Even small differences can lead to big issues when it comes to website usability and customer experience.

People can view your site in many ways, and it's up to you to make sure that it looks good and functions well in the most popular browsers and devices. Many free and low-cost tools make it easy to check your site's compatibility in different versions of various browsers and devices, including mobile devices, such as Android, iPhone, and the iPad or other tablets. For example, we used the testing tools at SauceLabs to test how a website appears in a popular browser (see Figure 6-1) and on an Android phone (see Figure 6-2). Sometimes the differences can be subtle, such as how much information appears on a typical screen. If your site is not optimized for mobile devices, however, the differences can be extreme.

Figure 6-1: Compare your site in more than one browser and device.

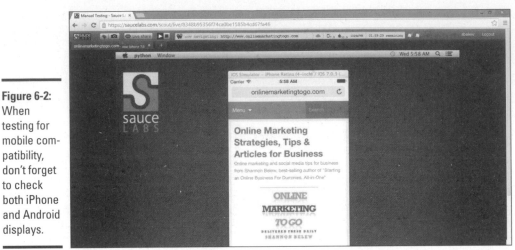

Figure 6-2:
When testing for mobile compatibility, don't forget to check both iPhone and Android displays.

Checking it out

How do you check for browser discrepancies? The obvious answer is to install every possible browser (or at least the mainstream ones) on your computer and run a trial version of your site on each one. Because you can download browsers for free, the only cost to you is your time. However, you could spend weeks manually checking hundreds of different browser editions. Instead, use a testing tool. For a small fee, tools such as GhostLabs (www.ghostlab. vanamco.com) test for browser compatibility and other functionality important to the overall user experience, such as links, downloads and forms. Free tools, such as Browserling (www.browserling.com), also quickly test for browser compatibility.

No matter which tool you use, look for glaring inconsistencies that make your information difficult to read, prevent images from loading, or omit information completely.

Another issue to test for is screen resolution, or how your site looks in different resolution settings. (Don't confuse this term with the physical measurement of your monitor's screen.) By *resolution,* we mean the number of pixels (or miniscule dots) that make up an image on the computer screen. Standard resolution settings are 640 x 480, 600 x 400, and 1024 x 768. Within each resolution is a designated amount of viewable space, which can affect how your website looks on a computer. Computer users can choose which resolution to use on their computers.

Testing on Mac, Windows, or whatever

If checking for browser compatibility and screen resolution isn't enough already, another major element is involved in testing your site. You have to test your site on different operating systems. For example, you might wonder what your site looks like using Macintosh OS X when you designed it on a PC using Windows XP. And we haven't even mentioned Linux!

Keeping people in mind

Even if you know the basic information to test when you're launching your site, you always have to consider a growing list of issues. For instance, your site should be accessible for viewers with disabilities, according to the World Wide Web Consortium (W3C) Web Content Accessibility Guidelines (WCAG) and other government regulations. Complying with these guidelines involves using slightly different coding, color contrasts, and text options for images, for instance.

Web-based services, such as CynthiaSays (www.cynthiasays.com) or WAVE (http://wave.webaim.org), can quickly scan your site to confirm accessibility. Both services check the code behind your design as well as the viewable areas to check for proper functionality according to WCAG standards.

Although you might not want to hear this advice right now, you should routinely test your site for these and other issues, long after you pass the initial launch stage. Keeping your site current and easy to use for the largest possible number of people is standard in the world of online business.

Taking a Trial Run

When a major company releases a software program, game, or website, it often has a limited distribution in a beta version. *Beta* means that the work is in test mode and is subject to change. A beta test, or a product in *beta mode,* is typically released to a large segment of the general public. As for *your* site, we suggest showing a beta version to a limited group of users in a trial run.

You can push your trial site *live* (make it available to the public) and not worry about lots of people finding it because it takes search engines a little bit of time to index the site. However, to be safe, you may prefer to keep the trial version a bit more private and difficult to find so that you can continue testing and making changes. Simply place all the HTML files for your site under a subfolder of your domain, such as www.mysitenamehere.com/testing/index.html. Google also provides some great tools and information on when and how to index your site and how to remove a URL from the search engine; check out Google Webmaster Tools, at www.google.com/webmasters. Or try Bing Webmaster Tools at www.bing.com/toolbox/webmaster.

These users include (ideally) friends, family members, and a few prospective customers who are willing to provide you with honest feedback. Upload the site and run a live trial version for a day or two. Everyone then has a chance to visit the site several times before you take it down again for final changes.

Your site launch checklist

Before you click that last button to make your website live, be sure to check off each box (as it applies to you) on this list:

❑ My site map (or the layout and structure of all my web pages) is complete.

❑ The site map matches my web pages — exactly.

❑ Each website page is displayed and is fully accessible.

❑ Each link works properly and takes me to the appropriate page.

❑ All graphics and photos are loaded quickly and completely, and the images are crisp and clean.

❑ My content is free of misspellings and grammatical errors.

❑ Pricing information and product or service descriptions are correct.

❑ Pages with online forms or registration information function when I click the Submit button, and the information is sent (in the specified format) to the designated point of contact.

❑ Text boxes or drop-down boxes on forms and other pages work correctly.

❑ Buttons for top-level menus function properly on every page.

❑ Special commands that are spelled out with coding language (HTML, CSS, or PHP, for example) show up properly when the site loads.

❑ My credit card processor or other payment service option is in place and working.

❑ All functions related to e-commerce, such as my shopping cart, operate correctly.

❑ I've included any appropriate membership icons, logos, or emblems (such as the ones used by members of the Better Business Bureau or Chamber of Commerce).

❑ I tested the site for browser compatibility and screen resolution.

❑ I tested the site using a dial-up connection and a broadband connection.

❑ My contact information (e-mail address or phone number) is clearly displayed and easy to find.

❑ The copyright symbol and current year, as well as a link to my privacy policy and website terms, are prominently displayed at the bottom of every page.

Your beta users should be on the lookout for common errors you might have missed, features or links that don't work correctly, videos and graphics that load improperly — or not at all — and the general appearance and overall ease of use of the site. (For instance, the site should be intuitive to visitors, and the names of the page links and buttons must make sense to other people, not just to you.)

Three, Two, One — Take Off!

NASA launches its space shuttle missions at certain times of the day and under the most forgiving weather conditions. Although we guarantee that the weather outside isn't a concern for your launch, certain times are better than others for sending your site out on the Net.

Particularly when you're using a freelance website designer, you should have input about when your site launches. Because that person usually sends the files to the server on your behalf, request that your site be launched early in the week. That way, if a problem surfaces, you have plenty of time during the workweek to fix it. Frustration is quick to set in when you launch a site on Friday afternoon and shortly thereafter you discover a problem that you have to live with for the entire weekend.

When you use an outside developer, you're asked to sign a waiver when the project is finished. The waiver says that your site is accurate and that all requested changes were made. You get a sense of finality when your site comes off a project-management list. Sign the waiver only when you're completely satisfied. The web developer is then released from additional work after the site is launched. If your provider charges for maintenance (or changes) to the site, the signed waiver signals that the provider can switch you from the development stage to the web maintenance stage, which can cost you.

Avoid launching the day before a long holiday weekend, regardless of whether you or someone else designs your site. Of course, larger websites might find that launching a site over a holiday is advantageous. The slower period gives the company an extended shot at a trial run — and one more opportunity to correct errors. If a site has been well marketed, the opposite effect can occur: It can be a hit by a large amount of traffic because more people are home and spending time online. However, unless you spend a lot of money and effort investing in prelaunch publicity and advertising, high traffic flow shouldn't be an issue for you at the beginning — holiday or not.

Nothing has to be forever on the web. If you discover a mistake after your website goes up, don't panic. You can easily make a correction. The web is certainly not static, so updates are usually a snap.

Plenty of excitement should accompany your site's sendoff to the web. This major accomplishment is the start of something potentially lucrative. Celebrate!

Book IV
Online and Operating

Providing your customers with several payment options is critical to a successful online business. Go online at www.dummies.com/extras/startingan onlinebusinessaio to find out how to increase the payment options for your business with one of several mobile credit card readers.

Contents at a Glance

Chapter 1: Determining Your Revenue Model

In This Chapter

✓ Acquiring and reselling tangible products

✓ Finding revenue-sharing opportunities with affiliate sites

✓ Selling your professional services

✓ Distributing information for profit

✓ Creating a revenue stream by placing online advertisements

✓ Incorporating multiple sources of revenue for a healthy bottom line

F ace it: Whenever you start an online business, you must answer one question before you answer any others — how will you make money?

You can have the most brilliant, original, or quirky idea ever conceived, but the concept doesn't hold water if you don't have a viable plan to bring in dollars. The good news is that, as the web continues to mature, a number of viable ways to make money have emerged. In this chapter, we break down the various revenue models on which you can base your online business.

Selling Tangible Products

A natural choice for making money online is to sell some sort of product. You might already have a fantastic product, or you might need to search for a mix of products that you can buy and resell to others over the web. Either way, selling a tangible product over the Internet has proven to be a successful online earnings model ever since e-commerce began taking off in the early 1990s.

Projecting how you'll make a profit

When you deal in tangible goods and services, the question of how to make a profit often boils down to a simple four-word phrase: "Buy low, sell high." As entrepreneurs have always known, you have to sell something for more than you originally paid for it to make money. Even if you're able to catch fish from the sea and sell them to big food suppliers, or if you're able to create works of art with the fruit of your talent, you still incur business expenses. A fisherman has to pay for a boat, fuel, and equipment. An artist has to buy paint, brushes, and canvas. No matter what you sell, you have to project how much you're going to spend in acquiring or producing the product, and how much you can reasonably get for it in the marketplace. The difference is your profit.

Before you even spend your first penny buying or producing tangible products to sell, take a moment and ask yourself some basic questions that will help you project your potential revenue:

✦ What does it cost to produce or purchase my product?

✦ How much is my overhead: the cost for utilities, rent, salaries, and transportation, for example?

✦ Can I price the product in such a way that it covers my overhead and purchasing costs and still remains competitive with similar products?

✦ Will added shipping costs skew (or diminish) that competitive price point?

✦ What volume of products do I need to sell each month to reach my desired profit margins?

✦ How much traffic (how many visitors) must I drive to my site *and* convert to customers in order to reach those sales goals?

✦ How much do I need to spend on marketing to attract that level of traffic?

Write all the projected expenses and income on a piece of paper or using your computer. Do some in-depth thinking about whether you can make your business plan (that's what this is, after all) work successfully. If your profit isn't enough to make a living or at least make enough for your immediate needs, make adjustments now. That might mean finding more products, raising prices, reducing expenses, or all these. Run the numbers past any experienced businesspeople among your family or friends who can serve as mentors.

Knowing for certain whether a product-based revenue model will meet your financial needs is difficult — a lot depends on the product itself. In Chapter 6 of this minibook, we show you how to research and further test your product ideas — whether you created the item or are buying products for resale.

Manufacturing and selling your own goods

In terms of sheer profit margin, you can rarely do better than creating your own products for little money and selling them online. If you're creative and enterprising, you can sell your own work by using e-commerce sites, auction sites such as eBay, and websites that have been set up to market a particular type of item (such as Etsy, at www.etsy.com, where artists and hobbyists can list their own handmade or vintage works for sale).

The kinds of items you can sell online is limited only by your imagination. You might sell delicately smocked dresses for children or funky, hand-strung beaded jewelry. Or maybe you want to develop an original board game or peddle custom-designed iPad covers. Rest assured that all these products have a place on the innovative Internet.

As you might expect, a few characteristics give your personal handiwork a leg up on the competition, including

✦ **Quality:** Without exception, consumers expect a product that's worthy of its price tag. When you're creating your own products, you have total control over quality. Make sure your designs are finished and your workmanship is of a high level before you put items up for sale.

✦ **Originality:** If your handmade product is a unique twist on a mass-marketed type of product, you can have rewards. Internet shoppers are always looking for products that are slightly different from the items available in most retail stores.

✦ **Appeal:** Maybe your handmade product isn't unique but is part of a specialized, hard-to-find or popular group of products (such as personalized cellphone or Android phone cases). Narrowing your product's appeal by audience is a good way to increase revenue potential. We discuss niche markets more in depth in Book X.

✦ **Built-in customer base:** Perhaps your product is designed to appeal to a specific group of people, such as a religious group that makes woven altar cloths for churches. Having a clearly identifiable existing customer base that you can market to makes selling your product that much easier.

When you're making a product from scratch, the way in which you earn money can vary. If your product meets one or more of these descriptors, chances are good that you will do well. At least you're off to a good start!

Buying tangible goods and selling them online

Even if you don't have the creative ability to craft your own products, you still have plenty of options for making money online. The overwhelming majority of online entrepreneurs are people who buy tangible goods at low prices and sell them online for a profit. You can either sell directly from your own website or allow another website to market your products.

Selling directly online means that customers come directly to you (by way of your website) to buy an item. There's no middleman. The marketing, publicity, and fulfillment are up to you — in other words, it's a lot of work, but the rewards can be great. If you don't have any experience selling, it makes sense to allow other websites, such as eBay, to market your products. The website brings you customers and provides you with systems for creating sales descriptions and receiving payments. Your host website charges fees for its services, but you don't have to do all the work.

Whether you sell directly or sign up with another website to sell your goods, you have to find a source for your products. Three of the most popular options — finding your own merchandise, finding a wholesale supplier, and finding a drop shipper — are described in the sections that follow.

Finding your own merchandise

Many people who sell online begin at home or close to home. They clean out their closets, their garages, and their attics, and then sell the extra merchandise. Then they move on to the homes of their relatives.

Others scour flea markets, estate sales, garage sales, secondhand stores, dollar stores, and many other marketplaces, looking for treasures they can sell online at a profit. Sellers who are lucky enough to find a reliable source of desirable merchandise can make part or perhaps even all of their income. The problem is that the time spent searching, hauling, and bringing home the items to sell is considerable. Not only that, but there's the question of where to store all the products and the boxes used to ship them: You either have to delegate a room in your house for this purpose or rent warehouse space. It's hard to build up a sufficient inventory to make a living at selling online.

Buying wholesale

Owners of traditional retail stores are accustomed to buying their inventories wholesale or becoming distributors for particular products or brands. The same option is available for your online store. When you buy wholesale, you purchase products at a discounted price and then resell them to your customer base at a marked-up price. You're responsible for ensuring that these tasks are completed:

✦ **Purchase inventory in bulk.** You can't buy just one hair dryer. You have to commit to an entire case (or several cases) to get a discount.

✦ **Warehouse the inventory.** Wholesalers don't let you keep all those cases of products at their place. You're expected to store the inventory you purchase for your site, even if you have to keep it around for several months. You have to find space for it in your home or rent a warehouse, and because online merchants tend to buy higher quantities of merchandise at wholesale than they do scouring flea markets, this proposition can turn into an expensive one.

✦ **Ship the products to your customers.** Because you keep the merchandise at your place of business, you have to handle packaging and shipping each item (unless you hire employees to help you). See Chapter 7 of this minibook to find out more about packaging and shipping your products.

✦ **Handle returns and exchanges from customers.** If a customer is unhappy with a product or the item is damaged, it has to be shipped back to you to be dealt with accordingly.

The drawbacks for a small online business are probably obvious. Among the biggest is that your out-of-pocket cash commitment is hefty. If you're just starting out, you take a financial hit right off the bat.

Of course, you have to have a place to store all these products, too. A garage or spare bedroom might suffice for some, but others will eventually need to rent storage space. That overhead expense certainly eats into your profitability. Many online merchants find that the third option listed for sourcing merchandise to sell — drop shippers — enables them to market their products without having to deal with having to store and handle inventory.

When you purchase merchandise from a wholesaler, you typically must provide some form of proof that you're a legitimate business (and that you're not buying for personal use). Wholesalers might ask you for a state-issued reseller's certificate or a federal tax ID number. And if the wholesaler doesn't require these items, you might not be paying truly wholesale prices.

Going inventory-free: Drop shipping

For many online entrepreneurs, the ideal setup is working with a *drop shipper,* a company that sells you merchandise at wholesale prices but only when you sell to a member of the public at a retail price you specify. You don't need to spend lots of money building inventory with a drop shipper; you're billed only when you make a sale. And the drop shipper stores the inventory for you and ships your products as you sell them. Drop shippers are ready to provide you with a steady stream of merchandise, and you don't even have to worry about warehouse space. When you use drop shipping, you can select products from other manufacturers, set a price for each item, and then turn around and offer the products for resale on your site. You're able to focus on presenting and marketing the products while the drop shipper handles fulfillment.

The factor that makes this model especially attractive is that you don't buy or hold any inventory. Instead, you wait until a customer places an order from your site. After the payment has cleared, you forward an order to your drop shipper and pay for the product. (You're charged a wholesale or discounted price, whereas your customer pays you full retail price.) The drop shipper then sends the product directly to your customer. You make money on the difference between your cost for buying the product from the drop shipper and the price you charge your customer. As far as your customer knows, the merchandise is coming directly from you. Other perceived benefits include being able to offer excellent customer service and concentrate

**Book IV
Chapter 1**

**Determining Your
Revenue Model**

on marketing, rather than on manufacturing, the product. You don't have to deal with the headaches of managing inventory and shipping products. You can focus on the front end — the sales process.

What's the downside? Lots of companies claim to be reputable drop shippers, but many aren't trustworthy. You have to scrutinize certain issues to create a realistic picture of your income potential:

✦ **Lack of control:** When you work with a drop shipper, you don't control how the merchandise is packed or shipped or how quickly it arrives. Discuss with the drop shipper which shipping method should be used.

✦ **Possible inventory problems:** You depend on your drop shipper to have the inventory in stock when someone purchases it. If it's not there, you have to explain delays to your customers.

✦ **Return policies:** Make sure your drop shipper accepts returns. If the drop shipper doesn't, you'll be stuck with the bill when the customer expresses dissatisfaction and wants to send something back.

✦ **Dealing with a lack of volume discounts:** Because you're not purchasing products in bulk, the discounted retail price is typically higher than when you buy wholesale. This price difference can translate to lower profit margins for you. If you sell consistently, you may be able to negotiate a lower price eventually, but at first your profit margin is less than if you purchase at wholesale and sell directly to the public.

✦ **Handling less-competitive pricing:** To offset lower profit margins, you might be tempted to mark up the product's price significantly. The risk is that your product might not be price competitive in the marketplace. That's not a bad thing — as long as you can balance it with another value proposition (such as excellent customer service or a huge product selection).

✦ **Balancing demand and value:** With profit margins a little tighter, you might search for drop-shipped products sold at the deepest discounts. Although your profit margin can rise because of this factor, the product won't sell if it doesn't have mass appeal.

✦ **Driving traffic:** When you pay more for a product (in exchange for the convenience of on-demand ordering), your profit becomes a true numbers game. You have to attract a much larger number of visitors to your site and increase the rate of conversion to realize the same, or similar, profit margins as a site that's buying wholesale (see the preceding section) or selling custom products.

Identifying drop shippers and wholesalers is the first step when using this strategy to earn revenues online. Several reputable resources for product sourcing, or locating a drop shipper, are available — at a price. For access to a directory of drop shippers and wholesalers, you may pay a one-time fee or a monthly fee that also includes access to various support and marketing tools. Some drop-shipper resources also allow you to integrate with your eBay store, letting you push product descriptions and listings directly to the site. The same type of integration is sometimes available for e-commerce solution providers and storefronts, such as Shopify (www.shopify.com), 1ShoppingCart (www.1shoppingcart.com), and BigCommerce (www.bigcommerce.com). You can learn more about using storefronts in Book VIII. Here are a few good resources for finding suppliers that drop-ship products:

✦ Doba (www.doba.com)

✦ Inventory Source (www.inventorysource.com)

✦ SaleHoo (www.salehoo.com)

✦ Worldwide Brands (www.worldwidebrands.com)

Selling Your Professional Services

Sometimes the issue isn't which types of products you have to offer. Instead, you have to ask, "What can I *do* for you?" Another source for making money online is selling your services. Most online services fall into one of four key areas:

✦ **Creative:** These products are delivered as a service. For example, you might be a graphic artist who develops logos, a writer who is paid to create ad copy, or an artist who paints portraits from photographs that customers upload to your website.

✦ **Organizational:** If your site is an organization based on paid memberships, we consider it a service website. Typically, your members pay for access to a group of services in exchange for a renewable fee.

✦ **Professional:** These folks are accountants, attorneys, public relations agents — you get the idea. Whatever the service, not only do you market it online, but your customers can purchase the service over the Internet.

✦ **Software-based:** A variety of websites provide software online that their visitors can use with their web browsers. Sometimes called an application service provider (ASP) or software as a service (SaaS), it's almost a hybrid of a service and a product. A company uses a website to sell software or a process that's delivered or managed as a web-based service. Some examples are an online payroll-processing firm, a website hosting service, and a shopping cart program.

Whatever service you want to promote online, you need to have a clear picture of the benefits and downsides so that you can maximize your chances of success.

Understanding the pros and cons

You gain a distinct benefit, geographically speaking, from offering any type of service-driven revenue stream online. For example, if you're a graphic artist living in a small rural town, the number of people who regularly need your service is limited. By selling your services from a website, you can quickly broaden your prospective customer base.

Selling your professional services online has a downside, too. As you know, revenues from most service-based business are limited by the products you can produce — there are only so many hours in a day! Your final output (and income potential) is based on your, or your staff's, available billable hours. You can take the following actions to minimize this type of effect on your revenues:

✦ Increase your hourly rate

✦ Hire additional staff

✦ Replicate your service as a web-based deliverable product

✦ Add complementary sources of revenue (other services or products) to your site

For many professionals, the added visibility that comes with a website outweighs the disadvantages. And these days, professionals need to be on the web just to keep up with the competition.

Building credibility

One of the most important issues for anyone who sells his services online is *credibility*. What experience or credentials do you have that help you stand out from the crowd? Although you can reach a larger number of prospective clients on the web, you're also up against more competitors. And when people purchase services over the Internet, they look for indications that you're legitimate and skilled.

Unlike meeting with a potential customer in your offline business, you don't always have the opportunity to establish a direct relationship with a prospective client. Your website serves as that introduction and relationship builder. If information about your service isn't available (or obvious), your potential customer will click through to a competitor's site.

Establishing your credibility isn't difficult. Your website can feature any or all of these items, to help solidify your reputation and put potential customers at ease:

✦ **Degrees or certifications:** Adding this information to your bio on the About Us page gives prospective customers a sense of security. If you have certifications in niche areas, this information is especially effective for building credibility.

✦ **Company history:** The issue of the number of years you've been in business is especially important if your website services are new but you've been in business offline for quite some time.

✦ **Clients:** Even if you don't have any heavy-hitter clients on board, a short list of named clients illustrates your legitimacy (and the fact that people hire you).

✦ **Case studies:** Describing how your service was used to help solve a customer's problem is an effective way to communicate a success story. A case study demonstrates the different ways your services can benefit someone.

✦ **Testimonials:** Whenever you finish a project that has gone well, ask your client to provide a testimonial. One or two sentences are plenty to let others know that you did a good job.

When developing client testimonials and case studies, consider delivering the information by using videos, which continue to increase in popularity. The most effective videos are short (under 90 seconds) and easy to consume. Plus, you don't have to pay high production costs — with inexpensive equipment, you can easily make low-budget but professional videos.

✦ **Social media endorsements:** Sites such as LinkedIn offer the opportunity for clients and customers to recommend you. The process is simple and is much like a traditional testimonial that happens to be accessible online. Don't hesitate to ask for that recommendation. Similarly, use other social media sites, such as Twitter, Facebook, Google+, and YouTube, to spread the news of your successes. Or eavesdrop on these open communications and find people who are already saying good things about you.

✦ **Recognition:** Any awards or kudos you receive definitely build confidence in your capabilities.

✦ **Press clippings:** Don't be shy. If you appear in a newspaper or magazine article, shout it from the rooftop or from your home page. Links to this type of publicity serve as validation from a third party.

✦ **Referrals:** Similarly, if other experts, service providers, or organizations tout your skills, let site visitors see that you're considered a leader in your field.

Add a link to your membership organizations at the bottom of your website's home page. Making these elements highly visible on your front page can encourage a new visitor to your site to hang around a little longer.

Adding the items in the preceding list to your site also helps you deal with another issue: When you run an online service company, you have to *market yourself,* just like you would market any product. Being hesitant about promoting your talent affects your earnings.

If you're not comfortable blowing your own horn or you just don't have time, hire a professional. Count it as part of your marketing expenses, as you would when you buy banner ads or Google AdWords.

Selling Information

The Internet holds so much information that simply finding the data you need the most is a time-consuming process. Some of the most successful businesses on the web got their start by simply organizing the mountain of online content and making key information easier to find. The two most notable examples are Yahoo!, which developed one of the first indexes of websites, and Google, which created one of the most effective search engines ever.

When it comes to content, though, *almost anything* can be converted and packaged into some sellable format. More and more newspapers, such as *The Wall Street Journal* (www.wsj.com), charge a subscription fee for accessing some or all of their articles, including articles from their extensive archives. Well-known magazines are readily following suit. But not just words are being sold. It's possible to charge money for music, games, videos (film), research data, mobile applications, and, well, you name it.

The subject of providing saleable content online holds so much promise that we dedicate an entire chapter to it. If this area interests you, check out Chapter 3 of this minibook to find out how to transition your expertise into e-books, webinars, and other online content-based products. Whether you create a website that organizes information or you sell articles or other information online, developing marketable content requires only four initial steps:

1. **Originate.**

   In this step, you create the product. Converting and saving your words, music, or images to a media format is a fairly simple and straightforward process.

2. **Replicate.**

   After you have an information product, your next step is to package it for resale by converting the content into a type of downloadable file distributed over an Internet connection. The file might be a PDF document, an image file, or even a link to a password-protected website that contains the information.

3. **Disseminate.**

   After the content is stored in the preferred format, you're ready to put it up for sale. You have lots of ways to make the content available for download: You can use standard shopping carts that integrate with content products, or you can use web-based services that distribute content on your behalf.

4. **Update.**

    Making minor revisions or updating content is a matter of returning to the original document or file. After the corrections are made, you save the changes and then replace the old media with the most recent version.

Ease of production aside, you're probably curious about how much you truly can earn. That number is hard to pinpoint because you can charge in several ways and because getting consistent numbers for this new industry is challenging. That said, from year to year, analysts gauge a steady increase in revenues from paid content, with totals reaching several billion dollars. Consider that Huffington Post, essentially a news-style blog site, was sold for $315 million. And in 2013, Yahoo! purchased Tumblr for $1.1 billion — the micro-blogging site is filled with user-generated content and attracts a heavy stream of traffic.

Equally encouraging are reports from industry analysts showing that global revenues from mobile apps continue to grow, having reached $26 billion in 2013. In 2017, that number is expected to hit nearly $76 billion, including app purchases, advertising, and in-app purchases. Moreover, social media heavy-hitters Facebook and Twitter have paid millions — and even billions — for start-up app companies and sites that focus on all types of content.

Companies such as YouTube, Apple, Netflix, and even traditional media sites for major networks have expanded the meaning of *content.* Apps, videos, and music have already skyrocketed into the arena of sought-after content. The new demand has caused a tug-of-war between two strategies: offering paid content versus offering free content subsidized by advertising. (We think paid content will continue to grow.) Prominent media organizations are leading the way and establishing a legitimate (and lucrative) market.

Perhaps responding to growing preferences, content distributors big and small are also offering content in single quantities. One of the best known examples is the Apple iTunes store, which struck a chord with fans when it started selling downloadable songs for 99 cents apiece. Online bookstores, such as Amazon and Barnes & Noble, also offer paid content that's immediately downloadable for use with their respective media or e-readers. Note that your price point and potential revenue for this model largely depend on three factors:

✦ The type of content you're offering (and how it is traditionally packaged)

✦ The popularity of your content

✦ The way your content is being sold by your competitors

**Book IV
Chapter 1**

**Determining Your
Revenue Model**

Placing Ads for Profit

Although paid programming is undoubtedly expanding on the web, it's not the only game in town. Content is being used to sustain another tried-and-true web business model: advertising. When you attract enough visitors to your website by providing marketable content, you can place advertisements and earn money from advertisers.

Looking at sites that sell

We know that you recognize the online billboard model of providing content, attracting visitors, and then selling advertising space on the site (thus, the term *billboard*). In this model, the content is typically good quality and free. Articles, tips, videos, and other types of content are used to draw visitors to a website. Typically, the more eyeballs the content attracts, the more money that can be earned by selling ad space. Sometimes, websites offer niche content to a targeted audience may be able to sell advertising even if the site doesn't have a high volume of traffic. Either way, the right type of free content is turned into money in the bank. Several popular types of sites support earning revenues from ad dollars:

✦ **Community:** The online community is modeled after one of the original web business models, the website portal. This type of site provides a host of information, articles, and resources on a specific area of interest, usually to a targeted audience. For example, The Knot (`www.theknot.com`) provides information to engaged couples and newly married couples. Mashable (`www.mashable.com`) provides information and resources for people focused on digital innovation. The site attracts more than 34 million unique visitors each month, and has over 14 million followers in social media.

✦ **Classifieds:** Personal ads are among the fastest-growing categories in this market. Sites that promote listings for jobs, household goods, or businesses for sale (such as Craigslist) also attract visitors.

✦ **Video channels:** Video content has become increasingly popular. YouTube reported that 6 billion hours of video were watched each month during the first quarter of 2014, and the video site has over 1 billion users. While YouTube is the obvious leader in video consumption, almost any type of video-centric site is ripe for high traffic and ad-based revenues.

✦ **Information exchange:** This area includes blogs, user groups, and review sites such as Angie's List (`www.angieslist.com`).

The online ad-based business model has been around practically since the birth of the Internet. As the industry has matured, it has become standardized to a large degree (although it continues to evolve). Today, the ad-based business model has generally accepted rules or guidelines concerning advertising, such as

✦ Which forms of online advertising are acceptable

✦ How results of an ad campaign are measured

✦ Why and how a site should be audited by a third party to validate its traffic

✦ How much advertisers are typically prepared to pay for ad campaigns

To discover more information about current advertising guidelines and standards for the web, we recommend visiting the Interactive Advertising Bureau (IAB) at www.iab.net.

Analyzing traffic patterns

After you examine websites that attract ad revenue, you need to improve your own website and analyze it so that you can determine whether it's attracting enough attention to make ad revenue a viable proposition. For the most part, your income is connected to the level of *traffic*, or number of unique visitors, your site receives. The level of traffic you receives depends on two factors:

✦ **Value:** The quality and appeal of your content have a direct effect on the number of visitors your site receives. Sites that have engaging content or deal with highly popular subject matter are more likely to attract and retain visitors.

✦ **Promotion:** Because even good sites can go unnoticed, your number-one job (following content creation) is to market your site. This task runs the gamut from search engine optimization to public relations. You have to attract eyeballs to make money. (When you're ready to get serious about boosting sales by promoting your site, check out Book VI.)

If your site has been up and running for a while (preferably, several months), you can use your traffic analysis data to gauge future traffic patterns. This strategy works even with a limited amount of historical data. Specifically, look at the percentage of growth in the number of visitors from week to week or from month to month. By multiplying this figure over several months, or even a year, you create a baseline calculation of the growth you can expect — assuming that no negative trend in visitor traffic takes place. This calculation doesn't account for spikes in visitor traffic following a higher search engine ranking or from marketing activities to promote your site.

How do you know when you reach a number of hits that's sufficient to start generating revenue from ad sales? Consider that most online *ad networks* (organizations that sell ad inventory on behalf of web publishers) require that you meet a minimum traffic count before they will work with your site. For most websites, this cutoff is between 3,000 and 5,000 unique visitors per month. That's an average of approximately 100 to 166 visitors per day to your site.

With a start-up business, you obviously don't have the hard, cold data to estimate when you might hit those magic numbers, so you need to project your site traffic. How? Take a look at the traffic patterns of sites that are similar to the one you're building. You can find some of this information from a third party, such as Alexa (www.alexa.com). This site, owned by Amazon, provides traffic rankings as well as fee-based tools for competitive intelligence and on-site metrics and monitoring (for your own site). To access the information on Alexa, you must sign up for a paid account, which ranges from $10 to $149 per month.

Alexa offers a free one-month trial of its low-end basic plan. However, the trial should provide enough information to offer some initial competitive data.

After signing up for a paid or free trial account, you can compare sites by following these steps:

1. **Log in to your account at www.alexa.com and go to My Dashboard.**

You see different sections featuring tools you can use to track information on your website as well as tools to compare other sites.

2. **Under My Site Comparisons, click the + New Comparison tab.**

The Site Comparisons page appears.

3. **At the top of the page, enter the URL of the website you want to compare.**

For this example, we used the Small Business Administration site at www.sba.gov.

The report is run and you see a six-month graph detailing historical traffic trends for the site, as shown in Figure 1-1. (With a Pro account, you can adjust this timeframe.) Available traffic trend information includes Alexa traffic rank, page views, and time on site.

Figure 1-1:
Check traf-
fic pattern
results.

4. **If you want to compare multiple sites, enter the URL for the next site in top-left Enter Site box.**

   For this example, we compared the IRS website (www.irs.gov) to the SBA website. You see a graph detailing recent traffic patterns for both sites, as shown in Figure 1-2.

Figure 1-2:
Compare
the traffic
history of
sites.

**Book IV
Chapter 1**

**Determining Your
Revenue Model**

Having access to competitive information provides a good overview of traffic patterns for sites similar to yours. These results are in no way a guarantee of *your* level of visitor traffic. Many other factors influence the results, such as

✦ Age of the site

✦ Organic search rankings (in Google and Yahoo!)

✦ Amount of marketing designed to drive traffic

Additionally, keep in mind that the figures from Alexa are only estimates.

Choosing ad formats

The types of advertising formats you choose to offer influence your ad revenue. Although a banner ad continues to be an old standby, savvy advertisers (and experienced media buyers) expect a variety of ad format options so that they can mix and match to find the best value for their investment. These ad formats include video ads, social media ads, and mobile-ready ads. Here are some common ad types:

✦ **Banner:** This standard boxed ad appears almost anywhere on your website, including at the top of your home page, in the sidebar of your site, or embedded in content sections on your site. Dozens of ad sizes are available; you can see samples of the most basic banner-ad sizes in Figure 1-3.

Figure 1-3: Common banner ad sizes.

✦ **Rich media:** Displayed like a banner ad, rich media uses images, Flash, or other dynamic programming (including video) in the ad. Rich media is sometimes referred to as an interactive ad.

✦ **Display:** This type of ad uses visual imagery. Rich media can be used as a display ad. Display ads also can refer to ads that can be shown in Google's display network (which is made up of a variety of websites across the Internet).

✦ **Pop-up:** This type of ad appears on the website page that your visitor is viewing.

✦ **Pop-under:** This type of ad opens behind, or underneath, your primary website. Visitors usually don't notice that a new window is open until they close or minimize the browser window.

✦ **Native ads:** Rather than offer a standard banner ad, your content-rich site can allow advertisers to sponsor certain sections. For example, on a site about raising children, a diaper company might want to sponsor the section targeted to infants or toddlers. The ads are considered part of the user experience and are in context with the content being consumed by your website visitors.

✦ **Text link:** You can embed a paid text link anywhere in your site. A visitor who clicks the link goes directly to the advertised site or product page.

✦ **Takeover:** This type of ad is focused on one product or brand. It is usually a collection of ads (including everything from banners to integrated content sponsorships) that uses up all ad inventory on a single page (often the home page). In other words, anywhere an ad is usually placed on the web page is now dedicated to one product. The entertainment industry often uses this approach to promote a new movie or television series.

✦ **In-stream:** These ads are shown within a video.

✦ **Referral:** Also called a lead generator, this format is usually set up as a form page that a visitor from your site completes and submits to the advertiser. The form information indicates further interest in the product and provides a sales lead.

✦ **Retargeting:** This type of ad targets website visitors after they leave a site and follows them to other sites (including social media sites) they visit. For example, someone visits your site and views content about a particular product but leaves without taking any action. Next, the visitor goes to Facebook, where he or she sees an ad related to the product viewed on your site.

Naturally, you might ask, "How much do I charge for ads?" Answering that question is tricky: Rates vary tremendously for the different online ad formats and your site's advertising clout. We can tell you that all formats are typically sold in one of three ways:

✦ **CPM:** Cost per thousand impressions. An *impression* is a single appearance of an ad in someone's Web browser window.

✦ **CPC:** Cost per click, or click-through. A *click-through* occurs whenever someone clicks an ad and goes to the advertiser's website.

✦ **Flat rate:** A fixed dollar amount that's paid regardless of results or number of click-throughs.

Although it's nearly impossible to say how much your specific site can charge, we can give you a typical range. For example, an average rate paid on a cost-per-click basis can run from several cents per click to a few dollars per click-through. A text link might bring in a flat fee ranging from $25 per month to several hundred dollars per month, regardless of the number of impressions. On the other hand, sponsorships or takeover ads might net anywhere from a few thousand dollars to six figures.

The magic variables to a profitable ad-based site seem to be both *traffic* and *site topic*. The more visitors you have and the more popular your site's topic, the more people pay for advertising on your site.

According to some industry reports, smaller sites, those with fewer than 1 million page views per month, can earn as much as three times that of large, high-traffic sites with more than 100 million page views per month. The smaller sites are typically niche sites with highly targeted content that reaches a targeted audience who are more likely to click through on ads. You can find out about what it takes to start a niche site in Book X.

Estimating your revenue potential

To find the ballpark amount of what you can eventually earn, we recommend researching your closest competitors. Although this method is far from scientific, it's a start.

Begin by checking out your competitors' ad rates. You can usually find a link from the site's home page labeled Advertise with Us or similar wording. The link helps you find information that advertisers need to know, such as

✦ Number of unique visitors

✦ Visitor demographics

✦ Size and cost of available ad formats

Also note the type and number of ads running throughout the site. A quick calculation (multiply the number of ads by the ad rate) provides a *general* estimate of possible ad revenues for that type of site.

Managing ad space inventory

You can choose to sell your site's entire advertising inventory. Nothing's wrong with managing that kind of campaign yourself, but companies (especially agencies) purchasing ad space from you expect the process to be smooth. They want verifiable data that the ad ran and the impressions were served by your site to those who visited it. You therefore have to

✦ Place the ads efficiently.

✦ Monitor the campaign.

✦ Report your progress to your advertiser.

To make this process easier to manage, you need to implement a good ad server program for your site.

An ad server program can be software that you install or a web-based product supported by a third party. To make your task as simple as possible, we recommend the latter.

One ad server program for publishers (or website owners) that has been around for a while and is well respected is DoubleClick, now owned by Google. By using this hosted ad server program, you can manage and serve ads on your site. You can find more information at www.google.com/doubleclick/publishers/solutions/ad-serving.html.

Another alternative is using a service we like from ValueAd (www.valuead.com/adserving). It offers two products, ValueAd Network (for global audiences) and AdXpress (an enterprise ad-serving network).

Selling the space

Of course, part of handling your site's advertising involves selling it. You're completely responsible for these tasks:

✦ Seek advertisers.

✦ Respond to ad inquiries.

✦ Manage the back-end functions of each campaign that's run on your site.

You might also have other responsibilities, such as

✦ Negotiating ad rates

✦ Invoicing advertisers

✦ Seeking renewals for ad campaigns

If your time is scarce or you would prefer to not handle these functions, you can contract with an *ad network,* a company that handles the advertising for your site from start to finish. Most networks work with you only if you provide a minimum number of page views per month, usually starting at 3,000 to 5,000. If you're interested, check out these established ad networks:

✦ **AdvertisingZ.com:** www.advertisingz.com

✦ **BurstMedia:** www.burstmedia.com

✦ **BuySellAds**: www.buysellads.com

✦ **Chitika:** www.chitika.com

✦ **Media Net:** www.media.net

✦ **VigLink:** www.viglink.com

As long as you can attract the eyeballs, using an ad network can be an effective way to increase your revenue potential. That's certainly the name of the game for using an ad-based earnings model.

Establishing an Affiliate Advertising Program

One of the most effective ways to take advantage of online advertising to enhance your income online is to set up an affiliate program. An *affiliate* agreement enables other sites to refer traffic to your website, usually in exchange for a small commission on each sale that originates from its referral traffic. You can set up an affiliate program based on one of these methods:

✦ **Pay per click:** You pay each time a link to your site or product is clicked.

✦ **Pay by lead:** You pay whenever a referred customer completes an online form, for example.

✦ **Pay by flat rate:** You pay a set fee as opposed to a percentage of each sale.

You might be interested in becoming an affiliate for others as a way to earn revenue, too. In Chapter 2 of this minibook, we show you how to start adding existing affiliate programs to your website.

A big benefit of establishing your own affiliate arrangement is that you maintain control over how your product is distributed to your customers. You're still the one handling and shipping the product, even though both you and your affiliate are likely to have contact with the customer. Another inherent benefit is that affiliate programs serve as a cost-effective marketing tool for building awareness about your product or website.

Setting up an affiliate program isn't complicated, although you're responsible for keeping up with some critical functions:

✦ **Create and review affiliate guidelines.** You establish your terms and conditions as part of a legally binding affiliate agreement. You also must review affiliate sites to make sure that they comply with your guidelines for affiliates.

✦ **Track affiliate sales.** Providing working links for routing and tracking affiliate traffic is an essential part of your offering. You also need to keep up with ongoing totals of affiliate sales.

✦ **Report affiliate income.** In addition to providing regular earnings reports to your affiliates, you have to report their income for tax purposes. That process requires sending 1099 forms to affiliates each tax year and reporting their income to the IRS.

✦ **Offer marketing materials.** An affiliate program is more effective when you provide your resellers with enthusiastic support, including everything from banner ads to electronic newsletters advertising special promotions.

✦ **Keep in touch.** Affiliates are like any other type of customer: If you want them to keep doing business with you, you have to service them. Your job is to communicate with your affiliates to keep them interested in, and (you hope) successful in, your particular program.

Setting up and maintaining any one of the preceding items for your affiliates can appear daunting at first. Dozens of legitimate companies are available, however, to manage affiliate programs for you. These pay-for-performance marketing firms not only run your program but also actively solicit and qualify new affiliates on your behalf. Of course, they also take a cut of your sales in exchange for this service.

If you prefer to manage an affiliate program in-house, plenty of software programs can make your job quite easy. The affiliate-management software available from AffiliateWiz at `www.affiliatewiz.com` has lots of features, and installation support is included when you purchase the software license. Its software starts at $699.

If $699 is a little steep for you, consider an alternative, such as iDevAffiliate, available from `www.iDevDirect.com`. This company offers its basic affiliate-tracking software starting at $149 with no monthly fees or setup charges. You can also get a hosted plan (run on their servers) for $30 a month.

You can set up an affiliate program for any type of product or service your website offers. As long as you can afford to offer a percentage of sales anytime a "buying" visitor is referred to your site, affiliate programs can be effective.

Putting It All Together: Multiple Revenue Streams

Online ad revenues have continued to soar over the past few years, reaching a record-breaking $42.8 billion in 2013, according to a report from the Internet Advertising Bureau (IAB). This steady growth, up 12 percent over 2012 revenues, helps to prove that online advertising is an exciting business model for your site. Who says that you have to choose only *one* source for earning the big bucks, though? Merging different online business models is smart business. The catch is deciding when and how to add different revenue streams to the mix. In our experience, you start by striking the right balance between your core customer base and your primary earnings strategy. At the same time, remember not to bite off more than you can chew. Also focus on the sales strategies that you can handle comfortably so that you don't become overwhelmed.

Begin by identifying your *earnings anchor*. This primary moneymaker provides you with a steady source of income and is the type of business most closely linked to the identity of your site — and your target audience.

After you establish an anchor, you can look for *complementary* products or services. These items extend the value of your site and increase your earnings potential.

When you're determining what revenue streams to add to a site, and when, we recommend these two philosophies:

✦ **Any added sources of income should complement, rather than take away from, your core business model.** Always remember your target audience, and make sure that you're appealing to their preferences or needs.

✦ **Although a single earnings source might be necessary initially, it pays to diversify.** For example, try not to depend on one revenue stream (or product or service) for more than 60 percent of your total sales. If one of your sources suddenly takes a nosedive in its earnings potential, the rest of your revenue mix can compensate — at least temporarily.

Chapter 2: Making Money with Affiliate Programs

In This Chapter

✔ Setting up affiliate programs that match your site's objectives

✔ Recognizing and avoiding rogue revenue streams

Affiliate programs, or revenue-sharing plans, have been around for quite some time, both online and off. Online versions became more than a passing fad when companies such as Walmart, Target, and Best Buy started offering them. A big-box retailer doesn't set up this type of program unless it has something to gain — usually, money. As online ads and paid searches became more competitive, the door for affiliate programs was opened even further. Affiliate programs, in a nutshell, pay you to send them customers. If a purchase is made by one of your referrals, you receive a small percentage of the profit.

Brand-name retailers aside, some affiliate programs are good, some are (admittedly) a little cheesy, and others are an outright bust. In this chapter, we help you sort out the winners from the losers so that you can earn affiliate income from your own website.

Looking at How Affiliate Programs Work

Revenue-sharing programs are simple to set up and easy to run as a sideline to your existing website. No kidding: Earning money through an affiliate program boils down to five steps:

1. Find a program that offers a product or service you like.

2. Sign up online by completing the affiliate agreement.

3. Place links to the program on your existing website.

4. Actively promote the affiliate program through banners, newsletters, and other suggested online marketing tactics.

5. Collect revenue.

On the surface, these steps are exactly what's required of you. Revving up the revenue stream takes a little more of your time and energy, of course. The amount of effort is minimal, though, compared to other online money-making strategies you might try.

Affiliate marketing can also be more than an add-on revenue stream for an existing site. As with any type of website, your success as an affiliate marketer depends on your ability to drive traffic to your site. A serious affiliate marketer may build and maintain multiple sites. These sites are often product review sites with lots of product comparisons and reviews and affiliate ads or links to the products or product trials. Serious affiliate marketers also spend thousands of dollars on pay-per-click advertising (such as Google AdWords), but the return on the investment can be well worth it. As the popularity of the concept has grown, it's become a competitive (but still extremely profitable) industry.

Whether you want to be an aggressive affiliate marketer or just use affiliate marketing for a secondary revenue stream for an existing website, here are the secrets to building a lucrative affiliate-marketing program:

✦ **Find a good match.** Think about your site's audience and the type of information they're looking for. Finding affiliate programs that offer products and services that appeal to your built-in customer base gives you a head start toward success. Similarly, if you plan to create a website around affiliate programs, match your marketing efforts to that prospective customer. If your site is marketed to business owners, an affiliate program for a toy store doesn't go over well with your customers. However, a site created to appeal to the demands of working mothers or home-based working moms is a much better fit with a toy store. Matching the products and services to your site is especially important because the type of content on your website is a tool for driving traffic. The people searching for your content should be the same target customer for the affiliate products and services you choose to add to your site.

✦ **Drive traffic.** One reason why the affiliate program creator offers the opportunity is to increase the number of potential customers who see its offering. How? By driving website traffic from one site (your site) to another (its site). For you, making money as an affiliate marketer depends on your ability to create large continual streams of qualified visitors to the affiliate link by using a variety of marketing activities.

Notice that we didn't mention one word about finding a *quality* product or service. Sadly, that's because a lot of people have made good money with lowbrow programs. We're not saying that the programs were illegal or even deceptive. Rather, a few e-books weren't well written or were filled with old, outdated information. For a few software products, you could have found shareware equivalents and downloaded them for free. Still, all these items appeared to sell like hot cakes.

For whatever reason, quality isn't always a critical factor in the world of affiliate marketing. Or at least it's something that can be overlooked. For the record, we believe that finding an affiliate program with a product or service that you would personally buy is important. Selling something that you believe in is so much easier than selling something you don't like.

Understanding some affiliate terms

When you're shopping for affiliate programs, you run into words or phrases associated with the affiliate process. Some you may recognize, and others are probably new to you. Become familiar with these concepts so that you can understand what's involved in participating in a successful affiliate program:

✦ **Advertiser:** A company or site that wants other sites (affiliates) to sell its merchandise

✦ **Affiliate:** An individual, a company, or a site that's paid money to promote another company's products or services

✦ **Affiliate network:** A single company that oversees affiliate programs for multiple vendors and then recruits and approves affiliates on behalf of the companies they represent

✦ **AutoRenew:** A feature that automatically renews an affiliate's account upon expiration of the original term or length of time

✦ **Cookies:** Technology used in coordination with web browsers to store information about a specific user

✦ **Cost per click (CPC):** An amount of money an advertiser pays a site each time a visitor responds to an ad (specifically, by clicking a link or an ad)

✦ **Creatives:** Advertising material (usually such items as banner ads, links, e-mail content, and pop-up ads) that you, the affiliate, use to promote items to visitors

✦ **Merchant:** Another term for advertiser

✦ **Pay-for-performance:** The process of rewarding a company or website (usually with money) for driving traffic to another site

✦ **Publisher:** The company or site that wants to be an affiliate

✦ **Qualifying link:** An approved link given to an affiliate to place on a website to earn commissions

✦ **Required URL:** The specific website address where affiliate links must point to earn commissions for referred traffic, or visitors

✦ **Subaffiliate:** Another site that's managed under a single affiliate account; anything other than your primary website that's added to your account

✦ **Tracking tag (or tag):** A device, usually a link, given to an affiliate to keep up with the success of a campaign; allows visits to be tracked

✦ **Unique visitors:** A specific number of individuals who visit a site within a certain period, usually counted in a daily or monthly timeframe

Types of affiliate payments

Not all affiliate income is equal. You can add different types of links or offers to your website, and each translates into a different level of payment. In other words, some actions are worth more money to advertisers. Here is a breakdown of the common affiliate payment types:

✦ **CPA (cost per action):** Just like it sounds, CPAs are determined by some sort of predetermined action that a visitor takes in relation to the affiliate promotions you offer on your website.

✦ **CPC (cost per click):** This payment is based on the amount of traffic you send to the advertiser's or merchant's website after the visitors clicked a link on your site.

✦ **CPL (cost per lead):** Often associated with product trials, you are paid when someone completes a form and becomes a lead for the merchant. Leads are particularly important for B2B (business-to-business) companies and, depending on the type of offer, CPLs can have a high payout.

✦ **CPS (cost per sale):** You are paid when someone purchases a product or service after clicking a link or an ad from your website. CPS payments are also usually higher because they result in a sale.

Finding an affiliate program

Affiliate-marketing programs are broken into three common sources, or places where they originate:

✦ **Retail sites:** Plenty of traditional retailers offer bona fide affiliate programs. Among some of the bigger names are Target, The Container Store, Nordstrom's, and Lands' End. Of course, each one is using an affiliate program to drive sales of its *online* business, not its bricks-and-mortar version. One way to locate stores with affiliate programs is simply to make a list of your favorites and do the research. The process takes time, but it's worth it. Alternatively, you can search for your favorite retailers in an affiliate network (which manages affiliate programs for many different businesses). Most major retailers use an affiliate network to manage their program.

A store with an affiliate program may identify the opportunity on its website. Look for the Affiliates tab on a site's home page, or sometimes on the About Us page. (Figure 2-1 shows the Nordstrom affiliate program.) However, some large retailers may not publicly promote their affiliate program. For those, you'll have to depend on finding them listed in an affiliate network site — keep reading to learn more about these.

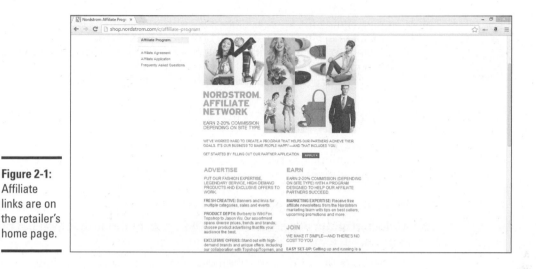

Figure 2-1:
Affiliate
links are on
the retailer's
home page.

✦ **Established online vendors:** Many branded names that are best known for delivering products through their Internet presence cater to affiliates. Topping the list are e-commerce giants Apple iTunes and Dell (computers).

✦ **Pay-for-performance networks:** In addition to searching independent sites, all-in-one sites can save you time. Pay-for-performance networks have assembled hundreds or thousands of affiliate-marketing programs under one roof.

An advantage of using a network is that you can apply for multiple programs at one time, and you can manage an unlimited number of your affiliate accounts in one place. Because major retailers often use networks to handle their affiliate programs, you're privy to exclusive promotions reserved only for the networks' affiliates. Networks are also a good way to locate category-specific programs, such as security software or gardening supplies, or to find lesser known products and services, such as e-books targeted to small businesses or coupon offers for pregnant women.

The networks on this list offer affiliate programs for just about everything under the sun:

- *Clickbank:* www.clickbank.com
- *CJ Affiliate by Conversant:* www.cj.com
- *ebay enterprise:* www.ebayenterprise.com/marketing_solutions/ affiliate_network
- *Amazon Associates:* http://affiliate-program.amazon.com
- *Rakuten LinkShare:* www.linkshare.com

**Book IV
Chapter 2**

**Making Money with
Affiliate Programs**

When you're signing up as an affiliate, visit any community message boards set up for affiliates. Find out what tools other affiliates found successful. If you're assigned to an affiliate-marketing manager, don't hesitate to drop an e-mail and ask for suggestions based on your site's core audience.

Signing Up for an Affiliate Network

After you locate a specific program or an affiliate network that appeals to you, you can sign up. The process typically takes fewer than ten minutes. For example, follow these steps to sign up for the LinkShare program:

1. **Go to the site's home page at** `www.linkshare.com`.

2. **At the top of the page, click the Affiliate tab. In the drop-down list that appears, click the Publisher Solutions link.**

You see a page that describes how to monetize your website traffic.

3. **Click the Publishers Join Now button at the bottom of the page.**

Joining is free. A new page opens, as shown in Figure 2-2, with a form for you to fill in basic information.

Figure 2-2:
Sign up
to earn
money as an
affiliate.

4. **Fill in your company and account information, and click the Go to Step 2 button.**

   The form contains standard questions, such as company name, address, and employer identification number (EIN) or Social Security number. You're also asked to read the affiliate agreement, ensure that you agree with the terms, and provide an electronic signature.

5. **Enter the information about your website and click Continue.**

6. **Watch for an e-mail message from the company and follow its instructions.**

   The e-mail also contains information about your new affiliate account.

Your approval for participating in an affiliate program may not come quickly because every legitimate program has criteria for eligibility, although some are more lenient than others. For example, many affiliate programs don't process your application unless you have an active, or live, site. Others, such as AffiliateFuel, also require a minimum number of unique visitors.

Some affiliates review your site in detail and may take several days before approving your application. Other programs provide immediate electronic approval as long as you meet basic requirements, such as

✦ An active website

✦ A valid Social Security number or employer identification number

✦ Verification that your site doesn't violate any of the network's terms and conditions

After your approval with an affiliate network is confirmed, it's easy to apply for as many individual programs as you like. At LinkShare, for example, the merchants are separated by categories. After you select the boxes of the programs that interest you, your application is submitted automatically. You then receive notification of acceptance (or not) in your e-mail.

You can join multiple affiliate programs as well as programs run by different affiliate networks.

Book IV Chapter 2

Making Money with Affiliate Programs

Scouring for details

When you're perusing an affiliate-marketing program that interests you, note the following before signing up to participate.

- **Commission structure:** Review the payout system for the program. Commission is usually calculated as a percentage of sales or as a flat dollar rate. However, the amounts may be based on minimum sales levels, which isn't a best-case scenario. Alternatively, programs that reward you with larger commissions as your volume increases are beneficial. Or if a product requires a recurring fee (such as a monthly subscription), you may receive a one-time payment rather than residuals. Knowing the payout rates comes in handy for comparing programs.

- **Method for payment:** You may get to choose how and when to receive payment. Look for details, including the currency used for payment; a set dollar amount accumulated before being paid (often, a $25 minimum); monthly or quarterly distributions; and the option for direct deposit into your account.

- **Refunds:** Find the program's policy for handling customer returns or refunds. Understand how and when that money is taken out of your account.

- **Recordkeeping:** Established affiliate programs typically offer a simple but sophisticated accounting system. You can view your complete commission history in addition to what's in your account. Always confirm that the program provides this type of account review, and find out how frequently it's updated (in real time, daily, or only at month's end).

- **Tracking:** One frustration occurs when an affiliate program doesn't provide an effective way to track statistics for your affiliate link. The best programs make it easy to understand how many click-throughs you get in addition to final purchases.

- **Cookies:** For well-known sites that receive plenty of traffic on their own, having a cookie tracker in place for affiliates is important. You know that someone will inevitably go to a site after clicking your affiliate link and then leave without buying anything. The following week, that person might be ready to go back and make a purchase. With affiliate link cookies in place, the site can monitor the visits and offer credit for your original referral. Most cookies are good for 10 to 14 days.

- **Limits or exclusions:** Larger programs may have restrictions on what products or services are included in an affiliate program. Or you may have to follow strict guidelines for promoting certain products or using product images. Always read the fine print so that you're not caught off guard.

- **Penalties:** Even an unintentional violation can lead to a slap on the wrist (such as a small monetary fine or a scathing letter) or to having your account turned off. Read the terms and conditions document carefully to understand how and when you may be penalized.

- **Restrictive marketing strategies:** Affiliate marketers commonly specify how affiliates can and cannot market their programs. Most restrictions refer to e-mailing strategies that can lead to trouble for the affiliates as violations of antispam laws. Companies are cracking down on this issue because they're the ones being held responsible (legally) for your (the affiliate's) actions. To avoid having your account closed over a simple mistake, look closely at which marketing strategies are prohibited or considered offensive.

(continued)

(continued)

✔ **Logos, banners, and content:** Affiliate programs want you to do well, so they typically provide you with marketing tools. Before signing up for a program, peruse the marketing collateral that's at your disposal. Is it enough? Is there a variety? Are they quality pieces? Would you, or could you, really use them? This issue is important because you may be restricted from creating your own marketing materials and have to use theirs.

Avoiding Scams and Questionable Content

As you now know, even something as popular as online poker can come with serious legal strings attached. After you join an affiliate program for something like that, you're at risk of paying the price if things aren't on the up-and-up. Last time we checked, claiming ignorance doesn't get you a Get Out of Jail Free card.

Illegal affiliations

Participation in any illegal affiliate programs is limited by the governing laws of your home state or country. You must know the law and then abide by it. To avoid becoming an outlaw, follow these safety tips:

✦ **Always read the terms and conditions of the affiliate agreement.** Affiliate programs might disclose legal caveats to you in easy-to-find warnings on their sites, but more than likely you find them in the fine print. Read agreements carefully to determine your potential liabilities for participating.

✦ **Look for clues to the country of origin.** Affiliate programs run from foreign countries, or without a U.S. base of operations, may be a sign that the activity isn't permitted stateside. Or when you sign up for an affiliate program, you may be asked to enter your country of origin. After doing so, watch for a message or special instruction that serves as a disclaimer about doing business in particular countries.

✦ **Conduct a search.** Although this tip isn't foolproof, you can start verifying the legitimacy of a program by doing a simple search. Enter in a search engine the name of the company you want to do business with or the type of program (online games, for example). Especially if it's a hot topic, you quickly find any red flags.

✦ **Investigate the company.** Although some specific products or subjects may be off-limits, sometimes you run into blacklisted companies. Participating in an affiliate program with one of these companies can label you as "aiding and abetting." If something seems questionable, don't hesitate to check out the company further. Start with the Better Business Bureau Online at www.bbbonline.org.

✦ **Check with authorities.** The U.S. Department of Justice has information on a handful of questionable Internet activities, including online gambling and selling prescription medication online. Visit the site at `www.usdoj.gov`. The Federal Trade Commission is another source for validating illegal affiliate operations. You can access it at `http://www.ftc.gov`.

Questionable affiliations

Affiliate programs that are technically legal but considered somewhat shady or distasteful are a sore spot. The "shady or distasteful" part of that description may sound like a line from the *Leave It to Beaver* generation, but it holds true.

These affiliate-marketing programs aren't completely on the up-and-up because of the validity of their offerings or their operational practices. For example, if a program has a long list of complaints registered by unhappy customers and affiliates, this company is skirting disaster. Or maybe the program is connected to obscene or pornographic products and there's a question about how the material is being distributed.

For lots of reasons, think twice before affiliating with these types of organizations. Be aware that your site's name and reputation become linked with any program you promote. With that advice in mind, here's a list of red flags to watch for when you review affiliate programs:

✦ **No money-back guarantee is offered.** Be wary of programs that don't provide product guarantees or some form of money-back guarantee to customers. As a prospective affiliate, this one definitely presents a red flag. You can get stuck holding the bag and taking the blame when your referred customers get burned.

✦ **Returning a product is especially complicated.** Nobody likes to deal with returns, but reputable companies offer return policies. Usually, you don't need an act of Congress to make the exchange!

✦ **Corporate information isn't readily available or verifiable.** Legitimate companies place contact information prominently on their websites. You can also cross-reference and verify company information by using domain-registration services and other affiliations.

✦ **Affiliates or customers are unhappy.** Monitor the parent site's message boards, or other community message boards, for tales of broken promises and disastrous customer service.

✦ **No support is offered.** The purpose of an affiliate program is to use other sites to drive more traffic and customers to your product. A company with that goal in mind provides resources and support to help affiliates be successful. Newsletters, contact information for technical support, links, banner ads, and other marketing materials are the norm in legitimate affiliate programs. If these items aren't mentioned, trouble might lie ahead.

✦ **A sign-up fee is required.** Signing up for most affiliate programs is free. If you have to pay to join or have your application "screened," run!

✦ **Scam associations are obvious.** You may find a company with no complaints that promotes the type of material that is often labeled as a scam or shows up on consumer watchdog lists. Work-at-home programs and business opportunities are often among the list of top offenders (although plenty of legitimate ones exist, too).

✦ **Legal proceedings have been initiated.** Although you might not have any concrete information, check for lawsuits that have been filed against a company or any pending legal proceedings that might point to fraud in the making. You can check with the Better Business Bureau online or call your state's attorney general's office. This information might also show up in an Internet search.

Another source of telling information is a company's affiliate agreement, along with its policy for accepting affiliate marketers.

Look for affiliate programs that adhere to strict guidelines. A legitimate program typically turns down approval of a site or cancels an affiliate agreement that has any of these characteristics:

✦ **Inactive URL:** Because your site cannot be verified, the domain may not match what you entered or your site may be under construction.

✦ **Trademark infringement:** You have references to registered names or logos on your site.

✦ **Mismatched information:** The information you provide doesn't match your tax information, business license registration, or domain registration from other, legitimate resources.

✦ **Questionable content:** Your site contains pornography or obscene information; contains hate-oriented information; distributes or links to illegal substances; promotes gambling activities; or is otherwise deemed questionable.

✦ **Questionable recruiting:** Affiliates who plan to market a program by using aggressive e-mail campaigns can violate anti-spamming laws.

Based on your state of residence, you may not be eligible to participate in an affiliate program. California passed a law requiring the collection of taxes on all online sales, regardless of whether you have a physical location in the state — and they extended this law to cover affiliates. For that reason, major online retailers (such as Amazon) have pulled eligibility of affiliate participation to businesses and individuals residing in California. Doing this helps Amazon avoid penalties for tax collection oversights and the creation of complicated tax collection procedures to cover all their affiliates.

Book IV
Chapter 2

Making Money with
Affiliate Programs

Chapter 3: Turning Information into Profit, from E-Books to Webinars

___

In This Chapter

✔ **Creating an information product**

✔ **Finding hot topics to write about**

✔ **Writing, formatting, and distributing an e-book**

✔ **Earning revenue from informational videos on YouTube**

✔ **Developing and promoting a webinar**

___

Many people think that online sales involve physical products, where you put something in a box and ship it off to Jane Smith in Iowa, who ordered your product online. These eager sellers sometimes overlook the most valuable "product" they can offer the buying community: their knowledge. The adage goes "Knowledge is power." Well, if power leads to wealth, knowledge also leads to wealth. Thanks to many of the technological advances of computers and the Internet, it's now much easier to build a system and earn money by sharing your information, knowledge, and techniques with people who desperately want to learn.

Information products are becoming one of the hottest categories of products you can find on the Internet. Unlike a physical product that has material costs (such as the cost of the paper for a book or the cost of microchips and a metal case for a computer), an information product can have zero physical costs. Unlike a television or car that has to roll off an assembly line and requires a certain amount of labor to produce one unit, you can make infinite copies of an information product — instantaneously — and meet whatever demand you have for your product. In the past, information products required printing, postage, transportation, and other fees to distribute information. Now you can send an electronic version of your information product anywhere in the world through an e-mail message.

In this chapter, we talk about the world of information products and how you can create, benefit, and profit from them. We show you how to create your information product, research and refine your topic, and lay out the information in a clear and concise format. Then we show you how to make your information available to customers by putting it into an *electronic book* (or *e-book*), an online video for websites such as YouTube, or a web seminar (*webinar*).

Creating Your Own Information Product

The best example of an information product is something you probably have in your car: a map. A map is simply a physical representation of highways, streets, intersections, and landmarks that tells you about a detailed but specific topic: how the roads in a certain area are laid out and intersect with each other. You then read and interpret the map to solve a specific problem — namely, how to move from point A to point B. Your information products should work in a similar manner. You simply organize a specific, complete set of information about a given topic, present it in a clear fashion, and collect money for distributing the information.

Finding hot topics

Which information should you sell? The answer varies, depending on your knowledge, experience, and goals. The topic of your information product is essential, so ask yourself a few questions to get started:

✦ **What am I good at?** Suppose that you're at a party or get-together and a friend or an acquaintance hears about your job and life story and asks, "Hey, how did you do such-and-such?" or "What did you need to know to get that opportunity?" That's a source for your information product.

If your life experience has trained you to excel at a difficult topic, such as assembling a complicated piece of equipment or laying out an interior design for a new home, you can capture and record that experience to help others and profit from the experience. People pay for experience all the time — if they didn't, every consultant in the world would be out of a job!

✦ **What are people having problems with?** If you notice that a number of people are having the same problem in one area, an information product to help solve that problem can be quite profitable.

Sometimes, the information is out there but it's hard to find, it's packaged poorly, or it isn't explained well. For example, someone who had attended driving school for a traffic violation found out how to legally challenge traffic tickets in court, exploit the most common loopholes that cause tickets to be dismissed, and inform drivers of all their legal rights when investigating and disputing traffic tickets. He wasn't a born expert, but he learned what he needed to know and made money by presenting that information in an organized and clear fashion.

✦ **What areas of service does my business provide?** Sometimes, the best way to explain what your business does is to transfer some key functions or knowledge areas of your business into an information product, and use it to introduce clients to your business or get noticed in your community.

Real estate agents commonly package small information packets describing the top ten things that new homeowners should look for in new homes. By distributing this packet, an agent can provide instant value to a potential client, show experience in an area, and, hopefully, gain some business beyond what the packet explains.

Put together a focus group consisting of your family members and friends. Ask them which books they bought recently, which magazines they subscribe to, and which television programs they watch. It doesn't hurt to expand your reach by talking to your customers or people in your field and asking them similar questions. Understanding your market is critical for any product, including information products.

Researching the information

After you know what area you want your information product to focus on, you have to research the information. In some cases, even though you may know everything you want to say, that doesn't mean you're done with this step. You should always start by making a list of everything you need to complete this product, even if the only thing you need is your experience.

As you prepare your list, you may want to start by creating the outline of your information product and matching up your research with sections of the product. For example, if you know that part of your product will include a contact list of professionals, one research item should be "Compile list of professionals." Every section of your product should have at least one research task, even if that task is "Think about it and write it down."

Before you finish your list, make sure that you cover the three Cs:

✦ **Current:** Make sure that your information is current. Even if you're an expert in a certain area, the rules may have changed since you last looked into it. If you're writing a guide for self-employed people doing their own taxes, for example, brush up on the new tax laws. If you're writing a guide to hot travel sites, revisit those sites and make some phone calls to make sure that everything is still open and accessible. Add a task to your research list to do follow-up, or *fact checking*, as they call it in the media.

✦ **Competition:** See what else is out there, and read up on other information products in your area. Find out what areas are covered, the length of the product (in pages), how much is being charged, and the means of distribution to sell it.

Don't copy other people's paragraphs word for word. Just get an idea of the scope that they cover, and make sure that your product is competitive with (and, you hope, better than) those other products.

✦ **Content:** What's the meat of your information product? What's the substance of the information you will charge for? Sure, you might copy some background information, some examples, and some information from a third-party source (such as the address, phone number, and mission statement of a business that someone needs to call as part of your product), but the specialized information you're adding is the reason that people are buying your product. Sometimes, the value of a product consists of the random pieces of information gathered into one document; at other times, the value lies in a streamlined set of instructions that nobody else has provided.

Organizing your thoughts

Even if you know your topic backward and forward, can you convey this information so that anyone can understand it? Some of the most brilliant people in the world may specialize in their areas but cannot commit that information to words and pictures to explain it to others. Explain the process or product in a clear and straightforward manner.

The best way to organize all your information into a product is to imagine that you're the customer for this item. Determine which information you would need to see first. Think about what state your customers are in when they start reading your product. If you have any assumptions about what your customers have done before they start reading, make those assumptions clear from the beginning. For example, if your information product is only for people who have already signed up with a particular web host, make sure that you state up front: "Do not read any further until you select your web host and sign up for an account."

Many people organize their information by using this structure:

1. **Explain the problem.**

   Summarize why someone bought this product, the situation they're in, and what this product provides. "Still on the lookout for a great apartment near your work? If you're ready to find that perfect apartment, this 10-page guide walks you through all the steps and puts you on the right track."

2. **Lay out the solution.**

   Start to give the "meat" of the product as you lay out the core of your information.

3. **Give examples.**

   As you're explaining the situation, be sure to give lots of examples and hypothetical situations of how your information is used in practice.

4. **Summarize with a conclusion.**

   Give a concise overview of what you just presented, remind readers of the most important points you brought up, and give them an action item showing what they can do after they read your product.

Use figures and illustrations to make your point. People respond to visual cues better than they do to words, so be sure to include illustrations in your information product to drive home your point. You can use computer screen shots, drawings or blueprints, or photos relating to your topic. Take a look at one artist's use of images to explain his point in Figure 3-1.

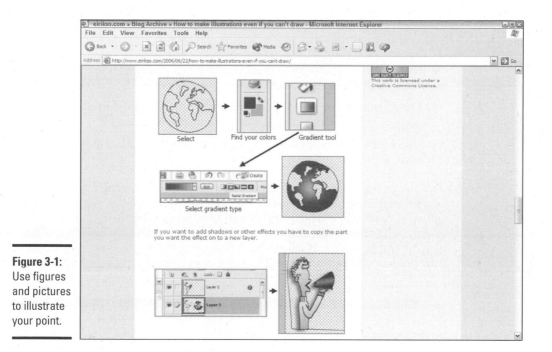

Figure 3-1:
Use figures
and pictures
to illustrate
your point.

As you lay out your document, make sure that the sections make sense in the order you present them so that readers can logically understand the points being made. Research has shown that people respond well to a story format, with these three parts:

+ **Beginning:** Explain the problem.
+ **Middle:** Describe your solution.
+ **End:** Give examples of using your information.

Use appendices, glossaries, and indexes to help people find specific facts quickly. This way, people can use your product as a reference guide after they initially read it.

Providing E-Books

One common way to capture and present an information product is in an electronic book, or e-book. Unlike a physical book you hold in your hands, an *e-book* is simply an electronic version of a book that you read on a computer screen, a specialized reader device (Amazon Kindle, Barnes & Noble Nook, Sony Reader), or your favorite mobile device (iPad, tablet computer, smartphone, iPod touch). Because the content of an e-book is stored in an electronic file, you have several options for storing it.

The great thing about an e-book is that you, as the creator, can choose a style for setting it up:

✦ Use chapters such as the ones you find in a physical book, with a beginning, a middle, and an end.

✦ Style your e-book as an academic term paper composed of page after page of prose, with examples, figures, and appendices.

✦ Use a long table with rows and columns of information in a directory-style format.

As you put together an e-book, its structure depends on the information you're presenting. Some e-books read like miniature books, with their own tables of contents, indexes, and chapter headings, like the e-book shown in Figure 3-2. If your e-book is long, consider breaking the content into clear, easy to-find headings. If your e-book is shorter than a typical chapter, an introductory paragraph is usually sufficient to explain its flow and structure.

Figure 3-2:
This e-book is set up like a printed book.

Creating the document

Because most people use computer programs such as Microsoft Word to write their documents, creating an e-book is easy. You can simply convert your document file into an e-book in a few steps. Then again, if you write everything using pen and paper, the first thing you'll need to do is enter all that information into a word processor, such as Microsoft Word.

One format for an e-book is Portable Document Format, or PDF. This technology was developed by Adobe so that people could exchange documents without losing their style and formatting. Adobe has provided free software, the Adobe Reader, which allows anyone to read a document by using the PDF standard. Businesses around the world have adopted PDF as their standard for reading and exchanging documents. One great thing about PDF is that you can lock your PDF file so your customers can't change or edit the document. After the text is created, it's locked into place and your formatting decisions don't get lost or changed. Every customer sees the same page layout.

PDF refers to a specific kind of computer file that stores formatting information along with text and graphics. When you send the file to other people, it appears the same way to them when they view or print the file.

You have different ways to create a PDF file. Microsoft Word has a built-in feature that will convert your document to PDF. You can also find software on the Internet whose only function is to convert different kinds of documents into PDF files or to print your files as PDF output instead of sending the files to the printer.

If you plan on creating a steady stream of PDF files, check out Adobe PDF Pack, an Internet-based utility at `www.acrobat.com/createpdf`. You can pay for a monthly or yearly subscription that allows you to create unlimited PDF conversions.

You can store your e-book in formats other than PDF. As of this writing, the Amazon Kindle is the number-one handheld book reader, so many e-book authors are converting their e-books to the Kindle format to be sold in the Amazon Kindle store. The Barnes & Noble Nook e-book reader supports the ePub format, which allows authors to protect their digital rights. Some people use scanners to take pictures of the pages in their e-books and save each page as its own image file. The most common picture formats are JPG, GIF, and BMP. By using image files, you (the creator) can lock in the text and formatting, just like in a PDF file.

Distributing your e-book on e-shelves

You created your e-book; now you might wonder how to hand it to your customers. In most cases, you also want to collect payment before you send the e-book to them. You can use one of these methods to distribute your e-book:

✦ Sell it directly on your website.

✦ Auction physical (printed) copies or digital copies saved on a CD-ROM on eBay.

✦ List it on Amazon.com, BarnesandNoble.com, or Apple's iTunes store as a product.

✦ Sell it on an information distribution website such as Lulu.com or ClickBank.com.

✦ Find a partner business that reaches the same customers as your target audience.

After the payment is collected, you can offer your customers several options for delivering the e-book to them:

✦ **Download:** Store your e-book on an Internet web server and tie it into a web page on your server or a third-party server (see Figure 3-3). When people use a web browser to go to the web page and click a special link, the browser asks whether they want to open the file or save it to their computers. The main copy of the e-book always remains on the server; each time a customer clicks the link, however, a new copy is created and sent from your web server to your customer's computer.

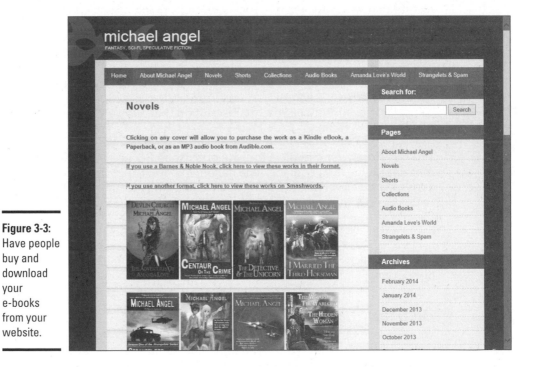

Figure 3-3: Have people buy and download your e-books from your website.

✦ **E-mail:** Most e-mail programs allow you to attach an e-book file to an e-mail message. After you collect payment, you create a message to send to your customer, attach a copy of your e-book, and send off the message. Just like in the download method, your original, or *master*, copy of the e-book never leaves you. Instead, a new copy is made and attached to the e-mail sent to your customer.

✦ **Flash/USB drive or CD/DVD disc:** Even though you're dealing with an electronic product that requires no physical media, you'll find that certain customers still want to buy something they can hold in their hands. Many e-book creators burn their e-books to Flash/USB drives or CD/DVD discs and then sell those physical objects with the e-books on them. Some sites, such as eBay, require you to have a physical item to sell or auction, so you have to create a drive or disc if you want to sell your e-book on those sites. This method can be especially effective if you're selling a large e-book that requires a long download time over the Internet. You can package your e-book with other documents or holders, to add some weight to your product.

Burning refers to the process your computer uses to store on disc the information that makes up a file. A special type of drive receives an electronic file from your computer and starts engraving, or burning, the information on the disc so that information can be read later by another computer.

Creating Informational Videos for Profit

Nowadays, when people want to learn more about a topic, they might type their question in a search engine such as Google and read up on the topic. Others learn better by having someone explain that topic in a lecture or demonstration format, such as a live tutorial or a PowerPoint slide presentation. With the explosion in popularity for video web sites such as YouTube, many people who want to see someone explain a topic look for short informational videos on these sites.

Many entrepreneurs are taking advantage of this medium and creating special content for sites such as YouTube and profiting in several ways:

✦ **Embedded advertising:** YouTube has a program in which they will insert an advertisement that viewers have to watch to see the video. YouTube shares the revenue from this ad with the creator of the video in a 70/30 split (70 percent for the creator, 30 percent for YouTube). A lot of money can be made here. For more information, check out YouTube's Partner Program website at www.youtube.com/account_monetization.

✦ **Website referral:** Many online videos have an embedded URL that points viewers to the speaker's website. Sometimes, the video is a simple commercial or preview for a more expensive information product on the person's website; other times the video is meant to explain the usage of a product for sale on someone's website.

✦ **Affiliate and Google ads:** You can use videos to promote affiliate products and make money when someone clicks your video to go directly to that affiliate to buy that product. Also, you can incorporate Google advertising inside or beside your video when it plays.

✦ **Educational revenue:** People who like to learn by watching longer web videos can subscribe to sites such as Lynda.com and pay one monthly fee to watch any video from their catalog. Teachers who are chosen to create classes for sites such as Lynda.com earn a percentage of the revenue collected each month, depending on the number of views of their class compared to the total monthly viewership of that site's customer base.

Putting Together a Webinar

Although e-books and short videos can be effective in teaching people valuable information, sometimes customers require a detailed explanation of a more complex topic, with live voices or slides or drawings to complement the information. Thus, the multibillion-dollar seminar business was formed. With technology now making it easier to transmit audio, video, and text all at once, education and technology have melded into the *webinar,* or web seminar.

Think of a webinar as watching a seminar on your computer or other Internet-connected device. During the seminar, you might

✦ Watch an audio feed of the instructor talking.

✦ View Microsoft PowerPoint slides on your screen.

✦ Read an outline of the presentation.

✦ Write some text notes.

✦ Use a chat window to ask the instructor some questions (or talk to your fellow seminar attendees) at the end of the presentation.

This technology is possible on a large scale because of the number of people who have broadband connections to the Internet using cable modems from their cable TV companies, DSL connections from their phone companies, or high-speed data connections through their smartphone's data provider. These connections allow that information — the audio, video, and text — to be carried to someone's computer or other Internet-connected device live, in real time as the presenter is giving the seminar. After the presenter has recorded the information, the webinar can be viewed any time, instead of requiring a live real-time connection, so the same seminar can be sold and viewed by an unlimited amount of customers.

The easiest way to decide whether to create a webinar is to ask yourself whether the video and audio add value to the presentation and whether the entire presentation is necessary to teach the subject matter, rather than one video or a series of short videos. Does the presence of video add to the value you're giving your customer? Does your point come across better if people can see you or a live demonstration of what you're trying to do? For example, if you're selling an information product about how to assemble a motorcycle, a live video demonstration of the bike being assembled can demonstrate the process better than any book can.

In case you're not sure whether a webinar is the right choice, take a look at your competition in that area. If everyone else is presenting webinars, you need to create one to compete. Conversely, if no one is creating webinars

and no videos are readily available in that topic area, you can stand out by creating one. Whoever first invests the time and resources in this newer technology will be rewarded.

Your recording session

If you've taught a class or presented a lecture or seminar, you have the ingredients for creating your own webinar. You can simply have someone record you as you give your next seminar and then edit the video and audio to create your webinar file. If you make your own PowerPoint slides, you can simply record yourself explaining the information and then add the PowerPoint slides to the audio file to create a basic webinar. In this situation, you simply indicate when during the audio file to move ahead with a new slide.

One company that can help you develop your webinar is WebEx, which handles live meetings and webinars for a variety of people and companies. It can provide the tools and assistance to combine your video recording, audio recording, and slides to create your webinar. WebEx employees can also help you create a webinar to deliver information live from your laptop to an eager audience. Your customers then can connect to you by using WebEx and watch the proceedings from their Internet-connected device. You can find more information by going to www.webex.com/products/elearning-and-online-training.html and reviewing their Training Center features, as shown in Figure 3-4.

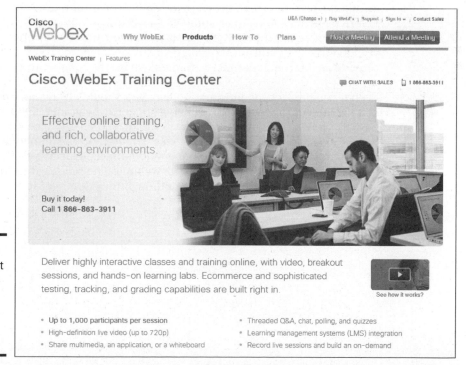

Figure 3-4: Learn about WebEx's different training center options.

Book IV
Chapter 3

Turning Information into Profit, from E-Books to Webinars

This popular trend has attracted software companies such as Adobe, which created the Adobe Connect program to help people meet virtually with integrated audio and video conferencing, an enhanced online whiteboard for collaboration, and the capability to write notes and questions back and forth, so that they can conduct meetings without face-to-face interaction. You can go to `www.adobe.com/cfusion/adobeconnect/index.cfm?event=trial` to sign up for a free trial version of Adobe Connect software.

Finding your audience

You have two main ways to reach your customers with a webinar:

✦ Customers can watch you deliver the webinar live.

✦ You can record the webinar so that customers can download it and view it later.

Based on how you present your information, you need a specific strategy for finding the right audience for your webinar.

If you're presenting a webinar live, recruiting customers is similar to finding students for a live class. Choose a date and start advertising it weeks in advance. Then plan a day and time that's conducive to the audience you're reaching. If it's a business crowd, target sometime during the week and during the workday, perhaps a lunch seminar or an afternoon meeting. If you're targeting a consumer audience, a weeknight after dinner or a weekend might be more appropriate. You charge admission to your webinar just like you do for a class, but rather than give out a conference room number, you provide an Internet link that customers can use to connect to your webinar.

Even if you present the information live, you should always record it to sell to students down the road. Selling a recorded webinar is like selling an e-book. The date of purchase isn't as critical, and all the necessary information is available at the time of purchase, so focus on the immediate sale. At the moment of payment, the buyer should receive access to the special Internet link to start downloading the webinar. The recorded webinar gives customers immediate gratification, although they don't get to ask questions while they're watching it.

Chapter 4: Paying with the Right Payment Options

In This Chapter

✔ **Taking credit cards**

✔ **Obtaining a merchant account**

✔ **Setting up your gateway and payment processor**

✔ **Understanding the cost of providing convenience**

✔ **Offering payment options beyond credit cards**

✔ **Avoiding fraudulent charges and other online credit risks**

*O*ne indisputable fact about running an online business is that you can't very well sell products over the Internet if you don't have a way to accept money from customers. You have a bevy of options, however.

One common solution is to accept credit cards, just as any bricks-and-mortar store does. With credit and debit cards most commonly used for online shopping, customers expect to be able to pay this way. Fortunately, the acceptance and growth of e-commerce have simplified the process for online merchants. In less than a week (and sometimes within 48 hours), you can be ready to accept your first online credit card order.

Then again, not all customers have credit cards ready at their fingertips. Or perhaps they don't want to use credit cards online for security reasons. As an e-commerce merchant, you should provide those customers with an alternative payment solution.

In this chapter, we tell you about all the payment options available to your online business, and we show you how to start setting them up on your site.

Accepting Credit Card Payments

Enabling a website to accept credit cards is one of the most misunderstood functions of e-commerce. A shopper understands that she has to type her credit card number into a box on her computer screen and then click the Purchase button. And she knows that, after a few seconds, she receives an approval (or not) for her purchase. Although everything that happens between these two points comes across as a mystical unknown occurrence, not a drop of magic is involved in this simple process (see Figure 4-1).

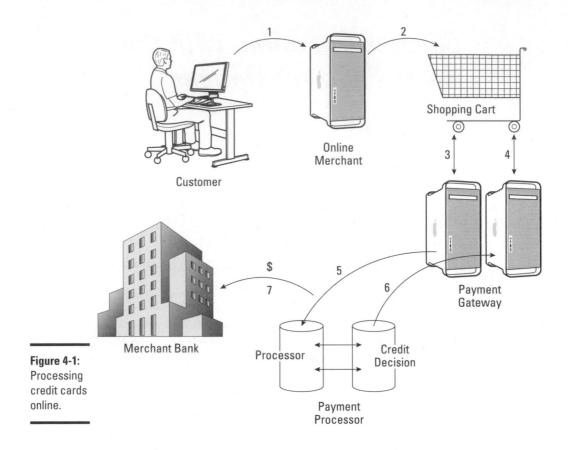

Figure 4-1:
Processing
credit cards
online.

Here's how it works:

1. **A customer goes shopping on your site and puts products into a virtual cart.**

   Shopping cart software that you add to your site allows customers to select products for purchase. When customers are ready to check out, the shopping cart starts the process of ringing up the sale.

2. **The customer pays for the product by using a credit card.**

   Your shopping cart program should provide an online form for the customer to complete, including personal information, shipping details, and a credit card number with expiration date and, possibly, a verification code from the back of the card. (An expedited checkout process may be used for returning customers.)

3. **Your site sends that credit card information to a payment gateway.**

   The *gateway* is a virtual gate through which information is transmitted, or passed between your site and a credit card processing site. The gateway, like the little box you use to swipe your card when you're shopping in a traditional store, is a tool for communicating information between the store and the credit card company.

4. **A payment processor receives and verifies your customer's information.**

   The processor's job is to talk with the company or bank that issues the credit card. The processor ensures that the card is valid and that it has enough credit to cover the purchase.

5. **The processor sends a credit decision back to the gateway.**

   The processor finds out whether your customer is approved or declined for the purchase and transmits that data right back to the payment gateway.

6. **Your gateway passes along the approval decision (approval or denial) to your shopping cart and finalizes the shopping transaction.**

   Your customer sees a final message saying that the purchase is approved (or not). From there, your shopping cart program can provide a receipt, shipping details, and an invitation to shop again.

   Steps 2–6 take only a few seconds, and then your customer's purchase is complete.

7. **While your customer is receiving an approval message, the processor is sending the money to your bank account.**

   After the credit card issuer says that credit is available, the processor makes sure that money is sent to your bank and deposited into your merchant account.

Although this process is happening within milliseconds of the approval process, you might not see the money in your account for two to three business days.

Securing a merchant account

Now that you better understand the process, you're ready to get it set up on your site. The first step is to secure a merchant account. You can choose from several resources:

✦ **Bank:** You can turn to your local bank to set up a merchant account. After all, your business checking account resides there. Most banks now offer e-commerce merchant services as part of their standard small-business service packages. However, be aware of a few issues. Banks often

   • Have a more rigid approval process for online businesses because they're still considered high-risk ventures

   • Pass your application to a third-party company for approval (as opposed to processing and managing it internally)

   • Increase your costs for a merchant account because the bank is essentially a middleman and receives a commission on the referral of your account

✦ **Direct provider:** You can access many of the same direct merchant account providers that your local bank might use. By going directly to a processor to set up a merchant account, you can cut out some of the initial costs. You can set up a merchant account with one of these processors:

- *Chase Paymentech:* www.chasepaymentech.com

- *Flagship Merchant Services:* www.cardservicesales.com

- *Merchant Warehouse:* www.merchantwarehouse.com

- *National Bankcard:* www.nationalbankcard.com

✦ **Third-party processor:** This type of company or independent agent offers the following types of merchant account services:

- *Broker:* This person is usually an independent sales rep who makes a commission from brokering or signing up new customers. A broker who represents more than one company can help you compare and find the best rates available. (Brokers are not as common as they once were, given the increased access to so many online options.)

- *Online service:* Companies that once offered a primary service, such as a shopping cart program, are now including bundled access to multiple companion services. Setting up merchant accounts is among those services. Network Solutions, originally best known as a domain registrar, is an example of an online company expanding its e-commerce service offerings to include merchant services (http:// merchantaccounts.networksolutions.com). Similarly, store-fronts or e-commerce solutions, such as Shopify (www.shopify. com), act as a third-party processor for their customers, so all your back-end operational and processing functions are tied with your online store — in one place.

- *Online specialist:* Possibly considered an online service provider, PayPal (www.paypal.com) is slightly different because the company specializes in online payments. Through its PayPal Payments Pro program, it offers e-retailers a complete solution that includes a merchant account and payment gateway for a low monthly fee, plus credit card transaction fees. Alternative or nontraditional services include Square (www.squareup.com) and Stripe (www.stripe.com). These hybrid online specialists are similar to PayPal, but the setup to start accepting credit card payments takes just minutes and does not require the setup of a separate merchant account. In the case of Square, you automatically use their gateway processing partner, Chase Paymentech (mentioned previously). Strip is unusual, in that it bypasses the payment gateway — to accept payments with Stripe, all you need is a Stripe account. These alternative online specialists also allow you to accept credit card transactions on mobile devices.

If you deal with one of the larger online services or online specialists, you can take advantage of their economies of scale and find a better deal on some items. For example, these sites may have inexpensive flat monthly service fees and no set-up fees or application fees. They also tend to have lower rates as well as higher approval and acceptance rates for online businesses because they target that customer base.

If you reside outside the United States or you expect to have a larger international customer base, make sure the merchant account can meet your needs. European countries in particular have different regulatory concerns than the U.S., and your merchant account provider should understand and meet those requirements.

Choosing a payment gateway

As soon as you receive the go-ahead to accept credit cards, your next action is typically to choose a payment gateway, unless you're using an alternative online specialist that doesn't require a gateway.

The gateway talks to the credit card companies, your banks, and your website. Needless to say, the gateway plays an important role in your e-commerce equation.

If you're receiving bundled services from one source, your merchant account provider might already have a designated gateway for you to use. That's good news because it indicates that a relationship is already established. Both ends know how to successfully come together in the middle, so to speak. Alternatively, the provider might have partnerships set up with several gateways. They simply let you select the one you want to use. Or you might be left to search for a payment gateway on your own.

You can choose from hundreds of payment gateways, and hooking up with the wrong one can bring your sales to a halt (sometimes before they get started). Don't worry, though: You should have no trouble finding the right match. Look for a payment gateway that has these characteristics:

**Book IV
Chapter 4**

✦ **Diversity:** To be effective, your gateway needs to work with all major credit cards, including MasterCard, Visa, and American Express.

✦ **Compatibility:** One of the most important requirements is that the gateway integrates with your shopping cart software. Although major gateways are already set up to talk with the majority of off-the-shelf shopping carts, it never hurts to verify that your gateway is compatible.

Paying with the Right Payment Options

If your shopping cart is custom designed or is a lesser-known software, you might have to do a little programming to make your gateway communicate with your site.

✦ **Timely payments:** Each gateway has its own rules for when and how to make payment to your bank. Choose a gateway that deposits your money within a few days at most (as opposed to once a month or so).

✦ **Support:** As with any service provider, make sure that your payment gateway has customer service support, including tech support available at any time of the day or night.

✦ **Accessibility:** You should be able to view the status of your transactions in an online report, along with other management tools.

✦ **Feature-rich:** Payment gateways have a surprising number of features you can use (or add for a fee). Allowing for recurring billing and additional payment options on your customer accounts and fraud-protection tools for you are desirable features. Even though these options might not be a big deal now, you want them available as your site grows.

With the increasing demand for mobile payments, look for payment gateways that offer secure payment processing from mobile devices.

Today, you can choose from dozens, if not hundreds, of payment gateways. When you're ready to get started, here's a list of some better-known payment gateways you can contact:

✦ **Authorize:** www.authorize.net

✦ **Cardstream:** www.cardstream.com

✦ **Chase Paymentech:** www.paymentech.com

✦ **MerchantWARE:** www.merchantwarehouse.com/merchantware

✦ **PayPal Payflow:** https://merchant.paypal.com

✦ **2Checkout:** www.2checkout.com

When you're comparing the cost of payment gateways, be sure to look at gateway resellers, too. Some offer a limited number of transactions for free when you sign up. In some cases, you don't have to pay additional fees on your first 1,000 transactions.

Reading the fine print: Fees

When you're applying to become an authorized credit card merchant, be sure to compare service providers. Although base rates might remain similar, other unexpected fees could swing the pendulum in favor of one over another. To compare apples to apples, you need to understand the different types of fees you might encounter:

✦ **Application:** Some agents charge a nominal fee for processing your application. Expect to pay at least $100.

✦ **Setup:** This fee covers the cost of establishing your merchant account and can range from $200 to $1000 or more. A typical fee is $200 or $300.

✦ **Discount rate:** Each time one of your customers makes a purchase with a credit card, your merchant account provider takes a cut of the sale. The amount varies based on the type of card that's used but is usually between 2 to 4 percent.

Your account should specify Internet, mail order, or telephone sales. Because you can't swipe an actual credit card, rates for these types of transactions are typically higher (sometimes by as much as a full point) than those for offline retailers.

✦ **Terminal cost:** When you're swiping credit cards or manually punching in account numbers, you need a small electric terminal or box. You might have to lease or purchase this equipment, which can add several hundred dollars to your annual costs. For e-commerce sales, a terminal usually isn't required. In some cases, you can use a phone app to swipe credit cards.

✦ **Statement:** This monthly fee covers the merchant account provider's cost of compiling, printing, and mailing a monthly statement of your account. The fee can be several dollars.

You might be able to eliminate this fee by choosing to access your reports online rather than on paper statements you receive by postal mail. When you ask your provider whether you have this option, also confirm how long online statements are available for viewing. (You print your own copies to serve as a permanent record, if needed.)

✦ **Transaction:** You pay a small processing fee for each credit card transaction. This nominal amount is usually less than 25 cents per transaction. And yes, it's in addition to your discount rate.

✦ **Monthly minimum:** If you expect to have a limited number of sales (maybe your business is new or you just don't expect a lot of traffic early on), your merchant account provider might establish a minimum charge level. If your sales, number of transactions, or combined discount rate and transaction fees don't exceed that minimum, the company tacks on an additional charge. In other words, the company is counting on you to process lots of orders so that it makes more money. You pay for it either way, though.

✦ **Charge back:** Whenever a customer disputes a purchase with the credit card company, the dollar amount of that purchase is taken from your bank account. Your merchant account provider might also charge you an additional fee for processing this transaction. Online orders that don't require signatures (or the physical cards to process) are especially susceptible to charge backs.

✦ **Termination:** Whether you're switching merchant providers or closing up shop, your original contract might contain a termination fee. Sometimes this fee can be as much as $1000 or more.

**Book IV
Chapter 4**

Paying with the Right Payment Options

Before signing any agreement, seek out the clause that details the steps you have to take to cancel the agreement. If early termination is expensive, make sure that a companion clause specifies that you can upgrade when new features are released. Today's version of the latest and greatest feature can be quickly usurped in a few months. You don't want to get stuck paying big bucks for features that don't keep pace with your growing business. Some competitive providers don't lock you into long-term contracts, so take the time to compare the pros and cons of each provider.

Offering Alternative Payment Options

You might think that credit cards have a hold on the online shopping market. Indeed, the majority of customers prefer paying that way. Yet online security concerns and the demand for flexibility are driving the need for alternative options.

You receive a definite benefit when you expand your customers' payment choices. Online stores that offer only credit cards as a payment source can still get a substantial number of their visitors to purchase something. But by adding PayPal or eChecks, you can sometimes boost that conversion rate by nearly 25 percent, according to research by PayPal.

Gaining more customers by being flexible is a no-brainer, as they say. As luck would have it, you can offer customers more than a handful of alternative payment solutions:

✦ **PayPal:** One of the most popular alternatives is allowing customers to pay by using a PayPal account. As we mentioned when discussing merchant accounts, PayPal specializes in online payment processing. It offers many options, is a one-stop shop for all your e-commerce payment needs, and is widely recognized. To start using this option, go to www.paypal.com.

✦ **Electronic checks:** This service, also called *ACH (Automated Clearing House) processing,* allows a customer to use funds taken directly from a personal or business bank account. The funds are then deposited directly into your bank account. For you, this service represents lower processing fees per transaction than with credit cards. Fees can range from 30 cents per transaction to more than a dollar for each check. Increasingly, payment gateways are making electronic check processing available for your website. Or you can use a third-party e-check provider, such as

  • *iChex:* www.ichex.com

  • *PaySimple:* www.paysimple.com

✦ **Gift cards:** Offering gift certificates or gift cards on your site is an easy way to extend payment options while increasing your sales.

✦ **Instant credit:** If your customers could buy now and pay later, don't you think that it would help prevent shopping cart abandonment? Well, companies are now providing online retailers a way to do just that. At the time of checkout, your customer essentially receives approval for the dollar amount of the purchase. This process usually takes no more than 15 seconds. Then the customer has a set amount of time to make the payment. Don't worry: You receive the funds immediately, as you would with any other type of payment. A third-party company handles everything for you. Bill Me Later (`www.billmelater.com`) offers one such solution.

✦ **Offline payments:** An option that's sometimes overlooked is allowing customers to send in payments by using a less technically advanced method. Although only a small percentage of shoppers are likely to use these options, it could be worthwhile. After all, it's certainly not cost prohibitive to extend these options:

  • Send payment though Western Union.

  • Mail checks through the U.S. Postal Service.

  • Pay by phone (requires a credit card, but some customers feel safer this way).

Managing the Payment Process to Protect Your Income

Believe it or not, one day you will receive a fraudulent charge back from a customer. You lose the money, plus handling fees charged by the credit card company. Of course, a charge back is only one type of online fraud you have to worry about. Dealing with stolen credit cards is another common headache.

Don't despair yet. Credit card companies, payment gateways, and processors are working diligently to help protect your online business from thieves. All you have to do is choose to implement their protective services. To help minimize your risks, search out these standard security features from your payment gateway provider:

✦ **Address verification service (AVS):** Each time an order is placed, the physical street address on file with the credit card issuer is compared to the billing address the customer gives you with an order.

✦ **Card code verification (CCV):** Customers must enter both a credit card account number and a special three- or four-digit code called the CCV. The code is usually on the back of the credit card.

✦ **Filtering:** You can use several security filtering tools. One type allows you to set a monetary limit for additional security checks on orders that exceed that amount. Other filters screen for suspicious orders and identify IP addresses that have excessive amounts of purchases within a short period.

✦ **Address blocking:** By using this tool, you can block IP addresses from your site. In this case, the addresses are known sources of earlier fraudulent orders.

✦ **Authorized AIM IP:** When you submit Advanced Integration Method (AIM) transactions, you can designate a server's specific IP addresses that are allowed to transmit transactions.

As a smaller online business (generating fewer than $5 million in annual sales), you typically have a lower fraud rate than large online retailers. That's because smaller businesses process fewer transactions, validate orders manually (usually), and fight charge backs by calling customers personally.

Chapter 5: Putting the (Shopping) Cart before the Horse

In This Chapter

✔ Identifying must-have shopping cart features

✔ Using hosted shopping carts

✔ Finding software for your server

✔ Developing a customized solution

Do you absolutely need a shopping cart? No. If you sell only a few items, you can easily get by with using an online order form. Customers making a purchase can print the form and then fax it to you (yes, some people still do that). Or, after customers fill out designated boxes on the online form and click Send, the results arrive in your inbox for manual order processing.

With that in mind, here's the real question: Do you *want* a shopping cart for your website? Absolutely — especially if you sell more than a handful of items. We encourage you to use a shopping cart regardless of how many products you plan to sell.

Assuming that you're serious about making money online and growing a viable e-commerce business, a shopping cart is an essential tool. For starters, it speaks to the credibility and security of your website. From a customer's point of view, using an antiquated, form-based process on a website can give the impression that the site is a small, mom-and-pop type of business. A lack of a fully functioning shopping cart may also cause concerns about the site's security. If customers think their credit card information won't be handled properly, you could lose sales.

Additionally, a good shopping cart makes doing business with you easier — and makes managing and growing your online business easier as well. This chapter helps you sort through all the latest options so that you can start selling like a real pro.

Not All Carts Are Created Equal

Today's sophisticated applications have grown into more than simple shopping baskets for online customers. You can also incorporate quite a few tools into your shopping cart program. Your job is to figure out which features you need most, right now — and which features will serve you best in the long run. Before you can do either, you have to understand what's out there and what's important to use. Changes in shopping behavior and the e-commerce market make this knowledge critical to your business success.

A shopping cart with mobile commerce enabled, for example, is now more than a nice-to-have marketing feature. According to a 2014 global survey from PricewaterhouseCoopers, nearly 30 percent of U.S. online shoppers make purchases from their mobile phones (and this doesn't include the use of other mobile devices, such as tablets). In countries such as India and China, the percentage of online mobile phone shoppers goes way up, to as much as 77 percent. Usage of mobile devices for e-commerce continues to skyrocket, so a mobile-ready shopping cart is a must. Speaking of international online shoppers, global sales are increasingly responsible for driving a great deal of business for all types of e-commerce sites. If you plan to sell internationally, choosing a shopping cart that handles multiple currencies and integrates with payment gateways from countries beyond North American borders is critical.

As you can see, you have a lot to consider about the necessary functionality and features of a shopping cart. To make this process easier, we divide the most sought-after features into four standard categories:

✦ Back-end management

✦ Customer-centric elements

✦ Integration and maintenance

✦ Promotion and marketing

Back-end management

Each shopping cart program has a set of administration tools. Although the specifics can vary among types of software, ultimately these tools give you control of your shopping cart. Here's a list of features to look for in admin tools:

✦ **Administrative functions:** Passwords, pricing changes, and options such as font size or number of items to display on a page are examples of the most basic settings that an administrator controls. Other admin functions should allow for easy management of order processing, inventory, shipping, returns, and more.

If you're not the type to be tethered to a desk, or you travel a good deal and don't have staff to stay behind and manage your business, look for shopping carts that can be managed from mobile devices. You may need an app for your iPhone, iPad, or Android device that gives you mobile-ready access to the administrative features in your shopping cart.

✦ **Customization:** Choices, choices — this factor is important when you're using a shopping cart program. The more you can change colors and fonts, for example, the more likely you are to create a shopping cart that melds with the rest of your site. Some shopping carts offer ready-to-use templates for simplicity, but you still want the capability to make small changes.

✦ **Exporting:** Always confirm that you can export your products from the shopping cart. This feature is critical if you end up using a different shopping cart down the road and need to transfer your inventory.

✦ **Importing:** Having to enter your products into a shopping cart one by one is the last thing you want to do. If you have dozens of product numbers (similar to bar codes), you would be typing at your keyboard for several days. Look for programs that allow you to import your products from an Excel spreadsheet (or a similar method).

✦ **Inventory:** If your shopping cart feature is integrated with your inventory system (if you already have one), you can easily manage your offline stock from your website.

✦ **Taxes:** A critical component of an e-commerce business is proper tax calculation on orders. The shopping cart needs to be easily configured to calculate local and state taxes.

✦ **Currencies:** Can the shopping cart handle more than one or two currencies? If you're selling internationally, you want to make to be able to accept money in multiple currencies.

✦ **Shipping:** You'll probably use more than one type of carrier, such as UPS and FedEx, for your shipping needs. The shopping cart should not only integrate with multiple shipping carriers but also give you flexibility in determining and calculating shipping rates. For example, you may want to offer flat-rate shipping for some items but tiered or location-based shipping rates for others. Some shopping carts can also get automated shipping rates calculated directly from the shipping carriers.

✦ **Recurring billing:** Do you sell web-based services in the B2B (business-to-business) market that are charged monthly? Or perhaps you offer membership-based product sales, such as a cheese of the month club, in the B2C (business-to-consumer) market? If you offer a subscription-based service, you may need a shopping cart that can handle *recurring billing,* or the capability to process payments more than once over a period of time. Look for shopping carts with a recurring feature that allows you to set time intervals (such as every month) and terms for billing your customers.

✦ **Payment gateways:** Hundreds of payment gateways exist, so make sure that your shopping cart integrates with and supports the gateway you selected to process credit cards. This capability can be especially important if you're selling internationally. If a list of supported payment gateways is not readily available for the shopping cart you're considering, talk with a salesperson and get written confirmation of the gateways supported.

✦ **Wizards:** Use these tools to customize your shopping cart and integrate it with your website. The wizard walks you step by step through the entire process. You may also see a wizard referred to as an easy or simple GUI (graphical user interface).

**Book IV
Chapter 5**

**Putting the
(Shopping) Cart
before the Horse**

Customer-centric elements

Which features are most important to your customers? When you're test-driving a shopping cart demo, try to view the experience from the eyes of your shoppers. Does the cart help your customers process their orders quickly? Or does it leave them frustrated and stick your site with a bad case of shopping cart abandonment? Here are some additional elements or features you can include that can benefit your customers (sometimes these features are considered add-on features or widgets and you must pay more to have them included in your shopping cart):

✦ **Product views:** Customers can't touch or feel your products when they're shopping online. The only qualities on which customers can base their purchasing decisions are the images and descriptions you give them. Be sure to use a shopping cart that allows you to upload multiple images for one product.

✦ **Save settings:** Can your customers save products in their shopping carts and then return later to make purchases? The capability to save these settings and others makes the shopping experience more pleasant.

✦ **Store data:** Does the cart give your customers the option to store their data? This feature prevents returning customers from having to reenter account information repeatedly. Having the option to save the data (especially credit card information) is equally important, however. Some customers would rather not sacrifice possible security risks in favor of convenience.

✦ **Wish list:** Some customers like to be able to designate products of interest that they're not ready to buy. Try to find a shopping cart that lets customers save favorite products to wish lists that can be shared with friends and family.

✦ **View order:** Your customers should be able to view complete orders as they shop or when they check out. Having to view a series of pages before they can see their total shipping costs, for example, is particularly frustrating.

Integration and maintenance

For your shopping cart to work optimally, it has to become a seamless part of your overall site. If it doesn't work, you need to be able to get help. Along these lines, you have to consider several critical integration and maintenance factors:

✦ **Access to support:** When and how is support available if you have trouble with your shopping cart? The best-case scenario is to have access to live support seven days a week. If you have to wait to get help, *your customers* also have to wait, and they aren't fond of waiting. Don't forget to ask whether you pay an extra fee for all that technical support.

✦ **Accommodation of other customer accounts:** Your shopping cart should have the flexibility to handle all types of orders — from wholesale orders to affiliates. Even if you don't need the flexibility today, you want to know that it's already built into your cart for use as you grow.

✦ **Communication with shipping and handling:** In addition to integrating your shopping cart with major shipping providers (such as UPS), you have to look closely at how orders are relayed for shipping and handling. Can you customize how and where the order requests are sent? For example, each time an order request is forwarded to your shipping department, can you have a duplicate copy e-mailed to another department?

✦ **Integration with third-party applications:** Your shopping cart needs to fully integrate with the other components of your business, including accounting- and inventory-management systems and your CRM (customer relationship management) software. One of the stickiest points of integrating any type of third-party business system with your shopping cart software is how well your shopping cart can relay information to the other system. If these two programs can't function together (or integrate with each other), your workload doubles.

Some shopping carts may offer an API (application programming interface) or a set of APIs that allow you access to the shopping cart for further customization or integration. Keep in mind that using APIs may require hiring or contracting with a software developer (or someone with development or coding skills).

Promotion and marketing

Of all the benefits a shopping cart can offer, the area of promotion and marketing usually receives the least amount of scrutiny before the purchase. Your first inclination is probably to look at how many products a shopping cart holds. Then you find out how much it will cost you. Marketing is one of the last items you consider, perhaps because you don't realize a shopping cart can offer that feature.

Think again! The following list of marketing and promotion functions is a small sample of how your shopping cart can help you increase sales. See how many features are built into your shopping cart of choice:

✦ **Bundled products or services:** Based on a customer's buying preferences, put together groups of products offered at a slight discount from what your customer would spend to purchase each item separately.

✦ **Shopping cart abandonment deterrence:** Customers often add products to a shopping cart only to leave the site before finalizing their purchase. Many reasons exist for this behavior — everything from a complicated checkout process that frustrates the customer to the customer simply changing her mind and leaving the site. Look for shopping cart abandonment features that not only capture the data of the lost sale but also let you easily send automated or customized e-mails to try and re-engage the customer.

✦ **Coupons:** Set up coupon codes to be entered by customers at the time of purchase.

✦ **Cross selling:** Suggest similar or complementary products that customers might like when they view certain products or check out.

✦ **Data feeds:** Your shopping cart should communicate your product information with other comparison shopping sites, including Google Product Search, Shopping.com, Shopzilla, Shop.com, and Yahoo! Shopping.

✦ **Discounts:** Set up different types of customer groups (such as wholesale or frequent buyer) to give a discount based on buying behavior. Or offer limited-time discounts by product.

✦ **E-mail communications:** Send newsletters or specials to your customers by e-mail. You would do this in addition to e-mails used as a result of shopping cart abandonment.

✦ **Featured products or specials:** Highlight certain products or limited-time offers throughout your website.

✦ **Free-shipping option:** Offer free shipping as a marketing special. This feature can be an important competitive advantage during busy shopping seasons.

✦ **Gift certificates:** A helpful seasonal (or year-round) tool is to offer the option of purchasing and using gift certificates, or virtual gift cards.

✦ **On-site search capability:** A good search tool helps customers easily find products based on several search criteria, such as brand name, category, or generic product name.

✦ **Product reviews and ratings:** Feature additional information on product pages to increase credibility and boost the potential for purchase.

✦ **Search engine friendliness:** Use the shopping cart built-in features to better market your products in major search engines. A shopping cart might offer `<TITLE>` and `<META>` tags for every product page or `<ALT>` tags with keywords.

✦ **Social commerce:** Integrate with social networking sites such as Twitter, Facebook, Instagram, and Pinterest. This type of feature provides a way to promote specials, coupon offers, and other discounts; to share customers' purchases with their friends; and to spread positive reviews of your products and customer service.

✦ **Survey tools:** Find out what customers are thinking by displaying a brief survey before checkout or whenever a customer abandons a shopping cart.

✦ **Tell-a-friend functionality:** Enable customers to pass along product pages to friends and family members.

✦ **Upselling:** Offer an incentive to purchase more products by upselling — for example, "Buy one, get one at half price" or "Buy two and get one free."

You don't have to use all these marketing tools. They might even feel overwhelming at first. Don't worry: That's perfectly natural. However, we recommend using a shopping cart that has a variety of promotional features. Then, as you become more comfortable, start testing the waters and increasing your sales.

Shopping Around for the Best Hosted Solution

Marketing features and administrative tools aren't the only features that can sway your decision in selecting a cart. You can make your decision based on how the cart is delivered to you (or set up for use). For instance, one easy alternative is to use a *hosted* solution. The shopping cart is stored on someone else's server and you pay to have access to it.

Hosted shopping carts have four specific advantages:

✦ **Cost:** A hosted solution is a more affordable option, especially for a first e-commerce endeavor. For a small monthly fee (sometimes for less than ten bucks), you gain access to an extensive set of shopping cart features.

✦ **Simplicity:** Because most shopping carts easily integrate into existing websites, theoretically they should be easy to get up and running.

✦ **Support:** You get access to customer and technical support, usually around the clock. When your learning curve is still steep, it's nice to know that you have a place to turn for help, any time of the night or day.

✦ **Flexibility:** When you use a hosted solution, you don't have to make a long-term commitment. Try it and see whether you like it. If you're on a monthly plan, you can terminate the agreement fairly easily. As long as the shopping cart has a good exporting feature, you can move your products to another solution if your current one isn't working.

Today, most people go with a hosted shopping cart (probably without even thinking about it as an option) because it is the prevailing method for delivering most e-commerce services. Start-up online retailers find it easy to turn to a single hosted vendor for everything from their domain name and hosting to a shopping cart and payment gateway. In this section, we describe a few popular shopping carts to start you on your search for the perfect hosted shopping cart solution.

You might instead decide to use a *storefront,* an all-in-one e-commerce solution. If you do, a hosted shopping cart is included with your storefront as part of the complete package. If you go this route, remember that each storefront has its own shopping cart with different features. We include a popular storefront shopping cart in this section, too, to give you an idea of what to consider. If you want to know more about using storefronts, you can discover all the details in Book VIII, Chapter 1.

1ShoppingCart

The 1ShoppingCart shopping cart has been around for a long time and has a large fan base. Before, it was a hosted shopping cart, but now the company now bills itself as a complete e-commerce solution. You can choose from several plans. The basic Plus plan is $59 per month and is limited to 500 products. You can get support for an unlimited number of products with the Premium plan ($99 per month) or Ultimate plan ($299 per month). The biggest differences between the monthly plans are the number of user licenses and products supported. Transaction fees also decrease from 1.25 percent in the Plus plan to .75 percent in the Ultimate plan. As for shopping cart features, you get the same features in every plan, except that affiliate management functionality is available only in the Ultimate plan.

1ShoppingCart has an extensive set of shopping cart features, with great flexibility and choice. For example, 1ShoppingCart supports up to six shipping methods, in addition to international shipping, and provides a variety of ways to calculate shipping (including the option for free customer shipping). It also has a robust recurring billing feature and an impressive set of upsell features customized to the buyer's shopping history. On the downside, 1ShoppingCart supports only 50 payment gateways; other shopping cart and e-commerce solutions support 70 or more payment gateways.

You can get a four-week trial of 1ShoppingCart shopping cart for free, but you must provide credit card information. (Your credit card is charged after the four-week trial ends.) If you decide it's not right for you, make sure to cancel the service before the trial period ends or your credit card will automatically be billed monthly (until you cancel the services).

You can compare popular features and pricing options for each plan by visiting www.1shoppingcart.com/packages. You can also see the complete list of features, as shown in Figure 5-1.

Figure 5-1:
Compare all features to find the best plan for you.

FoxyCart

FoxyCart (www.foxycart.com) is a true hosted shopping cart, but several things make this solution unique. For starters, FoxyCart promotes itself as being only one thing: a secure e-commerce platform — *not* a jack of all trades or a turnkey solution — and they mean it.

Unlike many typical shopping cart solutions, FoxyCart does not attempt to include other back-end functionality, such as accounting, CRM (customer relationship management), or affiliate marketing. Although we usually suggest that start-up online retailers choose a shopping cart with more functionality, FoxyCart is an exception. It is set up as a solution for developers to use on behalf of online retailers. Yes, this means you need to work with a developer if you do not have certain programming skills. Again, this seems contrary to our typical advice, but in certain circumstances, FoxyCart makes it worthwhile to pay someone.

If you need a fully customizable shopping cart and the ease of a hosted product once customization is complete, FoxyCart is the ideal fit. It is fully customizable and can integrate with just about any third-party software, from QuickBooks to Salesforce. The shopping cart features one-page checkout, guest checkout, coupons and discounts, international shipping, tax calculations, and unlimited shipping options, including multi-shipping (shipping to multiple addresses from a single order), free in-store pickup, and free ground shipping. You see an example of the simple checkout process in Figure 5-2. FoxyCart also supports integration with over 70 payment gateways and allows for alternative payment methods (including Bitcoin). The most important take-away when considering choosing FoxyCart for your shopping cart is remembering that it is a fully customizable, hosted solution.

Figure 5-2: FoxyCart provides a simple, customer-friendly checkout process.

How much does it cost? FoxyCart uses a combination of monthly and per-transaction fees. The standard plan is $15 per month, plus a transaction fee of .5 percent (up to a maximum of 15 cents) with the first 100 transactions free. A custom SLL certificate costs $100 annually. The advanced plan is $250 per month with the same .5 percent transaction fee (up to a maximum of 5 cents), with the first 1,000 transactions free. The advanced plan does not charge for a custom SSL certificate.

You may be scratching your head and again asking, "How much does it cost?" Here's an example to help explain their pricing model. On the standard plan, if your average order is $25 and you have 200 transactions a month, you would pay approximately $28 per month. If you sell less than 100 items in a month, you only pay $15. This pricing model is beneficial if you stay under the maximum allowed number of free monthly transactions, or if your number of transactions fluctuate based on seasonality, for example. In that case, you are not locked into paying a high monthly fee just because you have a peak selling season each year.

When considering using FoxyCart, you can take advantage of their *unlimited* free trial period (see Figure 5-3). The shopping cart solution allows you to take as long as needed to set up a trial of FoxyCart. You don't have to pay anything until the site goes live.

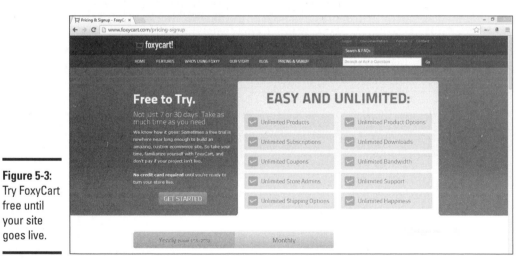

Figure 5-3:
Try FoxyCart free until your site goes live.

Shopify

Shopify (www.shopify.com) is not only a hosted shopping cart but also a complete e-commerce solution that has received rave reviews since launching in 2006. With Shopify, you get access to a long list of shopping cart features at a price ranging from $29 to $279 per month. In addition to varying bandwidth limitations, the biggest difference between monthly plans comes down to some important shopping cart features. Abandoned cart recovery, gift cards, and real-time carrier shipping calculations (from UPS, FedEx, and USPS) are available only in the two more expensive monthly plans. In addition, some key administrative-tracking and -reporting capabilities are available only in the most expensive monthly plan.

The shopping cart integrates with over 70 payment gateways, including several popular European payment gateways. If you're selling internationally, Shopify's shopping cart is particularly useful because it supports website checkout in more than 50 different languages. It also handles multiple currencies and automatically calculates major county and state tax rates.

A mobile version of the shopping cart is included free with all monthly Shopify plans, which means your customers can buy products from any mobile device. Shopify also provides an app that enables you to manage orders from your mobile phone. Because Shopify is a complete e-commerce solution, it offers lots of free and low-cost templates for your online store, including some that are *responsive* (mobile-ready), helping to ensure that your complete site (including your shopping cart) is displayed properly on every mobile device. Customers are more likely to not only browse products from their phones but also drop items into the shopping cart and complete the purchase. In Figure 5-4, you see an example of a clean, simplified shopping cart that also works well on any mobile device. For a complete list of features included with the Shopify shopping cart, visit www.shopify.com/website/shoppingcart.

Figure 5-4: Shopify is a hosted e-commerce solution with a feature-packed shopping cart and a simplified checkout process.

Finding Stand-Alone Shopping Cart Software

Before so many hosted shopping carts flooded the market, stand-alone or off-the-shelf software was your best bet for a quick, inexpensive solution. The software was available from an Internet service provider (ISP), or you could license the product yourself. A stand-alone shopping cart allows you to add the software to your own server. Many web developers pursue this option and then become resellers of their particular shopping cart programs.

When you use this type of shopping cart, one big advantage is that you aren't tied to a specific web host. In theory, that feature makes managing your store easier if you switch service providers. However, with importing and exporting functions now a common tool in most shopping carts, where your site is hosted is less of a concern. Other advantages include control and price. For larger stores, the price issue is particularly important. Whereas you might pay $250 to $2500 per month (or more) for a hosted shopping cart that supports an unlimited number of products with complex back-end and feature requirements, you might find that paying a little more up-front makes it easier on you as your company grows.

In general, we recommend stand-alone shopping carts for larger retailers who have an existing website. If you're just starting out or are a small online retailer, it's hard to beat the convenience, support, and savings of either a hosted or an all-in-one e-commerce solution. In fact, many stand-alone shopping cart software providers are now hosted or storefront solutions, including Miva Merchant (`www.mivamerchant.com`) and Volusion (`www.volusion.com`).

If you want to get your hands on one of the remaining stand-alone shopping carts, you can approach it in two ways:

✦ **Purchase:** You can buy software outright. Depending on the shopping cart, the price can range anywhere from $499 for a basic program to more than $2,000 for a more dynamic software product.

✦ **License:** More often than not, software vendors require that you license the use of their products. The process is like leasing a car: You pay a monthly or an annual fee for the right to use the software, but you don't own it.

When you're purchasing or licensing a shopping cart, technical support may or may not be included in the price. You might have to purchase a separate technical support package, which adds to your overall cost for the product.

Here are a few remaining providers:

✦ **ShopFactory (`www.shopfactory.com`):** Provides the capability to create ready-to-go storefronts with shopping cart systems included (or sold separately).

✦ **X-Cart (`www.x-cart.com`):** A PHP e-commerce software that you can buy and download, it includes many standard shopping cart features, is mobile-ready, and can be customized.

✦ **PDG (`www.pdgsoft.com`):** Shopping cart systems with built-in search engine capabilities.

If you run your website using WordPress, the popular (and free) blogging software, you can use a free WordPress plugin to add a simple shopping cart to your site. Simply search the WordPress plugin directory, at `http://wordpress.org/extend/plugins/`, using the term *shopping cart*.

Before purchasing an off-the-shelf shopping cart, find out whether your preferred payment gateway is supported by the shopping cart. Conversely, after you buy the software, know which gateways are compatible before selecting one for your store. If you happen to choose one that's not supported, extra programming might be required.

Designing a Cart

Custom cart development takes place when you program (or someone you hire programs) a shopping cart unique to your needs. You are truly building a shopping cart from the ground up!

On the bright side, you can get a program that meets your specifications in every way. And if you know how to program or have someone willing to donate the time (or give you a steal on the price), this option can be less expensive than an off-the-shelf, or hosted, solution.

Then again, hiring someone can get expensive fast, especially if you require a good amount of customization. (Remember too that you can get an incredibly robust hosted shopping cart for less than a few hundred dollars per year.) Another problem is that a customized solution can be difficult to integrate with payment gateways or will involve at least some additional coding. Perhaps the biggest drawbacks are the limitations on support and ease of scalability. Every time you hit a snag, you have to go back to the developer for help. If your needs change or you discover a feature you want to incorporate, you're again dependent on your developer, which can get expensive.

If you do hire someone to build a custom solution, you'll have a wide variety of options. With access to developers around the world, you may find some good deals by outsourcing the work to firms in other countries, such as India. The cost of a custom project can vary widely (as can the level of skill or customer service you get from contractors), so shop around for the best option. Be sure to compare the details between multiple quotes for your project, so that you understand what is or is not included in the bid. Also ask for a few customer references. If you have a large enterprise, these issues might be small deterrents. For a small online business, your money and time might be better spent elsewhere.

If you decide to delve into the custom route, you will need to take the following actions:

+ **Get bids and quotes.** Gather at least three bids before selecting a developer. Then ask for a final quote delivered in writing before you begin the project.

  To ensure that you can compare apples to apples, provide each prospective programmer with the same list of specifications. Ask each company to develop a bid from *your* list.

+ **Define support.** Discuss what types of setup and ongoing support are available, including when support is available and how soon a support issue will be addressed. (Support might be available only during weekdays, for example, and processing your request might take three business days.) The cost of the support should also be included in the final quote.

+ **Determine the timeline.** Be specific about the length of time involved for any type of software development project. Set a series of targets or objectives that should be completed by a certain date. This guidepost ensures that the project stays on track.

+ **Get the details.** The more nitty-gritty specifics you can nail down, the better. Find out how many programmers typically work on a project. More programmers can result in faster delivery of your system but can also add to its overall cost.

Lots of reasonably priced hosted and off-the-shelf shopping cart solutions are available, with impressive lists of features. With so many options at hand, consider whether custom features or unique needs are really worth the delay in time and the amount of out-of-pocket cash necessary to implement a custom cart.

Chapter 6: Taking Inventory

In This Chapter

- ✔ Taking stock of the items you should make available for sale
- ✔ Using your research to validate decisions
- ✔ Choosing price points that move merchandise
- ✔ Creating a winning selection with the right number of products

You probably know someone who is a fantastic salesperson. Usually, this person is described as being capable of "selling anything to anyone." Well, the Internet is similar to that top-notch salesperson. It can sell just about anything to almost anyone around the world — with your help, of course. As any good salesperson knows, however, you have to know a few tricks of the trade. The same statement holds true for selling online: To do well, you have to know a few tricks. In the case of choosing inventory, you simply need some additional information to give your business a boost.

How do you decide what to stock up on to give your business a leg up? To create the ideal inventory for your online business, always keep in mind these three points:

- ✦ **Product:** The goods or services you sell should be readily available for you to purchase and stock and reflect items of interest to your customers.

- ✦ **Pricing:** The amount you charge for your product must make it attractive to customers while providing you with a reasonable profit.

- ✦ **Selection:** The range of products you offer your customers is more than a matter of quantity. Offer variations of the same product so that your customers can choose from alternative sizes, colors, and styles.

Fortunately, deciding which type of product to promote — and at which price — isn't complicated. In fact, several useful tools and methods can help you determine potential sales-chart-toppers.

Finding Out What's Popular

One thing is certain, the world loves data — and there's plenty of it to be had. You may have heard terms such as *business intelligence (BI)* and *big data.* Both involve tracking, collecting, and analyzing all sorts of metrics or data points to form a more detailed picture about what's happening in a particular area, such as what items are selling well during a specified time period. You can access this type of information from various sources, and sometimes it's free. One place to turn for high-level sales data on a wide range of product types is Amazon. The mega online retailer moves a lot of products and readily shares which ones are selling best at any given time. Using Amazon Best Sellers, you can explore any of its product categories to see which individual products are climbing up or down the chain of most-wanted items. Although you can't access specific sales figures, you can see the following information:

✦ Numeric ranking of 1 to 100 in top sellers list

✦ Number of days in the top 100

✦ Recent movement up or down the list

Within each product category, you can also access a list of top 100 sellers based on categories such as Hot New Releases, Movers and Shakers, and Top Rated. Figure 6-1 shows you a view of an Amazon bestseller in its Camera and Photo category. You could drill down to something even more specific in this category, such as Accessories or Camcorders.

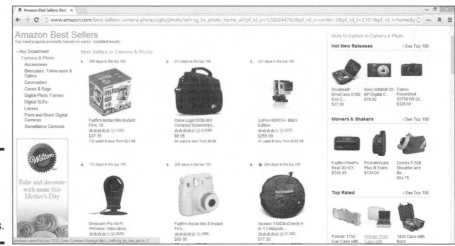

Figure 6-1: Find what's hot on Amazon Best Sellers.

Although this view is limited, you can still get a good sense of what people are buying because of the amount and diversity of products sold. And if you dig into the buyer reviews for the top sellers, you can possibly get more granular product detail and why people bought the product or why they like it. Granted, it takes a good bit of time to read product reviews, but the task is worthwhile when you're building an inventory of online products for your business.

Hot tips for choosing the right products

When you're deciding which products to offer for sale online, ask yourself these questions:

✔ Will shipping the product be difficult? Large, bulky products can add to your shipping woes.

✔ Will larger products, which are expensive to ship, deter customers from making a purchase online?

✔ Are you selling perishable food products? If so, do they meet federal food handling, storage, and shipping guidelines?

✔ Is the product fragile, and does it require special handling?

✔ How much product does a supplier require you to buy at one time to receive the best price?

✔ Where will you keep the inventory? Do you have suitable storage facilities, or do you have to pay for (rent) additional space?

✔ If you have to store the inventory, is it important to you that smaller products, flat products, and information products take up less room?

✔ If you're making custom products by hand, how long do you spend fulfilling an order? Can you keep up with demand?

✔ Are you familiar with the product?

Two other popular websites can provide a glimpse of the types of products that are selling well. Etsy (www.etsy.com), an online marketplace for handmade and vintage items and craft supplies, and eBay (www.ebay.com), the online auction site, attract lots of buyers for a variety of products. Both sites are good sources for helping you decide what types of products should be in your inventory.

A third-party site called Craftcount (www.craftcount.com) uses an API (application programming interface) from Etsy to track top Etsy sellers and top products by category. Stores with more than 1,000 sales are tracked, and the information is updated every 24 hours. If you think information about handmade items couldn't possibly help drive your own inventory decisions, consider this: Large retailers have started turning to Etsy to look for popular products to stock in their own stores. Big-box retailers often work directly with top-selling Etsy store owners to reproduce their handmade bestsellers. If you happen to sell similar types of goods — from apparel to home goods, this type of report could prove to be a good source for beefing up your store inventory.

To research a much wider variety of products, you can turn to eBay. To access the sales data, however, you need to invest in a tool called Terapeak (www.terapeak.com). This tool provides a detailed view into the most popular products selling on eBay over a given period of time as well as which listings are resulting in sales. You can also access pricing recommendations. Although Terapeak is designed for current eBay sellers, it is also a source of insightful data for building a sought-after inventory of products for your online store.

**Book IV
Chapter 6**

Taking Inventory

Terapeak pricing plans start at $30 per month, but you can access a free trial, which may be enough to give you helpful information. As a bonus, Terapeak includes more detailed data about Amazon sales, too.

Putting Together All Your Research

When you're starting a new business, it's comforting to be able to validate your decisions. That's exactly what market research allows you to do. If your searches show that a potential product or service is in high demand, it's a signal that you're on the right track. Or if you're having trouble selecting products to stock your web inventory, the popularity listings in your research can spur your imagination.

Some established companies specialize in market research. Their background work is summarized in concise reports that forecast trends and buying behaviors. For the best results, search each company's data bank of reports for titles or topics such as e-commerce, online retailing, and e-business. Although some resources provide free information, others are paid services. Reports can range from several hundred dollars to more than a thousand dollars. For that reason, take extra care to read the descriptions and the date of the report to make sure they have the most accurate and current information for your purpose.

The following companies specialize in market research:

✦ **eMarketer (`www.emarketer.com`):** Specializes in providing data and analysis on trends in e-business, online marketing, and emerging technologies. The site also offers free articles for limited periods, so check it frequently.

✦ **Forrester (`www.forrester.com`):** Offers information specifically about technology and business. Product areas and services include data and research reports, consulting services, and community programs.

✦ **Internet Retailer (`www.internetretailer.com`):** Provides a series of Top 500 guides for e-retailers, including the top 500 sites based on annual sales and the top 500 up-and-coming sites based on sales. Internet Retailer also offers free articles detailing online trends and news.

Pricing Your Products

After you decide which products or services you're most interested in selling, it's time to price your merchandise. Having delved into the results of your research, you probably have a good idea of which items have the best chance of selling. However, no matter how trendy or in demand your products are, setting the wrong prices might leave you with unsold inventory. In this section, we take a look at some pricing strategies and considerations to make sure that you move the merchandise directly into your buyers' hands.

When you're tagging your merchandise, the following factors are the most probable *price influencers,* or factors that affect your sticker price:

✦ **Demand:** Whether customers are seeking out your product because it either meets a need or is thought to be a desirable or trendy item.

✦ **Competition:** Not only who, but also *how many,* competitors you have, and what *prices* they have established for the same or similar products you're selling.

✦ **Market position:** How you want your business to be perceived by customers in the marketplace. For example, an upscale store with high-end products might influence pricing strategies in one direction while a larger, warehouse-type of image might warrant a more competitive pricing strategy.

✦ **Cost:** How much you pay (your expense) to create or purchase the product before reselling it to your customer.

✦ **Profitability:** How much money you want to make each time an item is sold, after you've considered all expenses or costs associated with selling the item.

Product pricing is one of the most critical business decisions you make. Researching all the advice and pricing models offered in textbooks or by economists, however, can leave your head spinning. Keep it simple. The basic number for you to grasp is the product's cost, which incorporates every expense associated with your item, including the wholesale price you paid (the raw costs of materials to make the product); overhead costs ranging from utilities to Internet service fees; commissions; and packaging and shipping costs to deliver the product to your customer.

Costs or expenses that don't fluctuate are *fixed costs* and are often considered overhead (such as rent). Expenses that might change periodically are *variable expenses.* The price of your product should cover all variable expenses and help contribute toward your fixed costs.

After you understand the cost of what you're selling, you can begin making pricing decisions. Use one of the following common pricing strategies:

✦ **Cost plus:** This method requires you to total the costs of your expenses associated with the product and then add an amount you want to make as profit. The resulting dollar amount represents the pricing *floor,* or the lowest price you should charge.

✦ **Value based:** With this strategy, you're setting a price that reflects the highest amount you believe your customers are willing to pay for the product. Unlike the cost-plus method, this one considers market conditions, such as demand, competition, and the perceived benefits (or value) of your product's features.

For example, if your cost for selling a coffee mug is $4.50, should you turn around and try to sell it for that same price? No, you have to make a respectable profit. That amount depends on how much you want — within reason, of course. If you decide that you have to clear $5.50 on every mug, for example, your price is set at $10.00 per item (cost-plus pricing).

By using value-based pricing, you might be able to set a higher price based on consideration of other factors. For example, how much are customers *willing* to pay for a coffee cup? In other words, what cost does the market bear? Perhaps, in the case of an Elvis mug, its perceived value is much greater than the perceived value of other styles of cups. You might be able to sell each mug for $15.00 or more. Of course, even if your customers are willing to pay that much, they might find a better deal elsewhere. Your next consideration is to find out how much your competitors are charging for the same or similar products. If $9.99 is the top price on other sites, it might be unreasonable for you to expect to set a much higher price.

Now that you have the basic information needed to determine a baseline price for your product or service, you have to consider one more factor: your inventory.

Building Your Inventory

Choosing the best products and prices for your online business is certainly an important factor in starting your new business. You have to consider another issue too: Exactly how much inventory you should keep on hand, or how many different products you should have available for sale. The answer depends on not only the type of products you're selling but also the type of business strategy you want to execute.

Savvy online shoppers are accustomed to an endless array of choices because they can easily jump from one website to another. These customers are quick to make a decision about whether your site's inventory meets their expectations.

To keep the attention of most online shoppers, have a clear strategy for the type and amount of product you choose to offer.

We don't mean that you have to carry hundreds, or even thousands, of products to find success online. But you can follow a few distinct strategies for building an appropriate online inventory. Each one comes with its own advantages and disadvantages, as discussed in the following sections.

Stocking up as a low-price leader

Competing based on price can be a tricky situation, although it's certainly one option for an inventory strategy. If price is the primary decision-making factor in whether your customers buy, keep this advice in mind:

✦ **Provide many choices.** Offer lots of choices. Your customers are looking for good deals, and might not even have a specific item in mind when they're shopping. You have to stock up.

✦ **Change products often.** Another consideration with this type of inventory is how often you need to change out products. Even if your site doesn't see large volumes of traffic, returning customers expect a revolving inventory. If they discover that your inventory stays pretty much the same after several return visits, they'll stop coming back.

To help avoid the *click-through syndrome* (customers quickly view all your products without stopping to make a purchase), make sure that your site offers a large variety of products that are rotated or switched out often.

Becoming all things to all people with trial-and-error inventory

This strategy is a category that swallows up many first-time online entrepreneurs. You don't truly have a strategy. Instead, you end up offering a little bit of everything, until you can form a better idea of what sells. This trial-and-error method, often referred to as offering a *chaotic* variety of products, can be cumbersome but necessary. To reduce stress and quickly try to find the best products to keep in stock, consider these tips:

✦ **Showcase a variety of products but in limited supply.** Nothing is wrong with offering a large variety of products. To keep expenses and storage issues to a minimum, maintain a relatively low level of inventory on all products.

✦ **Rotate featured products often.** Because you're testing the waters with customer preferences, highlight different products daily or weekly. Featuring or spotlighting select items helps you quickly narrow which products your customers respond to most.

✦ **Track your results to find out inventory needs.** You want to see which types of products your customers respond to most, so maintain thorough sales records. After you have more information about your visitors' buying habits, you can begin scaling down the number of products and adjusting your inventory to provide a better selection.

Specializing with limited inventory

Specializing in a field usually leads to the best inventory strategy. And doing so provides the most likely chance for success when you're building your online business. You might decide to deal exclusively in English teapots or maintenance supply parts for the army. Artists and craftspeople are usually in this category, too. They typically work in only one medium, such as black-and-white photography or high-grade wood carvings. If specializing sounds like your cup of tea, consider the following advice when building your inventory:

✦ **Offer a select number of products.** Focus on the quality or uniqueness of the products rather than on mass quantity. You can afford to keep relatively low levels of inventory, as long as you're always searching for new items to replenish your stock.

✦ **Position yourself as an expert.** Because you deal in a narrow type of product, visitors are more likely to seek you out for your expertise. You can keep inventory levels low and charge a finder's fee or consulting fee to help customers locate similar products on request.

Keep inventories low and establish an active network with others for quickly locating similar products. Being able to direct customers to other resources, or locate special pieces in a timely manner, provides a valuable service that can also keep customers returning to your website.

If you're an artist selling handmade goods or crafts, you can test market conditions by first selling on Etsy. With this strategy, you don't have to invest in your own full-scale e-commerce website with lots of inventory. Or you can maintain an Etsy shop in addition to your full website, and test new inventory on Etsy.

Chapter 7: Fulfilling Expectations and Orders

In This Chapter

- Planning the logistics of your operation
- Setting up an in-house fulfillment system
- Outsourcing your shipping area to someone else
- Learning the rules of shipping and handling
- Maintaining your information as you pack up and ship out

Setting up your online business can be full of excitement and milestones. The true payoff, though, is best realized when that first payment rolls in for something you sold. Seeing a paper check or an electronic deposit right in front of you helps cement the idea of what you're doing and provides validation of the business you created. Even though you may feel satisfied when you see the money, don't think you're done.

After the order is completed and the payment has cleared, you still need to handle one area of the sale. *Fulfillment,* or filling the order, is simply the practice of delivering the product to the buyer after payment has been received. In a retail store, fulfillment is easy: You hand your customers a shopping bag with the purchase and the sales receipt, and they walk out the door. In an online business, you need to perform a few steps to make order fulfillment happen. Thankfully, with all the advances in Internet technology and shipping services, achieving this goal is easier than ever.

Of course, planning for order fulfillment doesn't start when the money comes through your door. In this chapter, we talk about the elements that can affect fulfillment, starting with how you set up your business. We talk about strategies you can implement to handle your product storage and organization, and how to pack and ship your items. In some cases, the best step you can take is to turn shipping over to another company and pay it to deliver your products to the right customers.

The moment you receive that payment, the clock is ticking and your customer is eagerly awaiting the item. A customer who experiences a bad fulfillment process will remember nothing else about your business, even if your website is well designed and the ordering process was easy to complete.

Figuring Out the Logistics of Shipping

How do you set up the entire flow of your business? Start by thinking about the operations and daily tasks that make your business work. Then lay out everything and decide how the business can best operate. To help you plan all these tasks, ask yourself these questions:

✦ Does my online business operate from my home or a dedicated office space?

✦ Should I buy products for resale or have someone else ship the goods?

✦ Does a physical store or presence have to work with my online business?

✦ How many employees need access to the merchandise and system?

Track the flow of one of your items for sale from beginning to end:

✦ Receive the product from your supplier.

✦ Prepare the product for sale.

✦ Store the product while it's up for sale.

✦ Pack the product after it's sold.

✦ Ship the product after it's packaged.

Think about when and where these events take place, so you can plan the logistics of your business. *Logistics* simply refers to how you manage the operations of your business. You might need to dedicate a room in your house, or you might need to coordinate products and shipments through a warehouse that has different vendors and manufacturers.

The key is to set up a model that fits your business. You have no reason to buy an expensive software inventory program if you sell 10 or 20 items per month. Likewise, don't expect to run a multimillion-dollar venture with a pencil and pad of paper. Choose a system that lets you know at any given time where your inventory is in the process, whether it's receiving, photographing, listing, packing, or shipping.

Developing an In-House Fulfillment Model

Many small businesses take care of their own fulfillment, which means that they pack and ship their own products and send them out the door. Doing so allows these businesses to control the quality of their shipments so that they know that their customers are being served. Typically, doing so makes sense: Because the inventory is on-site, orders can be packed at the source and sent out rather than relayed to some far-flung warehouse.

Setting up an in-house fulfillment model requires first having enough inventory on hand and available at your location. In the beginning, you need to estimate orders and decide how many different products to carry in your store. Be sure to have enough on hand to fill initial orders. After you're in business a while, you'll know from your average order level how much inventory to have. After you know how much inventory you need to have in stock, you can plan for the space required to hold this inventory.

Don't let a lack of available space be the reason that you don't carry more inventory. Different fulfillment models, both in-house and outsourced, allow you to hold more products than your current available space allows.

Your relationships with your vendors help determine the amount of space that's required. If you receive shipments in batches, make sure that you have enough space available to take in a shipment and hold it until sales for that order come in. If you have a responsive vendor that can ship items in a just-in-time approach, your space requirement can be much lower.

In *just-in-time* inventory management, vendors deliver their products to you just before you need them for listing or shipping out. If you're receiving shipments just in time, you don't need to have a big warehouse to store upcoming orders. However, if your just-in-time vendor is late with a shipment, you have nothing to sell or send out to your customers.

If the space you require is more than the available space at your location, either look at temporary storage, such as a storage locker, or rent dedicated industrial or warehouse space for your inventory. If you acquire additional storage away from your location, make sure that you keep at least one sample of each product close at hand, so you can take photographs, write descriptions for your website, and refer to the item when necessary to answer customer's questions.

If you rent a storage locker to hold inventory, ask the management team whether it can accept packages for you and place them in your unit. This way, you don't have to be present when your shipments come in or worry about sending them to storage from your home.

After your space requirement is resolved, think about labor: Who will pack and ship your products? The number of orders to be packed and shipped can help determine the number of fulfillment workers required. If you're packing only a few orders a day, you or one of your employees might handle the task. As the number of orders continues to grow, consider hiring a dedicated employee to perform the fulfillment or reassign someone to focus only on fulfillment.

**Book IV
Chapter 7**

Fulfilling
Expectations and
Orders

Deciding to Outsource Fulfillment

Most people have a passion for the businesses they want to create. Whether someone is turning her knowledge of, and experience with, a hobby into a business or solving a need and providing a product that people want, a business owner dreams of turning a business idea into a reality. A business owner usually doesn't dream, however, of a massive shipping-and-warehouse operation (unless that person is in charge of UPS or FedEx). Therefore, many business owners choose to outsource their fulfillment operations to someone else so that they can focus on the most important element: their businesses. After all, just because you're good at selling widgets doesn't mean that you're good at packing and shipping them.

Contrary to popular belief, you don't need to have a Fortune 500 corporation to outsource fulfillment. Small businesses around the world outsource this process. This action not only reduces the amount of space you require but also frees you and your employees to work on other aspects of your business.

Enter the *fulfillment house,* a business whose sole job is to handle the packing and shipping of other people's goods. By grouping multiple clients' shipping operations, a fulfillment house can employ fewer people to handle the volume of goods than individual companies who hire their own staffs. These fulfillment companies create state-of-the-art, computerized inventory-management systems and train their employees to be efficient in this process.

Outsourcing companies also offer specialized and enhanced service in these other areas that affect your business:

✦ **Customer service:** Every time a customer calls to ask a question about an order, make a special request, or have a product returned, someone has to handle the call. Fulfillment houses typically employ their own customer service teams to manage these calls. The houses worry about hiring, training, and maintaining the calls and about handling the request so that you don't have to.

✦ **Reporting:** As your business grows, you need to keep track of how many orders go out for each product line and then analyze that data. Most fulfillment houses have some sort of tracking and reporting capability built into their systems so that they can deliver reports and let you know what's going on, to help you plan for your next phase.

✦ **Scalability:** Suppose that you operate a seasonal business, such as stocking Christmas gift items, and you have to quickly grow and expand your inventory space to meet demand. Doing it yourself means worrying about reserving temporary space in September that you need to give up in early January. If you use a fulfillment service, you can draw on its resources and let it worry about finding the space. If your business grows quickly, a good fulfillment partner accommodates that growth easily.

Outsource some and keep the rest

Many online business owners dive into the fulfillment outsourcing question by giving up only a part of the fulfillment process and keeping the rest in-house. After all, their business reputations are on the line. Start with a test situation (one small function), and see how your outsourcing partner handles it.

Consider hiring a college student to help you a few times a week to pack and ship orders.

It's a quick way to bring on some additional help and free up some of your time. If things work out with the student, you can bring him onboard for more hours per week. Additionally, you can hire more students or part-time help and soon have your own shipping department filled with extra help.

Finding an outsourcing partner

When you're ready to outsource the fulfillment process, you're probably wondering what the first step is. After all, you probably don't just flip open the Yellow Pages and go to the *O* page, for *outsourcing*. Every business magazine and talk show discusses the effect of outsourcing for bigger corporations, but what about small businesses? Some outsourcing companies are targeted to small-business accounts, especially online businesses.

After all, these companies know that if they can pool several inventories of small businesses, they can manage those accounts with a smaller team of trained personnel and one warehouse. In other cases, your outsourcing partner can be a similar business that has its fulfillment process down to a science and has decided to use that expertise to make money for other companies by solving their fulfillment headaches.

As you look for a fulfillment partner, keep a few guidelines in mind:

✦ **Know your budget.** Some companies can complete a part of your fulfillment process, and others assume control of your entire shipping department. Know how much you can afford to spend, to guide yourself to a partner that's right for you. Understand that you're saving employee labor time and salary when you're outsourcing your fulfillment, so factor those into your budget.

✦ **Shop around.** Just like shopping for any other type of service professional for your business, get two or three estimates. Develop a feel for the service levels each offers, and see whether one company is willing to match another's price.

✦ **Factor in all the costs.** You can easily see a price quote from a company and think that it shows the total cost. Before you sign anything, make sure that you understand all the requirements you will have to provide to the fulfillment partner and factor in all the costs. One quote might be cheaper because your company is still handling part of the fulfillment process, for example.

**Book IV
Chapter 7**

**Fulfilling
Expectations and
Orders**

When you're ready to look for a partner, start by asking around: Ask your vendors, manufacturing partners, and even fellow business owners in places such as Chamber of Commerce get-togethers, small-business workshops, and online forums. Internet searches on Google and Yahoo! will turn up lots of leads, so do your research. See what other business owners say on message boards and in forums.

Here are some Internet companies to get you started:

✦ **E-Fulfillment Service:** www.efulfillmentservice.com

✦ **Fulfillment Works:** www.fulfillmentworks.com

✦ **Strategic Fulfillment Group:** www.strategicfulfillment.com

✦ **Webgistix:** www.webgistix.com

Look for a company that specializes in your area (such as Webgistix for e-commerce, as shown in Figure 7-1) or provides the reporting features you need, such as Strategic Fulfillment Group and its real-time system.

Figure 7-1: Webgistix helps you fulfill your inventory.

You can even turn your shipping company into your outsourcing partner. UPS Contract Logistics, for example, helps businesses around the world coordinate their supplies, orders, and product flow. The company's range of

supply chain services and business technology services help take care of your fulfillment headaches. Go to `ups-scs.com/logistics` for more information.

Establishing your outsourcing relationship

After you find the outsourcing partner you want, it's time to create an agreement and determine the terms of your relationship. You have to agree on terms such as service level and the rate of customer response. You need to know how quickly the company ships your products, what materials it uses to pack them, and how quickly it responds to customer requests.

Here are the factors in this relationship that should concern you:

✦ **Reputation and service level:** Even though the outsourcing company is doing the work, *your* name and reputation are on the line with your customers. If something goes wrong, guess who gets blamed? Yep, you do! Make sure that your partner is willing to commit to a service level that doesn't embarrass you or annoy your customers.

✦ **Scalability:** As you grow, your outsourcing partner must be able to grow with you. After all, you're turning to your partner to smoothly handle a part of your business so that you can expand the operation. If the company is struggling to keep up the pace of your business, you run the risk of your whole operation falling apart.

✦ **Experience:** Your outsourcing partner's management team needs to have the right experience in the right areas to lead that company. You're paying for experience, so make sure that team members are well versed in controlling

 • Back-end computer systems

 • Customer service

 • Inventory management

 • Logistics

✦ **Subject matter knowledge:** A product is a product is a product. It helps, though, to find a partner that can understand your specific product line, whether it's computer chips or dried fruit. See whether this partner has ever handled an account similar to yours and understands some of the nuances of your product line, to better anticipate any problems or questions that might arise.

Operating with an outsourced fulfillment house

When you're ready to start working with a fulfillment house, don't just sign the lowest-price contract and begin transferring inventory to it. You need to talk about how your relationship will work, what expectations you have for the company, and — believe it or not — what expectations it has of you. After all, even though you might have hired the fulfillment house to do "all the work," you, as the client, still need to provide these items:

✦ **Inventory:** Most fulfillment houses take on your inventory and warehouse it at their locations. Decide how much inventory to transfer, when to do it, and when and how replacement inventory should funnel in. Make sure that you carefully assess your inventory before it leaves your business, and double-check the inventory list when it arrives. Some fulfillment companies provide the trucks and labor to move inventory; others need you to make the arrangements.

✦ **Order information:** When orders come in, find a reliable and automated way to move that order information over to your fulfillment house. Depending on how you capture orders and which computer systems your fulfillment house uses, you can transfer orders as they occur or as a group of orders every day (in a *daily batch*). In some cases, you can have the fulfillment company operate the order-collection part of your business so that the order goes directly from the customers' computer screens to the company's databases.

If the fulfillment house is taking your orders, make sure that you receive a detailed report containing all customer data and order information. After all, customer orders are the building blocks for a customer list that helps your business thrive.

✦ **Payment:** Fulfillment houses don't pack and ship your orders out of the goodness of their hearts, so they need to get paid. You have several options for handling this cost:

• Build the extra cost into the shipping amount of your orders, and have that money transferred each time the company fills an order.

• Instead of transferring money each time an order is filled, have the company invoice you for a couple of months' worth of orders as a reserve or retainer. (You may be required to pay a reserve amount anyway to cover initial orders.) As you see the costs accumulate, you should begin to estimate the monthly cost better and can arrange payments that better fit the cash flow of your company.

• If the company is taking your orders and payment, it can keep its portion of the shipping amount and pay you for the goods it ships out.

After a certain length of time, you should receive a report detailing the activity your fulfillment house has performed. Never just file the report without looking it over. This report gives you a revealing look at the flow of your business and shows you how products are moving out the door. If you're concerned about the quality of the fulfillment house's work, compare the ship dates of those orders to the times you received them, and calculate how quickly this company is processing your business orders.

As your inventory level goes down at the fulfillment house, you need to have an event that triggers the transfer of more inventory. This *inventory replenishment level* is the point at which the inventory on hand is projected to drop to zero before the next delivery from your business would usually occur. Many fulfillment houses can help you calculate this number because they use sophisticated computer tracking systems that monitor shipment levels and predict how long it takes to ship all inventory in their possession. They usually factor in some time to cover unexpected delays in inventory transfers or unusual bumps in your orders. When you negotiate this cushion of products with your fulfillment house, choose a level that keeps orders flowing but doesn't back up the warehouse.

If your fulfillment provider is far away from the location of your products, calculate the cost of transferring inventory versus storing that inventory at the warehouse. Reducing a long, expensive inventory transfer by one per year can save you more money than the storage fees you pay at a warehouse.

Assessing the quality of the fulfillment work

When you get a sense of the quantity of work that your fulfillment partner is performing, look at the quality of its work also. Most important, determine whether your customers are happy with the packages they receive. Were the items well packed? Did packaging materials withstand the pressures of being shipped cross-country? Did your customers receive their orders in a reasonable amount of time?

The easiest way to find this information is to provide a phone number that your customers can call to report any problems. In some cases, the fulfillment house can also be your customer service partner. This way, if a problem with a customer's order occurs, a fulfillment person can go into your inventory on-site, pull a replacement set of products, ship it immediately, and let the customer know that the replacement is on its way. Make sure that you receive a monthly report of any customer service calls, and see whether that number goes up or down.

You can also go one step further: Rather than wait to hear whether a problem has occurred, reach out and ask your customers in the form of a survey. You don't want to bother them too much, but sometimes a simple survey packaged into each order can elicit some helpful feedback. Give prizes (such as gift certificates) or guaranteed discounts (such as free shipping on future orders) to customers who respond. You can partner with a company (for example, Shopzilla; see Figure 7-2) that coordinates online surveys of customers and gives you the results. This way, you can uncover any problems before they get out of control.

Figure 7-2: Hire a company such as Shopzilla to coordinate surveys of your customers.

If you notice a problem, talk to your fulfillment partner. Be direct, not confrontational. Find out the cause of the problem, see whether it can be fixed, and inquire about how your partner will ensure that it doesn't happen again. You can never prevent all problems, but you can help make sure that they don't happen as often.

Shaping Up and Shipping Out

The immediate gratification that customers feel when they order something from your business applies also to the fulfillment of those orders. Customers want to hold a product in their hands as soon as possible, and some customers are willing to pay even more to receive their order faster. Customers often have a favorite shipping carrier, or a carrier that they don't want you to use.

When those same people hear the term *shipping and handling,* they usually envision you performing these basic steps:

1. Pull an item off the shelf.

2. Put that item and a packing slip or invoice in the box.

3. Add packing material to fill up any empty space in the box.

4. Seal the box with tape.

5. Put the customer's name and address, and your business return address, on top of the box.

6. Ship the box.

Even though these steps demonstrate the basic flow of the shipping process, you can make it happen in many ways. If you're handling the shipment of your business orders, you can take advantage of some existing systems to make your life easier.

Giving your customers shipping options

In the end, the best way to satisfy both your business goals and the customer's shopping goals is to offer multiple shipping options to your customers.

Giving customers options can mean that you offer a variety in

+ **Shipping carriers:** You're willing to ship something by using FedEx, UPS, or the U.S. Postal Service.

+ **Shipping methods:** If your only carrier is FedEx, for example, customers can pay for Next Day Air, 2-Day Air, or Ground (with an average delivery time of one or two weeks).

+ **Order mixing:** A customer who orders multiple items can choose which items get which type of shipping. For example, a customer who orders a heavy computer system and a light book about computers can have the book delivered to start reading the next day, and have the heavy computer system delivered by ground in two weeks.

When you offer customers these options, you (as either an in-house or outsourced business) have to be ready to use each service whenever it's needed. You have to know the common rates and link to their websites to find updated pricing quotes based on different weights and sizes. You also have to update your shopping cart with these different options so that customers can pick and choose.

The rewards of these efforts are best expressed in terms of customer satisfaction. Giving your customers shipping choices is like giving them product choices; they feel more in control of the shopping experience and that your business is willing to cater to them. Often, an online business charges a flat fee for the lowest shipping rate and slowest delivery service. Although that strategy might work for some customers, you're missing the customers who need items immediately or by a guaranteed date.

The best example of the power of multiple shipping options is Amazon. To spur sales, it offers free shipping if you spend at least $35 on an order, and it ships items by U.S. Postal Service Ground Mail. However, customers can specify all or part of their orders to be sent a certain way, and they can pay the appropriate rate for faster shipping, such as Next Day Air or 2nd Day Air.

Setting up accounts with carriers

Two truths apply to shipping companies:

+ They always seem to break even the most carefully packed items.

+ They're always competing for your business.

The amount of gross revenue generated by shipping online orders has become a primary means of producing revenue. Therefore, carriers are fighting to keep customers by virtue of their service — and adding new features and adjusting prices whenever necessary to succeed.

Because the shipping companies' goal is to maximize revenue, they cater to higher-volume customers. They're usually online businesses, like yours, that have a number of orders to be shipped each day, week, or month. Online businesses that are setting up accounts with one or more carriers are finding, therefore, that they have some negotiating power for better rates or more services.

To sign up for a business account, choose one of these methods:

+ Contact the company by phone and work with a sales representative to set up your account.

+ Go to a shipping company's website and look for a Business Accounts link for the appropriate forms to fill out.

+ Go directly to a shipping company's office and ask to speak to a representative to set up an account.

When you start to talk to these companies, they ask you a number of questions to gauge your level of shipping. Determine your answers to the following questions before you start calling:

+ How many packages do you expect to ship in a month? How many do you send in an average week? What are your high and low numbers for a week?

+ What size and weight are the packages you typically send?

+ Are your customers mostly in the United States, or do you send a mix of domestic and international packages?

+ What percentage of orders do you ship by using an air option, such as Next Day, 2nd Day, or 3 Day? What percentage do you send by ground?

If you're setting up your shipping system from scratch, be sure to tell the company that you're providing estimates based on your initial research and by talking to fellow business owners in your field. Although you aren't bound by these numbers, the company needs an estimate to be able to set up your account.

When you start reviewing these details with the company, ask about rates and price breaks for certain shipping levels. Find out whether your current level is close to a certain price tier for shipping, and see whether you can raise your order shipments to meet that new level to save money for your business. Meeting a goal is easier if you can aim for a measurable number.

An account with a shipping company is typically free of monthly charges, unless you add a special service. The company keeps a payment method on file so that you can accrue shipping charges and make one monthly payment. That way, you're not always paying out when you want to ship a package. Your shipping department then runs much more smoothly and you qualify for corporate rates.

After you sign up for an account with a shipping carrier, always remember to review your monthly bill. Never assume that the carrier automatically screens your bill or lets you know when you've been overcharged.

Creating online postage and labels

One of the best developments in Internet technology over the years (especially if you're in the fulfillment field) is being able to print postage from your computer and create your own shipping labels. Although you can still stand in line at the post office, now you can prepare packages at home or at your business and drop off addressed packages with your carrier.

If you need to buy postage for various sizes of letters or packages, you can print postage by the package or join a service such as Endicia (see Figure 7-3) and pay a monthly fee to print all the postage you need. You sign up for an account and provide a credit card number. When you print postage, these services charge your account and send to your printer a special coded label that acts as your stamp. Every month, you pay for only the stamps you print.

Here are some of these services:

✦ **Endicia:** www.endicia.com

✦ **Pitney Bowes:** www.pb.com

✦ **Stamps.com:** www.stamps.com

✦ **USPS Click-N-Ship:** cns.usps.com/labelInformation.shtml

For example, rather than print the stamps for a customer's order, you print a prepaid label that has all the customer's address information, your return address, and the postage paid. You stick this label at the top of the package and hand off the package to the shipping company. Every month, your account is charged for the shipping costs of all the labels you prepared.

Figure 7-3:
Endicia helps you print your own postage and labels.

Virtually every big shipping company can now generate these shipping labels from their websites, including FedEx, UPS, and the U.S. Postal Service. You simply log in to a company's website with your account number and then start specifying customer addresses and the weights and dimensions of each order.

> **TIP** If you're using these online shipping tools to create labels, invest in an accurate scale that measures as close to the ounce as possible. Make sure that the scale's capacity can accommodate a large order. If you're selling only light items, such as stamps and coins, a scale that measures by the ounce, up to 25 pounds, is fine. If you sell electronics and computers, buy a scale that can measure up to 150 to 300 pounds instead.

Having items picked up for delivery

After you do all the work to prepare your packages, they still have to move from you to your shipping company. In the past, you had to load your car or company van, drive down to the shipping company's office, fight for parking, and then stand in line to unload your vehicle.

Almost all the big shipping companies now come to you to get your items:

✦ **U.S. Postal Service:** If you print your shipping labels in advance and pay for your postage online, a postal employee can pick up the item on her normal route. When you schedule a pickup (shown in Figure 7-4), someone picks up all your Express Mail and Priority Mail packages in a two-hour period that you specify.

Figure 7-4: Schedule your mail carrier to pick up your packages whenever you want.

✦ **Other carriers:** Carriers such as UPS and FedEx work more on demand. If you're receiving a package from one of these carriers, you can hand off your completed packages when the driver arrives, but you have to know that the shipment is coming. For business accounts, these carriers typically offer weekly or daily pickup, based on the needs of your business. If you have a low-volume account, you're charged for this feature, and the rates vary. Depending on how many orders per month you can guarantee, however, one item you can request during your account setup is a free daily pickup. Ask your shipping company for more details.

If you're printing labels online for a given company, you can usually ask for a pickup when you create the label.

Shipping international orders

Customers around the world are communicating with each other instantaneously by using the Internet, fax and data lines, and cellphones. These methods have allowed online businesses to reach millions of new potential customers. Shipping companies have responded by beefing up their international shipping options, which gives you more options for servicing your customers.

**Book IV
Chapter 7**

Fulfilling Expectations and Orders

The only shipper that reaches most countries in the world is the U.S. Postal Service. The U.S. Postal Service offers air-mail service, which can take at least a week to reach its destination country. Although the USPS offers insurance for packages to most countries, it typically doesn't provide any tracking capability. The only service it offers that guarantees a tracking number and insurance is its Global Express Mail service, which is expensive.

To see a list of countries and services that the USPS delivers to internationally, go to pe.usps.com/text/imm/immctry.htm.

If you want to use UPS, FedEx, or other carriers such as DHL to ship packages, you have to send them by some form of air mail, which can be quite expensive for heavy items. Although these services automatically issue tracking numbers, in some cases their tracking capabilities end when the packages enter their destination countries. Each country also places specific limits on package weight and dimensions. Consult each company's website for specific information about country-specific limits.

In all cases, you're required to fill out a customs form to document the following information about an item:

✦ The country of origin

✦ The quantity

✦ An item description

✦ The value of each product in the package

Shippers such as UPS and FedEx incorporate the customs form information into the label-creation process so that when you create your label, the appropriate shipping documents are created alongside it. The USPS uses two customs forms:

✦ **Form 2976:** For packages that weigh fewer than 4 pounds (see Figure 7-5) and have no insurance

✦ **Form 2976-A:** For packages that weigh more than 4 pounds or have insurance

You can fill out USPS customs forms online by going to www.usps.com/send/customs-forms.htm.

In some cases, the destination country requires you to complete a certificate of origin or a signed affidavit that certifies the origin country of an exported item. Some countries also require that you

✦ Have your goods inspected by an independent, third-party organization

✦ Include a certificate of inspection with your label and customs forms

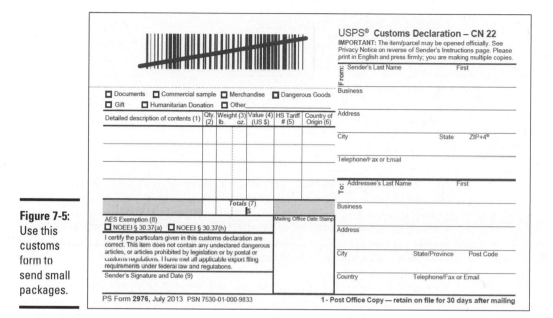

Figure 7-5:
Use this customs form to send small packages.

For more detailed information on how to send large shipments overseas, consult the International Chamber of Commerce website (www.iccwbo.org).

For smaller shipments that you send directly to customers, you typically need to classify your shipment in one of four categories:

✦ **Commercial sample:** Samples or free product trials

✦ **Documents:** Catalogs and paperwork

✦ **Gift:** Products that customers didn't pay for

✦ **Other:** Most other types of shipments

An international customer might ask you to classify a package as a gift and specify a lower amount for the value. Be aware that you can insure a package for only the value you state and that falsifying a customs document can result in fines and penalties levied against you and your customer.

Maintaining the Back End

As you expand your business, keep track of how your fulfillment operation works so that it can grow with your business. Investing in good recordkeeping enables you to not only provide customers with tracking numbers and copies of invoices but also see what's working and what's not so that you can make necessary improvements.

Deciding on a database

You have several choices for storing your business information. Many online businesses create one or more databases to store these types of data:

✦ Customer information

✦ Order information

✦ Payment information

✦ Product information

Sometimes a business owner chooses a database solely because it can "talk to" the shopping cart or website software that the business uses. At other times, the database was installed first and the business owner wants to ensure that all other products can communicate with it. Other small-business owners organize their information by using spreadsheets in a financial program such as Microsoft Excel.

The key for you is that your database — in whatever form — needs to be accessible and searchable. You and your employees need to be able to see your data easily. You use your database to answer questions about your business (such as "How many customers do we have?" or "Which orders are ready for shipment?" or "Who still owes us money?") and to store information about how your business is doing financially.

Your order-information database should list not only the products that someone ordered but also these items:

✦ Carrier name

✦ Internet link, if possible, to monitor the shipment

✦ Invoice number

✦ Order-packing date

✦ Shipment date

✦ Tracking number

As you're setting up your business, here are some questions to help you determine which database program to use:

✦ Is a database program in your budget?

✦ Which programs work well with your other software systems, such as your web server or electronic shopping cart?

✦ How many people need access to the database? Are all the people in one building (or on one internal computer network), or are they spread out around the world?

✦ Which software programs do you have access to?

Using handheld scanners and bar codes

Inventory tracking is a process that even a small online business can afford to implement. You don't have to be Walmart or Home Depot to use technology to help organize your inventory. You just have to spend some time setting up the equipment and codes to make it work. You can use handheld scanners (or newer smartphones that support the RedLaser app, such as the Apple iPhone) to read bar codes identified on your products to help keep track of your overall product inventory.

Here's how inventory tracking works:

1. **Make sure that each individual product for resale has some sort of bar code on its box.**

   The bar code can be either the Universal Product Code (UPC) that comes with the product or one you provide by using an inventory-management program.

2. **Decide where in your warehouse or inventory area you want to store the product.**

3. **Scan a special bar code that represents the shelf or rack number.**

   Use a handheld scanner (like the ones used in grocery stores or by delivery personnel) or a smartphone equipped with the RedLaser app and an inventory app.

4. **Scan the bar code of the product.**

5. **Sync your scanner and inventory-management software.**

Syncing occurs when two sources of information "talk" to each other electronically to ensure that both sources have the same up-to-date information.

Developing a shelving inventory system

Many online businesses buy industrial-strength racks and shelving systems for organizing their products. You can find these systems at most hardware stores, such as Home Depot and Lowes, for a couple of hundred dollars apiece (with some assembly required). After you buy and set up these racks, label each shelf properly and start storing your products on these shelves. Then, whenever you need a product, you can just walk over to your shelves and look to find the product you need. If you keep similar items together, locating and retrieving the product you need is that much easier.

Some popular ways of organizing your shelves involve grouping items by category, size, or color on one shelf or in one area. Keep different items that look similar far away from each other so that you don't mistakenly grab the wrong item for order fulfillment.

Feeding orders into the shipping department

You might think that when you receive an online order, red lights should start flashing and sirens should sound to announce its arrival. Although that level of drama isn't necessary, you need to make sure that your orders are being properly funneled to your shipping area so that they're packaged and sent in a reasonable length of time. You can

✦ **Print orders from a printer automatically.** Then, whoever is in charge of fulfillment can grab the printout and start pulling the inventory.

✦ **Print manifests or invoices (known as *pick-and-pull sheets*) from the preceding day's orders.** Items are picked off the shelves in your warehouse area and pulled into the packing area.

If you're outsourcing your fulfillment operation, you can specify that customers receive an e-mail every time they place an order. A duplicate of that e-mail is sent to a specific e-mail account for new orders at the fulfillment house, and the employees monitor and print an order every time an e-mail is received or print a batch of e-mail at certain times during the day.

After an order is prepared and packed, the last pieces of information to capture on the back end are the package shipment date and tracking number. If you're using online postage creation tools, that information is already captured. If you're creating your own postage and labels, be sure to keep a copy of every tracking number and shipping date and then feed that information into your order database.

Book V
Internet Security

Visit www.dummies.com/extras/startinganonlinebusinessaio to discover three easy methods that you and your employees can follow to increase the online security of your business.

Contents at a Glance

Chapter 1: Understanding Security and Your Risks

In This Chapter

✔ Recognizing your liability

✔ Establishing written guidelines

✔ Setting up secure ordering

✔ Gaining third-party approval

*N*early 3 million Internet-related crime complaints have been received by the Internet Crime Complaint Center (IC3), since its founding in 2000. The organization received more than 289,000 complaints in 2012 alone — and over $525 million in reported financial losses from consumers. Although the number of cyber-related complaints was below 300,000 for the first time in four years, the dollar loss increased by almost 10 percent. The IC3 is a join effort with the Federal Bureau of Investigations (FBI) and the National White Collar Crime Center, established to track cybercrime.

As both a consumer and an e-commerce merchant, you are vulnerable to becoming a victim of cybercrime. Each year the IC3 receives a large number of complaints involving identity theft and nondelivery of payment or merchandise, including credit card charge backs. Complaints from both buyers and sellers continue to grow for online auction sites (for example, eBay) and sites such as Craigslist. JP Morgan's 2012 Cyber Source Online Fraud Report estimates a total loss of $3.4 billion in Internet-related fraud, with merchants losing approximately 1 percent of their total online revenue to fraud.

None of these stats and online crime reports include more recent large-scale fraud affecting merchants such as Target (and an estimated 110 million customers) and Neiman Marcus (and an estimated 1 million customers). In each case, some type of malware or online breach was suspected in the compromise of customers' credit card data. Initial estimates put losses at nearly $4 billion for Target, alone. Any merchant (and their customers) is susceptible to cyber-related crime. The burden *always* falls on you, the online business owner, to provide a safe, secure shopping environment for your customers while protecting both your customers and yourself from potential financial losses.

In this chapter, we talk about what you can do to keep your customers as safe as possible so that they continue shopping with you.

Legal Responsibility: The Merchant and the Customer

As the owner of your business, you're responsible for protecting your customers. With identity theft and fraud continuing to rise at alarming rates, credit card companies and regulatory agencies are saddling e-commerce merchants with the bill (including shipping fees and the costs of the goods). You can prevent your customers from being victims of identify theft and fraud — and stay in business yourself — by being vigilant about the credit card payments you accept and keeping your customers' information as private as possible.

Avoiding charge backs

Most of the time, fraud comes in the form of *charge backs*. Customers using credit cards and other online forms of payments (that access credit cards and bank accounts) can request that charges be removed. The Fair Credit Billing Act (FCBA) allows consumers to dispute purchases.

A customer can request that a charge be removed for two reasons:

✦ The card is stolen or otherwise used without the legal cardholder's permission.

✦ The customer doesn't believe that you fulfilled your obligation in delivering the product. (You either didn't deliver it or delivered a different product from what you promised.) Mistakenly delivering an incorrect product isn't a true case of fraud, but it does lead to charge backs. It becomes fraud if you did indeed ship the correct product but the customer insists that you did not.

Unfortunately, charge backs happen frequently, and proving a customer wrong is difficult — and expensive — for an online business. LexisNexis reports that online retailers lose $279 for every $100 in fraud, due in part to charge backs and their related fees and costs. Because you simply don't have the same ability to authenticate or verify a cardholder's identification as you do in a bricks-and-mortar environment, you get stuck with the cost of the merchandise, the shipping fees (possibly), and the processing fee that your credit card vendor charges for every transaction. Those amounts, as estimated by LexisNexis, add up quickly.

Fortunately, you can minimize your risk of excessive charge backs. To avoid them, use some basic security strategies for your site:

✦ **Verify the cardholder's address.** Credit card merchants offer an address verification service (AVS) that compares the billing address a customer provides with the cardholder's name. You're notified immediately if the billing address and name don't match the information associated with the account. You can also make this comparison manually if AVS protection isn't included with your online merchant account.

✦ **Get the card verification value.** When you're completing an order from a customer, make sure to ask for the card verification value (CVV2). Because this set of numbers appears only on the customer's credit card, the customer must have physical access to the card to see the numbers. This set of numbers appears as four digits on the front of an American Express card or as three digits on the back of a Visa, MasterCard, or Discover card.

✦ **Process only approved transactions.** If a card is declined for any reason, don't process it. Although this advice seems obvious, you might be tempted to believe that the message is a mistake and try to process the order anyway.

✦ **Scrutinize e-mail addresses.** Always ask for a customer's e-mail address at the time of purchase. If the address looks suspicious, don't hesitate to call the customer and verify the order.

✦ **Be wary of excessive orders.** Buyers using stolen or compromised credit cards sometimes purchase extremely large orders or purchase several units of the same item. Call the number on the billing address to verify unusual orders.

✦ **Maintain good records.** Keep copies of an online order transaction, verification e-mails, and records of any other communication you might have with the customer.

✦ **Keep your end of the bargain.** If you experience a delay in shipping the product or the product is out of stock, notify the customer immediately and do not make any charges until the product ships.

✦ **Clearly post your return policy.** Preventing or fighting a charge back is tough if you're not clear about your return and shipping policies. Having this information readily available to customers makes it difficult for customers to use the lack of information or lack of a formal policy as a reason to decline a payment to you.

✦ **Follow merchant-issued policies.** Whether you use PayPal or a credit card vendor to process customer transactions, be aware of its charge back policy. Always make sure that you're following the vendor's recommendations for the prevention and dispute of charge backs.

You can dispute any charge back by contacting your credit card vendor directly. Before calling, be prepared to show how you complied with verifying the card's authenticity at the time of purchase. Hang in there because you might have to wait several months for a claim to be settled.

Keeping your customer information secure

Charge backs aren't the only issue you have to worry about with online purchases. The second part of your security obligation to your customers is proving that you consistently handle their private information with the utmost care. Specifically, customers want to know how you collect and store sensitive data, including credit card numbers, Social Security numbers, birthdates, and even phone numbers.

Somewhere on your website (usually in a privacy or security policy), you should explain how and why you collect and save customer information. Here are the questions your customers want answered about how you hold on to their data:

✦ Do you see customers' credit card numbers before they're processed?

✦ Are credit cards processed in real time, which means that you might have access to only the last four digits of an account? Or are they processed manually, which means that you see and have access to the full account number?

✦ How many people have access to the information?

✦ How are customer files stored? Are they recorded only as electronic files or printed for filing and storage?

✦ What precautions do you take to keep data secure? Are paper files locked away? Do you have a firewall or other security layers to protect electronic files?

✦ Are your computers password protected? Who has access to them?

✦ If you assign passwords to customer data, how are they maintained and secured?

The Federal Trade Commission and other agencies offer information to help your business comply with e-commerce policies. You can access the information from its website, shown in Figure 1-1, at www.ftc.gov.

As part of the Payment Card Industry Data Security Standard, an alliance of the leading credit card institutions created a policy designed to provide some level of compliance with how your customers' personal data is processed and stored on your site. Depending on the number of online transactions you process each year, compliance can be either mandatory or self regulated (if you have fewer than 20,000 transactions per year). As with other government agency policies, failing to comply with this enforceable standard can cost you a fine of as much as half a million dollars. Book II, Chapter 1 covers this standard.

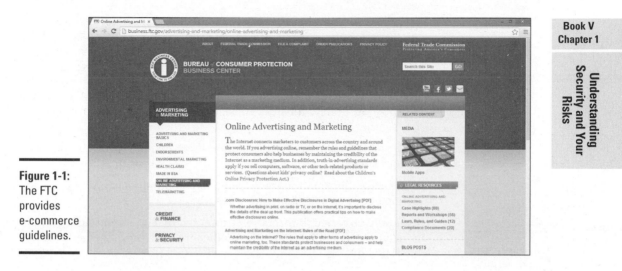

Figure 1-1:
The FTC
provides
e-commerce
guidelines.

Fortunately, certain organizations are dedicated to helping protect you and your customers from all types of online fraud. Check out these two membership-based groups:

✦ **Merchant Risk Council (www.merchantriskcouncil.org):** Provides access to articles, tools, and vendors that help you secure your site. Membership fees start at $500 per year for online businesses with annual revenues of $10 million to $75 million. The fee covers membership for two people.

✦ **Merchant 911 (www.merchant911.org):** Educates small, online merchants about credit card fraud protection. Membership is free and the organization offers information on everything from credit card fraud prevention to PCI (Payment Card Industry) compliance and security.

Defining Your Privacy Policy

When you're tackling security concerns, you have two goals as an online merchant: Do everything possible to make your site secure and safe for both you and your customers, and promote buyer confidence by letting visitors know that you take all necessary precautions to keep the online shopping experience safe.

One of the best ways to stay ahead of the security game is by being clear about your online policies. Also, regulatory agencies might want confirmation that you're looking out for your customers' best interests. Here are two types of policies you can institute:

✦ **Security:** A security policy should explain what protection is in place when you're processing customers' orders. You want to educate visitors on how information is collected, stored, and protected.

✦ **Privacy:** This type of policy was once best known for letting customers know whether their e-mail addresses were shared with or sold to third parties. Privacy policies are now much more inclusive: They include details on which information is collected and why; how customers can update, change, or delete stored information; and how they can notify you if they believe that their information has been breached. When you develop your policy, consider these three categories, which can be areas of concern:

  • *Personally identifiable:* Information that connects your customer to your site

  • *Sensitive:* Information that's private to customers, such as transaction histories or e-mail addresses

  • *Legally protected:* Information protected by law, including credit card numbers, financial accounts, medical records, and even education-related details

Privacy and security policies are the two types most prevalent to your site. Don't forget that online fraud and charge backs are always at issue, too. You need to include or refer to other types of policies, especially when a customer makes a purchase. Don't hesitate to direct buyers to policies that spell out conditions relating to shipping, back orders, returns, and even customer disputes. (Book I, Chapter 5 covers these policies in depth.)

Keeping Your Website Secure

No matter how much online security and privacy policies are heightened, buyers are still uncertain about their online security and privacy. Research shows that people are hesitant to give out personal information or credit card numbers to websites, even though e-commerce has become accepted as a viable alternative to storefront shopping. The risk of online fraud and identity theft are two big factors that make consumers skeptical, but lots of other issues keep online shoppers frustrated. Figure 1-2 shows a snapshot of the top complaints for online shoppers in 2012, according to the Federal Trade Commission (FTC). You probably aren't surprised to see that the figure includes things such as never receiving merchandise, not having refunds honored, and other misrepresentations by online merchants.

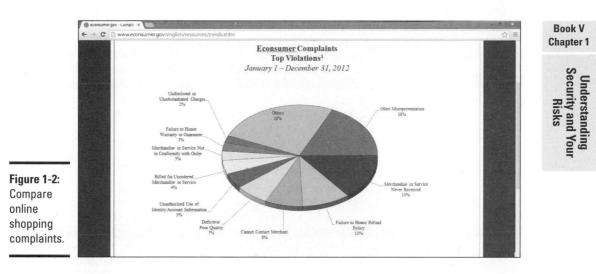

Figure 1-2:
Compare online shopping complaints.

The FTC also keeps track of which online products or industries warrant the most complaints, as shown in Figure 1-3. Such products as shop-at-a-home or catalog sales account for 17 percent, while Internet auctions add up to only 5 percent. As you can see, the largest source of complaints (34 percent) falls into the Others category. Although these complaints don't seem to keep everyone from buying, they provide another reason to go out of your way to make your site secure. One of the easiest and, possibly, most expected ways to do this is by using Secure Sockets Layer (SSL) certificates.

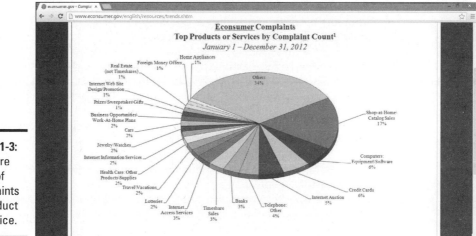

Figure 1-3:
Compare types of complaints by product or service.

SSL is a protocol, or method of communication, for scrambling information as it travels across the Internet. Any type of data, whether it's a medical record or credit card number, can be encoded so that only the authorized sender and receiver can view it. Without this protocol, the sending process would be similar to stuffing all your private information into a clear plastic bag, sealing it, and passing it around a crowded room. Even though the bag is tightly closed, anyone who has access to it can see everything inside.

Having an SSL certificate for your website lets customers know that their confidential information is protected when they send it over the Internet for you to process.

Using SSL is just a matter of licensing the right to use the protocol through an approved vendor and having it installed on your server. You can get a certificate directly from a private company, such as Symantec (previously VeriSign), or (usually) from your web hosting or domain registration company. Some e-commerce and shopping cart providers now offer basic SSL certificates for free as part of their monthly or annual service plans. If buying one directly, prices vary greatly. Some are advertised for less than $10, but a more typical range is $50 to more than $1,500 annually. The difference in price depends on the type of certificate you choose and the level of validation attached to it. For instance, the SSL certificate on the low end of the range may validate only your site's domain name. The more expensive certificates often provide financial warranties of varying amounts and validate these factors:

✦ Domain name registration

✦ Business owner's identity

✦ Company identity and address (possibly requiring copies of business licenses and incorporation documents)

The more expensive SSL certificates also claim to provide a higher level of encryption. The industry standard is 128-bit encryption, and an advanced 256-bit version is available. A higher level of encryption just makes compromising (or hacking) data a little more difficult — but recent attacks, such as from the Heartbleed bug, have shown almost every level to be vulnerable. Still, it's best to have some protection, rather than none at all.

If you're not certain what level of encryption you need for your SSL certificate, or how those levels may affect your customers when they visit your site, check out the great resource page on the Symantec website that discusses these SSL certificate related questions, and more: www.symantec.com/verisign/ssl-certificates.

After you purchase your SSL certificate, you're given instructions on how to activate it on your site's server. However, in many cases, your web hosting company or a professional website developer can install the encryption certificate for you.

If you use an e-commerce–enabled server that's shared by others or you sign up for a storefront, you might not have to purchase an individual SSL certificate. Some companies provide encryption service to all their customers by using a single server.

Displaying Seals of Approval

When most people shop at a store online, they look for signs that the business is legitimate — particularly if it's new or located in a different city or if they're just not familiar with it. Offline, people look for a valid business license hanging behind the counter or a local Chamber of Commerce sign.

The online equivalent of the local Chamber of Commerce is a seal of approval from one or more third-party organizations. Customers feel safer shopping online with you when you post a seal of approval on your site. Table 1-1 lists organizations that provide seals. Although these seals aren't requirements, they definitely boost buyer confidence.

Table 1-1   Organizations Providing Reliability and Privacy Seals

Organization	Seal Type	Reliability	Fees
BBB www.bbb.org	BBB Accredited	Member of Better Business Bureau; in business one year	Membership fee; licensing fee based on size of company
Guardian eCommerce www.guardianecommerce.net	Safe Site or Approved Site	SSL certificate and other site information submitted for review	Annual fee of $19.99
TRUSTe www.truste.com	TRUSTed certifications for websites, apps, cloud, downloads, and more	Pass site audit	Annual fee

You can apply for the following types of seals:

✦ **Reliability:** Posting this type of seal on your site confirms that its sponsoring companies have verified information about your business. Additionally, it confirms that you agree to abide by certain online advertising and operating standards and dispute-resolution guidelines. Often, part of the qualifying process for the seal requires that you be in business for a certain length of time (usually, a minimum of a year).

✦ **Privacy:** You're eligible to display a privacy seal on your site if you meet stringent guidelines. You usually have to create, post, and adhere to a privacy policy, along with other industry standard recommendations. The organization issuing the seal is likely to conduct a security and privacy assessment on your site before giving you the seal.

✦ **Kids' privacy:** The Children's Online Privacy Protection Act (COPPA) hands out a seal of its own. Check out Book X, Chapter 2 for more information.

Because application and licensing fees can range from slightly less than a hundred dollars to several hundred dollars for each seal, you might not be prepared to apply for them when you're just starting your business.

Chapter 2: Developing a Security Plan

In This Chapter

↳ Forging a realistic plan

↳ Making an investment in security

↳ Tapping into the experts

You've heard the drill: Plan, plan, plan! The first step in protecting your business from an unwanted computer invasion or an IT catastrophe is developing a plan. Your plan doesn't have to be complicated or expensive. However, you do need to give your security strategy more than a passing thought. In fact, put your plan on paper so that you and your employees have a written plan of action.

The fun of thwarting a cybercrook doesn't stop here, though. After all, what good is a plan if you don't implement it? You also have to invest in a decent online security system (or two) and maybe even bring in a few professionals to ensure that you're properly prepared. If these upfront considerations are ones you've thought about — but haven't gotten around to accomplishing — this chapter has your name on it.

Making a Plan

As Paul Simon says in his classic song "50 Ways to Leave Your Lover," it's time to "Make a new plan, Stan." Only in this case, it's time to find 50 ways to leave your computer protected.

Where do you start? Whether you rework an old plan or build one from scratch, the six major components to an effective security plan are

+ Policies and procedures

+ Inventory and skills assessments

+ Risk analysis

+ Existing security measures

+ Action plan

+ Resources and follow-up

In the following sections, we guide you through the details to include in each of these components for your plan.

Policies and procedures

If you're part of a larger online business, you might already have a book of policies and procedures carefully spelled out, tightly bound, and neatly filed away in every employee's desk. The reality for a smaller online company, though, is that you probably haven't had time to think about formal procedures. If you're working solo, you might still be skeptical about needing to write these types of policies.

As an online business owner, the purpose of your security plan is to protect both you and your customers. By establishing and implementing written security policies, you reduce the risk of overlooking holes or flaws in the plan.

Honestly, the amount of information that has been published about how to write a security policy could fill a small room. No wonder the task of writing one has become cumbersome. However, in a smaller company, you can concentrate on the basics.

Here's a baseline rule for establishing your security policies: The magnitude of how much policy you need should fit the breadth of your organization and the depth of the risk factor you want to protect.

In other words, IBM might require several hundred policies whereas you might need only five policies. At the end of the day, if either you or IBM suffers a substantial security breach because a policy wasn't effectively in place, you're both in the same boat. And we don't mean in a good way.

With that in mind, follow these steps to create your own policies (however many you might need):

1. **Write your overall goals or objectives for your security policy.**

   Break down the big-picture goal of protecting your online business into a few smaller chunks of information or goals. Maybe you're more concerned with outside threats or establishing guidelines for employees. Or you might be most interested in protecting yourself legally and need written policies in place to set precedents.

2. **Create a list of areas in your organization that require protection.**

   After each item, make a notation of which ones are better served by the implementation of a formal policy. Use the checklist in Table 2-1 as a guide to the areas that are open to possible security risks.

Table 2-1	Security Coverage Checklist	
Security Risk	*Currently Secured*	*Requires Formal Policy*
Desktop computers	❏ Yes ❏ No	❏ Yes ❏ No
Laptop computers	❏ Yes ❏ No	❏ Yes ❏ No
Employee devices	❏ Yes ❏ No	❏ Yes ❏ No
Mobile devices	❏ Yes ❏ No	❏ Yes ❏ No
E-mail	❏ Yes ❏ No	❏ Yes ❏ No
Bank or financial information	❏ Yes ❏ No	❏ Yes ❏ No
Server	❏ Yes ❏ No	❏ Yes ❏ No
Wireless network	❏ Yes ❏ No	❏ Yes ❏ No
Firewall	❏ Yes ❏ No	❏ Yes ❏ No
Cable modem/Internet connection	❏ Yes ❏ No	❏ Yes ❏ No
Software	❏ Yes ❏ No	❏ Yes ❏ No
Customer data and credit card numbers	❏ Yes ❏ No	❏ Yes ❏ No
Social media accounts	❏ Yes ❏ No	❏ Yes ❏ No
Passwords	❏ Yes ❏ No	❏ Yes ❏ No
Database	❏ Yes ❏ No	❏ Yes ❏ No
Cloud-based applications and services	❏ Yes ❏ No	❏ Yes ❏ No
Inventory	❏ Yes ❏ No	❏ Yes ❏ No
Products	❏ Yes ❏ No	❏ Yes ❏ No
Back-end system	❏ Yes ❏ No	❏ Yes ❏ No
Offices or other facilities	❏ Yes ❏ No	❏ Yes ❏ No
Other physical properties or facilities	❏ Yes ❏ No	❏ Yes ❏ No
Files or other miscellaneous	❏ Yes ❏ No	❏ Yes ❏ No
Intellectual property	❏ Yes ❏ No	❏ Yes ❏ No

3. **Determine the *scope* (number of policies) that is legitimately warranted for the size and need of your organization.**

In reviewing your list of goals in Step 2, you might find that it makes sense to combine several components into a single policy. Conversely, other areas might produce larger or more frequent risks and require a stand-alone policy.

4. **Starting with your first policy, write its purpose and provide an overview of its importance to the organization.**

   For instance, you might create a policy about who can access your primary e-mail account. Your goal might be to restrict usage to only designated personnel — and doing so is important so that confidential communications aren't compromised.

5. **Detail the scope of your policy.**

   Specify which employees or level of employees the policy applies to. Also indicate which locations, systems, and data are affected by the policy. Refer to your list in Step 2 to make sure that you include all areas that might be affected.

6. **Write the operational guidelines of the policy.**

   The guidelines are the cold, hard facts. Be specific about which actions and behaviors can and cannot happen under the policy.

7. **After the guidelines are in place, write a paragraph about how the policy should be implemented.**

   In this part of the policy, provide information such as how employees are to be notified of the policy as well as specific penalties for not enforcing the rules.

8. **Document the date when the policy was created.**

   Every time you update the policy, add the next revision date. Leave the earlier version dates so that you have a running history of the document.

9. **(Optional) Add details to the policy.**

   You might include a glossary of terms or cross-reference additional procedures and policies that might also intertwine with this one.

10. **Repeat Steps 4–9 for each policy.**

After you finish writing all your security policies, you're ready to place them in the front section of your written security plan.

Inventory and skills assessments

One helpful component for your overall plan is to create a catalog, or *inventory*, of your equipment and the information that you're protecting. Table 2-2 serves as an inventory assessment guide, and we tell you in this section how to fill it in.

Table 2-2	Equipment Inventory Assessment Guide					
	Description or MAC Address of Computer	*Registration*	*Username*	*Travels Off-Site? Y or N*	*Security Risk: High or Low*	*Other Information*
Hardware						
Software						
Peripheral compo-nents						
Servers						
Cloud-based applications						
Documents						

When you're filling in the guide, your final inventory list should capture the following information:

✦ **Hardware:** Record a complete list of your laptops and desktops, including supplemental information, such as their serial numbers and the names of people who use each machine. Also list any warranty information per machine. Denote which systems have DVD and other components. For laptops, note whether the equipment is carried off-site.

✦ **Software:** Log an inventory of your company's software. Include details such as user registration information, licensing restrictions (single or multiple user), and registration numbers. If possible, note which software is loaded on the computers.

✦ **Peripheral components:** This list might include data drives; printers; scanners; tablets, iPhone, Android, and other smartphones and mobile devices; handheld devices; portable memory storage devices; extra monitors or keyboards; networking equipment; and even plain old cellphones.

Employees frequently want to use their own smartphones and mobile devices for both personal and business use, which is referred to as the bring your own device (BYOD) trend. You should include BYOD policies and procedures as part of your overall risk analysis and planning.

Break out your inventory by each individual piece of equipment or software program. That way, you can compile serial numbers and registration numbers or other unique identifying factors for each piece.

✦ **Cloud-based applications:** Make an inventory of any cloud- or web-enabled programs and services that your business uses, whether for delivering customer surveys, printing online postage, managing customer relationships, or providing business phone service. Detail which computers maintain licenses for each application or have access to web-based solutions.

When creating an inventory of applications delivered over the Internet, don't overlook instant-messaging programs and music or video-related applications. You might not use them, but your employees probably have them installed. Increasingly, these programs are becoming an easy delivery method for viruses, worms, and other malicious activity. You want these programs accounted for in your inventory so that proper security measures can be applied.

✦ **Social media:** Although social media is not a tangible or hard asset, we recommend including a detailed log of all your business social media accounts as part of your inventory list. Social media accounts have increasingly proven to be vulnerable to security threats, especially if passwords are used across multiple accounts. As part of your inventory assessment, keep track of which platforms you use, associated passwords, and those in your organization who have access to the accounts.

✦ **Documents:** This group includes not only critical files but also your intellectual property, promotional materials stored on your computer, financial data, customer data (contracts and invoices), and current and archived e-mail messages.

After you complete this equipment assessment, turn your attention to a skills inventory. (You can add it to the bottom of your inventory assessment.) Compose a paragraph or a complete list of the security expertise that you and your employees have. You can include certifications or other applicable training, too. By conducting a skills assessment, you can see when you need to call in outside security consultants — or how much of that expertise you might need.

A skills inventory can further help you determine points of educational training needed for you and your staff so that you can develop more internal expertise.

Risk analysis

One of the most important pieces of your plan is the *risk analysis* portion, in which you identify possible security threats. This important exercise forces you to evaluate the factors that hold the most potential for harming your online business. Your first action is to make a list of all potential threats that can compromise your security. Classify these security occurrences, or *events,* under the following categories:

✦ **External threats:** Include any risk that originates outside your business. You typically have no control over these events (other than being prepared to combat them if they occur):

- *Viruses and worms:* Also group Trojan horses and other harmful programs in this category.

- *Malware:* Include any type of malicious software that can be unknowingly installed on your computer from an outside source, such as spam, adware, and spyware.

- *Phishing:* Add this popular method of tricking and defrauding employees to your analysis. A phishing scam is an e-mail that looks like it comes from a legitimate source but is from a fake company. This type of scam can add up to lots of lost dollars if an employee reveals sensitive data (credit card number, password, and more) to an online scammer.

- *Malicious intruders:* Consider any type of activity originating from another individual that's meant to harm you. Include hackers, former employees, competitors, and thieves. Don't forget that theft can occur on-site (at your place of business) or off-site (such as at airports and coffee houses). Comparatively, hackers steal intellectual property and data by way of an Internet connection. Hackers can also do damage by shutting down your network or your website.

- *Disasters:* Address floods, tornadoes, hurricanes, and fire as possible external risks.

✦ **Internal threats:** Although not always intentional, these incidents occur from within your own operations. Internal threats can do serious damage as well as expose your vulnerabilities:

- *Malicious intent:* Employees or other people might have somewhat unlimited access to your assets. Unfortunately, not everyone is as nice or honest as you want to believe. Consider the possibility that a serious — and intentional — breach of security can occur right under your nose.

- *Accidents and user error:* Think of any accidents or human errors that can occur. Coffee spills on laptop computers, accidentally deleted data, dropped monitors — the list is endless.

- *Failures:* Specifically, these failures are system failures. Whether your computer crashes, your software bombs, or your Internet connection or server goes down, these failures are all part of an unwanted security risk.

After you put on your doomsday hat and identify all possible threats that can take you down, go one step further and prioritize each one according to its level of risk. You can do this by using a hierarchical ranking system. Or you might prefer to assign a low, medium, or high risk value for each of your items.

Ranking your risks is a subjective process that requires you to be open-minded and honest in evaluating the security of your business. If you don't feel that you can be objective, consider bringing in outside help.

If you find that a risk analysis shows your business to be at a medium- to high-level risk for attacks, accidents, or failures, consider inviting a paid technology consultant to evaluate your business and offer solutions. The costs of improving your security will be paid back in the long run by reducing the odds of your losing data, damaging your reputation, and putting customer information at risk.

Existing security measures

Unless you're in the planning phases for a new business, you probably already implemented some level of security. Here's the appropriate place in the plan to specify which actions to take.

You want to describe firewalls, antivirus software, and other basic security measures that provide some level of protection. However, you can add any routine security-related systems or functions you conduct. For example, you should plan to

✦ Change passwords regularly

✦ Back up your data regularly

✦ Perform routine system maintenance and software updates

✦ Implement physical security measures, such as alarm systems or fire-proof safes

✦ Minimize access to servers and business-critical computers by storing them in a secure location, such as a controlled server room or lockable closet

No matter what, be honest. If the last time you backed up data was several months ago, don't include it as a security measure that you can check off your list.

Action plan

To some degree, you can consider the action plan the meat of your document. After all the assessments, inventories, and analysis, you're ready for a true plan of action.

Based on the information you collected (see the earlier sections of this chapter), you can readily spot your strengths and weaknesses in the realm of security. And now you can focus on what we like to refer to as your *points for improvement (PfI),* or the specific areas where you find weaknesses that should be corrected.

By concentrating on your PfI, you can create a step-by-step plan of action to beef up your security. In each step, be specific. Here are examples of some of the steps that you might include in your own plan of action:

+ Purchase and install external security locks for all laptops.

+ Turn on the Automatic Update feature on all desktop computers to activate a fixed schedule for installing all new software updates.

+ Purchase a password generator and choose quarterly dates for changing passwords.

+ Create a scheduled backup, specifically for customer data such as order historics.

Find an online service for an additional backup so that your data is stored off-site yet still readily accessible if your on-site files and backups are destroyed.

Your plan of action might include a couple dozen steps or only a few. You have a thorough action plan when all your PfI are accounted for and the security holes are plugged.

Compare your action steps with the security policies and procedures you already created. Your plan of action for security should take into account those policies and contribute to each one being effectively implemented.

Resources and follow-up

The final component of your security plan addresses the resources (and budget) that are required to put your plan into action. Make a list that identifies all the purchases you need to make to fulfill your security plan. Include a price estimate for each item. If your total is hefty, prioritize which ones fall under the must-have category as well as which ones can wait.

In addition to the resources that require cash, you should include all other resources used in your plan. For instance, budget the time for yourself or employees to attend an Internet security class. Even if a vendor offers this type of training session for free, attendance still requires a small investment in human resources capital.

The last piece of this section should include a timeline for change. Assign both a reasonable date for completion and a person who's responsible for each action item. Schedule a recurring date for reviewing the progress of your plan's implementation, too.

No matter how many action items you develop or how many pages your security plan turns out to be, its true worth is measured in one way: Does it work? If your plan is thorough and realistic, your answer should be a resounding "Yes!"

Creating a Budget for Your Plan

Developing a written security document is an investment in itself. If nothing else, it bears the cost of your time. But as the resources and follow-up section of your security plan indicates, that step is only the beginning when it comes to paying the price for security. You probably already put down a fair chunk of change but haven't tallied your investment. The typical places in which you probably already spent money include insurance for your computer equipment, antivirus software, and a good firewall for your network.

Determining how much more you need to spend depends on your circumstances. The ongoing threat of cyber-related crime, in addition to the number and magnitude of actual incidents, has kept businesses spending a expanding portion of their IT budgets on security. Research from Canalys indicates that security spending continues to grow by 5 percent, year over year, and is expected to reach $30.1 billion (globally) by 2017. Executive surveys conducted by Gartner previously found that businesses were probably spending approximately $500 per employee, but recent IT spending trends show that that number is now most likely low.

To come up with a reasonable and effective budget for your business, take another look at your resources list from your security plan and determine the total value of the resources you're protecting.

Figure out how much a security breach can cost if you *don't* make that investment. Roughly calculate the value of your equipment: all your hardware, software — everything. Then assign a value to the intellectual property you need to protect. It's probably a whopping number. For e-commerce sites, another financial factor is identity theft. You have to consider the potential dollar value of your loss if a hacker gains access to your customer information. Lawsuits and insurance aside, consider it from another perspective: If your site has a major compromise of customer data, those customers must be notified. That situation can be a public relations nightmare — and can result in the loss of future orders.

When determining your security budget, be sure to include the cost of compliance. As the owner of an online business, you may be required to implement and maintain additional security procedures to protect customer data as part of government regulations or private industry standards. Examples of these compliance issues include the Health Insurance Portability and Accountability Act (HIPAA) and the Payment Card Industry Data Security Standard (PCI DSS).

No one can tell you how much you need to spend, or should be willing to spend, on security. When deciding how much to invest for security, ask yourself these two questions:

✦ What's the value of the assets I'm protecting?

✦ Is that amount worth the cost of security?

After you list the value of your assets, give this detailed inventory list to your insurance company to verify that you have the proper type and amount of coverage for your business. Don't forget to save a copy of this list for yourself in case disaster strikes.

Finding Security Resources

After you commit to your security budget, you can find plenty of outside resources that are happy to assist you in spending it. And you have lots of do-it-yourself opportunities, too. You have to decide when — and whether — an outside source is warranted. Then you should determine which resource is the best one for you to use.

When searching for help with security issues, you have many choices. More than likely, they fall into one of these categories:

✦ **Consultants:** Often specializing in a particular area of security, a consultant can be hired to offer an initial assessment or to assist with the complete solution. Most consultants bill in one of two ways:

   • *Hourly:* Some consultants charge by the hour, which typically ranges from $80 to $300 (or more) per hour, depending on your geographic location and on the consultant's specialty.

   • *Flat fee:* A consultant can also bill you a flat fee based on the scope of the project. As a general rule, the more complicated your issue — or the more specialized the expertise of the consultant — the more you can expect to pay.

✦ **Experts:** Experts can be individuals who work in a technical-support environment or who have full-time jobs in a related subject area (and advise informally or on a part-time basis). You can find experts in your vendor relationships or in community service programs for businesses (such as Service Corps of Retired Executives, or SCORE). The cost of an expert's time varies widely but usually is on the lower end of a consultant's fee. You might even find volunteers.

When paying for an expert or hiring a consultant, check out the person's certifications and ask for references. You should ask even if you're getting help for free (although it's more difficult to be selective if you aren't paying someone).

✦ **Training programs:** Call them seminars, training programs, or webinars, these resources provide information from a classroom perspective. Rather than provide individual support, these types of programs are targeted for a large group of people. Cost for this type of instruction varies. A one-day seminar might cost $300 or $400; a webcast or an online class might be free.

When attending a vendor-sponsored training program or seminar, the solutions that are offered tend to focus on that particular vendor's products. If you want unbiased guidance, make sure that someone other than a vendor or distributor teaches the session.

✦ **Self-help:** As in a training program, you can go the self-help route to seek out the knowledge base you need to educate yourself. The cost ultimately is a result of your time and any resources you purchase.

You have to decide which solution is right for you, and knowing when to go somewhere else is usually pretty clear. It's determined by these four key factors:

✦ **Budget:** You might have the money to spend on outside assistance, or you might be particularly budget conscious. As with the issue of time, hiring someone else and spending your labor dollars on other projects might make more sense.

✦ **Expertise:** Either you have the knowledge to resolve the issue or you don't. If you don't have the expertise, you must have the ability and the time to learn.

✦ **Scope:** Determine how serious the problem is and whether it's limited to your immediate network or reaches outside it.

✦ **Time:** If the issue is critical or you're reacting to a problem that already occurred, you probably want immediate action. Or you might be taking preventive measures. If so, time is on your side. Even if you have the time, consider whether it's best spent somewhere else. You might prefer to call in the experts.

Chapter 3: Attacked! What to Expect from the Net-Thief

In This Chapter

⤺ **Shutting down your site**

⤺ **Breaking through security barriers**

⤺ **Spreading Internet illnesses**

⤺ **Derailing your traffic**

⤺ **No phishing allowed**

A n estimated 3 billion people will use the Internet worldwide in 2014. In fact, 40 percent of the world's population now has an Internet connection — compared to less than 1 percent in 1995. With so many people and businesses online today, the Internet has ushered in a gold rush (of sorts) for cybercriminals, or what we refer to as the *Net-thief.* Estimates provided to the United States Congress showed that global losses from cyber-related crimes have surpassed the $1 trillion mark.

Given that figure, if you haven't been on the receiving end of an online security threat, consider yourself lucky. As an online business owner, your vulnerability to cyberattacks increases. Studies show that companies suffer from multiple security incidents per year from hackers, viruses, worms, spyware, and other malicious efforts. And when companies are suffering from Internet-related attacks, they can lose an average of $1500 per attack in small incidents, and potentially millions, or even billions, of dollars in revenue in larger, more severe attacks.

As an online business owner, you need to minimize the opportunity for any type of security interference that threatens your success. Before you can defend yourself and your computer, though, you need to know what to expect. In this chapter, we review the security threats that are most likely to take a bite out of your business if you let your guard down.

Fending Off Denial-of-Service Attacks

Any time an Internet thief, or Net-thief, can prevent you or your customers from accessing websites and other online information or applications, it's a *denial-of-service (DoS)* attack. Okay, maybe you don't think that your website is large enough or popular enough to interest someone in disrupting it. If you think DoS or distributed DoS (DDoS) attacks are no longer as prevalent, think again! DoS attacks are still considered one of the top Internet security threats. In 2013, several very large DoS attacks affected government sites as well as business and e-commerce sites. Previous DoS attacks have gone after major sites, but this type of malicious action can affect smaller businesses too. Some research indicates a growing trend of targeting smaller businesses (websites) with all types of cyberattacks because they have less sophisticated online security and are easier to breach.

Even if your site is fairly secure, consider this: What if the company your business uses for online payment transactions is attacked? Or maybe your online banking site is hit? Worse, what if the company that hosts your website falls prey to a DoS attack? You and hundreds of other small sites can be wiped out for several hours — or an entire day or more. Each of these is a real possibility and is an example of how easily a DoS attack can prevent you from being productive or possibly even hurt your company financially.

The hard truth is that your small or midsize business is more likely to experience a DoS attack these days because it is most vulnerable. As we mentioned, the Net-thief knows that online security is often at the bottom of a long list of concerns for smaller e-commerce sites, and you're also not investing much money in sophisticated security tools, like the big corporations are doing. That situation translates to opportunity. Intruders troll the Internet every day, looking for sites that offer security holes. Plus, DoS attack-launching tools are now fairly cheap and easy to come by, so instigating an attack has become easier. An intruder can divert legitimate traffic away from your site and drive it to other sites. The attacker may be paid every time your customers visit the rogue site, whether or not they intended to go there. With lots of dollars at stake, you can understand why the frequency of DoS attacks has spiked.

Fending off a DoS episode isn't easy. After you're under attack, your choice of responses is limited. However, you can take certain steps to reduce the chances of an attack occurring and to minimize the damage that can be done if your site suffers from a DoS attack:

✦ **Know your host.** When selecting a hosting company for your website, understand which security measures it has in place. Ask how your host would work with you if your site experienced a DoS attack as well as whether security experts are part of its support staff. The more prevention at the network level, the better.

✦ **Update the basics.** Individual users and their computers are also responsible for creating security holes. The best defense is to continually update antivirus and spyware programs as well as download the most recent patches (or fixes) for your computer systems. Keep your browsers updated, too — especially Internet Explorer, which has proven to be quite susceptible.

Book V
Chapter 3

Attacked! What
to Expect from the
Net-Thief

✦ **Report attacks.** If your site comes under a DoS attack, report it to the FBI. Attackers often use Yahoo! and other free e-mail services; the FBI might be able to trace these accounts. The FBI has created a special division, the Internet Crime Complaint Center, to address these concerns, as shown in Figure 3-1. You can access the division at `www.ic3.gov`. Additionally, the United States Computer Emergency Readiness Team (US CERT), which is part of the U.S. Department of Homeland Security, monitors, tracks, and responds to cyberthreats. You can report attacks on the US CERT website at `https://complaintic3.gov`, as shown in Figure 3-2.

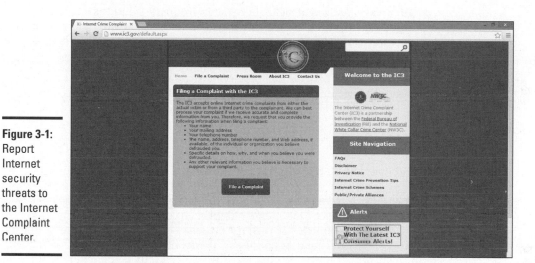

Figure 3-1:
Report
Internet
security
threats to
the Internet
Complaint
Center.

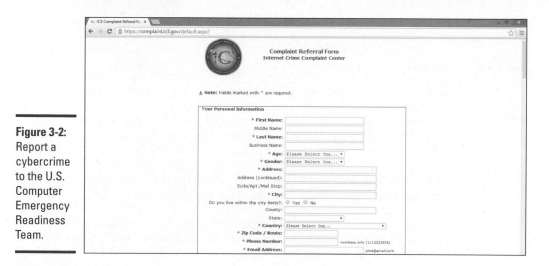

Figure 3-2:
Report a
cybercrime
to the U.S.
Computer
Emergency
Readiness
Team.

McAfee, an online security company, offers a Threat Center that provides updated information about the most recent cyberthreats (for both businesses and individuals). This resource also provides online security tips and risk assessment tools to help reveal your potential online security vulnerabilities. You can access this portal at `www.mcafee.com/us/threat-center.aspx/`.

✦ **Block traffic.** You can work with your host company to block traffic coming from suspicious or malicious IP addresses. Although you run the risk of also blocking legitimate users, this choice might be your best option.

✦ **Be aware.** As DoS attacks increase in frequency and type, you must stay up-to-date on security issues. Your best defense against any attack is to be aware and knowledgeable of current threats and recommended preventive measures.

To stay ahead of potential cyberthreats, get tips to keep your business secure by visiting the tip site from US CERT at `www.us-cert.gov/ncas`.

Deterring Hackers

Behind every DoS attack or any other harmful Internet-related threat is usually a single person or group of people responsible for starting the malicious activity. Discovering the identity of these electronic thieves isn't easy. Recent data suggests that roughly 25 percent of hacking incidents originate from the top 15 countries known for attacks — and while the United States is considered one of those 15 countries, it was responsible for just over 1 percent of known attacks. So, what — or who — exactly is a hacker? In general, a *hacker* is anyone not authorized or given permission to intrude on or to gain access to your information systems. Hackers are basically opportunists.

Some hackers are motivated by the challenge of merely trying to break through a security system and then bragging that they did it. Those hackers are typically attracted to large high-profile sites or government sites. In another growing trend, *hactavism,* the hacker purports to break into sites for a greater good or for some cause that the hacker believes needs attention. For example, Julian Paul Assange, the editor of the online site WikiLeaks, gained worldwide attention as an Internet activist who hacked into websites of governments, politicians, and major corporations to illegally obtain potentially scathing documents that he, in turn, leaked to the public. Your organization can be vulnerable to hackers not only for financial gain but also to get access to your company data or to draw attention.

For most online businesses, the threat of hackers is simply based on the possibility of making money from your site. The "rewards" for this type of action can be enormous for a hacker. One notorious hacking incident in the last few years occurred when Sony's online game network, Playstation, was breached, resulting in hackers gaining access to confidential information (such as credit

Book V
Chapter 3

Attacked! What
to Expect from the
Net-Thief

card numbers and passwords) of millions of Sony customers. The network was shut down for 23 days, for a staggering financial loss of more than $171 million. Again, big or small, online companies have a lot to lose to a hacker.

Among the most popular methods of hacking-for-pay are stealing these elements:

✦ **Keystrokes:** This kind of attack might not seem like a big deal, but even inexperienced hackers can monitor and record the keystrokes on your computer. By using a keystroke logger tool, hackers capture your data, making it a snap to gain access to your system.

✦ **Sales:** Hackers divert your traffic to a rogue site (which might even look like yours), where customers spend money, in the belief that the site is legitimate.

✦ **Data:** By obtaining passwords to your or your customer's secure data, hackers can build a lucrative business. With passwords, hackers gain access to pertinent information, such as bank accounts, birthdates, and Social Security numbers.

✦ **Credit card numbers:** Hackers relish the chance to obtain your customers' stored credit card numbers. These days, those numbers can easily be resold for cash — and before anyone realizes that the accounts have been compromised.

As we've shown, your data is worth a lot of money to a Net-thief. Sites that fall prey to this type of hacker are vulnerable because they're easy targets. Think of this type of breach in terms of your home's security: Although locks and alarms don't always stop thieves, they deter them. Given the choice, most bad guys break into places that are easier to get into and out of without being noticed.

If a hacker sees that you're sloppy with security, he doesn't waste any time taking advantage of you. These days, computer programs allow a hacker to scan the Internet and look for vulnerable sites.

Implementing firewalls and antivirus software certainly helps deter a hacker. You can take some additional measures to irritate a cybercrook:

✦ **Use uncommon passwords.** Yes, using uncommon passwords is good ol' common sense, yet most people choose passwords that are easy to remember or have special meanings, such as birthdates and anniversaries. Instead, use a nonsensical or complex mixture of words and numbers. Be sure to create a different password for each application or program that you access.

For added security, you can get help creating unique passwords by using a *password generator.* This software creates random passwords for you. Free password-generator programs are available, or you can purchase programs for $15 to $75, depending on whether it's for personal or business use.

✦ **Change passwords frequently.** Merely creating good passwords isn't enough. You have to create them repeatedly. Generate new passwords every three months (depending on the sensitivity of the information being accessed) for applications you use all the time. Change other passwords annually for low security-risk applications or websites.

Remembering unique and constantly changing passwords is difficult. And keeping written records of your passwords defeats the purpose of changing them. Now you can get help remembering passwords by using a password manager. KeePass is a free, open-source application that keeps all your passwords locked away, so to speak, in a secure database with only one master key, or key file. You can get started creating a secure password manager by visiting www.keepass.info.

✦ **Keep data out of site.** Hackers can originate close to home. Whether you're working from home or an office surrounded by employees, get into the habit of protecting your information. Don't leave account numbers, passwords, and other pertinent data out in the open. Thieves lurk everywhere.

✦ **Shut down your computers.** In this 24/7 world of the Internet, you're always open for business. It's tempting to leave your computers on around the clock, too. A better idea is to shut them off at the end of day to limit the possibility of unwelcome access to your system. This advice is especially good if you have a home-based business and use cable modems to access the Internet. The shared bandwidth makes you much more vulnerable.

✦ **Update your computer system automatically.** Configure your computer for automatic updates to your operating system.

Avoiding Viruses and Other Malware

According to the McAfee security firm, hundreds of thousands of active virus threats are invading computers right now. Named for the germ-like nature of an illness that rapidly spreads, viruses were originally a nuisance more than anything else. Similar to thwarting hacking, programmers face the challenge of preventing the spread of irritants from one computer to another.

A *virus* is a program or piece of programming code and is usually spread by way of e-mail attachments. The attachments can be Word documents, photos, games, or other types of applications. By opening the attachment, you unknowingly unleash the virus onto your computer and possibly help spread it to others. Viruses are almost impossible for you to detect without using some type of antivirus software.

The capability to hide a virus combined with its ease of distribution makes these attacks increasingly more threatening to the health of your computer and your online business. Some computer experts now refer to viruses as a part of *malware*, short for *mal*icious soft*ware*. In 2014, a powerful form of

Book V
Chapter 3

Attacked! What
to Expect from the
Net-Thief

malware, called Heartbleed, struck fear in the hearts of many. The bug affects a popular open-source (free) software called OpenSSL, which is used by web servers of all sizes to encrypt information and make the transfer of data more secure. Normally, OpenSSL is used as part of a limited exchange of data, but the bug in the software allows for the malicious retrieval of additional pertinent data, such as passwords. By the way, the Heartbleed bug was the result of an accidental security flaw originated by developers contributing to the OpenSSL code. Nonetheless, the bug caused much concern for businesses and organizations worldwide, and eventually required an update in the OpenSSL code. Customers of websites using OpenSSL were also encouraged to immediately update their passwords.

Here are some other types of malware, viruses, and annoyances to be aware of:

✦ **Worms:** Unlike most viruses, worms don't need your help to spread. You don't have to open an attachment or accidentally launch a harmful program. A *worm* simply replicates itself and then spreads to other computers over a shared network. TheMoon is a worm that garnered attention in early 2014. Named after the 2009 movie *The Moon,* this worm infected various routers that were part of the Linksys product line for the E-Series. After the worm compromised a router, it would scan for other vulnerable devices on the network and replicate itself to infect those devices. Other than spreading across devices, the worm didn't cause any particular problems — unlike other well-known worms in the past, which would continuously shut down infected computers.

Worms have also been used to infect mobile devices. In 2014, the Samsapo worm used malicious text messages to infiltrate Russian Android phones (yes, these were geographic-specific worms). The worm would access an infected phone's SIM card and captured personal data. The worm was also able to trigger a text-to-pay system and steal money, which was charged to the mobile phone owner's cellular bill. Worms are not only infectious but also potentially costly.

✦ **Trojans:** A computer Trojan employs the same type of subterfuge as the Greek Trojan horse. Delivered in a seemingly harmless package (usually by e-mail), it sneaks onto your computer system. Then, without your permission, it opens and performs some type of unwanted activity, such as shutting down your computer. Unlike some other threats, Trojans do not replicate themselves.

✦ **Adware:** This phenomenon started out as annoying pop-up windows that disrupted your computer surfing with unwanted ads. Now adware is big business. Someone makes money every time this advertising software displays ads.

✦ **Spyware:** Much like adware, spyware is a type of malicious software that plants itself deep into your computer system, posing as a legitimate program. It wants to stay around as long as possible so that it can collect information about you. Spyware can redirect you to certain websites or track and record your personal information and send it back to the spyware's originator — without your knowledge.

✦ **Botnets:** When your computer is infected with malware, it can also become the unknown host that helps spread malicious software to other computers. Essentially, your computer becomes part of a robot network called a *botnet,* which is made up of thousands of controlled computers that instruct your computer (and other vulnerable computers now in their network) to send out infected e-mails, without your permission.

✦ **Hoaxes:** It isn't unusual for rumors about false virus threats to circulate around the Internet. Although these little pranks don't infect your computer, they waste your time. You can tell whether a threat is real or a hoax by noting these characteristics:

   • *Source:* If an e-mail alert came from your antivirus software provider or another trusted source, it's probably real. If it's part of a chain of e-mails being circulated by friends and family, it's more likely to be a fake.

   • *Participation:* An e-mail alerting you to this latest threat and prompting you to send it to everyone you know to spread the news is a classic sign of a hoax.

   • *Authority:* If the e-mail contains a link to a recognized antivirus software vendor or a legitimate Internet security source, it's probably real. If not, you might be participating in a virus hoax.

If you receive an e-mail virus alert and suspect that it's a hoax, check out VMyths at `www.vmyths.com`. This site tracks hoaxes and other over-hyped computer threats.

Keeping Your Domain Name Safe

Ever since the Internet started gaining in popularity, devious minds with a creative bent have found ways to cause problems. In addition to the other methods that hijackers use to derail your sales and your business — such as virus and DoS attacks — a determined Net-thief has one more trick: stealing your domain.

Domain slamming occurs when you're tricked into moving your registered domain from one registrar to another. In this scenario, you receive an e-mail saying that it's time to renew your domain. It even appears to be from your legitimate registrar. Unfortunately, a competing registrar has gained your information and is waiting to collect a domain renewal fee from you. Although domain slamming might be more economically detrimental to your originating domain registrar (they lose your business), it's still a hassle for you, too.

Somewhat more disturbing is the opportunity for a hacker to take over your domain by using the registration process. When a thief takes possession of your domain, you can spend years trying to get it back. Some documented cases show that small e-commerce companies never recover ownership. Whether your domain is hijacked for a day or an eternity, here are some common problems that occur when your name is stolen out from under you:

**Book V
Chapter 3**

Attacked! What
to Expect from the
Net-Thief

✦ **Reselling:** Your domain name can be resold to an unsuspecting third party. Popular names can fetch millions of dollars, making domain hijacking a lucrative career for a thief.

✦ **Lost sales:** If you have an active e-commerce site that's taken over, you lose sales during the time it takes to regain ownership. Some companies have lost thousands of dollars in sales, not to mention the legal expenses involved in recovering the domain name.

✦ **Damaged reputation:** Even if you regain your site domain, you might be stuck convincing customers that it's safe to shop with you again. In some cases, stolen domains are used to redirect visitors to sites that download adware or spyware onto computers. Unsuspecting customers might be hard-pressed to return to your site.

Here's how domain stealing happens: If hackers can find enough personal information about your account, they can transfer your registered domain into their name and basically take ownership of your domain in a few short hours. Most of the information needed to achieve this process can be found by simply viewing the public records of the WHOIS directory.

To prevent having personal or business information readily available for public viewing, choose to make your contact information private. The WHOIS directory then shows a third-party vendor — a *proxy* — as the point of contact and lists its information rather than yours. Your domain registrar offers the private registration service for a small annual fee, usually for as little as $10 per year.

Sadly, domain stealing is becoming more common. Domain registrars and the Internet Corporation for Assigned Names and Numbers (ICANN) continue to put policies in place that prevent or limit the damage. Still, no policy is foolproof, so here are some other tips you can follow to minimize the risk of domain hijacking:

✦ **Lock down:** Registrars offer the simple and free service of *locking down* (restricting others from changing) your URL. When registering your domain, select the check box indicating that you want to lock the domain name. If you have an active domain name, you can change its lockdown status by using account-management tools or sending a lockdown request by e-mail (or phone) to customer support.

✦ **24/7 support:** Use domain registrars that offer 24-hour support or give you access to support after business hours. This strategy is important so that if you discover that your domain has been hijacked, you can start the investigative and recovery process immediately.

✦ **Standard notification:** Choose domain registration services that state standard methods of contacting you for changes or that will agree to contact you by using multiple methods (such as by both phone and e-mail).

✦ **Review status:** Frequently check the WHOIS directory to ensure that you're still listed as the owner of the domain and that your contact information is current and correct.

Glossary of security threats

Do you recognize all the threats that can pose a hazard to your computer and your business? Test your security knowledge by checking out this list:

- **Adware:** This type of software displays ads and pop-up windows on your computer. More than just annoying, adware includes code that tracks your personal information and shares it with third parties without your knowledge.

- **Blended threat:** Just like it sounds, this attack incorporates several types of threats to maximize the damage in one shot. For example, a virus might be distributed by e-mail while a Trojan horse hides in an attached file to cause further damage to your computer.

- **Data-driven attack:** Seemingly harmless, this threat is encoded with data that you, the user, unknowingly executes to launch an attack. This type is dangerous because it can sneak through your firewall.

- **DNS spoofing:** This process happens when a hacker assumes the DNS name of another system but redirects you to an unauthorized site. The domain name of the legitimate site appears just as it should, but you're now on a different site.

- **Flooding:** Flooding happens when a large amount of information is directed to a particular system, contributing to a denial-of-service (DoS) attack.

- **Pharming:** This strategy tries to obtain personal data, such as credit card numbers, by using domain spoofing. Pharming poisons your DNS server by infusing false information that then redirects your customers elsewhere. As far as the customers know, they're still on your website because the domain doesn't change. Any information they provide during the visit is pharmed by the attacker.

- **Phishing:** In this ploy, you receive what looks like a legitimate e-mail from a large, recognizable site, but the e-mail is actually from unknown sources. The hope is that you respond to their request to update and verify personal and financial information.

- **Smurfing:** This type of software mounts a DoS attack by broadcasting large amounts of data.

- **Botnet:** This form of malware is unknowingly placed on your computer, which then becomes part of an army of thousands of computers that are controlled and instructed when and where to send infected e-mails to other computers, without your permission or knowledge.

- **Spyware:** Any software that uses your Internet connection without your knowledge or permission is spyware. It's usually distributed by using free or unknown programs that you download from the Internet. After the spyware is installed, it watches your activity on the Internet and transmits that information to other Bad Guys.

- **Identity theft:** In this method, a Net-thief uses any number of security threats to gain access to your personal information, or that of your customers, for his or her own financial gain. Most commonly, the type of information consists of bank records, credit card numbers, Social Security numbers, and any other data that would allow someone else to assume your identity for financial gain.

To discover more security-related terms and find information on protecting your computer, visit the National Cyber Security Alliance at its website, www.staysafeonline.org.

Staying Away from E-Mail Scams

Book V
Chapter 3

Attacked! What
to Expect from the
Net-Thief

You should be familiar with two schemes that affect the way you handle e-mail and keep your business safe: phishing ("fish-ing") and pharming ("farm-ing"). Both methods use unscrupulous means to find personal or private account information about you and then use it for a hacker's personal gain.

Phishing

Phishing occurs when you receive an e-mail that seems to be from a legitimate source, such as PayPal, Amazon, or even your bank. The e-mail usually requests that you immediately update your account information because it has been compromised or needs to be verified for other reasons. When you click the link (included in your e-mail notice), a bogus site opens that captures your personal information as you "update" the account.

Legitimate companies have done a good job of alerting users to potential phishing scams and making it easier for you to spot e-mails that don't originate with the company.

Generally, you should be aware of these details:

✦ **Account verification:** Most legitimate e-mails from a member-based company or financial institution now include the last three or four digits of your account number. If the e-mail doesn't have any highly personalized or account-specific information, it might be a fake.

✦ **Contact information:** Check whether the contact information at the bottom of an e-mail matches the source that it's supposedly sent from. E-mail contact information should come from the company's primary URL, such as `support@paypal.com` — not `support@paypalsecurity.com`, for example.

✦ **Collecting data:** A legitimate request should not ask you to submit, update, or verify private and confidential information by completing an e-mail-based form or replying to that e-mail. You should be able to visit the company's website (without using a link in the e-mail) to update account information.

✦ **Notice of urgency:** Most phishing scams insist that you reply right away or act immediately. Bogus e-mails scare you into the thinking your information is being compromised and that you must act right now.

✦ **Contact customer support:** If an e-mail looks legitimate but you're still not certain, play it safe and call the toll-free number listed on the back of your credit card or the one listed on the company's website.

Pharming

Suppose that you visit a favorite shopping site. You type the domain name, and the site pops up momentarily on your screen. You log in using your password, enter your credit card information to buy products, and perhaps fork over some personal information as part of an online giveaway. Everything seems normal. What you don't realize is that a hacker has rerouted you to a website that looks like the one you intended to visit, but this one is bogus. In the meantime, all the passwords and personal information you entered into the site are *pharmed* out and the data is used for malicious purposes.

You can fall victim to a pharming scam in a couple of ways. The first occurs when a virus, delivered by e-mail, compromises your computer's information. The virus can enable the computer to redirect you to a bogus site when you type a URL into your browser.

The second method is when a hacker uses *DNS poisoning,* which alters the string of numbers in your DNS (Domain Name System), causing the real URL to be redirected to a fake domain. Pharming that uses DNS poisoning is a little more destructive because it can affect a larger number of users. And that destruction becomes especially costly if you're an online business owner whose site has been poisoned.

Because no standard method exists for helping visitors confirm that a site is legitimate, it can be difficult to avoid becoming a victim. The best protection against pharming attacks as an individual user is to

+ Keep your firewall updated

+ Keep antivirus software current

+ Install patches and updates to your browser

In your Internet business, protecting your site from becoming a victim of DNS poisoning is much more difficult. In fact, no sure way to avoid it exists. The best defense is to talk with the company that hosts your site, to ensure that its servers are running the latest updates of DNS software and that all patches are installed. If you have an in-house server, you or your IT manager should be responsible for the same thing.

Chapter 4: Securing Your Site and Your Business

In This Chapter

✔ Securing customer data

✔ Backing up your own data

✔ Adding a firewall for additional protection

If you've spent any time on a computer, you know most of the security drills about spam, viruses, and other unwanted intruders. (If not, turn to Chapter 2 of this minibook to create a top-notch security plan for fending off online predators.)

As an online business owner, your responsibility to run a secure site is now increased in magnitude. In addition to watching out for your best interests, you must realize that your customers depend on you to take the appropriate precautions. In this chapter, we show you good security measures and provide information and tools so that you can increase protection for yourself and your customers.

Protecting against Credit Card Fraud

Operating an Internet business means that you're likely collecting, processing, and storing credit card data regularly. You therefore have to look at potential credit card fraud from two points of view: yours and the customer's.

Minimizing your financial losses

E-commerce sites lose billions of dollars to online credit card fraud every year. CyberSource Corp. states that online fraud reached $3.5 billion in 2012, according to its 2013 Online Fraud Report. The average online fraudulent order is $200 for e-commerce stores, but that's down 20 percent from the previous year. Even so, research from Avira shows that consumers are still wary when it comes to spending money online. Of those who do shop online, 20 percent choose to buy only from well-known e-commerce sites, such as Amazon. And, even in 2014, 20 percent of shoppers do not buy online because they are fearful of the security risks. These statistics add up to potentially less revenue for your online business.

You want to be aware of potential security problems so you can combat them and protect your prospective revenue. Here are just a few of the ways that your online business can get hit with fraudulent transactions — and end up losing merchandise and money:

✦ Customers buy a product but then claim that they didn't order it (or file a similar complaint), and the credit card company deletes the charge.

✦ You unknowingly process stolen credit cards.

✦ You process invalid credit cards or cards that you should have declined.

Although you might think that the big online retailers are most at risk, smaller sites are often more likely targets because smaller sites usually have less sophisticated resources for detecting fraud. Fraudulent credit card orders increasingly account for a larger percentage of all processed online orders. Although the percentage is still relatively small (less than 10 percent), that doesn't help if you're the one suffering a loss.

Protecting against online crime means that you have to stay alert, cautious, and informed. As with any security concern, seek ways to reduce your risk:

✦ **Validate credit cards.** Whether you process manually or in real-time, confirm that the credit card is approved. If a card is declined or shows up with a questionable item, resist the urge to process it anyway.

✦ **Verify suspicious orders.** Don't hesitate to contact a customer by e-mail or phone to confirm an order to validate a card number. If everything is okay, your customer will be impressed that you take this degree of precaution.

✦ **Fight excessive charge backs.** Even if a card is valid, a customer can steal from you by refusing to pay for the product or service after receiving it. If the customer gives a valid reason (such as the product was damaged or appears to have been used or refurbished), the credit card company removes the charge. Because you have no signature on file for an online transaction, you're stuck paying the bill — plus a charge back fee from your credit card company. You can challenge the claim by responding to the charge back complaint that the credit card company sends you. You need diligence and patience to fight this type of complaint, and you won't win them all. Still, you can recover some losses, making your time invested worthwhile. (For more information on fighting charge backs, see Chapter 1 of this minibook.)

If you suspect a problem or perhaps an honest mistake, call your customer directly to work it out. Keeping good records and documenting follow-up calls go a long way toward fighting charge backs.

✦ **Add fraud protection.** Online payment processors sometimes offer fraud protection programs for e-commerce sites. These services add screening features as well as links to fraud alerts to minimize the acceptance of bad orders. This service is considered an add-on, so expect to pay a monthly fee, plus a small transaction fee on every order.

✦ **Use card codes.** As part of your ordering process, ask for the credit card verification code, which usually appears as a three-digit number on the back of a Visa or MasterCard credit card, or a four-digit number on the front of an American Express card. Asking for this information requires that the user has the physical card in hand (or at least knows the number).

✦ **Accept online checks.** You can choose to accept electronic checks or Internet checks to provide another payment alternative with fewer fraud risks. On the flip side, restricting your payment options can hurt your sales. Limiting customers to only one form of payment (such as online checks) likely can turn off many customers.

Work directly with your online payment processor to see how to further protect yourself. When selling on eBay or other third-party sites, always read the fraud policies to understand your rights as a merchant — before a sale goes wrong.

Protecting customers' privacy and financial data

Luckily, only a small percentage of customers — if any — turn out to be thieves. A bigger challenge is protecting your customers' data from online crooks and potential carelessness. One of these violations can land your customers' data in the wrong hands — and also land you in a lot of hot water:

✦ **Online security breach:** A lone successful hacking attempt can leave your online database of records as open game. Names, addresses, passwords, and credit card numbers — some of the most sought-after information — is easily left at risk.

✦ **Offline theft:** Someone can break into your office and access customer files filled with personal financial data. Don't discount *internal theft,* where the thief is someone you knowingly invite into your office space.

✦ **Sloppy disposal:** Okay, maybe you have extra copies of customer data or you decide that the statute of IRS limitations has passed and you can now get rid of old files. How you dispose of this information can leave customer records vulnerable.

✦ **Vendor carelessness:** Your security and data storage practices aren't the only factors that can lead to a mishap. Any vendor that you partner with — and who has access to your customer data — can cause a security mishap. (Think about scandals in which credit card companies and delivery services have mishandled or lost customer information.) How they handle — or mishandle — data can affect your site's reputation.

The preceding list gives you some good ideas about how easily a problem can occur. Now all you have to do is make sure it doesn't. Take these precautions to minimize your risk:

✦ **Store data properly.** You probably have two basic methods of keeping data — hard copy files and online databases. Make sure that each one is tightly secured:

- *Hard copy:* Paperwork and hard copies of backup files that contain sensitive customer information must be kept in locked file cabinets or in rooms and storage facilities with locks and limited access.

- *Online:* Online information should be password protected and have the added protection of a firewall.

✦ **Dump your data properly.** When it's time to get rid of hard copy documents, these files must be thoroughly shredded. You can even hire a professional document disposal service that will come to your location to shred documents. How convenient is that?

 Before getting rid of old computers or disposing of any electronic files, erase or overwrite the machine or files (as opposed to simply deleting individual files). You can use a free, downloadable program from Active@ KillDisk at www.killdisk.com. Or try guaranteed erasure services from companies such as Shred-it (www.shredit.com) or Kroll Ontrack (www.krollontrack.com).

✦ **Add layers of security.** Be sure to protect any type of company information, not just customer data. Showing that you have multiple layers of security processes is important. Having only one type or layer of security can become a compliance issue if your data is compromised. Include these items in your layers, as shown in Figure 4-1:

- *Antivirus:* Keep antivirus software updated.

- *Backups:* Back up data regularly.

- *Checks:* Conduct regular security checks.

- *Encryption:* Use encryption tools to code information in case your data is compromised. Encryption lets you hide your data from hackers and other unwanted eyes. Only someone with the proper password can decrypt the information for proper viewing.

- *Firewalls:* Maintain active firewalls on your computers and servers.

- *Inventory:* Keep an inventory of your files.

- *Offline security:* Lock up data that's stored offline.

- *Security policy:* Write an official security policy to ensure that you cover your bases (see Chapter 2 of this minibook).

- *VPN:* Use a virtual private network (VPN) when sending information over a wireless connection (see Chapter 5 of this minibook).

LAYERS OF SECURITY

Proactive

Utilize Encryption Tools
↑
Enable VPN on Wireless Network
↑
Use Password Generator

Preventive

Activate Antivirus Software
↑
Install Antispyware & Adware-Blocking Software
↑
Enable Firewalls
↑
Secure Office Data & Hardware

Maintenance

Establish Security Policy
↑
Conduct Regular Security Checks & System Updates
↑
Maintain Inventory of Files
↑
Back Up Data Regularly

Figure 4-1:
Layers of
security.

✦ **Institute a notification policy.** Taking preventive measures also involves
planning for the worst. Follow up your privacy policy with an internal
policy describing how you will handle a security breach as well as the
process for notifying authorities and customers.

You might be a one-person show when you're starting your online business,
but the stakes for messing up are the same as they are for the big guys.
Mishandling, losing, or compromising customer information can cost you
thousands of dollars in fines, possible jail time, and untold damage to your
image as a reputable online store.

Backing Up Your Data

Stop. Take a moment and think about the information you store on your computer. Consider the amount of time you spend creating, updating, and maintaining your website. Now imagine that all that information disappears in a blink of the eye. Yikes!

Most of us go through our business day assuming that nothing really bad will ever happen. That's followed by the assumption that the contents of your website and your computer files are perfectly safe and always at your disposal. Guess again. You can lose data through human error (coffee splashed on your laptop, for example) or natural disasters, such as hurricanes.

You can prevent disasters from becoming cataclysmic by properly backing up and storing your data. Try these methods:

✦ **Store data on a removable storage device.** A common way to back up data is to save it to an external hard drive. You can also use a flash drive, as long as it has enough memory.

✦ **Partition your hard drive.** An easy way to back up files is to move them to a separate section of your hard drive. You do this by *partitioning* the hard drive, or dividing it into two or more sections. If one partition is corrupted or compromised, you can still access the second partition. Partitioning is also a good method for providing another layer of security (by limiting access) to certain files.

To partition your existing hard drive, use an off-the-shelf program to make the job easy. Try the EaseUS Partition Master for free at www. partition-tool.com.

One goal of backing up data is to have your information available in case of a disaster, such as hurricanes, tornadoes, and flooding — which we've seen plenty of in the last few years. If your computer is stolen or destroyed in a fire, having data backed up on a hard drive doesn't do much good. You can make a duplicate copy that's not backed up as often but is saved to disk and stored in a fireproof safe or in a safe-deposit box. Or you can keep your information backed up in a cloud solution for a few dollars a month.

✦ **Use a cloud-based or remote backup service.** One advantage of using a hosted or cloud-based backup service is that your data is stored off-site. If anything calamitous happens at your location, you can retrieve a copy from your backup provider and immediately restore your data. Backup services can cost as little as $10 per month and increase to several hundred dollars per month depending on the features you want and the amount of storage space required. Shop around for the best deal.

✦ **Back up your operating system.** If you operate Windows 8.1, Microsoft includes a few options to back up files and recover your PC. You can find out about your options at http://windows.microsoft.com/en-us/windows-8/restore-refresh-reset-pc.

In 2014, Microsoft discontinued support of its Windows XP operating system. If you're using XP, it is highly recommended that you update your PC to Windows 8.1 to avoid compromising your data with increased security risks.

If you're using an Apple Macintosh, Mac OS X includes Time Machine for free, which allows you to automatically back up your system. You can get the details, along with other options, at `http://support.apple.com/kb/ht1553`.

In addition to the data you keep on your computer, make sure that the web pages stored on your server are also backed up. Check with your hosting service to determine how and when backups are made and also what you must do to access them.

**Book V
Chapter 4**

Securing Your Site and Your Business

Adding Firewalls

One of the best lines of defense against viruses and intruders is having a firewall installed on your computer. Think of a *firewall* as a security guard standing watch at all the doors and windows of your computer. The firewall monitors the traffic, decides what's safe, and then gives permission to enter. If the firewall detects a threat, it shuts the door and blocks the intruder.

Firewalls are particularly important because hackers are aggressive creatures. They actively search for networks that are unprotected or have disabled firewalls. To a Net-thief, that situation is the equivalent of having an open invitation to browse through all the files on your computer. The lack of firewalls also make it easy to install harmful programs that infect or shut down your computer or — worse — scoop up and send out to the hacker pertinent information (such as passwords and bank account numbers) without your knowledge.

If a pesky virus manages to break through your front lines of defense, a firewall cannot remove or quarantine infected files. You still need to run antivirus software in addition to installing a firewall.

For added security, we recommend that you do the following:

✦ **Enable individual firewalls.** When your computer is part of a local area network (LAN), most routers have a firewall installed. For the best defense, though, enable a personal firewall on each computer.

✦ **Add an enhanced firewall.** Install a second dynamic firewall to gain protection from both incoming and outgoing traffic and to provide an additional layer of security. You can buy firewall software, often combined with antivirus software or other security tools, for $30 and up. One popular product is ZoneAlarm, which offers free and paid versions of its firewall solution at `www.zonealarm.com`.

Chapter 5: Overcoming Security Concerns in the Wireless World

In This Chapter

✔ Identifying the risks of Wi-Fi

✔ Discovering how to work through problems

✔ Blocking wireless threats

*W*ithout a doubt, one of the best parts of running an online business is that you aren't permanently tethered to one location. The wireless revolution allows you to work in almost any room of your home, outdoors on your back deck, or even at the neighborhood coffee shop. Even brick-and-mortar businesses are increasingly implementing or accessing wireless networks on a regular basis. The rising popularity of mobile devices, from smartphones to tablets, has only increased the appeal of the wireless world. Many e-commerce applications and solutions used to manage all areas of your online business now come with the capability of using the app or service via a mobile device. That means you can run your online business from almost anywhere.

Freedom of that nature comes with a price, of course — *security risks*. Like it or not, if you're using a wireless connection, you're vulnerable. The increase of mobile applications is undeniably at the center of many wireless security concerns. Whether you use an iPhone, an iPad, or an Android device, the projections for the use of mobile devices is staggering. Research indicates that 1 in 4 Americans now own a smartphone. In addition, the sale of mobile devices has outpaced the sale of desktop computers. As the use of mobile apps and mobile payments continues to increase, so does the opportunity for data breaches.

Another business and consumer trend that is raising the bar on security risks is the growing popularity of cloud-based computing. Also referred to software as a service (SaaS), cloud solutions are essentially the use of subscription-based or pay-for-use service over the Internet in real-time. This type of computing has become an affordable way for businesses of all sizes to expand their capabilities. For example, a business can host their phone system in the cloud and use cloud-based shopping carts. Most business services can be delivered from and managed in the cloud. Although cloud computing isn't strictly wireless, this "outside the network" approach to conducting online business introduces the opportunity for increased security risks.

As you see, plenty of opportunities exist to let intruders into your business when working untethered in a wireless world. In this chapter, we show you how to keep unwanted guests off your network so that you can work in protected solitude.

Understanding How a Wireless LAN Works

Before you can protect against a security breach of any kind, consider how a wireless network operates. In short, a *wireless local area network* (WLAN) provides access to the Internet without the need for cables or other wires hooking directly into your computer. Instead, an access point (AP) connects other wireless devices to your local area network (LAN). Then high-frequency radio waves transmit the signal from the LAN to your mobile computer. Figure 5-1 shows you an overview of this process.

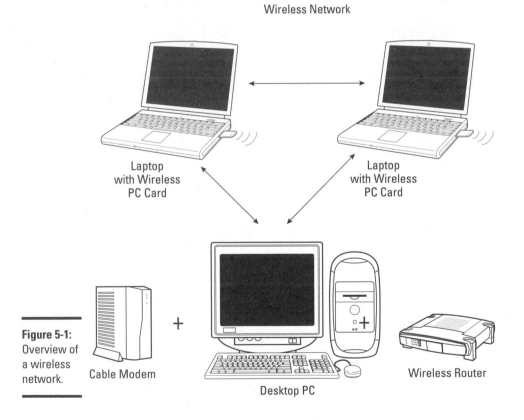

Wireless Network

Laptop with Wireless PC Card

Laptop with Wireless PC Card

Figure 5-1: Overview of a wireless network.

Cable Modem

Desktop PC

Wireless Router

Wireless connections are classified by IEEE 802.11 standards, commonly known as *Wi-Fi*. The original IEEE 802.11 now has lots of other versions, all bearing the number 802.11 followed by one or two lowercase letters. Each letter represents different features or speeds of the wireless network. For

Understanding How a Wireless LAN Works **347**

Book V
Chapter 5

Overcoming
Security Concerns
in the Wireless
World

example, 802.11b is a wireless capability that operates at 2.4 GHz. You find this capability built in to most laptops, which makes it possible for you to connect with public WLANs. When buying wireless equipment, be sure to match versions. Although you may still see 802.11a and 802.11b, 802.11g is now considered the most common version. In fact, most public wireless LANs (such as in coffee shops) now use 802.11g and are continually updating to the most recent versions of the standards.

Just keep in mind that whether the wireless LAN is set up in your home, in a hotel, or at a city park, the result is the same: You share a signal that's broadcast over public airwaves. Why does this matter to you? Think about your house as it sits in the middle of your neighborhood. Now imagine that your house has no walls. If you don't mind neighbors — or perfect strangers, for that matter — being able to walk through your house and root around in your drawers and file cabinets, you don't have a problem. However, if you have things you would rather not share (such as credit card numbers, passwords, and other sensitive data), being exposed to that degree can be harmful.

IEEE 802.11 standards

When you use wireless products, the following numbers describe certain attributes or features of that particular wireless network, as developed by IEEE (Institute of Electrical and Electronic Engineers):

- **802.11a:** Operates at 5 GHz with rates as high as 54 Mbps

- **802.11b:** Operates at 2.4 GHz with rates as high as 11 Mbps

- **802.11d:** Allows the wireless network to conform to networking rules in another country

- **802.11e:** Represents the addition of Quality of Service (or network performance levels) features and multimedia support to common wireless networks

- **802.11g:** Operates at 2.4 GHz Wi-Fi with rates as high as 54 Mbps

- **802.11h:** Allows Wi-Fi to work with different radio frequency devices at 5 GHz

- **802.11i:** Identifies security mechanisms used with any 802.11 network

- **802.11j:** Addresses Japanese wireless regulatory requirements

- **802.11n:** Improves network throughput and expands rates from 54 Mbps to 600 Mbps

- **802.11-2012:** Covers a variety of clean-up and maintenance issues for the various standards

- **802.11ac:** Addresses very high throughput of 6 GHz, building on the 802.11n standard

- **802.11af:** Addresses using TV white space for WLAN operation, limiting interference, and expanding possible range (referred to as *super Wi-Fi* and approved February 2014)

- **802.11ax:** Proposed standard for high efficiency WLAN, increasing throughput by four times that of 802.11ac

This might seem like a far-fetched example. However, someone using a laptop or any other wireless device (portable gaming devices come to mind) can pick up and use your wireless signal from outside your home or office — without your even knowing it.

The good news is that wireless networks come with some basic protection — Wired Equivalent Privacy (WEP) — which is simply an encryption method that scrambles the information being sent out on a wireless signal. The bad news (you knew it was coming) is that WEP is no longer considered secure given the decrypting tools readily available to thieves. A more secure option, and the most common, is Wi-Fi Protected Access (WPA) 2 with PSK (Pre-Shared Key) encryption keys. This authentication tool provides another layer of security and was designed to address the problem spots with WEP. Although WPA 2 with PSK was recently shown to also have some vulnerabilities, it is still thought to be the most secure option.

Any type of security measure is only a deterrent. If someone really wants access to your network, he or she will find a way. In most cases, though, online thieves and hackers take a more random approach. They look for someone who is careless or naive and then take advantage of that opportunity to intrude.

Unfortunately, wireless networks can leave plenty of doors unlocked to usher in a roaming thief. Check out some of the threats that leave your wireless network exposed:

✦ **Sniffing:** Hackers use software programs called *sniffers* that scan the activity (or traffic) on a network. When a sniffer detects a vulnerability, it grabs data that's being sent across the wireless network connection.

✦ **Sidejacking:** Using a program called Firesheep, essentially anyone can use an open Wi-Fi connection in a public facility to take advantage of another user in that same Wi-Fi environment. In this case, the unsuspecting user logs into a website, such as Amazon, and upon the verification of the user's name and password, a cookie is created for that and subsequent sessions. When sidejackers use Firesheep, they intercept the session cookie, basically snagging it as their own, and can then proceed to assume the identity of the original user and buy things under that name or account. In our example, the sidejacker now has the cookie and Amazon can't tell whether or not the legal member is using it.

✦ **Wardriving:** Using a wireless device, such as a laptop or smartphone, a person literally drives around picking up unprotected wireless signals from homes and businesses. The wireless identification information (service set identifier, or SSID) is documented along with your physical address. Your information is put into an online database that lets curious thieves know that your wireless network is accessible.

**Book V
Chapter 5**

Overcoming
Security Concerns
in the Wireless
World

✦ **Evil twin:** In this scenario, your access to a legitimate wireless access point is blocked or jammed. Then you're redirected to a second access point that's managed by a hacker. At that point, all the information you transmit is vulnerable, and thieves can even capture keystrokes to find passwords. This type of threat most often occurs in public Wi-Fi spots such as airports and coffee shops.

✦ **WiPhishing:** Similar to the evil twin threat, thieves basically lure you to what looks like a safe access point. By using common SSIDs of public hot spots, your computer connects to a hacker's network. Again, your information becomes readily viewable; in some cases, viruses and Trojans are unknowingly sent to your system. (Read more about viruses and Trojans in Book IV, Chapter 3.)

✦ **Snoopy:** With this threat, mobile phones and any other wireless devices with Wi-Fi enabled are at risk of being compromised by drones. It sounds like something out of a spy novel, but drones armed with computers programmed to track and profile wireless devices and intercept or spoof a network can capture your data. The attacker gains access to all types of data (such as passwords and credit card numbers) shared between the mobile device and the intended network.

Obviously, the real problem with these and other wireless network threats is that your bottom line is at risk. For online thieves, it's not a harmless hobby: It represents money in their pocket and out of yours. That's why investing in precautionary security measures is worthwhile.

Establishing Barriers

When protecting your wireless network, you can choose from a range of services, applications, and common procedures that can lower the risk of being compromised.

Following your common sense

Here are some basic rules you can follow to minimize your risk:

✦ **Shut down.** As silly as this method might sound, simply turning off your laptop when you're not using it reduces the chance for intrusion on your network. This technique also includes cutting the power to your cable or DSL.

✦ **Limit sharing.** Allow your networked computers to have shared access to only limited files or directories rather than to hard drives. In fact, you might want to disable file and print sharing.

✦ **Add a personal firewall.** A personal firewall installed on your laptop or on other individual computers provides another layer of protection between you and the wireless world.

✦ **Configure WPA2.** Ensure that all devices on your network are configured or set up to use WPA2, the enhanced version of wireless encryption. If not, the less protective WEP wireless encryption becomes the default.

✦ **Disable broadcast.** You can turn off the broadcast SSID feature that automatically searches for and logs on to a wireless connection. In other words, don't leave the Wi-Fi setting of your wireless device always turned on.

✦ **Change the SSID.** Wireless network devices that you buy are supplied with a preset SSID, which makes access convenient for thieves. Because this preset SSID identifies your network, you should immediately create a new SSID after installation of the wireless device. Create your SSID by following suggested guidelines for creating any password:

   • *Characters:* Combine letters and numbers.

   • *Length:* Use the number of characters allowed. (If the limit is 12, for example, use all 12 characters.)

   • *Uniqueness:* Your SSID should be different from any of your other passwords.

   • *Updates:* Change your SSID every three to four months.

To change your SSID, disable the broadcast feature, or configure devices for WPA, refer to the owner's manual supplied with your particular wireless router or access point.

✦ **Update your OS and apps.** Make sure you always install OS (operating system) updates, as well as any updates to applications you use, as soon as the updates are available. The updates frequently include patches or fixes to security flaws.

The increased use of social media networks, virtual games, cloud-based services, and other apps on wireless devices provides plenty of opportunity for security vulnerabilities. One of the best ways to fight it is to install the most recent updates, as soon as they are available.

✦ **Use two-factor authentication.** This security process requires two methods of identification, usually a password (something you know) and a physical token (something you have), such as your mobile phone. If Net-thieves get your password over a wireless network, they must still have the physical token before they can gain access to your online data.

Many websites provide two-factor authentication, and taking the time to enable it is worthwhile. Some of the most important sites where you should consider using it are Gmail, PayPal, Amazon Web Services, Apple, Dropbox, Microsoft, and WordPress. Because social media sites are increasingly vulnerable to security attacks, two-factor authentication is recommended for LinkedIn, Twitter, and Facebook. Keep in mind that if a site such as Yahoo! or Twitter gets hacked and passwords are stolen

Book V
Chapter 5

Overcoming
Security Concerns
in the Wireless
World

(which has happened several times recently), the stolen passwords are run through programs to find matches to other sites that use the same password. If you use the same password for multiple sites (a real no-no!), you could have a serious data breach on your hands.

To show you how easy it is to set up two-factor authentication, consider this example. If you're a Gmail user, authorizing use of the two-factor authentication mode enables Google to send a text message to your mobile phone that contains a simple numeric code. You must use both your normal password and the numeric code to access your Gmail account.

Set up your Gmail account for two-factor authentication by following these steps:

1. **Log in to your Gmail account at www.google.com.**

   Access your Gmail account by clicking your photo, which appears in the upper-right corner of the Google.com page.

2. **Click the Security tab at the top of the page.**

   Blocks with various security settings appear.

3. **Under the Password settings block, click the Setup 2-Step Verification link.**

   A two-step verification overview and sign-up page appears.

4. **On the right side of the page, click the Start Setup button, and then sign in to your account with your password again.**

   A Set Up Your Phone page appears.

5. **If your preferred phone number is not displayed, fill in the box with the phone number you want to use for Google to send verification codes.**

   Choose to receive either text messages or voice calls.

6. **Select the Send Code button.**

7. **After you receive a code from Google, follow the onscreen instructions to complete the next three steps of the verification set-up process.**

Setting up a virtual private network

When you use a *virtual private network* (VPN), you create a protective tunnel around your wireless connection. The VPN keeps your transmission secure and also keeps out anyone not specifically granted access. To set up a VPN for your home office or small business, you can purchase a wireless VPN firewall from companies such as Netgear (www.netgear.com).

If you plan to work frequently at hot spots, consider signing up for a subscription-based VPN service. As we mentioned, one of the biggest threats when working from free Wi-Fi hot spots is Firesheep. Because Firesheep is so easy to access and use, the chances of becoming a victim of this threat are super high. So far, one of the best protections against a Firesheep attack is having a VPN. You can connect to a VPN for added protection in restaurants, hotels, airports, or any other Wi-Fi hot spot. Check out providers such as Private Internet Access (`www.privateinternetaccess.com`), which costs as little as $7 per month or $40 per year. TorGuard (`www.torguard.net`) offers two kinds of VPN services, starting at $5 per month.

Keeping an eye on your connection

No single method is best for protecting against wireless crimes. Instead, use a combination of security measures and common sense. You can never be too secure — the more the more measures you take, the better off you are.

Book VI
Boosting Sales

Contents at a Glance

Chapter 1: Driving Traffic, Driving Sales

In This Chapter

✔ Calculating the visitors-to-sales ratio at your site

✔ Discovering your high-volume traffic periods

✔ Marketing your site to drive traffic through the roof

✔ Getting customers to make the decision to buy

You've probably heard the old saying "Build it and they will come." And you probably know by now that this particular theory doesn't necessarily apply to your website. Instead, your site is competing for visitors with hundreds of thousands (if not millions) of other sites. If that's not intimidating enough, consider that you have to not only figure out how to get people to come to your website but also convince them to stay long enough to buy something from you.

Both challenges pretty much boil down to your conversion rate — how many browsers become buyers. In this chapter, we show you why your site's conversion rate matters, provide instructions for calculating it, and then describe some strategies for increasing it.

Calculating Your Site's Conversion Rate

In any retail business, the goal is to *convert* a window shopper to a real buyer. For online businesses, you can use a simple formula to determine how successful you are at converting shoppers to buyers. The formula, called your *conversion rate*, is the number of visitors that come to your site and then buy from you for a given period of time. For example, suppose that on one day, 15 people buy something from your website and you get a total of 1,500 unique visits to your site. You calculate your conversion rate by dividing 15 by 1,500, for a 1 percent conversion rate for the day. That's simple enough. The concept becomes complicated, though, when you try to pin down exactly which number represents a good conversion rate.

Before we try to identify a healthy conversion rate, note that many types of conversion rates are worth tracking, and lots of factors influence the final number. For starters, in this book we often talk about conversion rates in terms of e-commerce, or B2C (business-to-consumer) sites, but B2B (business-to-business) sites must consider conversion rates, too. What's the difference? In B2C, the ultimate conversion is the online purchase of the product you're selling. In B2B, you may have a more involved sales process where customers buy from a salesperson, instead of online. In that case, your conversion rates may track your online lead generation (submitting a web form or downloading a white paper, for example). Whether you're an online retailer selling B2C or you have a B2B website that needs to generate leads, here are some other conversion rates that may matter to you:

✦ **Format:** An action, or conversion, occurs not only in a shopping cart but also on a non-e-commerce web page, on a landing page (that may reside off your primary website), or in an e-mail. You'd need to monitor conversion rates for all these types of pages.

✦ **Device:** Conversions and what they mean or how they are made may differ by the type of device from which they originate, such as a desktop, a tablet, or a mobile device (smartphone.) Note that the mobile device category may include both smartphones and tablets.

✦ **Visitor or source:** You may have one ideal conversion rate for North American website traffic and a separate rate for international traffic. Depending on your data's *granularity,* or the level of detail you have available about your website traffic, you might be able to track conversion rates in more specific ways. For example, you might have a conversion rate by customer type (new customer or returning customer), or by visitor type (new site visitor or returning visitor), or industry.

Understanding that a one-size-fits-all conversion rate does not exist is important — and necessary when evaluating how to improve that rate! When you dig deeper, the details or data behind a single conversion rate number can reveal very different information.

Experts cite different acceptable conversion rate percentages. You often hear an average conversion rate of 2 to 4 percent for e-commerce sites. We've seen everything from .05 percent to nearly 8 percent, depending on the type of site. For established, larger online brands, a conversion rate of 20 percent or more is not unusual. With B2B sites, conversion rates are often cited as being even higher, sometimes close to 30 percent.

Before benchmarking any of these conversion rates against your site, make sure you know exactly what those percentages represent. Is the percentage an across-site average or does it apply only to shopping cart conversions or to a particular type of offer? Is the percentage for a particular day, for one event, or across a year? For example, a popular e-commerce conversion rate for researchers to track surrounds Cyber Monday (the Monday following Thanksgiving), which is typically thought to be the busiest online shopping day of the year. In the past, for this one day, conversion rates for new customers have tracked close to 5 percent for online retailers, but these numbers don't always reflect Cyber Monday conversion rates for small online retailers with less than a million dollars in revenue.

A report that we like to follow because of its level of detail is the IBM Digital Analytics Benchmark, Black Friday Report. (Although this report is not for Cyber Monday, it is specific to online retailers and applies to the same busy online shopping weekend.) Again, it tracks data for a single day of the year, but it divides the information into numerous segments, such as U.S. retail as a whole, health and beauty, home, and department stores. The report also breaks out conversion rates for each of these categories based on new visitor, shopping cart, and mobile conversion rates. This type of report gives you a much clearer understanding of how your similar conversion rates may then compare.

When researching conversion rates, use industry data that most closely matches your type of online business and know exactly what type of conversion is being tracked. For our purposes, let's consider 2 percent a good conversion rate for first-time visitors to your e-commerce site throughout the calendar year.

What if your site has 500 visitors per day? At a 2 percent conversion rate, that's about 10 sales (500 × .02) per day. That number seems a little depressing — unless you have some incredibly high profit margins! Based on this equation, one way to drive up sales is to drive more traffic to your site.

To figure out how many visitors you need for a healthy 2 percent conversion rate, follow these steps:

1. **Determine the number of sales you need per day to stay in business.**

2. **Divide the number of sales by .02 (the 2 percent conversion rate).**

This number becomes your targeted goal. For example, if you want 100 sales per day, your target goal is 5,000 visitors per day.

Before you get too comfortable, keep in mind the following factors that influence your true conversion rate:

✦ **Qualified traffic:** If you're shooting in the dark for traffic, that conversion rate becomes a sliding scale. However, by identifying visitors who are most likely to become buyers (a higher quality of site visitor), you can put your efforts into targeting this demographic. Theoretically, you attract fewer visitors, but more of them buy.

✦ **Site construction:** Everything from the layout and navigation of your home page to your search feature and shopping cart affect the probability that your visitors will be converted to buyers. The more intuitive, attractive, and useful your site, the better your likely conversion rates.

✦ **Quality product or service:** If you have a product or service that nobody wants, the number of visitors you can attract to your site doesn't matter. The conversion rate will be zero!

✦ **Content:** Your website pages may be designed to attract visitors but not designed to immediately convert buyers. A blog, for example, may be written to gain exposure for your brand or website, but you don't expect first-time visitors to your blog to become buyers. A sitewide conversion rate (based on total number of visitors) can be misleading; tracking conversion rates for specific pages may be preferable.

✦ **Price point:** You can drive up conversion rates by using pricing strategies. Unless you can maintain price-based leverage in the marketplace, however, consider these rates falsely inflated.

Considering all these factors, another method for increasing sales is to increase your site's rate of conversion. We'll address that topic in a moment. First, let's look at what you can do to increase your traffic.

Figuring Out When You Get the Most Traffic

In addition to increasing the sheer volume of traffic, you have to look at the whole picture to increase your sales numbers. Part of navigating that landscape involves figuring out what time of day you're driving the bulk of your traffic to your site.

The average day is divided into several important time segments, called *dayparts*. This concept is important if you happen to own a business — even an online business that's open 24 hours a day, every day.

For example, a restaurant typically receives the majority of its sales at three specific times during the day: breakfast, lunch, and dinner. It works almost the same way with the Internet, where five specific dayparts represent typical patterns of online traffic:

✦ **Early morning (6 a.m. to 8 a.m.):** Fewer people shop during these hours. Research indicates online retail buying drops by half in most cases.

If you sell to an international audience, you may have customers who are buying during a daypart that is considered slow for your location. Typically, this customer segment or daypart should be a very small percentage of your overall site visitors.

✦ **Daytime (8 a.m. to 5 p.m.):** This period is one of the busiest online times for 25- to 54-year-old professionals. Conversion rates for online retailers often peak between 10 a.m. and 1 p.m. That's right: Your customers typically spend their lunch hours checking out your site. Not only that — they're also willing to make a purchase.

✦ **Evening (5 p.m. to 11 p.m.):** Between the time folks arrive home from work and the time they go to bed, they apparently have enough downtime to do a little more online shopping.

✦ **Late night (11 p.m. to 6 a.m.):** This period isn't a busy one. Sure, some night owls are still looking for deals, but they're in the minority.

✦ **Weekend:** Yes, Saturday and Sunday get their own daypart! The conversion rates vary for the weekend daypart, but you can count on the peak periods being somewhat similar to weekday buying habits.

Does all this mean that you should close shop during the wee hours of the dayparts? Of course not! You may have an online business that doesn't match these typical buying patterns. The Internet is always open and you can potentially have customers during any daypart. To make the most of marketing to your prime dayparts, here are some strategies you can explore:

✦ **Balanced ad spending:** If you know when your customers are most receptive to your ads, that's when you want to spend the largest amount of money to get your ads shown. Similarly, you may want to decrease spending amounts during downtimes.

✦ **Increased ad revenue:** Alternatively, if you sell advertising, you may be able to make more money per impression during busy dayparts.

✦ **Targeted specials:** Don't just run more ads during your slow periods. Create offers and time-sensitive pricing specials targeted to the frenzied shoppers from your busiest dayparts, too. With the right offer, you may be able to bump an already strong conversion rate into an outstanding conversion rate. You can also use a retargeting strategy to target ads to site visitors no matter what time of day they visit your site. Retargeting is a way of continuing to show ads to visitors even after they leave your website (tracking capabilities allow the ads to follow your visitors to other sites and be displayed on those sites).

You should also think about your specific site and to whom it appeals most. If the majority of customers are teens, for example, the likelihood that they will buy from you during the weekday lunch hour drops. Evening and weekend dayparts may be busier for you because your customers aren't in school during these periods. However, lunchtime may present an opportunity to reach out to their parents (or to other secondary customers). Consider promoting your site's gift cards to this customer.

Balance the daypart information with what you already know about your customers. Always ask these questions:

✦ Who are my primary customers?

✦ Based on my their lifestyles, when will my customers most likely visit my site?

✦ How can I serve my customers better during the specific dayparts when they're most likely to be ready to shop?

✦ What new, or secondary, customer base can I reach by taking advantage of peak dayparts?

✦ What type of offer or incentive can I create to attract new customers?

✦ How can I better serve my customers during the least-busy dayparts?

✦ What can I do to improve traffic and buying during nonpeak dayparts?

Getting Customers to Notice Your Website

Getting prospective customers to stand up and take note isn't of your website isn't difficult, but you have to be consistent, thorough, and unrelenting. Take a multipronged approach that includes both online and offline marketing efforts. You can use the following techniques to increase traffic and bump up conversion rates:

✦ **Keyword searches:** Paid keywords, such as Google AdWords, have been proven to be a cost-effective method of driving targeted traffic to your site, if you budget wisely and target the right kinds of keywords. Although the cost per click (CPC) rate has gone up significantly in the past few years for popular search terms, plenty of keyword search phrases are still affordable — especially long-tail keyphrases. For example, the term *flower pots* is a broader term and may therefore be more expensive than *terracotta flower pots.* Check out Chapter 6 of this minibook to find out more about paid keywords.

 Google offers lots of resources to help you learn everything from the basics of using AdWords to mastering advanced user strategies and tips. These resources are available in the Google AdWords Small Business Center at www.google.com/adwords/smallbusinesscenter/.

✦ **Organic search**: Considering web shoppers' dependency on Google, Yahoo!, and Bing, getting your site to rank high remains an important way to drive traffic. Search engine optimization is a critical strategy when driving *organic* (non-paid) search results. To gain organic traffic, you must optimize your site with the right content and appropriate keywords. We show you how to reach that all-important rank in Chapter 6 of this minibook.

✦ **External links:** Increasing the number of sites that link to your site is usually a safe bet for attracting qualified visitors. Similarly, getting link referrals from online custom reviews and blogs can greatly increase traffic to your site.

✦ **Affiliate traffic:** Setting up an affiliate program can also help direct traffic your way. (Of course, you may not want to take on this task until your site is more established.) See Book IV, Chapter 2, where we discuss affiliates in more detail.

✦ **Advertising:** Paid banner advertising, display ads, retargeting (showing ads in other websites or social media sites to people who have already visited one of your web pages or landing pages but did not convert), and even direct-mail campaigns can generate just enough interest to make a visit worthwhile.

✦ **Offline efforts:** Everything you do doesn't have to take place online. Promoting your site offline (such as on business cards and by networking) can help drive traffic, too. See Book VII, Chapter 4 for more offline advertising ideas.

✦ **Content:** Building content on your site gives customers a reason to check out your site and then hang around long enough to buy something. We cover the different content that you can provide (such as reviews) in Book IV, Chapter 2.

✦ **E-newsletters:** Whatever the method you use to reach customers, the idea is to connect with them. After they form a relationship with you or define a need that you can answer, they will follow your lead — right back to your site. See Book IV, Chapter 3 to find out how to put together an e-newsletter.

Getting Customers to Buy

Driving traffic is certainly one approach to increasing your rate of success. After all, if converting visitors to buyers is indeed a numbers game, the more site visitors, the more buyers you *potentially* will convert. Your actual conversion rate may remain the same, but if you now have 4,000 visitors per day (instead of the 500 we used in our earlier example), your 2 percent conversion rate should bring in 80 sales. Right?

Statistically, your odds for gaining more sales should increase with a greater number of visitors. But consider the cost of increasing those odds. Using paid keyword searches and online advertising, you could end up spending thousands of dollars for that increased traffic count. A different approach is to increase your rate of conversion by getting more of your visitors to buy. For example, by increasing your conversion rate to 4 percent with your existing website traffic, you essentially double your sales, without spending the money required to double your traffic.

How do you get people to click that buy button more frequently? According to research, the following factors influence the conversion of browsers to buyers:

+ **Your site's security:** Buyers prefer to make a purchase from the site that is most secure. This means keeping your SSL certificate updated and clearly displaying privacy policies and recognizable trust seals, such as those from the Better Business Bureau.

+ **Multiple options for payments:** Customers want and need choices when it comes to making a purchase. These options include credit cards, debit cards, PayPal, and extended payment option programs.

In addition, increasing conversion rates may also be a matter of making buying easier:

+ **Decrease clicks.** Reduce the number of clicks required to get from your home page to a product page, or from the product page to completing the purchase transaction.

+ **Minimize buying headaches.** Some research shows the rate of shopping cart abandonment at 75 percent! You can reduce that percentage by requiring only a few steps to complete a purchase, or by increasing the functionality of your shopping cart.

+ **Incentivize buying now.** Offer reasons for a customer to buy on the spot, such as a small discount, a freebie that comes with the purchase, or free shipping — but only if the customer makes a purchase on that day's visit to your site.

+ **Add online chat.** Include the opportunity for guests to receive real-time support using online chat. Having the ability to get product questions answered immediately can speed up a customer's decision to buy.

+ **Guarantee it.** Whether you offer a money-back guarantee or the manufacturer of a product offers a full or limited warranty, make this information readily available to your shoppers. Also include a link to your store's return policy. These pieces of information can put customers at ease and make them more willing to purchase an item from you.

+ **Display customer reviews.** It's no secret that as consumers, almost all of us are influenced by others' experiences and opinions, which is one reason why product reviews by customers are so popular. Your online customers may be more inclined to make a purchasing decision if they can see that other customers were satisfied with the product.

In addition, you should think like a customer. When making changes to your site, consider what factors influence your own decision to buy when shopping with an online retailer. Chances are, the things that encourage or discourage your buying behaviors are the same as your customers. And addressing these concerns is the first step to boosting your site's conversion rate.

Chapter 2: Special-Edition Public Relations for the Web

In This Chapter

- ✔ Writing product reviews
- ✔ Being a community leader by hosting web seminars and sharing information
- ✔ Distributing free articles to build your portfolio

Although *PR* stands for *press release*, you don't always have to draw attention to your business in the form of a press release. Publicity can come in many forms, and by using the Internet, you can differentiate yourself and your company to attract customers in lots of ways. You've probably heard the phrase "There's no such thing as bad publicity." Well, if your customers are unhappy and advise everyone they know to avoid your business, we're sure that it won't help your bottom line.

You must be out among the community you depend on to build a relationship for customers to connect and use your business. You not only gain a sense of what customers want and need in their lives but also connect with the community to help sell the story of you and your business. Consider the time you spend online reaching out to your community as an investment. You're building intangible relations, the goodwill that a positive company can generate, and the reason why these customers should shop with you and not someone else.

In this chapter, we focus on the publicity that revolves more around you and your product knowledge. We explore different ways in which you can indirectly promote your company while demonstrating your expertise and competence in your product's subject area. If you establish yourself as a leader or expert, customers will consider your business. One way is by using blogs, which we discuss fully in Book X, Chapter 3.

Every time you give, you receive in return. When you contribute information, opinions, reviews, or specific knowledge, people see that it's coming from the owner of Business X, not just from an individual. They believe that they can get to know both you and, through you, your business. Customers are looking for a connection, a bond, a reason to go with a particular business. Give it to them.

Writing Reviews

Most shoppers are used to seeing positive and glowing comments about a product clearly printed on the product box. They more highly value third-party independent reviews, however. After all, what company would slap the label *Worst Product Ever* on its product packaging? However, if thousands or millions of people are rallying because they're not happy with a product, consumers will give that action much more weight than a company's endorsements.

The independent testing organization Consumer Reports (`www.consumer reports.org`) rates everything from automobiles to computers to garden equipment. It has more than 4 million subscribers to its magazine and an estimated 2 million people to its subscription website, where thousands of reviews, statistical test data, and evaluations are available for members to see. When customers are shopping online, they don't have the option to ask their local shopkeeper what he or she thinks about an item or to hear about how that shopkeeper helped a customer with an item that worked well (or not so well) at home. Customers turn then to reviews written online about the product, which is where you can make your entrance.

As someone with access to these products, and a history with them, you likely know more than the average person about some of the products you sell. Although you might not have used everything you sell, you have a better idea about how to evaluate a product or you gathered enough customer comments to form an opinion based on a fact.

When you write reviews, readers typically can access your profile and find out more about you. You might be surprised at the number of people who take the time to do so. Maybe they were impressed or intrigued by your comments about a product and want to learn more. Or maybe they're impressed by your depth of knowledge and want to know what else you approve or disapprove of. After customers identify you as knowledgeable, your opinion takes on greater weight, and so does your business.

In this section, we show you how to put those thoughts together and write some reviews of the products you sell.

Finding the best places to post reviews

The most valuable place your reviews can be posted is on your own website. After all, you're contributing this value to help your online business succeed and empower your customers to make better decisions. Therefore, you should incorporate any reviews you write to appear alongside the products you're selling on your own website.

After that, you want to spread the word about your knowledge and demonstrate to the larger community your experience with, and the professionalism of, a given product, to raise your profile as a product expert and expose new potential customers to your company. Start by doing some investigating online, and look for websites that offer reviews of products you carry.

These major online sites offer reviews:

✦ **ConsumerSearch (www.consumersearch.com, owned by About.com):** Using human editors who gather information without regard to advertising or commercial considerations, ConsumerSearch (see Figure 2-1) collects the best reviews they can find on the web and provides analysis and recommendations on what to buy, in categories that range from health and beauty to electronics and more.

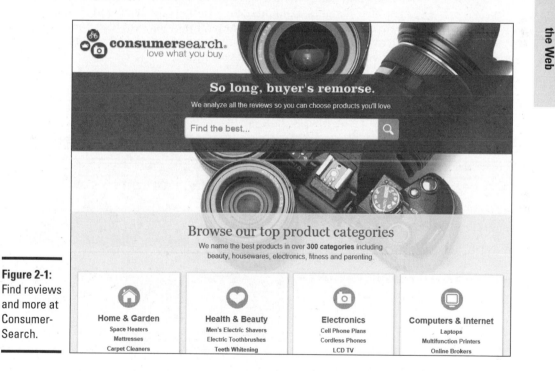

Figure 2-1: Find reviews and more at Consumer-Search.

✦ **Amazon (www.amazon.com):** The world's largest online retailer offers a wealth of reviews for its growing catalog of items. These reviews and comments are some of the drawing points for customers to this site.

✦ **eBay (www.ebay.com/gds):** The world's largest online trading platform has been incorporating reviews and guides that its members provide. When eBay buyers are looking around for their favorite merchandise, they can read reviews and buying guides written by other eBayers about those same products, to help make up their minds about whether they should bid on them.

✦ **CNet Reviews (www.cnet.com/reviews):** This online technology news site has amassed a growing array of product reviews for computers and consumer electronics and even services such as web hosting. Below the editor's reviews is a section where all user reviews are grouped and averaged per product.

✦ **Epinions (www.epinions.com):** With more than 30 categories of products, Epinions (see Figure 2-2) has collected tens of millions of product reviews and can generate personalized recommendations and provide customer insights. Epinions offers unbiased advice and in-depth product evaluations. Along with the reviews, Epinions provides complete pricing and availability options from a number of online merchants who have been verified and rated by the website.

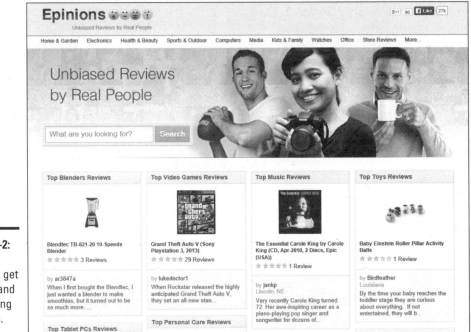

Figure 2-2: Read reviews, get advice, and shop using Epinions.

Other places cater to different niches, such as Growing a Green Family's Product Reviews (`www.growingagreenfamily.com/green-product-reviews/`) for ecofriendly products and *PC Magazine* (`www.pcmag.com`) for computer components. If necessary, ask some of your customers where they do their research before they buy.

Every once in a while, you should check up on your product reviews to see what other readers are saying in response. Reader feedback can provide invaluable advice about whether your reviews are hitting the mark or are too confusing. Keep an open mind about their comments, and treat this strategy as another learning exercise.

In the end, you should be persistent and not overbearing. Allocate a specific amount of time per week to contribute reviews so that you don't spend all your time filling up page after page. Stay current, and approach new avenues as you have time. If you deal in new products, make sure that you're one of the first people to review a product. That way, you lend greater authority to your opinion and provide your own helpful early warning if you review an item you sell that customers have a frustrating time using properly.

Writing the review, section by section

After you know where to post your review, it's time to write one! You don't need an English degree to write reviews, and you don't have to carefully research, document, and stamp each one for approval. Most people are looking for honest, candid, easy-to-understand information that breaks down the essentials about a product. The best way we have heard someone describe how to write a review is this: "If friends asked you what you thought about product X, you could hand them your review as the answer."

Have the product in front of you when you start writing. Being able to hold up the product, scan its box, read its specifications, and experiment with the product can trigger thoughts and confirm suspicions when you're writing a review.

When you're ready to write a review, make sure that it has these basic sections:

✦ **Initial impressions:** Start by writing your initial impressions of the product. What were your initial thoughts the first time you saw the product? What did you think about the first time you used the product? What were you hoping the product would provide, and what did you expect it to be?

Don't worry about immediately assigning a product a number between 1 and 10 or coming up with a title. These issues should be the last ones you write about, because writing the rest of the review can lead you to the ultimate ranking answer.

Your initial impressions should provide a quick summary of the product, your impressions, and a sense of whether you favor it. Someone reading only your first paragraph should see all the basic information and know whether you approve or disapprove.

✦ **Pros:** Write the reasons you like the product, no matter how big or small the issue. Include the ways that this product is better than similar products on the market, and describe its best features.

✦ **Cons:** Write the reasons you dislike the product. Think of the features you're not happy with or that you wish could be changed. Note whether the problem prevents you from using the product correctly or just bothers you individually. Obviously, rank the problems that affect your usage higher than your personal opinion.

✦ **Experience with the product:** Regardless of whether you love the product or hate it, does it do what it's supposed to do? If it's a digital camera, for example, does it take high-quality photos? Even if the camera is hard to use and its battery life is low, does it perform its main functions? Most products have a purpose or a use, and people want to know how this product can help them. A great-looking item might be completely useless, or an item that solves a big problem might be difficult to use.

Talk about your experience with your product in a positive, nonconfrontational way. Don't say that you love it because it sells well. Say that you love it because the product is so solid that your customers love it and that's why it sells well.

✦ **Recommendations:** Would you buy your product? Would you recommend it to someone? Would you recommend it only for a specialized need or a certain kind of user?

After you complete all these areas, you should have a good idea of how you would rank the product on a scale from 1 to 10. You might be asked to rank certain individual characteristics on some websites, so consider them last too, after you think about the good, the bad, and the ugly.

The title of your review should be a one-sentence summary that captures the essence of what you're saying. The easiest titles to write are for products you absolutely love ("This product is the best thing since sliced bread!") or absolutely hate ("Don't buy this product, even if they're giving it away!"). For most reviews that lie between these two ends of the spectrum, choose a good point and a bad point, and emphasize the one you most agree with. For example, say something like "Good product for the money, but don't expect full features!" or "Product X: Adequate but in need of improvement."

Make sure that your reviews are sincere and honest. Don't rave about a product just because you sell it and hope that a good review will boost sales. Readers will see through an insincere review, and your plan could backfire because they will go online and warn other consumers not to trust you or your reviews, opinions, or business.

After you have completed your written review, you can also turn it into a video review. Record yourself in front of a computer webcam, a handheld video recorder or tablet device (such as an Apple iPad), or even certain smartphones, and then upload the product review to popular video-sharing sites such as YouTube. Don't forget to brand your review by embedding a link to your website. Video allows you to visually demonstrate a physical product, which will only add to your review's effect.

Becoming a Community Leader

Building a business is not only time-consuming but also rewarding and educational. Your work, however, doesn't end with your own website. Interaction with the community is essential for any business, whether you hang a shingle or code a web page. On the Internet, you have ways to participate as a business owner that lend credibility and raise the collective energy of your community, who will remember those qualities when it's time to buy.

Speaking out with webinars

In the past, you could make connections with potential customers by agreeing to speak at their Rotary Club or Chamber of Commerce meetings about your chosen subject area. The Internet and high technology have combined to create a way for you to deliver that same talk — without the rubber chicken and the echo from the borrowed sound system. A *webinar* (short for *web* sem*inar*) combines video, audio, and graphics to give the audience an experience similar to sitting in a lecture hall.

When you prepare and deliver a webinar, you can give the same set of information to an unlimited number of people and at any time of the day. You control the message, the delivery of that message, and all the accompanying information that goes with the message. The formatting of your presentation is always the same with a webinar, and your presence cannot be deleted, because your image, voice, and slides drive the presentation.

One leading company that produces web seminars is WebEx, shown in Figure 2-3. Founded in 1996 and acquired by Cisco Systems, WebEx focuses on ways to provide videoconferencing and other technologies to connect multiple people to one event. A section on its website is dedicated to creating these web seminars. You can read about WebEx services and prices by going to `www.webex.com/howto/index.html`.

You don't necessarily have to worry about the technical aspect of producing a webinar. See whether you can partner with a company that can handle the technical tasks so that you can focus on speaking. You're giving the company the benefit of a webinar that it can include in its portfolio, and you can unburden yourself from the technical process of creating the event. In this case, definitely make sure that your profile is front and center on the webinar.

Figure 2-3:
Expand your business by using WebEx web seminars.

Organize your thoughts for a webinar as though you're speaking in a big lecture hall. The only difference is that people are watching on their computer screens, not from chairs physically positioned in front of you. A webinar presenter can host a question-and-answer session with a live audience, so it can be an interactive experience, not just another lecture.

Book IV, Chapter 3 provides more information about how you can turn a webinar into its own profit center rather than just a mechanism for raising your profile.

Billing yourself as an expert

Given the immense amount of information and options for consumers, the easiest way for them to cut through all the noise and presentations of the high-tech world to find what they're looking for is to rely on the low-tech, time-tested tradition known as *word of mouth*. Most customers make their decisions based on recommendations from family members and friends. In the absence of a friend or family member, however, online consumers look for an expert in that area. That's where you come in.

Expertise isn't a degree that a university can confer on you; it's the real-world experience you build up in a given subject area or product category. It's up to you to share that information in a constructive way so that customers see you as the expert. After customers start asking you for advice, they also find out about your business. When it's time for them to buy a product, they're much more likely to choose someone they consider an expert over a nameless, faceless website with a slightly lower price.

To become an expert, spend some time in the places where your potential customers congregate and ask questions about your area of expertise. Three of the most popular places to frequent are Twitter, discussion groups, and mailing lists. Follow these general steps:

**Book VI
Chapter 2**

**Special-Edition
Public Relations for
the Web**

1. **Identify the discussion groups or Twitter topics that pertain to your area.**

   Dig around, do some research, and use search engines or your favorite websites to see where people are gathering online to discuss topics.

2. **Join the designated groups, and find out how to participate correctly.**

   Take the time to complete the registration processes at each of these sites, and choose usernames that advertise you, not your business. If people see that a corporate name is contributing information, they might see it as an invasion for sales only. (For Twitter, see what topic names, or *hashtags,* are used consistently, and be sure to use the relevant hashtag in your reply.)

3. **Set up your profile and signature file.**

   Make sure that your business and website address are clearly mentioned at the bottom of your signature file and Twitter Profile Bio field, so that people can follow up if they're interested.

   In your profile and signature page, always reference one landing page, or a web page that will consistently reference all your online articles, websites, and online references.

4. **Start looking for discussions and questions that you can contribute to easily.**

   Start by monitoring conversations to develop a sense for the tone that people use in their responses. Don't feel that you have to dive in right away. Start by providing a comment here and there, and take some time in the beginning to observe the atmosphere and get to know the major contributors.

   Don't use these places for blatant self-promotion. Participate in a healthy manner, and make sure that your signature file contains a line or two about your web business.

5. **Set up a regular schedule to contribute to one or more discussions.**

Include this process in your weekly routine so that you don't forget about it as time goes on. Maybe you spend a half-hour each Tuesday logging in to see the most active discussions. You can spend a few minutes each day and look for the most relevant discussions for your area. Find something that fits your schedule so that you have the time to participate without feeling rushed.

 Make sure that each posting is free of any obvious spelling and grammatical errors. Use a word processing program, such as Microsoft Word, to write your post so that you can easily check and correct mistakes. Then copy and paste your words into the listing.

Writing Articles

When people share information, they don't limit themselves to just one or two channels. Countless sites are set up to satisfy people's need for more information, organized around every imaginable subject, discipline, passion, hobby, and criteria. Although these sites are good at organization and attracting traffic, they all usually want help with one particular area: content.

People who contribute content gain lots of exposure by sharing their information. The exposure comes from one simple requirement that you tie in to your free articles: Your name, as the author, contains a profile that links to your website. You allow anyone to publish, reprint, or distribute your article, as long as your profile information is attached. That way, everyone who reads these articles knows that you're the source of that information and is inclined to check out your company's website to see what else is out there.

Free distribution of your articles has other important benefits. As more and more websites pick up your article and publish it, more search engines pick up the link in your profile. Many search engines, especially Google, now rank search results based partially on how many people make references to a given web page. Your articles create more references on the web, and ultimately raise your ranking, so you naturally appear in a user's search results and don't have to pay as much in search engine advertising. (See Book VI, Chapter 3 for more information on search engine advertising.)

Tailoring your article topics

When you were told to write a paper in school, you probably didn't have much choice about the topic. Now you have complete control, so be sure to write articles that appeal to your customer base. You can easily fall into the trap of writing only what you know, even if that topic is nowhere near what your customers would be reading.

Writing what you know about works in the beginning, if you need some motivation to start writing articles.

As a business owner, you're already looking to stay ahead of the curve to see where your market is heading. Now you get to use that knowledge to help tell customers what to expect. You can choose from a variety of angles for your article, including these:

✦ Provide straightforward, concise explanations and examples of a new technology.

✦ List four or five nonobvious ways that a product or service can be beneficial.

✦ Create a step-by-step guide for accomplishing a specific task.

✦ Describe how to improve a (popular) way of doing something.

✦ Specify what not to do in a given area.

✦ Create a case study showing someone's right and wrong actions, and then explain why.

The best topics, sometimes, are about issues you just faced with your business or your personal online adventures. Think about how you handled a given situation. Did you learn a new trick or two along the way? Did the recommended solution pan out? Did an unorthodox method (or even the tried-and-true method) produce measurable results? If so, ask yourself this question: "Would other people benefit from what I just learned?" If so, and if you're not revealing a competitive advantage, start making notes to turn into an article.

Putting together your article

Don't be afraid to brainstorm and jot down ideas to revisit later. Your articles have to capture readers' attention, even if it's just for the first paragraph, so it has to be relevant, useful, and interesting. Most people — whether they're reading newspaper stories, magazine features, or online write-ups — see a headline, read (maybe) the first paragraph, and then move on. That's why articles have to grab you in the first paragraph.

Put together your articles in this fashion:

✦ **The first paragraph** presents the overall picture. You need to accurately and vividly describe the situation you address in your article. If the article is about a solution to a problem, first discuss the problem. Remind readers about how much of a headache this problem can cause, and detail the pain, so to speak. If you're writing a step-by-step guide, use the first paragraph to talk about the problem this guide will solve. Then make sure that you end the first paragraph by telling readers what you will say in the rest of the article.

✦ **Middle paragraphs** contain the "meat," or the essence, of the article — namely, the information that readers want to read. Stay away from technical jargon or low-level details or specifics, and provide an overview in plain English of what readers should do, look into, or implement themselves. Let them do the additional research of finding the specifics. Your article should identify the solution path and give readers enough information to continue investigating.

✦ **The last paragraph** wraps up your article with a summary of what you presented, and shares either a success story or a result that readers can expect afterward. If readers need to take action after reading your article, you want to leave them with an important reason to get started, even if it's an obvious reason.

The average length of an article is about 300 to 600 words, or one or two double-spaced pages in a word processor. If you're direct and to the point, don't worry about sending out a 280-word article. Conversely, if your article continues page after page, it had better be useful and not repetitive or fluffy.

Even though you're not being graded on your work, be sure to check for any spelling or grammatical errors before you send it out. Mistakes detract from the professional image you want to convey in your article, which would defeat the purpose.

If you're curious about whether your article is ready for distribution, use a small group of friends, employees, or customers as your test market by sending them a copy and asking for honest feedback. Don't expect them to correct any mistakes — just listen to their feedback and consider their comments. A peer review usually makes a piece stronger, and a stronger article is more effective.

Handing out your articles

After you write and prepare your article with the correct profile and web link, you need to distribute the goods. You can submit your articles to dedicated online article directories and e-zine newsletter sources, which then do the work of disseminating your article to various sources. These directories stay in business by providing content to hungry websites and newsletters that need content to attract visitors.

Most directories have a submission process that's available on their websites. Submit your article to as many sites as you want. You can find a good list to get started with in Table 2-1.

Table 2-1	Online Article Directories
Name	*Submission URL*
Amazines	www.amazines.com/register.cfm
Articlesbase	www.articlesbase.com/submit-articles.php
Ezine @rticles	www.ezinearticles.com/submit
GoArticles	www.goarticles.com/submit
Isnare	www.isnare.com/members.php

**Book VI
Chapter 2**

**Special-Edition
Public Relations for
the Web**

 Don't be afraid to mention the release of a new article in your blog, Facebook business page, or Twitter stream (see Figure 2-4). You gain publicity and reinforce the image you're presenting to your audience. Every reference to a new article shows how you're working to keep the community informed and gives you a great reason for a new, current blog entry.

Figure 2-4: Promote your articles using sites such as Twitter.

 If you're already a member of niche news sites, check into submitting your article directly to them. Look for an e-mail address of the editorial director or a reporter in the About Us section of that website, and send an introductory letter along with your article. You might be offered a column or contributor status, or you can serve, at the least, as a good source to find quotes for the site's upcoming articles in your area of expertise. The effort of sharing these articles all goes back to raising your exposure and achieving expert status. After all, you never know who might read your article next.

Chapter 3: Web Marketing at Work

In This Chapter

- ✔ Implementing a total marketing strategy
- ✔ Creating a long-term conversation with customers by using social media
- ✔ Offering newsletters to lure in potential customers
- ✔ Advertising through a pay-per-click strategy
- ✔ Marketing your business in nonelectric ways

Regardless of how big your online business is or will become, the power of the web is a far-reaching and low-cost way to effectively turn people on to what you provide. One reason for the effectiveness of web marketing is the power of *one-to-one marketing*. Rather than create TV ads that speak to tens of millions of people during a popular sitcom, for example, web marketing speaks directly to your interested customers and builds a one-to-one connection between a potential customer and your business. These first-time buyers can become repeat customers who spread the word about your company to new customers; your business continues to grow with each wave. Online sites such as craigslist grew in popularity because people came together not just to buy and sell stuff but also to find jobs, apartments, romance, and events in their geographical areas.

Many people believe that web marketing works for only the big companies that can rent banner ads and host lavish websites with large e-mail distribution lists. The truth is that small businesses and entrepreneurs, just like yourself, can benefit from the same techniques that the larger companies employ, by investing your time and effort along with your dollars. In this chapter, we show you how to use these marketing techniques to reach potential customers.

Developing a Marketing Strategy

In the early days of the Internet, you could build a website, get mentioned in the right places, and instantly receive a stream of customers, whether you sold sweaters or homemade apple butter. You didn't have much competition, and a hungry audience would soak up whatever they could find. Now, websites and online commerce companies sell everything that's legal (and a few things that aren't), and competition is fierce and ever-present. The days of building a website and receiving instant traffic are mostly over. In this section, we show you how to use branding and a targeted advertising strategy to spread the word about your business.

Hit the right concept at the right time, however, and you might find early success. When people heard of Google, a search engine that provided relevant results, they started using it more and more. When anyone could create a video file and share that video on the Internet with other users, who could rate and comment on those videos, YouTube jumped to the top of the charts of the social networking trend.

Devising your brand

To get your business noticed, you need to come up with a basic, all-encompassing strategy. This strategy defines and drives your marketing efforts. Always send the right message from the start so that you don't confuse your customers and waste your money.

The first part of your strategy is to create your brand image. Your *brand image* is the message that your company portrays in everything you do, from telling people about your business to treating its customers a certain way to providing value through your products and services. It's not one piece, but rather the overall sense that customers and your general audience get when they think of your business. Your brand is shaped by the successful combination of a memorable logo, a catchy slogan, a distinctive color scheme, and more. These elements all influence how your customers view your business, but individually, these elements are not your brand. Your brand is the impression your customers have of your business, and that impression is triggered by seeing the memorable logo, catchy slogan, distinctive color scheme, and more.

What should your brand be? Consider these points to get you started as you devise your brand:

+ **Competitive prices:** Because you have an online business, you're not paying for expensive retail space and a carpet for customers to trip on as they walk through the front door. You can therefore offer lower prices than your offline competitors.

+ **Convenience:** Your customers can interact with the business even when they're wearing pajamas.

+ **Customize requests:** You can provide each customer's specific request or match people with similar interests.

Although we could give you more examples, the lesson here is that you have options. Choose the brand that fits with your company.

Working the brand

After you have an idea for an appropriate brand, it's time to share it with the world. Because your business operates online, you can easily promote your business online. Billions of dollars are spent each year on web advertising (just look at Google's numbers), and the numbers increase each quarter.

Rather than pay for a billboard that you hope people see on their way to work, make your web advertising stare customers in the face — literally. You're speaking to a captive audience because the advertising is part of the screen, built into the web page in a variety of ways. In addition, you have a better chance of having the right ad reach the right customer because you can better target who receives which ad.

Because many companies offer advertising opportunities, you want to find the markets that best push your brand. Think about whom you want to reach with your brand. If your brand involves power tools and improving the home, maybe a website that offers cooking tips isn't the right place for you to advertise. If your company appeals to the teenage consumer, Cartoon Network, G4, and extreme sports websites are good places to start.

You can reach out through the web and advertise your brand and company in many ways:

✦ **Paid advertising:** Many sites offer options, such as banner ads, center ads, and paid-placement spots where you can rent space based on how many people click through to your website. This way, you can track the *click ratio* to see how effective certain sites are to your brand, and pay only when someone who wants to find out more clicks your link.

Click ratio refers to the percentage of people who click a specific ad based on the total population who saw that ad. You calculate the click ratio by dividing the number of times someone clicked an ad by the number of times the ad was displayed. On average, click ratios can range from 0.5 or 1 percent to 5 or 10 percent on specialized sites.

✦ **Social media:** Businesses of all sizes are using social media websites, such as Facebook and Twitter, to reach out where their customers are hanging out. These businesses use the sites to stay relevant, broadcast important information, and create a long-term connection with potential and existing customers instead of just trying to sell one product. With social media, you're selling the customer on your business, not a particular product.

✦ **Partnerships:** Rather than pay outright to be on someone's website, come up with a partnership deal in which you and another company promote each other to your users. You can make

• *A simple deal:* You and the other company put each other's banner ads on your own site.

- • *A complex deal:* You and the other company create joint promotions and provide links back and forth.

✦ **Classified advertising:** Rather than place banner ads that advertise your company, you can take out classified ads that market a specific product or sale item. Many sites allow you to post free ads, such as craigslist (`www.craigslist.org`), shown in Figure 3-1, eBay Classifieds (`www.ebayclassifieds.com`), and even some local newspaper online classifieds sections.

✦ **Product placement:** In this form of advertising, you arrange to get your products mentioned and your website referenced by someone else. You can do it through a blog, or someone can feature a review of your product on a website after you send a sample.

✦ **Keyword searches:** Search engines offer advertising that can appear on the same web page as search results. You can bid on the right to have your ad appear for a given keyword that someone types. See the "Searching for Traffic with Search Engine Advertising" section, a little later in this chapter, for more information.

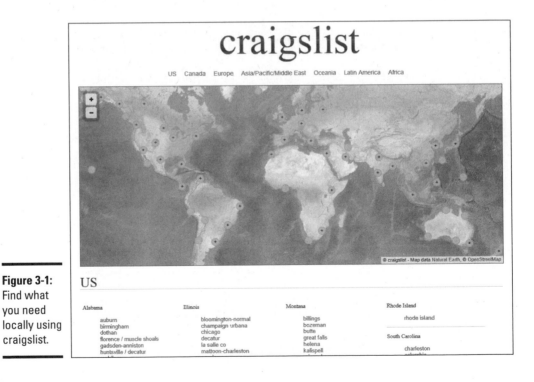

Figure 3-1:
Find what
you need
locally using
craigslist.

Big advertising campaigns don't necessarily mean big budgets. You need to think about every move that you make online, and the best campaigns start at home. Your own website needs to reflect the brand that you want to present to your customers. Every e-mail you send should mention your business and website address. When you contribute to any online discussions, chat rooms, or groups, make sure that your business and website are carefully displayed at the bottom of any posting you make. Small actions like these can lead to name recognition, which can lead to customer recognition and acquisition.

Gaining a Following with Social Media

Someone once said, "Go where your customers are." When people started using social media websites such as Facebook to keep in touch with each other and share updates, businesses quickly followed, building their own presences and business pages where fans of that business could stay in touch with that business; hear about contests, promotions, and sales; and have direct communication when there was something they liked (or disliked) about the business.

Today, websites use social media for various purposes. Some websites maintain Facebook and Twitter accounts simply to broadcast upcoming sales, specials, and Facebook-only or Twitter-only discounts or deals. Other websites have an expanded presence that includes social media sites such as Google+, Instagram, Pinterest, and Tumblr, where they share photos and new content, host unique contests, gather feedback on new products, and handle customer service inquiries. Some businesses go one step further and create original content for their social media presence or partner with other companies via social media to promote nonprofit causes or to create media events.

Using social media properly

A common mistake many businesses make with social media is to sign up for an account with these websites, set up some basic information initially, and then ignore or forget to use or update these accounts on a regular basis. Social media requires a long-term commitment, not a short-term promotion window. The most successful social media presences for businesses are updated regularly and contain useful, interesting, and helpful information not necessarily tied to the specific products or services of that business.

The other big mistake that businesses make with social media is to treat this avenue like other forms of advertising (such as search engine paid advertising) and try to make sales immediately from their social media audience. These companies talk only about products and specific sales on specific SKUs, and answer every question with "Well, we recommend the XJ9000 for that, because . . ."

When businesses understand that their social media presence needs to be a long-term, non-sales-focused, ongoing discussion between them and their customers, they begin to see the following benefits:

✦ **Build trust and connections:** People like to shop with companies they know and trust. As your social media users interact with you on an ongoing basis, they get a feel for your company, see updates from your company, and begin to include your company in their daily activities. They gain a higher sense of trust because they know you're a real company with real people instead of some "faceless" website that treats them like a number.

✦ **Learn about problems before they explode:** Social media is immediate, so customers can write on Facebook or tweet about your product as soon as they receive it. When you have an ongoing presence, your customers can contact you immediately or you can monitor discussions regarding your brand. If some dissatisfaction or trouble is brewing online, you can respond right away and try to resolve open issues before letters are written and angry mobs show up on your doorstep.

✦ **Turn customers into ambassadors:** The real power of social media comes from people passing along links, pictures, and information to their own networks immediately. When you announce something through your Facebook, Twitter, Google+, or other accounts, your current users can send the announcement to their own networks, so their friends see your updates as well. Information can be rebroadcast multiple times on multiple networks — suddenly, your update can go viral and gain exposure to thousands or even millions of potential customers overnight, mainly because the update came from a friend, not from some anonymous business.

Social media has other benefits as well, but we hope the core message is clear: Social media allows you to create an ongoing, one-on-one connection with your customers so that they can interact with you whether or not they're shopping, which leads to greater loyalty and more frequent purchases. As we discussed, the best way to proceed is to first do some planning, which we'll discuss in the next section.

For specific help in setting up your two most important social media accounts, check out *Facebook Marketing For Dummies*, 4th Edition by John Haydon and *Twitter Marketing For Dummies*, 2nd Edition by Kyle Lacy.

Determine who will administer your social media accounts

When you decide to use social media for your business, your first job is to determine who will administer the social media accounts for your business: perhaps someone in marketing, sales, public relations, IT, or a dedicated social media coordinator. You want to be consistent, so rotating the responsibility to different staff members is probably a bad idea.

In this section, we walk you through the steps of setting up a Facebook business page. The process is simple:

1. **Go to the Facebook home page at** www.facebook.com.

    The screen shown in Figure 3-2 appears.

2. **Click the Create a Page for a Celebrity, Band, or Business link.**

    You see the Create a Page screen shown in Figure 3-3.

Figure 3-2: Click the link to create a business page.

Click this link

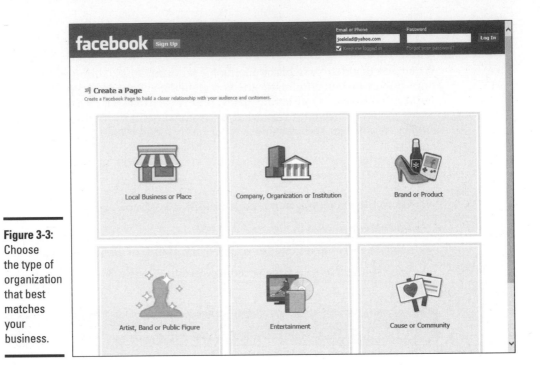

Figure 3-3:
Choose the type of organization that best matches your business.

3. **Select a page option.**

   For example, depending on your business, you can choose from Local Business, Company/Organization/Institution, or Brand/Product.

4. **Select the category of your business and provide some basic information.**

   Examples of categories are automotive goods, bookstore, and shopping or retail site.

5. **Click the Get Started button.**

   Facebook wants to know whether to tie this new business page with an existing Facebook user account.

6. **Provide Facebook user account information for your business page:**

   • *If you already have a Facebook account,* log in and associate your user account with this new business account.

     Don't worry, your personal info will not show up on the business page. This information lets Facebook know who will be the administrator of the business page.

   • *If you don't have a Facebook account,* provide an e-mail address and password that you'll use to log in as your business.

7. **Follow the prompts to start customizing your Facebook page.**

   Facebook begins with an empty page, like the example in Figure 3-4. Simply click the buttons in each section to add elements such as a photo or logo, to invite friends to connect to your business page, and more.

Book VI
Chapter 3

Web Marketing at Work

Figure 3-4: Customize your new Facebook page.

After you build your Facebook page, add a link to it from your website. Many companies, such as Dummies.com (shown in Figure 3-5), use a clickable Facebook (f) button to signify their Facebook page link. If you're using other social media sites, such as Twitter, don't forget to send an update with your new Facebook page URL. Use any other means of communication with your customers — a newsletter, e-mail marketing, marketing literature, or a sign in your store — to let them know about your Facebook page.

Figure 3-5: Add a link from your website to your social media sites.

Reeling in Customers with Newsletters

You enticed someone to visit your site and maybe even buy something. What you really want, though, is a repeat customer. Studies have shown that getting an existing customer to return to your site is as much as six times more effective than getting a brand-new customer. You have to give people reasons to come back, and a newsletter gives them an added benefit of shopping with you and a reason for them to consider your business for their next purchase.

Newsletters are quickly becoming one of the most popular ways to promote a business. Think of a newsletter as a souped-up church bulletin or PTA announcement, made over for the Internet. Most newsletters are a combination of articles and information, with definite *plugs* for, or mentions of, specific products, sales events, or company news. Figure 3-6 shows a newsletter for Lynn Dralle, the Queen of Auctions. She gives helpful tips for selling with auctions, but also plugs her books and upcoming seminars.

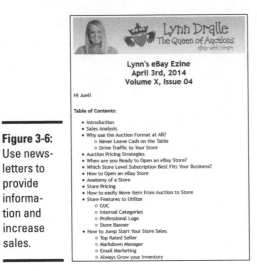

Figure 3-6: Use newsletters to provide information and increase sales.

A regular newsletter to which people can subscribe has many benefits. You can

✦ **Communicate with your customers.** Newsletters give you the opportunity to share why you're in business and what you can offer your customers. Although most people have trained themselves to skip pure advertisements, reading stories or tips can break down customer defenses so that they listen and find out more.

+ **Share information.** The products you sell have a specific use, so helping customers use the products more effectively gives your business an added value. If you sell cooking supplies, provide recipes and describe how your products help make different foods, for example. If you sell books in a specific genre, post customer reviews of the newest releases so that customers can decide whether they want to buy the latest Stephen King horror novel or "ripped from the headlines" legal thriller.

Don't just fill a newsletter with product announcements, sales offers, and discounts because then you have a flyer, not a newsletter. Carefully balance the content and promotion that goes into each newsletter. Although some people recommend a specific balance, such as 30 percent sales and 70 percent information, the key is to provide enough good information to make the newsletter worthwhile to the customer.

+ **Build a connection.** If consumers become accustomed to receiving from you a regular newsletter that they find helpful, they build a connection in their minds that you're now a trusted source and will consider your business more carefully. They might think, "Oh, yeah, that's the company that sends out the Top 10 Tips that I read every week. Those people know what they're talking about, so I'll use them to order my next batch of supplies."

Creating your newsletter doesn't have to be a large and complex project full of deadlines and drama where you yell "Stop the presses!" whenever a new idea comes in. You do, however, have to do some planning, be consistent, and follow some guidelines. In the following sections, we discuss the planning you need to do.

You can also check out the excellent *E-Mail Marketing For Dummies,* 2nd Edition by John Arnold for more information on developing and distributing your newsletter.

Decide who will write your newsletter

Many business owners think that their job is to create each newsletter and come up with all its fabulous content. If you have a staff, that shouldn't be the case. As the owner, you might want to have your own newsletter column or introduction to which you sign your name, and then have different people contribute different parts of the newsletter. Decide in advance who will produce which section because it's better to have that system in place than to scramble every time a newsletter needs to be created.

Don't forget about your customers. They can help you write your newsletter. You can include a Letters section, where customers get to share their experiences, ask questions (that you can answer in the newsletter), or be honored by you, the business owner, for reaching a certain milestone. Customers love to see themselves in print, and it shows potential customers that real people use your business.

Decide what your newsletter will cover

You need to provide different, fresh, and relevant content every time. Stay current on the issues affecting your industry by reading newspapers, magazines, and press releases in your subject area to help generate ideas.

Don't include news stories from other sources in your newsletters without their express consent. If you or someone on your staff writes the articles, you can refer to quotes or statistics from articles, as long as you cite the source in your articles.

Decide when to issue your newsletter

You need to decide at the beginning how frequently your newsletter is released: weekly, monthly, or yearly. Make sure you publish the newsletter on a consistent schedule. Readers lose interest with late or varied schedules, so choose a publishing time that you and your business can handle without much stress. You can publish on a less frequent schedule as long as you're reliable.

You also need to decide on which day of the week you will publish. Some companies target the day of new product releases to send out their newsletters. A movie and music seller might choose Tuesdays for its newsletter release because new movies and CDs hit stores that day. Another site might choose a weekend day so that its newsletter can serve as a weekly summary of events and readers can follow up when they're not at work.

Decide on a format for your newsletter

You can use a number of different computer programs to create a newsletter, although you can present it in only two main formats:

✦ **Plain text** has words and web links but no graphics. Although plain-text newsletters can be read by anyone and are quick to send and receive, they look, well, plain, like the newsletter shown in Figure 3-7.

✦ **HTML** has words, graphics, and design formatting to look exactly like a web page. HTML newsletters can look cool and sophisticated but can't be interpreted by every e-mail system and can take a long time to show up onscreen.

You can create two different versions and ask your readers during the sign-up process which version they want to receive. If you want to be safe, create just a clean, plain-text format, which everyone can enjoy.

```
USED COPIES FOR SALE AT AMAZON

Think twice before sending out f.ree review copies all over the country
-
especially New York. Here's why: They can all end up for sale on
Amazon.com by second-hand dealers--your f.ree books competing against
you.
If you are small and your pockets are not deep enough to produce enough
copies for an established distributor, be careful and selective with
review copies you send out.
--Gary N. Bourland

There is more to this phenomenon.

Many books sent to reviewers in NYC are ripped off in the mailroom and
sold to the Strand bookstore. To the basement denizens of large
buildings,
packages with books are windfall occasions.

But, the books offered at Amazon, may not be ripped off, may not be
review
copies and may not even exist.

Dan Foynter sent out just over 100 copies of The Book Publishing
Encyclopedia in PDF form via email ONLY. Within hours of the book being
posted at Amazon.com, some resellers were offering it in the paper
edition. The catch?--The paper edition did not exist.
```

Figure 3-7:
Plain-text
newsletters
display the
facts plainly.

Decide how to distribute your newsletter

After you create your newsletter, you have to get it to your readers. After
your customer list grows beyond a few people, you can't just open an e-mail
window, insert your newsletter, and send it to thousands of people at one
time. You need to talk to your Internet service provider (ISP) to make sure
that you can distribute the same newsletter to hundreds or thousands of
people. By notifying your ISP, you ensure that it doesn't just shut down your
newsletter when someone suddenly sees the increased traffic.

Send your newsletter only to people who specifically request it. Don't just
spam everyone you've done business with in the past.

If you have trouble sending the newsletter through your normal ISP, you can
contract a company to manage the newsletter distribution for you. This way,
its computer systems handle the mailing of your newsletter and can coordinate the automatic subscriptions of new readers or the *unsubscriptions*
(removals) of customers when they want to stop receiving the newsletter.
Table 3-1 lists a few of these companies.

Table 3-1	E-Mail Newsletter Distribution Services
Name	*URL*
Campaigner	www.campaigner.com
Constant Contact	www.constantcontact.com
Delivra	www.delivra.com
iContact	www.icontact.com
JangoMail	www.jangomail.com

On your website, maintain an archive of all past newsletters, which simply adds more content for your customers. Not only can new and existing customers read your newsletter online, instead of relying on an e-mail program, but the search engines scan your newsletters, which can lead to more customers finding your website. Just make sure the archive is easy to find on your website.

Automating Routine Tasks

How many times have you tried to reach a company through a toll-free hotline only to be put on hold or made to listen to an endless array of recorded messages? Have you pressed a number on the keypad so many times that the number has now rubbed off the button? If you're like us, you hang up and never do business with that company again.

Guard against this situation when customers interact with your online business. If they can't quickly add or delete themselves from your newsletter mailing list or respond to an e-mail or banner offer, they get frustrated and leave. They might never come back, no matter how many offers and deals you throw their way.

Enter automation. By setting up automatic processes, your marketing campaign can go 24/7. And with automation handling routine tasks, you're free to handle more business deals (such as finding the right merchandise, analyzing your sales numbers, or hiring the right staff to increase your business).

Here are some tools you can use to automate parts of the process:

✦ **Autoresponders:** This tool automatically generates an e-mail response based on an incoming request, such as when someone joins your newsletter mailing list. An autoresponder can add that person's name to the database and send him or her a welcome message (full of information about your company) and maybe even an introductory newsletter issue.

 Don't abuse the autoresponder with every process you have in customer interaction. The last thing customers want is form letters every time they send you e-mail, especially if the form letter response has nothing to do with their original question. Reserve the autoresponder for situations that have only one expected response, such as addition to or deletion from a mailing list.

✦ **Ticklers:** Send out *ticklers* (automatic reminders or updates) every few weeks by using contact managers such as ACT! or Salesforce. Include a variety of offers in your tickler to slowly but surely encourage these contacts to try out your company and your products.

✦ **Archived information:** Sometimes, the best way you can help your customers is to enable them to help themselves. Dedicate a portion of your website to hold all your marketing collateral and information. Put the most frequently asked questions (FAQs) in this help section, and make sure that it's accessible from any page of your website.

Try putting your marketing material in different formats to appeal to different customers. You can turn a brochure into an audio file sales pitch, a PowerPoint presentation into a YouTube online video file, or a meeting into a downloadable webinar, for example. Each new format serves as a hook to a portion of your audience. See Book IV, Chapter 3 for more information on creating different products.

Searching for Traffic with Search Engine Advertising

If you were building a gas station, would you have it on a rural country road or a freeway off-ramp? The answer is simple: You want to position your business where your customers are located. The best businesses in the world can't succeed if their customers can't find them. That's why location and access are so important, even for an online business.

You want to position yourself where the traffic is, and nowadays most people find websites through search engines. Therefore, set up shop right on a search engine page with advertising, and benefit from that "drive-by" traffic.

After all, one big benefit of search engine advertising is that you know in advance what the target consumer is looking for. Search engine advertising works like this: You tie your products or website to specific keywords. When someone types those keywords in the search page, your ad is displayed. Suppose that a potential customer is doing a search on Google for a certain brand of golf clubs. If your business sells that brand, your ad can appear next to the search results, as shown in Figure 3-8. Because the ad is targeted only to people who demonstrate that interest, your rate of return is higher than in a generic ad.

Google and Yahoo! are the two biggest companies in the area of search engine advertising, but they are by no means the only game in town. Table 3-2 lists the major companies that offer search engine advertising. We show you in the following section how to sign up for Google AdWords.

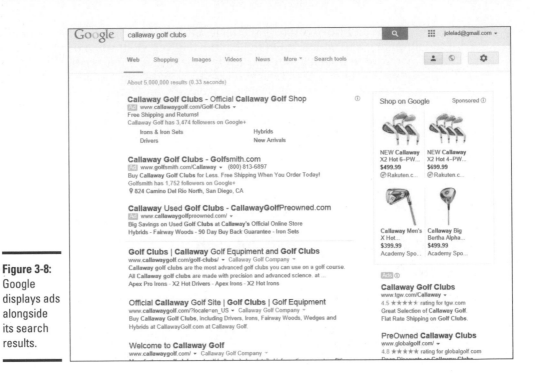

Figure 3-8:
Google displays ads alongside its search results.

Table 3-2	**Search Engine Advertising Companies**	
Company	*Service*	*URL*
Google	AdWords	`www.google.com/adwords/`
Marchex	Search Advantage Network	`www.marchex.com`
MSN (Microsoft)	Bing	`advertising.microsoft.com`
Yahoo!	Yahoo! Advertising	`advertising.yahoo.com`

If your products appeal to a certain niche audience, check to see whether news or portal sites that cater to that industry also accept search advertising on their sites. Although some of these websites have outsourced their advertising to companies such as Google or ValueClick, the sites still control the ads that are displayed and are usually open to a partnership or paid arrangement.

Signing up for Google AdWords

The leader in search engine ads is Google AdWords. You can use this program to create your own ads and to bid on keywords that trigger the display of those ads. When a Google user types your keywords during a search, your ad appears as part of the results screen, with a yellow Ads identifier above the ad (refer to Figure 3-8).

You pay only for the times your ad is clicked, not the number of times your ad is displayed on the screen. Like other services, AdWords lets you set a budget, so you pay only for the ads you can afford. When your budget is used up, your ad doesn't appear any more. You even specify a daily budget so that your ad campaign can't be spent in the first day.

Book VI
Chapter 3

Web Marketing at Work

A Google AdWords *campaign* doesn't refer to a politician's run for office; it means running a specific ad for a given budget. Your ad campaign might consist of one ad running on Google until you spend $100, or a series of ads running for several weeks to promote a new product.

Your customization of the campaign isn't limited to just the keyword. Using Google AdWords, you can choose your target area (a city, territory, or country), and Google targets where the search user is from, whether it's from the search itself, the specific IP address of the computer, or the preferences that the user has set up. By using this targeting, you can show different ads to different territories, offer specific ads and promotions to specific areas, or even create your own test markets where only a specific group of computer users is presented with a given ad.

We discuss Google AdWords because it's popular and easy to use. All the services work similarly, so just choose the one that works best for you.

Setting up a Google campaign

If you're interested in setting up your own AdWords campaign, type your keywords and look at the ads that already appear on Google for your targeted subject area. Get an idea of the ads that you're competing against and the words they use to craft their ads. This strategy should give you some ideas for your ad.

For a complete guide on how to set up and maintain Google AdWords campaigns, check out *Google AdWords For Dummies,* 3rd Edition by Howie Jacobson and Kristie McDonald.

Write your ad copy and have two or three people proofread it before building your campaign. Also take the time to think of the right keywords to use in advance so that you're not guessing when it's time to build the campaign.

When you're ready to build an AdWords campaign, just follow these steps:

1. **Go to www.google.com/adwords/ and click the Get Started Now button.**

2. **Tell Google AdWords about your business so it can help build your first ad campaign. Then click Continue.**

Google asks for information about your business, as shown in Figure 3-9. Provide your e-mail address and website URL in the boxes provided, and keep the check boxes selected if you want Google to send you tips, best practices, and surveys with more information.

Figure 3-9:
Tell Google AdWords some info about your business.

3. **Tie your AdWords account to an existing Google account or create an account. Then click Continue.**

To create a Google account, enter an e-mail address and a password plus some key personal data.

4. **On the Your First Campaign screen, shown in Figure 3-10, start setting up the parameters for your campaign:**

a. Click the Set Your Daily Budget link to determine the maximum amount of money you're willing to spend per day on this campaign.

b. *Decide on the locations for your ad.*

c. *Select the networks that can display your ad.*

**Book VI
Chapter 3**

Web Marketing at Work

Figure 3-10:
Start your
Google
AdWords
campaign
here.

5. **After selecting your networks, click the Select Your Keywords link.**

6. **In the window that appears, specify the keywords that will trigger your ad (see Figure 3-11). Then click Save.**

   Specify one or more keywords related to the product you want to advertise. AdWords will fill in the some of the more popular keyword phrases related to the website category that Google thinks best matches your website. The search popularity appears next to each prefilled phrase. You can remove any of their choices and add your own keyword phrases to the list.

7. **Set your bids:**

   a. *Scroll down and click the Automatically Set My Own Bids link.*

   b. *Let Google set your bids or set your own bid price manually.*

   c. *Click the Save button.*

Figure 3-11: Choose the keyword phrases to associate with your ad.

8. **Compose your ad:**

   a. *Scroll down and click the Write Your Ad link.*

   b. *In the Landing Page box, enter the URL that will take your new customer to your website.*

   Make sure you put any promo codes or tracking words in your landing page URL.

   c. *In the Headline box, enter up to 25 characters.*

   d. *In the Display URL box, enter a URL that will be visible in the middle of your ad.*

   This URL does not have to be the same as the landing page.

   e. *In the Ad Text Line 1 and 2 box, enter up to 35 characters per line.*

   f. *Click the Save button.*

   g. *Click the Save and Continue button.*

   You don't have to link your ad to your home page. Instead, you can specify a web page on your website that presents a special offer to only those people who click your ad. In this way, you can track the number of people who view that page.

9. **Provide your billing information, and then click Save and Continue.**

   Enter your billing country, account type, and payment information.

10. **Read and agree to the terms of the Google AdWords program.**

11. **Review everything you've entered and then click Save.**

Your ad begins to appear on Google almost instantly. Go to the main Google page and perform a few searches to see where your ad ends up on the results page.

Determining the right amount per click

After you set up your account, you want to know where your pricing is positioning you on the page. Follow these steps to check on your pay-per-click rate:

**Book VI
Chapter 3**

Web Marketing at Work

1. **Go to www.google.com, type your keyword phrase, and click the Google Search button.**

   On the results screen, look for your ad in the list just below the Search box. If it doesn't even appear, you're not paying enough to appear on the first screen; you have to click the See More Sponsored Links link to see your ad.

2. **Log in to your Google AdWords account, and click to the specific campaign.**

   Look for your campaign name among the list of campaigns (see Figure 3-12).

3. **Raise the maximum amount you're paying, and click Save.**

4. **Go back to the Google results screen and refresh it.**

   You can refresh screens in most web browsers by pressing F5. See what position your ad moves to on the page. If you see a jump in the placement of your ad, you have an idea of what your competitors have spent to get their positions, and what it will take to keep this new position. If your position hasn't jumped, your competitors are paying even more than your new amount to keep their top spots.

5. **Repeat Steps 3 and 4 to fine-tune the position of your ad on the page.**

   The top spot is the costliest to own, so consider whether a healthy positioning on the first results screen — albeit a few spots down — is the best economical solution for you.

Figure 3-12:
Access
your Google
AdWords
campaigns.

When you fine-tune your campaign, don't expect those price levels to be in effect forever. Your competitors are fine-tuning their campaigns, too, so be sure to revisit your campaign from time to time to achieve maximum effectiveness.

Deciding when to use pay-per-click

Search engine advertising is one popular way that you can drive traffic to your storefront, although it's not necessarily the right way for every business. You need to consider a few elements of your business that will affect your advertising efforts:

✦ **Your marketing budget:** If you have an unlimited marketing budget, pay-per-click is an ideal solution to generate subscribers and sales. If your budget is small, you might be better off sticking to other marketing techniques and adding pay-per-click ads to your strategy as your budget increases.

Dedicate a small portion of your budget to experiment with pay-per-click, and be ready to analyze the results after your test to see whether the results justify the cost. See the nearby sidebar, "Doing the math on pay-per-click," to figure out how to interpret the results.

✦ **Your product:** Are the products you're selling in demand and hard to find? Or are they steady products with a limited audience? If your products sell well to anybody who can find you, pay-per-click is the way to go. If the awareness of your company is already high, however, pay-per-click might be effective only during limited promotional periods in which the combination of a pay-per-click ad sending a user to your website and a special sale greeting can result in customers who place an order.

✦ **Your product margin:** If your product sales are slower but with a high profit margin, a pay-per-click ad can be effective as long as you get a decent conversion of browsers to buyers. Basically, if you make enough money from the sale of a product, you can afford to go find ten leads, for example, if one of those ten decides to buy. If you're operating on a razor-thin profit margin, however, you need quantity, not quality, and a targeted approach such as pay-per-click might cost too much in the long run.

Doing the math on pay-per-click

One way to determine whether a pay-per-click ad campaign will be effective is to study certain numbers related to how your online business now operates. You need to know three numbers:

✏ **Your average profit margin per sale:** The difference between the price the customer paid for a product and the price you paid to obtain the product.

✏ **Your site's *conversion ratio:*** The percentage of people who order something from you, based on your site's total number of visitors.

✏ **Your site's *click-through ratio:*** The percentage of people who have clicked a link to get to your website, based on the total number of people who saw that link.

Suppose that your average profit margin is $20, your conversion ratio is 5 percent, and your click-through ratio is 4 percent. If 20 people click through from an ad, one person should order and generate $20 in profit. Each click-through visitor is then worth $1 to you (or $20 × 5 percent); if you can achieve that click-through rate for $1 or less, you should have a profitable campaign.

If you're paying for the total number of ads displayed, you can calculate the value of getting 1,000 impressions (a common measurement for these types of ads) by using these numbers again:

✏ 1,000 impressions * 4 percent click-through ratio = 40 visitors

✏ 40 visitors * 5 percent conversion ratio = 2 paying customers

✏ 2 paying customers × $20 profit margin = $40 profit

✏ $40 profit / 1,000 impressions = $40 CPM (cost per thousand — M for the Roman equivalent of a thousand)

These results demonstrate why you need to know how your online business is performing before the ad campaign, and why monitoring the results after the campaign tells you whether to continue doing campaigns.

✦ **Your competitors:** Keep an eye on your competition, and see how they're attracting customers. If your customer base is more of a niche than a mass market, you definitely have to adopt similar marketing techniques to divert those customers to your website rather than to someone else's. If your competitors are using pay-per-click, you might find that outbidding them is worth the price to convert a potential customer.

Marketing Your Company Offline

Even though you're running an online business, you don't have to do all your marketing online, too. Any communication that you do on behalf of your business should feature your online store and web address. Here are some offline media you can use to advertise and spread the word about your online business:

✦ **Business cards:** Add your website address, e-mail address, and website slogan to each of your business cards along with your name, address, and phone number. You never know who might learn about your website from seeing your business card.

✦ **Company letterhead or stationery:** Whenever you send a letter of some kind, whether it's a request for information, an explanation of a situation, or a thank-you note to a customer or vendor, include your website address at the bottom of the letterhead (see Figure 3-13).

Figure 3-13:
Work your website address into every document you send.

NEW**Comix**©com

Dear John Doe,

Thank you for your payment. It has been recorded.

Joel Elad

Owner
NewComix.Com

http://www.newcomix.com

✦ **Business flyers and brochures:** Whenever you hand out any form of paper that explains your business, you should include not only your website address but also a description of what the website adds to your business. Even if you're just reminding people that your website acts as a support site after a customer buys your product, the inclusion of your website in the brochure reinforces the website's importance.

✦ **Catalogs:** Something about a printed catalog encourages customers to browse and shop. Even some of the most recognizable e-commerce companies, such as Zappos, will send out printed catalogs to remind people of the goods at their online sites. Although a catalog reinforces the product line, your website should always be mentioned in any catalog as another easy way to order from you.

✦ **Invoices and purchase orders:** Putting your website address and a mention of your site features on your invoices and purchase orders can remind your suppliers and vendors to check out your website and maybe even recommend ways that they can transact with you online.

✦ **Voice-mail greetings:** As customers call to ask questions or place orders, part of your on-hold message or initial greeting can gently remind them that they can find more information on your website.

✦ **Company vehicles:** If you have company trucks or vans making deliveries for your company, why not use that big space to remind passersby that your business is now online? You might be surprised at the potential for orders to come in with the comment "I saw your website when your truck drove past me."

✦ **Boxes:** One way that Amazon distinguishes itself is by plastering the Amazon logo on its customized boxes and mailers. Not only do customers know instantly that their orders have arrived, but anyone around them is also gently reminded of the Amazon brand. Other retailers, such as Zappos (a big seller of shoes), have followed suit, with their web addresses clearly marked.

If you own a retail store along with your online business, check out Book VII, Chapter 4 for more ideas on how to market the online part of your business in the bricks-and-mortar counterpart.

Chapter 4: Converting Browsers to Buyers

In This Chapter

✔ Providing content to keep your customers coming back

✔ Figuring out what your customers want

✔ Creating a website that users enjoy

✔ Tempting your customers with good offers

People measure online businesses by using different statistics (such as total revenue, total profit, and total number of customers). Another measurement, however, exists in the online world that doesn't exist in a bricks-and-mortar business: *Stickiness* indicates how many minutes a user stays at a certain website.

Stickiness is measured from the moment online users first load your website on their screen to the moment they either move on to another website or close the web browser, including the time spent browsing around the site and deciding what to do there. The longer the average time, the stickier the web business. The more time that people spend on your website, the greater the chance that they will purchase one or more of your products or interact with other customers.

Some online businesses are stickier because of their purpose. Compare businesses such as eBay or Facebook to a business such as MapQuest. Facebook and eBay offer lots of reasons for users to browse around, but MapQuest offers only a couple of reasons (maps and driving directions).

Strive to make your website as sticky as possible. Customers who keep coming back are more likely to buy your products — which is, of course, important to your bottom line. In this chapter, we show you how to keep your website fresh and buyer friendly, and how to make your customers feel important so that you can convert browsers to buyers.

Giving Customers a Reason to Stay on Your Site

To increase your website's stickiness, give customers a reason to hang around, come back, or participate more in your business. Here are some ways you can make your online business stickier:

✦ **Provide original content.** This information can come in the form of articles, tips and tricks, reviews, or opinions. You can write about the hottest new product, list ten ways a customer can use a product, or share stories about how customers use your products. In today's multimedia age, you can include videos and podcasts on your website as well as on sites such as YouTube, which then point people to your website.

Two ways to reuse your original content are to put that information into newsletters to keep your customers informed and to repeat the information on your social media outlets, such as your Facebook business page and Twitter feed.

✦ **Create discussion boards.** Allow customers to talk to each other, ask and answer questions about your product line, and get to know each other and your staff.

✦ **Keep your content up-to-date.** Create a blog, maintained by either yourself or one of your employees, to provide in-depth, always changing content for your customers. Insert sections of your Facebook page onto your website, so customers who are Facebook users can see their friend's likes and comments. Stay active on different social media sites such as Twitter, Instagram, Google+, and Pinterest.

✦ **Encourage your customers to provide and share content.** Ask loyal customers to write reviews, guides, and anecdotes that you post on your website or they post on your Facebook page. Some businesses even have contests where the contributor of the best story every month gets a gift certificate. In addition, think about adding Share buttons on your website so your customers can share your content with their friends on their favorite social media networks.

✦ **Publish help and product support.** Make items such as the following available on your website (see Figure 4-1):

• A FAQs (frequently asked questions) section

• Support documents

• Downloadable computer programs (known as *drivers*) that help certain products talk to a computer

• Articles and schematics that describe how to install, assemble, or fix problems with your products

Figure 4-1:
Provide a
resource for
customers
to get online
support.

Providing your own content on your site

Regardless of what kind of business you're running, you should offer content to the buyer. Buyers want original information that they can't get anywhere else. It's like visiting a local store and persuading the owner, an expert in the field, to tell you all about products for sale and how to use them. One reason that Amazon is so successful is that it provides tons of customer and editor reviews, how-to guides, and bestseller lists.

Providing information can lead to more sales and happier customers. Start with information that matters to your customers. If you sell books, have your employees provide short reviews of their favorite new releases for the month, or write the reviews yourself. If you sell consumer electronics, perhaps you can write a guide for shopping for the best digital camera and then compare some of the top brands and discuss their features.

When you provide content for your website, don't forget to include links and references to the products you sell. Avoid flashing banners and loud sounds; instead, post a thumbnail picture of the product you're discussing, set up so that the customer can click the thumbnail and go straight to that product page.

You can also go above and beyond by providing information that anyone would want, not just your core customers. Provide links and sources to general news stories or local city guides, for example. You can specialize in an area and become the ultimate authority on it, in the hope that when people come to your site to read your content, they will stay and check out your product selection. Some financial websites are popular and ranked highly on search engines, for example, because they provide interactive tools such as rate calculators, which enable people to calculate the lowest interest payments necessary on a loan or a mortgage, for example.

Getting other people to provide your content

As the person maintaining your business, you might think that you have to provide all your content, although that might not be the case. Some of the biggest online businesses rely on others for the content their users depend on every day! Tap into that global community, and encourage these people to contribute to your business:

✦ **Customers:** Besides you, who knows more about your products than your customers? Encourage them to provide stories, reviews, and opinions regarding products you sell and similar products in your area. You gain the content, the authenticity of a real customer, and the support of that customer, who feels even more invested in your business. Figure 4-2 shows a section of reviews and information provided by readers and customers of CNet.

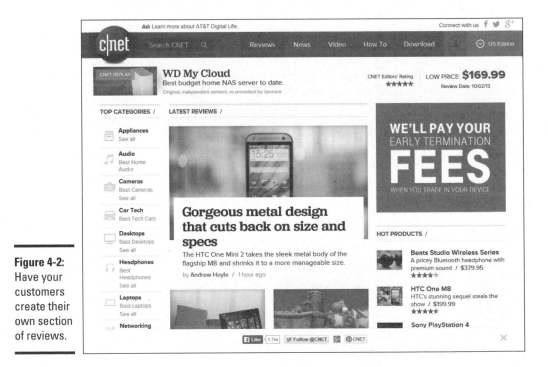

Figure 4-2: Have your customers create their own section of reviews.

If you have a well-known or experienced customer, see whether he or she would be willing to write a weekly or monthly column for your website. Promise a featured spot on your site and maybe some credit toward purchases, and give customers a fun reason to come back regularly to your business.

If you run online contests or have discussions with your customers and fans on a social media site, such as a Facebook business page, a Twitter account, or an Instagram account, include that content on your website or add a link to your website. Companies big and small are running photo or anecdote contests that gather tons of interaction from their customers. For example, the Pilot pen company held a contest in which they asked customers to write a handwritten note, take a photo of it, and post the photo on Instagram with the #PowerToThePen hashtag. This contest was tied in to the Pilot website and their social media channels.

✦ **Suppliers:** The manufacturers, distributors, and suppliers you work with are usually trying to build their brands, too, so involve them in your online business. Let your customers know the newest and greatest things coming from your manufacturer, even if it's just links to its website and announcements about contests, promotions, or events your customers can participate in.

✦ **Media sources:** A ton of organizations can happily feed your website with articles and information you can post for free on your website. Try one of these sources:

- Articlesbase (www.articlesbase.com)

- eZine @rticles (www.ezinearticles.com)

- GoArticles (www.goarticles.com)

- Isnare (www.isnare.com)

Anticipating Customer Needs

Veteran business owners can tell you that to succeed, your goal should be to not just meet your customer's expectations but to also anticipate and respond to those expectations. Online retailers are no different: You need to read buyers' minds and figure out what they want so that you have the products to meet their demand — rather than watch your competition make off with your customers and your revenue.

You have a few ways to figure out what your customers want:

✦ **Take a look at your sales data.** Watch the purchases made through your business to see who's buying what and how much customers are spending per order.

✦ **Monitor your customers' questions.** Whether customers communicate by e-mail, phone, Facebook or Twitter posts, or a web form, if they're starting to ask for similar products, investigate!

✦ **Check out your competition.** See what other sites are providing, putting on sale, raising prices on, and carrying in their stores.

✦ **Look at other resources that talk about your product lines.** See what websites are promoting or hyping as "the next great thing" (see Figure 4-3). Read magazines, books, and newspapers, and watch TV shows about your product areas, to see what people are talking about, preparing for, and predicting for that industry.

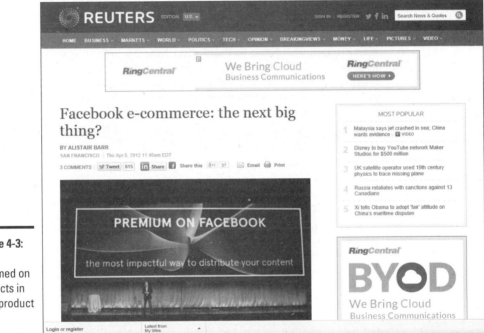

Figure 4-3: Stay informed on subjects in your product area.

✦ **Go to trade groups, conventions, or organizations.** Attend trade shows for your product area, whether it's Electronic Entertainment Expo (E3) for video games, Consumer Electronics Show for general consumer electronics, or American Toy Fair for the newest action figures, to get an idea of what your buyers want next. Subscribe to these organizations' newsletters to get up-to-date information. You should always order catalogs from manufacturers that belong to these groups and ask to be on their mailing lists.

Watching customer logs

Customer orders aren't the only evidence of what customers want from your business. Because you're online, you can keep track of the different web pages that customers view. A *customer log,* or *web server log file,* contains information about particular pages your customers are looking at. Every time they look at another page, a new entry is created in the customer log. You can open your log and see all customer activity.

The web server log file is a text file that your website provider automatically creates and maintains for you. It keeps track of all the web page requests your customers ask for when they browse your website.

When you're reading through your customer log, ask yourself these questions:

✦ What pages are looked at the most? The least?

✦ How many pages does the average customer look at?

✦ What's the last page that customers look at before they leave? Is it an order confirmation page, or did they give up before ordering?

✦ Are customers following the same flow through your site? That is, do they typically look at the same web pages in the same order as everyone else?

✦ Are customers viewing the newest web pages you provide? Are they sticking to the same core pages regardless of whether those pages are updated?

After you know this information, you can update your website by deleting the pages (or content) that no one is looking at. By streamlining the buying process this way, you continue to meet your customers' expectations and keep them returning.

Predicting future purchases

Mutual fund companies are notorious for this disclaimer: "Past performance is not an indicator of future returns." In the e-commerce world, however, past purchases are an excellent indicator of what customers will buy next — so much so that a company such as Amazon tracks every single activity (not just purchases) performed by customers on its website. Your customer logs are good indicators of what your customers are looking at, but you should also look at what they're buying.

One benefit you enjoy in an online business is not being limited by physical shelf space and, in some cases, the cost of carrying the products before purchase. So, you probably offer an expansive array of products. After your orders come in, though, you want to see which products customers are ordering the most. Are these products concentrated in one or two subcategories, or are they spread out among your catalog of goods?

Obviously, if a product line is flying off the virtual shelf, you should restock it as soon as possible. If the product is a fad item, however, such as the Rainbow Loom (a crafting kit to help kids make rubber band bracelets) or the Shake Weight, you don't want to get stuck with a warehouse full of that item after the fad ends.

To choose future products to stock and to anticipate your customers' wants, look at what they're willing to buy from you today. As you examine past purchases, consider these dimensions:

✦ **Average price per sold item:** At what price levels are your highest-selling products? This price gives you an idea of whether limited, high-priced items or mass-quantity, low-priced items would work better for your business. After all, if your customers are used to buying the hottest computer accessories for less than $50, selling a $2,000 laptop might be out of their reach.

✦ **Average order size:** The average amount of money spent per order doesn't necessarily correspond to the average price per item. Although your customers might love your site for inexpensive items, they could be willing to purchase multiple items, resulting in a big order. They might be occasional buyers who buy expensive items. Find products that fit into your customers' average order and get them to exceed this number. Offer free shipping on a larger order, for example.

If you increase your customers' average order amount, you're increasing their value to your business. Consider new products that meet or exceed your current average order size. You want this number to go up, not down.

✦ **Luxury or necessity:** Are your customers buying entertainment products with their disposable income, or are they purchasing everyday items that they need continually? Look beyond the fad or trend, and figure out what part of their budget you're reaching. Continue to stock products that are so cool, so cheap, or so easy to use that customers *have* to have them, or stock products that customers need or see as automatic buys. Then they will continue to buy from you rather than look around for someplace better.

✦ **Technology items:** If you're selling items with lots of technology built in (even if they're kitchen appliances), always have an eye on the next model, iteration, or version. Keep enough on hand to satisfy current demand and also acquire newer models so that customers can stay ahead of the curve or stay where they are until they're ready to buy the new model.

✦ **The 80-20 rule:** Are 80 percent of your orders coming from 20 percent of your customers? Chances are, 80 percent of the products sold come from 20 percent of the category areas. The way to make the biggest effect on your business is to increase the 80 percent of sales, so be ready to continue serving the customers of that 80 percent group.

Organizing a Buyer-Friendly Site

For a regular business, being friendly to buyers means saying "Hello" when they walk through the door, shaking their hands, and smiling at them. For an online business, friendly means creating a buyer-friendly site that makes sense to buyers and makes their lives easier. After all, they're coming to you partially because they don't want to get in their cars, fight traffic, battle for parking spots at the mall, and navigate their way through the sea of humanity just to get a new pair of jeans.

When buyers come to your website, provide them with a few basic pieces of information right off the bat, or else they will click their way to the next business. Go to your home page, and make sure that it answers these basic questions:

✦ What is your business?

✦ What's the primary focus of your business?

✦ What does your business offer consumers?

✦ What makes your business good enough to earn a customer's trust and, therefore, an order?

✦ How would a customer start shopping on your site?

If your opening page can't answer these questions, your website isn't buyer friendly. You want to be straightforward and direct with your buyers because, in essence, your business reason for existence is to help a customer with a specific need. In this section, we talk about what you can do to spiff up your website to offer customers a satisfying shopping experience.

Streamlining the shopping process

All-night convenience stores can charge two to three times the grocery store price for items for a good reason. People want convenience, especially online, so being able to grab an item and leave is crucial.

An example of an easy-in-easy-out website is the Amazon 1-Click system. For returning customers, Amazon fills in all their information ahead of time so that they can choose their items, make an immediate purchase with the click of a single button, and leave. Customers return to Amazon because they know that Amazon's 1-Click system works right every time and they don't have to retype their credit card number, shipping address, and other information. Their accounts are already created, so they can pop in and get what they need. That's great service.

On your website, make sure that your shoppers can always

✦ **Reach their shopping carts and accounts:** No matter where on your website shoppers might be, they should always be able to look in their shopping carts or check their accounts. We recommend including links to these two functions along the top of every web page so that they're always just a click away.

✦ **Understand the total costs of their order:** If customers can't figure out what the shipping cost will be for their order before having to enter credit card and full address information, many will abandon their shopping cart. The same concept goes for customers who get hit with taxes or extra fees on the final screens of the order process instead of before payment information is required.

✦ **Access any product specials you offer from the home page:** The less hunting buyers have to do, the quicker they can add your specials to their carts and continue shopping or check out.

When you're designing the page flow of your website, reduce as many in-between steps as possible. If the majority of your shoppers pay by credit card, don't ask customers how they will pay. Display a page where customers can either fill in their credit card information or choose other forms of payment.

✦ **Search for a specific item:** Your customers can use the search function to interact with your business by telling you exactly what they want to buy. Add to your navigation section a search box or link that appears on every page of your website.

Check whether the software or web host you're using to create your website offers a search function. Make sure that the search offers customers a focused set of results or the most relevant product.

✦ **See the content on a page at a glance:** We can't stress enough the importance of clear headings and labels. Your customers are drawn to the biggest type on the page. Every page on your website should have a clear and relevant heading at the top, and subheadings throughout the page if you're presenting a long list of products. Look at how CNET organizes its site (see Figure 4-4) with red tabs on top and navigation icons near the bottom of the page.

As simple as it sounds, make sure that headings correspond to what customers are seeing on the page. If a heading talks about clearance items and you're displaying new, full-priced goods, you'll lose your customers fast as their trust in you starts to evaporate.

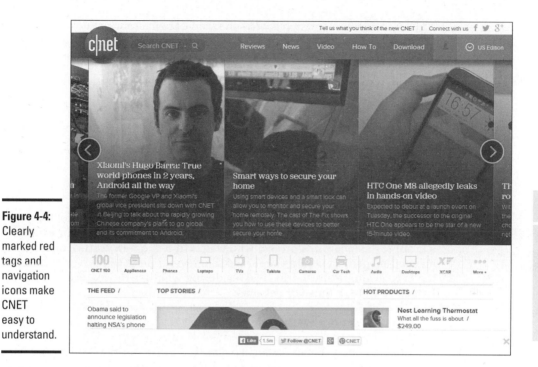

Figure 4-4: Clearly marked red tags and navigation icons make CNET easy to understand.

Toning down the bells and whistles

Although you might want your website to look as nice as possible, cool features such as Flash movies, JavaScript programs, sound files that play automatically, or scrolling banners can slow down the buying experience and make shopping harder. Although buyers might find such effects cute the first time they visit your website, the effects can quickly become annoying. If a Flash movie serves as your home page, you ruin your chance to be seen by search engines and customers who have to wait for a function to load might feel frustrated and try a competitor's website instead. Although some customers might enjoy these extra effects, others will abandon your website in search of a less annoying business.

Flash movies are animated movies or introductions you sometimes see on websites. By using Flash technology (which is controlled by Adobe), you can create moving animations with sound in one file that an Internet browser can easily display.

A Flash movie or animation is only one kind of bell and whistle you can add to your website. Businesses use all sorts of additional features to draw attention to their online sites or spice up the user experience. Some of these include

✦ Sound files that play when a visitor arrives to the website

✦ JavaScript functions that load a miniwindow of information on the page

✦ Java functions that load a fully functional application into the web page

✦ Pop-out menus that cover part of the screen with a new window (also called *DHTML menus*)

✦ Animated graphics or large, fancy graphics on the page

Some businesses, however, simply throw in these "cool factor" features without thinking about how they can affect their bottom lines; for example, a graphic designer on a project who wants to test a new feature or work on an exciting project would encourage the development of these features. Your job is to evaluate any extras by considering whether the feature is worth having in spite of these drawbacks:

✦ **The feature is memory-intensive.** Most U.S. buyers have broadband (fast) Internet access in their homes. However, some people still use dial-up (phone) lines, especially in other parts of the world, or are using a mobile device that may have a lower bandwidth. For these customers, a graphics-intensive website, a video or large audio file, or a large animation graphic can slow down their experience. Customers who get put on hold when they call a company "drop off" after they have to wait a while, and the same thing happens online.

✦ **The feature might display your content incorrectly.** Many of the newer features used in HTML web pages, such as layers or JavaScript, strictly control how the content is laid out on the page. The problem with this strict control lies in older computers or different web browser software that interprets these new commands inconsistently. Your result is that some customers may see a distorted and, at times, unusable website because the pages aren't displaying correctly — some elements, such as an Order button, might not even be displayed on the page. Other features, such as Flash, can't run on devices such as the Apple iPad, which could make your website unusable to iPad users.

Keeping Your Shopping Cart Simple

Most studies about online shopping include the percentage of online e-commerce shopping carts that are left abandoned by their users. Some statistics state that customers abandon anywhere from 45 to 90 percent of all shopping carts, for a variety of reasons:

✦ They're turned off by the high cost of either the item or the shipping and handling.

✦ They can't find all the information or functionality that they need to finish.

✦ They're uncomfortable registering or handing over credit card data online.

✦ They're unsure how to completely check out with their items and pay for their purchases.

✦ They're afraid to place their final orders.

For these reasons, keep in mind some helpful tips and avoid the common traps of having shopping carts on your e-commerce site:

✦ **Make the shopping cart easy to find.** Sometimes, the only way for customers to even access their shopping carts is to click a link that's available on only certain web pages. At other times, they see their shopping carts only after adding items. Put the shopping cart link at or near the top of every web page (as shown in Figure 4-5). Create a second browser window that's small or always minimized, and put the shopping cart information on that screen.

Figure 4-5:
Put your
shopping
cart in a
consistent
location
on your
website.

Shopping
cart link

✦ **Make the shopping cart updatable.** Your customers should be able to add, update, and delete products in their orders at any time. When they make changes, they probably want to see their updated totals. If customers change shipping options or choose an out-of-state address, they want to see any total changes. Make sure that any change to an order triggers your software program to recalculate the order amount and display the revised order with a revised total.

✦ **Require no upfront information to use the shopping cart.** If your customers can't easily add items to their shopping cart first and give personal information later, you might scare them off by forcing them to register or type lots of data first. Enable them to shop, and then require the other information before they place orders.

At some point before an order is complete, don't forget to ask "How did you hear about this site?" Provide a box for the referral name, e-mail address, or promotion code so that you can better track your marketing efforts.

✦ **Provide help from the shopping cart page.** Always have available on the shopping cart screen at least one web link to a list of frequently asked questions (FAQs) about how to use the shopping cart. Nothing is worse for customers than getting stuck when they try to add something to their shopping carts and can't find any help. Don't leave customers wandering around your store aimlessly; throw them the virtual rope in advance.

You can also offer live help with chat technology. When buyers click the chat link, they can chat with your customer service representatives (or you, depending on the size of your business) and have their questions answered on the spot. Several companies offer software that augments your website with chat technology, such as

- RealChat (www.realchat.com)

- ProvideSupport (www.providesupport.com)

- ParaChat (www.parachat.com)

✦ **Allow customers to easily add or remove items.** Customers make multiple decisions, usually when they're deciding what to order. They need the flexibility to update, add, or delete any single line item in the shopping cart without affecting the rest of the order. Customers who have to delete everything and start over are likely to just "walk out."

✦ **Protect customers' information.** When you collect sensitive information — such as credit card numbers, birthdates, or bank account information — make sure that your shopping cart is using a safe technology, such as Secure Socket Layers (SSL). A customer should see a URL starting with https:// or a closed-lock icon in the lower-right corner of the web browser (see Figure 4-6) to indicate that data can be safely entered on the page. If the URL starts with https:// or the lock is open, entering data isn't 100 percent safe on that page. Pages containing data about your products don't have to use SSL; when in doubt, though, secure the page. (See Book V for more information about security.)

Don't just secure customers' information; tell them about it! Create a special window or web page detailing how you're protecting their vital information. When you reassure customers that you're looking out for them in the beginning, they're more likely to buy.

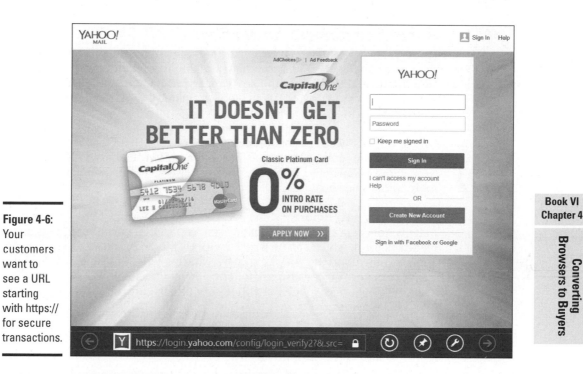

Figure 4-6: Your customers want to see a URL starting with https:// for secure transactions.

Avoiding Assumptions about Your Customers

You have to make plenty of decisions every day, and you can easily fall into the trap that you have to know everything to make your business work. You don't have to know everything, although you do have to know whom to ask or where to look.

When you're wondering whether the actions you're taking in your business are truly converting browsers to buyers, step back a moment to see what's going on. Pull up your website and click through the pages yourself. Just because the pages and offers grab *you* doesn't necessarily mean that customers will react the same way. It's a good start, though. In this section, we show you ways to see your site from the customers' perspective so that you can provide them with exactly what they need.

Asking customers for feedback

Many times, your buyers know what they want — sometimes before you do. They're the ones using your products, talking to each other on your discussion board, and looking for the next great product. You should always provide a way for your customers to give you general or specific feedback using a feedback form.

One of the best ways to encourage regular, ongoing feedback is to participate in social media sites such as Facebook or Twitter. Encourage customers to become followers so they can share experiences, ask questions, or learn more about your business.

Most websites incorporate some sort of feedback form, whether it's part of a help system or a contact system or even as part of a guest book. This simple feedback form, which can be written with HTML code, allows customers to send comments to the website owners, sharing what they like and dislike about the site. You can also ask for specific feedback on your product line or ask how a customer found out about your site. Figure 4-7 shows an example of a feedback form.

[en] Customer Evaluation -#- 003 - Customer Satisfaction with Product/Service

Thank you for purchasing from [COMPANY]. Please take a moment to tell us about your experience and how well [PRODUCT] has been meeting your expectations.

Overall, how satisfied are you with [PRODUCT]?

○ Very satisfied
○ Satisfied
○ Neutral
○ Dissatisfied
○ Very dissatisfied

If you are dissatisfied, why?

How satisfied are you with [PRODUCT] regarding the following items?

	Very satisfied	Satisfied	Neutral	Dissatisfied	Very dissatisfied
Overall quality	○	○	○	○	○
Value for the price	○	○	○	○	○
Purchase experience	○	○	○	○	○
Installation experience	○	○	○	○	○
Usage experience	○	○	○	○	○
After purchase service	○	○	○	○	○

How often do you use [PRODUCT]?

○ Daily
○ Several times a week
○ Once a week
○ Several times a month
○ Once a month
○ Several times a year
○ Once a year or less often
○ Do not use

Figure 4-7: Make it easy for your customers to communicate with you.

If your most loyal customers are asking for a particular product, consider stocking it so that you don't lose them to your competition.

If shoppers want a fad item, especially one that requires a large investment, stock only what you feel that you can definitely sell. If the shelf life of a product could become very short, you don't want to blindly act on your customers' inquiries. (Just ask the businesses that are sitting on a warehouse full of Neopets.)

Make sure that customer inquiries and feedback are fed into the inventory acquisition phase as quickly as possible. You have no excuse for not considering a new product line if your customers have given you notice about the item. Some items sell more quickly than others, and you need some time to find the right distributor or manufacturer and set up an account.

Test a new product line on a subset of customers before investing too much of your inventory budget on one item. Buy enough of the product to get it in stock quickly and serve a subset of customers. Send a targeted e-mail or direct-mail piece to assess the response for the test audience. If the numbers are good, reorder more and repeat the test, or integrate the new product into your catalog.

Book VI
Chapter 4

Converting
Browsers to Buyers

Encourage customers to help keep you on the cutting edge by rewarding them for their feedback. Include surveys, links to social media outlets such as Facebook or Twitter, toll-free hotline numbers, or follow-up e-mail in your communications with buyers. Make contacting you as easy as possible for them, and use giveaways, promotions, or incentives to push these customers into giving you their valuable advice.

Create a buyer council or a volunteer group of buyers that you can poll regularly to find out what customers know about a product area. Choose some steady customers with whom you've built relationships, and ask whether they're interested in joining. Most will accept to get a feeling of ownership and to get their opinions heard.

Remembering your customers

Many online business owners get started in areas they know well and are passionate about. Then they fall into the trap of assuming that they're the perfect target audience for their own online stores, and their own preferences get in the way of doing business. If this happens to you, your bottom line — and the future flow of customers to your site — could be harmed.

When you decide which products to carry in your store, ask yourself "Am I choosing these items because I like them — or because I think that my buyers will like them?" Put your customers' needs and desires ahead of your own. Even if you're putting yourself in the role of a potential buyer, you carry certain biases that your customers might not carry.

Put your buyers' interests ahead of your own. You're not selling to yourself — you're selling to your customers! Offer products that they want to buy, at prices they're willing to pay. See the section "Anticipating Customer Needs," earlier in this chapter, for tips on finding out what people are buying.

Be open to what your customers, and the orders they place, are telling you. We have met enough business owners who were too afraid or too ignorant about venturing outside their known worlds to try new product lines. Those folks usually lost great opportunities to expand their business.

If you don't have the items buyers want, they will go somewhere else to find them. And chances are good that they won't come back to you. Buyers remember who serves them best. Respond accordingly.

Encouraging Viewers to Buy

Being available to your customers is important for people who stumble across your site while searching for something. To generate sales, however, you need to encourage those people to take action and buy something from your site. You can build a clean and robust website, full of exciting products, and then wonder why you aren't making sales. In the world of e-commerce, building your website isn't enough. You have to close the deal. Encourage buyers to place your products in their shopping carts and then commit to placing orders. You created your website to give them the means to do so, and now you have to give them a little nudge. In this section, we describe two techniques to convert browsers to buyers: Give them a time-limited offer, and then reinforce that offer when they're leaving your website.

Offering deals and promotions

Special deals and promotions are the most common way to ask for the sale because you're giving buyers a specific buying proposition. You're offering something to sweeten the deal, whether it's a discount, a free additional item, or an extra service. Usually, though, a successful deal or promotion has that all-critical time limit. You can limit these elements:

+ **The length of time that an offer is available:** "Good for only the next 24 hours."

+ **The number of people who can take advantage of the offer:** "Only the next 25 customers can act on this deal."

+ **The specific outlet you use to make your offer:** "Like us on Facebook to qualify for an exclusive offer."

+ **The supply of the product:** "Order now — supplies are limited."

A time limit spurs customers to act. Otherwise, if an offer is always out there, it's a regular deal, not a special offer. Figure 4-8 shows a time-sensitive, one-time-only offer for a product.

Figure 4-8: Make sure your offers include some form of time sensitivity.

STOP Stop! You can Take 40% Off The Price of Your Crazy Egg Subscription... Right now

Here's why we're doing this...

When a Crazy Egg customer purchases our one-year plan, we're getting paid in advance for 12 months' worth of service. And that's good for us because it allows us to spend more (and faster) on developing the Crazy Egg app for its next killer upgrade.

That's why we're willing to test this idea and let you take 40% off the regular price of our one-year subscription. There is a catch, but it is a reasonable one.

→ This is the ONLY time you will see this offer. Ever. It's a one-time opportunity.

You can choose from a number of events that can trigger a special deal or promotion:

✦ A customer registers for the first time.

✦ A customer adds a second, fifth, or tenth item to the shopping cart.

✦ A specified length of time (15 or 30 minutes, for example) has elapsed and the customer still hasn't added anything to the shopping cart.

✦ The customer visits your website by using a special web address.

Pushing to make a sale works: It forces a buyer to make a decision, and if the customer is getting a good deal, the impulse to buy can kick in and seal the deal. Although you don't necessarily want to be overly aggressive, you can't just believe the line from *Field of Dreams:* "If you build it, he will come." Customers might come, but they might not shop. You have to encourage the sale.

Sending one last reminder

Many shop owners never think of the one instance in which they can ask for the sale: when a customer is leaving a website and moving to something else. Some special web programming language commands in the customer's web browser kick into gear when the customer chooses a different website or closes the web browser window.

Some business owners think, "Well, if they're leaving my store, they definitely don't want anything." Your customers might not be able to find the deal they're looking for. Or they might want to comparison-shop before making the purchase. Maybe they just got bored because nothing unusual popped up or happened while they were shopping at your store.

The moment customers leave your site, you know a few things about them:

✦ **They just spent some time in your online business.** They browsed, looked at some products, and read some pages. Your business is now on their mind and they have at least considered your offerings.

✦ **They had some specific interest in browsing your site.** Maybe they were looking for a product, an ad caught their eye, or they were a referral. These buyers are interested.

✦ **They're leaving your website, so you have little left to lose.** After all, if you present them with something more and they don't want it, what are they going to do? Leave? They already made the decision to leave, so what does it hurt to give them one final offer?

Your browsing customers are knowledgeable about, and interested in, your business and your products, and they're motivated and ready to leave. It's a perfect time to make a final offer. Call it your goodbye offer or your before-you-go offer. Display a pop-up or pop-under window that encourages your viewer to consider a new offer or discount (such as the one shown in Figure 4-9). Now is your last opportunity to make an impression (during this particular shopping session), so make it count.

Figure 4-9: If you know someone's leaving, ask one more time for the sale.

Pop-up (and pop-under) ads are annoying, so use them sparingly on your website. You can reserve the use of pop-up ads for goodbye offers. This way, you're not annoying customers while they shop; you're just offering one last reminder as they're going out the door.

If your browsing customers are dead set against shopping, they will close this offer window just as fast as they left your site. If they were tempted to buy but remained on the fence, this goodbye offer might be enough to swing them back your way. Remember the adage: You never know until you try. The same concept holds true when you're asking for the sale.

When you implement this offer, make sure that it appears only if the browsing customer hasn't purchased anything. You don't want happy buyers to suddenly realize that they could have saved money if they had just tried to leave your site first. In this case, your goodbye offer should be a chance to add to an order or receive faster shipping for a lower price.

To add a goodbye offer to your website, add lines of code in these places:

✦ **On every web page at your site except the order confirmation screen, add the following lines of code to the <HEAD> section:**

```
<SCRIPT LANGUAGE="JavaScript">
function goodbye(){
        alert("Before you go, consider our final
    offer!");
        open("finaloffer.htm");
        }
</SCRIPT>
```

**Book VI
Chapter 4**

**Converting
Browsers to Buyers**

You should also create a special web page to correspond to the second line in the goodbye function that contains your final offer.

✦ **On the web pages that contain an order confirmation screen, add the following lines of code to the <HEAD> section:**

```
<SCRIPT LANGUAGE="JavaScript">
function goodbye(){
        alert("Here's a special offer just for our
    loyal customers!");
        open("extraoffer.htm");
        }
</SCRIPT>
```

You should also create a special web page to correspond to the second line in the goodbye function that contains your extra offer.

✦ **Add the following block of text to the <BODY> tag on all your web pages:**

```
<BODY . . . onUnLoad="goodbye()">
```

You should add the onUnLoad section at the end of the <BODY> tag.

When your goodbye offer is in place, you can study your website statistics to find out if your offer is effective by comparing your success rate with your normal customer conversion rate. Just like with any other deal or promotion, you can make changes or even remove this offer based on customer results.

Chapter 5: Analyzing and Monitoring Your Customers

In This Chapter

✔ Monitoring your website traffic

✔ Interpreting the records left on your web server

✔ Using software to assemble reports on website usage

✔ Implementing techniques to gain more information from your visitors

✔ Asking your customers the right questions

✔ Updating your website to correct or improve performance

*A*fter you build your website, your next step is to ask, "How can I make my site better?" Your initial version is rarely your current version. You create your site, watch how users interact with you, make changes, watch how users react to those changes, make more changes, watch some more, and then repeat the process. This process is ongoing as you evolve your site to meet the changing needs of your customers.

Analyzing your website can tell you a lot about your business that other metrics (measurements) — such as sales volume, average order amount, and repeat customers — cannot tell you. You can figure out exactly which web pages on your site are the most and least popular. You can see how many people start with your home page, and then calculate the average number of pages a user sees before leaving. You can even find out where users come from when they arrive at your website and determine the last thing they see before they leave.

In this chapter, we look at the field of website analysis, from traffic monitoring to gathering customer feedback. We help you break down the massive amount of raw data you have on your site and turn it into useful statistics that can change your business — by using either log files or a software program. You find out which pieces of information are more important than others and how to focus your analysis to study individual user behavior. You can then use this data to make useful updates to your website and study the immediate and lasting effect of your changes.

The best changes that come from website analysis are gradual, or *evolutionary,* changes. Look at how sites such as Amazon and MSN handle changes. Their interfaces don't radically change every week, although subtle and gradual changes are always being introduced, to respond to customers and enhance the shopping experience.

Tracking Trends

If you sit at an outdoor café and watch traffic drive by, you begin to get a sense of patterns. You can estimate the number of cars that drive by; determine the most popular makes, models, and colors; establish whether the cars are zooming past or crawling by; and ascertain whether they're coming in groups or as a continuous stream.

You can apply the same techniques to monitoring your website traffic. If you want to understand the behaviors of the traffic, you need to know basic information and understand the trends that are occurring:

+ The number of visitors coming to your website

+ The number of *unique* visitors coming to your site

+ Which websites are referring viewers to your site

+ Which web pages are the most frequently viewed and the least frequently viewed

+ The number of web pages that the average visitor sees in one visit

You can track this usage without monitoring direct website traffic, although this method mainly involves direct customer interaction. You can contact a research group to find sample visitors and perform *usability testing,* where the research group introduces visitors to your website, asks them to interact with it, and then studies their activities to see whether they can intuitively find their way around your website, place an order, and perform basic functions. Based on these user interactions, the research group makes recommendations to you about changes you should make to your website to make it more user friendly or easier to use.

You can also solicit direct customer feedback through surveys, follow-up phone calls, or e-mail response forms. Many websites gather this feedback by contacting past customers or people who have just ordered something from the website, and then getting their opinions about a variety of issues. This method is useful for identifying issues that need correcting or promoting, or to add insight or qualitative information to the level of your website's usefulness, beyond what the quantitative information is telling you through trend analysis. Find out more about adding qualitative information in the section "Getting to Know Your Customer," later in this chapter.

Measuring Website Traffic

Every time your web server receives a request from a visitor and displays a web page for that visitor, it creates an entry for the request in a log file on the web server. The log file records all the activity your website experiences. The server captures a lot of information in this file that you can then use to get a better idea of how your website is being used and operated by visitors and customers.

A *log file* is just a text file stored on your web server that receives a new entry whenever your web server has to fulfill a request from a web browser. Sometimes, the log file is called the *access log file* (see Figure 5-1). Other times, the web server breaks the log file into different files, for example, an error log, a request log, and a referrer log.

Figure 5-1:
Your access log file shows you all the visitors and what they saw.

Your log files tell you a lot about your website:

✦ The popularity of various pages in the site

✦ The usability of your site

✦ The types of visitors that come to your site

✦ The capability of your site to present your web pages effectively

Defining the terms of traffic analysis

Your website measures a *hit* whenever a piece of your website, whether it's a web page or a graphics file or another object, is sent over the Internet to someone's web browser. You might hear this activity described as "My website got a million hits last month." That statement is saying that your website handled a million different requests for everything from text to images to audio tracks.

Although some people think of hits purely as visitors, a web page might have nine different graphics and generate ten hits every time it's accessed. Why? When a visitor wants to view the web page, the web server sends out the HTML code of the page as the first request, and then the server sends nine separate graphics files, one by one, and records each of those transmissions as a separate hit.

This process is the reason that measuring hits isn't as important as other metrics, although it does give you a good baseline to understand the level of demand. When you're talking to advertisers, finding funding, or planning a marketing campaign, a high hit count doesn't spell success on its own.

A *page view*, on the other hand, happens when a visitor views a particular page. This number, which is independent of the number of elements that might be present on a web page, usually correlates to the number of visits to a particular page, especially on your home page.

Because most websites have multiple pages, you want to determine the number of visits, or *unique visitors,* to your site. Look at the log file for some identifying information, such as an IP address, and correlate that information to your page views. If you see the same IP address viewing multiple pages, you get an idea of the average number of pages viewed per user.

An *IP address,* or *Internet Protocol address,* is a series of four sets of numbers (in a range from 0 to 256) defining a computer's location on the Internet. An example of an IP address is 207.171.166.102 (which belongs to Amazon). Each IP address is unique to one computer at a time. Many users are assigned an IP address *dynamically,* which means that they're assigned a unique set of numbers the moment they sign on to the Internet, and they lose the right to those numbers when they're done. Some people, like those using cable modems or university computers, have the same IP address, or *static IP address,* all the time.

Most investors, suppliers, and employees, including you, are interested in knowing the number of unique visitors to your website. The easiest way to figure out that number is to implement a system where you place a text file (a cookie) on each user's computer. Turn to the later section "Storing data using cookies" to find out how to use cookies.

Public computers skew the data

Shared (or public) computers, like those you find at public libraries, Internet cafés, schools, and even some workplaces, are always on and always connected to the Internet, and they always use the same IP address to access the Internet. For this reason, your website log file shows every request coming from a shared computer as the same user. If you see 50 page views coming from the same IP address, you don't necessarily know, therefore, whether the page request is coming from one person or ten people.

As a result, you have to look at other elements, such as the length of time a page is served, to figure out the average number of page views per visitor. When you know an average, you can break apart a heavily used IP address to represent an average number of users. If you know that a visitor will view, on average, 5 web pages and you get 50 page views from one IP, you can assume that the IP address represents 10 unique visitors.

Looking at your log file

Your log file resides somewhere on the hard drive of your website's server. Depending on the operating system that your web server uses — whether it's Windows, Unix, Mac OS X, or a version of Linux — you can use a regular text editor to open and view the log file.

Inside your log file is a long list of entries made up of the different requests that your web server has received and the file or information that it has sent back to the user requesting it. A typical entry looks like this:

```
208.215.179.139 - - [06/November/2013:06:01:16 -0400] "GET /
    index.html HTTP/1.1" 200 32768 "http://search.yahoo.com/
    search?p=ecommerce+products" "Mozilla/4.0 (compatible;
    MSIE 7.0; Windows NT 5.2; DigExt)"
```

✦ `208.215.179.139`: Corresponds to the IP address of the computer from which the request was made. When you see multiple lines with the same URL, you know that either one person is requesting different files or multiple people are using the same computer.

If you want to know more information about the computer, you can do a reverse lookup of the IP address to see whether it relates to a known *URL,* or web address. Some websites, such as `www.dnsstuff.com`, offer reverse URL lookup services for free.

✦ `[06/November/2013:09:01:16 -0400]`: Shows the exact date and time of the request. The `-0400` at the end refers to the offset from Greenwich Mean Time. In this case, the time is marked as the U.S. Pacific time zone.

✦ `"GET/index.html HTTP/1.1"`: Refers to the item being requested and the method used to transfer that file from your web server. Here, you see web pages (`.html` or `.htm`), graphics files (`.gif` or `.jpg`), or other content, such as JavaScript programs (`.js`), audio files (`.mp3` or `.wav`), or video files (`.mov`). Most of the time, files are transferred by HTTP (HyperText Transfer Protocol), which is the standard protocol for web pages, although occasionally large files are sent by FTP (File Transfer Protocol).

✦ `200`: Represents the result code for the request, or the initial response that your web server sent back to the visitor when the request came in. The number `200` means that the request was successfully processed, or you might see `404` instead, which means that the file wasn't found.

If you're seeing numerous entries with the result code `404`, check your web links to make sure that you're not referring people to a *dead link,* or one that no longer exists.

✦ `32768`: Indicates the size, in bytes, of the file that was sent back. If you have lots of graphics, audio, or video files, this number is large.

✦ `"http://search.yahoo.com/search?..."`: Shows the *referrer URL,* or the URL from which the request originated. In this example, the visitor was doing a Yahoo! search and clicked a result link to reach your website. You can see the search terms used. See the next section for more information on referral links.

✦ `"Mozilla/4.0 (compatible; MSIE 7.0; Windows NT 5.2; DigExt)"`: Represents the name and operating system of the web browser program your visitor is using to make the request. In this case, you see either a user browser, such as Mozilla (which is the Firefox web browser — running on Windows XP) or a search engine robot, such as Googlebot.

As you can see from these entries, you can find lots of information in your log entries. As you manually search the listings, you begin to see certain trends, such as which web pages show up most often as `GET` commands or which IP addresses come back week after week.

Manual scanning, however, can tell you only so much, especially if your log file measures in the thousands, or hundreds of thousands, of lines. Later in this chapter, in the section "Jam Packed: Traffic Analysis Software," we talk about computer programs that read these log files for you and break down the information into easy-to-read statistics.

Referring to your referrer file

In some cases, a separate log file (a *referrer* file) on your computer contains the sources of all your web page requests, as shown in Figure 5-2. The sources you see are mostly other websites that link to you or search engine links where a visitor has typed certain keywords and found your site as one of the results.

Figure 5-2:
See where your website visitors are coming from.

For example, a referrer entry like this one

```
"http://www.somewebsite.com/links.html" - /
```

tells you that a specific web page (`links.html`) on a certain website (`www.somewebsite.com`) is offering a link to your website, and that's where your visitor was when he clicked the link to reach your website.

The referrer entry

```
"http://search.yahoo.com/search?p=ecommerce+products"
```

tells you that the visitor came from the Yahoo! search engine. The beauty of this link is that you also see the keywords (`ecommerce` and `products`) that the visitor typed to eventually end up on your site. This information alone can be invaluable when you're planning web-marketing campaigns. (See Chapter 3 of this minibook for more information.) If you see specific keywords or phrases in your referrer file, you know that those words are powerful terms that bring people to your site.

If you're running a web-marketing campaign, you should distinguish search result referrals from sponsored ad referrals. If you include a keyword at the end of the link you provide for the sponsored ad, the keyword shows up correctly in the referrer file. For example, if you're linking to your home page and creating a Google AdWords campaign, you can add the link `www.yourwebsite.com?google` to help interpret your results.

You might also see links that come from your website, like this one:

```
"http://www.yourwebsite.com/page1.html"  - /page2.html
```

This line indicates that the user is on Page 1 of your website and is clicking to move on to Page 2.

You might also see entries like this:

" - "

Typically, this entry means that users just typed your URL directly into their web browser or has your website set up as a bookmark in their browser so that they can go directly to your site. This entry is a good thing to see because it indicates that people are being drawn naturally to your website without having to find it from another website.

Examining error logs

Error log files keep track of errors that are sometimes generated when people access your website. Different web servers keep different fields of information: Some keep the date and time, the client IP, and an identifying field, such as `info` or `error`. Figure 5-3 shows an error log. You're interested in the last field on each line, which indicates the reason for the error.

Figure 5-3:
See which page requests are causing errors on your website.

Watch out for these messages:

+ **Send aborted:** A visitor has stopped the transfer of the file from your web server to his or her computer. This situation occurs mainly when large graphics files (or other media files) are taking too long to load on a visitor's machine, so the person stops the process and moves on. If you see this message repeatedly, you need to condense the files and optimize your web page for faster loading.

+ **File does not exist:** Someone is linking to or looking for a specific file on your web server and the web address the person is using is no longer valid. Perhaps a search engine is referencing a page that's no longer on your website or you advertised a specific web link and misspelled it in the ad. When you see this message, create a web page or file and put that file at the specified web location or create a catchall link that points any incorrect references to the home page or a special error page.

Book VI Chapter 5

Analyzing and Monitoring Your Customers

When a search engine robot finds your website, it looks for a `robots.txt` file in your main website directory, to see whether you put any restrictions on its indexing of your site. When the robot can't find this error, you see an entry in the error log, although it doesn't mean that a problem occurred. In the absence of this file, the search engine robot program searches the entire site.

File stopped transferring: If no mention is made of the client stopping the transfer, you might have a faulty connection between your web server and the visitor.

Although a transfer stoppage occasionally happens, if it happens repeatedly, your web server's Internet connection isn't as reliable as it needs to be. Consider changing Internet service providers.

Checking abandoned shopping cart logs

Typically, an e-commerce shopping cart creates a text file that contains a customer order. As the customer makes changes to that order, the shopping cart program adds or deletes from the file. When the customer checks out and pays for the order, the shopping cart converts the file into something else and deletes it from memory.

However, numerous studies indicate that website visitors abandon their shopping carts as much as 90 percent of the time. By looking at the shopping cart files that don't get ordered, you get an idea of how many people start the process but don't finish. You can compare this number to the number of orders you receive to calculate the percentage of potential customers that complete an order.

Suppose that you receive 50 orders for products in a month and then search for your shopping cart files and find 150 that were never processed. Your result means that 200 customers started the process, but only 50 finished, which is a 25 percent completion ratio for your visitors. When you know your ratio, you can start to take steps to improve it; we show you how in the section "Using Your Data," near the end of this chapter.

You can also find out which products are more popular by counting which ones get added to the carts. If someone took the time to physically add a product to his or her shopping cart, there is intent and demand for the item. You can use this information to help guide future product orders.

Scrutinizing the most common entry- or exit-page logs

Usually derivative files of the log file, the most common entry pages and exit pages focus on where people are specifically entering and exiting your website. In a sense, these entries tell you how your website functions when people use it.

Your *entry* pages detail the areas that draw people to your website. Maybe a product page that you thought wasn't important shows up repeatedly in this file. This information indicates that people are interested, and that you should use similar pages to bring in more people. If you're not seeing targeted landing pages that you created specifically to bring people to your site, something you did there isn't working.

Your *exit* pages show you the point in a customer's path where the person gives up and goes somewhere else. Sometimes, it's the final order confirmation screen, which is what you want to see. Most times, however, you see another page, which should encourage you to investigate why that's the case. Maybe that page gives a negative impression of your website. Perhaps you're encouraging your customer to check out another website and he or she is following that link rather than continuing with you. A page on your site might contain invalid, outdated, or useless information and links. This log identifies the *where;* you have to determine the *why.*

Measuring Traffic against Activity

Your website traffic data shows you a lot of information. To give these numbers some perspective so that you can make higher-level decisions, you have to match the traffic with other indicators of activity on your website:

✦ Number of orders

✦ Average order size

✦ Number of registered customers (if you offer registration)

✦ Total sales volume

✦ Average number of products per order

✦ Most common search terms (if you have your own site search engine)

The reason to compare these numbers is to give you an idea of how much your traffic is influencing your sales. Suppose that your website gets 1,000 unique visitors one month and you see that you're getting 250 orders from 200 unique customers that month. Theoretically, if you can double the number of visitors you receive in a month, you should see a similar increase in your orders and unique customers. Perhaps it doesn't double, but if you can estimate the benefit of bringing in more people, you can estimate the amount of money you can spend to increase traffic.

Putting together all this information gives you a complete picture of how your business is operating. Knowing these factors helps you make dozens of decisions that affect your entire business.

Jam Packed: Traffic Analysis Software

After you get your website up and running, you can expect your log file to generate massive amounts of data as it records every interaction between your visitors and your web server. As the number of visitors grows, so does the number of lines in your log file. It eventually grows to the point that you can't manually analyze the information to get your statistics. At that point, traffic analysis software enters the picture (such as Google Analytics, which you can find at `www.google.com/analytics`).

Traffic analysis software build a summary of your website traffic criteria. These software programs

✦ Break apart each log file entry

✦ Group together similar entries

✦ Factor out known entries, such as search engine bot programs

✦ Calculate totals and averages

You can choose from different versions and levels of traffic analysis software: basic, detailed, and enterprise or big business.

Basic analysis software

When you're using a basic analysis tool, you're looking for a program to create summaries of traffic information for a given period. Some tools, such as AngelFish (`analytics.angelfishstats.com`), run on your self-hosted server. Others, such as Deep Log Analyzer (`www.deep-software.com`), Google Analytics (`www.google.com/analytics`) or Mach5 FastStats Log Analyzer (`www.mach5.com/products/analyzer/`), present data in both columnar and graphical formats for easy viewing.

Here are some statistics that every program should produce or estimate:

✦ Total number of visitors and unique visitors

✦ Average number of daily visitors

✦ Total and average number of page views

✦ Total and average number of hits

✦ Average length of a visit (in minutes or number of page views)

Although the software you use might produce additional results, you can usually count on these categories being calculated. As an example, if you're using a free tool that creates a text summary and you requested a summary for your November 2013 traffic data, you might see results like this:

```
Period: Fri-1-Nov-2013 12:00 to Sat-30-Nov-2013 23:59 (30
    days).
Total successful requests: 2,221
Average successful requests per day: 74
Total successful requests for pages: 948
Total failed requests: 75
Total redirected requests: 349
Number of distinct files requested: 42
Number of distinct hosts served: 618
Number of new hosts served in last 7 days: 72
Total data transferred: 25,349 kbytes
Average data transferred per day: 844,967 bytes
```

This data gives you some important numbers for future demand. By looking at the total and average amount of data being transferred, you get an idea of the bandwidth you need to purchase for your website. You can see how many different web pages are being looked at on your site. In this example, 42 different web pages were requested. If your website has only 50 or 60 total pages, your customers are using a wide range of your site. If you have 200 or 300 pages, you need to see which pages are being loaded and figure out what to do with the rest.

You can also see more detailed information with a more powerful program, such as Webalizer (see Figure 5-4). Webalizer provides bar graphs and summary tables to draw a detailed picture of your website's usage statistics, broken down by month and arranged by different criteria.

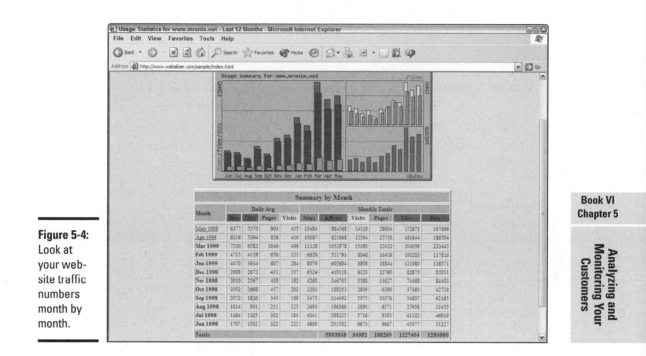

Figure 5-4:
Look at
your web-
site traffic
numbers
month by
month.

Detailed analysis software

At some point, you want to see more advanced information about how your
website operates so that you can make targeted changes and updates to
improve performance. At this stage, you should look into buying a tool such
as WebTrends (www.webtrends.com), Mach5 FastStats Log Analyzer Gold
license (www.mach5.com), or SmarterStats (www.smartertools.com/
smarterstats/) to analyze your log files and provide more defined criteria,
such as

✦ A detailed breakdown of page views

✦ The most common referral links used by your visitors

✦ The pages from which users are most often exiting your site

✦ The number or percentage of return visitors

✦ The most popular web browsers used by your visitors

✦ The most popular search engines that deliver your traffic

✦ The amount of nonhuman traffic (such as search engine programs)

✦ The busiest and slowest parts of the day for your web traffic

These tools come with a number of predefined reports that help you understand your visitors' and customers' sophisticated interaction with your website. Figure 5-5 shows a report from WebTrends that provides a series of dashboard reports. As you change the dates of the period you want to analyze, the graphs are updated automatically. This way, you can compare traffic levels for different weeks, months, or even seasons.

Figure 5-5: WebTrends provides a series of reports to understand your website traffic.

Upload your log files or grant access for these analysis software programs to read your log files automatically. You might have to install these programs on your web server to get them to work properly. Follow the setup instructions and talk to your web-hosting provider if you need specific path or filename details.

Enterprise or big business

As your business grows, you might want to move up to an enterprise-level solution, such as one of these programs:

✦ Adobe Marketing Cloud Analytics: `www.adobe.com/solutions/digital-marketing.html`

✦ Google Analytics: `www.google.com/analytics`

✦ IBM Enterprise Marketing Management (formerly Coremetrics): `www.ibm.com/software/marketing-solutions/coremetrics/`

In this case, you want to install the service on your web host. The key to using these programs is being able to write your own queries to the database, which means that you come up with your own specific requests for summary data.

Some programs require that you know a specific computer language, such as SQL, to create your own reports. If someone in your business is focused on information technology, have that person help you develop the language necessary to build these reports.

Collecting the Correct Information

After people start taking advantage of website traffic analysis, they sometimes fall into the trap of believing that the software does all the work of collecting the right data. You have to realize that although your web server collects some types of information, you can collect other types yourself. In this section, we discuss how you can use your website to reach out and collect more specific information without your customers having to cough up their Social Security numbers.

Storing data using cookies

Any web server can create a standard file on a visitor's computer, to keep track of that visitor's activity and interaction with the web server. That file is known as a *cookie* because it leaves "crumbs" of information that the web server can access when the user visits that website. A cookie is a website owner's friend in many respects because it can show him or her what an individual user is doing on the site. You can track individual behavior and calculate unique visitors and session length much more precisely than by using log files. You can focus on one user for any length of time, from a few days to a few months, to see what the user does on every visit. You can see which web pages the user looks at and the order of those pages and then correlate that information to the user's orders and sign-up activity.

Cookies help move your focus from a site-specific level to a customer level. When you add cookies to your server log files, you can gauge the efficiency of your marketing campaigns with precision. You can judge for yourself how effective your campaigns are so that you're not relying solely on your advertiser reports.

To turn on the use of cookies, ask your web-hosting provider to enable them for your web server. After you do that, tell your provider which basic fields you want to use and capture in your cookies, such as

✦ The visitor's IP address

✦ The visitor's username or account name

✦ The date and time of the visits

Your customers can refuse to have cookies stored on their computers, or they might use public computers, so their cookies won't be consistent. Even if you don't get a 100 percent view of your traffic, using cookies is much more precise than just analyzing your log files.

After you enable cookies on your web server, your last step is to ensure that your traffic analysis software can access the cookies that your web server leaves. That way, the software can incorporate that information into its reports and update its figures accordingly.

Adding information to your links

When you're looking at your log files, you see keywords in the string that represent a referral URL. (Refer to the section "Looking at your log file," previously in this chapter.) Sometimes, these keywords are search terms used by visitors when they're using search engines. At other times, however, those specific terms were created for the purpose of communicating information.

You can *tag,* or add keywords to, your URL to track the success of a marketing campaign. For example, you can tag your URL differently for your Facebook post, a specific tweet, an e-mail newsletter, and other marketing materials to judge the efficiency and reach of each announcement separately. Add the keywords after the name of the HTML file by typing a question mark (?) and then the keywords, like this:

```
<a href="http://www.yourwebsite.com/index.html?GoogleAd1">
```

This way, when someone uses your targeted URL, the traffic analysis software can determine the number of times the keyword (`GoogleAd1`, in this example) was sent in the URL as a percentage of the total number of requests and then calculate a percentage.

If you continue to include this keyword throughout the ordering process, your analysis software can determine the conversion rate of browsers to buyers by studying how many buyers used a keyword as a percentage of the number of the browsers who came to your website.

Studying the path analysis

Your customers eventually follow a path of specific web pages that take them from start to finish on your site. Although individual customers might check out different parts of your website along the way, they need to visit a minimum number of web pages to go from a browsing customer to a paid customer. This minimum number of pages is sometimes called the *critical path* of your website.

Suppose that your website targets different levels of customers and has a special section for small-business customers. Your critical path might look like this:

> Home page→Small-business home page→Small-business catalog page→Order review page→Order checkout page

When you identify the critical path for your customers, you can combine this knowledge with the traffic analysis you already completed to determine when and where people are dropping out of the order process. If you improve this process for your users, you should see an increased number of completed orders and a decreased number of abandoned shopping carts.

Suppose that you're studying the order checkout path. Here are some ways you can integrate all your research:

✦ If your report of the most common exit pages shows the order review page as a common exit page, something in the order review process might be confusing or counterintuitive to your users.

✦ If your referrer file indicates that a number of people are jumping to your frequently asked questions (FAQs) page or privacy policy page from your order review page, your customers most likely need or want more information before they check out. When they jump out of the critical path, a percentage of them never come back to the review or checkout phase. Therefore, you can integrate some of this content into your order review page and see whether fewer people exit before completing the review page.

✦ An order checkout page that involves multiple steps and shows people linking back and forth to the same pages could indicate that users are caught in a loop and can't break out to finish their orders. You might need to combine certain steps on one page or provide more clearly labeled links to convince customers to move forward.

Besides keeping your customers from dropping out of the order process, the other reason for studying your paths is to help you decide to redesign your website. Your customers eventually make their own path through your website, despite any warnings or guidelines you post. You can either continue to try to steer those customers or study their paths and incorporate that information into your site design so that the most common paths are recognized and supported by your website links and structure.

Just as a river cuts its own path through the countryside, your customers will cut their own path through your website. You should always support that path and optimize your site around it rather than fight it and prevent customers from moving around the way they want.

Getting to Know Your Customer

If you've ever walked into a store to buy batteries, you know that the store wants to know a lot about you. The clerk might ask for your zip code, and sometimes your address, even if you're paying cash. The people who run the company do this so that they can get an understanding of the customers who walk through their door and how those customers shop. Although you may find this process annoying or off-putting, you probably accommodate the request. The store can then accurately predict, for example, which customers from which zip codes will order the most batteries.

Gathering customer information is a delicate but ultimately profitable venture because analyzing that information gives you razor-like focus on how your customers interact with you. Just like supermarkets that encourage their customers to use loyalty cards when they shop, websites are now gathering information on a customer level, independent of the traffic information that their web browser leaves with your website. Because the customer is now signed in to the website, every activity is recorded and assigned to a customer account, which can be analyzed and aggregated without worrying about issues such as IP addresses and cookies.

As you understand your individual customers better, you move the focus of your data from your overall website statistics to your customers, where the common factor isn't your entire website but rather the average customer and what he or she does on your website. Begin by having your traffic analysis program identify a unique visitor and then summarize information, such as average length of a visit or session.

Your goal is to find customer-specific patterns, not overall site trends. Collect data from your customer interactions that allow you to gain insight into customers' browsing and buying behavior. At this point, you should add tags or information on pages that matter to your customers, whether it's the order process screen or customer login screen.

Your existing customers have already told you a lot about themselves, including their

+ Names
+ Mailing addresses
+ Credit card information
+ Order lists of products

At some point, consider signing up users when they arrive at your website or want to learn more or do more on your website. Then tie that information into both the traffic and order statistics, to give yourself a true customer focus on your website activity.

When a customer has to log in to your website to use it, you can track every movement and tie those movements to a specific user ID number. Typically, users need some sort of incentive to reveal their personal information and complete a sign-up process. Some websites offer their members exclusive, premium content that casual browsing customers cannot access. Other sites require accounts to be created before products can be added to their shopping carts. You need to determine which special features you want to give to people who sign up with you.

When you use a sign-up process, you lose a certain percentage of browsers who could have become buyers. If you see a big drop-off in activity after instituting a sign-up process, consider assigning a guest account to your procedures. A user who wants to shop can convert a guest account to a permanent account.

Most websites ask for basic information whenever someone signs up for an account:

+ User's name
+ Address
+ City, state, zip code
+ Phone number
+ E-mail address

However, if you think beyond these basic fields, you can ask users additional questions to draw a better picture of your customers, and even to gather ideas that can influence your website, such as these examples:

+ **Demographic information:** Gender, ethnicity, age, marital status, kids
+ **Psychographic information:** Likes, brand recognition, purchase reasons
+ **Lifestyle information:** Income, housing status, types of cars
+ **Interests and preferences:** Favorite subjects, products, and people

Use the data to better understand what customers want and to customize content to them. On the survey form shown in Figure 5-6, the company asks about the interests of its potential shoppers based on their recent order.

Figure 5-6:
Ask customers what they like to buy and use that information.

The options you present can be limited if your customers don't contribute information; if you make it required, however, you can lose a substantial number of potential and actual customers. Make this information-gathering process optional so that customers who don't want to reveal their information aren't blocked from using your website.

Using Your Data to Understand Your Business

Collecting your website traffic and usage data is important for understanding your business. The true value of all this collection and analysis becomes evident when you act on the data and implement changes to your site. After all, what good is learning about a problem if you don't correct it?

Watching trends to find out average behavior

After you set up and collect your data, you have to monitor the activity levels to see trends and behavior so that you have a benchmark for comparison when you're ready to make changes. After all, if you don't know the average behavior of your website, you don't know where it has room for improvement.

When you study traffic and usage patterns for a longer period, look for any big changes in the data. If you see that your traffic suddenly experienced a big increase or suffered a huge drop, ask yourself what is causing big spikes or drops in your activity. Determine whether they're related to a change you made (such as an ad campaign), overall traffic, or a random event.

To fully investigate, create or access reports that give you detailed information from around the time of the change. This way, you can hunt down big problems quickly. If the number of orders decreased and the number of error-log entries about pages not being delivered correctly increased, you know that your web server or Internet service provider was experiencing outages. If your website was unexpectedly mentioned as part of a big news article, you probably saw a spike in visitors to your site and (you hope) a spike in the number of orders placed on your site.

Other problems are less obvious to identify. Diagnosing these situations involves looking at web page activity and seeing which statistics have been affected by the change in activity. As you look at your site, be aware of any changes you made to the web pages, however big or small, and see whether the dates of those changes match up with the change in usage. Sometimes, a simple change disrupts an otherwise stable process and causes unexpected problems. If you watch trends, however, you can spot problems early and then fix them.

Identifying areas of improvement

You have many ways to know when something needs updating. When your car bounces over a pothole and says "ka-thunk," you know that it's time to repave the road. On your website, a report might indicate that traffic took a nosedive. Your e-mail account might be filled with customers screaming IN ALL CAPS that you can't keep operating a certain way.

You can also look at the data you're collecting to start making predictions before problems get out of hand. Find out which web pages your users

✦ Gravitate to

✦ Avoid

✦ View most often and least often

Sometimes, the problem is a factor that your data can only partially identify. Suppose that your traffic report indicates that people check your website every morning. In addition to having traffic data, you know that your product catalog is updated only at the end of the business day, when you hear back from your suppliers. Put together those two pieces of information, and you have a timing problem because your site isn't as current as possible when visitors check it out. They might move on if they see you as unresponsive. In this example, you have to figure out a way to update your inventory each morning.

Put yourself in the role of your customer. Start at your home page and try to place an order. Use your traffic and usage data to back up your assumptions about how to proceed. If you find a page frustrating to use and it shows up on your most common exit pages, you've identified an area to improve.

Don't overlook the importance of direct customer feedback for website improvements. Encourage regular dialogue, use follow-up surveys, and stay in contact with a portion of your customers at all times. They're usually up front about what can be improved and what has to be changed. After they identify a concern, you can research your data to choose your next step.

Deciding on a change

As you look at all your data and trends, identify an area that can be improved. Look at all factors that can influence its poor performance, and choose an element to change on your website that mimics a part of the site that performs well. Look at competitors' websites to see whether they handle the process differently. Ask customers for feedback on how you should handle the process.

When you're ready to update a part of your website, follow these steps:

1. **Make sure that you have a beginning set of statistics before you implement the change.**

   You need a set of data specifying how your website operated before the change, to use for later comparison.

2. **Make the change on your website.**

   Many sites post notices about maintenance periods, as shown in Figure 5-7, where their sites are temporarily unavailable while new updates are posted. Typically, these updates take place during the night for U.S. customers so that the updates have the least effect on traffic. Use the maintenance period to send new versions of your web pages to your web server.

3. **Gather your traffic statistics after the change is posted to your website.**

Watch the usage data after the new version is available, and notice whether traffic went up, as predicted, or down. Notice also whether other parts of your website were affected and whether orders increased.

Figure 5-7:
Use a
regularly
scheduled
maintenance
period
to make
updates
to your
website.

System Maintenance Announcement - Microsoft Internet Explorer

File   Edit   View   Favorites   Tools   Help

Back ·   ·   Search   Favorites   Media   ·   ·

Address http://www.newcomix.com/maintain.htm   Go

System Maintenance Announcement

This system will be undergoing general maintenance from
approximately 3 am to 5 am Pacific Standard Time on Friday,
June 30th.

During this maintenance period, certain site features and
ordering capabilities will be intermittently unavailable or slow.

We apologize for any inconvenience. Thanks again for shopping
here!

**Book VI
Chapter 5**

**Analyzing and
Monitoring Your
Customers**

Following up

Any change to your website can affect all your other processes. Therefore,
you must follow up any change you make to your website, to make sure that
you haven't disrupted anything else. You also have to study customer reaction to your changes and make sure that they benefit from them as much as
possible.

Sometimes, you need to *roll back* the change (remove the update or go back
to the old process). Although the techniques discussed in this chapter give
you lots of insight into customer behavior, traffic analysis doesn't predict
events with 100 percent accuracy. That's why you must stay flexible and
judge whether any updates still provide value after they're implemented.

Chapter 6: Mastering Search Engines, Optimization, and Rankings

In This Chapter

✔ **Understanding how search engines operate**

✔ **Convincing other businesses to link back to your website**

✔ **Telling search engines about your website**

✔ **Updating your web pages with the right keywords**

✔ **Arranging your web pages strategically**

✔ **Watching how websites are ranked**

✔ **Moving up in the search engine rankings**

✔ **Using your own knowledge and experience to help your business**

*I*f you earn prominent placement for your business where traffic is flowing, customers are more likely to stop by, look around, and buy something before they leave. Now, with the ever-growing and ever-changing nature of the Internet, many people are using search engines as their on ramp, or premier starting point for web browsing. After all, if potential customers think that they are going to end up at a search engine to find something, why wouldn't they start there? As a consequence, search results are becoming the gateway to the web, which is exactly where you want to be, offering your products.

In Chapter 3 of this minibook, we talk about marketing yourself in the sponsored ads that are part of the standard search results page. In this chapter, we put the more valuable real estate — the search results themselves — front and center and show you how to improve the quality of your search engine placements.

We also discuss the inner workings of the biggest search engines and then show you how you can influence those engines in your favor. Nothing about these tricks is illegal — you're just increasing your presence in the right areas to get noticed more easily. We also show you how to stay near the top and describe more direct ways to "wave people down" in those search engine results.

Navigating the Ins and Outs of Major Search Engines

When you open a search engine web page and type some words in the search box, do you ever wonder how the search engine produces your search results? Do you imagine a blindfolded person tossing darts at newspapers spread over a wall? Maybe a chicken is let loose to peck its way to a few sites that are then transmitted to you. Although the true answer isn't as comical, search engines use different procedures and methods to compare information against similar sites to come up with the all-important rankings.

Companies that figure out these procedures are the ones that continually find themselves near the top of the rankings. Other businesses, which might have well-designed websites that are chock-full of information, get buried on page 10 or page 20 of the results. A few years ago, human intervention could elevate worthy sites to the top and give them featured placement. Now, however, the placement process is almost all computerized — and because computers follow rules, logic dictates that if you follow the rules, the computers will follow you.

The full set of rules that search engines use to order all their results are tightly guarded secrets because those rules, known as *algorithms,* set companies apart in this area. Google, in particular, uses complex rules.

The words you enter into a search engine typically aren't ordinary words. They're *keywords,* or specific words tied to a particular subject you're interested in. When you go to a search engine, you should give that engine the keywords, or most targeted words, that describe your search.

Search engines work like this:

1. You go to your favorite search engine, type a search term (a keyword) in the text box, and click Search to see the results.

2. Your search engine matches your search term against its database to look for relevant mentions of that keyword.

   The database is made up of countless entries of different web pages that were gathered by either computer programs (known as *bots* or *spiders* in the technical world) or human editors.

The search engine doesn't analyze entire web pages by scanning every word in a page against the keyword you specified. Instead, the search engine looks through *notes,* or a shorthand representation of that page. These notes (which summarize the page) are taken from such elements as

✦ The name of the website and particular web page

✦ Words used in the *title* (or *head*) of the web page

+ The first paragraph or two of the web page

+ Words assigned by the web page to represent the title and description (by using the <META> tag, which we discuss in the section "Creating <META> tags," later in this chapter)

+ Internet web links present on the web page

+ Words used by other web pages that offer a link to the web page

In fact, the first page of the search results lists web pages that contain your search term. We discuss how to insert your keywords into these various places on your web pages later in this chapter, in the section "Placing Keywords in Key Spots on Your Website."

Book VI
Chapter 6

Mastering
Search Engines,
Optimization, and
Rankings

You're not limited to a single keyword. You can have multiple keywords or even phrases of keywords. However, you have a better chance of promoting a handful of keywords or phrases than trying to be the website that offers everything to everyone. Think about the most important or valuable phrases that your customers will use when they search for the products you sell.

Getting Your Website Noticed by Search Engines

Whether people are waving their hands in front of a crowd or smiling for TV cameras, they like to be noticed. To succeed in business, you're always told, "Stand out from the rest and be noticed." As business owners struggle with the notion of getting noticed on a finite budget, creative measures come into play.

As we discuss in the preceding section, increasing your website's visibility on search engines involves knowing the rules they use and ensuring that your site follows those rules. Search engines don't really base their rankings on keywords. If they did, a web page that mentions the same word a thousand times would be at the top of their rankings. Instead, search engines look primarily for content, or how much quality information you offer on your website. Websites with more content — articles, blog entries, calculators, reviews and guides, or plain text — are more useful to someone searching for information and are typically given higher search result rankings than sites with little content. That content, however, should be unique to your website, not just reprinted from other sites.

Some people have a goal of writing an article a day for their sites. In a year, you can turn 10 or 15 minutes of writing into 365 articles! Or you could hire someone to create content for you. Just make sure that the content is readable and not simply packed with the keywords you think you need on your site. Search engines penalize sites that are overloaded with keywords, also known as *keyword stuffing.*

Search engines also look for *references,* or how many other websites offer a link to a given web page. The more links that point to a particular page, the higher that page appears on the search engine rankings, especially on Google. If other websites are pointing their visitors to a particular page, that page must have more relevant content than other, nonlinked pages.

Having other websites link to your web page is the next step. Greater weight is given to a web page whose referring links use the main keywords for that page in the text for that link. Suppose that you're trying to promote a web page for Arctic Technology Solutions. You have the best URL you can get for the keywords in your company name, www.arctictechnologysolutions. com, and leading IT consultants link to your website. Now, tell these consultants to build the link this way:

```
<a href=http://www.arctictechnologysolutions.com> Talk to
    Arctic Technology Solutions! </a>
```

Notice that the clickable text that points to your website contains the same keywords as your URL. The search engines receive a double message that your website contains the text *Arctic Technology Solutions* because their computer programs read the keywords in both the HTML command and the clickable words.

Search engines look not just at the link itself but also at the website from where the incoming link is originating. Therefore, here are a few additional issues to keep in mind:

✦ **The more reputable the website, the higher value the link brings you.**
Search engines typically assign a higher value to links from websites that are highly respected. Therefore, an incoming link from Google, Yahoo!, or one of the top ten sites on the Internet helps your search engine rankings much more than a link from your friend's toy review website. Aim for known websites, educational institutions, if possible, or even government agencies when applicable.

✦ **Make sure that the referring website is relevant to your business.**
Getting reputable websites to link to you is important, but search engines also look for relevance. Does it make sense for them to link to you? Do your sites have something in common or something complementary? For example, having a technology review site link to your organic garden business may not be relevant, but having *Better Homes and Gardens* magazine link to your garden business is relevant.

Book VI
Chapter 6

Mastering
Search Engines,
Optimization, and
Rankings

✦ **The age of the website name may be a factor.** Search engines check for a website's age by looking at the date the domain name was created in the main domain name database. For example, a website created in the late 1990s has obviously been in the database longer than a website whose domain name was first registered two weeks ago. Therefore, aim for incoming links from websites with some history. Check WHOIS (`www. whois.com`) to find the age of a website.

✦ **The best links are incoming only, not reciprocal.** When two websites link to each other in the hope of raising each other's search engine ranking, the links are *reciprocal*. However, reciprocal links carry a lower ranking weight than incoming only links. If several websites create a looping chain of links, where Site A links to Site B, Site B links to Site X, and Site X links back to Site A, Google will lower the weight of all those links. If a website links to you without a link back to it, that incoming link helps your ranking a lot more.

Submitting Your Site to Search Engines

Don't wait for other people to reference your website. The most straight-forward way to make search engines notice your site is for you to tell them directly. Years ago, in the search engine submission process, website owners could file reports containing information about their sites and the URLs and content used on their sites. Although most of this information gathering is now done by the search engines' automatic programs, called *spiders* (because they crawl around the Internet looking for information), some search engines still allow you to submit your site.

Signing up with Google

Google sends its own programs, known as *Googlebots*, around the web looking for new sites to add to its index. There's no reason, however, that you should wait around and hope that a Googlebot will magically land on your website, especially when you're just starting out. Google maintains a simple, one-page web form that you can fill out to identify your site for its software programs to analyze.

You can identify yourself to Google by following these steps:

1. **Go to `www.google.com/addurl.html`.**

Google asks you to log in and redirects you to the Webmaster Tools page shown in Figure 6-1.

Figure 6-1:
Google
wants
to know
about your
website.

2. **In the URL text box, enter the full address of your website's home page.**

   Don't forget to add the `http://`. You don't need to include the home page name unless it's not `index.html`, `index.htm`, or `default.html`.

3. **Type the words shown in the big box.**

   Google adds a special "human detector" on this form to distinguish between humans filling out the form and special software programs that do it automatically. Software programs can't analyze this box because all they see is the generic name for the graphical image. Only human eyes can interpret the letters that are shown.

4. **Click the Submit Request button.**

   Google gets all the information you provided. Eventually, it may send a Googlebot to your website's home page to follow the links, read every page it can find, and store the results.

Signing up with Yahoo!

The roots of Yahoo! are in its category search, not just a general search. Every category has an index page that contains lists of websites that belong to that category. Each index page also points to subcategories, each of which has its own index page. Even though the Microsoft Bing network has acquired Yahoo!'s search engine, it has maintained the category approach to organization and also accepts submissions for its general search.

To guarantee that your submission is seen, you have to take the paid route. The submission process is still in human hands. Editors scan these submissions and decide what to include and where to include it. The human involvement in the inclusion process is one aspect that sets Yahoo! Bing apart from other search engines.

To sign up with the Yahoo! Bing network, follow these steps:

1. **Go to** `http://search.yahoo.com/info/submit.html`.

You see the page shown in Figure 6-2.

Book VI
Chapter 6

Mastering
Search Engines,
Optimization, and
Rankings

YAHOO! ⎯⎯⎯⎯⎯⎯⎯⎯⎯⎯⎯⎯⎯⎯⎯⎯⎯⎯ Yahoo - Help

Submit Your Site

The goal of Yahoo Search is to discover and index all of the content available on the web to provide the best possible search experience to users. The Yahoo Search index, which contains several billion web pages, is more than 99% populated through the free crawl process. Yahoo also offers several ways for content providers to submit web pages and content directly to the Yahoo Search Index and the Yahoo Directory.

Yahoo Search Submission

Submit Your Site for Free:
- Suggest your site for inclusion in Yahoo Search (requires registration)

Yahoo Directory Submission

Yahoo Directory Submit:
- Submit your site for review and inclusion in the Yahoo Directory.
- Editorial review of your pages.
- Intuitive categorization of your site in the Yahoo Directory.

Yahoo Standard:
- Submit your non commercial site for review and inclusion in the Yahoo Directory.

Yahoo   Help   Privacy   Terms   Advertise   Submit Your Site

Figure 6-2:
Take advantage of the different submission methods.

2. **Choose the type of content you want to submit.**

   Yahoo! Bing offers a few ways for you to submit site content to its engine. Click the appropriate header based on the program you want:

   - *Submit Your Site for Free:* Bing and Yahoo! don't guarantee that they will look at your site or include it in its search engine.

   - *Yahoo! Directory Submit:* Yahoo! will consider your site for inclusion in its category index within seven days. Although you have no guarantee that your website will be approved and added, it's reviewed. (Submitting for free carries no guarantees.) The cost for this program is $299; if your site is accepted, you pay an annual $299 fee to continue your inclusion.

   - *Yahoo! Standard:* You can submit your site for category inclusion in the Yahoo! main directory. This option is for noncommercial websites and does not include submission into the Bing directory.

3. **Enter the URL of the website you're submitting.**

   Regardless of the type of content you're submitting, you follow the steps presented and enter in the appropriate box the URL of the website you want to submit. After you enter the URL and click Submit, the address is sent to Bing and Yahoo! for inclusion in their next Yahoo! robot search of the Internet. (Although Bing owns the Yahoo! search engine, they have kept the Yahoo! directory distinct from the Bing directory.)

Don't forget about Yahoo! Local, especially if your business has a retail or local outlet that sells products. If you want to use this paid service, go to `http://smallbusiness.yahoo.com/local-listings` and select your area to begin. Inclusion in the local index ensures a higher visibility by potential customers who live in your specific area.

Submitting to other search engines

You might think that submitting your site and having it picked up by Google and Yahoo! are all you need to do. After all, who uses the other, smaller search engines? The answer is that search engines such as Google and Yahoo! do. By increasing your mention in all the smaller search engines, you get more referrals to your website, which leads to higher rankings on the Big Two search engines.

If you know from researching your logs that customers are using a particular search engine, you should definitely do whatever is necessary to be indexed by that search engine. See Chapter 5 of this minibook for more information on how to analyze your customer logs.

Following are some smaller but active search engines with free submittal pages:

✦ **Beamed:** `www.beamed.com/search/AddURL.html`

✦ **ExactSeek:** `www.exactseek.com/add.html`

✦ **WhatUSeek:** `www.whatuseek.com/addurl.shtml`

Many medium-size search engines — such as Ask.com and Lycos — have their own ways of accepting submissions (mainly by paid inclusion), and others no longer have a manual submission process. Search engines rise and fall in popularity, just like the results they display, so do your homework and follow up with any up-and-coming search programs.

Many businesses offer, for a price, guaranteed submissions to hundreds, or even thousands, of search engines. Many links that are offered are no longer valid because companies are absorbed or go bust. Do your research before signing up with a company that makes big promises about search engine inclusion.

**Book VI
Chapter 6**

**Mastering
Search Engines,
Optimization, and
Rankings**

Placing Keywords in Key Spots on Your Website

Content is important, but people also search the Internet with words, so understanding and using keywords is still an important part of preparing your website for search engine traffic. You can use different methods to incorporate on your web pages the keywords that will be viewed as the most relevant and important words that represent your page. The keywords must appear in multiple locations so that the search engine bots know that those keywords represent the content of your page.

The most important factor is, as they say in real estate, location, location, location. Sure, you can write a web page about the hundred greatest uses for a ball-peen hammer and use the words *ball-peen hammer* repeatedly in the body of the web page. But you can find better locations than the body of the web page to attract the attention of search engine bots more reliably and consistently. Some locations are invisible to the web browser, and others are hiding in plain sight.

Keywords that are invisible

Web pages are built on *HyperText Markup Language,* or *HTML.* Commands aplenty identify the information contained in a web page. For keyword purposes, the most important tag to use in your web page is `<META>`. It defines the name, purpose, author, and date of a web page. Search engines read this tag to catalog web pages more efficiently.

Because of this command's purpose, search engine bots are interested in knowing what information is assigned to <META> tags. They take that information with a grain of salt, however, because they know that the <META> tag info is being written by a biased source — the author of the page. Nevertheless, the <META> tag information is added to the formula for reading and interpreting web pages.

If you're having someone design your web pages, be sure to ask specifically whether he's defining <META> tags for every single web page on your site. These optional tags are commonly forgotten because they don't affect the performance of the web page on the server.

The <META> tag is specific to only the individual web page where the tag resides. Therefore, the information in the <META> tag for your home page is (and should be) completely or significantly different from an interior web page that focuses on one product line.

Creating <META> tags

For each web page, insert at least two <META> tags into the HTML for the page. More options are available, such as defining the author of the page or the last revision date of the web page. Although you might want to define these fields for other reasons, they're not as helpful for targeting search engines.

META tags can speak foreign languages

In this global era of the Internet, your audience is no longer restricted to one region or country. Similarly, your keywords are no longer restricted to one language. The <META> tag has the capability to assign keywords to a particular language set, so you can have a different tag for Americans who speak English, Britons who speak English, and almost everyone in Central or South America and in Spain who speaks Spanish.

You can define an attribute of the <META> tag known as `lang` (short for *language*). The search engines implement a filter if they see the `lang` attribute defined and then assign the correct keywords to the specified language in the web surfer's preferences.

If you sell soccer jerseys and sweaters, for example, your <META> tags might look like this:

```
<META name="keywords" lang="en-us" content="soccer, jersey,
   sweater">
<META name="keywords" lang="en" content="football, jersey,
   jumper">
<META name="keywords" lang="es" content="futbol, Jersey, sueter">
```

Include these <META> tags as part of the head of each web page, not the body section.

The syntax of a <META> tag works in two parts: You define which type of <META> tag you want to use by assigning a name to it, and then you assign the content for that <META> tag. For example, if you want to assign the keywords *Arctic, Technology,* and *Solutions,* your <META> tag would look like this:

```
<META name="keywords" content="Arctic, Technology,
    Solutions">
```

Unlike in other HTML commands, a closing tag isn't necessary. This line of code is sufficient. You need a separate <META> tag, however, for each type of information you want to define. Figure 6-3 shows how to separate the definition from the keywords by using two <META> tags.

Book VI
Chapter 6

**Mastering
Search Engines,
Optimization, and
Rankings**

Figure 6-3:
Use separate <META> tags for different types of information.

```
searchenginewatch - WordPad

View

<title>Search Engine Marketing (SEM), Paid Search Advertising
(PPC) & Search Engine Optimization (SEO) - Search Engine Watch
(#SEW)</title>

<meta name="description" content="The authoritative guide to
search engine marketing (SEM), search engine optimization (SEO),
paid search advertising (PPC) and social media marketing. News,
how-to and marketing strategy guides to succeed on search
engines." />

<meta name="keywords" content="search engine marketing, meta
tags, top search engines, search engine submission,
searchenginewatch" />

<meta name="google-site-verification"
content="7hLqnmqWjOBcrndic5oL0rSUP9-vEI3OxrsJhWYBS9U" />
<meta name="y_key" content="4ed89234c0c67468" />
<meta name="msvalidate.01"
content="A1B7CB550A813BCA5125257704A6D5CJ" />
```

The two <META> tags you need to include are keywords and description. For added effect, some people repeat their keywords as part of their descriptions. The search engines, though, are reading the <META> description and looking for context. A laundry list of keywords in the <META> description tag, therefore, doesn't improve your results. A creative integration can help your efforts, though.

If you're selling gourmet artichoke sauces, your <META> tags might look like this:

```
<META name="keywords" content="Gourmet, Artichoke, Sauces">
<META name="description" content="Our gourmet chefs have
    picked the freshest artichokes to create gourmet artichoke
    sauces sure to liven up any artichoke recipe!">
```

Note the repeated use of the targeted keywords as part of the context of a readable, legible sentence. Although the <META> description tag doesn't have a hard limit, using more than one or two sentences dilutes any meaning you hope to get from using the tag in the first place. Simply put, if you overload the description tag, you water down your results to the point that the search engines don't know any more what's particularly meaningful. Moreover, search engines can *lower* your search ranking result if they think that you're *keyword stuffing,* or putting too many instances of the keywords on your web page.

Adding ALT attributes

A valuable addition to the HTML image tag is the ALT attribute. This attribute is assigned to image files loaded onto a web page. The ALT attribute is a description of the graphical image that's displayed on the web page if the web browser cannot load the image properly on the screen. Additionally, in web browsers such as Internet Explorer and Netscape's Mozilla, a user can hover the cursor over the image to see the information assigned to the ALT attribute.

If you're using the basic Firefox web browser, don't expect to see any ALT text when you hover your cursor over the image. This program treats the ALT information as originally intended, and it's displayed only if the image doesn't load properly.

Because search engines cannot read text that's part of a graphical image, they read the ALT attribute, if it's defined, and give it some weight. Like the <META> tag, the optional ALT attribute is easily forgotten when a website is being designed. You should always take the opportunity to define your ALT attributes for your images; otherwise, you're missing an opportunity to promote your keywords.

The ALT attribute is added to the <IMG> tag that includes an image on the web page. If you're using a big logo image of your business that represents gourmet artichoke sauces, the command to insert the image looks like this:

```
<IMG SRC="logo.jpg" ALT="Gourmet Artichoke Sauces Logo">
```

Keywords that are visible

Although search engines rely on HTML commands such as the <META> tag to gain an understanding of the purpose of a web page, their computer programs are more interested in divining the "natural" meaning of a web page, by interpreting the text visible on the page and understanding what the page itself is trying to convey to users. Therefore, make sure that the keywords that best identify your web page are clearly used in some visible — but not obvious — locations:

✦ **Page name:** Every web page is simply a file containing HTML commands and text, and each file has to have a name. The last three or four letters of the filename after the period must be `htm` or `html` because of web standards. Everything in front of the period in the filename is up to you. If you set up a page to sell tennis equipment, for example, don't use an abstract name, such as `order.html`. Instead, name this special page `tennis.html` or `tennis-equipment.html`.

If you're designing your website for optimal search engine recognition and one web page offers two or more categories of products, divide the product line and dedicate a single page for each one. This way, you can gear everything on each page toward the specific product the page represents.

**Book VI
Chapter 6**

**Mastering
Search Engines,
Optimization, and
Rankings**

✦ **Page title:** Every web page on your website should have a title, regardless of the purpose of the page. Search engines pick up this valuable space.

The worst thing you can do is leave an empty title. The second-worst thing you can do is use a vague or meaningless title, such as "Welcome to my website!" or "Stuff for you." Make sure that each title has the important keywords for that page.

✦ **Page headings:** Human eyes pick up headlines quicker than any other text on the page. Computer programs read headlines and assign a greater weight to them than to the text on the page. You can be more specific in the headings than in the title — just focus the headings on the page content, not on your overall site.

✦ **First sentence:** The first sentence on the page is typically a summary or an overview of what the page offers. Because some search engines don't index an entire page of text, make sure that the first sentence draws a clear picture of your intentions for the page.

✦ **Text inside links:** Search engine bots are hungry for web links, so make sure that any clickable text contains the right keywords for that link. The bots assign weight to those keywords because they're being referenced by the link.

In addition to adding keywords in these locations, you should still fine-tune your pages to mention your keywords throughout the text, as shown in Figure 6-4. Work these keywords into the flow of the text in a way that isn't jarring to readers. Don't just offer strings of keywords that don't form complete sentences. Search engine bots pick up on context, so they flag as non-essential any out-of-place lists of keywords they find.

Don't display any valuable keywords as graphics files on your web page. Search engine bots can scan only the text in the HTML file (or the `ALT` attribute for an image) — not the contents of a graphics file. If you have to use graphics, for a navigation menu or header, for example, complement that menu with a text menu at the bottom of the page. This way, you're using the keywords as text and the keywords are clickable text, which improves your site's ranking.

Figure 6-4:
See how important keywords are used throughout the page.

Arranging Your Pages Strategically

Your website is simply the collection of various web pages that make up your overall business. Therefore, you want every web page in your business to be well defined and serve a specific purpose. You don't want to create web pages whose only goal is to attract search engines with keywords and defined tags. Instead, you want pages that make sense to users and search engine bots.

Keep the following rules in mind when you're constructing the web pages in your business:

✦ **One page, one focus.** If one web page contains two or more product lines, consider breaking up that page so that each line has its own page. You can still have a category index page, which you can optimize with your overall business mission, and each product page can then be a launching pad for that subset of your business. The web page shown in Figure 6-5 concentrates on one product — corrugated mailer boxes.

**Book VI
Chapter 6**

Mastering
Search Engines,
Optimization, and
Rankings

Figure 6-5:
Give every
important
product its
own product
page.

✦ **Define your page.** Make sure that all your definitions, tags, and keyword mentions are at the top of your HTML source code for your web page. Some search engines limit the number of characters per page they take, and you don't want to lose out because you added a lot of comments or JavaScript code first.

✦ **Think about keyword density.** Focus each web page to target a select group of keywords and phrases. This technique increases the weight of each of these phrases more than when you try to use every keyword in every page (a practice known as *keyword density*). When the same words are used repeatedly, search engines see this density of words and assign greater weight to the few words that are used than does an average website that tries to be popular for every popular keyword.

✦ **Put away the bells and whistles.** If your web page excessively uses elements such as graphics, animation, and video or audio files on the same page as valuable product information, separate the extra features into their own section of the website or create two versions — one with just text and basic graphics and one with all the extras. The search engine bots give up on loading a page if it takes too long, and so will your customers.

Watching Your Rankings

Although website pages might last forever in a search engine's database, the website's importance or relevancy doesn't carry over. As website owners try to figure out ways to improve their positions in search engine results, search engines update their systems and algorithms to reduce the effect of specific popular tricks.

One such practice is *keyword spamming*. Website owners hide paragraphs of targeted keywords by matching the color of the keyword's text with the color of the web page background. For example, the owner of a website using a white background might put in a block of keywords using white text. These keywords are invisible to customers browsing the website because the white text doesn't show up on a white background. The spiders that download the information from the web page can see the keywords, however, and they assign weight to those keywords regardless of whether they're relevant. Search engines now compare the colors being used and eliminate those keywords, even if the colors being used are slight variations of each other.

As a business owner, you need to stay informed of the changes the search engines make to their programs, and then update your website accordingly to take advantage of whatever the new rules enforce. The last thing you want is to optimize your website based on one set of rules and then have your website ignored because the rules changed and you didn't update your site.

A variety of websites provide news, updates, columns, and information about major and secondary search engines. If you want to stay up to date with search engine techniques, follow some of these sites:

✦ **Search Engine Watch:** This site, shown in Figure 6-6, calls itself the "Source for Search Engine Marketing," and many users agree. The company uses a variety of mechanisms — such as news articles, blogs, discussion boards, and a marketplace for vendors of search engine optimization (SEO) products — to spread the word about search engine marketing. It offers a wide variety of free content and a reserved Members section (which has premium articles written by experts), an extensive archive of information, and a private newsletter. It even sponsors the Search Engine Strategies Conference and Expo, in different cities around the world, to promote the same concepts as the site. Visit www. searchenginewatch.com.

✦ **Seochat:** If you're looking for a particular discussion area that covers either a general search engine (such as Google, Yahoo!, or MSN) or a discussion about a particular topic (such as link building), Seochat (www.seochat.com) is the place for you. It has a number of discussion boards — including a section dedicated to e-commerce development — that provide help and discussion for online-store professionals or the graphic design or database work that your website requires.

✦ **Search Engine Journal:** What better way to find out what search engine optimization professionals are thinking than to keep up with their journal? Search Engine Journal provides in-depth guides by subject, reports breaking news, and has expert guest contributors review and comment on the newest and most popular events in the SEO space. They even provide perspectives targeted to entrepreneurs, ad agency professionals, content marketing professionals, and more. Visit their site or subscribe to their newsletter at www.searchenginejournal.com.

**Book VI
Chapter 6**

**Mastering
Search Engines,
Optimization, and
Rankings**

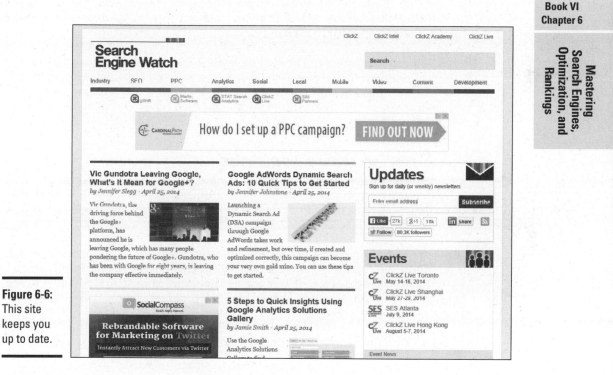

Figure 6-6:
This site keeps you up to date.

Moving Up in the Rankings

The key isn't always to be in the top spot. Considering the enormous amount of new information that becomes indexed every day — not to mention the continual updating of search engine algorithms — you can waste a lot of time trying to stay on top by retaining the top search engine result for your important keywords.

You should have two goals for your ranking in the search engine results:

✦ A position that's high enough on the list before a potential customer sees your competitors.

✦ A position among the first page or two. (Keep in mind that a person using a smartphone to conduct a search will have fewer results per page, making a high placement even more important.)

Most people who are presented with multiple pages of search engine results typically skim the first page and try a few links. A few of them then go to the second page and try more links. After the second or even third page of results, however, if the destination sites aren't close to what the user is looking for, that person typically enters a new string of keywords, sees a different set of results, and tries again.

You can earn a prominent spot by using keywords in the right spots or partnering with a business to link to your website. If you're interested in staying ahead of your competition, though, read these next few sections. We show you how to find your rankings and then how to keep an eye on your competition.

Knowing where you stand

You can't know where you're going unless you know where you are. Your first job is to understand what the search engines know about your website. Search engines provide a growing number of tools that can open a window into their databases and show you what they know about you.

Internet company Moz offers the Open Site Explorer tool, which shows you all the information it can find about a specific website. Some information this tool provides is free, but you can get more information by subscribing to Moz's services, such as their Moz Pro program. Follow these steps to use Open Site Explorer:

1. **Go to** `http://opensiteexplorer.org`.

The opening page for Open Site Explorer appears.

2. **In the text box, enter the URL of the website you want to analyze, and then click the Search button.**

You don't need to enter the `http://` part of the URL.

After you enter the domain and click the button, the results screen is displayed.

3. **View all the inbound links for that website, displayed in their natural search order.**

The default tab view for the Open Site Explorer results lists all inbound website links that redirect people to the domain you specified. After we entered `www.dummies.com` in Step 2, we saw a page similar to the one shown in Figure 6-7. (The website adds the `http://` part when the screen is displayed.) The results include the first 50 links of the 53,797 links from 1,096 root domains (or unique websites) that link to Dummies. com. You can click the title and URL of the linking page to see the page where the link exists.

Book VI
Chapter 6

Mastering
Search Engines,
Optimization, and
Rankings

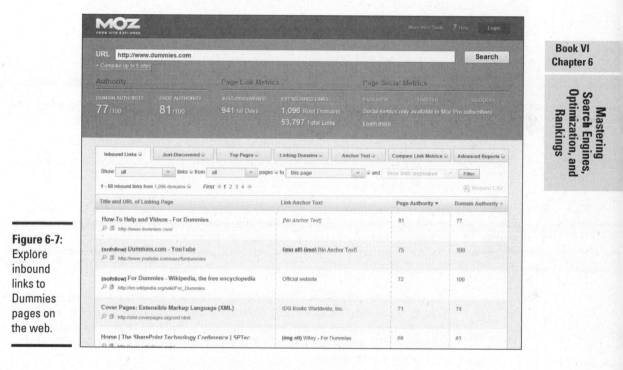

Figure 6-7:
Explore inbound links to Dummies pages on the web.

4. **Click the Top Pages tab to see which pages on your site are the highest-ranked pages for your specified domain.**

   The Top Pages view shows you which web pages in the specified domain have the highest ranking, based on a combination of factors including inbound links, the amount of linking domains, and content on that page.

Seeing what your competition is doing

No analysis of your website is complete without looking at your competition. If your website is the only one in your given area, this step is unnecessary. Chances are, however, that you have more than one competitor and you're trying to figure out how to steer customers to your site and away from the others. You have to recognize the difference between these two types of competitors:

✦ **Direct:** These businesses are the same size as yours and offer a similar (or almost identical) product mix to your target set of customers.

✦ **Indirect:** This type of competitor happens to sell some of the same products you sell (divisions of a big retailer, for example).

You can learn about your competitors by visiting their websites to see their web page design and find out what they offer to customers. Also ask yourself these questions about your competition:

✦ Which keywords are they using in their website names?

✦ Which keywords are showing up in their web page titles and headings?

✦ Which <META> keywords and descriptions are they using? (In your web browser, choose View⇨Source to see the HTML source code.)

✦ How many other links point back to their websites?

✦ Where does their content (website, social media sites, blogs, and so on) appear?

Don't cut and paste any info from a competitor's website. That site has an automatic implied copyright the minute it's created and posted on the Internet. Although you can observe and apply techniques or concepts, you cannot plagiarize the text or reuse a site's graphics or photos without permission.

As you're reviewing your competitors' websites, note the techniques they use that you don't implement. Then compare their search engine results to your results on multiple search engines. Concepts that work well on one engine might not be picked up on another site. Find out what works, and avoid what doesn't.

Creating your own referrals

Some website owners have decided that if they can't get other websites to offer a link to them, why not build their own links? The sole purpose of some websites is to serve as part of a newly built network to promote a central site. When you go to these referral sites, it's obvious in some cases that they're built for only one reason. As search engines have adapted their rules, they ignore sites whose only purpose is to link to someone else.

The right way to achieve your own network is to build a series of targeted, focused content sites, each of which feeds into your main e-commerce business. Suppose that you sell pet supplies. Rather than add original content solely to your e-commerce site, you can set up targeted websites about dogs, cats, birds, fish, gerbils, and hamsters. You can then focus on building up these websites by becoming an authority or expert in these areas. After you have fellow enthusiasts hooked on your information, you can refer those people to your e-commerce site when they're ready to buy something.

Getting another website to cross-promote with you is easier when you're exchanging links with a content site, not with an obvious potential competitor. You can always offer excerpts of your content on the e-commerce site, in case your repeat customers come straight back and want to read something first.

You can even promote your products on sale at places such as Facebook, Twitter, Instagram, Tumblr, Pinterest, and other social networking, blog, or profile web pages. Each third-party website has its own restrictions, so you may want to check the terms and conditions for these websites if you launch something with a questionable link.

**Book VI
Chapter 6**

**Mastering
Search Engines,
Optimization, and
Rankings**

Book VII
Retail to E-Tail

Contents at a Glance

Chapter 1: Knowing When to Put Your Store Online

In This Chapter

✔ Deciding whether a website can help your business

✔ Perfecting your timing when you're launching a site

✔ Building on your store's existing identity

✔ Mapping out the details for your online move

✔ Putting your inventory on the web

Today, rather than asking whether a retailer has a website, you most likely simply assume that they do. Why wouldn't a traditional bricks-and-mortar business also have a web presence, so you can purchase their products online as well? However, although significant numbers of retailers have moved online, plenty have yet to make the jump or have not made their complete inventory of products available on the web.

If you're in this group, don't fret. You might have put off launching a fully functional e-commerce website because of costs or other reasons, but believe us when we say that there has never been a better time to join the online revolution. E-commerce sales in the United States grew by nearly 30 percent in 2013, beating industry forecasts, according to Forrester Research. By 2017, online sales are projected to reach $370 billion and account for more than 10 percent of all retail sales in the United States.

In addition to gaining sales online, your web store is probably also influencing your offline sales. Forrester Research found that a larger amount of offline sales are driven or influenced by customers doing online research. By 2017, estimates predict that nearly 60 percent of retail sales will be influenced by the Internet, either in direct online purchases or indirect web-influenced sales.

The blurring of lines between online and traditional retailers got fuzzier during the holiday shopping season of 2013. While traditional retailers had a soft Black Friday (the major offline shopping day to kick off holiday sales), the bricks-and-mortar stores with e-commerce sites did exceedingly well on Cyber Monday (the online version of Black Friday), which usually benefits online retailers selling exclusively online. Through record-breaking sales in 2013, consumers sent the retail industry a strong message that they want to shop online — and they don't care if you are an online retailer or a traditional retailer. They just want to buy online.

What does this mean for you? Simply put, when moving your store online, you not only add new web sales to your revenue stream but probably improve or influence your in-store sales, too. What are you waiting for? Let's start helping you move your store online today. In this chapter, we explain what you need to do to make the transition from your bricks-and-mortar store to an online store.

Making the Decision to Move Your Store Online

While you're thinking of taking your business online, ask yourself this basic question: Why do I want to move my business online? If you're making the move only because it's expected or because everyone else is doing it, you might want to think about it a little more. Having an online presence is essential, but you shouldn't rush into it without a plan and without the proper resources. You should make the move for the right reasons — and be prepared.

You're ready to get serious about building an online site when that site can help you reach a specific goal that makes your business stronger. Typically, these reasons include

✦ **To expand:** Going online opens another channel for selling your products. If your site is executed properly, it helps increase your revenue and profit potentials — a standard goal for any business.

✦ **To control the cost of growth:** Expanding onto the Internet can be much less expensive than opening another physical location. Additionally, an online store potentially reaches a national or an international customer base rather than confines you to a limited geographic area. You reach more customers for less money. That's smart business.

✦ **To create awareness:** Your site is an extension of your marketing efforts. It becomes a permanent, online advertisement for your bricks-and-mortar store. Sometimes, you might have a site solely to support your other marketing or PR activities. If you're already getting a lot of exposure through your current marketing methods, you need a place to direct prospective customers for more information. Either way, customers won't easily forget about your store when you're continually communicating with them, both online and offline.

✦ **To drive traffic:** No matter how much, or how little, inventory you offer for sale online, you're ultimately building foot traffic to your store, too. Your site is an interactive marketing tool. For example, to attract new customers, you can use paid and *localized* (targeted to your local market) keyword searches and search engine optimization (refer to Book VI, Chapter 6). And online coupons, e-mails, and e-newsletters become incentives to purchase (online and off). You decide where you want to direct the traffic.

Ultimately, your reason for starting an online store must make sense as part of your business strategy. As with any other decision, this choice deserves your deliberate and considerable attention.

Unfortunately, some offline entrepreneurs haven't thought through their online strategies. In fact, they don't have strategies. This type of storeowner is chastised by customers for not having a website. Eventually, the storeowner gives in and decides to buy a domain name and throws something up there just so that he can say, "I have a site!"

Here are the four worst reasons to move your company online at any time:

+ **Your employees offer to build it:** Sometimes, employees and other well-meaning friends and associates insist that you must get online. They're even willing to create an e-commerce-enabled site for you. Maybe they truly want to help, or perhaps they want the opportunity to expand their own skill set. However, a hastily developed website won't appease your customers.

+ **Your competitors are online:** Feeling like the only retailer in your industry that hasn't moved online is frustrating. But if you're not ready to invest in the components that you need to create a quality online store, your customers will find your competitors more enticing anyway. The fact that your competitors are online shouldn't be the *only* reason you decide to make the transition.

+ **You finally have the money:** Saving up for the amount that you budget for a site is one thing. Haphazardly deciding to spend some of your profit just because it's available is another thing entirely. If e-commerce is an important part of your strategy, you can find the necessary money to fund it at the right time, according to your plan.

+ **Your business is failing:** If your retail sales are way down and you're on the brink of closure, you might think that moving your store online is the only answer. However, having a website isn't a cure-all for what ails your business. Instead, e-commerce is only an element within your business. Therefore, if your offline store is already flailing, your online version is likely to face equal — if not greater — struggles.

For the most part, the reasons in the preceding list represent pressure points. And when you can't take the pain any longer, you finally respond. Someone (or something) else is then calling the shots and deciding what's best for your business. Don't give in to this kind of pressure. Instead, think about the timing of your decision and take control.

Finding the Right Time

To find the right time to make the move online, you have to step back and analyze the situation as objectively as possible. Does creating an online store truly fit into your business plan right now? In what ways would an online store contribute to your short-term and long-term goals? Is there a better time to move your business online?

In addition to your internal store goals, you have to consider external factors. The presence of an online store doesn't mean customers will flock to it and spend, spend, spend! You have to market your online store just as you do your offline location — and external conditions can play a big role in your success. What are the current market conditions for your industry? In what general direction is the national economy heading? If your customers aren't spending right now, you might want to conserve the money that you originally budgeted for your site development. On the flip side, if market factors are pushing the demand for your type of products, you might want to bump up the development of your site by a few months.

Make time to track industry trends, both online and off. Regularly check out the issues by reading trade magazines and following industry-related research. Start with research from Gartner (www.gartner.com) and Forrester Research (www.forrester.com).

Taking into account seasonal latitude

As a retailer, you probably have a particularly busy season, when you earn the majority of your revenues. Your busy season might be the end of the year when most holiday shopping drives sales. Or, if you sell recreational items, such as bikes or swimming pool accessories, the summer is probably when you gear up for brisk business.

Your products are most in demand during this period, which can affect your plans for starting a site in two ways:

✦ **Development time:** Building a site takes time. Even if you're outsourcing the work, you're intricately involved in the process. Creating your first online endeavor during your store's most hectic time of year is a bad idea. If you're already loaded with work, you're likely to make hasty site-related decisions or drop the project altogether out of sheer frustration. You can offset this potential for disaster by planning around your store's busy time.

Start working on your site right after your busy season ends. Although you might anticipate a development timeline of only a few months, many events and circumstances can delay or extend that deadline. Even adding e-commerce to an existing site can take more time than expected, with all those pictures to take and descriptions to write. Beginning site construction (or expansion) at the close of your business's high point gives you plenty of cushion before that busy time rolls around again.

✦ **Launch time:** Planning to launch a site during your seasonal high point isn't a grand idea. You need time to test the site to see how it works and to find and correct errors. Sure, you and your developer test most of these items before you take the site *live* (the point at which you put it on the Internet), but plenty of minor glitches go unnoticed by everyone but your customers. If you launch the site before your busy season begins, you have more time to respond to these customer issues and resolve them. And because fewer customers are likely to be affected by the problems, you can keep the issues contained.

Don't be shy about letting your customers know that your site is new. Make a point to ask for feedback and suggestions for improvement or to be notified of trouble spots. Reward customers who send you information. You can give them coupons or other small gifts to thank them for their time.

Timing your launch around an event

Similar to seasonal timing, other events can influence when you decide to launch your site, such as an annual event that your store participates in. You might think that an event where all your potential customers are gathered is the perfect time to unveil your site. Keep in mind, though, that perfect timing isn't always as perfect as it seems.

If you insist on coordinating your site's debut with an event-driven date, keep in mind the following points:

✦ Double the amount of time that you think you need for your site's development.

✦ Add another six to eight weeks to that date for testing and customer feedback.

✦ Don't commit to using your site for event-related promotions (just in case).

✦ Avoid using event-specific merchandise in the launch of your site.

If your store's online premiere is tied to an immovable date, hope for the best — and plan for the worst.

Dedicating manpower

You need to find the time for a project the size of a website launch. Regardless of what else you have going on in your business (and your life), at the end of the day you have to dedicate your time to the cause.

Although you can hire out the bulk of the development work for your site, you need to be involved in a long string of commitments during the process, including these tasks:

✦ Find and hire a website designer (two to three weeks).

✦ Define the scope of the project (eight to ten hours).

✦ Decide on the site design (one to two weeks).

✦ Choose a shopping cart solution or e-commerce platform (one to two weeks).

✦ Coordinate payment-processing options (three to five days).

✦ Select inventory to stock your online store (ongoing).

✦ Create a site launch campaign (one week).

You get the idea — you're going to be busy!

Take a look at your average day and then tack on a minimum of another two to three hours for managing site-related tasks. The time that you devote to your site includes meetings with your design team and your staff as well as the time you need for decision-making. Block off at least half a day on the weekends for site work, too. You probably need to use this schedule for about three to six months.

Bridging Your Offline Store with Your Online Store

All too often, a retailer is eager to have an e-commerce alternative and then takes a somewhat haphazard approach. Most traditional entrepreneurs who are unfamiliar with the Internet tend to view the physical store and the online store as two separate, different entities. When you treat your bricks-and-mortar store and your online store differently, customers have two different experiences with your company — and become confused about which experience truly represents your brand.

Seamlessly bridge your bricks-and-mortar store (your company's history) with your online store (your brand's future). With this approach, you can provide a single, cohesive user experience. Focus on these three critical areas: identity, image, and integration.

In this section, we show you how one company — Williams-Sonoma — does an outstanding job of meeting these three objectives. Williams-Sonoma remains one of our favorite examples of how an established retailer keeps its website's design and functionality current while staying true to its brand's in-store image.

Finding your identity

Identity incorporates all the physical characteristics that your customers associate with your store. It's your logo, color palettes, store layout, and any other details that contribute to your store's distinctiveness.

When you visit the bricks-and-mortar Williams-Sonoma, you see a lot of natural, muted, neutral colors as a backdrop on the walls. The color scheme is simple and understated. The occasional pop of color springs from the products themselves, neatly arranged as part of the in-store displays. The online version of the store (www.williams-sonoma.com) has the same feel to it: A subtle white background lets featured products grab the spotlight. Product images are crisp and bright and reflect the way the company's high-end products shine in their stores.

Creating an image

Image incorporates not only the physical appearance of your store but also how customers perceive it. Is your store considered a high-end retail store with select but pricey items? Or is your store an eclectic mix of trendy yet unique gifts? Are you known for exceptional customer service? Or do customers enjoy browsing in a low-key environment? All these details contribute to your store's image, and you want that image to carry over to your online store.

One thing that sets apart Williams-Sonoma is the helpful information it provides, often in the form of in-store demonstrations and cooking classes. The store has created an image of being a solution provider for upscale kitchen products. It carried that image online by including recipes that incorporate cooking ingredients or products for sale on the site. The website also makes it easy to find in-store events (see Figure 1-1).

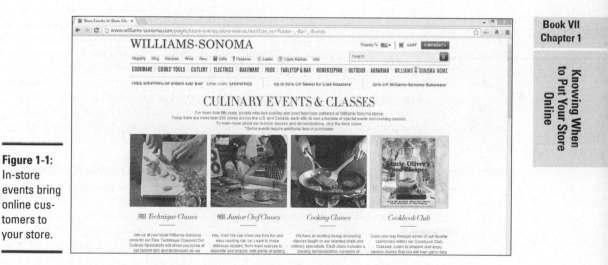

Figure 1-1: In-store events bring online customers to your store.

Book VII
Chapter 1

Knowing When to Put Your Store Online

Further keeping with its image of being helpful, the Williams-Sonoma website makes personal recommendations for other products and services you might like, based on your online browsing experience and matched to what customers with similar tastes have also viewed and purchased (Figure 1-2). It's all part of the brand's image of being your source for cooking needs — whether you shop online or in the store.

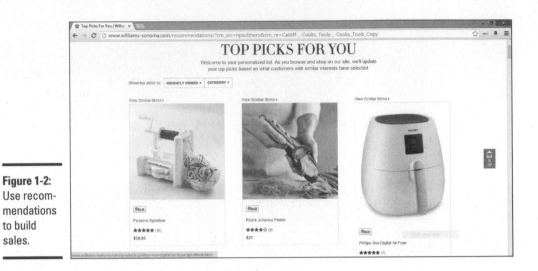

Figure 1-2:
Use recommendations to build sales.

Integrating your shopping cart

Less visible to the customer is the functionality of your site on the back end. In particular, you need to consider how your online inventory is managed. Your goal is to integrate the back end to work alongside your offline inventory system. For example, if a customer orders a product from your site, that product should be in stock. If it's not, you want that information to be available to the customer at the time of the order.

The technology choices you make (such as which inventory-management solutions and shopping carts you use) ultimately determine the types of buying experiences your customers have on your site. (For more information about shopping carts and inventory management, refer to Book IV, Chapters 5 and 6, respectively.)

We really can't tell you how or whether the Williams-Sonoma online shopping cart is tied into a particular store's inventory or whether it's integrated with a shipping warehouse. Frankly, as a customer, you don't need those details. The Williams-Sonoma website gives you a good example of shopping cart functionality, though. If the site has additional information about a particular product, a message appears at the top of your shopping cart before you check out. You can find out whether you need to expedite shipping for a holiday-themed item to arrive by a particular date or how long a product on back order might take to arrive. If you have an account, you have an express checkout option. Or if you don't want to take the time to register, you can check out quickly as a guest. These examples of making the buying experience as helpful and frictionless as possible are part of the many reasons we appreciate this brand's online store.

Making a Flawless Transition

Granted, a national retail chain has a much larger budget for a website than you do. Even so, your smaller store can embrace the same concepts that the big boys use for a smooth, effective online transition. The best way to make this transition is to plan.

Adding an e-commerce component to your store is similar to planning a big party or a major event. Part of your plan is already in place: You have an approximate timeframe for making your project a reality. To make that time-table more manageable, break it into three smaller chunks, or *stages:* orientation, implementation, and evaluation. For each stage, create a checklist of activities that should occur during that stage.

Stage 1: Orientation

When you're talking about moving your store online, the orientation stage includes everything from conducting initial research to evaluating and choosing the best vendors and software applications.

Following are some of the tasks that you should accomplish in the orientation stage:

✦ **Identify and research your competitors.** Check out the competition's sites, and even purchase items to get a feel for how their shopping carts work. Put together a list of products and price points (refer to Book IV, Chapter 6). See the "Building an Inventory" section, later in this chapter, for more information about this step.

✦ **Set up your website.** Research a hosting solution, choose a domain, and set up your server. (To find out about these tasks, refer to Book III.) Then you're ready to begin integrating your existing back-end solution with your online processes.

✦ **Decide on payment options.** Determine which forms of payment (credit cards, PayPal, or gift certificates, for example) you want to accept on your website. Contact your bank provider and ask about its options for online transactions. Or choose from the options provided with your e-commerce platform.

✦ **Evaluate shopping vendors and other customer service.** Decide whether you're going to provide live or e-mail-based support.

Take a look at Table 1-1 to get an idea of how to start a checklist of the tasks you need to accomplish during this stage.

Book VII Chapter 1

Knowing When to Put Your Store Online

Table 1-1	Orientation Checklist		
Action Item	*Result/ Resources*	*Decision*	*Notes*
Identify all competitors			
Research competitors			
Study their sites			
Purchase their products online			
Test their customer service functions			
Return a product to check the process			
Maintain list of similar products and price points offered by competitors			
Review industry trends			
Check for domain availability			
Determine options for hosting solutions			
Compare third-party hosting versus internal servers			
Locate top three shopping cart products or e-commerce platforms:			
Compare prices			
List capabilities			
Note limitations			

Stage 2: Implementation

In the implementation stage, you move from just thinking about your website to making it happen. You're building the site, integrating your back-end systems, and creating offline and online marketing tools to use.

Take a look at all the research you compiled in the orientation stage, and start making some decisions:

✦ **Set a budget and a schedule.** Create these items to keep track of your money and your time.

✦ **Approve the site design.** Create the *copy* (text) for the site and gather any content from other people, such as reviews and testimonials.

✦ **Go live with the site and register with search engines.** Start making your URL visible to the public.

Table 1-2 shows how to set up a checklist to keep you on track while implementing your site.

Stage 3: Evaluation

Technically, after your site is up, the evaluation stage never ends. You need to continuously test, review, and revise your site to maintain its functionality and appeal.

Here are some elements that you want to keep your eye on after your site goes live:

✦ **Site performance:** Check how long individual pages take to load, how many page views you're getting (refer to Book VI, Chapter 5), and whether all your links are working.

✦ **Shopping cart:** See whether the cart is working as it should.

✦ **Shipping and handling:** Make sure that orders are being fulfilled in a timely manner and that customers are happy with your service.

Table 1-3 gives you an idea of how to start a checklist for this stage.

Table 1-2	Implementation Checklist		
Action Item	*Status*	*Implementation Date*	*Completed?*
Set budget			
Create development schedule			
Develop marketing plan			
Register domain			
Contract with SEO specialist (if applicable)			
Approve site design			
Approve site map			
Obtain web hosting service			
Purchase additional hardware (if applicable)			
Initiate vendor agreements (payment processors, fulfillment, and so on)			
Select shopping cart software			
Create product list for initial launch			
Set prices			
Complete product details			
Choose product images			
Add image tags			
Write product descriptions			
Upload products to shopping cart			
Create all web copy			
Develop FAQs			

Table 1-3		Evaluation Checklist			
Function/Area	*Last Update*	*Status*	*Problems or Concerns*	*Corrective Action*	*Complete By*
Site performance					
Load times					
Page view					
24/7 access (no downtime)					
All apps work					
Internal links work					
External links work					
Home page					
Info is correct					
Graphics load properly					
Policies current					
Individual product pages					
Product images					
Product descriptions					
Customer reviews					
Supporting content					

Book VII
Chapter 1

Knowing When
to Put Your Store
Online

Building an Inventory

A big part of planning for a successful transition online involves selecting the right inventory from the start.

The pressure of choosing the best products to sell on the Internet might seem like a daunting task. Unlike other e-commerce sites that are starting from scratch, however, you have a distinct advantage: product mastery. You not only have an existing inventory but also know it intimately. You understand exactly what sells and what doesn't, and you have an established sales history with actual data to prove it.

Consider the number of conversations you've had with customers over the years. Because of that feedback, you have a firm grasp on why your customers like a product and what they might need to know about it before making their final purchasing decisions. That's exactly the information you need to move those same products online without missing a beat.

Follow these steps to begin building your online inventory:

1. **Pull together a list of your current inventory.**

   We hope that you have this list already. If not, you need to create an up-to-date and complete inventory list.

2. **Separate your current inventory into categories.**

   For example, you can group products according to which areas will help or hinder how well they sell online. These categories include

   - *Top sellers:* Items at the top of your moneymaking list.

   - *Exclusive items:* Unique, hard to find, or handcrafted items.

     If you're an approved reseller or licensed dealer for a particular product or brand, check your agreement for any conditions or terms on how or where you can sell.

   - *Shipping weight:* Heavier or bulkier items that are more expensive to ship.

     You don't have to eliminate items that might be too bulky, and thus too expensive, to ship. Instead, make those items special orders and have customers e-mail or call for quotes that include shipping. Or make the products available only for in-store pickup.

   - *Availability:* Items that are in stock or readily accessible from the manufacturer or supplier.

   - *Drop-ship capability:* Items that can be shipped directly from the manufacturer or supplier, which saves your inventory space.

3. **Rank your inventory.**

   List items in order from those most suitable for selling online to those least suitable. Suitable items are easy to ship, not unusual in size or shape, and nonperishable. Food items and products such as flowers that are perishable can sometimes be unsuitable for online sales unless you use the fastest delivery methods possible.

4. **Go online and find as many websites as you can that sell items similar to those in your inventory (starting with the products at the top of your list).**

   Make a record of these sites so that you can watch them as you prepare to build your store. Study the sites and determine how they compare to your store and future site. How are the competing sites branded? Are they easy to find in the search engines? Do they ship globally? What advantages and disadvantages does your store have in comparison to these stores? What do you like or dislike about how they promote the products?

5. **Compare the sticker prices of the actual products. Mark on your inventory list the products that are price competitive.**

   When you're comparing prices, factor in all the pricing considerations, including sales tax and shipping and handling fees.

6. **Review your inventory list and reprioritize, if you need to.**

   Move or drop those items for which you don't have a strong competitive advantage. Bump to the top of your list the products that make your store shine.

   Keep this data because it not only helps you decide which items are ideal for your online inventory but can also help guide you in promoting your products later.

7. **Determine the number of products you want to sell online.**

   Revisit your strategy. If the purpose of your site is to sell merchandise, the more products, the better. If you're just promoting your brand, starting with a smaller amount of products might work fine. Or you might be limited in the number of products that your shopping cart program allows (without investing more money in a shopping cart).

   Rather than delete items, consider adding ones that aren't part of your current store inventory. Nothing is wrong with adding to the list, if it makes sense and especially if vendors can *drop-ship* (pack and mail the product directly to your customer).

8. **Apply the *customer factor* (any customer-related information that can influence an online purchase).**

   Here's where your years of customer interaction come in handy. Evaluate the products through the eyes of your customers. Which items are difficult to sell because customers need additional information?

Can you present that information in an online product description? (Or maybe the product sells even better online because you can give the customer additional product detail.) If the customer might see some aspect of your product in a negative way, now is the time to delete an item from your online inventory.

9. **Delete any products based on their image — or, rather, lack of one.**

Sort through your inventory and figure out which products have photos available from a vendor or manufacturer. The quality of the product images on your website directly reflects the image of your store. If a high-resolution quality photo doesn't exist, you have two choices:

- Drop the product from your online inventory.

- Spend the money to hire a professional photographer.

Although amateur pictures taken with a digital camera might work on eBay, customers expect higher quality from a retail store. Hiring a professional photographer is worth the investment.

Ask your vendor whether any marketing program incentives are available that could help offset the cost of a photo shoot. For example, you might agree to feature certain products on the home page of your site or use them in your store's offline marketing materials. In return, you might be eligible to participate in a vendor's marketing reimbursement program (which can equal several hundred dollars for a small retailer).

You need to take pictures that feature several different angles of the product. Most products sell better if a customer can see multiple views of the item; if the site offers the option to show a product being used or positioned in a setting; and if a customer can zoom in on the picture for a more detailed view. You must have permission to use photos that are not your own, unless you've paid a fee to license the image. When it comes to product photos, your vendor or supplier may provide you with the right to use various images.

Chapter 2: Understanding the Differences between In-Store and Online Customers

If you expect your in-store customers to be identical to your online customers, you may be setting yourself up for a nasty fall. Sure, the two types of customers have some similar characteristics. But the reasons why someone buys from your retail location can be quite different from how, why, and when that person chooses to shop with you online.

Perhaps you're wondering whether these differences really matter. The short answer is yes! Your job is to entice customers to buy. To do that, you have to get to know your customers — both online and offline. In this chapter, we cover the differences between offline and online customers and how you can accommodate both.

Comparing Online and Offline Customers

When you launch an online store, your ultimate goal is to change the way your customers shop. Whether that means getting them to buy more or buy more often, you're hoping that your online store provides the incentive to make that change. A recent survey of online retailers with at least $25 million in annual sales indicated that the average purchase was more than $150. Repeat customers, which made up approximately 40 percent of their online business, spent at least $178 per order. As you can see, spending time growing your online business is worthwhile. But before you can change your customers' behaviors and get that high-dollar repeat business, you have to understand them, especially in the area of e-commerce.

Once accidental or happenstance, most online shopping is now quite purposeful. Your customers are making a conscientious decision each time they make a purchase online. To better understand their decisions, compare some of the reasons why your customers might shop in your store (real customers) as opposed to shopping online (virtual customers).

Customers showing up in your bricks-and-mortar store expect these features:

✦ **Security:** Your customers may think that shopping in your store is more secure than giving out credit card information on your website.

✦ **Guaranteed delivery:** Sometimes, purchasing a product is a time-sensitive issue. If customers need an item in their hands by a certain time or date, shopping online may become an afterthought. This need-it-now mentality is especially true during a holiday rush.

✦ **Instant gratification:** Waiting for a product to ship isn't everyone's idea of shopping. Sometimes, customers need or want an item immediately, and shopping in a store gives that instantaneous gratification.

✦ **Loyalty:** Customers who are familiar with your store feel a connection. They often translate that into a perceived relationship with you and your employees. These customers are loyal and expect loyalty from you in return.

✦ **Service:** Having access to personalized service is a big plus for many traditional shoppers. These customers typically believe that shopping in a store is the only way to find that level of assistance, and they don't realize (or believe) that they can find quality sales support online.

✦ **Only option:** Some customers simply don't consider other buying alternatives. They may think that in-store shopping is the only option because they aren't comfortable or familiar with the Internet, don't have online access, or aren't aware that they can shop online with your store.

✦ **Try it before you buy it:** Some customers need to see, touch, or try on products before making a buying decision. In this case, shopping over the Internet doesn't do the trick.

✦ **Avoid extra charges:** Shipping cost is the main factor working against online shopping. Many customers decide to shop offline simply to avoid additional shipping and handling fees tacked on to their purchases.

Online shoppers who do not want to pay shipping costs are more likely to buy offline, from your local store, if you offer price matching to the online store's price. Price matching can give your store a competitive advantage, if you can afford to discount some or all of your merchandise. If you decide to promote price matching in your store, make sure you clarify any exceptions of products or brands you cannot discount.

Virtual customers have the following expectations from your online store:

✦ **Research material:** Shopping online provides the opportunity for detailed research before making a final purchasing decision. Shoppers can find product reviews, read customer feedback, compare brands and prices, and then make a purchase — all in a matter of minutes. Research shows that male customers are especially prone to do a little digging before they start buying online. Some mobile-savvy customers now stand in a store and use their smartphone to compare prices and styles or to check availability of products online. (This type of behavior can work for or against you.)

✦ **Hard-to-find items:** An item may be out of stock in a store or may not even be available locally. Shopping online provides access to products that aren't otherwise readily available.

✦ **Niche or specialty items:** Customers are frequently drawn to online stores because those stores provide access to specialty items, including vintage goods, collector's items, or any other type of exclusive or niche product.

✦ **Convenient store hours:** Round-the-clock shopping is tough to beat. These customers enjoy the flexibility that comes with virtual shopping — and knowing that the store is never closed.

✦ A **better value:** Although shipping costs may be of concern to an in-store shopper, an online buyer may factor in the cost of gas and time.

✦ **The best price:** Comparing prices and finding the best deal online is a snap these days. That ability to get the lowdown on a price for any given product is the reason that many buyers head straight to the Internet to shop.

✦ **Extended inventory:** Retail stores traditionally have limited shelf space, but a website can house a lot more. (And products can often be *drop shipped* — ordered and shipped directly from a manufacturer or a supplier.) Because many web shoppers believe that they have access to a wider product selection online, e-commerce stores are often their first stop for shopping.

**Book VII
Chapter 2**

Understanding
the Differences
between In-Store
and Online
Customers

What Your Online Customers Expect from You

Customers shop online for many reasons (see the preceding section to read about some of those reasons). But you need to recognize another underlying difference between real and virtual shoppers: Online customers have great expectations for your online retail location. Sure, all customers are particular and — dare we say — demanding, but the Internet has raised the bar. It's up to you to make sure that your online store performs. In the following sections, we talk about what online customers expect of you.

Round-the-clock hours

Most customers expect your store to be open 24 hours a day, 7 days a week. Granted, meeting this need seems like a cinch. After all, after you put your site out on the web, it's . . . there. Right? Unfortunately, running a store 24/7 involves a little bit more work. Your customers are used to having 100 percent access to online stores, whether it's midnight or midmorning. Here are a couple of site-related tasks that you may want to consider:

✦ **Customer support:** Can your customers contact you in the middle of the night and expect to receive an answer? Or will prospective buyers receive help only during normal business hours? Ultimately, that's your call. But you have to decide the rules up front and then let your customers know.

✦ **Routine maintenance:** Maintenance includes any factor from your server going down (and your store being temporarily offline) to a glitch in your payment gateway provider that may prevent credit cards from being processed. When you're open for business around the clock, it helps to have a backup plan for all the things that could go wrong when you're not at the helm. For example, while shopping on a niche retail site one weekend, a glitch in the shopping cart prompted it to ask for a password before finishing the checkout process. Weekend assistance was unavailable, so the online retailer lost our sale — and countless others that weekend. It's just as easy for a customer to sail over to a competitor's site to find what they want when they need it.

A variety of payment methods

Accepting multiple forms of payment is a necessity online. Customers may be more forgiving when they shop in your retail location, because they can whip out a checkbook or cash. In the world of web retail, customers simply leave your store and surf to a competitor. See Book IV, Chapter 4 about the wealth of payment options you can make available to your customers.

Everything a customer could want, plus the kitchen sink

Virtual inventory is a big component in e-commerce. It doesn't matter whether you store all your products in a warehouse behind your retail location or have orders drop-shipped from a supplier. Customers want you to provide a large selection of choices, including everything you have available in your retail location. In addition, customers expect your store to be well stocked — at all times.

If a product is on back order or temporarily out of stock, your customers expect to be notified before they start the checkout process and preferably when they try to add the product to their shopping cart.

Some shopping cart programs have a feature that displays a message when a product is running low, such as "Only 2 Left." If your software can't display such a message, manually add the disclaimer "Almost Out" to your product description when inventory of your best sellers gets low.

Details, details, details

Savvy web shoppers are spoiled by the amount of information they can find with the stroke of a key. But too much information can overwhelm customers and distract them from purchasing. Thus, your challenge is to anticipate which information a shopper really needs (and wants) to know about a product and then provide that info (and only that info) in a succinct and accessible manner. The following list gives you some of the most sought-after product information:

✦ **Product descriptions:** Listing the color and style of a coffee table is helpful, but if you leave out its dimensions, customers will hesitate to make a purchase. You need to make all the details of a product available to your customer. The trick is to offer the information in layers. In other words, give a brief description of the product, along with a photo, but then give customers the option to click a link for more details or additional photos.

✦ **Visual information:** You can't try on different sizes or styles of clothing in an online store. Even the best photos may make it difficult to see other details that make a product special. Increasingly, online retailers are turning to the power of video to give that almost-in-person experience. Videos that demonstrate the product in use or display it on a real person provide a better view of the product and may prompt a purchase.

✦ **Reviews:** Customer reviews came into vogue after Amazon made them popular on its site. Providing easy access to reviews by experts or other credible sources (such as magazines) is also a hot demand from online customers.

✦ **Delivery options:** Customers want to understand, at the absolute least, the different methods of delivery your site offers. This information includes the provider of the service (U.S. Postal Service, UPS, FedEx, or some other shipping company), the delivery options (for example, Express or Ground), and the cost. In addition, customers want to have access to a shipping number and a direct link to track the delivery status of their packages.

When searching for an e-commerce solution, look for the ones that already integrate with the leading shippers (such as UPS) or offer a feature that allows customers to track shipments.

✦ **Contact information:** Make sure that customers can easily find your phone number and e-mail address. (And then make sure that you respond when a customer contacts you.)

Book VII
Chapter 2

Understanding
the Differences
between In-Store
and Online
Customers

✦ **Return policies:** Online shoppers want to know return and exchange policies before they make that final purchase. Especially when buying clothing or perishable items, your customers want to be reassured that they can get a fair deal if something goes wrong when they receive the product. Keeping your return policies clearly posted on your site not only helps make the sale but also reduces confusion later.

Methods for coping with the holiday rush

Having your return policy clearly accessible is certainly a plus during a busy holiday season. But that's the bare minimum. Keep in mind that customer expectations peak during holidays and high-demand seasonal periods. Whenever your rush occurs, you can prepare for it in the following ways:

✦ **Offer rush deliveries:** Your delivery company may not have a problem with rush delivery, but you need to make sure that you can get the items packed and out the door to meet the hectic pace. Several online stores, such as Amazon, help customers know exactly when they can expect their order to arrive based on when they place it. For example, a message appears that says if you order by a specific date, you will receive your order by a specific date. This message helps customers decide what type of shipping option they should choose.

✦ **Extend delivery times:** Again, you just need to handle those last-minute orders that arrive the day before (or the day of) the major holiday. Whether or not you can extend your delivery times often depends on whether you have enough help behind the scenes to keep filling those orders.

✦ **Prepare for backups:** Even if everything goes smoothly on your side, the delivery company might drop the ball. We saw this happen during the 2013 holiday season when extreme weather conditions, along with a surge of online sales, prevented major delivery companies from making deliveries promised by online retailers to show up in time for Christmas. You can't always predict this type of widespread delivery failure, but you can prepare for it. Make sure your policies clearly state how failed deliveries will be handled, even if they're not your fault. Sometimes, reimbursements or offering a special discount on the next purchase can go a long way in creating goodwill.

✦ **Stock up on inventory**: Nothing is worse than running out of a hot item and finding out that you can't get more in until after the holiday. You may want to go a little heavy on your inventory or alert your suppliers to the potential of increased demand.

✦ **Bulk up on service representatives:** Customers don't hesitate to ask for help when it comes to holiday shopping.

Although the busiest retail season is typically November and December, other holiday periods also drive sales. According to recent research, online sales also heat up during Valentine's Day, Easter, and Mother's Day (for example).

Superior customer service

At the heart of the difference in shopping online, as opposed to in a store, is the customer service. The level of support that you provide your online customers is one of the single most influential factors in whether those customers return to your site to buy again. You probably don't doubt that superior service is important in your store. But a high level of service is even more important online because customers are limited in their ability to interact with your products. Customers depend on you to provide as much information about a product as you can so that they can make an immediate buying decision. They can't pick up a product and examine it up close. If you don't have enough detail on your website or a customer has an unusual question, you want that customer to be able to reach you.

Fortunately, offering exceptional customer service from your site has become pretty darn easy. The technology is readily available, and implementing it doesn't cost you an arm and a leg. Here are a few of the ways you can reach out to your customers:

✦ **E-mail:** One of the easiest ways to provide customers with information about your products is by letting them contact you by e-mail. You can make shopping easy by posting a customer service e-mail address throughout your site. Remember to respond in a timely manner. Just a few years ago, it was acceptable to respond to e-mail within a 24-hour period, but customers now expect much faster response times — usually within a few hours.

Use an automated responder to automatically generate a return e-mail that notifies your customer that you received the e-mail he or she sent. Acknowledge their request while providing a time for when you will contact them. Also give them alternative options for reaching you faster.

✦ **Phone:** Clearly posting a direct phone number so that shoppers can access customer support is an absolute must. If you can swing it, get yourself a toll-free number. If you don't have a 24-hour support line, be sure to post the normal operating hours of customer service.

✦ **Social media:** Customer service no longer originates only from your website. The proliferation of social gives customers another way to get the attention of online retailers, especially if customers think they are being ignored or are not getting help quickly enough. Many online retailers are frustrated because social media has become another place where they have to service customers — and those customers expect a response in minutes, rather than hours. In addition, customer service through social media occurs in an open forum that exposes problems to the public. However, for online businesses that embrace customer service and do it well, social media has proven to be a terrific way to turn unhappy customers into loyal brand advocates. As a small-business owner, be prepared to monitor social media for customer concerns and address them as quickly as possible.

**Book VII
Chapter 2**

Understanding
the Differences
between In-Store
and Online
Customers

✦ **Live chat:** Although some online shoppers like the anonymity that the Internet provides, many more demand instantaneous support, such as they might find in your bricks-and-mortar store. To answer that need, consider offering standby customer support representatives through live-chat technology. This tool helps customers immediately connect to a person who can answer their questions (through either an instant-messenger-style format or audio over the computer). Some companies tout that live chat has increased online sales by 20 percent, increased average order values, and decreased customer support costs. If you decide to use live chat, look for software that enables integration with mobile devices and social media.

Most live-chat software providers offer a free trial, and in some cases you can get started with the service for as little as $35 a month. Check out live-chat services from LivePerson (www.liveperson.com), which offers pricing based on your website's traffic (a great feature for smaller sites), and BoldChat (www.boldchat.com), which integrates with mobile devices and starts at $600 per year.

Figure 2-1 shows the extensive customer service options available from Zappos. It offers support via e-mail, live chat, and a toll-free number. Customers can get help 24/7. They also offer free returns if products don't fit or aren't what you expect — return postage labels are automatically shipped with every product.

Figure 2-1:
Zappos provides exceptional customer service options 24 hours a day, 7 days a week.

Establishing Patterns

Getting customers to buy from you (at any location) comes down to establishing buying patterns. You take part in forming your customers' buying patterns by helping them develop the habit of coming to *you* as opposed to a competitor. After you understand your customers and what they want, you're in a position to start creating that pattern. To establish a buying pattern with your customers, you need to provide three things as an online retailer:

✦ **Information:** Your site is a place to shop, but it's also a resource for product information. After you establish yourself as an authority on your product lines, customers begin making a conscious decision to go to you first.

✦ **Buying opportunities:** Experienced web shoppers aren't looking strictly for information. They want a reason to buy, too. You can give them access to regular specials or limited-time-only offers, exclusive sales, and select or new merchandise to convince them to buy.

✦ **Reliability:** In addition to providing a good inventory and terrific customer service, the entire buying process at your site has to pass muster — from the time your customers pull up your home page to when the purchased product is delivered to their doorstep. When you have the opportunity to prove yourself as a reliable retailer (and use that opportunity), customers get used to coming to you to shop.

**Book VII
Chapter 2**

Understanding
the Differences
between In-Store
and Online
Customers

Chapter 3: Window Dressing for the Online Display

In This Chapter

↙ **Revealing your store's unique identity**

↙ **Organizing your store so that customers can find anything**

↙ **Designing a site that convinces your visitors to become customers**

As a bricks-and-mortar retailer, you probably gave a great deal of attention and thought to your store's appearance — the selection of paint colors, the placement of shelving, and even the way each product is positioned. You probably agonized for days, if not weeks, over each decision — and for good reason, too.

Major retailers spend a substantial amount of time and money sorting through the same details. And when they find that perfect look, it becomes a blueprint for every store that follows.

Why go to all this trouble? Your goal in creating a positive shopping environment is to increase sales. That process begins with the look of your store. The way products are arranged contributes to an overall feeling or mood. Customers will buy more if they're comfortable shopping in your store, can find what they need, and are treated well. Retail merchandizing experts have shown that careful attention to in-store displays can have a direct (positive.) effect on your sales.

The same concept holds true for your online store. In one e-commerce case study, a global online retailer experimented with how they featured a group of lighting fixtures on their website. They claimed to see an increase of 30 percent in their online sales for one particular product grouping. Similarly, other functions or features of your online store can make a difference in sales. For example, enabling additional product views and providing the capability to zoom in on product images for a closer look contribute to sales increases of as much as 15 percent, according to industry research.

The result is clear: The way you position or feature your products online could mean earning several hundred dollars (or more) a day in online retail sales. That's worth it, in our opinion. With that result in mind, in this chapter, we show you how to map your very own online-store blueprint.

Creating the Right Look for Your Online Store

Imagine for a moment that one of your customers is blindfolded and brought into your store (without knowing where she is being taken). After the blindfold is removed, the customer should be able to tell that she's in your store. For example, do you carry specialty products or a line of signature items? Do you use bright, unconventional colors on the walls?

Transferring your physical image, or *identity,* to your online store is a major part of creating the right look for your site. As with anything else, you can go overboard. That's why we recommend starting the process by choosing a single element that you believe customers most readily identify with your store. The main factor that makes your store special may be one of these features:

✦ **Architectural element:** Maybe the shape of your store's building makes it stand out. Or perhaps you designed the interior with special features, such as high vaulted ceilings, curved walls, or dramatic windows. Sometimes, the physical appearance of your location leaves a lasting impression.

✦ **Color scheme:** The interior and exterior of your store may be filled with soft, muted tones or wild, bright, eye-popping colors. Either way, these telling color combinations may provide your customers with a strong association with your store.

✦ **Location:** Some stores take their images directly from their surroundings. For example, you may be located in a trendy, upscale part of your city. Or maybe you're part of an eclectic revitalization of a downtown area. Then again, your customers may know you best as "that shop by the beach." Your store may be associated with a vacation hot spot or a well-known tourist destination.

✦ **Theme:** Your store may be created around a particular theme, such as birthday parties or business travel.

✦ **Event or activity:** Perhaps you hold an annual event closely tied to the image of your store. Or maybe you have certain ongoing activities that draw attention.

✦ **People:** Every once in a while, a store is less about the products it sells and more identifiable with the person who owns it. So maybe you're a pseudocelebrity — or an outright famous person. Either way, if that's the case, your personal image may be most closely tied to the image of your store.

✦ **Selection:** Superstore retailers are known for offering a wide variety of products. Although you may not compete at that level, you may be best known for your extensive selection of a particular brand or type of product.

✦ **Price:** Ah, price. You may be on the superexclusive high end or the rock-bottom low end.

✦ **Customer service:** During a time when many stores compete on price alone, retailers (particularly smaller ones) that focus on customer service receive lots of attention. If customer service is your forte, that may be what customers remember most about you.

✦ **Niche:** Maybe you specialize in Mexican pottery, collectible Disney products, or nostalgic items from the 1950s. If you have a streamlined product base that appeals to a highly targeted customer audience, you can bet that this specialization makes up your total image.

Your offline store identity gives you a starting point for your website design. As you build your site, this element gives you a clear place to return if you get off-track from the image you want to project. Your store identity is a guideline.

Similarly, after you begin promoting your online store, having a single element related to your image gives you a useful tie-in for advertisements, promotions, and marketing materials. And even though this identifier is what you're best known for in your local (offline) market, it can become a unique selling point in a crowded online marketplace.

Creating the Perfect Shopping Experience

The right image is just the beginning. The look of an online store can be nearly flawless, but after you open the door (or enter the website), you may find a different story. Regardless of your store's image on the outside, if customers have difficulties with the actual shopping experience inside, you can quickly lose those customers.

As a shopkeeper, you have to make great strides to carry your complete image from the outside in. For an online store, that inside image is all about organization.

For example, any large bookseller probably has thousands and thousands of books packing the shelves and tables of its store. Yet every book has its place. Each one is neatly categorized according to subject matter, release dates, clearance items, sales, or even product type (books, magazines, greeting cards, and gifts, for example). With all this managed chaos, the store still has room for wide aisles, chairs and sofas, and an entire coffee shop.

When you visit the online version of the bookstore, you should find the same strategy at play. The navigation should provide clear choices that mimic the categories you find in the store.

To achieve this level of detail online, start by taking a tour of your bricks-and-mortar location. Think about all the ways that you categorize products to make shopping (and inventory management) easy. These categories often include

✦ **Brand name:** People shop by designer labels and other recognized brands.

✦ **Product type or style:** These distinctions can even be product categories within categories. For example, a drugstore might carry makeup, books, and school supplies. You can divide the categories further by lipsticks and eye shadows, bestsellers and bargain books, and pens and notebooks.

✦ **Price:** Although it may be more difficult to do in your offline store, you can allow online customers to sort products based on price (from high to low or from low to high).

✦ **Sale or clearance items:** Everybody likes a bargain. Your customers are no different, and they appreciate when a bargain is easy to spot.

✦ **Discontinued items:** These products won't be produced any more, and especially with collectibles, customers want to know that they won't be able to find these items on the shelves (real or virtual) any more.

✦ **New release (or just in):** Books and DVDs aren't the only items that are classified this way. Products are continually being updated, or new items are introduced in a product line. Even if an item isn't hot off the press for the manufacturer, it may be the first time you have it in your store.

✦ **Solution:** Increasingly, products are categorized by the problem they help customers solve. In books, for example, you can find an entire section of self-help categories. You can probably categorize your products in a similar fashion (for example, kitchen tools and bathroom cleaners).

Organizing your products in categories

However you categorize products, carrying your retail store's organization through to your online store isn't difficult. It just takes some, well . . . organization.

You may not realize (or may have forgotten) how and why you placed your products the way you have in your bricks-and-mortar store. Follow these steps to refresh your memory and come up with a plan to organize your online store:

1. **Draw a diagram of the inside of your retail store.**

Your diagram doesn't have to be drawn to scale. But the drawing should clearly show the layout of your store, including shelving units, display cases, and doorways.

2. **On a separate piece of paper, make a corresponding list of all the items you have displayed.**

   This step helps you make an inventory of everything that's placed out on the floor (where customers shop) and detail where it's displayed. Label shelves and tables in your store diagram with numbers or letters. The corresponding list should indicate which products are stored where; note why you organize them that way.

3. **Create a list of top-selling items.**

   Pull this list from your store's inventory and sales reports. When you have your list, look to see where those top-selling items are located in your store. Do you see any noticeable patterns?

4. **Identify your merchandising hot spots.**

   Your *merchandising hot spots* are the places that receive the most attention because of their physical location in the store. Items next to your cash register, in your front window (if you have one), and near the front door where customers can see them when they walk into the store are all examples of merchandising hot spots.

5. **Group products into categories that you want to use online.**

   Take your preferred product groupings and incorporate them into your website's site map. Basically, you're merchandising your online store by using the identifiable trends from your offline location.

One product can appear in several categories. Your shopping cart software should allow you to easily cross-reference items in multiple categories.

Offering a search function

In addition to creating a plan for the layout of your online store, you can offer customers another critical organizational function: a web-based search tool.

You're probably familiar with using Google, Bing, or Yahoo! to search the Internet for keywords. Well, online stores have found that the same kind of tool is a true boon to business. Think about search tools in comparison to your store: A customer can come in and ask a sales associate where something is located in your store. Online shoppers, however, have to depend on using the clues on your site's menu bar. Including a search function on your home page eliminates customers having to guess in which category they can find a certain product.

Not all search functions are created equal, especially when your online store deals with thousands of products. Make sure that customers can search by using the smallest detail (such as a brief product description, a brand name, or even color) and still find what they want.

Look for a search tool that

✦ **Searches by a specific keyword term:** If you type a keyword such as *shelves,* the search returns all similar items. Figure 3-1 shows the search results on the Organize website.

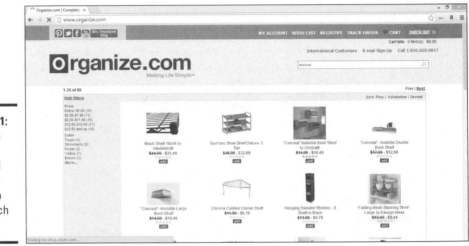

Figure 3-1: A search should return all products similar to the search term.

✦ **Sorts the results:** Customers should be able to further sort their search terms. Macy's allows customers to further search or filter by such things as price, brand, color, customer product reviews and ratings, and even special discounts or offers (see Figure 3-2 for examples of some of these). The additional sorting function prevents a large number of results from overwhelming customers.

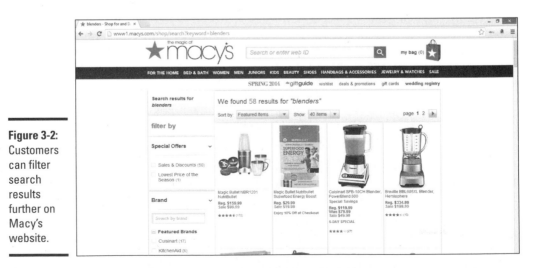

Figure 3-2: Customers can filter search results further on Macy's website.

✦ **Displays similar or complementary items:** When customers click a product, they should see a list of items that they might be interested in buying, based on the original search term.

✦ **Allows exclusions:** Site searches that allow customers to specify certain words or terms that should not be included in search results are helpful for returning more accurate results.

✦ **Shows customers specific ads or promotions:** Customers should see ads targeted to them, based on the results of their keyword searches. Targeted ads can convert visitors to buyers.

Beyond Window Shopping: Designs that Lure Traffic

A good site design makes attracting buyers to your site much easier. The aesthetics of your site matter, but you also need functionality. These elements can keep your site's traffic flowing (and, you hope, convert that traffic to sales):

✦ **General appearance:** Research indicates that shoppers are more likely to purchase from a site that has a professional and trustworthy appearance. Although nothing's wrong with fun and wacky (if it fits your product), just make sure that you also show that you're responsible. For example, clearly display your terms of agreement, return policies, and contact information, and make sure that you have a reliable shopping cart program.

✦ **Uncluttered appearance:** Resist the urge to pack your site's pages full of information, promotions, and product choices. When a site has too much going on, customers become overwhelmed. Rather than buy, they flee.

✦ **Simplicity:** Keep both the graphical design of your site and the information you provide simple. A popular design trend for making e-commerce sites more appealing is a simplified color scheme. The phrase "less is more" is one to take to heart when selling online.

✦ **Good navigation:** A sure way to convert visitors to buyers is with your site's ease of navigation. Shoppers should be able to move from one place to another on your site relatively easily. And your navigation system should be intuitive so that a customer clearly understands how your site is structured.

✦ **Special landing pages:** A unique landing page attracts buyers and increases your odds for a sale. A *landing page* is usually focused on one product or service and is used as a stand-alone web page. You might promote a link to that particular page or use that link in an online ad — and instead of new visitors coming to your home page, they "land" on this specific page first. (This type of page is also referred to as an *entrance page* because visitors enter your site from this special page instead of your home page.) If you want to promote a new high-end tent on your outdoors site, for example, you can create a page that's only about that tent. Visitors don't waste time sorting through your entire inventory when all they really want is a tent, increasing the likelihood that they will make a quick purchase.

✦ **Links:** Set up your site so that customers don't have to click many links to reach their destination.

✦ **Layered information:** You may want to give customers the option to go deeper into the site to find more detailed information. Simply provide the details in layers. Usually, you see layering when a product is displayed with a photo and a general description. If customers want to know the item's dimensions or see alternative views of the product, they can do so by clicking the next link (or layer) of product detail.

✦ **Cash register:** From an easy checkout process to the opportunity to *suggestive sell* (offer similar products or useful items, such as batteries), the function of the cash register — or shopping cart — program is one of the most important elements of good design.

✦ **Product display:** Provide customers with simple headlines, good images, and detailed information. The basic information, such as an item's price and how to purchase it, should be clearly displayed.

✦ **Special promotions:** Offering discounts or limited-time offers is a good way to convert buyers. But these specials don't do you any good if a person can't find those offers or the offers aren't in line with what a person is buying (or shopping for). Carefully place targeted promotions in your site to make them effective.

Having good design and the right image for your website isn't that different from what you already do in your bricks-and-mortar store.

Chapter 4: Making In-Store Customers Loyal Online Shoppers

In This Chapter

✔ Pairing your storefront and your website in your customers' minds

✔ Making in-store customers an online offer (they can't refuse)

✔ Supporting and informing your customers

✔ Giving customers a starring role

Some people who operate traditional bricks-and-mortar storefronts don't consider what others may see as obvious: the connection between their storefront customers and their online business. These store owners may be concerned that if the bricks-and-mortar customers start using the websites, customers may stop visiting the store, buy less often, or even forget about the store altogether.

A customer is a customer is a customer, whether he or she walks through your front door or pulls up the home page of your website.

The more options you give your customers, the better chance you have of keeping them. Having your in-store customers take advantage of your online business can increase revenues — both in-store and online — and create a longer-lasting, more valuable customer overall. Although some businesses have shut their doors permanently and moved online, most store owners find a healthy mix of the two venues. And the increased range of options that this dual presence offers customers makes ringing up purchases at both sites more appealing to those customers.

In this chapter, we describe how you can go about grooming your customers to embrace both in-store and online buying. Specifically, we tell you how to introduce your offline (in-store) customers to the power and potential of also shopping with you online. We detail some strategies and techniques you can use to take advantage of the dual mediums and how they can feed off each other.

Benefiting Customers (and Your Business) with In-Store and Online Synergy

Customers look at an online store much differently if they know that a physical storefront goes along with it. Sometimes, a customer just likes knowing that he can drive down to a building and talk to a person if something goes wrong with his online order. At other times, the cleanliness, professionalism, or range of options that your physical store shows off tells the customer, "Hey, Joel's Electronics knows its stuff. Buying online from the website is just like walking through the store." The goodwill that you generate in-store acts in your favor online, and these venues come together in your customers' minds in the following ways:

✦ **A physical presence builds customer confidence.** Your in-store customers form an impression about your business before they even walk through the door. The mere fact that you have a physical presence gives many customers the confidence that you're a reputable business, and that feeling can encourage them to trust your online business as well. Many stores, sometimes called *pure plays,* operate only online and don't have the chance to build up confidence until a customer completes a successful transaction with them.

One of the best examples of a successful pure-play online retailer is Amazon. Amazon built its online business from scratch and never allowed customers to interact with it physically. Because of this lack of physical presence, Amazon cannot expand its market share beyond Internet users.

✦ **Selling your goods online makes your store always open.** Customers can shop in your online store 24 hours a day and 7 days a week, from the comfort of their homes and their favorite pajamas, without the hassle of getting dressed, fighting traffic, finding a parking spot, and waiting in line to pay and leave (so they can get back in the car, fight traffic, unload the car — you get the idea).

Your online store has to be always on and available to take orders. Unlike your physical store, which has specific opening and closing hours, your online store must stay open to serve customers at their convenience. You can't close it for other than brief periods (which you may need to do to perform maintenance on your website software). Because your online customers may shop at nonstandard hours, you need to have your store hosted on an Internet server that's supported around the clock. If you run your online store from home over a high-speed connection, make sure to always leave that computer on and connected.

✦ **An online store gives your customers access to unlimited shelf space,** Anyone who has had to rearrange an in-store aisle display knows how valuable retail floor space can be. Most stores have to carefully plan how to use every last square foot without overwhelming the customer.

Online stores suffer from no such physical restrictions. You can offer one or one million items on the same site with the same amount of screen space, and you can store the actual inventory in less expensive warehouse or industrial space rather than in a costly retail space.

Enticing Customers to Your Online Offering

For your in-store customers to become online shoppers, they have to know about your new store location (online, that is!). So use the advantage of having that customer in your bricks-and-mortar store to advertise and promote your e-store. Whenever you make an in-store sale, you have the perfect opportunity to inform and entice that customer with the lure of the web.

Publicizing your web presence

Make a big deal about your move to the web by showing off the name of your online business — and the *URL* (web address) of your online store — in your physical store and in all the transactions that take place there. We're not saying that you have to draw six-foot letters on the wall or plaster the windows with gigantic URL addresses, but you should definitely incorporate your online store name and URL in all your store literature and promotional space. This opportunity to promote your e-store includes items such as

+ **Business cards:** Leave your business cards (with your e-store name and address highlighted) next to the cash register and throw one into the bag with every customer's purchase.

+ **Sales flyers:** Integrate your website address into every flyer, usually along the bottom. Add a blurb on the flyer that says "Check us out online at . . .." On the flyer, include online discount codes that allow the customer to shop online during the sale at the same discount.

+ **Cash registers and counter displays:** In addition to keeping your business cards prominently displayed next to the register, add a small sign to your cash register, and perhaps add a small counter display with a brochure or one-page flyer that someone can pick up and read while waiting to check out.

+ **Outside windows:** These panes of glass are always visible and can include a sticker or display mentioning that you're online. This technique is especially valuable if you get a lot of foot traffic, such as at a shopping center or strip mall.

+ **Receipts:** Customers may throw away your shopping bags, your business cards, and your sales flyers, but they're likely to look at their purchase receipts again — at least once. Include your web address on the receipt. Check out the "Showing shoppers the money" section, later in this chapter, for more ideas about using receipts.

✦ **Shopping bags:** When it's time to reorder those shopping bags with your name and logo, insert an extra line that includes your URL address.

✦ **Company delivery trucks:** Add an extra decal or section that features your URL address and your online store.

Mentioning your online store's name isn't limited to including it on literature and promotional materials. Train your sales associates to casually mention your online store when talking with customers. This reference can be a simple statement made to customers during checkout — for example, "Hey, you can also check out our Internet store at Myonlinestore.com." Or when a customer asks about an item, have your employees say, "You know, we're out of that item here, but you can order it from us on the web at Myonlinestore.com."

Some stores have developed mobile applications, or *apps,* that customers can download and use on their smartphones when they're in the store or at home. Several retail stores, such as Staples, offer special discounts to customers when they "check in" to their app while at the physical store. In this way, the store is notified that a loyal customer is in the store and can offer special deals. Put up signs with special QR codes that customers can scan with their phones to download your store's app to their phone.

Displaying your online goods in-store

Although promoting your online store presence is the first step, it surely isn't the last. Some store owners have an interesting tendency to hide their online-only merchandise at the back of the store because customers can't buy it immediately and take it home. We think that store owners are missing a valuable opportunity: Take advantage of your customers' immediate presence by showing off the items you have for sale online, whether these items are part of your online inventory or are unique items that you're selling on an online auction, such as eBay.

Make sure that any online-only items that you display in-store are clearly marked with a note along the lines of "Hey, find me online at Myonlinestore. com" or "This product is up for sale under my eBay ID myonlinestoreid." Some people print little cards or slips of paper with information on how to find that item online (perhaps a special QR code for easy scanning) so that customers can take the slip with them for reference when shopping at home. The physical presence of merchandise with the sign not only reminds in-store customers that you're online as well but also allows customers to see, hold, feel, move around, and inspect the item before they buy it. Besides, they might take out their smartphone or tablet computer and initiate an online purchase while standing in the store.

When creating these helpful shopping slips for your customers, don't forget to include directions to find items through the special links of your affiliate programs, as we talk about in Book IV, Chapter 2. You can earn more money when your customers follow these links.

Definitely pay attention to the reactions of customers who look at your online-only items. Here are some ideas for handling questions and gleaning information from these reactions:

✦ **If customers ask whether they can buy an item right away (in-store),** tell them why it's available only online. Online auction items are the easiest to explain because you can say something like this: "Well, this item is unique that I want all my customers to have an equal chance to purchase it. The fairest way to give everyone an opportunity is to list it in an online auction on eBay."

✦ **If you're selling something online that you pay for only after the customer has ordered it,** tell your customer, "I'm testing this new product by ordering it from someone on consignment. That's why you need to order it online." If enough customers insist on being able to buy this item at your store, their input becomes valuable sales data about which products to carry in-store.

The feedback and opinion sharing related to your online offerings can help both your real and virtual stores improve. And making improvements based on the feedback shows your customers that you're listening to what they say and using their input, which can lead to greater loyalty and enthusiasm.

Showing shoppers the money

Every store owner has an opinion about the value of coupons or special discounts. But most owners agree that offering special values definitely helps generate additional sales — otherwise, you would never see all those half-off sales or the gobs of weekly coupons that arrive in your mail. Generating sales for online stores is no different, and one of the best ways for you to introduce your in-store customers to your online store is to offer a coupon or special discount that they can use only online.

The following list describes a couple of ways you can offer specials that may entice customers to your online store:

✦ **Print a special card that you slip into every customer's bag.** Use this card to invite shoppers to check out your online store and save 10 percent on their first order. You can have your sales associates hand out to your best customers a special coupon offering free shipping if they buy from you online. Or place a display next to the cash register, telling people that your online store is offering a new product this month at a special price.

✦ **Print special discount or coupon information directly on your sales receipt.** We tell you to print your online store's name and web address right on your sales receipts (see the section "Publicizing your web presence," earlier in this chapter), and we think that you should do the same with online discounts or coupons. Check with your cash register's maker and find out whether your register has the capability to generate special codes or discount offers that print with a customer's regular receipt.

If you decide to print special discount codes on your in-store customers' receipts, don't forget to update your online store with the new discount code before you start handing out those receipts. Don't risk the wrath — or, worse, the lost confidence — of the online shopper whose discount code doesn't work.

Your discount or coupon doesn't have to be a complete giveaway. Many companies tie the discount to a form or survey that the customer fills out online. This way, you entice in-store customers to answer a few questions about your online store, and when those customers finish the survey, they receive a special code that they can use for their discount. A helpful example of this survey incentive comes from the fast-food industry: Restaurants print a special receipt with a survey URL and code, and everyone who fills out the survey also enters a drawing for money or earns free food on a future visit.

Providing a Positive Shopping Experience

The best way to encourage your in-store customers to also shop online is to make sure that all your sales processes work together. How customers buy goods from you — at the cash register or by way of an Internet web browser — shouldn't affect how they can interact with you. When you combine the capabilities of your in-store and online processes, you can offer some interesting advantages to your customers that an online-only store never can.

Keeping friendly, flexible policies

Making the sales process smooth for your customers and giving them options for how the process works are effective ways to cultivate customer loyalty. Make sure that your online shoppers can pick up at your physical store any (or most) items that they buy online. Although many people thoroughly enjoy the convenience of shopping online, a lot of them are unwilling to pay the shipping charges to have items delivered to their house.

For other shoppers, the emphasis is on immediate gratification. That is, they see items online, click the Buy button, pay for the items with their credit card, and want to receive the items right away. In-store pickup allows these impatient shoppers to do just that — and it gives you a chance to sell them more items when they arrive to pick up their online purchases. Even big businesses are encouraging in-store pickup. For example, Walmart provides free shipping when customers order products at Walmart.com and use the Site to Store option to pick up their items from their local store.

Offering impeccable customer support

You can never go wrong by keeping customer support and convenience in mind. Offer a return policy stating that customers can bring items they purchased online back into your physical store for a refund or credit. This way, you (or the customer) not only save the postage cost of having items mailed back to you but also gain the face-to-face opportunity to help customers and smooth over any perceived problems from the purchases they initially made. If you already have your physical store open for business, why not take advantage of it to offer superb customer support?

Some customers who shopped online for convenience don't want to get in the car and drive over to return the item. But at least you offer the option, and letting customers know that they have the opportunity for in-store returns is comfort enough. Who knows? They may walk in to return an item and walk out with a shopping bag full of new items.

Enlightening your shoppers

For many customers, in-store interaction is the best part of their shopping experience. They take the time to come into the store so that they can ask questions, gain knowledge and expertise, or hear the opinion of the "expert" in that field — namely, you as the store owner or manager. Online stores build that type of interaction through the use of newsletters, which you may already produce for your bricks-and-mortar store. These newsletters can be a mixture of articles, tips and tricks, featured items, information or responses from your social media sites (such as your Facebook business page) and anything else related to your store — whether it's an in-store promotional event or a feature on your employee of the month. Here are some ideas for promoting online activities with your newsletter:

✦ **Feature your online store and any special online promotions.** You may need to display the store's URL where customers can see it, and maybe print a discount code or highlight a special web page. If you want to expand your coverage to either increase sales for your online store or encourage a shift in offline shopping behavior, you can include profiles of online store items, online auctions for the store, or testimonials about an online sale. Doing so provides an important and powerful reminder to your customers about your online store.

✦ **Have printed copies of the newsletter available at the store.** You may want to include a newsletter with any in-store purchase. You're not forcing the interaction — you're simply making in-store customers aware of the different options they have when shopping with you.

✦ **Offer customers the opportunity to sign up in the store for a free monthly newsletter delivered to their e-mail address.** You can simply place next to the cash register or information desk a clipboard with a sign-up sheet for the customer's name and e-mail address. Or you can have the sales clerk ask for an e-mail address during checkout and receive permission from the customer to send out the newsletter. The best way to entice people to agree to receive your newsletter is by offering a discount, a "deal of the month" promotion, or special advice that they can find only in the newsletter.

Making Your Customer the Star

We encourage you to make your customers the stars of your show. One way you can encourage in-store customers to check out your online store (and, you hope, check out with some purchases in their online shopping carts) is to involve them in the online presence. Take pictures of your retail store and your in-store customers, and feature these pictures in your online storefront. Do surveys of customers who shop both in-store and online, and feature those testimonials on your website or your social media outlets, such as your business blog.

Most people love to see their name in lights — whether it's a neon sign or a backlit computer screen. If your customers know that they will be featured, they will not only log in to see their name and review but (chances are) also tell their friends, neighbors, coworkers, and even their daughter's soccer team about it.

Making your customers the "stars of the show" builds excellent word-of-mouth advertising, and the feedback that you receive from surveys and testimonials gives you valuable data about how to improve or update your online store. Putting your in-store customers in the spotlight also shows your online customers how fun, personal, and interactive your physical store can be, which may create the bonus effect of turning loyal online shoppers into loyal in-store customers.

Chapter 5: Expanding Close to Home with Localization and Mobile Marketing

In This Chapter

✔ **Understanding mobile commerce for traditional and online retailers**

✔ **Sending text alerts**

✔ **Building business with mobile coupons**

✔ **Targeting local customers online**

*I*n an increasingly competitive environment, you have to make every possible effort to reach customers and convince them to buy from you. For storefront locations, you need to not only reach out from your website but also draw local online shoppers to your location. Mobile commerce, or *m-commerce,* offers unique advantages to both online and traditional retailers looking to extend their brands online.

For the most part, m-commerce refers to the way companies use smartphones or other mobile devices, such as tablets, to market and sell to customers. If you own a cellphone, especially an Android or iPhone, chances are good that you've already experienced mobile commerce. For example, have you

+ Paid a bill by entering a specific code into your cellphone?

+ Voted for a contestant on a reality show by texting a short numerical message?

+ Entered a contest or giveaway?

+ Sent a short text (to request information)?

+ Checked into a particular store or restaurant using your phone and received a coupon in exchange for promoting the business in real-time to your friends?

+ Made a donation to the Red Cross or other charitable organization by sending a short text from your phone?

+ Received a text message from a favorite store, alerting you to an exclusive bargain?

All these examples demonstrate m-commerce, and more applications are on the way. Mobile commerce in the United States is expected to grow 50 percent by 2018, adding up to more than $46 billion in business, according to a report from Forrester Research. In the world of finance alone, the growth of m-commerce and related activities is taking hold at a phenomenal rate, from paying bills through your cellphone to depositing a check with your smartphone or tablet. These mobile banking activities are anticipated to expand to more than 1 billion users (globally) by 2017, according to Juniper Research. One reason for these staggering predictions is technology. Many smartphones can access the Internet and make transactions with speeds and functionality similar to those of a desktop computer.

You can find more about mobile commerce from the Mobile Marketing Association at `www.mmaglobal.com`.

In this chapter, we offer you a glimpse of how m-commerce is poised to change the way customers buy in the future and how you can capitalize on existing mobile applications to increase sales now.

Distinguishing Between Different Types of Mobile Commerce

As exciting as it is to see the use of m-commerce growing, online retailers should make a reality check, according to Forrester Research. Mobile conversion rates are typically small, averaging .6 percent for smartphones and 1.5 percent for tablets in 2013. The average amount of goods sold through m-commerce is also a low, with 56 percent of mobile purchase less than $50. And only 15 percent of m-commerce purchases (versus more than 30 percent for desktop purchases) are in the range of $100 to $500. Shopping from a mobile device is still difficult, and many shoppers will begin researching products on a cellphone but move to a desktop to make or complete the purchase. Even so, consumers are quite comfortable using their mobile phones for the following retail-related activities:

✦ View e-mails from online retailers

✦ Get information about retailers (such as directions, business hours, and contact information)

✦ Research products and compare prices

✦ Receive texts with codes for special offers

✦ Redeem coupon codes

The last two items on that list are especially good news for retailers online and offline because using m-commerce to deliver special offers and coupons helps drive revenue for your business. With that in mind, here are some ways you can now use mobile commerce, all of which we discuss in greater detail in the following sections:

✦ **SMS alerts:** Companies use SMS (Short Message Service) to send short text messages to their customers' cellphones. For example, Redbox, the video vending-machine company, sends daily or weekly messages about new video releases, movie trivia, and more to subscribers who have chosen to receive text alerts. The goal is to drive subscribers to the Redbox website, to keep them actively engaged, and to entice customers to go to a vending machine and check out a movie.

✦ **Text-to-buy:** Some savvy marketing companies are using an instant gratification type of application for mobile commerce. With text-to-buy, companies place traditional advertisements for a specific product on billboards, in television or radio commercials, in print ads, and online in social network sites. Included in the ad is a special numerical code (usually a short string of numbers or letters). The consumer enters the code into a cellphone and buys the product.

Text-to-buy ads are an effective way to strike while the iron is hot, or to get a customer to buy while he's thinking about the product he just saw in an ad.

✦ **Mobile coupons:** Some customers may still be reluctant to make a purchase by using a cellphone, but you can still reach out to them by sending them mobile coupons (m-coupons) by cellphone. Customers can then go online or to your physical location, provide the coupon code, and make a purchase. Just like that, the customer gets a good deal and you get a bump in sales.

✦ **QR codes:** These small graphic icons are about the size of a postage stamp. You see them printed in magazine ads and in books, on in-store displays, and online on websites. They allow your customer to use a smartphone to snap a picture of the image and reveal something of interest — from a coupon code to a how-to manual. QR (Quick Response) codes have dipped in popularity recently, but because they offer instant gratification and encourage more buying, we wouldn't count them out as an effective m-commerce tool just yet.

✦ **Check-in specials:** A growing trend is to offer coupons or other specials to customers who use social media (such as FourSquare or Facebook) to *check in,* or publicly announce that they are on-site at your location. The customer should be able to redeem your offer on the spot (not on a future visit). This reward seems counterintuitive because the idea of a coupon is to bring people to you who otherwise wouldn't be shopping with you. However, this on-the-spot reward is important because it encourages existing customers to let their friends and followers know that they are at your location — think of it as free advertising.

✦ **Mobile banking:** PayPal is among the financial service providers making it easy for customers to interact and get information, such as account statements, from their phones. Similarly, credit card merchants and

**Book VII
Chapter 5**

**Expanding Close
to Home with
Localization and
Mobile Marketing**

banks increasingly send daily account balances to your phone, or make it possible to swipe your phone to make a purchase charged to your credit card or to deposit checks to your bank account. As stated, this segment of m-commerce is expanding rapidly.

You may not want to use *all* these examples for your online store. But you can expect that customers will demand more options when doing business with your store through m-commerce, so you don't want to ignore this important industry trend, either.

Communicating on Twitter

Another increasingly popular way of using a cellphone to communicate with customers is Twitter (www.twitter.com). This social media platform has proven to be an industry heavyweight after quickly rocketing into the spotlight as a way for individuals and companies to hold and follow short conversations. Unlike having a conversation with just a single person, Twitter allows an unlimited number of people to follow your conversation and lets you follow or track dozens or hundreds (or more) of conversations by others.

Twitter was created based on asking the question "What are you doing?" Entries are short text messages — no more than 140 characters — which makes them easy to use with mobile devices. Users must register with Twitter and then identify conversations they want to follow or start their own conversations.

As an online or traditional retailer, your customers can follow frequent updates from your company on the status of a release of a hot new product, such as a video game. Or you might be opening a new store or hosting a special event (online or offline), and customers can learn about it or follow updates about it by using Twitter.

Most recently, Twitter has been introducing new ways to use the social platform for in-network shopping. Through Twitter Cards (a form of advertising), online retailers can expand their typical short tweets by using images, additional information, detailed lead generators (a call to action, such as downloading an e-book), or a buying incentive (such as a discounted price). The process is like adding a small virtual card or display area to your standard tweet. These advertising cards launch the buying process for your store. You can also use Promoted Tweets, another form of in-platform advertising, to target segments of Twitter users with special offers, including by way of Twitter Cards.

Amazon now gives Twitter users the opportunity to shop directly from the social media platform. By using the hashtag #AmazonCart with promoted products (as shown in the figure), consumers can respond to product promotions and have the featured item placed in their Amazon shopping carts for later checkout. As this form of *social selling,* or selling through social media, develops, look for innovative new ways to turn occasional customers into a community of loyal followers for your brand.

To find out who might be looking for information about your store or site, use the Twitter search function to track conversations by inserting keywords. For example, if your online store is MyPlace.com, just enter that name in the search box; Twitter pulls all current and archived conversations in which your site's name is mentioned. This feature is a helpful way to find out what customers are saying about you and your products.

Twitter is also a popular way for customers to voice dissatisfaction. Tweets from unhappy customers can attract negative attention to your brand, and can sometimes add up to a bevy of complaints about your product or service if other people start responding to or sharing the original tweeted complaint. Mobile phones make it even easier for customers to complain on social media, anytime and from anywhere. You need to pay careful attention to negative tweets about your business and respond to them quickly.

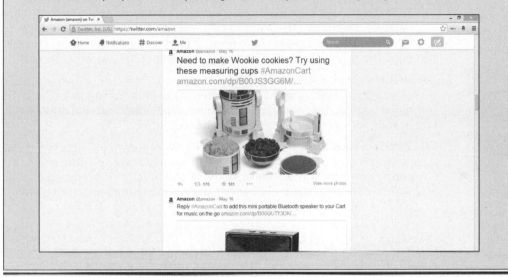

Book VII
Chapter 5

Expanding Close
to Home with
Localization and
Mobile Marketing

Sending text alerts

Sending short text messages (called SMS messages) over a cellphone is an easy and affordable way to communicate with customers. It works especially well for these tasks:

✦ Sending reminders about an event, a product, or a service

✦ Creating immediate awareness

✦ Hosting a contest, or sending information related to contests

✦ Sending special offers

Customers must opt-in, or choose, to receive text alerts. Similar to e-mail marketing, certain rules apply regarding how and when you can send messages via mobile phones to customers. Do not send unsolicited texts. Especially because customers can be charged a per-text fee by their cellular service provider, a business can get in trouble if they don't ask permission to advertise or market to a customer using SMS alerts.

A growing number of companies offer SMS marketing services. Try one of the following:

✦ **Cardboard Fish** (`www.cardboardfish.com`): Offers a number of marketing options for SMS services. Service is available to a large number of companies outside the United States. In some cases, a minimum purchase may be required.

✦ **EzTexting** (`www.eztexting.com`): With a host of different plans for businesses, EzTexting costs as little as a few cents per text (not exceeding 5 cents) in a true pay-as-you-go format. They also offer monthly plans, based on usage, that range from approximately $30 to $150 per month.

✦ **Red Fish Media** (`www.redfishmedia.com`): This company has a range of mobile marketing and SMS services. As m-commerce has become more popular, this company has expanded its offerings and now helps brands with all parts of mobile marketing.

✦ **WebText** (`www.webtext.com`): Offers pay-as-you-go pricing. Typically, pricing is on a per-message basis, with each message costing only a few cents. However, this business model is continually changing, so check with WebText for the most current pricing structure and service offerings for the retail segment.

Advertising with text-to-buy

Text-to-buy ads give customers an easy and immediate way to purchase your products by using their cellphones. Here are some companies that offer this service to online retailers:

✦ **4Info** (`www.advertising.4info.net`): Works with many large businesses and online retailers. Using this ad service, you can send customers text messages that allow them to do things such as

  • Make purchases

  • Link back to a live support person in a call center

  • Click to view a product video

✦ **Cross Link Media** (`www.crosslinkmedia.com`): Offers several solutions as an advertiser. They claim that 25 percent of people in the United States participate in at least one type of mobile campaign each month.

When you use any type of mobile campaign to promote your store, you should follow a few rules. Make sure that your mobile message recipient always opts-in to the campaign. Additionally, ask customers to submit a keyword or short code to signal their desire to participate. And, of course, never sell your mobile contact list to other retailers.

Distributing mobile coupons

It's hard to say what's driving the demand for mobile coupons, which were once thought to be a disruptive nuisance. Perhaps Americans are becoming more cost-conscious and are on the lookout for a deal. Or maybe they are simply curious as to how mobile coupons work. Whatever the reason, billions of mobile coupons are being distributed each year. According to research from Accenture (www.accenture.com), more than 70 percent of people surveyed showed interest in receiving coupons on their cellphones, and that percentage continues to grow as more people realize the benefits of mobile coupons.

More consumers are enjoying the delivery of mobile coupons to get discounts and perks while they are near a particular store, for example. Retailers (both online and offline) are finding that mobile coupons are spurring a type of spontaneous buying, ultimately driving more sales and greater revenue for their stores. Even so, other research reveals that a large percentage of mobile coupons go unused — but even if not used, they are influencing future buying decisions. The fact that so many mobile coupons are being distributed is a good indicator that the demand for them is likely to continue growing as they become more mainstream.

What's the big deal about having coupons sent to your phone? For starters, they are coupons sent to your phone! Seriously, as a traditional or online retailer, mobile coupons have been shown to

- ✦ Generate better engagement and response rates with customers
- ✦ Increase customer loyalty
- ✦ Cost less than traditional advertising
- ✦ Reach customers when they are near your location
- ✦ Be easier to administer than other advertising

Plenty of companies are set up to administer these types of services for your business. Following are some companies that provide m-coupon distribution services:

- ✦ **Cellfire (www.cellfire.com):** Cellfire works with very large retailers, not only to distribute coupons but also to use mobility to help further brand the company.

- ✦ **Groupon (www.groupon.com):** This volume-based coupon company was initially promoted via e-mail. The company eventually launched a mobile application that allows customers to use their mobile phones to take advantage of location-based deals in a particular city.

- ✦ **Plum Reward (www.plumreward.com):** Unlike some of its competitors, Plum Reward specializes in working with bricks-and-mortar locations. The company sells a small piece of hardware, similar to a debit or credit card scanner placed in stores. Customers then enter their cellphone numbers into the device to begin receiving offers specific to that particular store.

**Book VII
Chapter 5**

Expanding Close
to Home with
Localization and
Mobile Marketing

Although the service is free for customers, you pay an ongoing monthly fee in addition to the initial equipment cost. Having to purchase a particular piece of hardware to make this work may be a disadvantage for most retailers, especially when so many other low-cost solutions are available.

✦ **Proximity Media (`www.proximitymedia.com`):** This mobile coupon solution uses Bluetooth technology to deliver coupons to customers when they are near your store. This location-based marketing provides a good return by drawing customers into a store, on the spot.

Distributed commerce

An important component of both mobile and social media marketing and how it affects online sales is referred to as *distributed commerce*. This phrase describes the way that online shopping is distributed, or spread across, multiple platforms. Just as shoppers like to have a choice of whether to shop in your physical retail location or online, consumers now want even more choices for the way they shop and buy online. With distributed commerce, shoppers are extending buying options to mobile devices (including both smartphones and tablets) and to social media websites. Just as we discussed the capability to market to consumers through these platforms, you also want to offer the capability to shop, or buy, directly from the same platforms with the least amount of interference or disruption to the buying process.

Several companies are offering mobile shopping platforms that integrate with your online store or your social media profiles, such as Facebook and Twitter. Check out mShopper (`www.mshopper.com`) to see how a mobile store can be integrated with your existing website to offer a truly mobile shopping experience (see Figure 5-1).

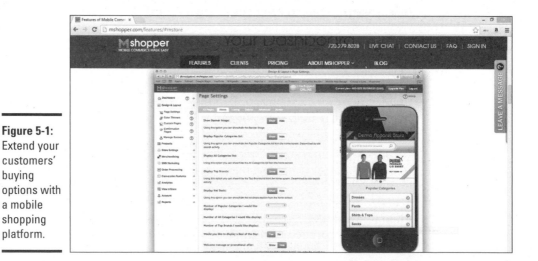

Figure 5-1: Extend your customers' buying options with a mobile shopping platform.

Localizing with Ads

As you saw with some of the targeted mobile coupons and ads, one advantage that mobile commerce offers is the capability to reach customers in a specific geographic region. The concept of *localization,* or local advertising, isn't restricted to mobile applications. If you're an online retailer who also has a bricks-and-mortar location, local search can mean big business for you. As competition and market conditions tighten, local paid search is expected to grow as an important advertising strategy for retailers. Spending for local ad revenues continues to rise, and projections show it reaching $183 billion by 2015. As targeting continues to improve and as mobile usage increases, localized search is expected to keep rising. In the next few years, an estimated 30 percent of all searches will be local.

In this process, also referred to as *geotargeting,* your business ads appear as part of search results that are based on a geographic location. The concept of local marketing is used by plenty of sites, such as craigslist and Angie's List. However, in the area of paid local search, the biggest contenders are Google, Yahoo!, and Microsoft (Bing). These search engine competitors have taken online advertising to a new level. Google remains the industry giant, accounting for more than 84 percent of paid searches. Microsoft and Yahoo! work to keep the 10 percent slice each currently owns, and have joined forces to try and be a worthy contender against Google's powerhouse. Yahoo! and Google both have geotargeting programs that provide paid search results based on a user's computer IP address, which can be associated with a specific physical location. Nearly 20 percent of Google's ad revenue came from mobile ads, and that number is predicted to grow to 30 percent by 2017. It's clear that businesses and consumers are responding to localized, mobile marketing.

Google AdWords

Using Google AdWords is comparable to placing an ad in your local newspaper. You purchase a specific amount of space (or ad size) for a set dollar amount to entice customers to come into your store. You can even specify a section of the paper in which your ad should appear. For example, if you have a sporting goods store, your ad might appear in the sports section of the newspaper. Google works almost the same way.

In this case, your ad is displayed in the search engine based on a prospective customer's search results. Suppose that someone uses Google to search for soccer balls. Your text ad, typically a few sentences long, shows up on the right side of the screen with other sponsored ads, or at the top of the search results as shown in Figure 5-2. Google continues to add more listing feature options, such as letting you include your phone number in the text ad (for direct-from-mobile calling).

**Book VII
Chapter 5**

Expanding Close
to Home with
Localization and
Mobile Marketing

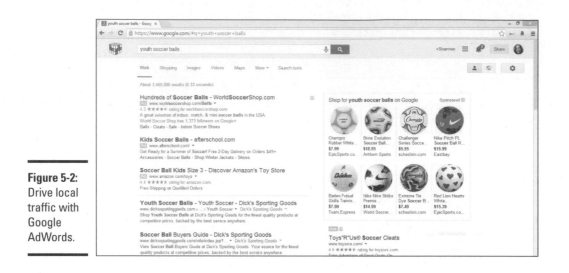

Figure 5-2:
Drive local traffic with Google AdWords.

Unlike with traditional print ads, with Google AdWords you choose the keywords that trigger your ad to appear and you decide how much you want to pay for the ad space. When you use AdWords, you aren't paying for a certain ad size but, rather, for a certain number of hits on your ad. In this process, known as *cost per click,* or *CPC,* you pay only when prospective customers click your text link. (Another common industry term for this type of marketing or advertising is PPC, or *pay per click.*)

Geotargeting takes CPC one step further. You also might decide that you want your ad to appear *only* when the prospective customer is searching from a specific location, such as a country or city. For example, if your sports store is based in Raleigh, North Carolina, and someone in that area searches for soccer balls, your ad appears. If the person clicks your ad, you're charged the amount that you agreed to pay. You can pay as little as a few pennies up to several dollars or more for each click. Google is also driving similar types of localized or geographically-based results in all their organic (non-paid) search results.

If you set the price, or CPC, that you're willing to pay (as we just mentioned), you may be wondering why you would ever agree to pay a high dollar amount. It's simple: Because you're basically bidding on the price of the ad, or in this case, the CPC, your price correlates with the popularity of the keyword on which you're bidding. The more popular your keyword or your keywords, the more people are willing to pay for them, which drives up the price and the competition for your *ad position,* or where it gets placed within search results. You might still choose to bid a smaller amount for your CPC, but that means your ad will appear fewer times or in a lower position on the page. To be competitive, you may have to pay a higher CPC.

You can limit the cost of your keywords by bidding on specific words or phrases, as opposed to choosing more general terms. Rather than bid on *soccer balls,* for example, bid on a specific type or name-brand soccer ball. Or use a phrase such as *soccer balls for kids* or *youth soccer balls.* You see fewer results, but they should also lead to a more qualified buyer for a smaller ad price.

Registration for Google AdWords is free, except for a minimal setup fee, and requires no contracts or minimum spending requirements. You're charged only when someone clicks your text ad. With Google AdWords, you can

✦ Create campaigns for multiple products or websites, using multiple sets of keywords

✦ Target multiple locations at once (instead of only one zip code, or city, for example)

✦ Use images, video, and audio with the ad, as opposed to only text

✦ Gain access to various advanced planning and budgeting tools

✦ Set daily budget limits (for greater control) versus monthly budget limits

You can extend the value of organic (not paid for) localized search results by taking advantage of Google's free local search placement, called Google Places. Registering with Google Places helps make sure that your business shows up (map and all) when a search for a local place or term is searched. To register for Google Places, visit www.google.com/places/. Did we mention this service is free?

We show you how to sign up for Google AdWords in Book VI, Chapter 3.

No matter which type of advertising program you choose to use, you can bet that spending money smartly on locally targeted ads is a good move. Increasingly, your local customers expect deals, discounts, and special incentives for choosing to shop with you — and they want to access these offers on the spot. You don't have to go overboard with localized or mobile promotions, but expect these types of advertising options to continue to grow in popularity.

**Book VII
Chapter 5**

Expanding Close
to Home with
Localization and
Mobile Marketing

Chapter 6: Troubleshooting the Transition to Online Retail

In This Chapter

✔ Developing a return policy and sticking to it

✔ Figuring out how to make your back end work online

✔ Bringing together your bricks-and-mortar and online stores

✔ Increasing service and sales with alternative payment options

As you move your retail store online, you can always hope that things will go perfectly. In reality, you can expect a few minor bumps along the way. This chapter talks about navigating over the bumps and avoiding the big potholes after your site goes live.

The good news is that your customers probably won't even notice most of the small issues that are to be expected when an e-commerce site launches. The secret to surviving is planning now for those situations most likely to cause you stress.

Handling Returns in the Store from Online Sales

Suppose that you have store policies already in place, but it's now time to update your return or exchange policy. Given today's high rate of fraudulent activity, you're probably already wary (if not suspicious) of customers who hightail it back to your store with merchandise in hand.

Now you have to add the return of online orders to the mix. After your online store is up and running, someone will certainly make a purchase on your website, and the purchase might be the wrong size, or damaged, or in a style that the customer doesn't like.

Before you can decide how to handle the return, you have to ask yourself how you want to respond to it. If your goal is to work with your customers and make them happy, you want to develop a customer-friendly policy. One of the leading online retailers best known for its customer-centric approach to business is Zappos. One example of how it strives to exceed customer expectations is in its shipping and return policy. The online shoe retailer ships all products free and allows you to return products (up to 365 days later) — for free! (Of course, the merchandise can't be worn.) The focus on free is readily promoted on its site, and they make sure the return process is simple for customers (see Figure 6-1). Not every online retailer, especially small start-up sites, can absorb shipping and return costs to this degree.

Figure 6-1: Zappos offers customer-friendly returns that are easy — and always free!

Or perhaps you are most interested in protecting your bottom line. In that case, you can approach the online return policy in a way that's most convenient for you. Don't worry. Lots of online retailers require customers to pay their share of return costs and put strict policies in place for managing returns. Just be aware that your return policy can be strategically used as a competitive advantage, as it is with Zappos, or it can be a status quo policy designed to protect your business.

Here are some decisions that you need to make about return policies:

✦ **Customer-friendly policy:** If you're taking this route, your policy might stipulate that you

- Pay for return shipping (or reimburse the customer for it) if a purchase is sent back by mail because the item is damaged or doesn't fit, for example

- Accept the return with no questions asked

- Give a complete refund or exchange the item

- Request (but not demand) a copy of the original receipt

✦ **Bottom-line policy:** When cutting corners is your biggest concern, protect yourself with these rules of return:

- No returns are made without an original receipt

- Issue only store credit or an exchange of equal value

- Limit the time for which returns are accepted (within 30 days from date of purchase, for example)

- Do not accept returns on sale, clearance, or discontinued items

- Returns must be made from the location where they were purchased (no in-store returns for online purchases)

You get to decide the terms of your policies based on what makes the most sense for your business. The preceding suggestions are just that — suggestions. You may want to use all of them or a blend of the two approaches.

When sending items to your customers, pack a return/item exchange request form inside the box. Make sure that the form provides complete instructions for returning an item and states your return policy. Customers wanting to return an item can use this form to provide basic information (such as name and address) and a reason why they're returning the product. Or you may want to allow the customer to complete this process online, through their customer account, if your back-end technologies allow this type of feature.

Merging Existing Back-End Systems with Online Requirements

By the time you launch your website, you typically already have a lengthy history. You have established customers, extensive sales data, an inventory-management system, in-store policies, point-of-sale systems, ordering guidelines, and a host of vendors and suppliers at your beck and call.

Having that much structure and information definitely plays in your favor because you're not starting from scratch when you move into e-commerce. But integrating all these systems and procedures to an online business can present a few challenges to your back end.

Garrison Confections, a successful bricks-and-mortar store, launched its e-commerce site with a nice look and a fairly standard back-end shopping cart solution. The online store, which sells luxury chocolates, worked fine initially. Its owner, Andrew Shotts, soon became recognized as a celebrity chef and judge on Food Network and for other highly regarded competitions, all of which brought more awareness — and traffic — to Garrison Confections. As the online site became more popular, it couldn't handle the increased traffic and the owner had to come up with a new back-end solution.

The company made two critical decisions about how to handle this transition period. First, the company outsourced the project to a local web development firm. The second part of the equation involved making the decision to invest the necessary money to make the upgrade happen. A small business (especially one trying to keep up with the demands from a national spotlight) can't easily spend thousands of dollars; but paying for a new back-end solution made sense as part of the overall business.

The changes paid off, and the site is better integrated with the company's back-end process. Small tweaks to the site's design and online ordering process keep the website fresh, on the front and back ends. Figure 6-2 shows a glimpse of the newest spin on the Garrison Confections site and ordering system.

Figure 6-2:
The Garrison Confections online store.

Garrison Confections is also a good example of an online store that has special shipping considerations that must be tied into the site's back-end functionality, as well as be visible to the customer. Because the company ships gourmet chocolate candies, summertime deliveries to some states can be difficult. For that reason, deliveries to most southern U.S. regions during certain months must be shipped overnight. Although this requirement is added to its checkout process, it is also clearly posted on the website's shipping policies. You can check out this gourmet chocolate site in full at www.garrisonconfections.com.

Managing inventory

One of the biggest headaches for an online retailer is handling inventory levels in a way that's least disruptive to both you and your online customer. At the heart of the matter, you need to make sure that your online store can communicate with your existing inventory system.

Here's an example of what typically happens when you have a kink in your inventory management. A customer goes to your site, places an order, pays for the order, and then expects it to be delivered according to your shipping policy. You receive the order and start filling it, only to find that the item is out of stock. Now you have to communicate with your customer to tell him or her that the product is on back order. As you know, this situation isn't ideal. For a better alternative, implement a system that communicates inventory levels with all your primary points of operations, including

✦ Point-of-sale system (your retail location)

✦ Online shopping cart

✦ Call center

✦ Warehouse

When investigating these different operations, make sure to determine whether each one can work with your inventory-management system. The best solution allows any (and possibly all) of these operations to communicate directly with your software inventory-management system to allow for a real-time updated tracking system of what you have in stock and what you need to reorder.

Fulfilling and shipping your orders

Chances are good that your store has already encountered the need to package an order and ship it somewhere. Depending on what type of store you have, you may do these tasks regularly (with catalog or telephone orders, for example) or only occasionally. But imagine that you suddenly have to ship out anywhere from 10 to 100 different packages every day. How does that affect your already hectic schedule? Do you have employees who can be dedicated to handling the process? Or does the idea of shipping orders evoke the image of you staying up late at night, digging for boxes, printing labels from your computer, and trying to meet last-minute pickup schedules?

Another concern with an increased number of shipments is space. Think about your existing location. Do you have dedicated space for packaging? If so, can in-store customers see the space or is it in a separate offsite warehouse? Regardless of where you ship the product from, how do you confirm that an order has gone out? Does computer software display that information, or are you keeping a manual checklist?

As you can see, you have a lot of questions to consider for what seems to be a simple process. Placing one of your products into a box and shipping it out to a customer isn't difficult but is more time consuming than you probably think.

One solution is to outsource the shipping-and-handling portion of the operation. Another option is to have many of your items drop-shipped to customers from your suppliers. However, you can also keep this function in-house, if you want. Check out Book IV, Chapter 7 to find out more about your shipping options.

Tracking your orders

You may already have internal systems for tracking customer orders. But now that you're selling online, you need to provide your customers with direct access to the status of their orders, particularly after those orders ship.

You can minimize the number of calls and e-mails that you receive from customers by allowing them to directly check on a delivery. Anything that helps reduce your workload is a good thing! The truly good news is that the major shipping companies provide free online order-tracking tools for you to incorporate into your site. Try these shipping companies:

✦ **DHL (`www.dhl.com`):** As a registered customer, you can use the DHL tracking tools and send automated e-mail messages to customers. The messages include information so that customers can track the status of their orders. DHL also offers a complete e-fulfillment solution for online retailers. You can get the scoop on all their e-commerce services at `http://dhl.com/en/logistics/supply_chain_solutions/`.

✦ **FedEx (`www.fedex.com/insight`):** Use the FedEx InSight tool to track shipments. You can see all your inbound and outbound shipments and get real-time updates of any potential delays. To let your customers track and manage their orders, encourage them to sign up for FedEx Delivery Manager. You can access other tools and resources at the FedEx Small Business Center at `smallbusiness.fedex.com`.

✦ **UPS (`www.ups.com`):** UPS also offers online-tracking tools for your customers. The delivery company has developed a set of applications that you can integrate directly into your website. By using UPS, you don't need to send customers e-mail messages with directions on order tracking or direct them to another site for tracking. Customers can check the status right on your site. You can check their list of approved vendors, including GoECart and GoDaddy, as part of their UPS Ready Program. You can also learn more about their e-commerce tools and solutions in the UPS MarketPlace Providers list. Find all these resources (and more) at `www.ups.com/smallbusiness`.

During the 2013 holiday buying season, extreme weather conditions across the United States wreaked havoc on shipping companies and prevented many online retailers, including mega ones such as Amazon, from making good on the standard holiday delivery promise, "Guaranteed to arrive by Christmas Eve" (when ordered by a certain day and time). Customers without gifts under their trees were furious, to say the least — but it was a problem outside everyone's control. Since then, online retailers have updated their shipping and delivery policies to note that they are not responsible for problems causing delayed deliveries that may occur on the shipper's end. We advise you to follow suit and add similar caveats to your shipping and delivery policies.

Maintaining site performance

Before you decide to sell your inventory online, you may already have some type of website. Sure, it's probably more of a brochure site that shows your logo and maybe a photo of your retail location and offers prospective customers a map to help them find your store. If that's the case, your site probably doesn't see a whole lot of traffic. And even you probably don't look at it that often. Well, after you enter the world of e-commerce, that situation is likely to change.

Now that you're an official online retailer, you need to understand your site's performance capabilities. For example, how much traffic can the site handle? If you exceed a particular limit of bandwidth usage, does your monthly hosting fee increase? What about the site design? Is it optimized for the best viewing in varying screen resolutions? Can a customer using a slower Internet connection shop your site as easily as a customer with a broadband connection? How well do product images load? These questions are just a sampling of the site performance issues that can surface as you begin selling online.

Deciding How to Handle Integration

Even if you're a smaller store, site-performance, inventory-management, and order-tracking solutions suddenly becomes major elements within your new business model. Even so, you probably start off needing to make only minor changes to your current way of doing business. That way, you have a chance to see what works and what doesn't, and you can then figure out what you need to change. This trial-by-error process is common.

However, if you already have sophisticated back-end processes or you're more of a midsize retailer, you may want to plan. In fact, you may find it worthwhile to hire a consultant to help you survey your systems and find the best hardware and software match to smoothly integrate your online operations.

No matter the size of your site, you can get a jump-start on the installation and integration of your hardware and software by using these four checkpoints:

+ **Review:** Make a list of all areas of your store operations, from your cash register (or point of sale) to your inventory system. Take a close look at how you currently handle each of these operations.

+ **Analyze:** You can begin deciding how, if at all, your current systems will translate to an online process. Can you use the software programs that you already have with your e-commerce site? Or is your software designed only for a traditional retail store? If you use manual programs, those programs can quickly get bogged down after your site experiences its first phase of growth.

+ **Decide:** After you have an idea of how well your existing procedures may or may not hold up, you have decisions to make. For example, are you ready to invest in new systems? Where will you get the money for upgrades? Are you comfortable managing your online retail operations in-house, or do you need to bring in the professionals?

✦ **Investigate:** If you decide that you need a new software program or want to outsource some of your operations, start looking at your options. Begin familiarizing yourself with current terminology, leading technology vendors, and the typical price ranges for various back-end solutions.

One thing is certain: You won't find a shortage of experienced vendors ready to help you transition into the world of multichannel retailing. The systems in the following list are worth looking into to help integrate your offline location with your online store:

✦ **CORESense (www.coresense.com):** CORESense offers multiple products that range from real-time inventory management to fulfillment and marketing.

✦ **Epicor (www.epicor.com):** Epicor retail solutions include a cross-channel order-management system, which helps you provide real-time inventory management between your store's inventory, website, catalog, and even kiosk. It can link your site and in-store point-of-sale (POS) system to a call center.

✦ **Celerant Technology Corp. (www.celerant.com):** Considered a multi-retail channel solution, Celerant Command Retail software integrates multiple key e-commerce and retail functions into one database that gives you a detailed, real-time overview of your business operations.

✦ **NetSuite (www.netsuite.com):** Using the SuiteCommerce cloud-based solution, you can combine all your e-commerce, in-store POS (point of sale), and order management with your back-end systems. SuiteCommerce is one of several products offered specifically for e-commerce businesses of all sizes.

Depending on the size of your business, you may be able to use an off-the-shelf, or web-based, e-commerce storefront solution, such as the ones we discuss in Book VIII, Chapter 1. These solutions are very powerful and sometimes more affordable.

A current trend with vendors is to offer an *omni-channel* retail solution, which takes cross-channel or multi-channel solutions a step further by seamlessly integrating or connecting nearly every component of the customer experience, including mobility. When shopping for solutions, make sure you understand exactly what areas of your business can be managed or integrated and how that integration is achieved because products described as being multi-channel or omni-channel are often two very different types of solutions.

Extending Payment Options to Virtual Customers

The goal of providing a variety of payments is to take away an obstacle that may prevent customers from buying from you. However, the increasing competition for online sales is forcing online retailers such as yourself to always be on the lookout for new payment options.

For a list of vendors for your online business needs, check out the Internet Retailer vendor list, which includes many payment processing vendors, along with other valuable resource categories. You can check it out at www. internetretailer.com/vendors.

Whether customers purchase from your store or website or by e-mail or phone, the future of online retailing comes down to two principles:

✦ Continually connect with your customers.

✦ Always give your customers options.

Buy now, pay later

Extended payment terms, deferred terms, or instant credit — call it what you like, this payment option is gaining popularity as an alternative online payment solution. This type of credit basically allows customers to delay paying cash out of their pocket at the time of purchase.

Deferred billing is the same as the offline promotion of "90 days same as cash." Allowing customers to take advantage of this type of payment can truly help your business if you sell higher-end items or want to increase your per-customer average sale. Customers often seek out this option during the holiday season, when they're already in a cash crunch. To set up a deferred billing arrangement, start by talking with your bank or merchant provider.

Another option that's exceeding expectations for online retailers is the Bill Me Later program offered by PayPal. This program acts as a fast and secure way to buy online but pay in the future. Plus, customers can take advantage of special financing options to spread out payments without penalty or interest. Your customer gets approved for a certain credit limit and then receives a billing statement. Customers like this approach for the following reasons:

✦ **Speed:** At the time of purchase, Bill Me Later asks your customers only for their date of birth and the last four digits of his Social Security number. (PayPal's banking partner uses this information to make a quick credit check.) Approval is returned in a matter of seconds, in most cases. Customers may also apply directly on the BillMeLater website before shopping with you. In that case, they come to your website, pre-approved to spend.

✦ **Security:** Because Bill Me Later doesn't require giving out extensive information or using credit cards, some customers view it as a safer way to make a purchase.

✦ **Linked to PayPal:** Customers link their Bill Me Later account with their PayPal account, giving them a hassle-free, alternative form of payment during checkout at your site.

As an online retailer, you're bound to like Bill Me Later for these reasons:

✦ **No risk:** PayPal accepts all the risk when extending credit to your customers, so you don't have to worry about losing anything if a customer doesn't pay.

✦ **Affordable:** When we last checked, the processing fee for a Bill Me Later transaction was still slightly less than for most credit cards.

✦ **Sales boost:** Based on what Bill Me Later says is the norm, online merchants are experiencing both higher ticket averages (customers spending more per visit) and increased repeat purchases from existing customers using the service.

Consider offering additional payment options similar to Bill Me Later, such as V.Me (www.v.me), established by Visa. Although V.Me doesn't offer a line of credit separate from the credit already extended through Visa, it is a fast, secure way to pay. And V.Me allows customers to link any other credit or debit cards to a V.Me account — again, as a means to provide more secure shopping.

To use Bill Me Later, customers can simply look for the Bill Me Later payment option during the checkout process on your website. Customers can also see a complete list of vendors accepting payment on the Bill Me Later website and may find your store listed there (see Figure 6-3).

Figure 6-3: Look for the Bill Me Later logo.

Check and cash alternatives

Another payment method involves your site accepting various forms of checks, or even money orders. With Internet checks, you work through an independent processor that accepts money from a customer's bank account and then deposits it into your merchant account, usually in fewer than 15 days. You can check with your payment processor to find out whether it offers this type of service. An even easier check solution is offering Automated Clearing House (ACH) processing that transfers money directly from a customer's checking account to your merchant account, usually within 48 hours. Many vendors offer eChecks, or ACH processing services, for your e-commerce site. Most charge a monthly fee, plus a small transaction fee each time a customer uses the service (similar to but often much lower than a credit card processing fee). Check out various monthly plans for ACH transactions from vendors such as First ACH (www.firstach.com), Forte (www.forte.net), and VeriCheck (www.vericheck.com).

An alternative payment solution that is gaining interest in the online world is Bitcoin. This Internet-based currency is, in general, an alternative to cash. Bitcoins are stored in virtual wallets — the equivalent to online banks. Where do they come from? Without getting too technical, bitcoins are virtually mined (like you might mine for coal, but using a sophisticated computer program). You can also buy bitcoins (using real dollars) on an open market, similar to the stock exchange market.

Because bitcoin is a digital currency, it is not backed by the Federal Reserve or any other institution. Bitcoins were designed to increase in value over time because a limited number are available, and they get more difficult to obtain after time. In other words, you need more computing power to mine for bitcoins as time passes. Why are we bothering to tell you all this? Bitcoins have become a recognized form of online payment, even by large online retailers such as Overstock. That said, bitcoins are still a novelty and the risks of accepting them as an alternative form of payment are different from accepting eChecks and delayed billing options such as Bill Me Later. For these reasons, we don't recommend adding bitcoins to your list of alternative online payments, just yet. But we do think it's worthwhile to be aware of how this virtual currency progresses in the world of e-commerce.

**Book VII
Chapter 6**

Troubleshooting the Transition to Online Retail

Book VIII
Storefront Selling

Continue your eBay success by using completed search results to understand how to best position each product you sell. Read the free article at www.dummies.com/extras/startinganonlinebusinessaio for tips, tricks, and techniques for conducting your eBay research.

Contents at a Glance

Chapter 1: Instant E-Commerce with Storefronts

*O*ne of the easiest ways to get started selling your products online is through an e-commerce solution. This type of online storefront, or e-commerce-in-a-box, provides all the components necessary to build, manage, and promote your store in one convenient location.

Selling products online has increasingly become the norm for all types of businesses, both new and established. As a result, e-commerce solutions have become more diverse, offer increased functionality and are much less expensive. This chapter explains the most popular — and most necessary — features available in e-commerce solutions and helps you make a decision about which storefront would work best for your business.

Some storefront solutions have recognizable names. In this minibook, we cover Amazon.com in Chapter 2, Yahoo! in Chapter 3, and eBay in Chapter 4.

Knowing What You Want: Features

When choosing your online store, make sure that the following three essential elements are included. Together, these functions help qualify the storefront as a true all-in-one solution:

✦ **Shopping cart:** This back-end feature allows customers to browse for, select, and purchase products. (If you want to know more, Book IV, Chapter 5 compares specific shopping cart features.)

✦ **Payment processor:** This feature is a virtual cash register. Of course, customers need a way to pay you during checkout for the products they want. A storefront solution should give customers multiple options.

✦ **Hosting solution:** You need a place to host your actual store. Your hosted shopping cart, however, doesn't have to share the service you use for your primary website. But one of the benefits of a storefront is that hosting is included in the deal, eliminating additional website hosting fees.

These bare necessities are just the tip of the iceberg when you're selecting features for your storefront. Most e-commerce solutions provide a long list of additional features and functionality. These features typically fall in three areas: performance; product merchandizing and marketing; and administration. All three are described in the following sections.

Performance

Unfortunately, performance is the area of a storefront that you don't always think about until something goes wrong or isn't what you expected, but it is truly the backbone of your operations. Paying special attention to these performance-related issues when selecting your storefront is ultimately worth your time:

✦ **Speed:** A lot of factors contribute to the speed of a storefront, and determining how the site's functionality will fare isn't always easy. The best way to find out is to visit some of your storefront's featured sites and see for yourself whether a lag in processing time occurs.

You can also sort through a storefront's community forum section to see whether other storeowners have complained about the storefront's *processing speed,* or the load time for pages.

✦ **Storage:** You want adequate disk space and bandwidth transfer available for your site. Even if your storefront starts small, you need room to grow without being immediately penalized with a higher rate. At a minimum, you should start with 1GB or 5GB capacity. Increasingly, the leading e-commerce solutions are offering unlimited storage and bandwidth in some or all pricing plans.

✦ **Security:** Proper security is an essential part of e-commerce. Before purchasing your storefront, understand what type of services or protections are offered to guard your store, and check for issues related to PCI (Payment Card Industry) compliance (we discuss these issues in detail in Book I, Chapter 5).

✦ **Product quantity:** Many storefronts place limits on the number of products you can sell. Which storefront you choose often turns into a price-based issue. The good news is that even with limitations on quantity, your monthly fee typically supports a substantial number of product listings. The lowest support level at most reputable storefronts is at least 100 products. As with trends in storage and bandwidth, some providers support an unlimited number of products across all plan options — the difference in price pertains to the features and support options available.

✦ **E-product delivery:** If your storefront supports electronic products (e-books, for example), they can be delivered by way of customer-initiated downloads. You can also sell *membership* (a service with recurring fees) electronically. The capability to download some products in digital format (such as PDF files or music files) or access digital services is growing, and you should definitely consider offering these kinds of products because they require no warehouse space and can offer substantial profit margins. See Book IV, Chapter 3 for more about selling e-products.

✦ **Import and export tools:** This feature lets you transfer large numbers of products into or out of the storefront. Storefronts with this feature commonly let you dump products into the storefront from an Excel spreadsheet, for example. This feature can be a timesaver if you have a lot of inventory.

✦ **Third-party integration:** Your online business will most likely use a number of different tools or software, from accounting to customer relationship management (CRM) solutions. Ideally, you want many of these tools to integrate, or work with one another, to maximize results. In particular, your storefront should work with as many of your other business tools as possible. In addition, many APIs (application programming interfaces) can provide access and integration to even more features and tools. When choosing an e-commerce solution, be sure to check which third-party solutions it supports as well as the diversity or expansiveness of its library of APIs.

✦ **Support:** Having access to the storefront's technical support team can be your only lifeline at times. In the best possible situation, full tech support is available 24 hours a day, 7 days a week. As we mentioned previously, some pricing plans vary based on the level of support you want or need. Paying an additional $20 or $30 per month to get increased support may be worthwhile, especially if you're a small-business owner with limited tech support knowledge or resources.

✦ **Templates:** One benefit of turning to a storefront is that you have access to templates. If you aren't a savvy web developer, predesigned web page templates are supposed to make it easy to open your store. To truly be of value, the storefront needs an extensive array of template styles to choose from and should also allow for some level of customization. You may find templates set up by categories or industries, such as sports or clothing store themes. This approach takes into consideration current design and color trends specific to that business type, so getting started is even easier.

✦ **Wizards:** The storefront solution should offer a setup wizard to guide you through the process of building and customizing your storefront. Ideally, the wizard takes your store setup from start to finish without any major headaches. A nonintuitive wizard or one that is difficult to work with negates one of the biggest advantages of using a storefront — simplicity!

Spend time on the storefront's demo section and tinker with the wizard before making your final decision. If the demo isn't fully functioning, contact a sales representative. Ask the person to give you live access to the store-building tools for a week or so. This access gives you a chance to test-drive the real wizard.

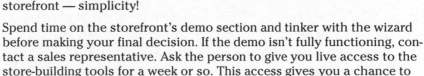

Book VIII
Chapter 1

Instant E-Commerce
with Storefronts

Product merchandizing and marketing

A stellar storefront solution should provide a host of tools that assist you in promoting products (offering ideas based on past purchase histories, for example), and marketing them (by offering promotion codes, for example) to your customer base. After all, these features ultimately help you move more products and bump up your sales revenue:

✦ **Product images:** Ideally, customers should be able to view multiple images of a product, including an up close or enhanced view, before making a purchase. To make several images of a product available on your site, the store's product gallery has to allow for more than one image to be uploaded and viewed per product.

✦ **Customization component:** One major online trend is letting customers customize products. You can customize a product by adding a monogram, engraving a message, or modifying a color or style, for example. Because customizing is potentially a persuasive purchasing feature, your storefront's shopping-cart program should allow customers to add customizing instructions.

✦ **Cross-selling (or upselling):** This feature allows you to promote similar products on a single page. In other words, when customers add one product to the cart, you can then recommend or suggest another product. Also referred to as *suggestive selling,* cross-selling occurs during the checkout process, where you recommend additional products or services to the customer, based on the existing purchase. Cross-selling is a standard technique to raise the amount a customer spends in one visit to your store.

✦ **Discount pricing:** You may want to be able to set up special groups that can be assigned different prices. For example, you may want to offer a 10 percent discount in February to active military members and their families. Or you may want to allow certain resellers to receive a different price than your public customers. This feature lets you distinguish among types of customers and charge them different prices.

✦ **Promotions:** Coupon codes, gift certificates, loyalty and reward programs, and any other special offers can be set up as incentives for your customers. The complexities of this feature vary, so take a close look at what each storefront solution can and can't do. As an example, some storefronts allow you to deduct only a certain percentage rate or a flat dollar amount. Other programs allow promotions such buy-one-get-one-free (or half price).

✦ **E-mail marketing:** Staying in touch with your customer base is a sure-fire way to drive up sales. Storefronts seem to offer wide variations of this feature. Some storefronts may offer their own e-mail function, while others may integrate with a third-party solution, such as MailChimp or iContact.

✦ **Search engine friendly:** Search engine optimization (SEO) is being continuously integrated into storefront features. Having your individual product pages (or the images) tagged or optimized with special meta descriptions is an increasingly important element to helping your pages show up in search engine results. See Book VI, Chapter 6 to find out more about search engine optimization.

✦ **Shopping feeds:** Similar to search engine marketing, your e-commerce store needs a way to hook into Google Product Search (Google's shopping comparison site) and other popular shopping sites. You use something called an *XML-data feed* to pull results from these types of sites into your own in the blink of an eye.

✦ **Mobile commerce ready:** Increasingly, online customers want to shop for and buy your products by using a smartphone or tablet, so your storefront should be accessible by mobile devices and *optimized* for (easily viewed on) an iPhone, an Android phone, and any type of tablet. This functionality is growing in popularity, but not all e-commerce solutions offer this level of functionality — or it may cost more for you to have access to this type of feature. We discuss the benefits of mobile commerce in Book VII, Chapter 5.

✦ **Social marketing:** Facebook, Pinterest, Instagram, YouTube, Twitter, and LinkedIn are among some of the popular social media sites today. Your customers want to interact with your brand using these sites; but how they do this is rapidly changing. Online customers now use social media to communicate with and about your business, receive special promotions and coupons, make purchases from your business, and even help sell your products to friends in their networks. Often customers want the opportunity to "like" a company on Facebook, follow them on Twitter, or add the company to a Google+ circle. An e-commerce solution should offer the functionality necessary to make most, if not all, these interactions possible. The types of social media sites and the ways in which they're used to reach different customers constantly evolve. For example, SnapChat and Vine videos have each been used by companies to engage teenager customers, in particular. Although social marketing changes quickly, this type of marketing can also have a big pay-off.

Administration features

To do your job properly, you have to manage some behind-the-curtain activity. Access to administrative tools lets you oversee these processes. The following list shows the most common features that you'll be grateful to have included with (or added to) your storefront:

✦ **Inventory management:** You need, at the very least, to keep track of your inventory levels and ensure that your existing inventory systems work cohesively with your storefront. Ideally, you should use real-time inventory tracking.

✦ **Accounting system integration:** Look for storefronts that can sufficiently communicate data between your storefront and your accounting package. If this option is available, it's typically set up to integrate specifically with QuickBooks (a financial software package).

✦ **Reporting functions:** Ah, the sales reports — and more. Your storefront solution should be able to track sales, returns, invoices, and more to provide you with the most *insight,* or business intelligence, possible.

✦ **Payment system:** Yes, a storefront needs a payment gateway. But perhaps equally important, your storefront needs to include a range of payment gateways for your customers. PayPal, Visa, MasterCard, American Express, and Discover Card are the basic options. Make sure that your storefront's gateway accepts multiple forms of payment because payment options can combat *shopping-cart abandonment,* the phenomenon that occurs when visitors leave your site without purchasing the items they placed in their carts (virtually abandoning their shopping carts).

✦ **Tax calculation and reporting:** Like it or not, you probably have to deal with taxes online. Taxes can be a complicated issue because amounts vary by county and state. By identifying storefronts that are already set up to add taxes when required, you can save yourself much trouble.

✦ **Multiple currencies:** You can use a feature that allows customers to make purchases with any type of currency. If you are selling internationally, this functionality is a must-have for your storefront.

✦ **Integrated shipping tools:** UPS, FedEx, and DHL are among the most popular U.S. delivery systems for packages. And to get your customer's product delivered, you need to ensure that your storefront can talk to one or more of these organizations. Your storefront doesn't have to integrate with all these shipping options, but it should work with at least the one your site uses most.

✦ **Analytics software:** Along with other tracking and reporting functions, your storefront should help identify your traffic patterns and data on how your customers use the pages of your site. A good analytics program built in to the storefront can give you many of those answers.

Realizing What You Can Have: Cost

Most storefront solutions claim that the sky is the limit on functionality and scalability. They're not far off. But as you probably realize, your budget ultimately becomes either the enabler or the deterrent.

Figure out what you can afford. After you do that, you have to decide which elements you can't live without. As you consider what's most important, keep in mind the way that storefront solutions are typically priced:

- ✦ **Monthly fee:** Most often, you're provided a monthly price for using the service, which should include your monthly hosting cost, too. You can cancel most monthly agreements at any time, as long as you follow the store's termination procedures.

- ✦ **Annual fee:** You have the option of prepaying for a year or more of service. You usually receive a slight discount for paying annually rather than monthly.

When you sign up for a storefront annual account, you're prepaying for a year of service in advance. You can always cancel your agreement before the 12 months end. But in most cases, none of your money is refunded, so you lose the money that you prepaid for the remaining months.

- ✦ **Tiered pricing:** Storefronts typically use a tiered pricing structure to suit all levels of need. They group benefits and features into different types of pricing plans. For example, if you need less disk space or fewer features, choose a basic plan for a lower monthly fee. But if you want the whole shebang, choose the more expensive plan (often called a gold or premium plan).

- ✦ **Product capacity pricing:** Similar to tiered pricing, some storefronts may divide plans by the number of products you want to support. So you may be able to get the benefit of all features in every plan and pay only according to the number of product listings.

- ✦ **Activation fee:** You may have to pay for some sort of setup or activation fee when you sign up for the service. Nowadays, this fee is not as common.

Activation and other service fees may be waived when you sign up for an annual account or premium account. In addition, you can sometimes convince someone to waive these fees by signing up over the phone rather than online. Let the customer service rep know that you're willing to sign today if he or she can drop some of the upfront fees. It never hurts to ask!

When deciding how much you can afford to pay (and the way you want to pay for it), determine what you need. Start by considering how many products you want to sell and the amount of disk space you may need. After that, choose the features that are most important to you.

You can also break down the numbers another way. Look at how many products you have to sell on a monthly basis to cover the cost of the storefront. For example, suppose you choose a mid-level plan that costs $149 per month, includes an extensive list of features, and supports as many as 10,000 products. You have only 75 products, and your average amount of profit for each one is around $9. That means you have to sell at least 17 products per month just to cover the cost of your storefront.

On the flip side, you might choose an entry-level plan that some providers offer to help get you started. These plans often support less than 25 products and have fewer features, but may cost only $5 to $10 per month. Using the same profit margins, you now have to sell only three products each month to cover your storefront costs.

So, if you're just starting out in e-commerce and don't have any built-in traffic, the lower fee means fewer monetary risks. Choosing the right storefront solution (and the appropriate plan) is often a matter of figuring out what's most important to you.

Shopping for Storefronts

After you know which features you want and figure out what you want to pay, you're ready to find a storefront solution. Here are some possibilities to look into:

✦ **Quick Shopping Cart:** You might not know it from its name, but Quick Shopping Cart is a complete storefront solution from GoDaddy. What makes this choice popular is its price. The economy plan is only $9.99 per month, including hosting, but it supports only 20 products. The next level supports 100 products and costs $29.99. For $49.99, you receive unlimited product support and 50 GB of disk space. There are no setup fees, and you get ad credits (or dollars) to spend on Google AdWords, Facebook, and others. All plans include mobile-optimized storefronts. The Quick Shopping Cart is a good deal for the price, but it doesn't have as many features as other solutions and the number of photos you can use per product is limited. Get the full scoop by visiting www.godaddy.com.

✦ **nsCommerceSpace:** Offered by Network Solutions, this is another e-commerce solution with an appealing price range from a recognized hosted provider. The base-level plan starts at $7.95 per month for 20 products, and the mid-tier plan costs $9.95 per month for 300 products. Even the premium plan is only $19.95 per month for up to 100,000 products. That's super inexpensive! Each level has setup fees. This solution includes mobile-ready templates, but some advanced features, such as bulk import and export and QuickBooks integration, are available only with the most expensive solution option. To find out more, visit www.networksolutions.com/e-commerce.

✦ **Volusion:** This storefront offers five pricing plans, ranging from $15 per month for as many as 100 products to $135 per month for unlimited products. All prices include hosting, unlimited storage, and no transaction fees. All plans also include mobile commerce and social media tools. You can check out this solution and the advanced features offered across price plans at www.volusion.com.

✦ **Shopify:** Launched in 2006, Shopify already serves more than 90,000 e-commerce sites. Shopify has over 100 design templates and include three primary pricing plans ranging from $29 to $179 per month. Each plan supports an unlimited number of products and provides 24/7 live support and mobile commerce functionality. Another interesting feature is Shopify POS, an Apple iPad point-of-sale system for your retail location. The list of features is too long to include here, but rest assured that plenty of impressive functionality and lots of marketing tools are included. The exception to this rule is a starter plan that costs $14 per month and supports only 25 products. To see all the options offered by this storefront solution, visit `www.shopify.com`.

✦ **BigCommerce:** BigCommerce has become an industry leader, gaining kudos for being a simple, powerful solution with an impressive list of features for the money. Plans range from $34.95 to $199.95 per month and support an unlimited number of products and unlimited storage and bandwidth. The list of features that apply across plans is impressive, including social media tools, real-time shipping quotes, built-in blog and SEO, over 60 payment options, and coupon and discount functions. The advanced plans do not charge transaction fees, include cart abandonment features, and provide a higher level of support. See the full list of features and pricing at `www.bigcommerce.com`.

✦ **WordPress e-commerce plugin:** If you use WordPress, the free blog software, for your site, you may also choose to use a plugin for your e-commerce solution, such as WooCommerce, WP e-Commerce, MarketPress, and Aptiva. Did we mention these are often free (or super cheap)? The downside of using a WordPress plugin is that it may have fewer features and payment gateway options than the non-free solutions and may require more work on your part for setup or customization (with limited, if any, technical support available). The best way to explore your options for a plugin solution is to do a search for *ecommerce* in the WordPress Plugin Directory at `http://wordpress.org/extend/plugins/`.

Chapter 2: Mastering the Amazon

In This Chapter

✔ **Listing items for sale in the Amazon Marketplace**

✔ **Going pro with a Pro Merchant seller's account**

✔ **Getting on board other Amazon opportunities**

It may be a jungle out there, but Amazon has strategically cleared a path for the willing online entrepreneur. That wasn't always the case. You might recall the days when Amazon was launched and the idea of putting an entire bookstore online to make a (substantial) profit garnered its fair share of skepticism. The only thing about the site that got any attention back then was the big, wooden door that the company's founder, Jeff Bezos, used as a desk! Well, a few things have changed.

Consider that Amazon earned around $74.5 billion in sales in 2013. That's not too shabby for a guy who didn't have a "real" desk. What's more exciting is that the site has continued to create business opportunities for people like you by selling products on Amazon. Having a slice of that billion-dollar pie probably sounds good!

Amazon has established multiple selling strategies for you to use: Marketplace, Pro Merchant, WebStore, and aStore, to name a few. In this chapter, we show you how to choose a sales model and follow the instructions that Amazon has carefully laid out for you.

Joining the Marketplace

Selling in the Amazon Marketplace as an individual seller is by far the quickest way to make some cash on Amazon. Considering its fee structure and setup, the Marketplace is a basic selling opportunity that will suit you if you want to sell only a few items. This clear-cut process has no start-up costs, which is an ideal way to get your feet wet if you haven't sold on Amazon previously.

After you register in the Marketplace, you can post a new or used item for sale. Your item is then listed alongside the same brand-new product sold on Amazon. Figure 2-1 shows an example of how used items appear on the same page as the new version of that item.

Figure 2-1:
Marketplace
items show
up on
Amazon's
product
pages.

Marketplace items

Customers can choose to buy the item from Amazon or you (or someone else). When a customer decides to purchase from you, the customer adds the product to his or her shopping cart and pays for it on Amazon (like a normal purchase). Amazon then sends you (the seller) the customer's order information and you're responsible for shipping the product. Your Amazon seller's account is credited for the purchase amount, and then you receive a direct deposit from Amazon for the items that sold. (Although total amounts show up in your account immediately, deposits are distributed every 14 days.) That's it!

Amazon doesn't charge you any money to list an item. But you pay a fee when the item sells. Here's a list of the fees that Amazon deducts from your sales price:

✦ **Referral fees:** Amazon bases referral fee (or commission) costs on the category in which your item is listed. The commission percentages break down like this:

  • *Automotive parts and accessories:* 12 percent

  • *Cameras and photos:* 8 percent

  • *Unlocked cell phones:* 8 percent

  • *Computers:* 6 percent

- *Consumer electronics* (such as printers, video game consoles, and scanners): 8 percent

- *Musical instruments:* 15 percent

- *Tools and hardware:* 12 percent

- *Watches*: 15 percent

- *Electronic accessories, entertainment or sports collectibles, and major appliances*: A sliding scale depending on the item price, starting at 15–20 percent and going down to 6–8 percent for higher priced merchandise

  - *Most other product lines:* 15 percent

✦ **Transaction fee:** Amazon charges a flat fee of 99 cents for each item sold. (This fee is waived for Pro Merchants.)

✦ **Variable closing fee:** This fee is the Amazon equivalent of a handling charge. The amount varies based on the shipping method and product category. For media items (books, music, video, DVDs, computer games, and software), the closing fee is $1.35 for standard or expedited shipping, or $0.80 for a Fulfilled by Amazon (FBA) order. (We explain FBA later in this section.) For other categories, the closing fee is $0.45 plus $0.05 per pound for standard shipping, or $0.65 plus $0.05 per pound for expedited shipping.

The advantage of shopping in the Marketplace is obvious for your customers: They receive the same product (used or new) at a discounted price. For you, the benefit is the ease of the selling process.

To get started with the Marketplace, first decide whether you want to start with a low volume (as an individual seller) or a high volume (as a Pro Merchant). If you want to be a Pro Merchant, see the next section for more information. Individual sellers should follow these steps:

1. **Go to Amazon at** www.amazon.com.

2. **Scroll down to the bottom of the home page and click the Sell on Amazon link, which is under the Make Money with Us header in the middle.**

   An overview page appears that briefly describes the options you can use when selling on Amazon (see Figure 2-2).

3. **Click the Sell as an Individual button.**

4. **Log in to your Amazon account.**

   If you don't have an account, click the I Do Not Have an Amazon.com Password button and follow the instructions for creating one. You will also have to agree to Amazon's terms and conditions.

   The Amazon Seller Central overview page appears, as shown in Figure 2-3.

Book VIII Chapter 2

Mastering the Amazon

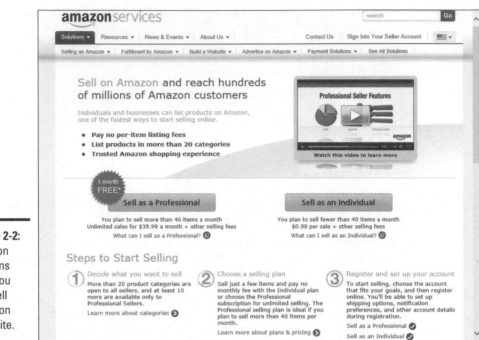

Figure 2-2:
Amazon explains how you can sell items on their site.

Figure 2-3:
Manage your sales at Amazon Seller Central.

5. **Roll your cursor over the Inventory link at the top of the screen, and then click the Add a Product link.**

   You can sell only products that Amazon sells. The screen shown in Figure 2-4 appears.

Figure 2-4: Amazon asks you to search for the items you want to sell.

6. **Search for the product you want to sell by entering one of the following in the Find it on Amazon text box:**

   • *Title or keyword:* Enter the title of your product or one or more keywords describing it.

   • *ISBN, UPC, or ASIN:* Enter an identifying code. You can find the International Standard Book Number (ISBN) or Universal Product Code (UPC) on the back of your product. Look for the Amazon Standard Identification Number (ASIN) on the item's product information page (see Figure 2-5).

7. **Click the Search button.**

   A results page appears that lists Amazon products that contain the title or search term you used.

8. **Identify the correct product in the list and then click the Sell Yours button to the right of the product.**

9. **Double-check to ensure that you have the right product.**

   Amazon requires that you sell the exact match to the product being sold on its website. For example, you should make sure to match items by the correct edition (for a book) or color (for a product).

10. **In the Condition drop-down list, select your item's condition.**

    Your choices include terms such as New; Used — Like New; Used — Very Good.

11. **In the Condition Note text box, enter a few comments about the condition of your product.**

    You can enter as many as 2,000 characters. Use this opportunity to further describe your product, as shown in Figure 2-6. The additional information can increase sales.

Book VIII
Chapter 2

Mastering the Amazon

Figure 2-5:
Find the
ISBN, UPC,
or ASIN
for your
product.

Figure 2-6:
Describe
your item's
condition.

12. **In the Your Price box, enter the price for your item.**

    For comparison, Amazon shows you its current price and other Marketplace prices for this item in the Competing Marketplace Offers section of the Product Summary box, at the top right of the page (refer to Figure 2-6). You can also click the Match Low Price button, above the Your Price box, and Amazon will automatically fill in the lowest price.

13. **Scroll down the page, and enter in the Quantity box the quantity of the item you're selling, as shown in Figure 2-7.**

14. **In the Start Selling Date box, enter the date you want to start selling your product (or leave this box blank if you want to start right away).**

15. **(Optional) Complete the information in the Country of Publication, Import Designation, or Country as Labeled boxes.**

16. **Select the check box next to each shipping method you want to offer.**

    The standard shipping method is already selected because it is required. The correct amount is credited to your account to cover the shipping method that your customer chooses.

17. **Scroll to the bottom of the page, and click Save and Finish.**

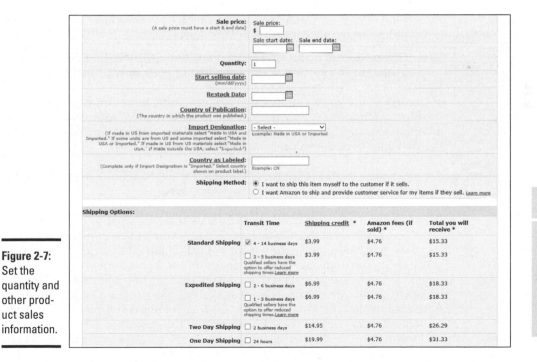

Figure 2-7: Set the quantity and other product sales information.

18. Enter your e-mail address and password in the appropriate boxes to register to accept payments from Amazon.

You have to provide this information only once. If you already registered with Amazon to accept payments, skip to the next step.

If you don't have an account, click the I Do Not Have an Amazon.com Password button and follow the instructions for creating one.

19. Follow the prompts for registration.

You have to supply a valid credit card number, a U.S. bank account number, a U.S. phone number where Amazon can reach you directly, and your billing address.

If you're already an Amazon customer, your customer account information is automatically used for the registration process, speeding up the process significantly. But you always have the option to change or update your information.

To complete the registration process, you must be available to receive a verification phone call from Amazon. You enter the phone number where you can be reached, and then you respond to the automated prompts when called. Completing the verification process takes about 30 seconds.

When the registration process is complete, you return to the final page to finish posting your listing in the Marketplace.

20. If you want to make changes to your listing, click the Edit Details button in the section of the page listing your new product.

Amazon sends you a confirmation of your listing to your designated e-mail address. Then you simply wait for the item to be sold. After 60 days, if the item doesn't sell, Amazon removes it from your listings. You don't pay any fees if your item doesn't sell.

If you have a Pro Merchant account (see the next section), you can leave the listing on Amazon until you choose to remove it.

If you have a large volume of similar items that you want to sell on Amazon, but you don't have the fulfillment capabilities to handle shipping your orders, you can request enrollment in the Fulfillment by Amazon program. You ship your items to Amazon, they store the items in their warehouse, and they ship the item directly to the customer when he or she orders that item from you. One of the biggest appeals of this program is that products that are fulfilled by Amazon qualify for free standard shipping (if the order is $35 or more) or free two-day shipping (if the customer subscribes to the Amazon Prime program). In addition, Amazon handles all customer service and return issues regarding these orders.

You can learn more by going to the Amazon Fulfillment Services home page at www.amazonservices.com/content/fulfillment-by-amazon.htm.

Manuals and videos in the Resources and Tutorials drop-down option explain the process and how to register.

Achieving Pro Merchant Status

Realizing that you might want to increase your sales potential by using Amazon, the site established the Pro Merchant account. You're a primary candidate for this type of account if you sell more than 40 orders per month. As a Pro Merchant, you're still selling in the Marketplace: The way your listings look, the options for where the listings appear, and the way you post your items for sale are the same (see the preceding section "Joining the Marketplace," for details about selling in the Marketplace).

When you become a Pro Merchant seller, you gain a few definite advantages:

✦ **Reduced fees:** The 99-cent transaction fee is automatically waived for all Pro Merchant accounts. All other commissions and fees remain, however.

✦ **Bulk listing capabilities:** Designed for sellers of large inventory, the Pro Merchant account provides tools that make it easier to load and manage multiple listings. Included among the tools are

- *Inventory Loader:* Modify, delete, and upload thousands of products at one time.

- *Book Loader:* Match and upload books considered to have pre-ISBNs. Rare, collectible, or out-of-print books are in this category.

✦ **Continuous listings:** Your listings never expire. You keep them posted until an item sells or you decide to remove them.

✦ **Management functions:** You gain access to various reports that show the status of your account at any given time. These reports allow you to view all account activity (including items that shipped) during the past 15, 30, or 60 days.

✦ **Fraud protection:** Amazon offers a payment fraud protection program to help eliminate fraudulent products. It also offers an A-to-Z Guarantee program that protects both the customers and you, in case something goes wrong with an order.

Unlike your basic Marketplace listing, opening a full account comes at a price. Amazon charges $39.99 per month for a Pro Merchant account (although it sometimes offers limited-time-only discounts for the first few months of service). Only Pro Merchants are allowed to sell in the beauty products, grocery and gourmet food, and health and personal care categories. Additionally, several categories require special approval from Amazon before you can begin selling. These categories include automotive parts, cellphones and accessories, clothing and accessories, jewelry, motorcycles, ATV and protective gear, shoes, and watches. If you're selling in the toys and games category, note that

Amazon doesn't accept new sellers in that category during the holiday season, which usually starts in late October and runs through early January.

Opening a Pro Merchant account can truly pay off. You have access to several types of inventory reports, including

✦ **Open Listings:** In this report, you view all items that are available for purchase, including the items you marked as Coming Soon. You can also make changes to this report, using an Excel file, and then reload your updated listings.

✦ **Open Listings Lite:** Sometimes, you don't need to see all the information — only a few key points. This report allows you to make updates to your listings quickly and then reload the changes. The Lite report shows you the *seller SKU number* (a unique number you use to identify a product you sell), quantity, price, and product ID.

✦ **Open Listings Liter:** The Open Listing Liter is scaled down even further than the Open Listing Lite report. One quick glance at this report provides you with access to only the seller SKU number and quantity.

✦ **Order Fulfillment:** Create a quick report of all products that have been purchased. You also see the buyer information (such as shipping address) so that you can send out the orders in a timely fashion.

✦ **Sold Listings:** You see an extensive report of all your product listings that have sold, even if payment is still outstanding.

✦ **Cancelled Listings:** Just as it sounds, this report shows which items are no longer "in the hopper" because Amazon has cancelled them. Not included are any items that may be sold out, that the Inventory Loader purged, or that you have nixed.

To sign up for a Pro Merchant account, click the Sell as a Professional button on the Sell on Amazon page (refer to Figure 2-2).

Although Amazon handles the payment process between you and your customer, you're responsible for any returns or refunds. If a seller requests a refund, he or she has to ship the item back to you, and you absorb the cost of shipping. All refunds can be handled directly from your Amazon merchant seller account.

Taking Advantage of Other Selling Opportunities with Amazon WebStores

Amazon has cleverly created several opportunities to make money using its site, products, and technologies. Truly, there's an opportunity for just about everyone. In addition to those we discuss previously in this chapter, Amazon has two other programs, or web stores.

The first, aStore, is the simplest way to get started. You don't even need your own inventory to sell using this method. Instead, Amazon allows you to examine its entire inventory of products and select which ones you want to sell. You sell them from a storefront that Amazon provides to you, at no charge. You can add the storefront to a website you already own or create a unique domain name (a *URL*) especially for your new web store. Did we mention that it's free?

What's the catch? Each time a product is sold, you earn only a small commission. In other words, you probably won't get rich serving as the Amazon middleman, but you can earn a few extra bucks.

Because the site has such an extensive selection of products, you can also use this option as a no-cost method of testing different types of products and how they might sell on your website, before investing in similar types of inventory. The aStore is also a useful quick-start way to start selling products on a new site or on a blog for an extra revenue source.

Figure 2-8 shows an example of an aStore that TypePad blog software added to help sell books by authors who blog on the TypePad platform. To start creating this basic web store and selecting products, go to `https://affiliate-program.amazon.com/gp/associates/astore/main.html`.

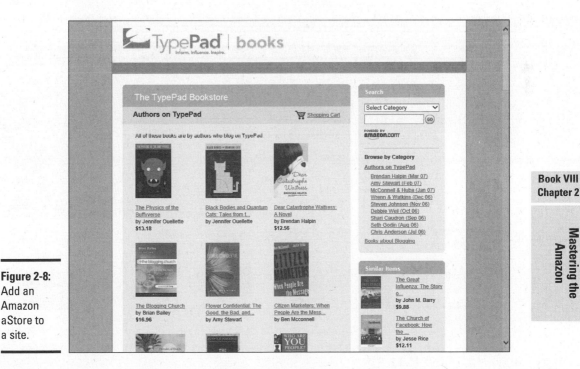

Figure 2-8: Add an Amazon aStore to a site.

Another selling opportunity comes in the form of the Amazon WebStore. This branded e-commerce store is complete with everything you need to sell online. It uses the same back-end platforms that power the Amazon site. In addition to selling your own products, you can extend your offerings and place Amazon merchandise for sale in your WebStore. Pricing starts at $24.99 per month, and Amazon charges a 0.7 to 2 percent commission on every item that's sold, plus a payment-processing fee. However, unlike selling in the MarketPlace, you face no setup or listing fees.

Basically, WebStore is an alternative to other storefront-selling solutions, but it comes with the name recognition of Amazon and allows you to piggy-back not only on its technologies but also on its promotional and marketing strength. Figure 2-9 shows how Samsonite (shop.samsonite.com) uses a WebStore for its e-commerce site. You can sign up by going to http://webstore.amazon.com.

If you're looking for the most up-to-date information and advice on how to sell on Amazon, check out Amazon's Seller Forums discussion boards by going to www.amazonsellercommunity.com.

Figure 2-9: Use a WebStore to sell online.

Chapter 3: Let's Hear It for Yahoo!

In This Chapter

✔ Setting up a Yahoo! e-commerce store

✔ Adding products to your store catalog

✔ Designing your store web pages

✔ Comparing package solutions

✔ Calculating the fees for using Yahoo! Merchant Solutions

✔ Using marketing systems to bring in more customers

✔ Evaluating the success of your Yahoo! store

*O*ne big advantage of using Yahoo! Small Business is how it enables you to easily create your own store. Yahoo! walks you through the steps necessary to create, design, fill, and maintain your own store. Over the years, smaller companies have folded or changed or were acquired by other companies, so customers of these companies aren't sure what to expect. With Yahoo!, though, you know that your website will be fully functional and available because Yahoo! professionals provide the technical expertise to keep all their websites running smoothly.

In this chapter, we talk about the many features that Yahoo! stores offer you, the basic platform of the small-business solution, and how you perform basic navigation and item creation. We cover the different packages and describe how Yahoo! makes its money with this service. Finally, you discover how you can make more money with your Yahoo! store through marketing, customer relationships, and data analysis.

We can't cover all you need to know about starting a Yahoo! business. To delve into Yahoo! web stores even more, check out *Web Stores Do-It-Yourself For Dummies*, by Joel Elad.

Why Open a Yahoo! Store?

Although you can order different levels of solutions with Yahoo!, a powerful base platform comes with every solution. Here are ten functions that every business can enjoy with Yahoo! Merchant Solutions:

✦ **Built-in shopping cart:** You can put an unlimited amount of products into your Yahoo! store. Its shopping-cart software presents those items to your customers and lets them add them to, or delete them from, their own shopping baskets. Then the software interfaces with shipping companies and tax tables to show customers their costs when they check out.

✦ **Customizable sales reports:** Yahoo! provides a set of customizable reports so that you can see what's selling, what's being clicked, and what's being searched. You even see which websites send you the most traffic and which web pages on your site are the most viewed.

✦ **Inventory tracking and alerts:** If you don't want to sell out of your hottest product or you need an e-mail alert when your available inventory gets too low, Yahoo! has you covered. It manages your inventory and automatically e-mails you if your inventory falls below a predetermined quantity.

✦ **Unlimited space and bandwidth:** If you have large image files or audio or video, you can relax. You get an unlimited amount of storage with each account and an unlimited amount of bandwidth to send those massive files each time a customer comes a-knockin'.

✦ **Your own subdomains:** Maybe you want to create distinctive names for parts of your website or add subdomains so that you can have `shop.`*yourwebsite*`.com`, `ebay.`*yourwebsite*`.com`, or even `customer.`*yourwebsite*`.com`. You get as many as 500 subdomains per account, so choose wisely to create a meaningful and intuitive set of subdomains that your customers (and search engines) will recognize.

✦ **As many as 1,000 business e-mail accounts:** Yahoo! gives you the power to create as many as 1,000 unique business e-mail accounts. Each of these accounts comes with an unlimited amount of storage. Now whoever needs a business e-mail from you — your employees, temporary employees, family members, vendors, suppliers, and more — can get it.

✦ **Secure technology:** With Yahoo!, your customers can enter information safely because you can create secure web pages by way of Secure Sockets Layer (SSL) technology that encrypts sensitive data (such as credit card numbers) when customers transmit that info to you.

✦ **Credit card verification tools:** If you're worried about credit card fraud, use the Yahoo! free Risk Tools to help verify whether the card is real or stolen — before you send your customer's credit card number to be processed.

✦ **Norton AntiVirus and SpamGuard screening:** To keep your files and e-mail as clean as possible, Yahoo! uses Norton AntiVirus and SpamGuard software to scan and destroy viruses, spam, pop-up ads, and other nasty annoyances of doing business on the Internet.

✦ **Automatic backups of your website:** Yahoo! takes a snapshot of your website at regular intervals and lets you go back and forth between those versions. If you accidentally lose data, you can restore the last version quickly. Yahoo! makes the backups without even asking or reminding you.

Setting Up Shop

When you're ready to set up a Yahoo! store, follow these steps:

1. **Go to the Yahoo! Small Business home page (`http://smallbusiness.yahoo.com`), and click Sell Online.**

   You can click Sell Online in the top navigation bar or in the bottom middle area, as shown in Figure 3-1.

   The Yahoo! Merchant Solutions page displays the three packages that Yahoo! offers: the Starter, Standard, and Professional plans. (The Standard and Professional plans are recommended for established e-commerce or offline businesses.) We discuss the prices and benefits of these packages later in this chapter, in the "Selecting a Yahoo! Plan" section.

   REMEMBER Yahoo! Small Business offers more packages than just its Merchant Solutions. If you want to build a regular website, buy a domain name, or sign up for online marketing services, you can do so at Yahoo! Small Business. Find out more at `http://smallbusiness.yahoo.com`.

Click here

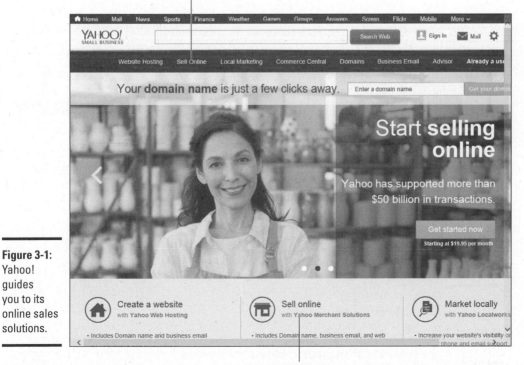

Figure 3-1: Yahoo! guides you to its online sales solutions.

Or click here

2. **Click the Sign Up button under the plan header that you want.**

3. **Enter a domain name for your Yahoo! store (see Figure 3-2).**

   If your first choice is taken, Yahoo! offers you suggestions of available domain names similar to your request. When you find an available domain, Yahoo! will prompt you with options for your order, such as private domain registration.

   If you already have a domain name, simply click the appropriate link under Already Have a Domain? section.

   Based on the promotion that Yahoo! is running, you may be prompted to pay for a full year of hosting. If you don't want to prepay for a full year, select the Order Summary box (to the right in Figure 3-2) to see your initial bill, and then click the Change link next to the plan name to change the billing to one month instead of one year.

4. **Log in to Yahoo! with your Yahoo! ID.**

   If you're new to Yahoo! or want to create a separate ID for your business, create a Yahoo! ID by clicking the Sign Up link. You see the Yahoo! one-page sign-up form. Enter your personal identification, such as name, birthday, e-mail address, gender, and phone number. Choose a user ID and password.

Figure 3-2:
Enter the domain name.

5. **In the Choose Payment Method section, enter your billing information.**

   You have to enter a credit card number to leave on file for Yahoo! to bill you monthly for your Merchant Solutions package. If you're new to Yahoo!, you need to verify your billing address for the card.

6. **Review your options (see Figure 3-3), agree to the terms of service, and select a category from the drop-down list.**

   The list appears under the question "Which category best describes your company's line of business?"

7. **To finalize your order, scroll down to click the Place Order button.**

   You need to select the check box to agree to Yahoo!'s terms of service and select your category.

Figure 3-3: Specify your options.

Managing Your Yahoo! Services

After you sign up with Yahoo! Merchant Solutions, you can control all aspects of your account. Go to http://smallbusiness.yahoo.com and sign in with your Yahoo! ID to open your account home page (see Figure 3-4).

Figure 3-4:
Access
all your
account
controls
from one
screen.

From the home page, you have access to the four main parts of your account:

✦ **Store control panel:** Use this main screen to build, maintain, and update your store.

✦ **Web Hosting control panel:** Find out about your web-hosting space and how much room you still have in your account. You can download the SiteBuilder tool from this link (see the later section "Opening Your Store for Business" for more information) or create a blog on your website.

✦ **Domain control panel:** You can handle all aspects of owning a custom domain name for your online business. Update your domain registration, add more unique URLs to your overall business, and organize the sections of your website to appear as subdomains on your site.

✦ **Email control panel:** You can manage all your business e-mail accounts in this area. Create an e-mail account, see how much space all your e-mail accounts are occupying, and set up a special e-mail account (a *catchall*) to receive mail that has been improperly addressed to someone at your business.

As your e-mail addresses are increasingly circulated, you run the risk that those accounts are being added to spam lists. The catchall can result in an overflowing account of spam; if that occurs, don't assign the catchall to any account.

Opening Your Yahoo! Store for Business

For your customers, your home page is their central hub. For Yahoo! Merchant Solutions, that launching pad is the Store Control Panel page. When you log in to your account the first time and click the Store Control Panel link, the Open For Business control panel page appears (see Figure 3-5) to walk you through the five main steps of starting your store:

✦ Designing your site

✦ Adding products

✦ Determining payment methods

✦ Setting up tax rates

✦ Setting up shipping

At any time, you can click the Store Manager link to go to your main hub. When you click the link, your main Store Manager page appears (see Figure 3-6), from which you can control almost every facet of managing your store after you've built it.

Figure 3-5: Get your store ready to open up for business!

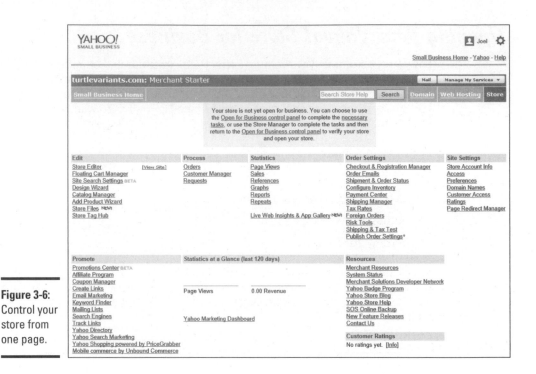

Figure 3-6:
Control your
store from
one page.

Constructing your catalog

Before we talk about designing your site, we want to focus on the core element of any vibrant e-commerce store, your catalog. What's a store without products? Yahoo! has the central program Catalog Manager, which lets you enter your products for sale and also tracks the inventory level as people place orders. You can update your inventory at any time, organize your inventory by different product tables, and even upload your entire product catalog at one time.

When you want to add a product to your database, follow these steps:

1. **From the Store Manager page, click the Catalog Manager link.**

   The main Catalog Manager page is displayed. If you use the Store Editor to choose a predefined template, Yahoo! will open an Add Products Wizard instead of the Catalog Manager page to assist you in adding products to your inventory.

2. **If the Products tab isn't selected, click it and then click the Manage Your Items link to add a new product.**

   If you already have a file (such as an Excel spreadsheet) that has your catalog inventory ready to go, you can upload the entire file and create your catalog in one step. Click the Upload Items link and then click the Upload button to send the file directly to your catalog database. Make sure that the file matches the Default table in your Store definition. See the tutorial at `http://ep.yimg.com/ty/cdn/vw/catalogtutorial.html` for more information.

The Default table of items that you defined in your store appears.

3. **Click the Add button.**

The one-page Add Item form appears.

4. **Complete these fields:**

   - *ID:* For this unique ID identifier, enter letters or numbers or both.

   - *Name:* Enter the name that you want your customers to see as the name of your product.

   - *Code:* This visible code identifies your product, like a UPC code.

   - *Price:* Every item must have a numeric price.

   - *Sale-price:* When you use this field, the sale price overrides the regular price and your customers see both prices, with a line through the regular price and the sales price highlighted.

   - *Orderable:* Set this option to Yes if you want customers to be able to order the product.

   - *Ship-weight:* Put the numeric weight of your item in this field. You can define the unit of measurement in your store settings.

   - *Taxable:* Set this option to Yes if you collect sales tax on this product.

5. **Enter the details of your product:**

   - *Image:* Specify the path where the digital image of your product is stored on your computer and upload it to your store.

   - *Options:* If you offer the same product in different sizes or colors or other options, don't create individual entries for each option. You simply enter your options, one line at a time, as a string of words with the option name and then the different options, like this:

     Size Small Medium Large

     Color Red Blue White Black

      Do not use any internal punctuation, such as a comma, between the options. Yahoo! is looking for a space between each option.

   - *Headline:* If you don't want customers to see the name of your product, you can add a headline here that replaces the name.

   - *Caption:* Enter all details in this field (similar to an item description).

   - *Abstract:* Think of the *abstract* as your summary, or a shorter version of the caption that your customers see when browsing your store.

- *Icon:* Specify and upload a thumbnail (picture file) to use when linking from category pages to your product page. This icon should be in GIF or JPG format only.

- *Inset:* (Optional) Specify a second thumbnail if you want.

- *Label:* Highlight a special feature of this item, such as a new arrival or a sale item.

- *Download:* If you're selling a downloadable product, such as an e-book or a music file, upload the file to your store so that Yahoo! can send it to your customers when they order it from your store.

- *Condition*: From the drop-down list, choose whether the condition of your item is New, Like New, Very Good, Acceptable, Used, or Refurbished.

- *Keywords*: You can define keywords to be associated with your item for search capabilities. These keywords won't be displayed to your shoppers on the product page.

- *Description:* Write a description for your product that you want customers to see when they're looking at your item on your store page.

6. **Click Save to store the item.**

   If you enter multiple items one at a time, you can click the Save and Add Another button instead to repeat the process.

7. **Repeat Steps 3–6 for any additional products.**

Opening the doors

As mentioned, Yahoo! will prompt you with their five-point checklist for building your store. You must complete all five steps before your store is live and open for business. Before you dive into all the steps, we recommend that you research and plan your store first. See what you like and dislike on other websites and come up with a plan for your website. See Book III, Chapter 2 for more information on developing a website design.

When you're ready to open your store for business, Yahoo! guides you through the following checklist:

1. Design your store. You need to construct the web pages that display your products. Building the actual store requires some design work, and Yahoo! provides three ways of building the pages you need:

   - *Store Editor:* Yahoo! has hundreds of special templates you can use to build all the necessary pages of your website. From the Store Manager page, click the Store Editor link; then choose from the pre-designed templates and assign the locations and attributes of your products to the page.

- *SiteBuilder:* You can download SiteBuilder software from Yahoo! to your computer and then use drag-and-drop technology to build your website. The SiteBuilder Store Products Wizard walks you through the process of creating individual product pages, multiproduct pages, and the overall category pages to hold your products. Use this software to create your thumbnail images and navigation bars, and then publish your work to your website with a few clicks.

- *Dreamweaver Extension:* If you or your professional web designer want to use advanced web design software such as Adobe Dreamweaver, download and use the special Dreamweaver extension. This plugin allows you to create store tags that you insert in your pages using Dreamweaver; those tags reference your catalog so that the page is automatically filled in with matching products whenever a customer views your Dreamweaver-built web pages.

2. Add products. We cover adding products to your catalog in the previous section, "Constructing your catalog."

3. Set up payment methods. You need to decide how you want to handle payment processing for your store. You can use an online payment-processing service (such as PayPal) or consult your bank to open a traditional merchant account to accept credit cards. You can find more about payment processing in Book IV, Chapter 4.

4. Set up tax rates. In today's age of Internet sales, you need to be aware of tax-collection policies. They vary from state to state, and new legislation is being considered as this book goes to press. Currently, in most states, you need to collect sales tax from customers who live in the same state as your business. And in a growing number of cases, you may need to collect sales tax from customers outside your business state. Consult your local Chamber of Commerce, accountant, or state government's business office for specific information. At a minimum, you need to set up the tax rate for your local business area.

5. Set up shipping rules. You need to define shipping methods and rates for your store. You can choose from vendors such as USPS, UPS, and FedEx. If you define shipping weights for each product in your store, Yahoo! can calculate shipping rates for each customer based on the weight of the items in the customer's shopping cart. You can also set flat shipping rates independent of the number or weight of items in the customer's shopping cart.

When you have gone through all five steps, click the Publish Your Order Settings link to set up your checkout form and run through a test order. The reason you have to publish your changes in Yahoo! is simple: When you're working on your store, customers don't see the changes until you're ready to publish them, whether you've updated the catalog, the store design, or the order settings. After you go through a test order, your store will be live and open for business.

Selecting a Yahoo! Plan

Yahoo! offers different levels of its Merchant Solutions service to coincide with the size and scope of your business. As your company grows, your Yahoo! plan can grow with it as you move up the scale to a more robust set of services.

With other services, you have to choose your features *à la carte* by cobbling together a plan. Yahoo! gives all its merchants a strong foundation, offering enhancements for its larger clients to fulfill the needs of a growing customer base. Yahoo! has years of experience in offering different tools — such as e-mail, web hosting, and marketing support — and those refined tools help make these packages that much more accessible.

Starter package: Starting out

Don't let the name fool you — the Yahoo! Starter package isn't a stripped-down, bargain-basement tool that holds only a few products. This package provides a rich set of features and is an excellent jumping-on point for new e-commerce retailers.

With the Starter package, you get the ability to build your own store, host any number of products, and design your site by using Yahoo! tools. Some of the more advanced marketing and reporting techniques are reserved for more expensive packages, but most small businesses don't need them.

Standard package: Moving up

The medium Yahoo! solution is its Standard package, which contains all the basic features of the Starter package but also offers more advanced features that bigger e-commerce stores need to run their enterprises.

Some of the benefits you receive in the Standard package mean that you can

- Export orders to outside accounting and order-management software in real time
- Access APIs to allow for back-office integration with your own databases or applications
- Export orders to UPS WorldShip shipping software
- View real-time advanced reporting using Yahoo! Web Analytics
- Offer gift certificates for your website
- Feature special software to cross-sell your goods on your website

Professional package: Building on solid ground

As e-commerce websites grew, Yahoo! needed a solution for its biggest customers, especially for store owners whose stores grew past the magic million-dollar number in sales per year. Although rich functions are important to bigger websites, you should care mostly about *scalability* — the capability to grow your website's capability to match an increased amount of customers or demand. Therefore, Yahoo! created the Professional package for its Merchant Solutions.

The Professional package focuses on providing the right amount of capabilities to make sure that the customer's website brings in millions in sales just as smoothly as they were bringing in their first few orders.

Breaking Down the Fees

With Yahoo! Small Business, you incur fees the moment you sign up and decide to use the system. Whereas some companies charge a one-time fee for creating an e-commerce site or provide free tools in exchange for ad placements or ownership, Yahoo! Small Business works on a subscription model. You pay every month that you use its solution. Your payment to Yahoo! consists of a few types of fees:

✦ **Setup fee:** Yahoo! charges a $50 setup fee regardless of the plan you select. Look for promotions in which this fee is waived. Check partner sites, such as PayPal, for special deals that waive the setup fee and deduct 25–70 percent from the regular price of your first 12 months of service.

✦ **Monthly fee:** Yahoo! Small Business charges a fixed monthly subscription fee for using its solution. A 1-month or 12-month price is available, depending on how long you sign up for initially. The price varies by plans:

- *Starter:* $19.95 per month or $10.95 per month if you sign up for 12 months.

- *Standard:* $49.95 per month or $25.95 per month if you sign up for 12 months.

- *Professional:* $299.95 per month or $254.95 per month if you sign up for 12 months.

✦ **Transaction fee:** In exchange for using its rich features (such as the shopping cart and the order-checkout system), Yahoo! takes a transaction fee for every sale you make in your store. The transaction fee is a percentage of your sales, depending on the package that you select. As your sales go up, the percentage goes down:

- *Starter:* 1.5 percent

- *Standard:* 1.0 percent

- *Professional:* 0.75 percent

**Book VIII
Chapter 3**

Let's Hear It for Yahoo!

This fee alone can determine your package level. For example, if you're getting at least $80,000 in sales per month, you should upgrade to the Professional package. The cost savings of the lower transaction fee easily pays for the extra monthly cost of the package.

Yahoo! provides a number of functions with its Merchant Solution packages, but the company charges extra for some added services. The following outlines some of these extras, which are mainly useful for larger or rapidly expanding businesses:

✦ Private domain registration (hide website ownership): 99¢ per month

✦ Campaigner e-mail marketing for your business: $10 per month

✦ Search engine advertising programs: Price varies by program

Growing with Your New Business Partner

After you use Yahoo! tools to build and run your website, you're probably ready to expand and grow your business further. That's why Yahoo! partnered with a number of companies that can help any online business grow, and those companies provide special discounts for Yahoo! Merchant Solutions members.

Marketing programs

You can spread the message of your business in many ways, through the Internet and in the physical world. Most people find that their biggest limitation is time because there are many more programs than there are hours in the day. That's where automation comes in. Yahoo! provides you with several ways to automate important merchandising features.

Shopping directory listings

If you're already using one of biggest search companies to manage your website, why not tap into its networks? Yahoo! has its huge Yahoo! Shopping powered by PriceGrabber, and you can pay to have your items listed as part of the Yahoo! Shopping network or Yahoo! Shopping and the PriceGrabber directory. Millions of unique shoppers use Yahoo! Shopping every month to find all sorts of products.

As a Yahoo! merchant, you qualify for a 20 percent discount when you submit your products to the Yahoo! Shopping directory. You then pay only when a potential customer clicks a product link of yours, whether that link showed up in its search results or after the customer read one of the Yahoo! Buyer Guides. Because Yahoo! can verify your status, it acknowledges your listings with a special Certified Merchant status and includes your items under the Buyer Protection Program for its customers. This way, the customers whom you reach are protected when they shop with you, which should encourage more spending. Yahoo! even bumps your text listings in its Buyer Guides to the top portion as a bonus, and lets you offer an express checkout so that these potential customers can shop quickly with you.

To sign up with Yahoo! Shopping, open your Store Manager page (refer to Figure 3-6) and click the Yahoo! Shopping Powered by PriceGrabber link in the Promote section.

Search engines

As we discuss in Book VI, Chapter 6, search engine advertising is important. You can position yourself at the right moment when a potential customer is looking for your products. Yahoo! offers you the chance to take out ads in its Sponsored Search program so that you can present targeted ads that link back to your Yahoo!-powered store.

On your Store Manager page, simply click the Yahoo! Search Marketing link in the Promote section. You have to sign up for Yahoo! Search Marketing, and choose a starting budget for your campaign. You then specify which key-words you want to bid on and how much money you're willing to spend per click. Yahoo! does the rest.

Why stop with paid search engine ads? Yahoo! automatically submits your website to its search engine, but at what speed? You can pay $299 to have your entire site submitted through the Yahoo! Directory Submit Service for inclusion so that people searching the extensive Yahoo! directory can see your website on the right category pages. Although Yahoo! doesn't guarantee absolute inclusion, it does guarantee speed: Yahoo! promises to review directory submissions within seven days.

If you sign up for Yahoo! Directory Submit Service, you must pay a recurring annual fee. Yahoo! then conducts a yearly review to see whether your site is in compliance with their minimum site criteria for inclusion in their directory.

Customer-relationship management

You can build connections with your customers in lots of ways. The power of an online business is that you can reach your customers directly, one by one, rather than rely on a network of distributors, middlemen, and retailers to connect products with customers.

Yahoo!'s Standard and Professional packages allow you to offer features on your store such as gift certificates. You can also provide automatic discounts to your customers, whether it's a one-time promotion, a reward for their first purchase, or an incentive to come back for a new order. Yahoo! keeps track of the logistics so that you can provide a simple code to your customers that acts as a gift certificate or discount coupon and also update your customer's orders when needed.

**Book VIII
Chapter 3**

Let's Hear It for Yahoo!

After you get to know your customers, you begin to see what else you can sell them. *Cross-selling* offers a complementary product that fits well with the original purchase. For example, when you see a customer buying a DVD recorder drive, you can reasonably assume that he or she needs blank DVDs to record on. Yahoo! has a special cross-selling engine that lets you decide which products are offered to your customers when they choose any product in your store.

This feature is available only with the Standard and Professional Merchant Solutions packages.

You simply click the Cross-Sell feature from your Store Manager page (under the Promote header). You then specify rules that display products that complement what a shopper is buying. For example, you can set a rule that your batteries should be displayed every time someone orders a digital camera.

Report results

You must think that we love reports, the way we talk about them repeatedly in this book. We are fans of reports for one basic reason: You don't know where you can go if you don't understand where you've been. Yahoo! offers a number of sales reports to help you track what's succeeding and what isn't, so pay attention to these reports and make smart decisions about how to increase your business.

Sales reports

The lifeblood of any online company is its orders. Your Store Manager provides easy-to-find statistics in the middle of its offerings. You can click the Sales link to display a chart of the orders you've received and the items that have sold. You can click the Reports link to see preformatted summaries of customers, orders, page views, and income from your store by the month, week, or day. You can even export that data to Excel if you want to do further number crunching.

If you're interested in doing your own data analysis with Excel, check out *Excel Data Analysis For Dummies*, 2nd Edition, by Stephen Nelson (Wiley Publishing).

After you see your customers' orders, you can then see how they found you in the first place. Click the References link to see a report of all visits your website has received. For each visit, you see the *referring URL,* which is the web address your customer was viewing before coming to your website. Yahoo! even ties together the orders that came from these links so that you can see the revenue per visit. This information gives you an idea of how valuable a new customer can be — so that you know how much to spend to get that new customer to return.

TIP

If the referral URL is from a search engine, pay attention to the URL closely. You see the exact search terms that the visitor typed in the search engine to find you. Knowing these words should definitely influence your search engine marketing campaigns.

One report that you don't see often on e-commerce platforms is the repeat customer report. The Yahoo! Repeat report tracks repeat customers, showing you how often those repeat customers come back to you and the items they ordered. After you know your core set of repeating customers, you can cater to them more effectively and increase sales through them. When you watch your repeat customers' orders, calculate their value to your business by watching the trends of which items move the best, what your active customers are buying daily, and the key ingredients of how recently they spent, how frequently they spend, and how much they spend.

Path reports

Your sales reports give you a useful picture of how your website is doing overall. Your next level of reports should tell you about the individual customer so that you can see what to update to appeal more to that specific sale. Therefore, Yahoo! gives its bigger merchants (Standard and Professional packages) the ability to watch customers and see how those customers use your site.

Imagine if you could follow a grocery store customer around the store. You could see which aisles she walks down, where she stops to examine a product, which items she scoops off the shelf and decides whether to put in her shopping cart, and whether she leaves the store after making a purchase or just walks out, leaving with a half-full cart in Aisle 7.

Yahoo! has a special Click Trails report that gives you the same ability to follow your website customers, if you have a Standard or Professional merchant account. This report shows you the exact path a customer takes in your store, showing you each page he sees as well as the link he clicked to open the next page. You can follow that path to understand which parts of your store enjoy the most traffic as well as which parts aren't seen. With this knowledge, you can put your valuable merchandise where your customers virtually walk.

Of course, some customers don't wander and browse. They type search words and try to go directly to the product page they need. To track this type of customer, Yahoo! also shows the most frequent words in your own website's search engine (not the main Yahoo! site). You see a ranked list of the top search terms that your customers use every day to find your specific products. You can then compare this list with your inventory. Investigating the search terms used by customers can help you match the right product with the right customer.

**Book VIII
Chapter 3**

**Let's Hear It for
Yahoo!**

Chapter 4: Making eBay THE Way

In This Chapter

✓ Figuring out the basics of eBay

✓ Gaining eBay experience

✓ Starting an eBay item listing

✓ Opening an eBay store

In the past 19 years, eBay has grown from a quiet, small online bazaar into the most powerful consumer trading platform on Earth. Although other Internet companies grew overnight into sensations and burned out of existence just as quickly, eBay has remained profitable from the first month it started charging users.

eBay is an effective way to gain customers, establish cash flow, and turn over some inventory. The beautiful part of eBay is that it takes care of many routine tasks that you need to handle by using e-commerce: the trading platform, website, and software needed to transact the sale. The one thing that eBay can't provide on its own, however, is a guaranteed stream of customers or income. Building an eBay business requires some work and effort, combined with a number of strategies and tactics.

In this chapter, we show you how to get up and running on eBay with auctions and fixed-price sales. Then, when you have your feet wet, we detail how to advance to the big leagues with a dedicated eBay store.

 Running an eBay business doesn't require that you focus all your efforts on eBay. eBay can simply be one channel for selling goods and making money, or you can use eBay to start your business before you launch your own website. In this chapter, we present a plan for building steady, constant sales through this channel. You decide how you want to use eBay, based on your total online business strategy.

Understanding How eBay Works

Online sales usually involve four key elements: product, price, seller, and buyer. On eBay, buyers can pay a fixed price or compete with one another to win the item in a bidding system. If you've ever been to a live auction, you know that buyers raise their bid price until one bidder remains, and then that highest bidder pays the top price and receives the item. On eBay, members place a bid electronically rather than raise a paddle.

Here's the basic flow of an eBay transaction:

1. List an item for sale on eBay. See the "Setting Up an Item for Sale" section, later in this chapter.

2. If you list your item with a fixed price, a buyer who is interested in your item at that price will click the Buy It Now button to purchase the item, and eBay sends an e-mail to you and the buyer.

3. If you list your item as an auction, a buyer places a bid on eBay for your item, indicating the highest price he or she is willing to pay. The buyer with the highest bid at the end of the auction's time period wins the item, and eBay sends an e-mail to you and the highest bidder.

4. You send the buyer an invoice, indicating the total for the item sold, including shipping, handling, and sales tax (when applicable) and whether you accept PayPal or a credit card.

    If you need to set up your accepted forms of payment, see Book IV, Chapter 4.

5. The buyer sends you payment.

6. You mail the item to the buyer. See Book IV, Chapter 7 for info on shipping products to your buyers.

7. You and your bidder can leave comments about your transaction, known as *feedback,* on eBay. See the "Leaving feedback for your buyer" section, later in this chapter.

Getting Started on eBay

Signing up for eBay is easy and free. Your account can be used to browse, bid, and sell on eBay. The main requirement is that you have to be 18 years or older. Just fire up your Internet browser and go to www.ebay.com and follow these steps:

1. **Click the Register link in the top-left corner.**

    The Get Started with eBay page appears, as shown in Figure 4-1.

2. **Enter your personal information in the fields provided.**

    You're required to give your full name and e-mail address, which eBay keeps on file if it needs to communicate with you. Your password must be between 6 and 20 characters. Choose a password that no one can randomly guess.

3. **Click the Submit button to continue.**

    Your eBay account is created and eBay assigns you an initial unique user ID (useus41), as shown in Figure 4-2. The ID is the name you use to do business on eBay. It can be a variation of your own name (such as john-doe1), the name of your business (mybusiness.com), or the name of a category where you plan to sell (buddyselectronics).

Figure 4-1:
Enter your information here.

Figure 4-2:
eBay creates your account and user ID.

You aren't stuck with your assigned choice. eBay allows you to change your user ID once every 30 days, which does not affect your user rating. Simply go into My eBay, click the Account tab, and then select Personal Information to change your ID.

4. **Click Continue.**

   The eBay home page and a confirmation message appears. Your eBay account is now active.

Check your e-mail for a message from eBay with links to pages explaining what you can do next.

After you register on eBay, you have to perform some additional details before starting your first auction or opening a storefront:

✦ **Sign up for PayPal:** PayPal, the eBay-owned division that handles online payment processing, lets you send or receive money based on your online sales, on or off eBay. You can maintain an account on PayPal for free — you pay only a transaction fee (typically 2.5 to 2.9 percent) when you receive a payment. Go to `www.paypal.com` to sign up.

You can also sign up for a merchant account from your bank, where you can process credit cards directly. You must have either a PayPal or merchant account if you want to sell on eBay; PayPal is the recommended payment method. According to research from eBay, 90 percent of all eBay auctions offer PayPal as a payment method, and 80 percent of all transactions are paid for through PayPal.

✦ **Set up a dedicated bank account:** Both eBay and PayPal require you to provide a credit card number and your bank account information to create an account. We recommend setting up a second bank account at a smaller bank and getting a Visa or MasterCard debit card through this account so that you can keep track of your eBay activity separately from your main banking transactions.

✦ **Set up an About Me page:** Use this page to advertise your own eBay store, talk about your online sales activities, and detail your reputation for doing business on the auction website. You can include a picture on this page, whether it's an image of your retail storefront, your company logo, or one of your products.

   To create your About Me page, go to `http://pages.ebay.com/community/aboutme.html` (see Figure 4-3). You can either insert your own web page HTML code or answer some questions and post a description, a photo, and information about yourself.

Figure 4-3:
Create your
own About
Me page.

✦ **Research your competition:** You can find out how to price your items, see which items are selling well, and determine which ones to stay away from. In the Search box, which is at the top of every eBay page, type the words that describe the item you want to sell and click Search. To see past sales, select the Sold Listings or Completed Listings check box after you perform your first search. You can then sort these past sales by price, from highest to lowest, and see a snapshot of how your item has sold on eBay in the past couple of weeks. You can also sort by distance to see how nearby competitors are doing, or sort by oldest or newest listings to get a sense of price levels over time.

Research not only shows you what to expect as a price for your item but also gives you the following useful information:

- Which keywords to use in describing your item

- Which category on eBay to place your item in

- Which features you should mention about your item

- The current level of supply and demand for this item on eBay

Here are the main questions you should answer while doing research:

- Are the items I want to sell doing well on eBay?

- Are the prices the items are selling for enough for me to make a profit?

If the answer to either question is no, you may want to find other items to sell instead, before you invest time and money on a product line that's wrong for eBay.

You can take advantage of lots of other eBay features and options that we don't cover here. Check out *eBay Business All-In-One For Dummies,* 3rd Edition by Marsha Collier for an authoritative and complete reference to using eBay.

Setting Up an Item for Sale

Many sales on eBay are auctions. You know the kind: *1, 2, 3, Sold to the highest bidder!* But rather than wave their hands enthusiastically, bidders place a bid on your auction by using their computers. On eBay, you have the choice of offering your item for sale as an auction or for a fixed price, so the buyer can click and buy immediately.

Either way, you set up an item listing by getting an item or a product you want to sell, writing a description of the product and taking photos of it, and creating a web page with all the basic information about that product.

When you're trying to decide whether to list your item as an auction or at a fixed price, here are some of the top reasons to consider an auction:

✦ **Auctions attract people's interest.** Shopping on eBay has become more than a matter of buying items. It's now a form of entertainment, with bidding, competing, and winning. After people bid on an item, they're more likely to follow the auction to its completion and stay emotionally invested in acquiring the item.

✦ **Auctions move merchandise faster.** When you sell items on your own store or by using an eBay store, it can take days, weeks, or even months to find the right buyer. With an eBay auction, you can sell an item in one to ten days and find your high bidder, and some interested underbidders, more quickly. Think of the auction as a call to action, where the buyers decide to respond.

✦ **Auctions cost the seller only money per item, not per month.** When you operate an eBay store, you're paying a monthly fee regardless of how many items you sell. In an eBay auction, you pay a small fee to list the item for sale, as low as 10 cents, and another fee if the item sells.

✦ **Auctions let you test the water.** Rather than launch a full-blown store for your items, you can run a few eBay auctions and gauge the interest of the buying community. You can get an idea of success before investing in website design and programming.

Of course, auctions have some drawbacks. The fees involved in running auctions can add up if you're continually trying to sell something that receives no bids. Although the short timeframe of the auction helps move inventory, it's also quickly forgotten in the minds of the buyer. You have to run a lot of auctions to build the constant presence needed to remind buyers of who you are. Without repeat buyers and the constant flow of goods, it's hard to build a sustainable flow of revenue by putting up random auctions every week. Still, auctions provide an excellent piece of the overall e-commerce business plan.

The easiest way to get started on eBay is to plunge ahead and set up an item for sale. Look around your business inventory for something that you want to sell and follow these steps:

1. **Click the Sign In link at** `www.ebay.com`.

2. **Enter your user ID and password, and then click the Sign In button.**

3. **Click the Sell link at the top of any eBay page.**

   If you're a new seller, eBay will ask for additional information, such as your address, postal code, and phone number, before you can sell an item.

4. **Type a few words that describe your item, and then click Get Started.**

   After you click Get Started, eBay prompts you with a list of the most likely categories where your item belongs.

5. **Choose your category and the appropriate subcategories.**

   The first step in selling your item is figuring out which category should be assigned to your item. eBay has more than 50,000 unique categories, organized in more than 30 top-level categories, such as antiques, art, and books. If the don't see an appropriate category, click the Browse Categories tab and search eBay's category structure yourself to find the most appropriate subcategory for your item.

6. **Click Continue.**

   Depending on the item you are listing, eBay may search their catalog and prompt you to *Create your listing from a similar item* and show you similar item titles.

7. **If you see your exact item listed, click the Sell One Like This link next to the item. If you don't see your item listed, scroll down and click the Continue to the Listing Form button.**

8. **Enter these elements:**

   - *Title:* Incorporate the most frequently used keywords about your item so that buyers who search eBay's database for items like yours can find it.

   - *Item specifics:* Enter specific details depending on what you're selling. (For example, every shoe has a size, width, and color.) The more details you enter in the boxes provided, the more easily buyers can find your item.

Book VIII
Chapter 4

**Making eBay
THE Way**

9. **Add photos to your auction as follows:**

a. Scroll down the page to the Photos section, and click the Add Photos button.

A second window opens, asking you to identify where on your computer the pictures for the auction are located.

b. Select the pictures.

You can attach up to 12 photos per listing, so don't be afraid to show off every angle, defect, or unique quality of the item.

c. Click the Upload button to send the pictures from your computer to eBay.

eBay requires at least one photo per listing, with a minimum pixel size of 500 by 500 pixels. Make sure your main picture is large enough to use in your listing.

10. **Scroll down to the Details section and enter a description.**

Remember to add not only a description of the item but also all your policies about payment and shipping methods, as well as a return policy. Use the buttons that eBay provides above the Description window to add bold, italic, or underlined text as well as bulleted or numbered lists.

11. **Decide whether you want to sell your item in an auction or with a fixed price:**

a. Scroll down to the next section, Select Format and Price, and click the Auction tab or the Fixed Price tab.

b. Enter your starting bid or a fixed price.

You can either enter the starting price of your auction (and assign a Reserve price or Buy It Now price or both) or click the drop-down arrow next to List As and select Fixed Price to sell your items for a fixed Buy It Now price. With a fixed price, you can choose to receive Best Offers, in which buyers can offer you a price below your fixed price and you choose whether to accept, counteroffer, or decline their offer.

c. Set the duration and number of items in your lot.

If you want to sell more than one lot at a time, you must use the fixed-price listing. eBay does not allow multiple identical lots to be auctioned at the same time.

12. **Scroll down to the next section and choose your shipping options (see Figure 4-4).**

For shipping options, you can sell your item to customers only in the United States or around the world. If you don't want to ship something (such as a heavy or fragile item), choose the Offer Local Pickup Only option.

How you'll ship it

| Select shipping for me | Select shipping myself | Offer local pickup only |

We'll apply this shipping option based on how similar items shipped. Learn more

USPS Priority Mail (1 to 3 business days) — Package (or thick envelope) — 1lb. — 7.0in. x 4.0in. x 4.0in.

$5.60 - $6.95 (varies by buyer's location)

☐ Offer free shipping to attract more buyers

☐ Add international shipping (optional) ⓘ

Need Help?

FAQs
▸ What are preferences?
▸ Why do you need my PayPal email address? What is it used for?

Contact us
We're here to help you
☎ Call us
💬 Live chat
📞 Call me

Review your preferences

* PayPal email address* ⓘ	order@newcomix.com
Item location ⓘ	90001
* Handling time ⓘ	2 business days ▾
* Returns	No returns accepted ▾

Listing fees

Insertion fees: Free

Total: Free

☑ Automatically relist this item up to 3 times if it doesn't sell — it's **free** to relist Learn more
  ◉ Relist with original prices
  ◯ Lower prices for each relist by 10% ▾

Figure 4-4:
You decide where in the world you're willing to ship your item.

You must enter a flat price for shipping or click the Select Shipping Myself tab and let eBay calculate your postage costs based on the weight and the buyer's zip code.

13. Scroll down to the last section and review your preferences.

Check items such as handling time and return policy. Provide instructions to automatically relist the item if it doesn't sell right away.

14. Preview your listing.

Scroll to the bottom of the page and click Preview to see how your listing will appear on eBay. Make sure that your title and gallery thumbnail photo appear correctly in the sample. Look over the information you entered and the choices you made.

15. When everything looks good, scroll to the bottom of the page and click List It.

Your listing goes live on the eBay site. If you want to fix something, go to your listing page and click Revise Your Item to return to the listing page and make corrections.

If you want to sell an additional similar item, you can click the Sell a Similar Item link to create a new auction, with all the information fields already filled in. You simply make the changes necessary for your second item and submit the new auction in a fraction of the time it took you to complete your first listing.

**Book VIII
Chapter 4**

**Making eBay
THE Way**

Maintaining your item listings

My eBay is your personal dashboard for monitoring your eBay buying and selling activity. You can get to that page by clicking the My eBay link, which appears at the top of any eBay page. Instead of clicking that link, however, roll your cursor over it to view an expanded list of the various sections on the My eBay page, including Bids/Offers, Purchase History, and Selling. Click the Selling link to display the Selling home page and its distinct sections:

✦ **Selling Reminders:** Your to-do list showing what to complete

✦ **Scheduled Items:** The items you're going to sell later

✦ **Selling Totals:** Your summary of sales

✦ **Active Selling:** Your items still up for bid on eBay

✦ **Sold Items:** Items that received at least one valid bid and are completed

✦ **Unsold Items:** Completed items that didn't receive any bids

When you click the Active Selling link, you see a live snapshot of all items you have for sale on eBay: auction, fixed-price, and store inventory items. This page shows you a lot of information about each item you're selling:

✦ Current high bid

✦ Number of bids that have been placed

✦ Amount of time remaining in the auction

✦ Number of people watching your item

✦ Number of questions people have

When your item has completed the bidding stage, it appears on another page in My eBay: Items I've Sold. This page provides you with a visual checklist of tasks you need to complete after the winning bidder has been determined. When you complete a step, its accompanying icon is colored purple. This way, you know what needs to be done for each item you sold.

Leaving feedback for your buyer

eBay buyers typically don't meet sellers, so these buyers require a level of trust to buy something sight unseen. eBay builds this trust by maintaining a feedback score, allowing the buyer to see the trading reputation of any eBay member instantly. Buying on eBay gives you a way to build a trading history and a positive reputation, which can help you as you start to sell on eBay.

For every transaction you participate in on eBay, whether you buy or sell, you're allowed to give feedback to the other party when the sale is completed. This feedback is aggregated into a numerical score for every eBay user, along with detailed seller ratings and a feedback record made up of comments from other users, as shown in Figure 4-5.

Success on eBay

Follow these guidelines to become successful on eBay:

- **Set up a template with your policies:** Use the description section of an auction listing to detail your policies for doing business. Mention the condition of the item, the payment methods you accept, how you plan to ship the item, any return policies you offer, and any other legal policies.

- **Write clear, organized descriptions:** Provide all the information your buyers want to know when they're making a decision about whether to buy your item. Make sure that your description makes sense and guides the buyer toward a decision. And make sure that any description of an item you're selling contains the condition of the item (its functionality, make, manufacturer, brand name, and model number) and its physical characteristics (color, size, and weight).

- **Define your shipping and return policies clearly:** eBay requires all sellers to specify defined shipping costs for all auctions, a defined handling time to process the auction, and a defined return policy for each auction. Therefore, think about your policies in advance, research the items your competitors are offering, and ensure that every auction you create has all its policies defined.

- **Add photos to your listings:** If a picture is worth a thousand words, it's worth even more on eBay because the buyer doesn't get to see the item until the bidding is over. Therefore, you want the best pictures you can produce: Blurry or dark photos just scare buyers away, and pictures that are too large take too long to appear can also turn buyers away.

Figure 4-5:
Feedback becomes your instant reputation on eBay.

Book VIII Chapter 4

Making eBay THE Way

As a buyer, you can leave three kinds of feedback for a seller:

✦ **Positive:** Increases the feedback score by 1

✦ **Neutral:** Doesn't affect the feedback score

✦ **Negative:** Reduces the feedback score by 1

The seller is allowed to leave only positive feedback for the buyer or to report the buyer for not paying for the item. The feedback system is a way to report whether people complete transactions reasonably and fairly. It isn't supposed to be a complaint or vendetta forum, although some users see it that way. Positive feedback is left when the transaction was handled satisfactorily or if both parties worked out an agreement to resolve the transaction. Neutral or negative feedback should be reserved for only those transactions where sellers grossly misrepresent themselves and do absolutely nothing to correct the situation.

In addition, buyers can rate their sellers on four different dimensions of the transaction, using a scale from 1 to 5. These detailed seller ratings, or DSRs, are designed to weed out bad sellers and reward good sellers. The buyer can rate the seller based on these criteria:

✦ **Item as described:** How closely does the item resemble its description in the auction? (A score of 5 means the same item, and 1 means grossly different.)

✦ **Communication:** Did the seller communicate with you, as the buyer, sufficiently during the process? (A score of 5 means yes, and 1 means silence.)

✦ **Shipping time:** How quickly from your payment (as the buyer) does the item arrive to you? (A score of 5 means a quick turnaround time, and 1 means that you waited a long time.)

✦ **Shipping-and-handling charges:** Did the seller charge you a fair price to package and ship the item to you, based on the category average? (A score of 5 means that it was reasonable, and 1 means that it was outrageous.) If the seller offered free shipping, this option is not available to the buyer.

Every buyer's rating is then aggregated and shown on the seller's feedback page as a set of stars, from 1 to 5, as long as ten buyers have responded in the past 3 or 12 months. Seller status and benefits are partially based on maintaining very high DSRs in all four dimensions.

Feedback is rarely altered after it's given, so think carefully before giving feedback. If you're having a dispute with the other party, try to work out the situation before leaving feedback.

Every member's feedback score is represented next to his or her user ID, along with color-coded stars after the score reaches 10. Multiple feedback from the same person in the same week increases the score by only 1, so if Aunt Sally buys ten items from you at one time, it raises your score by only 1 point. If she buys one item per week, you receive multiple feedback credit for multiple sales, even if it's to the same buyer.

Opening an eBay Store

An eBay store is an interesting combination of eBay sales and your own e-commerce store. Think of owning an eBay store as owning a small shingle under eBay's massive marketplace.

With an eBay store, you benefit from these features:

✦ **A dedicated e-commerce storefront:** You can direct your customers to one place, which you can advertise on any printed material you send to customers worldwide. Then you can see exactly which pages, which items, and which deals your customers looked at the most, so that you can see what's working and what's boring.

An eBay store can significantly increase your sales because it gives you another mechanism for reaching customers. Every time you sell an item on eBay, you can point the winner (and all your other bidders) to your eBay store to buy additional merchandise.

✦ **The chance to sell many items on eBay with a lower fee structure:** You can list thousands of items in your eBay store at a lower insertion cost than listing each item without an eBay store. In addition, you're charged a lower sales fee (or final value fee) when an item sells in your store.

✦ **Sales and marketing tools to sell your items:** If something doesn't sell right away, you can use a program called Markdown Manager to put an item (or an entire category of items) on sale by temporarily discounting the fixed price.

eBay Stores give you a place to sell your products online under a fixed address, but they also come with many other features to make your business more successful. Here's a look at five features that can assist you with running your eBay store:

✦ **Sales reports:** On a month-by-month or three-month basis, review key numbers such as average sales price per item, sold items percentage, and repeat buyer percentage.

✦ **Cross Promotion tool:** You can specify which of your items for sale is shown to potential customers when they're looking at one of your items. For example, if someone looks at a pair of your skis for sale, you can use the Cross Promotion tool to display boots, poles, and goggles.

✦ **Advertising templates:** You can download these templates to create business cards, stationery, envelopes, flyers, and more.

✦ **Coordinating active customer lists with e-mail marketing:** The e-mail newsletter function also helps you handle the mass e-mail of marketing items, such as your monthly newsletter or sales announcements.

✦ **Traffic reports:** Find out exactly which pages in your store receive the most traffic, which search words are used most often in store searches, and which inventory items are selling most quickly.

Have we sold you on running an eBay store? Well, before you do so, you need to know that you have to pay eBay some additional fees for the glory. Your very own eBay store costs from $15.95 to $299.95 per month, depending on its functionality and placement. If you're running a small business, you can do quite well with the Basic package or the slightly more expensive Premium package, which includes bonus features for marketing and tracking your store. If you want to list thousands of items for sale at any time and want the lowest insertion fee structure, you may want to consider the (pricey) Anchor store plan. After you pay for a store subscription, you can add a set amount of items to your store for no insertion fee. (If you exceed your set amount, adding more items to your store costs 3 to 20 cents per listing per month that it's listed.) When the item sells, you pay a commission to eBay based on the category of the item.

Setting up shop

You retain a lot of control with your eBay store. Plus, you can study your customer's shopping habits. If you're ready to have your own eBay storefront, here's what you need to know.

You have to have an active eBay seller's account, a credit card on file, and a PayPal Premier account in good standing to open an eBay store. Try to build up your feedback score and gain some experience before opening an eBay store.

Before you open your store, make sure that you have these items lined up:

✦ A good name chosen for your store; this name can be (and usually should be) different from your eBay user ID

✦ A store inventory sufficient to make having a store worthwhile

✦ The knowledge that you can handle the extra work of selling merchandise at any given time

When you're ready, go to stores.ebay.com, and follow these steps to open your store:

1. **On the Stores home page, click the Open a Store link.**

2. **Click the Subscribe Now button.**

3. **If necessary, log in with your user ID and password.**

A Subscription Level page opens, as shown in Figure 4-6.

Figure 4-6:
Choose
your store
subscription
level.

4. **Choose your subscription level.**

   Your buyers won't know your store subscription level because all the
   core functionality comes with the Basic platform. Most sellers who are
   starting out choose the Basic option ($15.95 per month) and move up
   to the Premium level when they want to do more online marketing with
   their stores.

5. **Scroll down the page, and enter your store name in the box provided,
   and then click Continue.**

   You can use as many as 35 characters for your store name, so choose
   wisely. Don't infringe on any copyrighted name, especially the word
   eBay, but make it memorable.

   The Review and Submit page opens.

6. **Agree to the terms and click Subscribe.**

   Your store is live!

Managing your store

After you sign up for an eBay store, it's time to get in there, spruce it up with some colors, logos, and products, and open it for business. At any time, you can manage your eBay store by clicking one of two links:

✦ From your store's home page, scroll to the bottom of the page and click the Seller, Manage Store link.

✦ From the eBay Stores home page, click the Manage My Store link.

The Manage My Store page opens, as shown in Figure 4-7. From here, you have access to the main features of your store, including but not limited to the ones in the following list:

✦ **Store design:** Use the Display Settings option to choose from many pre-formatted templates that you can use for your eBay store design. You can define as many as 300 custom store categories, such as Top Picks of the Month or Gifts Under $10. If you want to add several pages to your Store, such as a policies or shipping page, use the Custom Pages link.

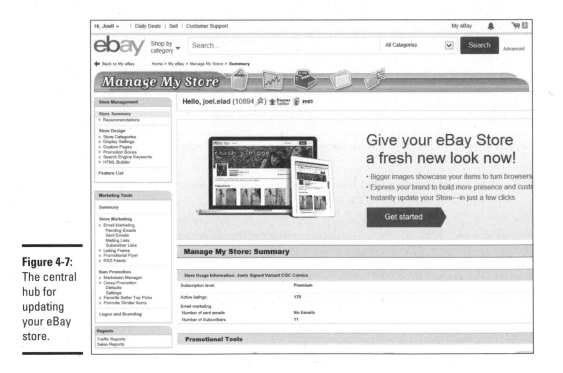

Figure 4-7: The central hub for updating your eBay store.

✦ **Store marketing:** You can control any e-mail marketing campaigns you want to run for your eBay store. eBay helps coordinate any customer lists you build, coordinates the mass e-mailings of newsletters and special promotions, helps design flyers, and distributes product information. See Book VI, Chapter 3 for more general information about running an e-mail marketing campaign.

✦ **Item promotion:** When you link your items and set cross-promotion rules, this function controls it all. You can specify rules and preferences for how your items should be cross-promoted throughout your store, and set up favorites to appear as featured items on your store's home page.

✦ **Logos and branding:** When you have a custom logo, use this function header to upload the logo to customized e-mail messages that you use to communicate with your customers.

For a full, in-depth explanation of maximizing your eBay store experience, you can't go wrong with *Starting an eBay Business For Dummies*, 4th Edition, by Marsha Collier. This book is full of tips, tricks, and techniques that you can use to make your eBay store shine.

Becoming a PowerSeller

eBay has a special term for people who sell a steady amount of merchandise every month, earn a high amount of positive feedback, and comply with all eBay listing policies: *PowerSellers*. eBay has different levels of PowerSellers, starting with Bronze ($1,000 per month) and going all the way up to Titanium ($150,000 per month). Every PowerSeller has to maintain at least a 98 percent positive feedback rating with a minimum of 100 feedback comments earned on their account, and create at least four listings per month. When you qualify, eBay sends you an invitation to accept your PowerSeller status. After you become a PowerSeller, eBay has another classification called Top Rated Seller, reserved for those PowerSellers with exceptional feedback and DSR scores. Top Rated Sellers qualify for special benefits, such as a discount on their sales (or final value) fees.

eBay uses a three-month average to calculate your sales level. If your average sales level drops below the PowerSeller minimum, eBay gives you one month to increase your sales; after that, you lose your PowerSeller status. You can be reinstated, however, after you increase your average sales.

Although not all PowerSellers focus on the same categories or use the same means to rack up impressive and steady sales, they typically share one bond (the reason that their sales jumped to the next level): "the sale."

Most PowerSellers can tell you about the single item they sold early in their eBay trading experience — usually an item that they had little faith in or little money invested in. Maybe the person watched the bidding every day or every hour, or maybe they forgot about it. But they never forgot the thrill of seeing the high bid when the auction was over, and that's how they became hooked. They then invested the time and figured out the different techniques to work their way up to PowerSeller status.

After you achieve PowerSeller status, your focus is on every sale, not just a single memorable sale. To keep track of the growing number of sales and customers, many PowerSellers look into using a third-party tool. You might try a program such as Auctiva (`www.auctiva.com`), which can help you manage listings and sales activities. If you carry a large volume, try an Enterprise solution from ChannelAdvisor (`www.channeladvisor.com`) to manage your sales across eBay and any other channels where you sell online, with every sale combined into easy-to-read reports.

For the ultimate source in third-party tools, check out eBay's Solutions Directory at `http://solutions.ebay.com`.

Chapter 5: New Storefronts, New Opportunities

In This Chapter

✔ **Discovering auction sites beyond eBay**

✔ **Creating and selling your homemade goods online**

✔ **Selling on demand with ready-made storefronts**

Selling online through storefronts has become second nature thanks to pioneers such as eBay, Yahoo!, and Amazon. These big-name storefronts quickly earned reputations as being online wealth makers. Although they continue to have the clout to help you pull in numbers and make the sale, bringing together buyers and sellers is only part of the equation in building a successful online marketplace. As online business models evolve and new technologies become available, traditional storefronts struggle to retain their appeal. That leaves the door open for new competitors, and new ways to extend the online selling landscape.

Sometimes, being successful comes down to your ability to spot the next big thing, such as storefronts with a social commerce element, which is simply e-commerce with an interactive component. In this chapter, we give you an overview of some lesser-known auction sites, several "crafty" storefronts, and a few other alternatives for those of you with an eye for design. It's worth your while to investigate each of these rising stars in the growing storefront community.

Flexible Bidding Takes All with Auction Sites

Online auction houses have certainly proven to have a viable revenue model. Admittedly, eBay has garnered the lion's share of the attention (as you find in Chapter 4 of this minibook). But the way customers prefer to shop on eBay is changing. The traditional bidding model, which drove nearly all the site's activity, has been eroded with Buy It Now listings, in which the seller sets a fixed price for an item. This model is similar to simply shopping online, except that sellers can extend the bargaining flexibility of a Buy It Now item by agreeing to accept a Best Offer bid.

For example, suppose you're selling a painting at a Buy It Now price of $250, but are willing to consider a lower offer. If someone offers, say, $175, you can accept it, reject it, or counter the offer. This new form of buying and selling on eBay is an indication of the type of flexibility buyers want when shopping online. The amount of competition across auction sites and storefronts provides plenty of new opportunities for both buyers and sellers. Several eBay competitors on that growing list are described in this section.

Bonanza

You might recognize Bonanza (`www.bonanza.com`), the eBay alternative shown in Figure 5-1. Bonanza is frequently voted by online sellers as one of the top sites (number one in 2014) in the annual Sellers Choice Awards for Marketplaces. The auction site boasts more than 5 million listings, which is still small compared to eBay, but Bonanza is winning fans because of its easy, simplified selling process and its listing fees, which can save sellers more than 50 percent compared to eBay's listing fees. That's a huge savings! Traffic from buyers is building, too, as shown in the site's 60 percent revenue increase, year-over-year. (An auction site doesn't keep making that type of money if there aren't enough buyers to keep sellers in business and profitable, too.)

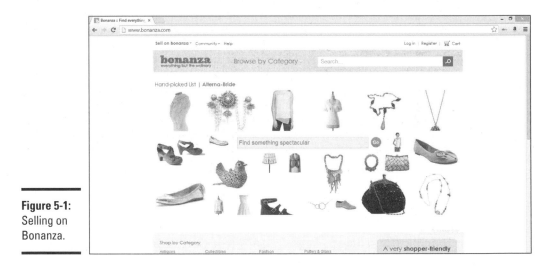

Figure 5-1:
Selling on
Bonanza.

Buyers like shopping on Bonanza because of the variety of merchandise and the flexible buying options that sellers can extend, such as best offers and discounts for buying multiple products, as you see in Figure 5-2.

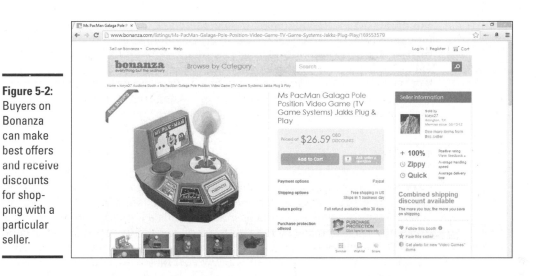

Figure 5-2:
Buyers on Bonanza can make best offers and receive discounts for shopping with a particular seller.

In addition to having a marketplace with a large variety of products and categories that attract buyers, one factor that further sets Bonanza apart from its competitors is its host of advanced features. For example, Background Burner removes backgrounds from pictures of items being listed for sale. Picture quality is a critical part of success on auction sites and storefronts, and the latest style trends lean toward keeping both websites and images clean and free from background clutter. Development-savvy sellers can customize the tool, for example, by integrating it with mobile commerce). You can also import items you have listed on eBay, Amazon, or Etsy as well as offer digital downloads for sale. The site also offers integration with social media with its Rich Pin for Pinterest tool, which allows products to be pinned (or shared) on Pinterest with accompanying product information, including pricing.

Saying no to listing fees

One hot topic that comes up when you discuss auction sites is fees. Listing fees, along with other pre- and post-sale charges, suddenly became more important when eBay aggressively began raising its own fees. Even sellers once loyal to eBay began looking for other online auction sites.

The following online auction sites have zero listing fees:

✔ Bonanza (www.bonanza.com) has no listing fees even with photos, and charges a value-based fee only when an item sells.

✔ eBid.net (www.ebid.net) charges a 3 percent fee when an item sells.

✔ MyAuctionPlanet (www.myauction planet.com) has free stores and no final value fee when an item sells.

You can find a lot of great scoop on online auction happenings by visiting AuctionBytes at www.auctionbytes.com. This online resource covers news about auction sites ranging from eBay to OnlineAuctions.

The total cost for listing items for sale, including unlimited photos, is zero! A modest Final Offer Value (FOV) fee of 3.5 percent is based on the final selling price or the accepted offer minus a shipping fee of up to $10. For products valued at more than $500, there is a flat fee of $17.50 plus 1.5 percent fee of the FOV amount that exceeds $500. The low fees and extensive features are helping Bonanza earn a reputation for providing true competition to once-loyal eBay sellers.

eCrater

The eCrater auction site (www.ecrater.com) launched in 2004, offering an interesting alternative to eBay and other auction sites. For sellers, the cost is almost free because eCrater does not charge a listing fee, nor does it take a percentage of final sales, unless eCrater sends a buyer to your listing from the general marketplace (the area on the main website where eCrater lists product categories and promotes products). In this case, eCrater charges a 2.9 percent fee. The trade-off for the low cost of selling in this marketplace is that the site's standard features — no bells or whistles here. However, you can list an unlimited number of products, with up to 10 photos with each listing. eCrater also lets you import items from eBay into your eCrater store. Sellers and buyers alike appreciate the simplicity of the site and the clean, open design style, which is shown in Figure 5-3.

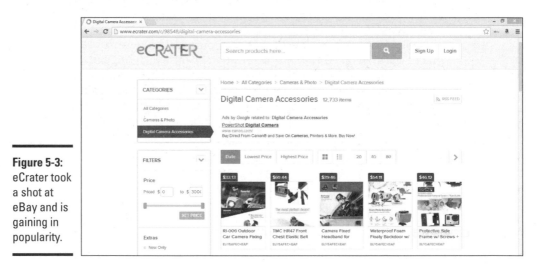

Figure 5-3: eCrater took a shot at eBay and is gaining in popularity.

Ruby Lane

Designed to provide an online marketplace for art and collectibles Ruby Lane (www.rubylane.com) has built a loyal following of buyers and sellers since its debut in 1998 (quite a track record for an e-commerce site of any kind). As of early 2014, Rubylane.com is still attracting more than 1 million unique visits to the site each month. The site, which is shown in Figure 5-4, offers an interesting and simple platform for buyers. Instead of starting items for sale in a typical auction format, Ruby Lane sellers offer items for a fixed price. However, buyers can submit a best offer for any listing, or a seller can use the Send to Auction feature to move an item listed on Ruby Lane to eBay or other sites to initiate an auction.

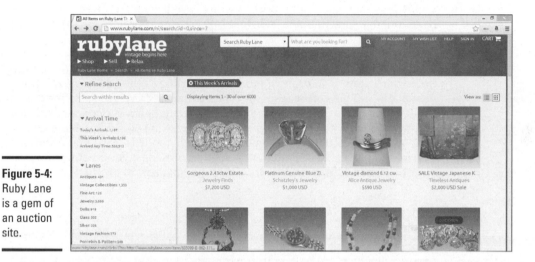

Figure 5-4:
Ruby Lane is a gem of an auction site.

Ruby Lane provides a simple, tiered pricing structure. Each listing is a flat 39 cents, which includes access to an advanced image-processing feature to clean up product images. The first of every month, sellers pay a maintenance fee based on the number of products they have listed at the time. The fee ranges from 30¢ per item for fewer than 150 items, to 1¢ per item for more than 1,000 items. The maintenance fee never exceeds $24 per month. Ruby Lane also charges sellers a $30 per month advertising fee (to help offset advertising and promotional costs). Sellers pay a one-time $100 set-up fee, too.

You may be wondering why anyone would pay all this money to sell on Ruby Lane when other online marketplaces strive to keep costs as low as possible. The answer is in the types of products you sell and the types of buyers you need to reach. For example, if you specialize in art and antiques, Ruby Lane can send targeted traffic to view your listings and has a team of in-house art and antique professionals who review and approve every new online seller to ensure quality standards. Ruby Lane prides itself on its excellent customer service and quality sellers and products. If you're looking for a high-end alternative to eBay with qualified buyers, visit Ruby Lane to learn more about its promotional tools and features.

Making Bank with Online Marketplaces for Handcrafted and Vintage Goods

Online auctions, particularly eBay, helped validate the Internet as a lucrative vehicle for selling everything from collectable Pez candy dispensers to used cars. In addition to auction sites, a growing number of niche storefronts are gaining in popularity. One industry in particular that has found a home online is homemade crafts. Both crafting enthusiasts and their customers have found it easy to make, sell, and buy custom products via the Internet.

Crafts and hobbies are a multibillion market in the United States, expected to exceed $30 billion by 2014, with more than 56 percent of American households participating in crafts annually (according to the Crafts and Hobby Association). This enthusiasm for crafts translates to a great business opportunity using online storefronts. Several storefronts have focused their efforts on providing an online marketplace for the crafting world and have even gone as far as restricting the types of allowed goods to handmade wares. The marketplaces described in this section provide a good vehicle for selling your handcrafted wares, artwork, and homemade food products.

Etsy

Etsy (www.etsy.com) has skyrocketed onto the e-commerce scene as a viable place to sell your handcrafted wares as shown in Figure 5-5. Allowable products include not only your homemade items but also hobby or craft supplies and vintage items (products more than 20 years old).

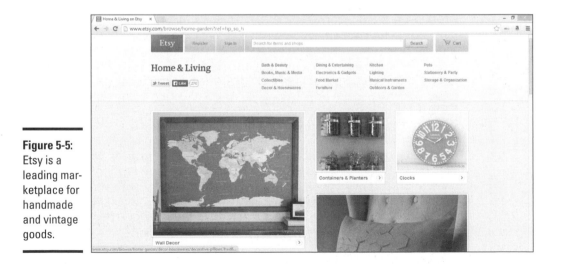

Figure 5-5: Etsy is a leading marketplace for handmade and vintage goods.

Fees are reasonable. You're charged 20 cents for each listed item, plus a final sales price, or final value fee, of 3.5 percent. Each listing can stay active for up to four months before you're charged another 20-cent listing fee. As the audience for this marketplace has grown (more than 30 million buyers and sellers), so too have the features and promotional benefits it offers sellers. For example, you can customize the functionality of your site by accessing Etsy APIs (application programming interfaces), access detailed statistics for your store, and utilize an on-site postage tool to make shipping easier for domestic and international orders. You can also integrate your Etsy shop with your Facebook account and provide coupon codes for special promotions. Etsy also offers a sellers-only app for managing your Etsy store from your iPhone.

In 2014, Etsy added the capability to wholesale items for an initial $100 fee plus 3.5 percent of sales. This move is a result of the interest Etsy sellers received from established retailers who are looking to extend their product selection with unique items sourced from the Etsy marketplace. The recent attention paid to Etsy shops from large brands is yet another sign of the power and influence of artisans crafting and selling online.

ArtFire

"Created by artisans for artisans" is the best way to describe ArtFire (www.artfire.com). This inspired storefront provides a place to sell fine art, homemade goods, vintage items, supplies, and media. Figure 5-6 displays examples of the type of artwork sold on ArtFire. The site does not charge listing fees or commissions. However, for a flat monthly fee of $12.95, you can have a Pro Seller account, which offers an unlimited number of listings with as many as 10 pictures per listing, the capability to customize your online storefront, access to various promotional tools — including a Facebook integration tool, coupon codes, and gift certificates — and participation in community-sponsored councils (groups formed from community members for the purpose of providing feedback about the site). ArtFire automatically pushes out your listings to Google, Google Shopping, Bing, and Yahoo! With all these features and millions of monthly visitors, ArtFire is a good deal if you're an artist looking for a professional online gallery.

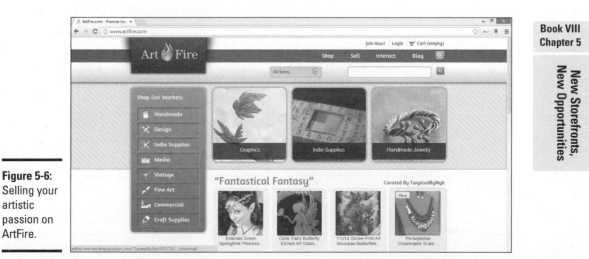

Figure 5-6: Selling your artistic passion on ArtFire.

Zibbet

Zibbet (www.zibbet.com) has been around since 2009, but you don't hear much (if anything) about this rival to the Etsy marketplace, even though it offers a sweet deal on listing and transaction fees. And by "sweet deal," we mean no fees. Your store is free, there are no listing fees, and you do not pay a commission on sales. What's the catch? Unlike other online marketplaces that operate strictly on listing fees and commissions, Zibbet takes an approach similar to hosted e-commerce solutions. As shown in Figure 5-7, Zibbet offers two plans plus a discount if you sign up for an annual membership. The basic plan is free, with product listings capped at 50 per month, one image per listing, and no access to advanced tools and features. For $10 per month (or an annual fee of $89), you get access to all features and marketing tools such as coupons, gift cards, and Facebook integration, an unlimited number of listings, and up to eight images per listing.

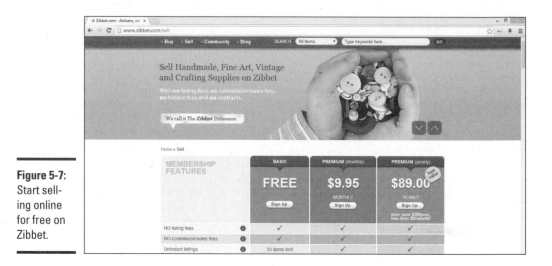

Figure 5-7:
Start selling online for free on Zibbet.

The site currently has nearly 300,000 product listings. The question is whether or not the site drives enough visitors to make selling on Zibbet worthwhile. After all, it doesn't do much good if you get a smoking hot deal on listing fees and commissions but never sell your items. You may take comfort in knowing that Zibbet earned a top place in the rankings for preferred marketplaces in the 2014 Sellers Choice for Marketplaces. Sellers voted it a top marketplace for profitability and ease of use. If you are getting started selling handmade goods, we think Zibbet is a good way to test the selling waters without investing much money.

Selling on Demand with Ready-Made Storefronts

If you don't have existing merchandise to sell at auction, you can create customized products by e-merchandising. Several sites, such as CafePress, have established themselves as proven leaders in this space, as described later in this chapter.

With *e-merchandising,* you still end up with products to sell, but you start with a blank slate (such as a standard white coffee cup or t-shirt) and then add unique artwork or text to put your own spin on the product. The result is a customized product — and you don't have to buy and stock truckloads of inventory. You can make multiple products and then sell them one at time — or, rather, on demand. (Naturally, customers can buy more than one item if they want.)

Discovering the benefits

The best part about e-merchandising is that the storefront solution takes care of almost everything for you, from inventory stocking to customer service issues. Other than uploading artwork to customize the products, your primary job becomes *marketing* your products — and most of the top marketplaces provide support to help with your marketing efforts. Here's what an e-merchandiser such as CafePress can do for you:

+ **Inventory:** Because the base products are bought and warehoused through the e-merchandiser, they're ready and waiting as soon as an order, however big or small, comes in from your store.

+ **Storefront:** You're given the tools to create a complete online store. You can usually use a URL with the CafePress server or get one of your own.

+ **Order processing:** When setting up a store, you have the option of using the e-merchandiser's built-in shopping cart and payment processors. You don't need to have a merchant's account to sell!

+ **Printing:** You don't have to worry about printing because the e-merchandiser prints your designated design on each item.

+ **Packing and shipping:** The site also handles all back-end functions for you, including shipping and handling.

+ **Customer service:** From fielding general questions to handling product returns, the e-merchandiser typically manages it all for you, often providing a toll-free number to customers. For example, if a customer wants to place an order by phone or isn't satisfied with a product and needs to return it, the e-merchandiser handles it all for you, in full.

+ **Reporting functions:** To keep up with sales, returns, commissions, and other functions, the site has an extensive online reporting function. You can access it at any time to see a snapshot of how your store is performing.

✦ **Payments:** Similar to an affiliate program, you track sales and earnings (the difference between the cost of the product and the price you set). After you accumulate at least a certain amount in your account (usually $10 or $25), the company sends you a commission check.

✦ **Marketing support:** You have access to several marketing tools, including ones for creating newsletters and e-mail marketing campaigns.

✦ **Traffic:** Because an e-merchandiser is also set up as a community of shopkeepers, your store is always listed on the site's marketplace. So customers can find you (by accident or on purpose) by visiting the main marketplace shopping pages. (Of course, your sales are always stronger when you market your site directly.)

Setting up your store

Getting started selling with an online marketplace is similar to selling with any storefront or e-commerce solution. The first step, after you register and create an account, is setting up a site from which you showcase the products you choose to sell. Setting up a store with an e-merchandiser offers several benefits:

✦ Free hosting

✦ Ready-made templates

✦ Customization

✦ Built-in reporting

✦ Integration with Facebook

Adding images to products

After you set up your store, you can start adding products. One of the most challenging parts of working with any e-merchandising solution is choosing the right high-quality images to use with the products you sell. Each e-merchandiser has different image guidelines, so review the guidelines carefully. The quality of your image greatly affects the quality of the final product — for example, using a grainy photo will appear grainy on the final product, too. The rule of thumb is to avoid using low-quality photos and JPEG images.

If you're not familiar with working with and manipulating images, start by uploading only one or two products until you're comfortable using the product features. You may want to start with a T-shirt or coffee mug because uploading images for each of those items is easy and will give you a good feel for what to expect when you start working with other products (which often require more image resizing to fit an unusual product surface or shape).

Most e-merchandisers provide an extensive image-creation and -sizing guide for their products. To help you out even more, the sites usually feature an online tutorial or image workshop to ensure that you use the properly formatted image for the best visual quality on your product. You can also check with the site's sellers' forum for tips from other shopkeepers about using and manipulating images for the best results.

Comparing features to find the best deal

More e-merchandising storefronts are popping up every day. For the most part, the features and benefits offered by all the sites are fairly similar. One site hasn't truly pulled enough ahead of the others for us to say that it's the one that will become the eBay of e-merchandising. Admittedly, many sellers prefer CafePress, but as that site matures and is considered mainstream, we see more interest in alternative or start-up options. In the following sections, we describe three of the top e-merchandisers.

CafePress

The site that is best known for e-merchandising (and has been around the longest) is CafePress (`www.cafepress.com`). CafePress provides you with a long list of products, such as T-shirts, coffee mugs, messenger bags, and other apparel — more than 250 products in all — and you can also sell books (self-published, printed on demand). You use your own graphical design and text to create a one-of-a-kind product. CafePress even hosts a complete store for you on its servers (see Figure 5-8).

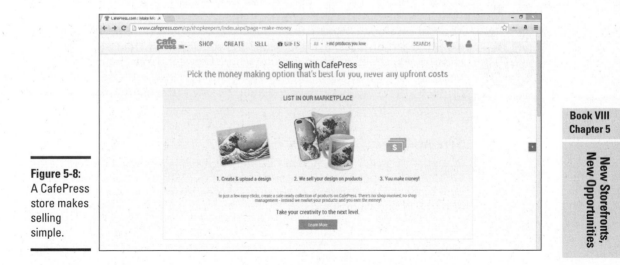

Figure 5-8: A CafePress store makes selling simple.

Book VIII Chapter 5

New Storefronts, New Opportunities

A big advantage of using CafePress is that you don't have to pay for the product until someone purchases it from you. And while you also pay no setup fees to get started with CafePress, some fees are involved in selling on this marketplace. You can choose from two plans:

✦ **No upfront costs:** You set up your store and pay zero fees, in advance. When you sell products, you essentially earn royalties — that's what CafePress calls your profit — and pay 10 percent of your monthly sales to CafePress.

✦ **Prepay:** You pay your fees as a set amount, ahead of time. You can pay $6.95 per month or receive a small discount for paying several months in advance. If you pay a full year in advance, you pay only $5 per month.

Let's take a closer look at the royalty model for CafePress. As mentioned, the e-merchandiser takes a 10 percent royalty fee from your sales each month. How much are your royalties? That's largely determined by you and how you choose to price the items for sale in your shop. Each product is associated with a base price that covers the cost of the product itself, the printing, and all other related services and overhead initially absorbed by CafePress. From that base price, you set the price to sell that product to your customers. For example, suppose that you sell a large coffee mug printed with your logo and a clever saying. CafePress sells the finished product to you for $12.99. You want to make $5 on each sale, so you would price the mug at $17.99. At the end of the month, you've sold a total of $395.78 in merchandise, which earns you $100 in royalties (after deducting the base price of $12.99 per product). CafePress takes 10 percent from your monthly royalties, so they get $10 and you get $90.

You can earn bonus money from CafePress by selling more products. If you exceed a certain sales level (for example, you sell more than $100 per month), you can earn a bonus of anywhere between 10 to 30 percent of your monthly base price sales. Or you can earn 10 percent on the sales of any products that you tag to be included in the CafePress marketplace. That's it! Sell more, earn more!

Spreadshirt

Spreadshirt, which launched in Germany in 2002, has opened United States and other European locations for its base of operations. Unlike CafePress, which offers a wide variety of products, Spreadshirt sticks to offering only apparel, as shown in Figure 5-9.

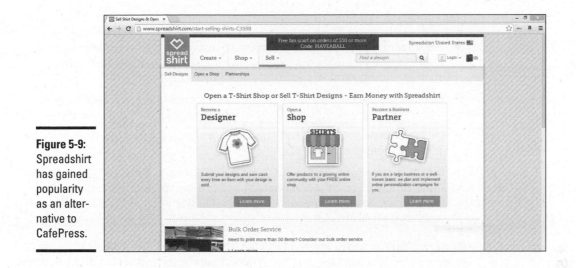

Figure 5-9:
Spreadshirt
has gained
popularity
as an alter-
native to
CafePress.

Spreadshirt has established several avenues for you to make money:

✦ **Open a shop:** You can create a fully functioning store for free, with access to all Spreadshirt apparel. You upload your own images to create truly customized products or commission artwork from one of the Spreadshirt designers for a small fee. You set the commissions you want to earn for each product, up to $20, which is added to the cost of the item. (Spreadshirt sets the base cost.) Spreadshirt suggests that the best commission range for success is between $8 and $10 per product. Because Spreadshirt handles all inventory management, shipping, and other back-end functions for your store, you have zero overhead and can afford a smaller commission! You can also open a Pro store account for $10 per month. In addition to removing restrictions from the number of products you can upload monthly, Spreadshirt also removes any advertising from your site.

✦ **Become a designer:** This option lets you share your creative designs with other members of Spreadshirt. Simply upload your artwork and set a commission that you want to earn. Each time a member of the Spreadshirt community uses your design on their products, you get a commission. According to Spreadshirt, the most successful commission is between $1 and $2.

✦ **Become a business partner:** This higher level marketing partnership is available only to established brands or personalities. Beginners (and all us non-celebrities.) should start with one of the other two options.

The Spreadshirt site has other advantages:

✦ **Brand-name products:** Your customers may be pleased to discover that your custom products are printed on established name-brand wares, such as Hanes, Fruit of the Loom, and American Apparel.

✦ **Extensive apparel options:** The Spreadshirt collection of T-shirt styles and other types of clothing are the mainstay of its product inventory.

✦ **Print on dark color:** You can choose to print on a variety of dark-colored T-shirts, including black, red, and gray.

✦ **Sell globally:** Because Spreadshirt has its roots in Germany, it's only natural that it provides a global sales strategy. You can choose to sell through a U.S. or European store. To sell in both places, you have to open two separate stores.

To start selling at Spreadshirt, go to www.spreadshirt.com. You can open a shop in only a few minutes, and then upload your own custom products to sell.

Zazzle

Zazzle (www.zazzle.com) is similar to CafePress in that it offers hundreds of products for you to sell, and your choices are not limited to apparel. You can place custom images on standard items such as magnetic buttons and coffee mugs, or on less traditional items such as ceramic tile coasters and upscale watches. You can also choose from a wide variety of colors and styles for the apparel products that are available for sale.

The model for making money with Zazzle is straightforward, as shown in Figure 5-10. You set up a free online storefront to display customized products for sale, choose the products to sell (based on the merchandise that Zazzle offers), and add an image, a design, or text to the product. Then you set the price you want to charge.

Figure 5-10: Zazzle rewards top sellers with access to promotional tools and tips.

Zazzle offers several options for earning money:

✦ **Royalties:** As with CafePress, Zazzle charges a base price for the merchandise, and you tack on the profit. Unlike other marketplaces, however, you decide the commission or royalties you want to earn and Zazzle adjusts the base price of the product accordingly. The e-merchandiser suggests a commission range of 7 to 10 percent. Zazzle uses a special royalty calculator in your store to help you price products.

✦ **Referrals:** This option works like an affiliate program in which you earn a commission on any type of Zazzle purchase that was made as a result of a link you shared. The referral fee is 30 percent, plus any additional volume bonus fee you many earn.

✦ **Volume bonus:** You can earn commission bonuses also based on your sales volume. After you sell a minimum of $100, you qualify for an additional royalty percentage ranging from 1 to 17 percent.

✦ **Pro seller status:** When your store hits certain annual revenue levels, Zazzle invites you to be a Pro seller. Although you do not earn additional royalties as a direct result of this program, your store probably qualifies for volume bonuses. As a Pro seller, you do get access to additional tools and marketing opportunities that help you sell more in general.

Zazzle boasts a traffic flow of prospective customers that exceeds 30 million visitors, monthly. That number represents a lot of eyeballs to potentially see your store and buy your products.

**Book VIII
Chapter 5**

**New Storefronts,
New Opportunities**

Book IX

Fundraising Sites

Contents at a Glance

Chapter 1: Raining Donations: Online Giving Is Big for Not-for-Profits

In This Chapter

⌐ **Increasing value with online and social giving**

⌐ **Spreading the message and convincing decision-makers**

Did you know that online giving has experienced *double-digit growth* every year, for the last four years? According to Blackbaud (www.blackbaud.com), online donations accounted for 7 percent of all giving for nonprofit organizations in 2012. In the next five years, online giving is expected to surpass 15 percent of total donations as more donors turn to the Internet as their preferred source for charitable giving.

Reports show that nonprofit organizations received more than $316 billion in total donations in 2012, even during a period of lower giving due to a sluggish economy. The portion of online donations topped more than $22 billion. Smaller nonprofit organizations saw the most growth in online donations, compared to large organizations. Even more encouraging is that new forms of online giving, such as crowdfunding, peer-to-peer online giving, and social (media) giving are fueling more opportunities for giving for organizations of all sizes.

One of the most successful and widespread online donation efforts occurred on Twitter and has since become an annual campaign for thousands of nonprofits. The #GivingTuesday hashtag was shared on Twitter, and people were encouraged to make an online donation to their favorite charitable organization. In 2013, Blackbaud processed more than $19 million in donations for 3,800 charities. #GivingTuesday donations were up 90 percent compared to 2012, with the average donation of $142 up 40 percent year over year. With donations made through social media continuing to rise and overall online giving exceeding expectations, one question remains: What are you waiting for?

Now is the time to bring your organization online, expand its web and social media presence — and its capability to capture the spirit of online giving. If you're unsure about how to accomplish these goals, we're here to help. In this chapter, we explain why online giving is appropriate for your cause and how to get everyone else in your organization on board.

Determining How Your Organization Can Benefit

Online giving, or *e-philanthropy,* refers to the concept of charitable organizations raising money from online donations. An evolving concept since it first came in vogue in 2000, online giving is no longer simply a means of asking for money over the Internet. In the past few years, online donations have skyrocketed following natural disasters in locations across the globe. Whether the catastrophe is an earthquake, a tsunami, or a tornado, the Internet has not only allowed organizations such as the Red Cross to collect much-needed donations but also served as a way to spread awareness and increase the generosity of giving offline, from clothing donations to blood drives. Online donations have had a powerful effect and are quickly becoming accepted as a mainstream fundraising method.

For those reasons, online giving is now a recognized strategic tool that you can — and should — use for your nonprofit. This method of marketing touches all outreach initiatives and specifically encompasses these six areas in an organization:

✦ **Awareness building:** An effective online presence targets your internal (or existing) membership base *and* your external (or potential) audience. You can increase awareness for a specific campaign or for your overall mission.

✦ **Donor development:** You're using the Internet to not only target one-time contributors but also build long-term donor relationships.

✦ **Membership retention:** The combination of targeted e-mail communications, a useful website, and active social media accounts is a proven means of generating membership renewals for your nonprofit.

✦ **Volunteer and client recruitment:** Your organization thrives on financial contributions and the support of volunteers. Fortunately, your site can serve as a recruitment tool for both entities. Additionally, if your nonprofit is service based (such as debt-management or tax-preparation assistance for senior citizens), an online strategy can help you reach the audience most in need of your services.

✦ **Board outreach:** Although your board members are technically part of your volunteer base, you should consider board outreach and development to be a distinctive area in your organization. A fully integrated and well-maintained Internet initiative is an increasingly important method for keeping your board committed to your cause.

✦ **Grassroots activism:** The Internet is increasingly used as a way to elicit action at the basic level. From online petitions to e-mail campaigns, response rates are rising among the masses, and the effort is paying off.

These are the key areas in which online initiatives should be regularly infiltrating your organization. Consider how each segment provides additional benefits to your cause, and then take a closer look at what your organization gains when it actively solicits online donors.

Savvy e-philanthropists have three characteristics in common:

✦ **Generosity:** Current research indicates that online donors are twice as likely to give to your cause, and they typically give twice as often as offline contributors.

✦ **Curiosity:** Online donors seek out information; they're eager to learn about your organization and its activities. Most important, these Net donors turn to the Internet for facts, figures, and general information before making their final giving decisions. In return, a donor who makes an informed decision takes the first step in forming a lasting bond with your organization versus a one-time random act of giving.

✦ **Loyalty:** The members of your nonprofit with whom you stay in touch over the Internet are highly likely to not only stick around but also make more (and larger) donations over time. Therefore, if you're fostering the relationship, chances are good that your multiyear renewal rates will increase.

Convincing Your Board of Directors

After you're committed to using an online strategy to grow your donor base, the next step is convincing the rest of your organization that it's the right thing to do.

Persuading your board that online giving is a timely solution is easier than you think. You might just have to spend a little more time moving progressive ideas through the approval process. Consider the usual reasons that board members tend to reject or stall a new idea:

✦ They're fearful of the unknown — especially where technology is concerned.

✦ They're convinced that the costs outweigh the benefits.

✦ They've decided that someone else has a more compelling argument against it.

If you understand these three points, you can arm yourself with the power of persuasion. People engage in many spirited debates over the proposal of innovative concepts, yet plenty of fantastic ideas are eventually rolled into action because someone embraced a plan of persuasion and stuck with it.

Not every board fights the incorporation of an extensive Internet strategy. Heck, people might even line up to take turns making this idea a reality. You may be one of the lucky ones with a board member who knows that

✦ Donating online is more widely accepted by donors.

✦ Security measures have made online giving a safer way to donate.

✦ Average per donor contributions could rise.

However, if your board tends to scrutinize a plan before rubber-stamping it, you might find the information in this section especially helpful.

Tying the Internet strategy into your mission

One characteristic that all directors of nonprofits share is their belief in an organization's mission. Because the mission is usually the catalyst that prompts a member to get involved, use that synergy in your favor. With every point you make in support of e-philanthropy, tie that initiative directly into your mission statement.

Developing an online strategy

Many organizations still view the Internet as a one-time fundraising shot and continue to treat their sites as separate entities. That's not a good argument to convince a board to invest its organization's precious dollars. Instead, if you're ready to get your board of directors on board, make sure that you have a plan with a detailed and all-inclusive strategy.

Use the six points we outline earlier, in the "Determining How Your Organization Can Benefit" section, and feel free to add others that might pertain specifically to you. Create an Internet marketing plan that incorporates each one. From donor development to member retention, don't hesitate to use them all. Your proposal is illustrating that the Internet is more than a single action item and proving it to be a component of the bigger picture. With this strategy in hand, you're ahead of the game when the board gives your plan the green light.

Providing a budget-friendly proposal

When you present your proposal to your board members, expect them to search for the price tag for implementing your project. That final number is often a deal breaker for an organization with a limited budget. (What non-profit does that statement *not* apply to?)

Be sure to take advantage of your organization's 501(c)3 status. Not doing so is the single biggest mistake that many organizations make when pricing technology.

Whether you're building or updating a website or purchasing back-end components to add to an existing site, follow these three simple rules:

✦ **Ask vendors for a discount or special pricing for nonprofit organizations.** Companies are usually willing to work with nonprofits, although it's not a price point that's typically advertised.

Always get multiple bids (from separate companies) for each service or technology, and use the same *specs*, or list of requirements. Then compare the prices, apples to apples, before making a final decision.

Never go with the first or only quote you receive. This may seem like commonsense advice, but we can't stress enough that shopping around can save you money.

✦ **Use your board of directors as a resource.** Board members might have access to the services or technologies you need through a company they own or work for, or because of their own special skills. Services and equipment are often donated or sold at rock-bottom prices.

When a board member performs a service, such as updating your website, ask for a written contract. The contract should specify, as with any other vendor, start and finish dates, the scope of work and project details, and a review-and-approval process for signing off on the finished project. In case something goes wrong, the contract protects both sides. Even better, it can help avoid an uncomfortable situation with a board member.

✦ **Check the Internet for organizations (both for-profit and not-for-profit) with technology programs specifically for nonprofits.** An untold number of resources offer free or discounted technology and related services to the nonprofit sector. In Chapter 2 of this minibook, we provide detailed information about several of these programs and the companies that sponsor them.

If you qualify for one of the technology programs, be sure to list your actual cost in the budget proposal. (Even if equipment is free, you might have to pay shipping or installation.) Then show a comparison of the bids you received from other commercial vendors. Board members appreciate seeing this type of cost savings. Just knowing that you found a good deal can sometimes sway the vote in your favor.

Offering case studies

Not everyone is a risk taker. In fact, most people tend to be conservative when they do new things. That's why boards especially love to hear other success stories before jumping into the unknown world of technology, and that's why we encourage you to find *case studies*, or examples of organizations, that benefitted from using an Internet strategy.

To increase the chances of your examples being well received, choose these types of case studies:

✦ **Mirror images:** Feature organizations that are as similar as possible to yours in size, budget, mission, or donor profile.

✦ **Matching projects:** Choose examples that use technology, or overall strategies, similar to what you're proposing.

✦ **Multipurpose:** Case studies should demonstrate more than a single point of success. Ideally, the strategy should result in multiple benefits. Even better, the study should also tout recurring, or lasting, benefits for the organization.

You can find technology case studies in several ways. Talk with other organizations in your community, read a few national newsletters or magazines targeted to philanthropic organizations, or check out the websites of nonprofit consultants who frequently list detailed case studies for prospective clients to view. Network for Good provides access to case studies, white papers, and best-practice research and tips for online fundraising at `www.fundraising123.org/nonprofit-marketing`.

Recruiting an expert

Plenty of experts specialize in both nonprofits and the design and implementation of Internet strategies. If you're uncertain about your own power of persuasion, consider inviting an expert to discuss the issue with your board. Even if you give an overview of the proposal, try to have a consultant on hand to answer likely questions.

A consultant who offers to speak to your board for free usually hopes to eventually be hired. If you have no intention of engaging the consultant's services (even if the technology proposal is approved), be honest about it. Instead, negotiate a reasonable hourly fee to cover the consultant's time.

Garnering positive peer pressure

Hiring a professional isn't the only way to find support for your proposal. Other board members or staff members might be willing to jump on your bandwagon. Identify possible candidates, and find at least one other person to help champion your cause. Finding someone whose opinion is respected, or who has a knack for generating positive peer pressure, obviously helps.

Getting specific

You know that more than one board meeting might be necessary to make a decision about something that encompasses a large strategy. To help your cause, offer to assign ownership to another individual or to a committee that can gather additional information between meetings. This strategy also helps spread the burden of conducting the final research. Additionally, suggest that the plan be implemented over a designated period. If you split the project into specific stages, the overall goal appears more attainable. Following is a sample timeline you can use for implementing a project:

> **February 1 (start date):** Confirm project goals and estimated completion dates.
>
> **March 1 (decision date 1):** Get board approval of budget.
>
> **May 1 (decision date 2):** Accept technology vendor proposals.
>
> **September 5 (decision date 3):** Get board approval of revised site and online giving campaign.
>
> **October 1 (implementation date):** Site goes live and first online giving campaign kicks off.

Following are the action items targeted by week:

Week 1: Assign ad hoc committee.

Week 4: Verify or define goals for Internet strategy; identify needs for updated or new website; finalize budget.

Week 12: Research desired technology solutions; identify possible technology vendors; request and review proposals from web developers; select web developer and technology vendors.

Week 16: Select first online giving campaign using updated site and technology solutions.

Week 18: Review first draft of proposed site revision (aesthetic design with site map).

Week 24: Give all approved content, photos, and graphics to web designer.

Week 26: Finalize marketing plan for online campaign.

Week 30: Present new or revised site, along with initial online giving campaign, for board approval.

Week 31: Develop all elements of campaign, including social media elements, e-mails, and offline marketing support materials.

Week 32: Implement final changes and corrections to site.

Week 33: Prelaunch site internally (not for public access); test all features and make necessary changes; announce upcoming public launch of site and fundraising campaign kickoff.

Week 34: Launch new site and begin first online giving campaign.

As you know, starting and managing a project of this magnitude is not easy and requires the support of many people in your organization (as well as partners and solution providers outside your organization). Use this project list as a springboard to put your organization's project on the right track.

Chapter 2: Adding Online Moneymakers to an Existing Site

In This Chapter

⮡ **Evaluating your site structure to decide which elements are plausible**

⮡ **Researching technology resources**

⮡ **Selling to the highest bidder as the ultimate e-fundraising tool**

⮡ **Adding easy fixes to increase online donations**

The Internet has provided a platform for a wide variety of organizations, causes, and trends. Since the early dotcom days, entrepreneurs and companies have blazed a trail of innovation, pioneering sites such as eBay, Amazon, Groupon, Facebook, and Twitter as well as smaller companies that have developed exciting and useful applications delivered online. At the same time, however, plenty of organizations have worked to simply keep up with current online technologies and trends, and others have, sadly, lagged well behind the rest. The laggards continue to resist current online solutions and resources — and it shows!

Unfortunately, this description also fits many of your nonprofit peers right now. An organization's online presence may suffer for many reasons. As with many important goals for a nonprofit, the lack of money and resources (staff) dictate when and how things get accomplished — even important things, such as the creation of a professional website. The good news is that you're committed to change. You're ready to bring your site into the next decade and fully embrace the opportunity of online fundraising. In this chapter, we arm you with information about your options and their costs so that you can make an informed decision and start raising funds and recruiting resources.

Determining Which Features Your Site Can Support

You probably have a basic website, with pages that explain your organization's mission, highlight a few of your annual fundraising events (along with some fuzzy photos), and list the names of your board of directors and officers. Then again, you might have developed a more detailed site structure and haven't yet implemented any type of online fundraising tools to go along with it.

Regardless, the first step in this process of adding money generators is to conduct a detailed analysis of all aspects of your technology, support resources, and site framework. Your primary objective is to realize current capabilities and address possible limitations.

If you've already implemented or designed a general technology plan, you can pull from it much of the information you need in this analysis. If you don't have this type of plan, the information you collect in this analysis can be transitioned into that document.

For this purpose, we recommend taking an inventory. Break down your situational analysis into the eight function areas shown in Figure 2-1.

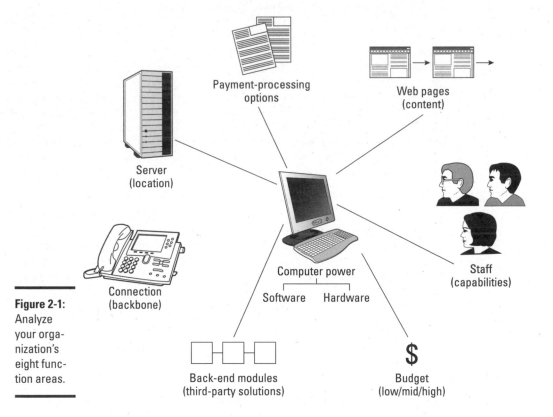

Figure 2-1: Analyze your organization's eight function areas.

Testing your backbone (connections)

Begin your technology analysis by taking a closer look at the power of your in-house computer connection. Are you still using dial-up to log on to the Internet? (We certainly hope that's not the case!) Or are you using a faster connection from a broadband-enabled service (typically, either DSL or cable)? Jot down the status of your current connection speed. If you're on a slower connection, note whether you can upgrade your connection.

Deciding on your computer needs

When it comes to hardware and software, a couple of main theories exist:

✦ **Buy only what you need and nothing else:** The idea is to buy items later when they become a necessity. You don't spend money on a larger display screen or a wireless mouse and keyboard, and you don't splurge for extra memory.

✦ **Buy as much as you can now rather than later:** In this theory, you get a better price by bundling all the components you need rather than buying them individually.

Both concepts are valid, and the one that you need to take into consideration depends on where you buy your hardware and software. Some vendors give discounts when you bundle printers, LCD screens, software, and other items with your basic purchase. Other vendors sell only bare-bones systems for extremely low prices, but these systems typically cannot be customized and are sold as is. Shop around with your list of requirements (divided into items you must have and the ones you can do without) and then do business with the vendor who can give you the best deal.

Locating your server

You need to identify the physical location of your site's server for your technology analysis. If your server is in-house, it's located on the physical premises you maintain. Otherwise, it must be hosted off-site, through a vendor, which is typically the case.

Now comes the tricky part. How much do you know about that server? For example, can you identify its operating system and whether it's Windows or Linux based? What you do or don't know about the server can hinder, or slow, the addition of fundraising elements to your site. Several small-business owners sign hosting contracts only to learn later that their company servers didn't support the specific language used to develop their websites.

Your answers to the following basic questions about your server can affect whether you can add future fundraising solutions to your site:

✦ **Is your server a database?** What type is it? For example, MySQL, Microsoft Access, and SQL 2000 are the more popular choices. Does the database have size limitations?

✦ **Which development languages are supported?** Does your server include ColdFusion MX7, .NET, Perl, PHP, CSS, or Java? Are you charged extra for supporting some of the languages, or are they all included in your regular fee?

✦ **What are the limitations on your server's disk space?** What's the cost to add space, if needed?

✦ **Do you have *root* (admin) access to the server, which allows you or your technical staff to make changes?** What are your host company's policies regarding technical support for changes that relate to the server? What are the tech-support fees for that type of assistance?

✦ **Is the host company partnered with other application vendors, such as shopping cart providers?** On the upside, your server might already be set up to handle some of these applications, perhaps even at a slightly discounted fee. On the downside, if the partnerships are exclusive, your host company might prohibit you from adding other (competitor) applications to the server.

Although you aren't expected to be the technical expert in this area, having this basic information written down and accessible is valuable as you begin evaluating applications from other vendors. You should have a good idea about whether the features are likely to be readily (and inexpensively) compatible with your site's server.

Look for cloud-based solution providers that allow the technical aspects of your server, or other applications, to be managed off-site. These types of services make it easy for your organization to access service, usually for a small monthly fee — but without the hassle of having to deal with the back-end maintenance and upkeep of the technology!

Processing payments

If you represent a nonprofit organization, you probably already accept donations. The issue for your technology analysis is *how* you accept them. If you accept only checks and cash, you should also have a merchant account with your bank or some other means of accepting credit card transactions. You might already accept debit and charge cards too, even if it's only offline. Well, your analysis is the place to spell it all out and put your cards (so to speak) on the table. Include a thorough description of the types of payments you accept, how they're collected and processed, and which company or bank processes them.

Use this part of your analysis to start conducting some research. For instance, maybe you have a merchant account but don't process payments online. Check with your merchant provider and your bank to explore what you have to do to collect payments through your website. If you're uncertain about which questions to ask or what your options are, check out the ins and outs of payment processing in Book IV, Chapter 4.

Tracking back-end modules

The module-tracking portion of your technology analysis is, more than any other part, a straightforward inventory. You need to know what types of applications and capabilities your site already has and whether to use these features.

In addition to considering the use of shopping carts, databases, and online form pages, think in broader terms to answer these types of questions:

✦ Do you use a contact-management system to keep track of donors and volunteers?

✦ Is a system in place for collecting and storing e-mail addresses?

✦ Is e-mail now gathered from visitors to your website, or do you only collect addresses offline?

Try to compile a thorough list of all back-end applications. Note whether you use each particular feature, detail how you use it, and identify the name of the vendor you obtained it from (if applicable).

One important reason for this part of your analysis is compatibility. As you add features, be sure not to replicate one that you already have.

Although we're specifically discussing the addition of online fundraising applications, a company might want to sell you, or encourage you to use, other services or features that are compatible with (or accessories to) the fundraising feature. Knowing what you already have helps prevent duplication and added costs. In addition, a vendor for one of your current applications might also offer fundraising applications. By checking with those providers first, you might be able to use those tools and receive a guarantee that they're compatible with some of your existing applications.

Mapping your site structure

Mapping your site structure is extremely easy. In fact, if you have a current site map of your website, this section of your technology analysis is partially complete.

Review your existing website page by page and create a site map of your pages, as shown in Figure 2-2. The map, similar in structure to an outline, uses hierarchical ranking to show how the site flows, or how subpages are linked to primary pages. Unless your site has hundreds of pages, this task isn't difficult.

Print a copy of each page of your site. The hard copy of your site is useful for reference and planning.

As you begin selecting online fundraising tools, use these pages to begin reconstructing your site to accommodate and promote the placement of those tools. Rather than completely reworking your site structure, you have to only identify the places where a visitor to your site is most likely to see and participate in the fundraising effort.

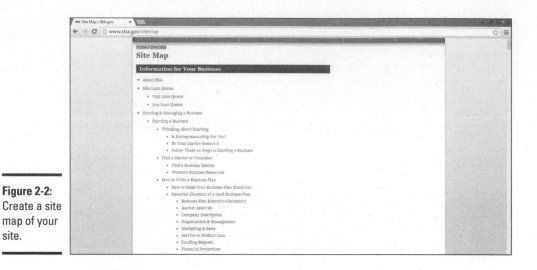

Figure 2-2:
Create a site
map of your
site.

Determining staffing capabilities

Your staff members and volunteers are an important resource for your
analysis. Not all organizations have a technical-support person on staff, so
here's your chance to thoroughly analyze the strengths and weaknesses
of your support base. Start this section of your analysis by making a list of
your staff members and regular office volunteers. List each person's skills
and educational background as they apply to technology. Although identifying people with highly technical skills, such as programming, web development, or IT maintenance is important, you should also reveal skill sets that
are useful in today's online environment. Look for staff and volunteers who
understand and regularly use social networking sites or excel in graphic
design, writing, and marketing. All these components will help support your
online fundraising efforts.

Even if you have a full-time technical-support position in-house, you should
still take an inventory of everyone's skill sets. Seeing a defined list of everyone's skill sets is a terrific opportunity to tap in to hidden talent or uncover
the need for a future training session.

Paying the piper: Your budget

The final piece of your analysis is probably the easiest to create. Identify
your current budget for technology and website development. If you already
have a line item in your annual report for this element, make a note of the
number. Don't stop there, though: Detail whether this money is truly available for use. Is it already spent or earmarked for another project? Are there
any restrictions on how the money can be spent? Be realistic about how
much money is available or when it might be available.

If you don't have money already designated for technology upgrades in your budget, try to calculate a workable amount. Rather than use an actual dollar amount, assign a range. If you're broke, call it like you see it: Give it a low-end designation and assign it a range from zero to a few hundred dollars. A good midrange amount is usually from $1,500 to $5,000. Consider the high end to be anything over $5,000 and realistically capping out around $10,000. Depending on the size of your organization, your numbers might be bumped up by several thousand dollars, especially if you are a larger, national non-profit with more intricate site requirements. You get the idea.

One reason that we prefer to assign a range for a budget analysis is that it makes a discussion with other people more palatable. If board members and other decision-makers know that you're looking in the low-end range of the scale, you're not immediately pinned down to a specific dollar amount. Likewise, when you're requesting price quotes from vendors, you feel less pressure to have to name the exact high-end dollar amount you can spend. Identifying a range that's budgeted for the project usually feels more comfortable.

Adding an Auction to Your Site

For individuals and businesses, online auctions continue to be a popular way to make money. (And as eBay has proven, there's no sign of these online auctions slowing down!) As an active part of the nonprofit sector, you probably know that onsite auctions have long been a staple of charity fundraising. Silent auctions are especially popular as stand-alone affairs or as add-ons to dinner galas and other live events. Thanks to the power of the Internet, the buck (literally) no longer stops there.

Your organization can increase the reach and earnings potential of your typical event-specific auction by putting it online. As with other fundraising tools, online auctions come in all shapes and sizes, so you can find the perfect fit for your organization. If you want to know more about eBay, turn to Book VIII, Chapter 4. In this section, we introduce you several online auction sites that may be beneficial to you.

Third-party auctions

From one point of view, a third-party auction — the "effortless" auction — is by far the easiest type for your organization to participate in. All you have to do is have your organization selected as a recipient charity. The auction itself is promoted and managed entirely from another company's website. These companies continually auction off items and then ration the proceeds to their approved nonprofits. Two examples are BiddingForGood and eBay.

The philanthropic auction service BiddingForGood is essentially an online community working for nonprofits. It promotes an ongoing auction of items that include furniture, clothing, collectibles, event tickets, and even celebrity items, which are sold from its website at `www.biddingforgood.com`. After the auction for each item ends, the proceeds go to the charity that provided the item or that was selected to receive the proceeds from the item. The site can host an entire auction for one charity or raise money from single auction items and donations. So far, the site has helped raise more than $238 million for schools, communities, and national charitable organizations.

The eBay Giving Works program is open to any approved charitable organization. To date, the program has worked with over 25,000 organizations and raised more than $375 million from eBay auction items. It teamed up with PayPal Giving — an independent 501(c)(3), formerly known as MissionFish — to handle auction-management services. For example, you must register and apply through PayPal Giving to be recognized as a legitimate charity. After you're in the system, eBay sellers can choose to donate anywhere from 10 to 100 percent of an item's winning bid to the charity of their choice. When a seller agrees to donate even a portion of the auction item's proceeds to your organization, a special ribbon icon is placed next to the item so that bidders know that the auction is part of a fundraiser or charitable donation. The ribbon icon is easy for bidders to spot, as shown in Figure 2-3.

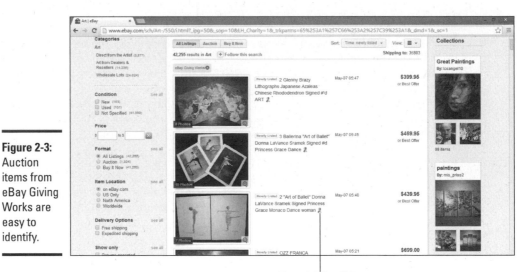

Figure 2-3:
Auction items from eBay Giving Works are easy to identify.

eBay charity ribbon

As a bonus, any seller can choose to donate to your cause by selecting it from a list of certified charitable organizations and then designating it as a donation item after listing it on eBay.

You don't have to depend on the generosity of strangers. You can encourage your own members and longtime supporters to auction items on eBay and then donate the proceeds to your organization. Or you can become a direct seller and hold your own auction and list items for auction on your organization's eBay page.

If hosting an online auction isn't in the cards for you, consider placing a Donate Now button on your nonprofit's page on eBay. You can allow cash donations of any amount, which are paid through PayPal.

When an item is auctioned for an approved nonprofit, eBay issues a credit for any listing fees and final value fees when the total donation is between 10 and 100 percent of the winning bid. A nominal administration charge and a credit card processing fee may also apply. Although this simple process is a favorable alternative to managing your own online auction, you have to consider a few other pros and cons:

✦ **Donation tracking:** eBay offers a password-protected web page that reports all fundraising activity for both the seller and your organization. Because not all auction websites offer a donation-reporting feature, though, decide whether it's a necessity for you.

✦ **Delivering donations:** Every auction site has its own policy about when and how to deliver funds to your organization. For example, eBay transfers funds to your bank account, but you usually don't see the donation for at least a month after the auction ends. Other auction websites send checks with final donation amounts, which are mailed either monthly or quarterly. Don't count online auction proceeds from third parties as immediate revenue.

✦ **Confirm receipt:** In most cases, the website (or a partner organization) that's managing the auction takes responsibility for issuing tax receipts. However, always confirm that this is the case, and keep the site's contact information nearby. If benefactors have trouble getting a receipt, you'll know where to direct them for help.

✦ **Promoting the auction:** As with any fundraiser, find out how auction items are promoted, and then ask whether the site offers other tools or resources to let your organization help promote the auction. Sometimes, you can do something as simple as add a logo to your website. Or perhaps e-mail-based tools can be used to prompt bidding.

eBay Giving Works offers several free fundraising resources, along with marketing tips to help increase online donations for your organization. You can access this information and learn more about how to participate in eBay Giving Works by visiting `http://givingworks.ebay.com/charity-information`.

Direct auctions without the middleman — almost

In the *direct-selling* form of the online auction process, *you* are the seller *and* the recipient. (One example is offered through the eBay Giving Works program.) You auction off your own items, such as excess inventory or old office equipment. On eBay Giving Works, eBay provides the auction structure and reporting features, and you handle the rest.

Of course, you can take the direct path and fully manage your own online auction. You still need the support of a vendor, though, at least for the back-end technology. In exchange for your use of the technology and other accompanying services, you can expect to pay a setup fee, a one-time usage fee, and a percentage of sales from each auction item.

Another growing trend is having an auction-management site oversee and promote auctions for multiple nonprofits. Specifically, these auctions let people bid on access to celebrities or other high-value, luxury auction items. CharityBuzz (www.charitybuzz.com) is one of these sites. The benefit of working with CharityBuzz, or a site like this one, is that it can promote your unique auction items to a wider audience, one that is prepared and able to pay top dollar for a special item, such as dinner with a celebrity. The downside of this type of service is that you often have to be a larger national nonprofit to participate, or you have to come up with a star-studded auction item! CharityBuzz helps your organization brainstorm unique auction items and make them a reality, taking 20 percent of the auction total (with funds delivered in 30 days of the auction). Realize that working with this high-profile type of auction does take a serious commitment, but the payoff is potentially significant. Figure 2-4 shows some of the exclusive offerings that CharityBuzz helps promote for nonprofits. Maybe your organization's auction item will end up on this page one day.

Figure 2-4: Exclusive, high-value auction items take the spot-light on CharityBuzz.

Of course, luxury auctions aren't for everyone. In fact, you may prefer to manage your auctions in-house. Fortunately, lots of other companies offer online auctionware and compatible services. The following companies can get you started:

✦ **AuctionAnything.com:** www.auctionanything.com

✦ **BenefitEvents:** www.benefitevents.com

✦ **CharityAuctionOrganizer:** www.charityauctionorganizer.com

✦ **DoJiggy:** www.dojiggy.com

✦ **WildApricot:** www.wildapricot.com/fundraising-software

Online fundraising doesn't have to have the same grand *scope,* or large scale, of an auction. But as anyone who has pulled off this type of event can tell you, online fundraising still requires lots of work.

Soliciting Donations on Your Site

Just as some sites manage auctions on behalf of different charities, other organizations solicit online donations for charities. Adding your nonprofit's name to the list takes only a few minutes.

Connecting with online giving sites

Online giving sites, or *charity portals,* typically work with thousands of types of charities. The portal actively solicits online donors, and then individuals choose which charities receive the donations. In some case, these sites also distribute their databases of nonprofits to larger entities, in an effort to increase giving potential.

A few of the largest and most widely recognized charity portals are

✦ **CanadaHelps:** www.canadahelps.org

✦ **JustGive:** www.justgive.org

✦ **Network for Good:** www.networkforgood.org

You pay no registration fee when you sign up with any of these three sites. However, they all deduct a small percentage of each donation (usually 3 percent) to cover their credit card processing fees. As for online reporting features and the transfer of donated funds to your organization, these items vary with each organization. You can check the FAQ section of each site to find more information on each organization's specific policies.

Adding your nonprofit's name to each site's list of charities takes only a few minutes. When you're confirmed as a recognized charitable organization (typically within 48 hours), you're automatically listed on the site. You can also place on your website a link that directs your members to the charity portal. Then, when visitors to your site want to make a donation, they just click the appropriate link.

To be able to participate in any of these three charity portals, you first must register with GuideStar, which is part of Philanthropic Research, Inc., a widely recognized nonprofit. Charity portals use GuideStar to certify nonprofits in good standing.

You gain other advantages by registering with GuideStar. Because sites such as JustGive, Network for Good, Schwab Fund for Charitable Giving, and American Express also use the GuideStar database of charitable organizations to supplement their online databases for giving, you can be automatically listed on several charity portals. The GuideStar site alone attracts more than 10 million visitors each year and distributed more than $1 billion to charities in 2013. That translates to a lot of potential donors (and dollars) for your cause.

Registering with GuideStar is a two-part process: You set up an account and list your organization in the GuideStar system. When you're ready to get started, follow these steps to set up your account:

1. **Go to the GuideStar website at** `www.guidestar.org`.

2. **At the top left of the site's home page, click the Create Account link.**

   You see an online form on a new page that requests basic information to set up an account.

3. **While logged into your account, click the Update Nonprofit Report button at top of the home page.**

   You will be instructed to learn more about the GuideStar Exchange, which allows you to access and update information on your nonprofit. You see instructions regarding how to register to "claim" your organization's report, along with a free web page on GuideStar. You first need to request permission to update the report for your organization.

4. **Click the Manage Nonprofits Report link.**

   A form appears, requesting the organization's Employer Identification Number (EIN).

5. **Enter the EIN and then click the Request Permission button.**

   Permission is typically granted within 24 to 48 hours. Once approved, you proceed with the GuideStar Exchange registration.

6. **Set up your GuideStar Exchange account by providing the following information:**

   - *E-mail:* Enter the e-mail address for your nonprofit.

   - *Contacts*: Enter the full name of the primary contact at the nonprofit and the name of the board chairman.

   - *Location*: Enter the geographic area served.

   - *Organization:* Specify which kind of nonprofit organization you are.

   - *Mission statement:* Provide your organization's official mission statement.

   - *Terms:* Accept all terms and conditions.

After completing the registration, you're an official bronze member with access to basic benefits. By completing more in-depth information about your organization, you become a silver or gold member, with access to additional benefits.

If your organization is an exempt nonprofit recognized by the Internal Revenue Service (IRS), you might already be listed on the GuideStar site. Although the basic listing is pulled from your IRS Form 990, it doesn't include full details about your organization. Update your report fully to ensure that as much information as possible is available about your organization.

Adding a Donate Now button

More than a dozen reputable sites provide you with the ability to accept online donations on your website without opening a merchant account for credit and debit cards. These sites work by providing you with a Donate Now button to place on your website. Visitors to your site click the button to contribute to your cause. The processing sites take care of the rest of the process on your behalf, by transferring donations into your account (in some cases, by mailing monthly or quarterly checks). Usually, these sites offer a range of online fundraising tools, and some sites make it easy to integrate a Donate Now button with your donor-management software for long-term tracking and nurturing.

Typically, the only fee for this service is a small percentage (usually no more than 6 percent), deducted from the donation total, to cover the processing fees charged by the credit card companies. Some sites may track these as two separate fees.

The types of additional fees charged by some Donate Now button services can include

+ **A one-time setup charge:** Can be as much as $1,500

+ **A monthly service fee:** Normally ranges from $15 to $25

+ **A transaction fee to cover individual charges:** Might be a percentage of the donation or a flat fee

Shop and compare services. Some fees might include services that you don't need, so you're better off selecting another, lower-cost provider. Here's a sampling of the Donate Now button service providers you can explore:

+ **Amazon (`https://payments.amazon.com/help/Amazon-Simple-Pay/Integrating-with-Amazon-Simple-Pay/Amazon-Simple-Pay-Donations`):** The Simple Pay service provides a Donate Now button, and users can make donations from their Amazon account

+ **Blackbaud (`www.blackbaud.com`):** Designs software for nonprofit organizations

+ **Donate.ly (`www.donate.ly`):** Provides online donation forms and buttons, including those optimized for mobile devices

+ **Network For Good (`www.networkforgood.org`):** One of the pioneer sites for digital giving

These types of sites often provide a range of services, products, and consulting help tailored to the needs of your nonprofit. Check out some of their other products while you're on their sites.

Revving up with mobile giving

A growing component of online fundraising is mobile giving, or the ability to make donations through cellphones or tablets. The use of mobile devices, particularly smartphones, continues to explode, do it's not surprising that mobile donations are rising, too. Mobile giving is now a necessary part of any nonprofit's fundraising strategy.

Mobile donations are effective, in part, because they are a convenient way to give. You don't have to write a check, mail an envelope, or attend a live event to make a donation. Mobile giving is as easy as tapping a few buttons! The ease of donating with a mobile device also encourages *impulse giving*, or that spur-of-the-moment decision to financially support a cause, even for an unfamiliar charitable organization. Mobile giving has also been an effective way to engage first-time donors and a younger generation of donors. Research shows that adults 18–34 years old are more likely to make a financial donation to a nonprofit if they can do so through a cellphones or even social media. Perhaps one reason why younger donors like mobile giving is because it often makes use of small or micro donations, in amounts as little as 50¢ or $1 and usually no more than $10 or $20. Mobile giving is a wonderful way to share your organization's cause with a new audience and help reach a broader base of potential donors.

How does mobile giving work? One method is the use of text messaging to send instant donations via wireless providers (such as AT&T and Verizon). This technique is popular following natural disasters, such as hurricane Sandy. With this method, donors simply enter a designated code and text it to a special number to instantly donate a small, preset amount (usually $10) to the charitable organization. The donation is charged to the caller's cellphone bill. For example, you can make a $10 donation to the American Red Cross Disaster Relief Fund by using your mobile phone to text *REDCROSS* to 90999. The Red Cross promotes this mobile donation code on its website, as shown in Figure 2-5.

Figure 2-5:
The Red
Cross lets
donors
contribute
by sending a
special text
message.

You may think this strategy works only for larger nonprofit organizations or is too difficult to set up or manage. However, local nonprofits as well as schools and churches can easily use text donations. Several online organizations make it easy to set up text-to-give campaigns. In addition to texting, plenty of mobile apps and websites encourage mobile giving. Some sites handle everything, including promotion. The nonprofit simply applies to get added to a list of qualifying charitable organizations. In other cases, your organization uses an app as an add-on to your website or live event; the app offers your existing donor base a more convenient way to give.

Check out some of these great mobile-giving tools, apps and websites:

✦ **Checking In for Good (www.checkinginforgood.com):** Local businesses make donations to a specific charitable organization each time a patron uses his or her mobile phone and social media to check in at that business. *Checking in is* a way to broadcast through social media that you are visiting a business, such as a restaurant. Nonprofits partner with local businesses, through Checking In for Good, to receive donations. Checking In for Good helps verify and track visits, and provides tools to both businesses and nonprofits to promote and manage mobile fundraising campaigns.

✦ **GiveMob (www.givemobapp.org):** This app, which is designed for the iPhone and Android devices, allows users to text donations in small amounts, ranging from $5–$10. Nonprofits must register to be included in the list of approved GiveMob charities. Registration is free.

✦ **Instead (www.instead.com):** This app is added to a donor's phone to enable micro donations of $3–$5 to registered nonprofits. The app encourages a donor to give $3 to a charity instead of buying a cup of coffee that day. To be included in the list of charitable organizations promoted through Instead, nonprofits must contact the organization via e-mail or Twitter. (See the website for contact information.)

✦ **mGive** (www.mgive.com): This service a range of fundraising and awareness building tools by using mobile technology. Services are available to IRS-approved 501(c)(3) organizations, and the use of tools is based on the nonprofit's revenue level.

✦ **OneToday** (https://onetoday.google.com): Using an app, Google sends messages to potential donors every day prompting them to make a small donation (usually less than $10) to one of the featured charitable organizations. The app makes giving suggestions based on the donor's interests, which helps increase the likelihood of a donation. Nonprofits register for free but must be an IRS-approved 501(c)(3).

✦ **SimpleGive** (www.simplegive.com): Designed for churches and other nonprofits, this service helps increase fundraising and tithing through one-time and recurring mobile donations. Free and paid versions are available, but there are no set-up fees or contracts.

✦ **ZipGive** (www.zipgive.com): This full-service platform helps nonprofits raise money through text donations, mobile web forms, and recurring monthly mobile giving, and includes campaign- and donor-management tools. Fees start at $99 per year, plus a one-time set-up fee.

Chapter 3: Getting the Donor Base to Come to You

In This Chapter

✔ Attracting visitors to start building a donor base

✔ Preparing your online strategy for attracting donors

✔ Moving your current supporters online and boosting activity

✔ Networking online for a good cause

Wouldn't it be wonderful if you could put up your site, post your mission statement, and then watch as the generosity of strangers poured in for your cause? Well, it can happen — but not quite as easily as that! Getting people to donate to your cause takes effort on your part, mixed with a little bit of time and skill.

Creating a healthy online donor base is similar to organizing any other major fundraising campaign or event: It requires event planning, the ongoing help of volunteers and staff, a good marketing campaign, and (almost) flawless execution. In this chapter, we show you how to transfer those offline fundraising skills to your online efforts.

Building an Online Donor Base from Scratch

As with any commercial website, your online success depends on attracting customers. In this case, those customers are your donors, supporters, or constituents. At the end of the day, your goal is to bring these qualified visitors to your site.

These people are actively interested in your mission and are prepared to invest money, time, and good will in your cause. To find and keep this online donor base, try these three actions, which we call the *G.E.E whiz factor:*

1. Get your site noticed.

2. Engage passersby.

3. Establish a relationship.

It sounds simple. In truth, it *is* simple. The only difficult part is that many fantastic causes reach donors by way of the Internet, and, ultimately, your organization is competing with each one of them. That's why the ones that are the most successful in e-philanthropy are the ones that best communicate the G.E.E. whiz factor.

Get your site noticed

Develop a strategy to put your web site on the map. This step requires actively promoting your site to existing members of your organization and introducing it to prospective donors from around the globe. The International Fund for Animal Welfare (IFAW) uses every opportunity to get supporters to help spread the word. For example, this nonprofit not only consistently provides opportunities across its website to donate or become active in their cause but also gets visitors to help them drive more traffic (and potential donors) to their site. How? IFAW invites visitors to place an IFAW promotional banner on their own website or blog.

With ad banners, there are no forms to complete and no waiting periods for approval. Visitors simply choose the ad campaign and size of the banner they want to use and place it on their own website. It's that easy! In a matter of minutes, the IFAW can have their logo, their name, and their cause on someone else's site, all in an effort to help drive traffic and increase support. IFAW also has a Get Involved web page that shows a variety of ways to get involved, including everything from asking visitors to share the cause on social media sites to writing to U.S. senators to ask for help (see Figure 3-1). As with the ad banners, the nonprofit makes it quick and simple to participate and help spread the word about their cause, while also attracting more visitors to their website!

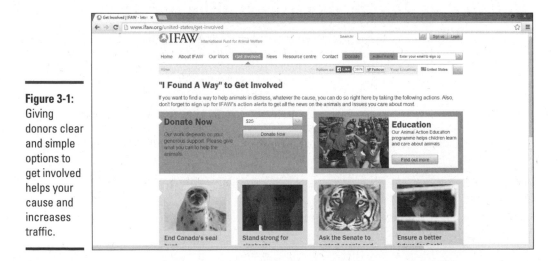

Figure 3-1:
Giving donors clear and simple options to get involved helps your cause and increases traffic.

Engage passersby

Give visitors to your site a reason to be involved in your organization *right now*. Rather than simply post your mission statement, use the site's home page to highlight one of your success stories. Show how other donors have made a difference, and then list specific actions that visitors can take to help create another success story. Your home page is a natural location for providing information that inspires people. And placing action buttons and links nearby offers site visitors an easy way to get involved after your stories have worked their magic.

Take a look at the home page for KIDS, Kids in Distressed Situations (`www. kidsdonations.org`), shown in Figure 3-2. As a nonprofit that assists children in need, whether as a result of poverty or illness or domestic abuse, this organization uses images and clearly posted tabs and links to draw your attention to the ways they make a difference in the lives of children. Without leaving the home page, Kids in Distressed Situations shows you multiple ways you can get involved and prominently posts the organization's mission statement explaining how they help "at-risk families and individuals." The home page also includes a How We Help section that shows how many companies have donated to the cause, the dollar value of product donations to date, and how many community agencies the organization has assisted through donations. These elements boost the organization's credibility and increase confidence that donations are getting to the intended recipients.

Figure 3-2:
Engage donors with multiple ways to get involved in your cause — without leaving the home page.

The home page also prominently shows donation buttons for both inventory donations and cash donations. Both a Donate Product button and a Donate Dollars button appear in the site's top-level navigation bar and in various places on the home page. Between the heartwarming photos of people in need and stories of what the organization is doing to change lives for the better, you can't help but want to at least find out ways you can help.

When visitors scroll down the page (which is also optimized for viewing on a mobile device), several places indicate the many ways to get involved with the organization, including:

✦ Giving cash donations through a Donate Now button.

✦ Providing donations of merchandise by completing an online inventory donation form.

✦ Finding a volunteer opportunity.

✦ Connecting with others who support the organization and staying up-to-date on events and news by participating in conversations on Twitter, Facebook, Pinterest, and YouTube. Because the site shows recent Twitter posts and provides links to these social networking sites, joining the online conversation is easy!

Establish a relationship

Getting people to take action once is a worthy goal; convincing them to become long-term donors is your real goal. To do that, use your website to keep people informed, to give them updates about how donations are being spent, and to expand their involvement into other areas of the organization.

The Humane Society brings home the G.E.E. whiz factor by establishing a relationship with its donors. The site invites donors to join its online community. Donors can sign up to receive regular information from the organization and also to customize their preferences. They can receive information that interests them, and the organization can keep donors informed about issues that they're likely to continue supporting and funding. The Humane Society provides another fun (and practical!) reason to keep donors coming back to the site through the site's shop, shown in Figure 3-3. The page lists their many corporate sponsors that give a percentage of purchases to the charity. It also links to the Humane Society's own online store, which offers a variety of products for sale. Donors may be more likely to give if they get something in return, such as a t-shirt for the donor or toys for their pet.

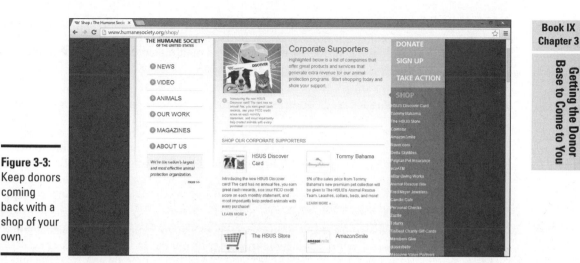

Figure 3-3:
Keep donors
coming
back with a
shop of your
own.

Putting Together a Plan to Reach Donors

After you have a good idea of what it takes to get your site noticed and to keep visitors coming back for more (see the preceding section), you can put together a plan for your own online efforts. Your plan should include these action items:

✦ **Identify your prospective donors.** Whom do you want to target? Be specific — an "everyone" response doesn't count. What does your typical contributor look like? Include descriptors such as age, gender, marital status, personal interests, or any other factors that typically reflect your most faithful donors.

✦ **Determine the desired donor actions.** What do you want people to do after they find your website? Are you interested solely in cash donations? Or are you soliciting in-kind donations and supplies? Perhaps you want to recruit volunteers, too.

When you determine all the possible actions, rank them in order of importance. Then you can decide how to place, or showcase, the opportunities on your site.

✦ **Describe the rules of engagement.** How can you capture (and keep) the attention of your visitors? For example, consider the content you use on the site. Have people shared testimonials or success stories of how your organization has helped others? Use these stories to pique visitors' interest, and follow them with instructions on how to get involved.

Visitor awareness building and education are probably expected at this point. In fact, now you want to use those objectives to help elicit a specific online action — whether that's making a contribution or having someone send your link to a friend.

✦ **Define your donor pool.** Geographically, where are your prospective donors located? Does it matter to you? Your organization might have a national or an international appeal, or your mission might benefit a regionalized population. Even if your scope is limited, other people might be interested in your cause. What about people who move away from your city and still have ties to the area? What about others who are simply affected by your cause? Deciding where your donors are likely to come from, or how far out you want to go to reach them, is an important element of your online marketing efforts.

The Internet readily allows you to localize your marketing efforts, if you choose. Or you can decide to cast your net far and wide. If this issue is important to you, use geographic descriptions in your <META> tags and page titles. That way, your organization is more likely to turn up in location-based results in search engines. Google also allows you to set a geographic target for your website to improve location-specific search results (for more information, visit https://support.google.com/webmasters/answer/62399?hl=en). Because IP addresses are used to help determine the location from which a person is searching for information, it's important to take the steps needed to help your website appear in localized search results. The increasing use of mobile phones for conducting Internet searches makes local search results even more important for your business.

✦ **Establish donor hangouts.** You want to create online marketing opportunities for your cause. To do that effectively, you need to know where your prospective donors are likely to hang out online. You can use these sites (social media sites or blogs, for example) to place banner ads, buy keyword advertising (paid searches), and post press releases.

✦ **List giving partners.** Exchanging links with sites that complement yours is an effective way to expand your reach. You can also partner with other sites by offering to provide content, place informational links to research, or simply promote a fundraising event.

✦ **Provide action opportunities.** Keep your donors involved by giving them lots of options to participate. Your plan should detail the ways in which someone can not only donate money but also take action that makes them feel connected to your cause for the long haul.

✦ **Specify follow-up.** Plan to stay in touch with your online donors. E-mail messages, electronic newsletters, podcasts, blogs, social networking sites — the list of ways to keep connecting is almost endless. You can use some or all forms of communication (online and offline) to stay in touch with donors and build lasting relationships.

Converting the Faithful

Although most online plans attack the issue of recruiting new donors, don't forget the ones who are already most familiar with you. Unless you have a recently launched nonprofit organization, you should have a fairly long list of existing supporters, which typically include

✦ Previous donors

✦ Full-fledged members or active donors

✦ Participants in, or attendees of, earlier fundraiser events

✦ Board members and volunteers (past and present)

✦ Community supporters and sponsors

If you played your cards right, you collected the e-mail addresses of these folks over the years. Even if you never had reason to use those addresses, you should still have them on file.

Your list of supporters and at least their current mailing addresses should be in a database. Regardless of whether you ever fully took advantage of this resource, you're now in a great position to do so. Obviously, these people represent a built-in group of followers. If nothing else, they're already aware of your organization and its mission. All you have to do is use your online initiative as a tool to step up their level of giving and involvement.

A great deal of recent e-philanthropy research indicates that people who give to charities over the Internet are likely to donate more — and do it more often. If you can convert a percentage of your offline contacts to online contributors, donations to your site might increase.

To see that happen, you have to reach out to everyone on your current list of names. Your objective is to get them active online.

Despite the fact that online giving continues to prosper, not everyone on your list is up to speed in Internet giving. Some donors are always more comfortable sending donations by *snail mail* (sent by way of the U.S. Postal Service) or being involved face to face, so continue to provide those options.

How do you decide whether someone is willing to receive your message online? You have to ask, of course! To start converting your faithful followers, do the following:

✦ **Send an electronic invite.** Use your data bank of existing e-mail addresses and send a request for donors to visit your website. Making them aware of the site — and the ways they can stay involved online — is the first step in conversion.

✦ **Reach out the old-fashioned way.** Send a postcard, make an announcement in your print newsletter, or write a letter. If all you have is a street address, reach out with traditional mailers and invite donors to check out your organization online — and include a postage-paid return envelope that makes it easy for donors to send a contribution back to you.

✦ **Register constituents online.** For your next fundraising event, let folks register online. You then have the opportunity to collect updated e-mail addresses and get them accustomed to communicating with you over the Internet.

A few issues are still at play here. What happens if that piece of snail mail sits in a pile unnoticed? Too bad you didn't have the recipient's e-mail address! Then again, maybe your list of contacts contains old, outdated, or incorrect e-mail addresses, which are useless.

One solution for these types of obstacles is to pay to obtain valid e-mail addresses from your list of constituents. Several companies now offer services in which they match information about your existing list of donors with their current e-mail addresses. You don't have to have existing e-mail addresses to use the service — this type of company can cross-reference information from other e-mail databases in order to find valid e-mail addresses.

You're likely to find one of these three types of services helpful in your online business:

✦ **E-mail appending:** You can cross-reference online databases to find someone's e-mail address when all you have is a name, phone number, or street address.

When you're choosing a company for e-mail-appending services, make sure that its process complies with guidelines issued by the Direct Marketing Association (DMA) and the Association of Interactive Marketing (AIM).

✦ **E-mail validating:** Your list of existing e-mail addresses might be outdated or invalid due to errors (such as typos). Companies can now verify e-mail addresses for you.

✦ **Reverse appending:** If you're collecting e-mail addresses online, the addresses might be all the information you have on prospective donors. A reverse appending service matches e-mail addresses with valid street addresses.

Dozens of legitimate companies offer e-mail appending and related services. Prices for these services vary; many charge based on the number of valid e-mail addresses they find. Blackbaud, a company that specializes in assisting nonprofits, estimates that organizations usually convert 20 to 30 percent of their total donor lists to valid e-mail addresses. DonorPerfect (at www. donorperfect.com) and DonorWorks (at www.donorworks.com) are also viable programs.

After you get someone's valid e-mail address, you still must obtain permission to send the recipient information about your organization (even if you already had the name in your records). The company performing the appending services should work with you to provide a final *opt-in,* or permission-based, list of valid e-mail addresses.

Reaching Out to People Surfing for Charities

Obtaining working e-mail addresses is only one component of building an active base of online donors. Regardless of how many names you already have, you want to reach out to as many potential donors as possible.

Fortunately, a growing online trend is opening the door to millions of socially conscious Internet users. *Social networking* is a form of socializing through virtual communities. Some of the most recognizable social networking sites started with a focus toward entertainment, dating, and fostering friendships. Today, however, many social networking sites, such as LinkedIn, Facebook, Twitter, Instagram, Pinterest, and YouTube, have a much wider audience and are often used for business and nonprofit purposes. Even so, a derivative group of social networking sites is geared toward charitable giving and philanthropy in general. These sites connect individuals or large groups who share an interest in various causes. In addition to highlighting current nonprofit news and topics of interest, members can share their experiences in community message boards. Social networking sites also allow members to create their own personal pages (for free) to discuss the causes in which they're active, to create and circulate online petitions, to donate to featured organizations, and to learn about different types of nonprofits.

Check out the sites in this list:

✦ **Care2:** With more than 25 million members, Care2 (`www.Care2.com`) is one of a growing number of sites that are proliferating social awareness online.

✦ **Charity Guide:** The website for Charity Guide (`www.volunteerguide.org`) is all about the organization's Volunteer Guide, which highlights how members can make a difference in 15 minutes, a few hours, or over several days.

✦ **Charity Navigator:** A special feature of this site (at `www.charitynavigator.org`) is that it rates charitable organizations from its database of more than 7,000 organizations. Members can even track and compare charities on their own personalized web pages.

You must understand what makes outreach through social networking different from other types of outreach. At these sites, you don't plaster Donate Now buttons across personal pages or aggressively solicit for paid memberships to your organization. Instead, these sites provide a forum to educate the public about your cause by interacting with your prospective donors and volunteers. Think of that forum as a low-key grassroots type of marketing tool, and get creative!

You can get involved with these types of sites and spread your organization's mission in several ways:

✦ **Sign up.** Become a member of the site. (Signing up is usually free.) Create your own personal page to discuss your cause, connect to similar groups, and send messages to friends in your online network.

✦ **Actively contribute.** Join the discussions on the message boards. Find out what people are talking about and, when it's appropriate, let them know what your organization does and how they can get involved.

✦ **Provide content.** Submit articles for the site's content, send press releases, and forward news briefs with information pertaining to your cause (such as the status of current legislation).

✦ **Become a sponsor.** With millions of active and vocal members, your site's marketing dollars are likely to go far when you become a sponsor or paid advertiser on these types of sites.

✦ **Submit your charity.** For sites that keep logs or reviews of nonprofit organizations, always send in the necessary information to keep your cause on the list.

With the exception of paid advertising, nonprofit organizations can face limitations on how, when, or whether they can actively or directly solicit for membership or donations. Always read the FAQs (frequently asked questions) section of the sites, and review their terms and agreements to ensure that you follow the rules for promoting a specific cause.

Chapter 4: More Online Marketing Strategies for Nonprofits

In This Chapter

↙ **Enlisting the help of others to ask for donations**

↙ **Simple solutions for collecting the dough (again and again)**

↙ **Strategies to pique curiosity, provide purpose, and elicit action**

In discussions of marketing strategies for nonprofit organizations, the term *marketing* can encompass many different activities, such as donor development, fundraising, education, awareness building, and public relations. For marketing purists, not all these items belong in a marketing discussion. Right or wrong, they all become part of a nonprofit's marketing mix.

In this chapter, we clarify what marketing means for nonprofit organizations, including taking advantage of opportunities that lead to growing your organization through online monetary donations and other contributions.

Asking for Donations

Online marketing provides more than one chance to ask directly for money (or whatever else your organization needs). You can even ask for donations repeatedly. The person on the other end won't even bat an eyelash. If you're uncomfortable asking people for money, the Internet removes that pressure of asking for donations face-to-face.

In fact, people checking out your website expect to be asked for donations. It's likely that they sought you out for the purpose of giving their time and money to your organization! It's time you become comfortable with the idea of using the Internet to ask people to give — over and over again. E-philanthropy provides a host of methods for doing so.

Multiplying donation buttons on your site

One of the most overlooked online marketing opportunities is the Donate Now button, which is typically a single button (or link) on the home page of a site. Clicking the button displays an online form page where a visitor can choose to contribute.

You can increase the potential for a donor response by increasing the number of places on your site that you ask for support. Note that we don't endorse randomly scattering Donate Now buttons throughout your site. Instead, take an integrated, thoughtful approach, and follow these pointers:

✦ **Be position-savvy.** Visitors to your site view numerous pages. Make sure that donation buttons or links appear in as many spots as possible (without going overboard, of course). Visible areas of your site include

- The navigation bar

- The upper-right corner of each page

- The lower-center of the page

- The top or sides of the site's pages, for banner- or button-sized ads

Ask in different ways. Rather than repeat the phrase Donate Now on every page, use different terms that draw attention, such as these examples:

- Make a Difference

- Help Change a Life

- How to Contribute

- Ways You Can Help

- Get Involved Today

- Click to Contribute

✦ **Latch on to content.** When you share a success story on your site or spotlight someone in need, ask for support. In addition to placing a button following the content, include links to donate within the article.

✦ **Associate with a specific giving opportunity.** Consider the types of visitors your site attracts and why they're interested in learning about your cause. Someone might be more likely to give if your request is tied to a specific area of help. For example, you can link a request for a donation directly to research funding or to provide meals for a family in need. Be specific.

✦ **Highlight alternatives.** Not everyone wants to, or can, donate money. You might offer information about how to participate in a fundraising event or write a member of Congress to speak out on an issue. The website for Surfrider Foundation, an organization dedicated to protecting oceans and beaches, has a variety of opportunities to help. For example, you can click a button to locate a chapter near you and get involved as a volunteer. In addition, the home page (see Figure 4-1) clearly shows you how to take action by contacting various agencies or Congress and asking for support or change to particular programs; provides a place for site visitors to take a pledge of support; and, of course, displays donate buttons. The organization does a good job of quickly providing you with options for getting involved and becoming a donor (via paid membership levels) by using clear calls to action and compelling images on their home page.

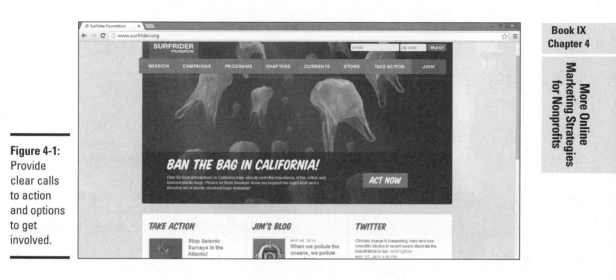

Figure 4-1:
Provide
clear calls
to action
and options
to get
involved.

✦ **Encourage social connections.** One of the keys to building an active, loyal donor base is staying in touch. Social media and mobile interactions provide the perfect opportunity to keep awareness levels high and to ask for donations, long after someone leaves your website. Just make sure that you provide plenty of opportunities while people *are* visiting your site to like your Facebook page or follow your organization on Twitter or Instagram (or any other social media platform in which your nonprofit is active).

✦ **Make a final plea.** Before a visitor leaves your site, display a final request for help in a pop-up window. Rather than ask for a cash donation at this point, ask the person to register to receive additional information on supporting your organization. Collect only a name and an e-mail address, to keep the process quick and unobtrusive. You can then automatically send e-mail with specific requests for donations.

This type of follow-up e-mail is the perfect time to spotlight a story about your cause and then ask prospective donors to sign up for your newsletter. Even if they don't donate directly from your e-mail request, you can keep them informed and grow their activity level.

Passing the hat (pass-alongs)

As you might know from working with volunteers, sometimes these people are passionate about your cause. Because their enthusiasm and dedication are infectious, not long after they start working for your cause, they recruit plenty of their friends and family members. In the corporate world, this concept is referred to as creating *buzz*, or word-of-mouth marketing; people in the nonprofit world call it *pass-along* marketing.

Suppose that 5 people who are drawn to your site discover something useful or important about your organization. They want to not only help but also share the site with others. If each of those individuals tells 10 more people they know and perhaps at least half of those people then choose to educate 10 of their friends, your cause has been shared with several hundred people just in that short cycle!

If your cause can motivate just one person to act, your site can also provide the tools to help that person spread the word to others. Here are three simple techniques:

✦ **Add a link or button on your site that asks visitors to send information to a friend.** A visitor who clicks the button can forward a message from you to a friend.

✦ **Provide social sharing buttons that allows visitors to share information on your website by pushing it out on social media sites.** With the click of a button, it's easy to share an article, a tip, an event notice, or any other information with friends by posting it to Facebook, Twitter, Pinterest, or other sites. Your site can even encourage visitors to post automated messages to their social media accounts when making a donation or a pledge to help. Their friends see a message such as, "I just made a donation to Surfrider to help clean up the ocean. If you want to join the cause, visit Surfrider.com."

✦ **Allow site visitors to start their own fundraising campaigns for your cause and invite their friends.** Peer-to-peer or friend-to-friend fundraising is a great way to let site visitors and loyal donors spread your organization's message. Organizations such as Charity: Water (`www.charitywater.org`) encourage visitors to engage their friends in fundraising through personal campaigns. The site makes it easy for visitors to set up their own fundraising pages and invite friends to donate or get involved. Charity: Water also lets visitors make a pledge to raise donations through Facebook on their birthday (see Figure 4-2).

Figure 4-2:
Let donors start personal fundraising campaigns and invite their friends to participate.

TIP

If you're already using a nonprofit service provider, such as Blackbaud (www.blackbaud.com), for various fundraising tools, they often offer friend-to-friend campaign tools. Other providers that also include integration with social media platforms are Razoo (www.razoo.com) and CauseVox (www.causevox.com).

Building personalized pages for events

Expanding fundraising tools for volunteers and event participants is part of the friend-to-friend fundraising trend. In this case, the personalized donation pages are used with specific fundraising events and may even be integrated with event registration, as opposed to the general fundraising campaign we mentioned earlier. For example, the easiest way to help volunteers reach their donation goals for your organization is to offer personalized web pages to promote a specific fundraising event (such as a walk-a-thon).

Personalized pages are typically miniature websites that constituents can build themselves by using templates (or a selection of preformatted web pages). A page usually includes an organization's logo, information about its cause, event details, and the personal story of the fundraiser, as shown in Figure 4-3. Pictures and the real-time tracking of donation goals can also be added to the site.

Figure 4-3:
Add your
own
fundraising
pages to
increase
donations.

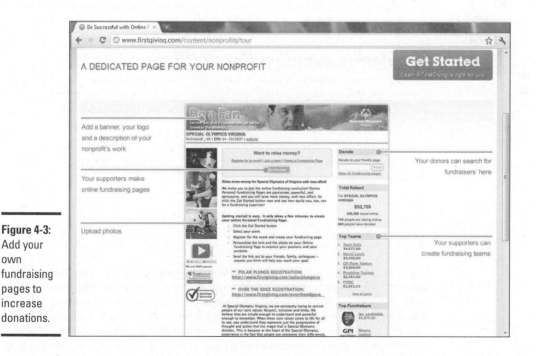

Firstgiving (www.firstgiving.com) offers this type of service. In this case, your nonprofit can access the personal fundraising pages for an annual fee. Two charges are incurred when donations are made: a 5 percent fee on the actual donation and another 2.5 percent credit card merchant fee. That means with a $50 donation, you still end up bringing in more than $45 to your nonprofit. There's no doubting the value of these services provided by Firstgiving:

✦ Creates on-demand reports showing the funds that are raised

✦ Collects donations and handles on-payment processing

✦ Provides unlimited support

✦ Manages online event registration

This unique solution helps supporters who are hesitant to fundraise in person.

Highlight your fundraisers' pages on your organization's main website, and provide prominent links directly to their personal sites. This way, you can easily offer prospective donors (visitors to your site) a specific, personalized way to give.

Because these personal fundraiser pages often contain personal information (including e-mail addresses), always get your volunteers' permission to post links from your site.

Circulating donation links offline

One way to increase the value of any type of volunteer effort (personalized fundraising pages or any other method) is to distribute your information by way of other established networks that your volunteers belong to, such as these examples:

✦ Churches

✦ Credit unions or banks

✦ Employers

✦ Member-based organizations or clubs

✦ Professional associations

Although most organizations and almost all companies maintain no-solicitation policies, you can occasionally find loopholes. For example, employers tend to make exceptions if their employees are contributing to good causes. Similarly, if an employee or a spouse suffers from a health issue (such as diabetes or cancer), a company is often willing to promote the nonprofit organization associated with that person's problem. Coworkers and peers are also more likely to donate to your cause when they're supporting someone they know.

Here are a few ways to circulate news about your cause and increase visits (and donations) to your website:

✦ **Create a newsletter.** Write a brief article about your volunteer and how that person is helping your organization. Your article can describe anything from raising money for a bike-a-thon to heading up a clothing drive. Include a web address where people can learn more and donate. If you create an electronic newsletter, provide an active link to your site.

✦ **Use the company's intranet.** An *intranet* is a private Internet site for an employer or organization that's unavailable to the general public. Employees or registered members access the intranet for news, general information, and critical updates. Provide a brief description (similar to a newsletter article) along with a button or link to your organization. You can then place the link in a prominent place on the intranet site so that other employees or members can reach you and make donations.

✦ **Get employees to like you on Facebook:** Social media provides another way to reach out to employees. If you have a Facebook page for your organization, you can encourage one or two employees who like your page to ask their coworkers to do the same. Getting people to join you on Facebook also gives you the opportunity to communicate with them frequently and provides a more direct way to share your organization's story.

✦ **Produce a member bulletin.** This regular e-mail notification goes out to employees or members of an organization. Or you might produce a non-electronic (printed) notice that's circulated in pay stubs or at meetings. Again, spread your message along with your website address to encourage others to get involved or make donations.

Cross-promoting

Not all donation requests have to originate from your site. You can take advantage of *cross-promotional marketing* strategies, too. In these programs, you work with another organization in a way that benefits both of you.

One type of charitable giving program, administered by major credit card companies, plays off the popular reward programs offered as incentives to cardholders. If you have a credit card, you know that many companies allow you to accumulate reward points based on a percentage of the dollar amount you charge to your card. For example, every $100 you spend may earn you 10 reward points. You could then redeem your points for a gift; for example, 2500 points might qualify you for a $25 gift card to your favorite spa. Several companies now allow you to trade points for a charitable contribution of a specific dollar amount. What an idea!

Unlike formal partnerships with card companies, some programs simply require you to enroll. The American Express donation site (shown in Figure 4-4) is an example. When you're ready to enroll, visit `www.americanexpress.com/give`. After you're approved, you can place a button or an ad on your site with the American Express logo. Visitors who click the button go directly to the card company's donation site to redeem reward points for your organization or to make donations by using the American Express card.

Figure 4-4:
Reward
points can
be donated
to your
nonprofit.

Before enrolling with the American Express donation site, you must be listed with GuideStar (see Chapter 2 of this minibook). You also need to have your employer identification number (EIN) handy to start the registration process.

Making Donating Easy

With a little help from your friends (and their friends), your online fundraising efforts are bound to be a success. However, it's ultimately your job to make it easy for people to get involved. The key is to not only get the attention of would-be donors but also eliminate any barriers that might prevent them from contributing. Your website provides a backdrop for combining simplicity with donor-building strategies. Look into these features:

✦ **Automated membership renewals:** When you're using your site to market for membership fees, do yourself and your new member a favor. Rather than ask for a one-time membership fee, give your donor other options, such as these:

  • *A multiyear membership with an incentive:* Ask your potential donor to pay now to sign up for a three-year membership, and you'll give a bonus gift or discount.

  • *Automatically membership renewal:* Gain permission for your organization to automatically renew the membership each year by charging the fee to a designated credit card.

✦ **Recurring donations:** Donating by credit card is one of the simplest solutions you can ask for in online fundraising. Another option for incorporating this service is to set up the processing of recurring donations. This set dollar amount is then regularly (weekly, monthly, or even semi-annually) charged to a credit card. Credit card companies sometimes offer this service directly from their websites, or you can manage the process internally.

Recurring donations via credit cards are terrific options, but only if you make it clear to donors that they are choosing to continue contributions on a fixed, recurring schedule. If donors do not fully understand this option, they are likely to be surprised and angry when the next charge appears on their card statement. And that means you risk losing the donor, permanently!

✦ **Simplified employee-matching programs:** When someone makes a contribution to your organization, doubling the donation can be a no-brainer. This option also serves as a strong incentive for people to give when they know their contribution is being doubled! All you have to do is

- Verify that the donor's employer has a matching program.

- Get the right form into the donor's hands.

- Make sure that the form is submitted.

- Ensure that the employer cuts a check to you.

Even if this process sounds simple, it can represent a lot of work that your supporters might not be willing to do. Or you might even overlook or forget the follow-up process. By implementing an automated donor-matching program on your website, you can immediately see your intake increase, in one of two ways:

- *Donor verification:* Provide a link from your site to an employee-matching database. The donor can verify that his employer participates, review the procedures for getting it approved, and review any conditions to the matching program.

- *Nonprofit verification:* Your organization verifies the participation of the donor's employer, *and* you use the information in the database to submit forms on behalf of the donor.

The DonorPerfect site (www.donorperfect.com) offers online software that enables you to track matching donations, pledges, grants, sponsorships, and even in-kind donations. You can choose from three versions, ranging in price from $59 to $264 per month (depending on the number of donor records you need to track and number of product features you want).

✦ **An easing of the burden of making nonmonetary donations:** Does your organization accept clothing, food, toys, or even cars? These items aren't easily collected from a website! You can simplify the donation process, however, by partnering with a third-party collection center to pick up donated items. Allow your site's visitors to schedule a pickup online, or at least fill out an online form to start the process. You can also list drop-off spots that accept these donations for you. Better yet, consider allowing visitors to make online monetary donations that are then used to purchase items you need.

It might seem like you're doubling your efforts to simplify the process of making online donations, even when they have to be made offline. Before you think that it's not worth your effort, take a look at how one nonprofit turns nonmonetary items into a big treat — literally — for everyone! The Second Harvest Food Bank in California (see Figure 4-5) provides food of all types, whether it is donated, surplus, purchased, or grown by local farmers specifically for the cause. In 2013, the organization distributed nearly 52 million pounds of food to low-income people. The many different ways to give food items has served the organization's recipients well!

Figure 4-5: Make it easy for donors to give more than just money.

Chapter 5: Legal Considerations for Nonprofit Organizations

In This Chapter

↳ Selecting a gatekeeper for online compliance

↳ Writing and posting important policies

↳ Handling must-do registrations and guidelines

↳ Signing up with a governing organization

*N*early 450,000 nonprofits have lost their exempt status because they failed to file a report with the IRS for three consecutive years. This small omission brings big consequences. As the owner of a registered nonprofit organization, you're accustomed to the issue of compliance. Filling out annual reports for the IRS, issuing tax-deductible receipts to donors, and distributing legal waivers to volunteers are all a small part of your legal duties.

Fundraising over the Internet is no different. When you go online to seek donations, certain responsibilities come along with it, and overlooking even a few of those responsibilities can have a significant downside for your organization. Some of the issues we discuss in this chapter are internal compliance activities. Even if an action item isn't mandated by a government entity, it's still something you should do. Other issues mentioned in this chapter are legal requirements. If you're venturing into e-philanthropy for the first time, this chapter is required reading. Even if you know that you're up to speed with the latest online regulations, consider this chapter a review.

Designating Responsibility

You know who takes the legal heat when something goes wrong: Your board of directors is ultimately in charge of the well-being of your organization. Even so, responsibility follows an internal chain of command. Depending on the size of your nonprofit, that chain of command might include an executive director, an entire paid staff, or a group of directors and volunteers structured by committees.

Now that you're entering the realm of online donations, similar legal responsibilities and consequences apply. Although your board accepts these legal responsibilities, you should assign responsibility for your Internet initiative to a designated individual or committee in your organization. By incorporating this position, you're developing both internal expertise and an internal watchdog for your online operations.

We recommend having an internal watchdog, for two reasons:

✦ **Branching out on the Internet is most likely new territory for you and your cause.** Initially, you might have to turn to outsiders for consultation and guidance. If you find good start-up assistance and develop a holistic Internet strategy, however, you find that online fundraising increasingly becomes a larger part of your overall revenues, resources, and image. Internet fundraising might grow from occupying 1 percent of your organization's pie chart to eventually meeting or exceeding the 50 percent mark. That amount is an extremely big piece of your pie to not have internal expertise assigned to it! Likewise, increasing contribution to that level takes a long time unless an insider is championing the initiative.

✦ **Industry watchdogs, individuals, the media, and the federal government are increasingly scrutinizing online fundraising.** That scrutiny is a good thing — you want the playing field to be as fair and ethical as possible. Otherwise, as donors see more scams and corruption from supposedly legitimate charities, they decrease their online generosity. Scams will happen to some degree, no matter what, which is why you have to go out of your way to promote your organization's high standards and continue building long-term, trusting relationships with online givers. By keeping pace with external watchdogs, changing policies and procedures will not catch you unawares.

You can assign the responsibilities associated with being an internal watchdog to an individual staff member, a director, or an ad hoc committee (that you hope will become a permanent committee after your by-laws are adjusted). Although a larger, national organization might have the funds to hire staff members for this position, a smaller organization can still build this internal expertise by giving an employee the added responsibility.

When you're selecting the appropriate person, you don't have to look for someone with existing or extensive knowledge of the Internet. The person should be comfortable with the Internet and technology in general, though. The biggest factor, by far, is that the person you choose should be willing, able, and enthusiastic to learn.

Try to recruit a person who can — and will — assist your organization for a lengthy period, to cut down the amount of time you spend continually reeducate and retrain. Some organizations are successful in recruiting permanent volunteers when hiring extra staff members is out of the question. Usually, these retirees, home-based parents, and professionals don't have full-time paid positions.

The designated individual should focus on keeping policies and procedures in compliance with any local, state, or national guidelines. An Internet strategy liaison can further benefit your organization by serving in these added capacities:

**Book IX
Chapter 5**

**Legal
Considerations
for Nonprofit
Organizations**

✦ **Point of contact (POC):** As the go-to person for questions regarding your online fundraisers, your designated POC should be responsible for overseeing or understanding all parts of your Internet strategy. The POC fills out the forms and updates any registrations on third-party sites, and assists your members, donors, and staff members with online fundraising issues.

✦ **Trainer:** As your organization adds online fundraising tools and features or participates in online events, your Internet strategy liaison should be available to train other staff members, directors, and volunteers.

✦ **Researcher and trend watcher:** In a quickly changing environment, having someone responsible for keeping up with the industry — from researching proposed policy changes to spotting innovative online tools for fundraising — is important.

✦ **Advocate:** Just as you or others in your organization are championing the cause of bringing your nonprofit into the area of online fundraising, the need for that advocacy will always remain. Having someone who's knowledgeable and excited about the role of e-philanthropy helps further your cause in the long run.

Creating Online Policies

When you shop online, on many sites you probably notice links to the legal section. You often see online privacy policies, user agreements, return or exchange policies, and other protective verbiage. After you begin your online fundraising endeavors, you too need to create certain policies to display on your site and to provide some basic information to visitors.

Include these items:

✦ **A privacy policy:** A privacy policy is a requirement. It's a statement that tells your visitors whether and how you collect information about them, such as e-mail addresses, names, and physical addresses. It's also the place to let people know whether you're tracking their visits to your site through the use of cookies or other tools. If you're collecting information, tell them how you use it and state whether you share that information with others. A link to your privacy policy should be clearly displayed on the home page of your website.

✦ **A security policy:** Similar to a privacy statement, your security policy lets visitors know how you store and protect their personal data. Although this policy is optional, you should use one if you collect donations online. In it, you explain how credit card data and other personal information are stored and protected. If you use a Donate Now button or an outside source to process online payments, let patrons know and then provide a link to that site's privacy and security policies.

✦ **A COPPA statement:** If your nonprofit appeals to children or if you suspect that children might visit your site, you need to comply with the Children's Online Privacy Protection Act (COPPA). Regulated by the Federal Trade Commission (FTC), COPPA helps protect children and dictates how or whether a website can collect information about children, particularly those under the age of 13. The FTC provides guidelines for compliance and a children's online-privacy statement to post on your website. You can find details at the FTC website at `www.business.ftc.gov/privacy-and-security/childrens-privacy`.

✦ **An explanation of funds:** Describe how donations are used in your organization and specify exactly where all the money goes. Online donors appreciate knowing that their charitable contributions are put to good use. If money can go toward separate endowments, lifetime giving opportunities, or other distinctive areas in your nonprofit, now is a good time to explain to donors. If donors can contribute in other ways (such as giving supplies, clothing, or food), break down those items into categories and display them so that donors readily understand their giving choices.

✦ **Form 990:** You might want to create a policy allowing visitors to view your IRS Form 990 online. Although you're not required by law to provide this information, it assures prospective donors of the legitimacy of your site. If you don't want to post this information on your website, provide a link to GuideStar, at `www.guidestar.org`, where visitors can view your form by searching the site's database. To find out more about GuideStar, turn to Chapter 2 of this minibook.

✦ **Contact information:** As the owner of a nonprofit, you must clearly provide contact information to your site's visitors. Providing an e-mail address is helpful; offer a phone number and mailing address, too. Then prospective donors can reach you if they have more questions. Seeing your full contact information prominently displayed on your website is also reassuring.

Registering Your Charity

The most critical registration task you can do is to complete the individual state registration process. If you collect donations from people outside your organization's home state, you must register with the other states. This procedure is part of the individual states' solicitation laws, and compliance isn't optional. A few exceptions exist because only 40 states now require charities to register individually. See `www.irs.gov/charities` to view the list of states. Each state differs in how it requires registration, so we can't give you details on how to do so. Try an online search using your state name and the search terms *register, donations,* and *charity.*

**Book IX
Chapter 5**

**Legal
Considerations
for Nonprofit
Organizations**

Fortunately, a collaborative effort was created to make filing a little less burdensome for nonprofits. The National Association of State Charities Officials, in cooperation with the National Association of Attorneys General, created a unified registration statement (URS) to make multistate registration simple. The organization provides a registration kit in PDF format, which you can download from its site at www.multistatefiling.org. After you complete the information, you can submit the form to multiple states to register your organization.

The unified registration statement kit isn't accepted by Colorado, Florida, or Oklahoma. If you use the URS kit, you aren't in compliance with these states and must register directly with each one. Other states that accept the URS kit may still require additional forms, and you will not be in compliance unless all forms are submitted.

If you use a Donate Now button service, participate in an online charity portal or solicit donations through social media, you may still need to register with *all 40* states. These methods for soliciting donations reach across the United States, in addition to Canada and other international locations, and may or may not be considered *passive* donations (which do not require multistate registration). If you don't register with all states, you can face serious penalties and stiff fines.

If you need more information about what you have to do to collect donations, the IRS website for charitable organizations (www.irs.gov/Charities-&-Non-Profits/Charitable-Organizations) has information on various tax and compliance matters.

Gaining Seals of Approval

Another step you can take to maintain compliance is to sign up with entities that govern charities. We discuss two in this section: the Better Business Bureau and Charity Navigator.

Although these programs might cost you additional time and money, they're well worth the investment. As a respectable charity, you want prospective and existing donors to know that you have high standards and are in compliance with mandated regulations. Providing this level of assurance only helps to expand the success of your online fundraising initiatives.

In addition to national ranking and approval systems, some regional and statewide organizations keep up with the progress of your charity. For instance, Maryland Nonprofits offers a certification program for participating organizations. It awards a Standards for Excellence seal to area nonprofits that qualify under its peer approval process.

To find out whether your state has a similar program through a recognized non-profit association, check with the National Council of Nonprofit Associations. Its website, at www.ncna.org, has a membership list of all state associations that you can view for free.

Better Business Bureau

The Better Business Bureau (BBB) is a nonprofit organization that works to monitor and improve the solicitation of funds. A few years ago, it developed the BBB Wise Giving Alliance (www.give.org). This online report and charity-evaluation system gives donors another reliable source for information about causes. The BBB offers the program to national organizations or organizations that solicit contributions in multiple states. If you're a smaller charity, you can still participate by way of your local BBB office. Register with the Wise Giving Alliance by clicking the Charity Reports and Standards link, on the right side of the page. Then click the Have Your Charity Evaluated link, at the bottom of that page, and provide the requested information for your local BBB.

The organization's website maintains an up-to-date database of reports and financial information on select national organizations. You or your donors can scroll through the list of archived charities on the Wise Giving Alliance website, as shown in Figure 5-1.

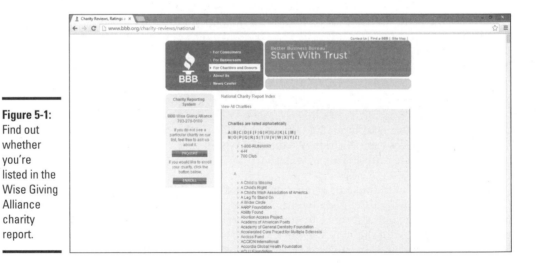

Figure 5-1:
Find out whether you're listed in the Wise Giving Alliance charity report.

An optional program you can participate in is the BBB Wise Giving Alliance Charity Seal Program. If you meet the approved accounting standards adopted by the program, you can post the Alliance's seal of approval on your website. The seal lets prospective donors know that you're in compliance with national giving standards. If you decide to apply for the seal, you must also sign a licensing agreement and pay a sliding-scale fee based on the amount of donations you took in during your last fiscal year.

**Book IX
Chapter 5**

Legal
Considerations
for Nonprofit
Organizations

Even if you don't participate in the seal program, your organization might still show up in the BBB online database of charity reports.

Charity Navigator

Although Charity Navigator (www.charitynavigator.org) doesn't hand out a seal for websites, it doles out stars in its rating system of U.S. charities. It helps people and businesses evaluate the reputation and financial well-being of more than 7,000 charities and is itself a nonprofit but doesn't accept donations from any of the charities it monitors.

The information is pulled from an organization's IRS Form 990. The nonprofit organization uses an established set of criteria to weigh first the financial side of your organization and then the administrative side. In other words, it assigns values to your financial statements, fundraising efficiency, administration overhead, and ratio of working capital, to name a few. Your scores are then combined into a ranking system based on stars. As with hotel rating systems, the more stars you receive, the better. Your organization is likely to be ranked by Charity Navigator, whether you want it to be ranked or not. If you aren't already listed, you can become a registered member of the site and request that your charity be reviewed. To become a member, click the Register Now to Access Expanded Features link to join.

For nonprofit professionals, Charity Navigator offers a guide to help you understand and improve your organization's ranking. You can access and download the Nonprofit Outcomes Toolbox by clicking the FAQ for Charities link on the home page and then looking for the guide.

Book X
Niche E-Commerce

Developing an e-commerce business around a niche market can be lucrative. Finding unique ways to reach and market to a smaller, niche audience is easier with social selling. To find out how to use social media to sell to a loyal base of online customers, visit www.dummies.com/extras/startinganonlinebusinessaio.

Contents at a Glance

Chapter 1: Discovering Niche Markets

*W*hen you start an online business, the Internet offers plenty of untapped markets for you to explore. These markets are segments within existing industries that have a lot of potential because they haven't yet become saturated by sellers. You can certainly find this potential in *niche markets,* which are smaller, more defined segments of an existing market. In this chapter, we provide a few basic guidelines for working with a niche product and also show you how you can access these niche markets and sell to their loyal customers.

Deciding to Sell a Niche Product

When thinking about a niche market, imagine the market in terms of a pie. The whole pie represents an entire market — one that's usually well established. But cut out one piece of that pie, and that piece becomes a smaller market on its own. Instead of concentrating on selling the entire pie, you narrow your focus to that single slice.

The pet industry serves as a real-world example. More than 68 percent of U.S. homes own a pet — that's more than 82 million homes with at least one pet. As you might imagine, that number adds up to a lot of potential when it comes to pet-related expenditures. Pets do indeed represent a multibillion-dollar industry, with nearly $59 billion expected to be spent in 2014. Of that amount, approximately $14 billion is expected to be spent just on pet supplies and medicine, according to the American Pet Products Association. Within that total market is pet insurance, which is a much smaller, but growing, niche.

Research shows that vet care adds up to $15 billion in that overall $59 billion pet market. Pet owners spend more than $1,000 per year, on average, on veterinarian bills. Moreover, surgeries or the need to treat serious illnesses can cost more than $5,000 per procedure. Pet insurance premiums continue to rise sharply, in some cases at more than 15 times the normal inflation rate, often due to a vast amount of technological advancements in the vet industry. Even with the growing expense, insuring pets continues to be a big trend because the cost of surgeries and medicines are rising at an equally startling pace.

However, only a small percentage (thought to be less than 4 percent) of pets in the United States are insured. These numbers show both a true demand and an opportunity for growth in this niche service offering.

To answer the demands of this customer base, websites such as Healthy Paws Pet Insurance (`www.healthypawspetinsurance.com`) and Petplan (`www.gopetplan.com`) offer online quotes and enrollment to pet owners. Pet insurance may be a relatively small piece of the industry, but for companies such as these, it also represents a significant amount of untapped potential. That's a niche market.

As you see, a niche market can be financially substantial, especially for a small online business. You enjoy the following advantages in a highly targeted market:

✦ **Defined customer base:** If you do your homework, you usually have no trouble identifying your customers. And because you're dealing with a narrow focus, you can get to know your customers extremely well. You can respond to their needs and wants much more easily, thereby creating loyal customers.

✦ **Customized messaging**: With a narrowly focused customer base and product or service type, creating highly customized content is easy. You can craft website articles, blog posts, videos, e-mails, and ads that have specific and highly relevant content matched to your audience or customer. Creating this type of customized content not only helps in marketing to potential customers but also can pay off with SEO (search engine optimization) because Google displays results with content specific to the search someone conducts. We explain this concept in more detail in Book VI, Chapter 6.

✦ **Bigger bang for your buck:** Because you're selling to a target group of people, you can stretch your marketing dollars further. Rather than invest in mass advertising, you can place less expensive banner ads on smaller websites that attract your particular audience. You also pay less for Google AdWords because you can use specific key phrases that may be less costly than general keywords (for example, *expensive vet bills* versus *pets*). Reaching a specific group of people using social media ads on Facebook or Twitter is also easier and less costly. Targeted e-mails and podcasts are definitely budget-friendly for sites of all sizes.

✦ **Pursued specialty:** When you provide products that are hard to come by, your customers often seek you out. In niche markets where there is less competition, the likelihood of people finding you online through organic searches increases. In other words, you can spend less in pay per click (PPC) advertising on search engines because your website may rank very high in search engine results.

✦ **Positive word of mouth:** Word-of-mouth marketing (WOMM) is powerful, especially in a tight-knit community of customers. When these niche buyers find a quality provider of products or services, you can bet that they will talk to everyone else in their circle of like-minded friends.

Not to burst your bubble, but you should consider these few disadvantages, too:

✦ **Limited customer base:** You're marketing to a much smaller group of potential customers. If the number of prospective buyers is too small, you can quickly reach market *saturation,* in which the pool of sellers is enough to satisfy the pool of buyers. Reaching market saturation levels is especially risky if you have a product or service that is likely to result in a one-time purchase.

✦ **Restricted product expansion:** Finding new products to sell that complement your niche can be challenging. In a specialty market, you may find yourself stuck with the same product, even as sales begin to taper.

✦ **Dreadful word of mouth:** Suppose that you make a few mistakes as you start growing your niche business. The same word-of-mouth marketing that could have been quite advantageous now becomes a killer. Because your customer base is small, negative comments can do a lot of damage to your site's sales. And the widespread use of blogs and community boards makes it especially easy to spread the negative online word to a connected community of buyers.

To offset bad word-of-mouth marketing, be even more aggressive in quickly resolving customer complaints. Follow up every order with a personalized e-mail. Invite customers to share the results of their online shopping experience with you. Become active on social media and engage with and respond to followers to create positive (and public) customer interactions. If a customer has a problem, your attention to him or her (even after the fact) mitigates the damage, and this attention often redeems you in the eyes of your customers.

The disadvantages shouldn't deter your plans for a niche business. The benefits far outweigh any of the minor risks involved. But those risks give you all the more reason to be thorough in selecting the right niche to pursue. After all, if the interest hadn't been there, pet insurance could have bombed. Instead, the timing was right, and this niche has left animal lovers begging for more.

Finding Your Niche

Almost every established industry has a single piece of pie waiting to be divvied up. When searching out your online niche, here are some general guidelines to follow (to help you remember them, notice that the first letter in each term spells out the word *niche*):

✦ **Notice:** All too often, niche markets are in plain sight — ripe for the picking. Some people see them, and others walk right by. So stop and pay attention to your personal interests and those of your friends and family. After all, you're consumers. Take a look at which services or products you want or need that larger companies aren't providing. Watch for new trends, too. Find out what people are talking about, and determine what's hot and different right now. Trends are often predecessors to an emerging niche.

✦ **Investigate:** If you think you've hit on a great idea, it deserves an adequate level of attention. Research the larger market from which your niche originates, and determine whether it's a growing market. Check annual sales and identify top performers (the large companies) in that market. Find out what analysts and researchers are saying about possible spin-off segments of the market, and determine whether these industry experts have spotted the same niche that you noticed.

✦ **Competition and customers:** As with any other market, you have competitors in a niche. Do a little digging to uncover how many others are already servicing the market. If you have zero competition, you may want to reevaluate the demand.

Put your prospective customers under the microscope, too, and find out who they are. Be specific. Note whether they're single men with dogs, for example, or working mothers with young children. Figure out their preferences, current buying habits, and available income. The more you know about the people you're serving in this niche, the better chance you have of successfully marketing to them down the road.

Find out whether your competitors are catering to only that particular niche or whether it's just one more piece of their overall businesses. If your niche is only a piece of the competitors' pie, you have a possible advantage. You can specialize in the niche and become the expert.

✦ **Hypothesize:** Before you launch your niche-focused site, you need to test your theory. Maybe you developed the perfect product. It answers a definite need, and research shows that there's money to be made. To be sure, you have to test, test, test. Conduct small samples to find out whether people are truly interested. You have to know whether they're willing to pay for it, whether it answers their needs, and whether they're ready to buy from a new online resource.

✦ **Execute:** Create a solid plan for selling to your niche market. Sometimes, reaching this type of customer proves to be more difficult than marketing to a broader customer base. After all, you're talking about highly targeted and specific customers. Not only do you have to work harder to locate them, but one misstep in your marketing efforts can also destroy your credibility. An effective selling strategy clearly communicates how your product answers a specific or unique need for that niche customer.

Niche customers are often quite knowledgeable and passionate about the niche that your product or service addresses. Can you speak their language? Talking the talk means being up to speed on current terminology, hot topics, and issues of importance.

Draw in your customers by providing timely, informative content on your website that supports the products and services you offer for that particular niche.

The Internet definitely provides an exciting opportunity to sell to a niche market, and often the opportunity is right under your nose. Many online entrepreneurs stumbled onto a niche market out of sheer necessity. In some cases, the market lacked a product that provided a much-needed solution. In other instances, a niche market started because an existing industry or market changed as the Internet matured. To stay ahead of the game, entrepreneurs identified smaller segments within their markets that weren't being served.

Tutor (www.tutor.com) is a shining example of how a need for a product can carve a healthy niche from a larger existing market. The kindergarten through 12th grade (K through 12) market represents billions of dollars, spent by both consumers and governments. In 2013, the market for *instructional resources* alone was $9 billion and was experiencing unprecedented 7 percent year-over-year growth. Combine that spending trend with the quickly rising cost of college and an increased emphasis on students obtaining academic scholarships to offset tuition and you have lots of reasons to be in this segment of the educational market. Tutor is taking advantage of that niche demand by providing online tutoring services for students. The website, shown in Figure 1-1, sells its online learning and tutoring services, in blocks of time, to parents and students all over the Unites States. Students aren't the only ones benefitting: Tutor has learned the value of launching an online business in a lucrative niche market!

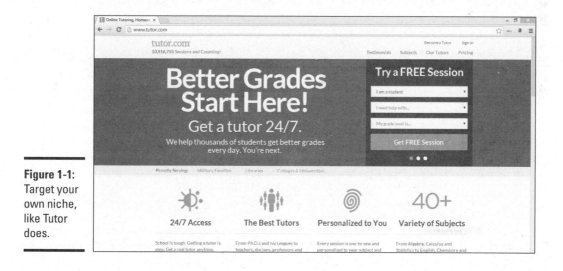

Figure 1-1:
Target your own niche, like Tutor does.

The following companies offer e-newsletters and other online resources that track trends and future niches to help get you started carving a nook for yourself:

- ✦ **CEB Iconculture Consumer Insights:** www.iconoculture.com
- ✦ **Pew Research Center:** www.pewresearch.org
- ✦ **TrendHunter:** www.trendhunter.com
- ✦ **Small Business Trends:** www.smallbiztrends.com
- ✦ **TrendWatching:** www.trendwatching.com

Chapter 2: Identifying Niche Markets That Keep Paying

In This Chapter

- ✔ Unlocking the minority report of the under-18 crowd
- ✔ Hanging out with the over-50 crowd
- ✔ Finding man's best (online) friends: pets and more
- ✔ Delivering niche goodness over-and-over again

In this chapter, we take a look at niche markets, or those segments within the marketplace that may be small but are lucrative. Some of the more popular niches that continue to withstand the test of time involve children, baby boomers, and pets — and each of these categories keeps spinning out even smaller niche opportunities within the niche! For the ultimate sweet spot of niche markets, you can keep your customers wanting more with subscription-based products and services.

Children make up a fairly large market of potential online customers, and there's no reason why you can't take a piece of that market — as long as you can keep them interested in what you have to offer. We show you how to tackle the marketing strategies that help you tap into the kids' market — and, most importantly, their parents' wallets.

Another growing segment of the niche marketplace is baby boomers. A record number of people were born between 1946 and 1964, and they eventually received the baby boomer label. Today, these baby boomers represent one of the fastest-growing markets and have enjoyed an overall level of prosperity that has made them a viable customer for the right online business concept.

Kids and boomers are not the only segments that can be credited as contributing to online wealth makers. Man's best friend (and all his four-legged cohorts) has proven to be a lucrative niche market. With nearly two-thirds of U.S. households purported to have at least one pet, you can imagine what that potentially translates to in dollars. We show you why this market continues to hold opportunities and what you need to know to capitalize on it.

There's no limit to the type of niche you can carve out in any number of mainstream markets.

Marketing to Children

Children are typically divided into the following three distinct groups, based on age:

✦ **Kids:** Although children who are 7 or younger don't always have enough independence to shop by themselves, they're influential in their parents' final purchasing decisions. Parents want to please their offspring and usually give 'em what they want.

✦ **Tweens:** Children between the ages of 8 and 12 are considered a target market unto themselves. These kids have outgrown "baby" items and are starting to emulate the trends made popular by their older counterparts (teens).

✦ **Teens:** Ranging in age from 13 to 17 (some marketers go all the way to 18), this group is typically more mature. Savvy-shopping teens usually have greater decision-making abilities with less adult input. And many teens have hefty amounts of money to throw around, from working part-time jobs or from receiving an allowance from their parents (or both).

All three groups share at least one characteristic: Many kids are adept at using computers. Tweens and teens are particularly comfortable surfing the Internet and embracing technology for multiple purposes — including shopping online, downloading apps and music, and playing online games. According to a 2014 *Taking Stock with Teens* report from Piper Jaffray Cos, 80 percent of teens (ages 12 to 17, with an average age of 16) shop online. That number breaks out to 78 percent of girls and 82 percent of boys with online shopping habits. One interesting differentiator between teen boys and girls is their preference for traditional retailers versus web-only retailers. Only 30 percent of girls shop with lesser-known e-commerce sites; the majority opt instead for online versions of well-known offline retailers. On the flip side, teen boys are pretty comfortable with either type of online retailer, with 41 percent opting for a variety of web-only retailers. As for as what teens spend money for online, here's a breakdown of their favorites:

✦ Apparel (29 percent)

✦ Footwear (22 percent)

✦ Electronics (20 percent)

✦ Accessories (13 percent)

✦ Other (11 percent)

✦ Personal products (6 percent)

Other interesting take-away points from this niche group of online spenders are the use of mobile devices and digital streaming. Approximately 55 percent of teens have an Apple iPhone, and 56 percent own a tablet. Mobile devices are an important part of teens' lives, and they use smartphones and tablets for everything from online research to online shopping. And nearly half of teens are equally passionate about downloading or streaming movies from the Internet.

Similar trends have been identified by Pew Internet and the American Life Project study, including these facts:

✦ More than half of teens using the Internet do so every day.

✦ When it comes to socializing, 73 percent of teens actively use a social networking site, such as Instagram.

✦ It's not all fun and games; approximately 62 percent of teens look to the Internet for news, current events, and political information.

Pew Internet has a lot of good research to help you better understand the market of kids and teens online. You can access more facts about teens and Internet usage for free on its website at http://pewinternet.org/topics/teens-and-youth.

Attracting a fickle customer

Perhaps one of the toughest challenges in selling to kids is simply keeping them interested. Kids are often among the first consumers to get excited about a new product and help it skyrocket to success. Unfortunately, their enthusiasm can pass quickly, and they're equally willing to shun an item after they tire of it. Their decreasing use of Facebook is a glaring example of the fickle habits of teens. Once considered the social network site for teens, as more adults and businesses embraced the site, teens began flocking to alternative social media sites such as Instagram and SnapChat. This behavior does not mean that an online store targeted to kids will be short-lived. Rather, it requires you to stay in tune to kids' interests and trends and be prepared to keep adding new products.

To decide which products your online business should promote to children, given this level of market uncertainty, you can search for items in one of the following broad categories. At least for the next few years, these product areas are expected to remain hot, hot, hot for kids of all ages:

✦ **Technology:** Kids love technology. Think about where iTunes would be today without its young audience of fans. The fantastic factor about kids and technology is that this relationship usually helps create other industries and products, too. You may not have created iTunes or the iPhone for that matter, but you can easily sell accessories or products to go along with these popular tech trends. In this example, think in terms of everything from custom cellphone covers to apps. Technology and anything related to it equals opportunity in the kid market.

✦ **Interactive services:** Kids use the Net in a big way. Their expertise and the amount of time they spend online will only increase over the next decade. That's why any service (for fun or otherwise) delivered by way of the Internet has a shot at success with kids. Online gaming, streaming videos, and binge-watching TV (on-demand) are all activities that rocketed into full-blown industries of their own, thanks in large part to the kid market.

✦ **Sports:** Kids and sports are almost inseparable. A record number of kids now play on local sports teams, and sports span the gamut of this market, appealing to young kids, tweens, and teens. Whether you sell sports gear online or promote e-books targeted to improving your game, even your most fickle kid customer can't resist this category.

✦ **Customization:** Kids like having the option to customize a popular product to their specifications. From shoes to jewelry, tweens and teens seem particularly fond of slightly tweaking a mass-produced item and calling it their own. This area has potential to grow, especially as more brand-name retailers offer online customization of products.

✦ **Decor:** This product category is definitely hot right now, including stylish home products to decorate kids' bedrooms or teens' dorm rooms, and fun accessories that dress up school lockers and a teen's first car. Decorating personal space feeds into the desire of children to make things their own.

Keeping 'em coming back for more

No matter what you choose to market to kids, you have to deal with the issue of how to keep those little shoppers coming back to your site. Follow these guidelines to help turn your young customers into repeat buyers:

✦ **Add products:** It almost goes without saying — introduce new products, and do it often. Period.

✦ **Offer a twist:** You can update older products by offering them in new colors or styles. Or after you identify a particular product that sells well, offer companion products.

✦ **Change your site:** In addition to the products you sell, the site itself needs a frequent facelift. You don't have to redesign your site. Instead, try adding fresh images, updating content, and switching colors occasionally.

✦ **Create a community:** As the popularity of social networking sites demonstrates, kids thrive on interacting with other kids. Sites that (safely) offer the opportunity for kids to communicate online or that can build a sense of identity for a particular group keep kids coming back.

+ **Let them socialize:** With 73 percent of teens regularly flocking to social media sites, keeping kids interested in your site means letting them connect and share the way they want. Integrate social networks into your site and provide a way for teens to share your site's information over these same networks.

+ **Grab opinions, give rewards:** You can include quick polls, top-ten lists, and other surveys that solicit the opinions of your customers on your site. (These features also help create a sense of community.) Kids also like to be rewarded for patronizing your site. Free downloadable games, coupons, loyalty shopping rewards, freebies, and giveaways are sure to please.

If kids like your site and your products, they tell their friends. Why not make it easy for them? Let your loyal customers pass along some of your site's freebies to their friends by way of e-mail, text, or social media. If you make sharing easy, you attract more attention — and future customers.

Book X
Chapter 2

Identifying Niche
Markets That Keep
Paying

Reeling in the parents

Like it or not, moms and dads continue to play a role in their children's purchasing habits, even as the kids approach early adulthood. How, or how much, you involve parents in the online selling process typically depends on two things: age and product.

Age

Exactly how old is your target customer? Generally, the younger the child, the more information you want to provide for parents:

+ **Kids:** Parents usually have the final authority on all purchases when young children are involved. But don't forget that these kids (especially as they reach school age) are fairly avid computer users. Have sections on your site that meet the wants of the children, as well as a section that addresses the needs of the parents. The Nick Jr. site (www.nickjr.com), for example, provides plenty of content, games, and interactive activities appropriate for its young fans in an effort to extend the brand of this successful children's television network. The site also has a separate section, called Family Life, which is filled with content, tips, and resources targeted to parents, as shown in Figure 2-1.

+ **Tweens:** After a child enters the tween stage, the parent/child relationship begins to change and your site has to respond appropriately. Parents still have a great deal of control, but their input becomes more of a filter. At this age, kids and parents are truly making decisions together. If you're marketing to tweens, you don't have to devote an entire section aimed at parents, but you may want to reassure adults that you're safely marketing to kids.

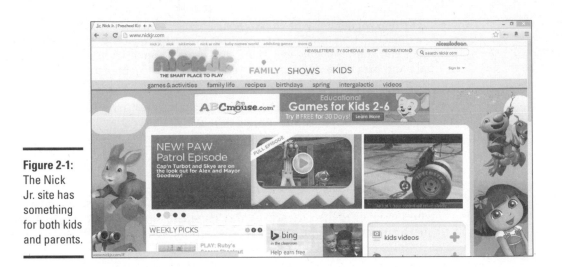

Figure 2-1:
The Nick Jr. site has something for both kids and parents.

✦ **Teens:** If teens are your market, you probably don't need any messages targeted to parents. WakeUpFrankie (`www.wakeupfrankie.com`) takes the approach of appealing only to teens. It specializes in linens and room decor for teen girls, and every part of the site's design is made to appeal to the 13-to-18-year-old market. The site uses bright colors and lots of images, and it incorporates content that speaks to its teen customers (see Figure 2-2). Similarly, the online website for *Boys' Life Magazine* (`www.boyslife.org`), targeted to teen Boy Scouts, is a great example of a site filled with age-appropriate content that doesn't require specific messaging to parents. Boys' Life has lots of photos and images to grab the attention of their young readers and also uses contests, jokes, games, and videos to keep visitors coming back to the site.

However, just because you're targeting the higher end of the kids' market doesn't mean you have to or should rule out parental interaction. TheSororityLife (`www.thesororitylife.com`) is targeted to older teenage girls getting ready to head off to college and join a sorority, as well as college students already active in Greek life. Parents often weigh in on their child's decision to pledge a sorority because it can add up to lots of time and money. TheSororityLife addresses those concerns not only by placing content for parents on the site but also by linking to a second website spun off just for parents, called SororityParents (`www.sororityparents.com`). Providing resources for both parents and their daughters helps provide both groups with a reason to keep returning.

Figure 2-2:
When targeting teens, your site should reflect their style.

> **TIP** If you have a product that appeals to more than one targeted age range, divide your site by age. Create sections for each age group so that kids and parents can quickly find the appropriate spot and start buying!

Product

The type of product you sell can determine how you involve, or market to, parents. One of the best examples of a product deciding the parents' role is clothing. Rarely do young children visit online clothing sites. In most cases, parents do all the shopping. Therefore, you might have a site designed in fun, age-appropriate colors because it matches the tone of the product line, but you're ultimately selling to parents.

Reading the small print: Important policies to consider

We can't cover the basics of selling to kids without sharing one of the biggest rules of running an online business: Always clearly post privacy policies and terms of agreement for your users. (You can find more details on these policies in Book II.)

Posting and following a privacy policy is the number-one rule when you're running a site targeted to kids. The Children's Online Privacy Protection Act (COPPA), passed by Congress in 1998, oversees children's privacy on the Net.

The primary goal of COPPA is to ensure that you're acting responsibly when you collect information online from children under the age of 13. In a nutshell, you can't request even a hint of personal information from a child without first notifying the child's parents and getting their permission. If you have one of the following two types of websites, COPPA applies to you:

✦ **Children's site:** You have content, products, or services specifically designed for children. Your site also

  • Is a *for-profit,* or commercial, website

  • Collects personal information from children under the age of 13

✦ **General site:** Your online business can offer any type of product or service, but COPPA applies if you

  • Have a section on your main site targeted to kids or specifically designed to appeal to kids

  • Knowingly collect personal information from a visitor under age 13

Generally, you have to follow seven basic requirements for communicating with preteens, using the COPPA rule:

✦ **Post your privacy policy.** Make your site's policy on protecting a child's personal information easy to spot on your home page. Don't be afraid to use a little extra real estate to make this policy stand out.

No matter which type of site you run, always clearly post a privacy policy on your site for customers to read.

✦ **Notify parents.** When children want to receive fun stuff from your site (or you want information about them), obtain parental permission first.

You're allowed to collect a child's name and his or her parent's e-mail address to request parental consent. Check the Q&A portion of the Federal Trade Commission's COPPA site for businesses (`www.business.ftc.gov/documents/0493-Complying-with-COPPA-Frequently-Asked-Questions`) for the lowdown on getting parental consent.

✦ **Protect data.** Any information you collect must remain private, secure, and protected. It's your obligation!

✦ **Offer a choice.** After you notify parents that you want to collect information about their children, make sure they know they can say no.

✦ **Provide access.** At any time, a parent can request to take a look at the information you have on file for their children. Be sure to open those files if a parent asks!

✦ **Keep in touch.** Stay in contact with parents. Give them the opportunity to *opt out,* or discontinue receiving information.

✦ **Allow participation.** No matter what, you can't restrict a child's access to your site if a parent doesn't want to give up personal information.

If you fail to comply with COPPA, you and your site can be penalized by the FTC. If you make the necessary changes, you still have to pay a fine. Previous cases have involved fines as high as $30,000 or more.

You can avoid tempting the Federal Trade Commission (FTC) to slap fines on you by deciding not to collect personal information. Instead, get parents involved. Communicate directly with moms and dads if you have messages for their children.

With everything that you have to worry about, selling to kids can seem a little overwhelming. If you take the time to plan your strategy, however, and make sure that your legal *i*'s are dotted and *t*'s are crossed, the kid's market is truly a fun one!

Understanding the Baby Boomer Market

After baby boomers hit the big Five-Oh, they became part of another interesting demographic — the over-50 market, with projections putting that total market size (not only baby boomers) at nearly 97 million in the United States. Most recently, the much-watched boomers hit another significant milestone in 2014. Nearly 20 percent of this closely monitored group have officially retired. And every month, more than 250,000 baby boomers turn 65, getting closer to the transition to retirement. The aging baby boomer market has both pros and cons for online businesses targeting this niche market.

On one hand, the boomer group has earned a reputation for spending billions of dollars — online and off. With more than 36 million of the over-50 market having computer access, that shopping bent bodes well for online businesses that court the boomer generation. However, some analysts wonder if this aging population, now headed into their Social Security–funded years, will still help fuel the economy with their buying habits or start to become a financial burden. So far, research indicates that the boomers' spending will remain strong, although what they buy may shift, which means yet another niche market opportunity.

What does this mean to you and your online business? Before targeting the over-50 customer base, you need to know some things about this group. Most importantly, you should monitor the changes in this group's traits and buying behaviors as the boomer population shifts and adjusts with time. For now, consider boomers to be lucrative customers, and take a look at these common traits. They are

✦ **Open minded:** Research indicates that boomers are willing to try new products, regardless of who makes them. Like everyone else, they have their favorites, but these consumers aren't bound by brand alone. This flexibility means that you have room to introduce alternative products or services to boomers, and they're likely to receive the message.

✦ **Value conscious:** Everyone likes getting a good deal, especially consumers over the age of 50. We're not talking about bargain basement shopping, though. Research shows that although this group is willing to spend money, they want to know that they're receiving a value in return. That value can range from a quality product for the price to a fantastic experience that makes the money worth spending. Again, consider that the tendency toward shopping for a value may only increase as this market segment reaches retirement age or if general economic conditions change for the worse.

✦ **Influenced by peers:** Friends tend to have lots of opinions about their buying experiences, and boomers seem particularly interested in hearing from their comrades. In fact, the over-50 market is quite receptive to opinions from their peers. And those opinions frequently influence the boomers' final buying decisions.

✦ **Self confident:** Friends and family aren't the only ones with valuable opinions. People over 50 trust themselves, too. A person's experience with a product or service greatly affects future purchasing decisions. That's not to say that you can't make an honest mistake and be forgiven. But this group thinks carefully before spending more money at your site if you've already let them down.

✦ **Research advocates:** Before buying, this market wants the scoop on products. And boomers are willing to invest whatever time necessary for a prepurchase investigation.

Make consumer research available on your site when targeting over-50 consumers. Add sections for product reviews and customer feedback. Then provide a Buy It Now button at the end of the review to make purchasing easier.

✦ **Embrace social networking:** Once a small segment of overall social media users, the older crowd has discovered the benefits of online communities. As of late 2013, the use of social networking sites among those 65 and older has tripled to 43 percent. For the 50- to 64-year-old crowd, more than 60 percent are on active on social media sites. Not only is it important for your niche business to advertise to boomers in these networks, but make sure your provide ways to share and connect in more meaningful ways from your website and your social media (business) profiles.

✦ **Willing to spend:** The over-50 market has plenty of disposable income (at least, for now). Even better, people in this group have a propensity to spend it — if they're moved to do so!

Designing your site to attract aging customers

As much as we want to give you a one-size-fits-all rulebook for targeting the 50+ market, we simply can't because this group of consumers is so diverse.

But you can rely on one undisputable fact about selling to the over-50 market: It's as much about having an appropriately designed website as it is the type of products you sell. By making a few conscientious decisions, you can improve your site's appeal to over-50 customers.

Background and colors

Research shows that your site for the over-50 crowd is better served by sticking to some standard color rules:

✦ **A white background color works best.** White is simple and crisp, and it makes text easy to read.

✦ **Certain elements need color.** Captions, headlines, and ads can use color — use brighter, bolder selections.

✦ **Black text reads well.** Stick with black text for articles and product descriptions.

✦ **Minimize your use of blue and green.** Avoid using too many blue and green tones, especially from the lighter color palettes.

✦ **Use only a few colors.** Keep the number of color selections to a minimum.

✦ **Maximize your use of contrasting colors.** They're more pleasing to the eye, and they make information on your site pop.

Text and fonts

The prevailing mindset says that if you target older consumers, you have to use huge text on your site. This idea isn't exactly true. The overall goal is to increase the readability of your site. Follow these tips for better readability:

✦ **Avoid placing text on top of blocks of color.** Use black text on a neutral (preferably white) background.

✦ **For primary text, such as main content, use a slightly larger font.** Try 12 or 14 point.

✦ **To grab attention in headlines and captions, use a large font.** Try 14 or 16 point.

✦ **Use case wisely.** Place captions in ALL CAPS for emphasis, but use low-ercase letters for other text.

✦ **Use leading appropriately.** Add extra spacing between lines of text so that your content isn't cramped.

✦ **Choose a sans serif font for your text.** Arial and Helvetica are good choices.

Although website styles can be adjusted for a target audience, such as baby boomers, you still need to put some style issues, such as optimizing for mobile devices, ahead of font type adjustments, for example. Try using only subtle design tweaks, and let your site visitors make adjustments to screen resolutions and font displays on their end. Readerwear (`www.readerwear.com`) specializes in selling reading glasses to a primarily older crowd. The site, as you see in Figure 2-3, makes small design adjustments for its baby boomer customer, but still keeps in step with current design trends of a clean and simple site.

Figure 2-3:
When designing for baby boomers, use a clean, simple website design that is easy to navigate and easy on the eyes.

Links and buttons

Every spot on your website serves a purpose, especially links and buttons. URLs placed on the site serve as links to help visitors move within your website. Buttons also guide people through your site's structure. You can enhance the functionality of these features, making it easier for boomers to get around, by using these tips:

✦ Visually differentiate between links that the user has or hasn't visited.

Having a link change color after a user clicks it is a common method to indicate a link that has been clicked.

✦ Place a series of links in a bulleted list.

✦ Be descriptive when labeling links. Use keywords and specific phrases to describe the link, as opposed to using the phrase *Click here*.

✦ Make the clickable areas of buttons and graphics larger than the button or graphic itself. A consumer should be able to click the mouse on a target area that surrounds the image (as opposed to clicking exactly on the image itself).

Site structure

The key word for organizing your site is *intuitive*. You want boomers to be able to easily (and instinctively) locate information and products throughout your site. To make your site structure boomer friendly, follow these guidelines:

✦ **Location, location, location.** Keep your most important information or content in the upper-middle areas of each page of your site, especially the home page.

✦ **Limit scrolling.** Not all online shoppers appreciate excessively long web pages.

✦ **Avoid excessive clicking.** Don't make shoppers click or double-click excessively to navigate through your site.

Try incorporating expandable menus in your site to show page options. Usually, these submenus appear whenever your mouse cursor moves over a specific button or link. Unlike with drop-down menus, you don't have to double-click to open expandable menus.

✦ Display a directory of topics (shown as a group of links) at the top of your pages. When you group link choices and make them all visible at one time, your visitors can easily move throughout your site.

Many of these design rules for the over-50 market translate to good design for everyone. For the most part, these guidelines come from a lot of research done on boomers. Organizations such as AARP now promote these design tools as recommended standards for this market.

Keeping baby boomers buying from you

As their active lifestyles demonstrate, boomers are far from decrepit! And although they may qualify for the classic senior discount at many businesses, you can use a number of better ways to reward those customers who fall in the 50-to-64 age range:

✦ **Provide enhanced service.** Excellent customer service is a plus for any age group. This market is no exception. Dazzling your customers with extreme care and attention is better than any $5-off coupon.

✦ **Offer targeted promotions.** Rather than give a general discount, you can create a personalized promotion that zeroes in on the interests and needs of each special consumer.

✦ **Give out loyalty rewards.** Boomers may be open to trying new brands, but don't hesitate to reward them when they decide to stick to yours. Frequent-buyer discounts, special giveaways, and other product-based rewards help convince customers to come back to your site.

Finding a niche in the baby boomer market

Accepting a gold watch upon retirement and settling into a comfortable recliner is no longer the status quo. This generation is bursting at the seams to stay active, fit, and involved. If your version of an online store for boomers is centered on denture creams and motorized wheelchairs, you'd better think again. Customized accessories for Harley-Davidson motorcycles and NASCAR paraphernalia are more likely the speed for this group. Here are a few other areas with great appeal to the over-50 market:

✦ **Business:** Boomers are working longer than their predecessors. They're also controlling their professional destinies by starting businesses of their own. Online sites that help boomers further their careers and businesses are finding a healthy niche.

✦ **Convenience:** The do-it-yourself (DIY) trend is passé for boomers. Many of them think that the convenience of having someone else do tasks is worth the price. Any type of product or service that saves time is a winner in this market.

✦ **Cosmetics:** On average, boomers consider themselves 12 years younger than their actual birth date indicates. Both men and women are willing to invest in helping their outsides appear as healthy as their inner selves feel.

✦ **Customization:** Boomers are a diverse bunch who often reject any type of labels. You can't pigeonhole this group into any single category. One 55-year-old may be retiring while another is launching a new business. Those two people may be the same age, but that doesn't mean that they're experiencing the same things. The good news is that this individuality opens up another lucrative online market opportunity for you. Customization, specialization, a niche within a niche — call it what you like. Focusing your product base to a boomer's current lifestyle circumstances, rather than to an age-based generalization, often equals profit.

✦ **Home decor:** Thanks to the interest in second homes and vacation properties, boomers have many houses to furnish. This demand creates a lucrative market for stylish household appliances, upscale linens, and many other decorative household items.

✦ **Recreation:** Boomers can always find time for play. Recreational items, ranging from RVs to Vespa scooters (and everything in between), fit nicely with the active, adventurous lifestyle of most boomers.

You don't have to sell a 16-foot RV to find success in the recreation category. Instead, focus on a smaller niche, such as specialized accessories for the large vehicles.

✦ **Romance:** Unfortunately, divorce for couples over 50 is on the rise. The number of newly single 50-somethings has led to an influx of increased dating among this age group. Online dating services are booming, along with other sites that help boomers explore a second (or third) chance for love.

✦ **Technology:** Many people believe that the over-50 market has a technology phobia. That may be true for seniors who are at least age 65. But boomers have been working with computers for a while now, and in the area of the latest high-tech gadgets, they have money to burn.

✦ **Travel:** Helping boomers explore exotic locations has proven to be a good strategy for several online travel sites. Any product or service that makes traveling more comfortable and enjoyable can result in a winning e-business for you.

The moral of this story is simple: You have an unlimited number of market opportunities when you're wooing the over-50 niche, so use your imagination and have fun with this exciting group of online consumers.

Selling the Goods for Pets' Sake

With nearly 62 million U.S. households claiming to have at least one pet, you can bet that plenty of proud pet parents are willing to spend money on Fido. According to the American Pet Products Association, pet owners are expected to expend more than $58 billion by the end of 2014 on everything from food and treats to boarding fees and healthcare — and that figure keeps increasing every year. Even in a recessionary type of economy, experts say the pet industry and its niche offspring businesses hold up well. Why?

**Book X
Chapter 2**

Identifying Niche
Markets That Keep
Paying

It turns out that people increasingly treat their pets like, well, people. Some of the recent pet business trends seem to back up this theory. Pet spas, organic pet foods, touch-activated pet toys, and clothing for the four-legged pets have all done well. Did you notice that if the word *pet* wasn't attached to some of these business categories, it would be nearly impossible to decipher whether they are intended for pets or humans?

Let's discuss why turning this lucrative niche market into a Net business is good for you. Consider that pet-related businesses

✦ Are part of a healthy and growing industry, even during a sluggish economy

✦ Have a relatively low entry cost

✦ Contain products and services that are easy to sell and deliver over the Internet

✦ Are part of a broad-enough market that makes it possible to identify a niche segment

When pursuing a serious online pet endeavor, we can offer an important piece of advice: Make sure you like pets if you're going to open a business targeting them! As mentioned, people treat their pets like one of the family and often refer to them as their kids. And, as with children, parents are particular about how their beloved pets are treated. Even in an online business, if you are not genuine in your interest and care for pets, this lack of enthusiasm tends to show.

Delivering Profit with a Subscription-based Niche

Speaking of pets, baby boomers, and children, a niche online business model exists that extends the value (and profitability) of any niche market. Subscription-based online businesses are making a splash in the world of e-commerce. For that matter, lots of offline businesses in both the B2B (business to business) and B2C (business to consumer) industries are extending their products and services to the online marketplace through a subscription-based selling model. And the returns on this niche delivery mode keep coming — every month!

For B2B companies, you often hear this type of niche service offering attached to cloud-based or hosted products and services. It's considered a software-as-a-service (SaaS) model, where customers access products from your website (or server) and pay a monthly fee for the service, which becomes recurring revenue for you. Throughout this book, we describe products and services based on this model. Hosted shopping carts, e-commerce solutions and storefronts, and website hosting are examples of subscription-based services you might use to run an online business.

This same approach to online business is a big trend, especially when you apply it to another niche market or specialty product. For example, when it comes to selling to pet owners, BarkBox (`www.barkbox.com`) figured out how to take advantage of subscription-based selling to a very lucrative niche market. Each month, BarkBox delivers a goodie-box filled with toys, treats, and gadgets for both you and your favorite furry friend. Customers choose a treat box based on the size of their dog and the frequency of deliveries (one month only, every month for a period of three months, or every month for a year), as shown in Figure 2-4.

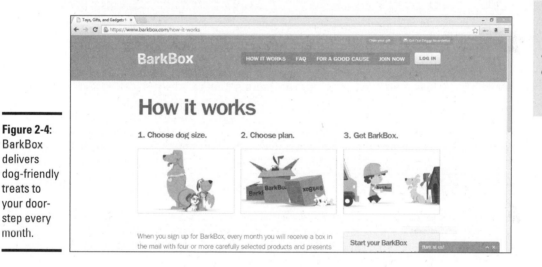

Figure 2-4: BarkBox delivers dog-friendly treats to your door-step every month.

Monthly treats aren't just for customers with four feet (or paws). Healthy living is another niche market that continues to gather steam, and it crosses almost all age groups. Typically, this niche contains products and services that promote a healthy diet and exercise. Naturebox (`www.naturebox.com`) delivers healthy snacks to human customers on a regular basis. The site, shown in Figure 2-5, lets customers customize selections based on the size of box (based on the number of snacks included in the box) and on self-selecting a type of snack or being surprised with new offerings each month. Or you can send a healthy subscription-based delivery as a gift. The fees range from $60 for a three-month subscription to nearly $200 for an annual subscription. The revenue from this type of online business adds up to a steady monthly stream.

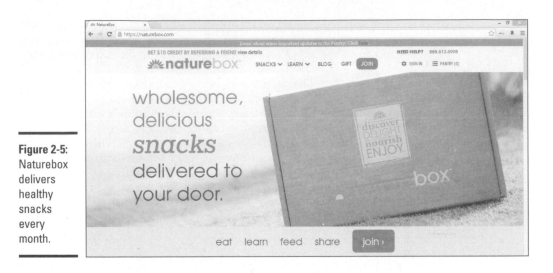

Figure 2-5:
Naturebox delivers healthy snacks every month.

You may notice that these types of businesses are reminiscent of the fruit-of-the-month clubs that were popular in prior decades. This is the same type of business, but the concept has been updated for the Internet and the business is no longer reserved for only fruits and cheeses. Some online businesses are creating their own niche with a very narrow product offering. One of our favorite examples is Foot Cardigan (`www.footcardigan.com`), shown in Figure 2-6, which takes a common product but specializes in *only* that one product — socks!

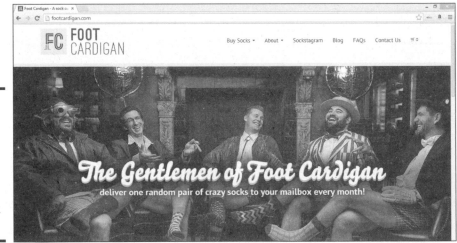

Figure 2-6:
Foot-Cardigan. com has a foothold in the sub-scription-based sock business.

The site gives customers a choice of subscription plans for receiving the monthly footwear, as shown in Figure 2-7. That's right. Customers purchase socks that are delivered to them on a monthly basis. How great is that for a niche online business?

Figure 2-7:
Subscription websites can still offer customers choices in how to buy.

We told you — there's no end to the type of niche you can create for your online business. But when it comes to creating a niche business using subscription-based products and services, offer the following:

✦ **Convenience:** Customers are drawn to subscription-based services or products because it's convenient. Often, these are items that they need on a regular basis, so having them delivered on a regular basis saves a trip to a traditional bricks-and-mortar store.

✦ **Savings:** More than saving the time it takes to go to an offline store, customers like subscription-based services that save money. If customers agree to receive products on a regular basis, they often expect to trim the normal price tag for the item.

✦ **Uniqueness:** Sometimes online subscription-based businesses are popular simply because they offer quirky, unusual, or one-of-a-kind products. Customers also like being able to get something that may not be available in their local geographic market.

✦ **Simplicity:** Especially in B2B markets, customers look for subscription-based services and products because they are easy to use. The same products, often technologies, may be difficult or expensive to maintain at the customer's business.

✦ **A treat:** Like the monthly delivery of fun, quirky socks, sometimes customers want to send themselves, or others, a treat. It may not be something they normally buy, particularly on a regular basis, but who doesn't love to come home and find a special box of goodies waiting for them every month?

No matter what type of product or service you consider offering, delivering it on a subscription basis can add up to a booming e-commerce niche business for you.

Chapter 3: Blogging for Profit

In This Chapter

↙ **Developing value with your blogging persona**

↙ **Identifying revenue opportunities**

↙ **Choosing the perfect blog platform**

*B**logs* originated as online diaries or journals of thoughts, observations, and comments about people's lives and the world around them. Today, blogs have moved well beyond the status of online journal and are considered serious business. Consider that WordPress, one of the most popular (and free) blog platforms, has more than 60 million published blogs. With estimates from other blog platforms, the total number of published blogs exceeds 200 million, with thousands of new blogs added, daily. Individuals, as well as the business world, have quickly realized the value of having this type of forum. Companies have adopted blogs for two reasons. Blogs provide a simple way to publish high-quality, helpful information that search engines (such as Google) use as a means of driving organic (non-paid) traffic to the site. Companies use blogs also as a way of promoting products and services.

Blogs are even being used as the foundation for a company's website. For example, WordPress can now be easily structured to look and function like a robust corporate site — and this area of WordPress is growing at phenomenal rates. The easy interface means that you don't have to know codes (such as HTML or CSS) or have graphic design skills to develop and maintain the site. WordPress, along with the availability of free design templates, makes it easy for the most novice users to launch a blog or a full website — adding content, photos, and other interactive features.

Aside from the ease of management that blogging software offers, another important factor for many companies that create and maintain blogs is the capability to enjoy a healthy financial return on their efforts. That's right: Companies and individual bloggers are making a lot of money for simply sharing their thoughts and opinions. That's not to say that you'll be making millions (or even thousands) of dollars overnight — or ever, for that matter. But with the right topic, the right tools, and the right level of dedication and hard work, you can create a healthy online income through blogging.

In this chapter, we show you how to turn a blog into a viable business. And with thousands of blogs and hundreds of tools now available to help any aspiring *blogger* (the person who writes a blog), getting started is easy.

Creating Value

The first rule of finding success as a professional blogger is to provide value for readers. WordPress indicates that every month more than 409 million people read 14 billion pages of WordPress blogs. It's encouraging to see high numbers of people engaging with so many blog posts, but it also points to the competitive landscape of blogging. For a blog to make money, it needs high traffic and loyal readers. To attract both, your blog must offer value. To better understand this concept, consider the top benefits that blogs offer to you and your business:

✦ **Current information:** Although websites are an effective way to disseminate information, their content doesn't change as often as people want. Magazines are published monthly, and newspapers (the ones that still exist, that is!) are now published only a few times a week. The Internet allows instant communication, and people want to hear the newest information immediately. Although many online news sites are now updated throughout the day, blogs enjoy the reputation of being the most actively updated news sources. A good blog posts multiple entries per day or even an entry per hour. (This frequency of updating information can also help your blog rank higher in online search results, provided the frequency doesn't erode the quality of the content.)

In addition to the frequency with which you post content to your blog, certain times of the day are considered ideal for attracting the most readers. According to Hubspot, a company that specializes in online inbound marketing, research shows that the best time to get views for your blog is early in the morning. This is also a good time to post because your content is more likely to get picked up by other bloggers and content (news) sites and receive traffic-generating referral links to your site.

✦ **The ability to connect:** The power of many blogs lies in the power of communication. On one level, bloggers are able to provide web links to articles, reviews, or even other blogs. The bloggers become an army of reviewers, by recommending to others which articles to read and which products, services, or trends to follow. In this way, blogs have significant influence. Research indicates that bloggers are among the most trusted online resources and blogs are the third most influential digital resource for influencing consumer buying behaviors. In other words, a good blog builds trust with its readers, and that type of influence is worth its weight in gold! Gaining that influence starts with good content and consistent engagement with readers. For example, bloggers and readers often communicate with each other by *commenting*, or leaving messages, following a particular blog post. This almost-instant two-way communication technique keeps readers engaged in a blog.

Readers who use the RSS (Rich Site Summary) feed on your blog can choose to receive updates from it as new posts are added. Promoting an RSS feed on your blog is another way to keep visitors engaged and coming back to your site. To get started for free, try using FeedBlitz (`www.feedblitz.com`), which is owned by Google.

✦ **Less filtering:** Blogs have sprung up to cover almost every topic imaginable. Traditionally, nonblog media organizations have to decide which stories to mention in a limited amount of space or time and don't always provide detailed information. On blogs, readers have a broader array of information to choose from, and it's often more in depth. Many successful bloggers focus on a particular niche, or a narrow set of topics, which makes it easier to deliver a steady stream of detailed content. Additionally, blogs provide links to other resources and background information.

One requirement of maintaining a blog is having extra time. Your blog readers expect that you will continually update your blog. If you create a blog with great fanfare and then wait weeks to post new entries, you quickly lose favor and even irritate your potential audience for wasting their time.

Finding your voice

When you create a blog, it needs two components:

✦ **Topic:** When you're selecting a topic, decide whether you want to share news and information about a specific industry, type of product, or notable trend. Or you might decide to make your blog more personal by selecting a topic such as the journey you're taking to run your business, by discussing health concerns, or by sharing ideas about raising kids. No single correct topic exists, so choose something you're passionate about. Of course, because you're planning to earn money from your blog, you should also choose a topic that has wide appeal to a large number of people. Along those lines, if you're adding a blog to an existing business site, blog about topics that relate specifically to that business (its products and services) or that matter to your target customer. Just because you sell accounting services to small businesses doesn't mean that's all you can blog about. You can write about any topic that helps your small-business customers better manage and grow their business.

✦ **Tone of voice:** Establish a tone of voice that's also unique to your blog. Keep in mind that blogs are conversations between you and your visitors. The information you post, or your blog entries, should reflect your own voice. In most cases, blogs don't abide by the typical rules of formal business writing. Instead, a blog's tone should be casual, friendly, informal, inviting, and informative — but use good grammar and check your spelling.

Write your blog as though you're having a one-to-one conversation with a friend. Your particular blog voice is then further defined by your personality. It may be a little more humorous, satirical, or to the point. Just make the voice yours.

Although one person should coordinate all blogging efforts, a good blog can and should have multiple contributors and even occasional guest bloggers. A good blog also includes feedback, or comments, from your readers. To encourage feedback, be sure to allow public comments on your blog.

Check out *Blogging All-in-One For Dummies,* 2nd Edition by Susan Gunelius, to find out how to build a blog, generate lots of visitors, and encourage them to contribute their voices.

Content, content, content

The best way to create and maintain value for your blog is by adding content. According to Neilsen and AOL, 27 million pieces of content are shared daily. That's a lot of information for readers to navigate through on a daily basis. But not just any type of content will keep readers engaged. ContentPlus found that having interesting content is one of the top three reasons consumers follow a brand or company in social media and on blogs. This information shouldn't come as a surprise. After all, who wants to read boring, uninteresting content?

So what makes a blog post interesting? Content that is useful or informative can be interesting. Content that is well written can make even simple facts seem interesting. The way the content is delivered, or the type of format used, can make content interesting (reading an infographic or e-book may be more interesting than reading an 800-word article). Including charts, graphics, or photos help make content more interesting. (Research shows that blog posts or articles with pictures accompanying them get 75 to 94 percent more views.) According to MarketingSherpa, content creation is ranked as the most effective SEO (search engine optimization) technique to help drive visitor traffic. Good content should attract site visitors. When they find your blog, how do you keep them interested — and keep them coming back? Content.

Blog posts

Adding new posts frequently is important. Although some people may encourage posting an entry at least once a week, we recommend a more frequent schedule. Blogs with heavy traffic, for example, may post a new blog entry three times a day. This number of entries may seem like a lot, but don't worry: The average blog entry is only 350 to 450 words. A larger post, the equivalent of an article (around 500 to 1,000 words) might be posted once or twice per week. Overall, it's not difficult to keep blog posts flowing.

Because blog posts are typically stamped with the date and time they go live, visitors can easily tell whether you're adding fresh content to your blog site.

Provide a balance in the type of content you offer readers. Here are some examples of different content you want to consider including on a regular basis:

+ **Feature story:**. A growing trend is posting in-depth, long-form articles (also referred to as *long-form journalism*), which can be 1,500 words or greater. This type of content is usually SEO-friendly (in that it may help your blog rank higher in search results). If taking on long-form content, once a month (or once every few months) should be plenty. Long-form content, or a feature story, may teach readers something or provide an informational deep-dive (detailed) look at a specific topic. Holding a reader's attention can be tricky on the Internet, so it's important that a longer article be especially interesting or useful. When you consistently provide good, usable content in this way, you may earn the reputation of being an expert in your field — which, in turn, helps increase your blog traffic!

+ **Current events:** In this case, the blog post is more topical and discusses news, popular culture, celebrities, or special events that are timely. Using information in your posts that are hot items and frequently being discussed is a good way to draw attention to your blog and attract new readers. Consider an important news story that people are discussing nationally or around the globe. Think about how often people search for that topic using Google or Bing. Now imagine your blog entry popping up in the search results. If a really hot topic is not directly related to your particular blog topic, don't be afraid to get creative and find a tie-in. For example, suppose you're a food blogger and a royal wedding is keeping the entire world buzzing. You might write a post about what type of royal-inspired recipes your readers could try at home while they watch the wedding. That's how you take a current story and use it to draw visitors to your blog.

Make sure that the content you post is relevant to your readers. Stretching your topic too far, just for the sake of tying into popular news, could backfire. If readers aren't interested in your content, they don't come back, no matter how many times you post.

+ **Evergreen content:** In addition to including topical posts, you should write about subjects that will remain relevant as long as possible and are not connected to a particular time. This type of content is called *evergreen* content because it lasts (almost) forever. Evergreen content is important for this reason: Suppose the year is 2015 and prospective visitors search for information on a particular topic and come across a link to your blog that references a date from 2011? They are less likely to read your blog because it would be considered out of date. Evergreen posts simply avoid referencing a date or period of time — so they always appears fresh.

+ **Infographics:** Having gained enormous popularity, infographics are the equivalent of having lots of images and graphics displayed on a single, very long piece of paper. Infographics is a way to visualize data in a series of simple, fun, or unique images.

✦ **Video:** Yes, video is considered content, whether you employ Skype and your laptop to conduct and record an interview, use an inexpensive GoPro camera (or use your smartphone camera) to conduct a how-to video, set up a Google+ Hangout On Air (that posts directly to YouTube), or have a professional video camera and editing system to create an entertaining piece of content. Video appears in search engine results, and adding video to your blog is another way to get found and bring new visitors to your site. The best part of putting video in your blog posts is that it doesn't have to be perfect. Keep videos short, usually between 30 seconds to 2 minutes. Your visitors will respond to video that is interesting, entertaining, and not too long.

✦ **Images**: As mentioned, images get a great deal of attention online and usually bring in more views to reach your post. Use a photo that is a stock image (an image that you pay for or access for free) and can download from a stock photo website), or one that is your own. You can also use graphs, charts, and other graphical formats that showcase data.

✦ **Short posts with links:** The goal of this type of content is to provide short, quick posts that are easy to write and simple to read. Then you provide a link or multiple links to more detailed information or articles. Although these links can go to content on someone else's website or blog, ideally they point to articles on your own site. Not only does this strategy keep visitors on your site, but the additional pages of content provide more opportunities for search engines to find your site, which translates to the possibility of earning more ad revenue. You must be careful to make sure the content is unique and not simply a duplicate of other content on (or off) your site. To find out more about search engines and how they help attract visitors to your website, read Book VI, Chapter 6.

Short, easy-to-write blog posts make it possible for you to post more of them. This tactic provides a way for you to keep fresh content on your site without draining all your time. As always, just because posts are short doesn't mean you should skimp on substance, relevancy, or good grammar!

Making Your Blog Pay, in Dollars and Sense

Spending a lot of time thinking about and planning a content strategy for your blog is not only necessary but also makes sense. Having lots of quality content leads to lots of visitors, which leads to the potential for earning lots of money. The most outrageous but authentic example we can offer of a rags-to-riches story is that of the Huffington Post. In 2005, Arianna Huffington cofounded the site on a shoestring budget. She convinced many well-known (and lesser known) writers to blog for the news and current event site. What developed was essentially a giant blog. The Huffington Post eventually became known as a controversial but well-trafficked media site filled with hundreds and hundreds of blog posts. Just five years after launching the monster blog site, it was sold to AOL for $315 million.

Many professional bloggers and online entrepreneurs are earning a steady (and respectable) income from their blogs. Others have built a large following of loyal readers and use the blog as a launching pad for other moneymaking endeavors, such as publishing a book, becoming a sought-after speaker, or creating a consulting business or research firm based on their specialized blog topic. An example of this type of success is Christy Jordan's Southern Plate (www.southernplate.com). Christy Jordan started blogging several years ago as a way to share family recipes and the art of southern cooking. Her site, shown in Figure 3-1, now gets 30 million page views per month, has more than 70,000 newsletter subscribers, and has a Facebook page with 115,000 fans. While she continues to blog, Christy has established herself as an expert in southern cooking with several cookbooks to her name and is a frequent speaker and on-air television guest.

Figure 3-1: Christy Jordan's Southern Plate is a popular blog for the cookbook author.

So, how do you get started down this path? Step one is building lots of quality content, as we've just shared. Step two is identifying and implementing money-generating opportunities for your blog.

Earning money with Google AdSense

One of the most popular revenue streams for blogs comes from Google and its ad-based moneymaker, AdSense. This program makes it relatively simple to display advertising throughout the pages of your blog. Ad formats include text links, banner and other display ads, and video.

Among the most popular, and easiest to display, are text links that complement your blog's topic, which are referred to as *contextual ads*. In other words, Google's AdSense crawls the content on your site and then matches it with ads that target related products or services. Not only is it easy to use (and requires no selling on your part), but the ads are also more effective and more likely to generate revenue because they're selling products that relate to your blog.

You can place the ads throughout your site, but they most often show up in the sidebar on your pages. The display and video ads work in a similar way, in that Google attempts to serve ads that match your site's content and audience interests. Setting up ads for your site is a matter of registering for the program, providing information about your site, getting approved by Google, and then placing code on your blog to get the ads to start showing. The hardest part is waiting for Google's approval, which can take anywhere from a few hours to a few days.

To sign up for AdSense, follow these steps:

1. **Go to www.google.com and click the Advertising Programs link in the lower-left corner.**

2. **Under the Make Money from Your Site section, click the Get Started button.**

   A new page appears that contains important information about AdSense and the sign-up process. Before proceeding to the next step, have your bank account information ready. Google requires a physical address that matches your bank account before you can complete the sign-up process.

3. **Click the Get Started Now button, or the Get Started with AdSense button.**

   You need a Google Gmail account before proceeding to the next steps. You can use an existing account or create one.

4. **Click the Yes, Proceed to Google Account Sign In button.**

5. **Sign in to the Gmail account you plan to use for AdSense.**

   You cannot change this e-mail address, so choose carefully.

6. **Provide the necessary details, such as the URL of your website where AdSense ads will appear, and the primary language of your content.**

7. **Review the AdSense policies, and then click the Continue button.**

   You're agreeing to Google's AdSense policies, along with other statements concerning your account. You can review AdSense policies in detail by visiting https://support.google.com/adsense.

   If you violate any part of the AdSense policy, you can be immediately and permanently banned from using AdSense. Google is notorious for having a one-strike-and-you're-out rule. In other words, no second chances — so read carefully!

8. **Complete the form, telling Google about your site's content, and then submit the application.**

   Within eight hours after submitting your application, Google sends an e-mail to tell you whether or not you passed the first part of the review process.

9. **Upon passing step 1 of the verification process, log into your new AdSense account.**

   You see a red bar on the page with code for AdSense ads.

   You must complete all payee or payment information before you get paid.

10. **Place the code from the red bar on a page of your site.**

    After the code is activated, Google conducts a final review of your website. The process takes three to four days. When Google gives you final approval, you can access your AdSense account.

If you're signing up for AdSense from a YouTube or Blogger account, you need to start and complete the registration process from that account. The application process is different than the one just presented.

**Book X
Chapter 3**

Blogging for Profit

Adding ad networks to your blog

Google AdWords is pretty much an ad network, but it's certainly not the only game in town. Other companies can serve ads to your blog and pay you, not only for allowing people to see the ads but also each time someone clicks the ad. Like AdSense, the process is simple. Best of all, you can run both AdSense and another ad network on the same blog. Here are some well-known ad networks:

✦ Chitika (www.chitika.com)

✦ PubMatic (www.pubmatic.com)

✦ Value Viglink (www.viglink.com)

Freelance blogging

One way to earn money as a blogger is to blog for someone else. For example, an investment firm may hire you to blog regularly about money-related topics, or a technology company may pay you to talk about a specific product. In either case, you might use your own name, or you might ghost-write the blog as an employee of the company.

Having your own blog is often the first step in being found and asked to contribute to other sites. One is not exclusive of the other; you can have the best of both worlds!

How much can you expect to earn? Companies pay as little as a few dollars per post, or pay by the word or the length of post, or pay a flat monthly fee of several thousand dollars. In other cases, blogging communities may also allow you to host a blog topic and pay you by sharing ad revenues. You earn a percentage of the company's ad revenue, which is influenced by the popularity of your topic is and how well you drive traffic to the blog.

If you prefer to work for yourself, you can earn money by selling ad space on your blog. This strategy is similar to the way you might use display ads as a moneymaker for any type of website. You can find out more about the process in Book IV.

Repackaging and selling your content

After you put in a great deal of time to make your blog shine with original, heartfelt pieces of content, it's a shame to let it sit and collect dust. Fortunately, you don't have to archive content and never let it see the light of day again. Put it to good use earning more money for you! Many bloggers have found financial success by repackaging their most popular articles into different formats and then selling them. Depending on the format and the popularity of the topic, you can charge as little as a couple of dollars to as much as a few hundred dollars. Good, quality content can take you far, online. Here are some of the most popular ways to repackage your content:

✦ E-books

✦ Videos or podcasts

✦ Research reports

✦ Self-published books

Earning money by speaking up

When it comes to earning money from your blog, all roads truly lead to content. We've said that before, and we'll say it again. High-quality, frequently updated content leads to more visitors, more opportunities, more money, and on occasion, more respect and notoriety. It's not uncommon for popular bloggers who are recognized as experts (or sought-after personalities) to be invited to speak at conferences and other events. Not only do conference organizers want to see you there, but they are often willing to pay you and pay your travel expenses, too. You may make two thousand dollars to many thousands of dollars for less than an hour of your time.

On the other hand, many successful bloggers decide to produce their own conferences based on or related to the topic they cover. In that case, the blogger becomes the conference organizer. You may make anywhere from a few thousand dollars to much more per conference. Granted, this method isn't the easiest of ways to make money, but it can result in substantial income.

Testing and reviewing products of all kinds

A type of blogger referred to as a *mommy blogger* can be credited with blazing the path for reviewing and recommending products to their many readers. This group of influential bloggers is also known for influencing the product development, pricing, and marketing decisions that come out of large, well-known companies who sell to parents. As companies realized that mommy bloggers had large, faithful followings of other parents who made buying decisions based on what the mommy bloggers recommended, well, Corporate America wasted no time responding. Mommy bloggers regularly received free products and services, as long as they agreed to try them out and then provide a review or buying recommendation to their loyal followers. In some cases, the bloggers received trips and other gifts.

Today, this technique is still a popular way for companies to spread the word about their products. In other cases, especially with tech-related products, reputable and influential bloggers may be paid to test one product, compare it to a competing product, and then write about the outcome. If the review is positive, a company has an independent, third-party person endorse their product versus a competitor's. Depending on the industry and the complexity of the texting method, you could earn several thousand dollars each time you conduct a test.

IRS tax laws require bloggers to report the value of all those free gifts and trips as income. Check with your tax adviser for specifics of how to report gifts.

Selling your stuff from the pages of your blog

Just because you have a blog and share your opinions doesn't mean you can't earn money selling stuff. As with a traditional website, you may choose to sell products that complement or tie in to the topic of your blog. For example, Invitation Crush, shown in Figure 3-2, is a blog about, you guessed it — invitations. In addition to sharing a love for all types and styles of invites, blogger Kristen Magee sells a variety of invitations for all occasions. It's a natural product extension for the theme of her blog. One day, for example, she may blog about the popular letterpress printing style used for custom baby announcements. After reading about this style of invitation or announcement, you can peruse the Invitation Crush shop and find letterpress cards for your own special occasion.

Figure 3-2:
Invitation Crush offers a range of invitation styles on its blog.

Regardless of the theme of your blog or the types of products you want to sell (handmade or store bought), offer complementary items, products that reflect the theme and style of your blog.

Choosing a Blog Platform

As with other online business opportunities, one of the biggest advantages of starting a blog is its extremely low overhead. In fact, many blogging software products and tools are free.

If you already have a website, talk to your hosting company to see whether you can integrate a blog into your website. This way, the blogging audience that comes to your blog can easily cross over to other portions of your website, which just might lead to a sale.

If you're starting a blog from scratch and don't already have a website, try one of the variety of free or modestly priced blogging tools.

Although plenty of free tools are available to start a blog, you might have to pay a small monthly or annual fee if you plan to use your blog to make money. You might want to start with a free version while you set up your blog and become comfortable using it, and then upgrade to a paid account when you're ready to build revenue for the blog.

Check out these free sites to start a blog:

✦ **Blogger (`www.blogger.com`)**, a free blogging site owned by Google, provides templates and has no restrictions on the number of blogs you can maintain. Blogger makes it easy to promote your new blog, too. See the next section to sign up for Blogger.

✦ **WordPress (`www.wordpress.com`)** is one of our favorite blogging tools and has become one of the most widely used blog software programs. WordPress is free. Although it occasionally runs ads on your blog, you can opt out of ads for a small annual fee. One WordPress feature lets you access your blog from your smartphone.

You can start with the hosted version (`wordpress.com`) and then upgrade to the self-hosted version (`wordpress.org`). In this way, you can grow into your blog and business without having to switch your blog to a different host.

✦ **TypePad (`www.typepad.com`)** is not expensive but does require a monthly plan. You can choose from several options, ranging from $8 to $50 per month. TypePad plans include access to most of the service's advanced features, widgets, and technical support. With a seemingly endless supply of template designs, this tool is ideal for starting a revenue-generating blog.

When selecting a blogging platform, check to see whether the tool lets you export content if you decide to move to another blogging tool. You don't want to build months, or even years, of posts, only to lose them if you find a better platform for your blog.

If you have an existing website, you may want to integrate a blog into that site rather than maintain a separate URL for a blog. When deciding on a blogging platform, see whether it can be easily integrated into your site. Most blogs can be added by using various levels of programming, but if you don't have that skill set and don't want to hire a programmer, make sure that the instructions for adding a blog to your existing website are clear.

Signing up with Blogger.com

One easy-to-use tool is Blogger (`www.blogger.com`), shown in Figure 3-3. Blogger provides a simple sign-up process for creating your blog and even has a detailed tour of how the system works.

Figure 3-3:
Get started blogging at Blogger.

Follow these steps to create a blog:

1. Confirm your blogger profile on the Blogger home page at `www.blogger.com`.

You can choose to use a Google+ profile that will be linked to your Google identity, or you can create a limited blogger profile. The limited profile lets you use a pseudonym but does not have all the benefits of using a Google+ profile tied to your actual identity.

Save time signing up with Blogger by having a complete Google+ account already activated. If you do not have one, Blogger requires that you go through a complete set-up (from adding friends to your circles to following other people).

After setting up your Google+ account, choose Continue to Blogger where you see a simplified dashboard to use for your Blogger profile account.

2. **Click the New Blog button and enter the following information the pop-up window:**

   a. *Name your new blog.*

   b. *Type the address or URL of the blog.*

      Start with `www.MyNewBlog.blogger.com` and then update to a customer domain name later. (Blogger lets you know if the URL you choose is available before you can continue to the next step.)

3. **Choose a template for your blog and then click the Create Blog button.**

   Blogger creates your new blog and then sends you back to the dashboard (refer to Figure 3-3), which now shows the name of your blog at the top of the page.

4. **Under the name of your blog, click the Start Posting link.**

That's it. You're ready to write your first post and officially launch your own blog.

Getting started with WordPress

Another powerful blog platform is WordPress, which provides access to many easy-to-use templates and features. One of the many advantages of WordPress is the capability to integrate the free version of the blogging platform into an existing website. The blog can also be your entire website, if you prefer. Websites such as Online Marketing to Go (see Figure 3-4) use WordPress to structure all the pages across their site, instead of using it only in a traditional blog structure.

Figure 3-4: More than a blog, WordPress can become your entire site.

To get started with WordPress, follow these steps to sign up for a blog:

1. **Go to the WordPress home page at** `www.wordpress.com`, **and click the Get Started Here button.**

   A new setup page appears.

2. **Enter the following information:**

   - *Blog name:* This name is also the URL for your new blog. You can host it for free on WordPress, in which case your blog name will be something like `www.yourgroovysitename.wordpress.com`. You can also choose to have the .com, .org, or .net extension, but you are charged $18. The upside is that your URL would look like this: `www.yourgroovysitename.com`. (You can choose to upgrade later.)

   - *Username and password:* The username, or the identity you create to access your blog in the future, is also used as the name of your blog and in the URL. For example, if you choose YourGroovySiteName as your site name, your URL becomes `www.yourgroovysitename.wordpress.com`.

     If you don't want to use WordPress to host your blog, you can upload the free blog software to your own server. Some hosting companies also sell inexpensive blog-hosting packages for WordPress. Be careful with those hosting packages because they may not include the necessary components to support all features of your blog (such as a database).

   - *E-mail address:* Use an e-mail address that you check often because WordPress sends you updates and other important information by e-mail.

   - *Legal agreement:* After reading the terms of agreement, acknowledge that you have done so and agree to the terms.

3. **Click the Create Blog button.**

   A new page appears to start the blog setup process.

4. **(Optional) Enter a tagline for your blog (this is optional).**

5. **Choose the language preference for your blog, and then click Next Step.**

6. **Choose a template style for your new blog, and then click Next Step.**

   WordPress has many templates to choose from, including free options.

   Start by selecting a free template. Later, you can peruse all the choices to find just the right fit. Selecting and applying a different template from your blog management dashboard is easy.

7. **(Optional) Share your blog with friends on Facebook and Twitter, and then click Next Step.**

You have the option to post an invite to friends on social media and let them check out your blog. We advise against this. Wait until you have completely set up the blog and added content before sharing with your friends on social media.

8. **Create your first post, or click Next Step.**

WordPress prompts you to immediately begin writing your first blog post. If you don't want to create a post just yet, click Next Step to continue to your WordPress dashboard, where you can write a blog post later (refer to Figure 3-5).

Figure 3-5:
Write your first post in the WordPress blog.

9. **Confirm your e-mail.**

When your dashboard first appears, you see a message at the top asking you to check your e-mail account and confirm that it is your e-mail. You need to complete this step before continuing to work on your new blog.

That's it. You're on your way to having your own WordPress blog.

TIP

To help search engines and other bloggers more easily find your blog post, add tags to it. *Tags* are keywords found in your post that someone may also search for when looking for information about a particular topic. For example, if you write a blog post about refrigerators you can keep in your dorm room, you may want to include tags for *refrigerators, mini-refrigerators,* and *dorm rooms.*

Chapter 4: Learning to Spot and Capitalize on Social E-Commerce Trends

In This Chapter

✔ **Connecting: the (virtual) reality of social commerce**

✔ **Getting ready for your close-up with video**

✔ **Gathering, sharing, and making a profit in communities**

Social networking and online communities continue to fuel opportunities in online niche markets. The surrounding niche opportunities that have sprouted up as a result of those first fertile sites have also proved lucrative.

You undoubtedly have heard of Facebook, which experts once predicted was worth $100 billion. In 2012, the social media heavyweight went public and its stock has since traded at a high of more than $70 per share. Its founders and key executives are said to be worth billions of dollars. The company has been on a long-running spending spree, snapping up Instagram (a photo-sharing app) for $1 billion, Oculus (a virtual reality company) for $2 billion, and WhatsApp (a mobile app) for $19 billion.

Although it hasn't been as aggressive in acquiring other companies, LinkedIn has found great financial success, too. The career- and business-focused social networking platform was the first social media site to go public. Its stocks have performed consistently well, even trading at a 52-week high of more than $250 a share. Twitter, the other leading social media site following in the footsteps of its peers, went public in 2013, trading at per share highs of more than $70. Even during the infamous dotcom boom, who would have thought Internet companies like these could hold their own against brand giants Coca-Cola, General Motors, and others?

By the way, all three social media sites had humble beginnings. Facebook was founded by college kids living on campus, LinkedIn was started in someone's living room, and Twitter got its start in a small apartment. Like other (now) giant technology companies born out of garages, spare bedrooms, and college dorms, social networking sites and online communities are experiencing the same opportunities for growth. And this is where you can find another option for pursuing your own success.

If you aren't familiar with the concept of online socializing, think of it in terms of attending a big networking event where hundreds or thousands of professionals might go to meet, mingle, build relationships, and drum up business. Lots of different types of online social networks exist, and they aren't always focused on business activities. Some communities are created solely for socializing, others are created for a specific group (such as business executives or hobbyists), and still others are developed as a support network for a particular group (such as moms).

Because these types of online networks attract so many eyeballs (or visitors), you can use them to make money, either directly or indirectly. Creative online entrepreneurs continually find innovative ways to monetize social networking — and so can you! In this chapter, we discuss the different types of social networking sites and online communities, along with some of the ways in which you can potentially profit from them.

Building Online Networks with Social Commerce

Although online communities are often lumped into the social networking category, they are much more than a social site. Each offers something different and has its own pros and cons, especially when it comes to using them to grow an online business.

In online communities, you interact with people from around the world, thus exposing yourself to virtual strangers. As a result, all these communities and social networking sites have had their share of problems. To reduce your risks, always read a site's policies, privacy statements, terms-and-conditions documents, and general member guidelines. Stay safe!

In its truest form, a social networking site provides a central hub where individuals or groups can exchange ideas, share information, and build relationships. We want to provide a brief introduction to some of the most popular and fastest growing social networks, and give you a glimpse as to why they may be important to you as you grow an online (or offline) business, or look for the next niche business opportunity. Here are the best known (and up-and-coming) social networks:

✦ **Facebook:** `www.facebook.com`

✦ **Google+:** `www.plus.google.com`

✦ **LinkedIn:** `www.linkedin.com`

✦ **Pinterest:** `www.pinterest.com`

✦ **Twitter:** `www.twitter.com`

Most likely, you want to use social networks (or social media) as a way to promote your business. We discuss this process in more detail in Book VI and illustrate how these sites help boost your business sales.

Facebook

Unless you've been hiding under a rock, you're familiar with the social networking giant Facebook, which was the first of its kind to carry social networking into the real world and get investors to see it as a business with potential. Facebook started with personal pages, which allow you and your (selected and approved) friends to view your profile and leave comments for you on your wall, but has expanded to include business pages. Companies are using these pages to extend their online presence into the social networking space.

What can businesses do with Facebook pages? Whether you have an e-commerce business or a bricks-and-mortar location, you want to create a profile of your business so that potential customers have an up-close look at what your business can do for them. In addition to the profile, fans of your business can leave a post or comment on your wall (or primary page), ask questions, seek out technical support, and share pictures of themselves using your product. Businesses use Facebook as a place to run contests, seek out information or research, and attract more customers by garnering more "likes." Facebook is also an ideal place to promote video content and other presentations or brochures in an effort to get your company in the face of those who count most — your customers. In addition to reading Book VI to see how to buy and run an ad and other ways to use Facebook as a marketing tool, you might want to check out *Facebook Marketing All-in-One For Dummies,* 3rd Edition, by Andrea Vahl.

Because deleting a Facebook page is extremely tedious, you should be prepared to always keep an eye on the posts. And should anything negative get posted on your wall, you want to be prepared with a policy or set of procedures in place to route and resolve bad comments. Otherwise, one or two negative comments that never get resolved could cost you lots of customers.

Google+

Sometimes, it feels almost impossible to keep up with Google. The Internet giant has a hand in just about every e-commerce pie. Its contender for the social media game, Google+ (pronounced "Google plus"), has had a bumpy ride since its debut. It boasts more than 500 million users and, its active members seem to consist largely of professionals from the technical industry and various tech-related hobbyists and enthusiasts. Although there has been much debate about whether or not its users are showing up and networking in Google+, the site is important for several reasons. For starters, Google wants to tie all your online activity to a single identity, which means it connects your Google+ profile with your Gmail accounts and your search activity. This strategy essentially forced people to have a Google+ presence (which boosted its members from the start). But more importantly, it's widely thought that Google+ profiles and activity contribute to search engine rankings. For that reason alone, spending time in your Google+ account could be especially beneficial when sharing blog posts, product updates, and other important information that can pump up your online earnings opportunity.

Another exciting part of Google+ that's ripe with opportunity is the Google+ Hangouts on Air, a video-based networking opportunity (think of a webinar where multiple people participate, each using the camera on a laptop to provide the video component). After the video meeting is finished, it's automatically recorded and saved to your YouTube account (which is also owned by Google). Hangouts provide lots of opportunity for online marketing and social selling.

Twitter

In 2011, after celebrating five years in business, Twitter exploded onto the social networking scene as a place to have real-time conversations. The object of Twitter is to build followers and have conversations — in 140 characters or less. After you sign up for this free web-based service, you can send as many (short) messages as you like.

Although it comes as a surprise to many, Twitter is a useful tool for business. For example, search functions make it easy to identify potential followers (and possible customers) based on your use of key search words. And, thanks to link-shortening tools, such as Bit.ly (`www.bit.ly`), it's easy to add a link back to your site to promote content such as blog posts, videos, and presentations, or to highlight your services and products. Using Twitter as a traffic-generating tool is one of the benefits it offers to your website. You can also use hash tags (the number or pound sign on your computer keyboard) to follow discussions on key phrases, promote key phrases, or allow others to discuss a topic relating to your business. Simply put the hash tag in front of the term you want to use and then tweet it. For example #socialmedia will bring up all Twitter comments on that subject.

Like Facebook, Twitter offers a promotional opportunity with paid advertising, called *promoted tweets.* The ad program lets you target a particular audience on Twitter (segmented by keywords used in user profiles and in tweets, and by hashtags and popular trending topics, for example). Your promoted tweet is labeled as such at the bottom of the tweet (see Figure 4-1) and is then inserted into the top of your target audience's Twitter stream.

Twitter has also started offering another way to advertise by using Twitter cards, which are shown in Figure 4-2. You add code to your website that allows images to be displayed with certain tweets. Or you can use a lead generation Twitter card, which lets you send tweets with images and allow a Twitter user to get a coupon or download an e-book directly from your tweet (without having to leave Twitter).

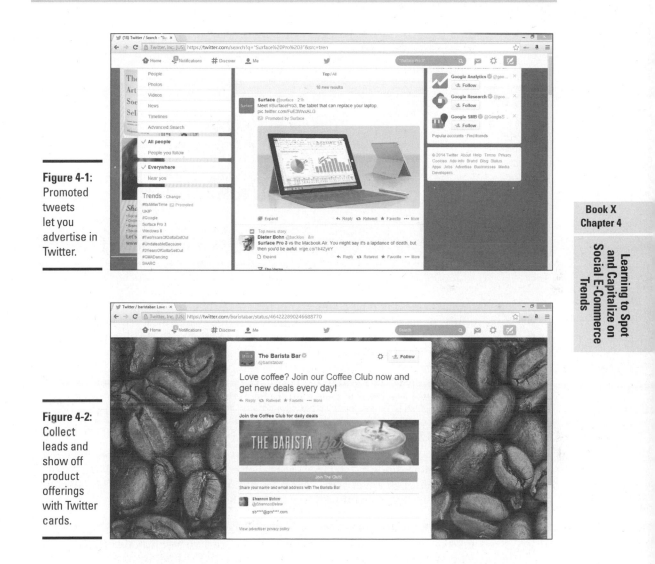

**Book X
Chapter 4**

Learning to Spot
and Capitalize on
Social E-Commerce
Trends

Figure 4-1:
Promoted tweets let you advertise in Twitter.

Figure 4-2:
Collect leads and show off product offerings with Twitter cards.

Another new opportunity for shopping from Twitter is being pioneered by Amazon. Using the hashtag #AmazonCart (see Figure 4-3), you can take advantage of special product offerings from Amazon's Twitter account and then add the product directly to your Amazon shopping cart — without leaving Twitter. The products you add to your Amazon account will be in your shopping cart and ready for check-out when you want to complete the purchase. This type of social media shopping is still new, but we expect lots of future opportunities for online sellers of all types.

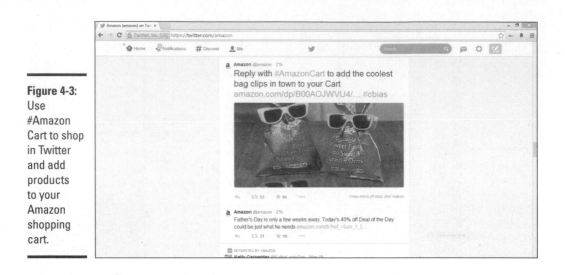

Figure 4-3:
Use #Amazon Cart to shop in Twitter and add products to your Amazon shopping cart.

Unlike Facebook posts, which stay prominently featured on a page for a while, posts on Twitter rotate quickly through your followers' feeds. To ensure that as many followers as possible see your tweets, you want to post similar tweets several times.

Twitter doesn't like you to tweet the exact message over and over again, so change your tweet message slightly each time you send it out.

LinkedIn

LinkedIn is one of the only (if not *the* only) social networking sites developed with businesses in mind. The site was also quick to develop a plan to earn money through advertising revenues and paid membership levels. They've also been successful at growing and maintaining their sales.

Although these details are nice to know, you're probably more interested in how LinkedIn can help you. LinkedIn is like a virtual Rolodex (filled with your professional contacts) that's been moved online and expanded to include everything about you and your profession (everything from a resume to your interests and most recent careers). Your first step in using the site is to create a user profile. (Your LinkedIn profile is scanned by all the major search engines.) Then you start building your network by adding people you know who are already on LinkedIn and inviting other people on LinkedIn who you would like to meet and add to your network.

If you're selling B2B (business to business), LinkedIn is an ideal social network for you. LinkedIn heavily promotes *social selling,* which is essentially finding and selling to customers through social media. It is continually updating its platform and tools to make it easy for you to sell or prospect in the platform. With LinkedIn, you have the opportunity to

✦ Expand your network through virtual introductions

✦ Post updates on projects you're working on and events you're attending

✦ Join groups with similar interests and participate in conversations

✦ Use your profile to help get found in search engines

✦ Use PDFs, PowerPoints, SlideShare presentations, and video to add to your profile information about your products or services

✦ Publish content to their Pulse platform, which is shared across the social network

✦ Promote events

Pinterest

Pinterest started out as just another social cataloging site (which we discuss at the end of this chapter). It's a collection of user-generated and user-shared images that members *pin,* or post, to personal boards — the virtual equivalent of posting something to a cork board. Pinterest has become one of the most popular image-sharing social networks. As a business or a blogger, your customers and readers can share images from your online store or blog directly to their Pinterest boards. In this way, your product images get shared across a huge network of Pinterest members, as shown in Figure 4-4. You can also add special tags to your images that include product information (such as price) and link back to your website so that people who see the pin can then buy the product. And Pinterest is not just for typical products such as clothing or home décor — you can promote books, services, and other digital products, too. This feature is a great sales promotion tool for online sales.

**Book X
Chapter 4**

Learning to Spot
and Capitalize on
Social E-Commerce
Trends

Figure 4-4: Pinterest is full of opportunity when fans share your products.

Each of the social networks we discuss in this chapter can be connected directly to your website. How? Twitter and Facebook both have plug-ins or tools that let you post real-time feeds of your social networking accounts (or pages) on your site. For example, visitors can go to your main website and see a sidebar that contains the most recent comments posted on your Facebook wall and a real-time streaming Twitter feed. Look for instructions on Facebook and Twitter on how to grab some simple HTML code to place on your website to get things started. Most e-commerce solutions, blog platforms, and website builders provide the capability for you and customers to share information from your site to social media. Customers can share products, articles, reviews, videos, and just about anything else on your site.

Visual platforms

Similar to Pinterest, several other visual-based social media websites hold great potential as moneymakers:

✦ **Instagram (www.instagram.com):** Instagram is social media platform that lets you post photos and short (15-second) videos. You can then share your images across your other social media networks, such as Facebook and Twitter. The twist that makes Instagram special is that it allows you to add special filters to your images to give them a more creative look. In other words, you can take a picture on your smartphone, upload it to Instagram, and then add a fun filter on top of the picture to give it a faded look, or change it to black-and-white, or make it look like it was a Polaroid picture taken in the 1970s. You can do the same to short video clips. Creative and entertaining people can build a following of thousands of fans and generate revenue (through brand sponsorships, for example) from the platform.

✦ **Vine (www.vine.com):** Vine enables you to create six-second stop-motion style video clips. These super popular mini-videos, called *vines,* are easily shared across other social media networks. People with a knack for entertaining or informing using this new medium have already proven that Vine can be a lucrative way to make a lot of money. One revenue opportunity is making vines for other companies and established brands. Understanding what works best on the platform and what engages viewers takes time. If you happen to be good at this task, you can earn thousands of dollars replicating your success for other companies. (Companies are clamoring to use Vine videos as part of their social media marketing, so they're willing to pay big bucks to have it done for them.) If your Vine videos are popular enough and you generate a large fan following, you can earn money through paid sponsorships and advertising opportunities.

The way social media is used and which social networking sites are most popular changes quickly. In addition, new social networking sites and new potential moneymaking opportunities pop up almost daily. (At least it feels as though new things evolve that fast!) Keep an eye on emerging visual-based social media sites, such as SnapChat, for ways to cash in on the site's sky-rocketing popularity.

Visual-based social media sites are extremely popular; and almost all other social media sites encourage the use of images and videos in posts. The use of images can help a social media post get more engagement — the post is more likely not only to be seen but also to get liked, shared, or commented on by followers. This resulting need for visual content presents another moneymaking opportunity for you. For example, businesses of all types need original images and photos (and content that uses lots of graphics, such as infographics) to use on their social media sites, websites, and blogs. If you can take good-quality photos or creative pictures, you can sell the rights to use those images. One place that promotes this service and connects amateur photographers with online buyers is Foap (`www.foap.com`). Check it out to see how you can trade your photos for dollars.

Book X
Chapter 4

Learning to Spot
and Capitalize on
Social E-Commerce
Trends

Creating Your Own Video Channel

Statistically speaking, there's a good chance that you watch YouTube videos regularly — whether you see them in YouTube or when shared on another social media site such as Facebook. This online video site claims over two billion video views per day, with an average daily viewing time of around 15 minutes. Since it hit the Internet in 2005, YouTube has changed the way we use video in our everyday lives — we want to video everything in hopes of being the next online sensation, or we can't wait to see what someone else does in their video to get everyone talking.

Basically, the online video pioneer has made it possible to monetize crazy, weird, funny, or even serious videos. You can make money from YouTube whether you are a professional filmmaker or hobbyist, or you just happen to have a video camera on your phone. The best way to explain these revenue-earning opportunities from YouTube is to look at a few examples.

Shopping haulers and vloggers

Hauler is the term used to describe people who love to buy things, bring them home, and then record and discuss their finds (or shopping hauls) on video. Hauling videos are a combination Home Shopping Network and online product review. Hauls started as a trend among teenagers, particularly girls. One of the most successful online haulers is Elle Fowler, who has the popular AllThatGlitters21 YouTube channel (`www.youtube.com/allthatglitters21`), shown in Figure 4-5. Elle and her sister started the channel in 2008. Since then, the beauty and fashion *vlog* (video blog) has expanded to more than 1.2 million subscribers and over 160 million video views. The AllThatGlitters21 brand also has more than 250,000 followers on Twitter, over 170,000 fans on Facebook, and nearly 243,000 followers on Instagram. Not bad!

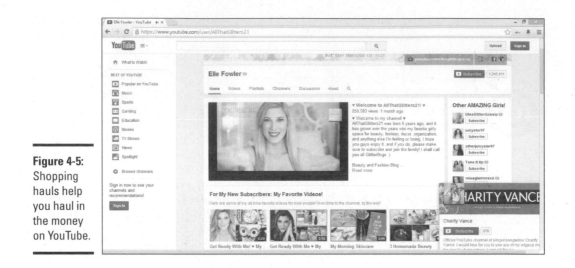

Figure 4-5:
Shopping
hauls help
you haul in
the money
on YouTube.

Figure 4-5:
Shopping
hauls help
you haul in
the money
on YouTube.

So, how do you make money showing off your favorite shopping finds? Most haulers earn money from advertising that appears on their YouTube channel (when people watch the videos) and from retailers paying for endorsements or product reviews. The hauling gig isn't only for teens. Moms, techies, and others are now in on the game.

As with any trend, this one has the possibility of diminishing. But that's no reason not to try it while it's still hot. And don't be afraid to use this trend as the basis for discovering the next big thing.

Instructional video

YouTube has a lot of content. Although the most viral videos are usually quirky or funny, other types of video are doing well online. And when it comes to making a profit from videos, instructional videos fit the bill. Think of a how-to format that teaches someone how to do something, or a travel video that showcases popular vacation destinations and gives tips or suggestions when traveling. Corporate-style training videos, geared toward more professional endeavors, are also a good choice. At the end of the day, video is still content. And if you offer quality content that people seek out, it's most likely content that sells.

Although YouTube provides incredible traffic and moneymaking opportunities, getting your videos noticed can be tough with so much competition. However, you can use other video sites, such as the following sites that are quickly showing promise:

✦ **Viddler** (www.viddler.com)**:** This video-hosting solution predates YouTube. Currently, Viddler provides several solutions, including a way to host or serve videos (other than on YouTube) so that they don't slow down your website's performance. Viddler also has a subscription service that helps you make money by selling subscription services to view or access your videos.

✦ **Vimeo** (`www.vimeo.com`): Vimeo is another hosted video service provider that offers tools, promotional assistance, and banner advertising options. These revenue-making tools are available only through their Vimeo Pro account, which costs approximately $200 per month.

✦ **DailyMotion** (`www.dailymotion.com`): Based on how it hosts and delivers user-generated videos on its site, this site is perhaps the closest competitor of YouTube. The site gets over 120 million unique visitors monthly. DailyMotion offers a couple of ways for you to make money. You can enroll in an affiliate-type program and earn money by sharing video links on your website or through your social media channels. Or as with YouTube, you can make money earning ad revenue with your videos.

Review sites

When was the last time you searched the Internet for product reviews before buying a specific product? Research shows that approximately 97 percent of online shoppers look to the Internet for recommendations and general product research before making a purchase. That's one reason websites that focus on product reviews are so popular. Of course, review sites focus on more than products. You also find reviews on places and services, from restaurants to day spas.

Regardless of what they're reviewing, these sites are yet another example of how social media influences behaviors — in this case, purchasing decisions. If you're selling anything, online or off, frequenting these sites is a good idea for several reasons. First, you can easily discover what customers have to say about the products you sell (or about your business). Second, you have the opportunity to interact with new and existing customers and get in on the discussion. On the other hand, if you have an interest in a niche market, you might consider launching your own review site. This strategy is popular when earning money through affiliate marketing programs, which we discuss in detail in Book IV, Chapter 2. Here are a couple of existing review sites to check for ideas:

✦ **Yelp** (`www.yelp.com`): Boasting more than 132 million unique monthly visitors in 2014, Yelp features reviews of all types of products, services, and businesses, and also allows business owners to respond to reviews.

✦ **CitySearch** (`www.citysearch.com`): Focusing on more than 75,000 cities in the United States, CitySearch provides reviews for services, restaurants, and other venues. Like Yelp, CitySearch lets businesses respond to reviews. Two interesting features are their mobile application and the promotion of local deals of the day. As for income, you can become a contributor and developer through CitySearch's CityGrid publishing program by using its SDK (software development kit). Find out how to participate and expand your network (and your revenue potential) by visiting `http://developer.citygridmedia.com`.

Many of the review sites, including CitySearch and Yelp, provide business owners with a free profile page. Taking the time to complete this quick overview of your business is a good promotional opportunity. In addition to providing details about your business type and location, you can use the profile page to post specials or coupons.

Social cataloging

Social cataloging sites are similar to a virtual catalog. You can identify images that mean something to you, group them in one place (sometimes called a board or collage), tag them, and promote them as things you like, as shown in Figure 4-6. In some cases, you can link product images directly to product pages.

Figure 4-6: Showcase your interest in brands and products and share with friends.

Although social cataloging sites are not considered a moneymaking platform yet, we think they have potential. Currently, your biggest benefit from these types of sites is likely to come in the form of brand recognition and possible traffic referral to your site. Traffic from social cataloging sites could possibly provide enough eyeballs to generate ad revenue or affiliate-style commissions from product referrals.

Keep the following social cataloging sites on your radar:

✦ Polyvore (`www.polyvore.com`)

✦ Thinglink (`www.thinglink.com`)

Presentation platforms

Plenty of community-based sites promote online socializing and sharing, but few of these networks, except LinkedIn, were created with businesses in mind. Given LinkedIn's success, sites that target the business customers and also provide a real service might just have potential as serious revenue generators. Presentation platforms are technically sites that offer a tool for businesses to publish, share, and archive business presentations. For example, a sales pitch developed in PowerPoint could easily be posted and viewed (publicly or privately) using one of these platforms.

Why classify presentation platforms as an online community? As mentioned, the capability to share, comment on, and circulate your published presentations in a defined space makes it a natural fit as a community. Your next question probably revolves around how to make money with this type of community. One possibility is that you could build your own niche presentation community and implement paid membership levels, similar to LinkedIn. But why go to all that trouble?

**Book X
Chapter 4**

Learning to Spot
and Capitalize on
Social E-Commerce
Trends

Instead, as a user of an existing presentation platform, you can use it as a tool to increase brand recognition and create your own presentation channel. From there, it's possible to capture leads (prospective customers!) and offer free or sample presentations as a way to send traffic to a site where your customers pay for access to more content. The following presentation platforms already attract lots of viewers:

✦ **SlideShare (`www.slideshare.net`):** Offering a free account, SlideShare (now owned by LinkedIn) lets you post presentations developed in PowerPoint, as a PDF, or even as video — and generate leads from within your presentation. You increase the capabilities of this presentation network when you choose to upgrade to a Pro business account. Note that SlideShare is in the process of updating this program, so expect to see lots of changes and expanded options for generating revenue. SlideShare easily integrates with LinkedIn, which helps generate even more views.

✦ **Prezi (`www.prezi.com`):** This presentation platform lets you create more of an interactive presentation that users can zoom in and out of, for example. The tool is easy to use and makes your presentation more engaging and user-friendly. Prezi offers different levels of paid accounts ranging from approximately $5 per month to $14 per month.

Both communities offers the potential to make your online business more professional and visible. Although the moneymaking side of social networking sites and communities isn't always obvious, explore the possibilities and get creative. The sky is the limit on how you use social networks for your online success.

Book XI

E-Commerce Advanced

Keeping up with the changing rules of search engine optimization (SEO) and understanding how a website ranks on a search engine results page (SERP), particularly in Google, is challenging. Hiring an SEO consultant can help boost rankings for an established e-commerce site. Before hiring a consultant, however, learn three important questions to ask by visiting www.dummies.com/extras/startinganonline businessaio.

Contents at a Glance

Chapter 1: Overhauling Your Business

In This Chapter

✔ Identifying when your business needs a change

✔ Inspecting falling numbers

✔ Taking your first steps toward renewed success

How do you measure the success of your website? As with any business, you should identify key performance indicators (KPIs) that closely match your primary objectives. These indicators may be based on profitability, sales revenue, or even customer service goals. According to a poll of small-business owners, two of the biggest indicators of e-commerce success are positive feedback from customers and the amount of *traffic,* or visitors, the site receives. Making the traffic to your site truly count usually means converting those visitors to customers. Perhaps that's why the survey also revealed that the number of sales leads and the amount of total online sales are important KPIs. However you choose to define success, understanding and tracking it is imperative.

Equally important is understanding that success has eluded you — and deciding that your online business needs an overhaul. This revelation is often the most important one you can make as a business owner and one of the most difficult to come to terms with. The sooner you confront the facts, the better chance you stand to reinvigorate sales. In this chapter, we show you the signs indicating that it's time for change, and we explain how to start putting your business back on the right e-commerce track.

Paying Attention to the Signs

Wouldn't it be nice if you could start your business, launch your website, attract lots of customers, make plenty of money — and never have to change a thing? If you've owned an online business for a while, you know that that's not the way it works. The Internet industry is constantly morphing, and so are the rules for growing a thriving online business. The secret of long-term online success is recognizing the signs of change — both good and bad — and being able to adapt.

If your website has any of the following characteristics, you might need to reevaluate your business:

✦ **A drop in search engine rankings:** A good, high-ranking position at Google, Bing, or Yahoo! is often the lifeblood of an online business. If your site begins to slip or inconsistently maintains its position after several years on top, something is wrong. The problem might be an optimization issue related to the many changes search engines make in their algorithms to determine rankings. However, don't discount the possibility that your site is losing relevancy.

✦ **An outdated look:** The visual look of your site doesn't have to be considered a design relic from the dot-com era to be outdated. Site design and design functionality change quickly in today's online business environment. Black backgrounds and plain fonts, for example, have long been stripped from sites in exchange for white backgrounds and clean, crisp images and font styles. Today's sites must also be mobile-ready and *responsive,* or capable of automatically shifting for display on multiple device types. In other words, it's time for you to make changes.

✦ **A lack of ongoing maintenance:** You can work in your business every day and still overlook the simplicity of good site-keeping. Broken links, expired coupon offers, and irrelevant or dated content are all indicators that you haven't been paying much attention to detail.

✦ **Fluctuating market conditions:** All types of issues in the world influence your business, either positively or negatively. The fluctuations that most closely relate to your industry or customer base obviously affect it the most. Some of these factors are increased competition, changing product trends, regional or national economic indicators, supplier costs, customer demand, and pricing issues. A significant change in your market space can dictate a change in your online business operations.

✦ **Overlooked technology upgrades:** Overlooking technology upgrades (whether you're updating antivirus software or installing a new version of a content-management system) is detrimental in the world of e-commerce. Allowing technology innovations to bypass you is a definite signal for change.

✦ **Nose-diving profitability:** This factor isn't one of the more subtle signs that it's time for Plan B. When revenue falls, overhead increases, and your bottom line pays the price for it all, you know that regrouping is a necessity.

✦ **A variation in visitors:** Is your site losing customers? Are your traffic counts falling or becoming less consistent? Or are you noticing an influx of visitors from a different traffic source, geographic region, or customer base — and you don't have products and services to relate to these new visitors? Fluctuations in site traffic and activity warrant a reaction.

This list of signs pointing to change isn't exhaustive. It's a starting point, though, for conditions to search for in your own business.

To make sure that you don't overlook anything, conduct a thorough *business change evaluation.* This system first establishes a baseline for your business, based on your KPIs (such as sales, visitors, and available products). Using the baseline, you then can evaluate other possible influences on your business.

Your goal is to take a snapshot of all your business indicators and determine which ones are driving change. Create a checklist by following these steps:

1. **Write a detailed description of your e-commerce business.**

   Include as part of your description the specific products or services you sell both online and offline. This description should provide a complete picture of your business.

2. **Describe your existing customers.**

   Be sure to include as much classifying information as possible about your customers. Details such as age and household income are bonuses. If you don't know those types of details, classify customers according to their product interests or purchases, or even by how they found your site (such as ads, other site referrals, or offline).

3. **Break out your revenue structure.**

   List the ways or places in which you earn money. Break down the list by month for the past 12 months. Then complete a year-over-year comparison for the past three years (if the data is available). Show the numbers in percentages of total sales. If you have a bricks-and-mortar store, include revenue from your offline sales too.

   If you're keeping up with your monthly profit-and-loss statements as part of your accounting procedures, you can pull these numbers directly from those statement histories.

   For a more immediate snapshot of what the numbers mean, show the results in the form of bar graphs or pie charts. This type of visual aid is often helpful for comparison purposes.

4. **Generate a traffic analysis of your site.**

   Break out the numbers in the form of a monthly comparison for the past 12 months, and then by year for the past three years. Include the total number of *unique* (different) visitors and *page views* (the number of pages requested within a particular period).

5. **Make a list of all areas that affect your business or influence change, either positively or negatively.**

   You can group the items by category as they apply to your site, such as marketing, sales, product development, or content.

6. **Categorize each item as positive or negative based on how it influences your site. Then explain why you chose that indicator. Beside the explanation, note whether you responded or reacted to the change.**

As you finish this section, you can identify areas where change is occurring and determine whether you have adequately adjusted to those new circumstances.

You might be tempted to believe that you already know this information or that this process is oversimplified. We can't emphasize enough the power of writing down this information in one place, for your review.

The purpose of making a meaningful evaluation is to help you identify holes in your current online business strategy. Then you use the information to target a market weakness or opportunity that you might have overlooked.

Keep this completed chart on hand as you continue through the overhaul process. Figure 1-1 shows an example checklist.

Business Change Checklist

Indicator	Type of Change (Positive/Negative)	Why?	Responded? (Y/N)	If Yes, How?
SITE				
Site design is outdated	_____	_____	_____	_____
Dated/old graphics	_____	_____	_____	_____
Broken links	_____	_____	_____	_____
Content not fresh	_____	_____	_____	_____
Expired coupons/offers	_____	_____	_____	_____
Defunct affiliate programs	_____	_____	_____	_____
New technologies released	_____	_____	_____	_____
INDUSTRY/MARKET CONDITIONS				
Increase in competition	_____	_____	_____	_____
Decrease in competition	_____	_____	_____	_____
Fluctuation in economy	_____	_____	_____	_____
Change in product/service	_____	_____	_____	_____
Change in consumer demand	_____	_____	_____	_____
Supply costs update	_____	_____	_____	_____
Pricing update	_____	_____	_____	_____
New vendors/partners	_____	_____	_____	_____
Customer (profiles) different	_____	_____	_____	_____
SEARCH ENGINE RANKINGS				
Dropped rank (out of Top 10)	_____	_____	_____	_____
Removed from rankings	_____	_____	_____	_____
Consistently moving down	_____	_____	_____	_____
Inconsistent rankings	_____	_____	_____	_____
Inconsistent rankings across various search engines	_____	_____	_____	_____
Keywords outdated	_____	_____	_____	_____
No active optimization activity	_____	_____	_____	_____
Variation in site visitors	_____	_____	_____	_____
Traffic/page views changing	_____	_____	_____	_____
MARKETING				
Offline advertising reduced	_____	_____	_____	_____
Less/more online advertising	_____	_____	_____	_____
Changed # of referring links	_____	_____	_____	_____
Updated promotions/offers	_____	_____	_____	_____
OPERATIONS				
Major fluctuation in profits	_____	_____	_____	_____
Outdated business plan	_____	_____	_____	_____
Revenue resources altered	_____	_____	_____	_____

Figure 1-1: Your checklist for evaluating change.

Qualifying for a Makeover from Lagging Sales

One no-fail indicator that your online strategy needs help is steadily falling sales. The issue always boils down to numbers — the number of products sold, the number of site visitors, and the last number on your bottom line. All these numbers are connected, and that connection has everything to do with sales.

The wonderful thing about the Internet is that you have immediate, and often real-time, access to online sales transactions. At any hour of the day, you can determine exactly how many dollars your website is generating. You then know whether your business is having a good day. What happens, though, when it's not a good day, or a good month?

If sales are down, start by asking yourself three basic questions:

✦ Do I need to pull in more visitors?

✦ Do I need to increase the amount of repeat visitors and buyers?

✦ Do I need to convert more visitors to buyers?

Sure, sometimes you answer "yes" to all three questions. Typically, though, your problem will stem more from one reason than the others. Addressing a sales decline most often comes down to an issue of acquisition, conversion, or retention. Either the number of people coming to your site has decreased and your sales are affected, or the proportion of sales to the number of visitors is off because people are leaving your site before making purchases, or you aren't getting enough repeat visitors and customers to offset the high cost of acquiring new visitors. After you decide which issue is most responsible for weighing down sales, you can begin addressing the problem.

Increasing the number of visitors to your site

If you need to increase the number of visitors to your website, concentrate on these areas to give sales a lift:

✦ **Search engine optimization (SEO):** Reexamine the search engine optimization techniques used for your site (see Book VI, Chapter 6). SEO is a necessary part of ongoing site maintenance. If your site isn't optimized correctly, its chance for a solid ranking in the search engines goes out the window. In addition, customers searching for your specific site can be disappointed when it doesn't pop up in their search results. Perhaps you haven't provided the best possible information to make a match during a typical search request.

✦ **Marketing strategies:** Letting routine marketing activities slip in priority in the daily chaos of managing an online business is easy. Diminishing numbers of visitors are a wake-up call to get back to basic marketing concepts. Create an online newsletter, or send out a fresh round of promotional e-mail to your existing customer database. You don't always have to dangle deep discounts in front of them. Sometimes they simply need a reminder that you're still out there!

✦ **Paid advertising:** Spend a little dough and pump up the number of site visits. Following are some areas where you should consider spending online advertising dollars:

- PPC (pay per click), such as Google AdWords or Yahoo Bing Network

- Mobile ads

- Display ads

- Retargeting ads

- Third-party sites, using banner ads, content sponsorships, or paid listings

If you're already spending money in these areas, look for new sites to place advertisements, or experiment with buying some different Google AdWords with new keywords.

✦ **Linking opportunities:** When was the last time you asked someone to exchange links with your site? Spending an hour or two per month searching for sites that are compatible with or complementary to yours is still considered worthwhile. You may find sites that have already shared information about your site or products but are not yet linking to your site.

Google continuously changes the algorithms that decide how sites are ranked in search engine results pages (SERPs). As part of those algorithms, if you break the rules or recommendations associated with SEO best practices, your website may be penalized, or dropped down in or booted out of the rankings. Link swapping is one of the areas that is affected by these changes, so it is important to always follow best practices.

Instead of swapping links, you can visit blogs that are applicable to your online business. Then leave comments to posts that include a link back to a specific page on your site (when allowed) or make sure your profile (that you set up to leave comments) references or links back to your website. The comments you leave on other sites may not rank high in search results, but they are a way to get awareness and possible traffic to your site from people reading the comments.

✦ **Public relations:** Are you creating awareness of your site by engaging in effective public relations strategies? What was the date on the last press release you distributed? Reach out to a few reporters and suggest a story relating to your business. When your site's traffic flow is slowing, now is not the time to be shy.

Not all news has to be based on good news. Think creatively and turn your *problem* into a relevant story idea that's timely and grabs attention. For example, a national report on decreased consumer confidence and spending could tie in nicely to a recent dip in sales for your site. Be sure to put a positive twist on how you're combating the issue. For instance, send the message that your site's competitive pricing is sure to win over customers now that they're more careful in their spending.

✦ **Social media expansion:** Spend some time building the number of followers you have on Facebook, Twitter, and YouTube. Social media provides a good opportunity to not only monitor real-time conversations that relate to your online business but also start conversations with customers and potential customers and keep people talking about your brand. You can find more information about using social-networking sites to boost sales in Book VI.

✦ **Offline promotions:** Whether or not you have a retail location, use traditional offline marketing to create an immediate boost in your online traffic.

Go to a networking event and hand out your business cards. Arrange for a speaking engagement at a meeting of a community organization or at a regional trade show. Create flyers or professional brochures and distribute them in stores that are complementary to (and not a competitor of) your site. Offline promotions also include the use of mobile marketing. Reach prospective buyers through their mobile phones and give them a discount code or other incentive to return to your website. You learn more about mobile marketing in Book VII, Chapter 5.

Converting more visitors to (repeat) buyers

Maybe the number of visitors to your site is on target. Instead, you need a boost in converting window shoppers into full-fledged buyers — and converting full-fledged buyers into repeat buyers. Focus on offering these features to start sales flowing in a positive direction again:

✦ **Functionality and usability:** You might be surprised to discover how cumbersome shopping on your website can be. Viewers leave sites if they tire of trying to figure out how to check out. At other times, the problem is all about site design. In Chapter 2 of this minibook, we explain how to update your site design and functionality to make it friendlier to customers.

✦ **Content and CTA:** One issue that derails a sale quickly is a lack of useful content properly placed with the appropriate call to action (CTA). Ensure that your content, or web copy, provides customers with enough detail to get and keep their interest. To help encourage a buying decision, use a CTA that makes it clear what action the visitor should take next.

✦ **Credibility:** Skepticism and uncertainty plague online shoppers, especially when buying from unfamiliar sites. Create trust and credibility by making customers aware of who you are and why your site is a safe place to shop.

Boost consumer confidence by displaying your contact information prominently throughout your site. Providing your phone number and physical address in addition to your e-mail address shows customers that you can be reached for questions. For an added vote of confidence, clearly post privacy policies, FAQs, and return and exchange policies. Be upfront with customers about what they can expect when they do business with you!

✦ **Customer reviews:** In addition to your own credibility, that same level of trust can be extended through the words of other customers. Data shows that the buying decisions of online customers are heavily influenced by the opinions of other buyers. When you allow buyers to rank the quality or value of a product (even if they didn't purchase it from you), write a review of the product on your site, or even link to a review offsite, other prospective customers will take notice.

Particularly if you have a service-oriented business, turn to the social-networking site LinkedIn to help boost credibility with recommendations. You can use LinkedIn to ask people in your network that have used your products or services to provide a written recommendation that remains on your LinkedIn profile — visible to the public. You can link to the recommendation from your website or place a duplicate of the recommendation directly on your website as an added testimonial. And don't overlook Facebook and other social-networking sites that allow your customers to leave comments and reviews.

✦ **Product selection:** Sometimes, declining sales are a result of an outdated or limited choice of products. In Chapter 3 of this minibook, we discuss in greater detail the idea of expanding your product lines.

✦ **Payment options:** Customers want not only a wider product selection but also payment options. Maybe your site is set up to accept payments only by PayPal. To attract and keep customers, you have to make buying easy and that often means you have to accept other methods of payment, such as credit cards, debit cards, and online check processing. See Book IV, Chapter 4 to find out the payment options you can offer.

✦ **Affiliate programs:** You might be used to signing up for other sites' affiliate programs to add a little revenue. Why not create an affiliate program of your own? Products and services with more forgiving profit margins are ideal ways to boost revenue for both you and your online allies. Or, if you don't want to worry about tracking specific products, offer a flat percentage (or referral fee) on *any* sales that come through one of your affiliates.

✦ **Pricing:** Drop by competitors' sites to find out what they're charging. A drop in sales can indicate that you're not keeping up with current pricing strategies.

To check out the competition, use online price-comparison guides such as PriceGrabber (`www.pricegrabber.com`) and ShopZilla (`www.shopzilla.com`). To more closely track sales from competing sites, check out competitor-price-monitoring software from PriceManager (`www.pricemanager.com`), Price2Spy (`www.price2spy.com`), and Profitero (`www.profitero.com`).

✦ **Buying incentives:** Whatever you call them — coupons, discounts, free shipping, limited-time offers, loyalty rewards, subscriptions, or special sales — incentives to purchase often nudge browsers to act and entice existing customers to buy again. Free limited-time trials are another type of incentive that makes it easy for visitors to decide to try your product or service and get one step closer to buying!

✦ **Upselling:** People in the restaurant business use this strategy to extract another dollar or two from customers at the time of purchase (for example, asking about dessert after a meal). You can do the same for online sales. Before a customer completes the checkout procedure, display another item and offer it at a one-time discounted price. You can use this same sales trigger to suggest products (based on prior buying preferences) to your returning customers as a way to increase the typical amount spent with your website. Impulse buys based on the power of suggestion are powerful.

Knowing Where to Start

When you're deciding which changes to implement, you can base part of your decision on an outstanding resource: your customers! Implementing a customer survey is a quick way to get the facts about your site. Keep these suggestions in mind when you're conducting this type of online research:

✦ **Identify the basics.** Choose only the most critical information that you want to discover about your site. An all-inclusive survey becomes long and complicated, so choose only three to five areas. Including more areas in your survey warrants bringing in a professional to administer it.

✦ **Keep it simple.** Web surfers have limited time and limited attention spans. Your best results come from keeping a survey simple and short.

✦ **Offer an incentive.** Always thank customers for taking the time to share their opinions. Better yet, offer a small incentive (a discount on their next purchase, for example) in exchange for feedback.

✦ **Select your customers.** Determine who will take your survey: potential customers or loyal customers who know your business.

Terrific online survey tools are available. Try SurveyMonkey (`www.surveymonkey.com`), which offers a full range of survey products and template options that start at less than $20 per month. The site also offers a free basic survey option that's ideal for quick surveys or for small sites. Another one of our favorite survey tools is SoGoSurvey (`www.sogosurvey.com`), which provides the ability to create surveys, polls, and online quizzes.

Chapter 2: Redesigning to Win New Customers

In This Chapter

↙ **Evaluating your website design for improvements**

↙ **Creating a plan to update your site**

↙ **Informing customers of proposed changes to gain feedback**

↙ **Making your site more accessible and user friendly**

↙ **Adding ways for customers to interact and learn**

*H*ave you ever visited a website and immediately thought that it was outdated or discovered that it was difficult to find what you need? The site may also have left you with the feeling that the information was no longer current and perhaps unreliable, making the products and service less desirable. Like it or not, prospective customers make buying decisions that are often based on a site's up-to-date appearance and functionality.

If your site appears dated and neglected, or lacks modern functionality and design elements, chances are prospective customers will quickly decide to head over to the site of one your competitors to make a purchase. These types of issues undermine your site's credibility, and often leave buyers wondering whether they can trust you to deliver reliable and high-quality products and services.

You may be wondering how you'll know when it's time to adapt. Well, web design is a continually changing and evolving concept. Despite the rumors, there isn't a single web guru who sits on a mountaintop and decrees, "This year, all websites will use blue Courier 12-point font with a polka dot background!" Instead, the collective nature of the Internet means that people look at each other's designs and, as time progresses and new styles are introduced, some are favored and mimicked while others stay on the fringe.

Other changes are dictated by functional requirements or consumer demand. For example, the rapid and widespread adoption of mobile devices (such as smartphones and tablets) spurred a change in how and where consumers shopped. Browsing and buying from a website on a smartphone is a different experience than searching and shopping from a desktop computer. The mobile trend not only altered consumer behaviors but also forced many changes in website design and functionality, which we discuss later in this chapter.

Whether a site refresh is based on actual needs or design trends, we advise you to scrutinize your website at least twice a year for possible updates. Some updates may be minor and can be implemented quickly. Other changes, especially those that affect the entire site, may take detailed planning and require you to roll out the updates in multiple phases.

As with most industries, each year the design community makes recommendations (and predictions!) about which web design trends are most important. Some businesses implement new trends faster than others. As an online small business, or one with limited resources and budget, it may make sense to wait a while before jumping on the bandwagon of the latest, greatest trend.

In this chapter, we describe those trends and how they should affect your own website. We show you how to examine your current design, compare it with the designs of your competitors' sites and sites in the community at large, and then adapt your site. We also describe the benefits of that adaption. You discover how to interpret new capabilities and decide what to include in your own site to stay current.

Updating an Outdated Look

Over the years, certain website themes have become the telltale signs of a site's age. These web page elements still exist (unfortunately) but should not be used on your website:

✦ Pages with a black background and white text

✦ Overused stock photo images (such as a group of people in business suits jumping excitedly in front of a computer)

✦ The Under Construction graphic, with a stick figure digging a ditch, or a "Hello World" blog post on your WordPress blog

✦ Long pages of endless text with few or no images

✦ Gimmicky graphics (such as giant starbursts), animated GIFs (pictures) and scrolling text along the bottom of the screen

✦ Splash screens (animated pictures) or Flash graphics that you have to watch before the home page is displayed

After you launch your website, keep an eye out for newer design trends. For an older, existing site, it's imperative to review your site regularly and decide whether to implement new design elements and functional features. Consider the task spring cleaning for your site: Throw out the old designs and try on some new ones.

If you wonder whether certain design techniques are becoming outdated, check out the websites of large, well-known brands, including competitors in your industry. The design techniques disappearing from or being added to those sites is an early indication that your site is in need of a change.

Giving your designs a purpose

When you evaluate the design elements of your website, keep the following questions in mind:

+ Does my website effectively communicate my business message?

+ What is the goal for each page of my website (or what action do I want visitors to take)?

+ Does my website design aid in the successful completion of these goals or hinder these goals?

+ Does my website design interfere with search engine optimization (SEO)?

Every design decision you make should revolve around these questions. After all, unless you're building a hobby site or an artistic site, your site needs to serve your business needs. Communicating your business message is particularly important when building credibility with new buyers. In the 2014 B2B Web Usability Report from Huff/KoMarketing, 43 percent of buyers said the lack of a clear message stating that states what the company does reduces credibility and causes them to click back out of a website. If your site isn't communicating clearly to your customers or isn't helping you reach and convert prospective buyers to customers, you're limiting your site's potential and harming its bottom line.

Design and functionality go hand-in-hand. You want to use design elements to clearly lead customers to take a particular action (your goal), such as purchasing a product, requesting additional information, or contacting you.

You might find that web designers and programmers are eager to implant the hottest new technology in your website, on the assumption that customers will want the technology because it's new. As time passes, these designers figure out that e-commerce design involves finding out what visitors want *and then* fulfilling those customer needs.

A perfect example is the Flash introduction, in which a company's home page displays an animated clip that resembles a movie trailer. Even if this introductory clip is slick and impressive, the Flash intro creates a barrier between visitors to the website and the information they are seeking. After numerous visitors and customers told site owners that they didn't want to see this feature, it started to disappear.

Changing the floor plans

Have you ever noticed that your local grocery store likes to move everything around from time to time, with no apparent rhyme or reason? You enter the store, ready to go to aisle 9 to pick up some rye bread and sourdough rolls, only to find salad dressing and olives. The store does have a rhyme and a reason for the move, and they have to do with learned patterns. Studies have shown that, over time, shoppers develop a specific path through a grocery store to pick up only the items they need and then head to the checkout stand.

When a store changes its entire layout, shoppers are forced to break their standard paths and evaluate every aisle again. In doing so, they are exposed to new items that they might now consider adding to their carts.

The same concept applies to website shopping: Your customers might learn a specific path to the products they always order from you and then head to the checkout line. By changing the navigation of your site, you force customers to browse a little while longer while they learn their way again. Then you introduce them (you hope) to products they didn't know about but simply must try.

Beware: If you change your flow too drastically or too often, resulting in customers not finding anything or adjusting too often to a new process, you may notice a lot of abandoned shopping carts and declining orders. Practice change in moderation.

Communicating your business message quickly, concisely, and cleanly on your company's home page is more important than ever. It's equally important to have that same clarity on your site's top *entrance pages* (pages, other than your home page, where visitors commonly enter the site). Web surfers spend only a few seconds evaluating a new site before they make up their minds and decide to stay or leave. Your home page and entrance pages have to catch a potential buyer's attention and give that person a reason to stay.

Changing for the sake of change

Suppose that you evaluate your website and that its design is still relevant and appealing to your customers. Because the web changes fast, however, you might want to redefine your site design simply to seem current in the eyes of your customers or to meet new functionality requirements. After a while, even the cleanest site interfaces can look old and tired because customers repeatedly see the same screens, buttons, and graphics. Sometimes, a company updates its site to give the impression that the company wants to keep its customer base interested.

These updates don't have to be radical redesigns of your current site. You can simply choose one facet of your site design to alter across the board, such as these examples:

✦ **Font type:** Change a font type throughout the site.

✦ **Color scheme:** Alter the color scheme enough to show a difference without making the site unreadable.

✦ **Navigation bar:** Update the navigation bar with a different visual template. Use tabs across the top of the screen rather than buttons along the left side, for example, or minimize the navigation bar.

✦ **Call to action:** Take a fresh approach to your call-to-action buttons and images. These are usually easy to update with new colors, fonts, or other graphical elements.

✦ **Shortcuts:** Add shortcuts from your home page to popular sections of your site.

Telling customers about the change

As you're redesigning elements on your website, remember that your customers will be on the receiving end of these changes. Keep customers involved when you're making significant changes to your design so that they know what to expect and when to expect it. Alerting customers to the change is particularly important if you have popular features or areas in your site that are frequented by returning customers, such as community pages or billing.

When a change is being made in road construction, road signs are clearly marked. Sometimes, signs are put up in advance to warn motorists of upcoming road or lane closures. Cones or guidance markers move vehicles away from and around areas of construction until they're ready for use.

We're not saying that you have to display bright orange signs on your web pages. Add an announcement to your site to let people know when to expect a new design. And include brief messages or links on the home page to let customers preview new designs.

A major redesign of your site can be a terrific marketing opportunity to existing (or previous) customers. Consider giving your customers the ability to vote on two or three samples of new home page designs. Use a poll on your company's Facebook page to let customers vote on what new design features or functions they most want added to the website. Or create a marketing campaign that offers visitors a tantalizing look at the new design, and then gives a special discount or coupon to celebrate the new site design when it goes live.

The more notice you give, the less shock your customers experience when the change occurs. Customers have certain expectations about doing business with you, even if they don't say it. The more feedback you solicit from them as you redesign, the less chance that you need to abort those changes if your customers disagree with your decisions.

Customers prefer doing business with people and companies that they like personally and can relate to on some level. On the web, customers can move around quickly from business to business because of the level of choice that's available. Customers stay, however, with companies that they identify with and companies that exhibit qualities (such as style, professionalism, quality, or friendliness) that they aspire to maintain in their own lives.

Deciding what to update

When you're ready to update the design of your website, here are some general guidelines you should follow:

✦ **Watch the competition.** Spend some time examining sites that handle graphical design well, to see how the sites are built. If the sites are using new techniques, take notes and find out whether the new design is showing up in more than one place. Check out your competitors' sites to see which designs they're using. Compare those designs to your site design, to see whether other designs look more appealing.

Your competitors can evaluate your site just as easily as you can evaluate theirs. Spend some time evaluating them routinely, to see how quickly they respond to a new situation. Your goal is to have other sites respond to your changes rather than play catch-up with their redesigns.

✦ **Check for consistency.** Go to your business home page and make sure that all your category and subcategory pages have the same design and graphics. As websites change, not every page is updated. You might have added to your website some new sections that don't incorporate the latest site design. If you don't check for consistency, you might have four or five versions of your design coexisting on your site and confusing your customers, which reflects poorly on your company image.

✦ **Test for compatibility.** If possible, test your current site on different devices and with different Internet browsers. Microsoft Internet Explorer is still used, but other dominant web browsers continue growing in popularity, including the Mozilla Firefox web browser (`www.firefox.com`), Google Chrome browser (`www.google.com/chrome`) and Apple Safari browser (`http://www.apple.com/safari/`). If you see errors while using an alternative browser, find out the cause and update your site accordingly. Similarly, you must test how your site appears on different screen sizes of desktop computers as well as on devices such as smartphones and tablets.

✦ **Familiarize yourself with new technologies.** Many times, the limitations your site faces are due to the technology available to you. As the web becomes more sophisticated and Internet browsers can handle new tools and devices, your options for implementing advanced design techniques on your site begin to expand. One example is the need for *responsive* web design, which allows your site to automatically change to fit the device being used to view it (such as a smartphone or a tablet). Talk to your website designer or do some research on the Internet to see which new technologies are reaching the mainstream. (The sites `http://webdesign.about.com` and `www.webdesignledger.com` have helpful articles.)

✦ **Talk to your customers.** If you truly want to know the current state of your website, talk to the people who use it all the time: your customers. Choose a subset of recent customers and send them a survey asking what they like and dislike about your site. Alternatively, you can include a comment area in the checkout process so that customers can write their comments as they're buying products.

The point is to identify what's working, what isn't working, and what's possible to implement in your site design. After you have an idea of what you want to do, you have to create some different scenarios for your redesign. They can range from simple page updates to a slightly redefined user interface to a complete tear-it-all-down-and-start-over total site makeover. Weigh these scenarios against your current available budget and your overall plans for the site. After all, if you're going to completely change your business model, for example, you might want to delay any site design changes until then.

If your resources are limited, focus immediately on any errors that are occurring and all wildly inconsistent web pages. When you have more time and resources, you can work on updating your web page styles.

Increasing Appeal

Have you ever walked past a storefront and wondered what was sold inside the building? A dimly lit store with an abstract name, a window covered in a painted design or a series of posters, or a confusing display can be quite misleading. Imagine the difference you experience if the store has a clear view inside, an inviting entrance that encourages you to walk in as well, and informative signs that clearly display pricing, selection, and store hours. A powerful redesign doesn't just look new — it's also appealing to your customers.

Although some websites are chock-full of information and deals, if users can't easily find what they're looking for — or understand what they're seeing — they move on to one of your competitors. Websites that appeal to customers make their information clear, concise, and easy to find.

Giving your site a fresh design

It's true that design trends change, but some trends clearly take hold and determine what makes a website modern and fresh. When looking for trends to apply to your own website, pay attention to elements that not only make a big splash but also relate to other widespread functionality changes (such as mobility and video). Here are a few examples of design trends that are defining a new generation of websites:

✦ **Hero image:** A large hero image on a home page is replacing the once popular sliding banner ad and carousel image. The hero image takes up a large portion of your page's real estate but also includes some text and important calls to action. The home page of ElectraBike.com, shown in Figure 2-1, is an example of how to make a big splash using a hero image.

Figure 2-1:
Large images become the hero of your site's home page.

✦ **Creative typography:** *Typography* is a fancy word for *fonts,* and the type or style of fonts you use is getting a lot of attention. Instead of using a plain style of text or using only one type of font throughout your website, online businesses are encouraged to get creative with font styles that have personality, such as the Berries website, which is shown in Figure 2-2. Being creative doesn't necessarily mean using crazy or comical fonts. Even if you have a B2B website with a more conservative tone or message, you can still use a variety of font styles or a more creative font style in some portion of your site to capture the attention of your customers.

Figure 2-2:
Font styles give a website more personality.

✦ **Videos instead of text:** We mention throughout this book that video is becoming an important part of website design — and marketing strategy. In many cases, video takes the place of lengthy text-based content. Packdog, shown in Figure 2-3, places the option to view a video prominently on its front page. As a bonus, notice that this site does a good job of combining all three design element trends: hero images, creative fonts, and video.

Figure 2-3: Give visitors the option to view videos instead of reading lots of text.

Some design trends have more staying power than others. Don't think that you have to immediately implement every trend that makes the rounds. Choose the ones that seem to have the greatest effect and endurance — and that work best for your website.

Adding content

People nowadays want to read good content wherever they go on the Internet. Quality content is also an important part of optimization to help your site rank well in search engines. E-commerce businesses that focus solely on selling products are finding that they have to add more information to entice people to check them out. But all online businesses must be mindful of the content they place on their sites — and today content includes not only words but also photos, graphics, and videos.

The key to satisfying both visitors and search engines is to provide meaningful and useful content. When placing words on the page, use clear, well-written, up-to-date, and accurate information that offers some value to the reader. Similarly, use good quality videos and photos that are helpful or interesting. Whatever type of content you use, it should contribute to (rather than take away from) the design and functionality of your website.

Look at the content on your site. Does it need to be updated? Could it be better written? Check out the information that people are reading on your site, and review the questions you receive from your browsers and customers. If you're not particularly skilled in editing, have some friends, employees, or colleagues look over your site and make suggestions. Does your site have dated or low-quality images? Does your site lack videos? Look for places on your site where videos and photos could add interest.

You should also look at potential ways you can add to your content, such as these examples:

✦ **Add a section featuring reviews and recommendations for your products.** When customers have to decide what they want to buy, they like reading about other people's impressions, experiences, and opinions. When you provide reviews, you give customers a reason to come to your website and one less reason to look elsewhere when it's time to buy.

✦ **Relate customer success stories and experiences.** When you highlight customers who have used your business, you provide a sense of validation to new customers by showing them that other buyers are happy with you. Videos are terrific vehicles for delivering customer testimonials or case studies because they can be quick, easy, and inexpensive to produce. However you feature these success stories, they also provide customers the opportunity to learn from each other, by sharing information on how they use your products. Sharing these customer experiences gives your business more value and helps you build repeat business.

✦ **Provide articles you wrote for other sites.** One way you can market your business online is to write articles that have the effect of referring people to your business. Why shouldn't those articles appear on your own site first? See Book VI, Chapter 3 to find out how to write well-written articles.

If you don't have time to write articles, tap into free and low-cost article databases and freelance-writing services, such as Scripted (`www.scripted.com`), Elance (`www.eleance.com`) and ODesk (`www.odesk.com`), to name a few.

✦ **Tell the personal story of your business.** Customers are always interested in knowing more about the people who work behind the scenes in a business. You create a sense of trust and purpose when you add some personal information, because then you're putting a "face" to your clean, well-laid-out online business. Adding short biographies of you and key employees is an effective way to build credibility, especially for B2B websites. Adding to the biographies the ability to connect, follow, and engage with you on social media, such as Twitter or LinkedIn, is another way to help build trust with new buyers. If people get involved after learning more about the people behind the business or after hearing your story and the reason your business was created, their purchase becomes a form of support because they're buying from a real person who has goals, desires, friends, and a family.

✦ **Add a blog.** If you have an e-commerce site or a service-based company, you might not think that a blog has a place on your website, but it's a natural fit for most sites. Blogs are a good way to keep a variety of content types (such as articles, videos, infographics, and photos) flowing on your website.

Creating a user community

You might have had the experience of turning to someone at a big department store and asking a question, only to find out that you're talking with a fellow shopper. Or maybe you overheard a conversation and you pointed another shopper to the correct aisle to find the item he was looking for that day. User interaction is a common aspect in the retail industry. Customers have a similar interest, which is why they're in the same store together. They can talk about their interests and how the products affect them, and even share advice about good and bad purchases.

In the online world, more businesses are adding virtual community meeting places to their websites or in social media sites. Mostly, these places take the form of forums, discussion boards, support boards, or full communities, where people can gather and discuss issues. Businesses provide a place for active discussions also by using social media, such as a Facebook page, a LinkedIn group, or even a Twitter chat group. For details on using social media to promote your website, see Book VI.

You, as a business owner, can enjoy several benefits by connecting your customers:

✦ Customers might be quicker to respond to a new customer's question or concern and can give detailed answers.

✦ Customers have one more reason to spend time — and their hard-earned dollars — at your site rather than at someone else's.

✦ As browsers and customers hear about potential uses of your products from other customers, they might be more inclined to purchase those products themselves. Because they're already on your site reading about a product, your site is their first choice for making a purchase.

✦ By keeping an archive of customer communications, you're building a knowledge database of questions, answers, and experiences that can help solve future customers' problems.

You can find several free forum and community software tools. Look on the major search engines for a tool that works on the operating system for your web server (search for *forum software* or *online community software*). Talk to your web designer or IT staff to see whether they have access to any ready-made discussion board or online community software.

One way to encourage people to become active right away is to create certain events that revolve around a specific day or time. You can unveil your new chat room software by hosting a "town hall" or open meeting with your CEO or a visible board member, where customers and general browsers can ask questions and receive immediate responses. You or an employee can host a workshop where you explain a new feature or product that's being rolled out on your website.

Running a poll

You can also offer polls or surveys so that customers can vote on questions of the week (or month) that you devise. Make polls fun by asking about customers' favorite stories in the news, or have the polls tie in slightly to your business by asking people about their favorite products.

Use your polls and surveys as valuable customer research. Present a few new product lines and ask customers to vote on their favorites, where the winner of the poll results in your new product line. You add excitement and involvement for your users, and they feel like they have some ownership in your business.

If you don't have a software tool available for offering polls, check out one of the free or low-cost options, such as www.poll-maker.com or www.polleverywhere.com.

Update your poll regularly, to avoid making your site look stale and outdated. A four-month-old poll turns off customers and makes your entire site look old and unprofessional.

You can add polls, community forums, social media platforms, and other customer-engagement tools in several ways. For example, if your website is built on WordPress, you can use free WordPress plugins to easily add these types of tools to your site. If your site uses an e-commerce solution (or shopping cart), it may provide free access to similar tools, or APIs (application programming interfaces), as part of its standard marketing and promotional features.

Making Your Website Functional

Websites used to be limited in the functions they could offer customers. You could display *static* (fixed) web pages, have forms e-mailed to you with text fields of information, and have customers sign a guest book. Now your site can be fully interactive, where each web page is built or personalized based on a customer's specific needs. Your site can talk to other computer systems automatically, link to your own database to read or write information, and process everything from data to audio and video.

When considering how to prioritize functional updates, especially those that are woven in with design updates, we recommend focusing on items that make your site more mobile-friendly. In the past, having a separate site for viewing on mobile devices was acceptable. Now, websites are expected to be designed for both desktop and mobile viewing, a process known as *responsive design.* Because a mobile-friendly site is critical to online business success, we discuss it throughout this book. But you can also learn more about responsive design in Book III, Chapter 2.

In addition to responsiveness, a site optimized for mobile functionality also means eliminating or reducing the number of pop-up messages and forms on your site. These pop-up, or overlay, features typically to do not function well in a mobile environment and interfere with the usability of your site. Another element of mobile-friendly websites is the use of long, scrolling pages that are divided into segmented blocks of short text. This design change improves the functionality of a responsive website, making it easier for customers to find and view important information on your site.

Just because websites can incorporate lots of complex functions doesn't mean that you should put all these functions on your site. Choose a series of functions that serve your business needs and your customer wants. The point of website functionality is to support the user experience and increase conversions.

Updating your website in a timely manner

As their websites become more and more complex, many businesses find that they rely on a single person or company to make all their site updates. This situation not only is a bad strategic decision (because it locks you into this entity if you want to keep using your own site) but can also seriously jeopardize your chances of keeping your customers.

Customers are looking for sites that are continually updated with fresh, important, current content. Businesses that want to succeed have to be able to respond to changes in the market quickly, go after new business opportunities, and satisfy a curious, fickle audience with varying demands. All these tasks require the ability to quickly update your site and its content, and relying on one person or business slows down the process. What if your web designer gets sick or is away on vacation? What if you have to post a critical announcement over the weekend and the web design company that handles your updates is closed? What if your designer is so busy changing someone else's site that your site isn't updated for weeks?

Your company should always be able to make some changes, especially content changes, to your own site. Why pay a web programmer lots of money to change some text? Instead, pay that person to develop a function where you and your employees can send changes to the site that are updated automatically. Or use a web-based site-building service or e-commerce platform that makes it easy for you to control most of your site's changes. Today's website solutions make it easy for someone with little or no knowledge of web programming and design to take a do-it-yourself approach with a professional result.

If you allow your employees to update your company site, be sure to install some sort of screening process, where a serious change has to be approved by either yourself or a manager. You don't want an angry employee's changes plastered all over your site.

Building smart navigation tools

We talk repeatedly in this book about the importance of a good navigation system on your website. Maybe you have a vertical row of links or buttons along the left side of your page or a series of tabs along the top. Take it one step further: Determine how sophisticated your navigation bar is and whether it helps customers move around the site. One trend in web design is to eliminate sidebar navigation. Before jumping on this trend, we suggest that you carefully consider the effect of removing navigation or links in your sidebar. Does it help or hinder your customer's experience when using your site? You may find that the sidebar is a distraction to your customers and decide to do away with it.

No matter where your main navigation is, it's important to focus on using it to help customers move to and from pages in your site in a way that helps the buying process. When customers use the navigation bar to go to a particular section, for example, does the navigation bar tell them where they are on your site? For example when you first arrive at the Jaxon website (www.jaxonhome.com), the tabs for navigation are the same color. When you click the Furniture tab and then click the Sofas tab, for example, a drop-down list appears and the Sofas tab is now underlined in a different color. If you hover your cursor over a list option, it is displayed in a different color to make it stand out, as shown in Figure 2-4. Your navigation system should make it easy for a customer to move anywhere on your site from any page on your site.

Figure 2-4:
Use color and other style options to differentiate between tabs in the navigation bar.

One way that websites show a shopper's progression is to display the current web page's context within the entire site structure, called a *bread-crumb trail* (see Figure 2-5). A user can return to a page by clicking the specific "crumb." Displaying a trail of crumbs shows customers how you group information on your site and how you establish a *hierarchy,* or order, of web pages. In addition, your customers can move up and down the hierarchy much more easily.

Bread-crumb trail

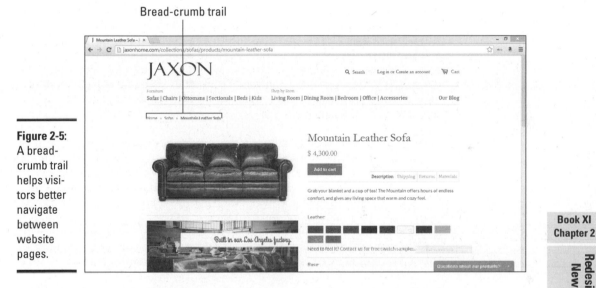

Figure 2-5: A bread-crumb trail helps visitors better navigate between website pages.

Your site navigation system should remain intuitive while being able to directly open the pages that customers need. They shouldn't need lots of explanation or training to navigate your site. A customer should be able to open your home page and instinctively know what to click or how to proceed.

As the owner or operator of your web business, you probably know your site by heart and can easily move around in it. What about new visitors, though? Gain a fresh perspective by having a stranger (or a friend who has never used your site) test your site. Or hire a company to handle this *usability study* for you. The point of a usability review is to gather a new visitor's impressions about what makes sense and what doesn't so that you can update your site and navigation system accordingly.

Usability, in the area of computer applications, refers to the effectiveness and ease of use that people find when they interact with the computer. If an element has high usability, people can easily learn about it and remember how it works, and they find it visually satisfying, efficient to operate, and helpful to use when things go wrong.

Building your customer history

One reason that people still go to local shops and pay higher prices for products is the familiarity they feel when they're shopping in a store. The owners or employees know their shoppers' faces and call them by their names, so they can recommend new products because they know the shoppers' purchase histories and likes and dislikes, and can recommend products accordingly.

This high-service model works for many small businesses, and you can convert this familiarity to your site with some added functionality. Basically, you want to make customers' previous purchases (perhaps within a time limit, such as one or two years) available to them after they log in to your site. If the purchases are available to shoppers, they're available to you, the store owner, and you can provide analysis. From analysis come recommendations and suggestions, perhaps tied into an automatic marketing offer based on the customer's purchase pattern.

For example, if you know what your customer's previous orders are and you see that he's ordering something you predicted, you can offer similar goods at a package discount to encourage sales. When your customers can go back to your site and view their past purchases, they can answer questions on their own without involving you as much. They can also look up their order histories, and your shipping department can record the tracking numbers in your software or website tools. If your customers can answer their own questions or find answers without hearing back from you, you can focus on other customer service issues more quickly and efficiently.

Implementing this function means that your website software has to have both a way for customers to create their own accounts and a database to store customer information and order information so that it's ready to be displayed on your own website. The customer account should have some form of password protection and should potentially store customer address and payment information. You can integrate this software by looking for customer relationship management (CRM) software that works with your e-commerce software, such as Salesforce (www.salesforce.com) or SugarCRM (www.sugarcrm.com). Or the e-commerce platform you use may already have this capability (as either an included feature or an API that you can add to the site), making it easy to suggest other products based on previous or current buying preferences.

Chapter 3: Expanding Products to Increase Stagnant Sales

In This Chapter

✓ Determining when to modify your line of products

✓ Restructuring your inventory

✓ Testing the waters for the best replacement inventory

*I*f you own a mature online business, you must master two tasks to maintain success. First, you have to nourish (or *feed*) your site in a way that keeps it healthy, productive, and growing. Second, you have to perfect your timing by creating a feeding schedule for your site and recognizing when it needs nourishment and care to expand.

The sale of products (or the lack thereof) is a good indicator of how well you're doing on both counts. If your site has been around for a while, you know that stagnant sales say a lot about your online business — and what they say usually isn't good.

If that's your situation now, this chapter is for you! We explain how to fine-tune the feeding schedule, adjust your inventory, and change your product mix to rev up your sales — at the right time.

Figuring Out When to Expand Your Product Line

With inventory, you're never deciding *whether* to drop a product; rather, you're deciding *when* to do so. Think about the last time you went grocery shopping. Did you notice that most food items had sell by (expiration) dates stamped on their packaging? If a product's sell by date has passed, the product shouldn't be purchased. Instead, it's eventually replaced on the store's shelves by a fresher product.

Most products (food or otherwise) have expiration dates, or at least life spans, because at some point, for whatever the reason, products are no longer valid. In marketing terms, a product's life span is referred to as its *life cycle* (see Figure 3-1).

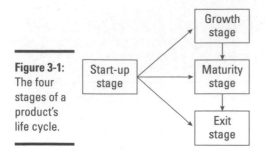

Figure 3-1:
The four
stages of a
product's
life cycle.

Typically, a product's life cycle is defined in four stages:

✦ **Start-up:** As you introduce a product to the market, you're defining the product's place among your customers and building awareness for it.

✦ **Growth:** In a product's expansion phase, you're increasing sales, developing the customer base, and exploring alternative markets for growth.

✦ **Maturity:** When a product hits its prime, you have to protect its market share. You might notice more competitors at this stage. After a product hits its peak, try to eke out profitability for as long as possible.

✦ **Exit:** In a product's stage of decline, its sales are steadily decreasing and interest in it has waned. You have to decide what to do with the product — eliminate it, repackage it, or update it.

Not every product experiences all four stages of development during its life cycle. A product can move directly from the start-up phase to the exit phase, for example.

You can follow the upcoming steps to plot revenue and help determine when to phase out one product and introduce another. You have to decide when to drop a product, however. Unlike food items, not all products have sell by dates stamped on them. *Your* job is to determine when a product is past its prime. A logical starting point for determining when a product has outlived its shelf life is to conduct an inventory analysis. When you're ready to start this process, follow these steps:

1. **Make an exhaustive list of all your current product offerings.**

   If you stock products, you can use a recent inventory list for this step. The most important task is to make sure that your list includes every product you offer on your site. Make a few notes about each product. You can include details such as

   • Product locations on your website

   • Product-specific promotional offers or coupons

   • Other sites that link to specific products

   • Ads or reviews that mention specific products

2. **Plot the sales history for each product.**

   You should chart sales weekly, monthly, or annually. We suggest review-ing monthly sales over the past year. For older products, you can then chart annual sales for the preceding two or three years. (Likewise, for newer products, you might want to break the total monthly sales into weekly figures.)

   When you're tracking a product's sales history, show the data in the form of bar graphs, line graphs, or other types of charts so that you can more easily visualize the product's progression in your overall inventory.

3. **Determine the percentage of sales for your inventory, by following this method:**

   a. *Divide the annual sale (in dollars) of the product by the total annual sales for all products.*

   b. *Multiply that number by 100.*

   Your equation should look similar to this one:

   $7525.00 (product X) ÷ $72,346.00 (total sales) = .10401 × 100 = 10.41%

4. **List the products in descending order.**

   The list is then organized from highest to lowest percentage of sales.

5. **Match one of the four stages of the life cycle to each product.**

   For example, products with sales that have steadily declined and account for a lesser percentage of your sales are probably in the Exit stage.

By the time you complete your list, you should see a clear picture of your inventory that shows how much, or little, each product has aged.

Limited appeal products

Just as some consumable products have a limited use, other products have limited appeal. Usually, you know that these products are temporary fads and that demand for them will wane after their novelty wears off.

Unless you're at least a certain age, you might not realize that someone once made millions of dollars by stuffing a rock into a box and selling it as a Pet Rock. Other examples of trendy products are T-shirts, bumper stickers, and coffee mugs printed with catchy phrases that reflect a current event. If you were selling a shirt with a witty slogan about the 2012 presidential campaign, for example, it naturally had a limited life cycle and should be replaced.

Limited-use products

Before you axe all the products classified in the exit stage, as we describe in the preceding section, you have to consider a few other factors. As you might expect, sales history isn't the only indication of how well an item is selling or why its popularity is declining.

Book XI
Chapter 3

Expanding Products
to Increase
Stagnant Sales

Some items — such as food, diapers, razors, or pet care products — have limited uses. After a product is consumed or applied, for example, it's all used up. Theoretically, this type of item should maintain a steady stream of sales because customers must replenish it.

If sales drop steadily, you have to consider the possibility that other factors are in play — for example, product quality, customer service, branding, or awareness (such as whether customers remember that they ordered a product from you).

Technology-based products

As technology advances, products become dated or defunct or their appeal lessens. If a new version of a technology-based product is released, the earlier edition can automatically be doomed for the clearance bin. Do your customers really want to purchase the Xmark1000 from you when they can have the advanced Xmark2000 for just a few dollars more?

Auxiliary products can force this change, too, as in the case of video games and game systems. The release of new games often coincides with the release of an updated game system. The catch is that the new games are compatible with only the new system. If the video games are popular enough, they drive sales of the updated game systems. In turn, the popularity of the earlier game system declines. Although the original system can take a while to become truly extinct, its value and marketability decrease.

You might decide that this type of product is in its final stage and should be replaced. Or, you might view it as a product entering its mature stage and decide to market the older system to a customer base that's more concerned with price and function than with the latest, greatest technologies.

Product marketing

Your marketing or promotional efforts can expand or shorten a product's life cycle. In fact, the theory of product life cycle is a marketing concept that's typically used in developing marketing campaigns for new products. By using the product life cycle concept, marketers can better respond to each stage of a product and increase (they hope) the overall product life cycle and its revenue.

Find out what you can do to prevent a decline in your product sales. Think about whether you actively promote products, and how often and in what ways you promote them. Before scratching a product from your inventory list, you might need to reevaluate your promotional strategy for that product.

Product positioning

Product positioning influences a product's sales and life cycle. Think about the physical location of an item (or, rather, its image) within your website. Do you rotate multiple products into premium spots on your site? Is a product positioned with similar items so that shoppers can easily find it? Or, is the product buried deep within your online store, waiting for someone to stumble over the right link? Even if a product is popular, if customers have trouble getting to it, your sales will suffer.

Price points

Setting the correct price for your product is essential. You can bet that a product that's priced incorrectly from the start will go straight to its exit stage in no time flat. As a product matures, though, its pricing also must be reevaluated.

Conversion rates

By using e-commerce (and effective analytic software), you're in the unique position of being able to track almost all your customers' movements, not just those initiating from ads. It's the equivalent of following someone around your store and watching as she picks up an item to look at it and then puts it down and moves on. You don't know exactly why she didn't buy it; you just know that she didn't. Online, when you direct a customer to a particular product page, you count it as a visit. If the visitor purchases the product, you count it toward a positive conversion rate.

You contribute to a higher or lower conversion rate for a particular product. Your site-design decisions, linking choices, and marketing efforts all factor into a conversion rate.

Suppose that your product has a history of low sales. You do a little research and find that even though the number of visitors to the product page is decent, the conversion rate is quite low. Do you cross the product off your list? Not yet.

Before you write off a product as a nonproducer, double-check all factors that affect the conversion rate. Here are two suggestions:

✦ **Take a closer look at the product page.** Determine whether the page has enough information to allow a customer to make the decision to purchase — whether size and color options and the price can be quickly obtained, for example. Some critical details might be omitted from the description, or the product photo might be small or fuzzy or cannot be enhanced. These factors can cause a potential buyer to remain a window shopper.

✦ **Track all pages that link to the product page.** Find out, for example, whether customers expecting to find one type of product are finding a much different product when they click through to checkout. You don't want them to believe that they were misled or oversold.

Take a look at Book VI, Chapter 1 to find out how to calculate the conversion rate.

Replacement or Expansion: The Art of Culling Your Inventory

When you decide to drop products that aren't selling well, you can take two approaches to adjust or refresh your inventory, as described in the following two sections.

Replacing one product with another

One strategy for refreshing your inventory is to replace nonperforming products: Get rid of one product and immediately substitute it with a new one. Your replacement products should meet these criteria:

✦ **They're complementary.** Look for items that are a good fit with the theme or focus of your site. You want products that continue to be relevant to your target customer.

Resist the temptation to add products that require marketing to an entirely different customer base. That's almost the same as starting a brand-new business, and it can permanently derail you.

✦ **They're price competitive.** The price points of replacement products should be within the range of your current pricing structure. You don't want to introduce a high-end luxury item if your site is more of a mid-range store. Similarly, you want to search for products that can be competitively priced on the general market. If you can find the product from other online sources for significantly less cost, you will have difficulty competing.

Always compare prices before adding products. PriceGrabber (`www.pricegrabber.com`) lets you view current rates online for a particular item. Or download a price-comparison toolbar, such as PriceBlink (`www.priceblink.com`), which you add to your browser. PriceBlink automatically displays comparison pricing and relevant coupons when you search for products online.

✦ **They're appropriate for markup.** Choose products that are priced right for you, too. An item can be costly to you if the wholesale price is too high, or if you have to buy a superlarge quantity to make the price feasible. These items throw off your normal markup strategy and leave you paying for it — literally!

✦ **They're deliverable.** When you search for products now, the world is truly at your feet. You can send anything from almost anywhere and then resell it. If delivering a product to your customer becomes difficult or takes too long, however, it costs you business. Your site should feature products that can be quickly shipped to customers without hassles or delays.

Expanding your product line

You can refresh your inventory by simply expanding it. Here are a few expansion tactics:

✦ **Concentrate on expanding a particular product line.** Perhaps your inventory analysis reinforces what you already suspected: One particular brand of products sells particularly well. Suppose that you're a reseller of spa products (hair and skin care) and you realize that the three Bumble and Bumble brand products on your site consistently sell well. After dropping your five worst-selling products, you decide to expand the Bumble and Bumble line. You have no reason to search for other brand-name products; just build on the one you already have.

Expanding on a popular line of products is also a useful marketing opportunity. Make the most of it. Promote not only the new products but also the fact that you're expanding the entire brand.

✦ **Accessorize your bestselling products by adding items that complement one of your top products.** Perhaps you sell electronics and games and find out that the Wii U game system by Nintendo is one of your three best-selling products. When you beef up your inventory, concentrate on Wii U companion products. You can expand your line of Wii U video games, memory cards, controllers, and any other items that work with it.

Accessorizing is similar to the promotional strategy of upselling. When you see a product that your customers want, add supplemental products that might also interest them.

✦ **Scale back the number of your products.** This strategy narrows your focus so that you can concentrate on a select group of your top sellers, no matter which brand or category they're in. In other words, eliminate the dead weight. Then start promoting the heck out of your best-performing products to increase sales.

For example, you might have 75 items for sale, and your inventory analysis shows that only a dozen of those products make up a clear majority of your sales. Combined, the other 63 items account for fewer than 15 percent of your total annual sales. If you get rid of the majority of your products and stick to the 12 bestsellers — along with marketing — you should see sales increase without the hassle of working with a large number of products.

Finding New Products

No matter what strategy you use to replace products, you first have to find new ones that shine. Fortunately, you can look in certain places to narrow your choices:

✦ **Vendors:** If you already work with regular suppliers, ask them what's selling. Your vendors know which items they can't keep in stock because of demand and which ones are lagging. Suppliers usually have a good idea of which type of new products are coming in, and can suggest ones that fit well with your site.

✦ **Customers:** Your customers know best. Or, at least they know what they're willing to spend money on. Do a little online polling or send a short e-mail survey to find out which products your customers want to see on your site. They're usually quite willing to share an opinion or two.

✦ **Competitors:** Check the clearance section of a competitor's site to see which items didn't sell, and take a look at deeply discounted items to see which items might be on their way out. Don't forget to see which items are being heavily promoted.

✦ **Online blogs and product sites:** A wide variety of blogs and sites are dedicated to every type of product. Often, these websites will include announcements about new products as well as rumors. Keep an eye on the conversations generated on these websites as well as their presence on social media sites such as Facebook and Twitter.

✦ **Trade shows:** These events are filled with product distributors showcasing their latest product offerings. Often, you can even detect a theme for upcoming releases. For example, you can see which colors are hot or which product categories distributors are pushing. Not surprisingly, manufacturers are all usually pushing the same items, so you can easily spot the next trend.

Trade shows and markets are also an opportunity to chat with suppliers and gather detailed information. The atmosphere is much more casual, and distributors and members of their sales force are eager to talk.

Of course, after you make your decision about which products to add, the real proof is in the pudding (as they say). With that proverb in mind, it certainly doesn't hurt to literally put your judgment to the test. You can run online tests for a product by using one of these methods:

✦ **Forced placement:** Try featuring only a single product on your home page. This strategy forces visitors to view the new product so that you can more easily monitor click rates and conversions when you're introducing a product. If you're uncomfortable promoting one item, you can also place the promotion in a premium spot on your home page.

✦ **Rotate promotions:** Alternatively, you can run internal promotions on your site and rotate new products with your popular staple items. Use banner ads, pop-up ads, product reviews, or testimonials, and then rotate the promotions throughout your site (not just on the home page).

✦ **E-mail customers:** Introduce new products in an e-mail campaign to your targeted customers. That way, you can quickly gauge customer reaction to your latest product selection.

✦ **Keywords:** You can also place external advertisements to drive visitors for product testing. The most effective method is paid keyword searches. Because these target visitors are already searching for your particular type of product, or something similar, this method is an effective way to test the waters for purchasing behaviors.

✦ **Sample offline:** Give a few samples to friends or family members, and ask whether they would buy the product or have bought one similar to it already. If so, find out where and for how much. You can even have an informal focus group check out your product online. You can watch as its members visit your site and search for the new product. Find out from them what they think of your product, whether the promotion you used was effective, and whether the product image on your site accurately portrays the product. Honest feedback offline can help put you on the right track online.

Even a well-researched and thoroughly tested product isn't a sure bet. However, implementing these strategies as part of your product expansion truly helps you beat the odds.

Chapter 4: Nurturing (and Bringing Back) Customers

In This Chapter

✔ **Understanding why loyal customers don't return to your site**

✔ **Creating offers that elicit a renewed response to buy**

✔ **Pampering customers with top-notch service**

✔ **Thanking customers for their loyalty**

"If you love someone, set them free. If they come back, they're yours." Hah! That quote might have worked for novelist Richard Bach in the 1970s, but it won't work for your site. When you're fighting for customer loyalty (and retention), nothing could be further from the truth.

In fact, keeping — or nurturing — good customers and enticing lost customers to return are not always easy tasks. Have you ever considered how much attention, time, and money businesses spend marketing to attract new customers? With ongoing efforts to grow your new business, it's easy to understand how your existing customers might get overlooked or taken for granted. But continuing to do so often leads to lost customers. And ignoring an occasional customer departure or two can be an expensive mistake for your online business.

Consider that gaining a new customer costs approximately five to six times as much as keeping an existing one, according to State of Retailing Online 2014, from Shop.org and Forrester. Online retailers surveyed for the report stated that an online order from a repeat customer was typically $178, which was at least $20 more than the average order amount, and that at least 40 percent of their business was from repeat customers. The report also indicates that less than 20 percent of marketing budgets go toward marketing to existing customers, even though the return on your investment (or ROI) for those dollars could be much greater!

So what happens when existing customers get fed up and decide to leave? Is it too late to show them you care? Not at all! This chapter describes how to take care of your good customers, woo back lost ones, and ensure that they all remain yours for keeps.

Figuring Out Why a Customer Left

Before you can hope to win back former customers, you need to understand what hastened their departure in the first place. Although you might think that every situation is unique, customers leave for a variety of reasons:

✦ **Product dissatisfaction:** Among the top customer frustrations is poor product (or service) quality, including a product with outdated or unsupported features, which is common for web-based services. In general, maybe the product didn't perform as expected, didn't fit properly, or was poorly made — the reasons are endless.

✦ **Poor service or support:** Customer service and support are among the most influential factors in maintaining customer loyalty. Allowing one bad service experience, or a string of experiences involving consistently mediocre service, is a sure way to drive away paying customers. Similarly, the lack of high-quality helpful support (especially for products that require ongoing technical assistance) is a pet peeve of many customers and makes it easy for them to walk away from your business.

✦ **High prices:** Technology increasingly allows online customers to compare price points with little effort. Customers who install price-comparison toolbars or check out online shopping sites that root out the biggest bargains can easily be lured by good deals — especially if no other compelling issue, such as brand loyalty or customer reward programs, makes them stay. Another price issue driving customer decisions is that if they can no longer afford your product, they search for affordable alternatives.

✦ **Difficulty in buying:** One of the biggest customer-loyalty roadblocks you can create is making it difficult to do business with you. Instituting changes that help you manage your online business can also inadvertently make buying more difficult for customers. An update can leave your site navigation cumbersome or make your checkout procedure more time-consuming.

✦ **Apathy:** You can lose customers because you fail to be memorable or to make them care. On the surface, you fail to create a sense of identity or loyalty to your site. Dig deeper and you find a lack of offers or promotions that prompt customers to buy. Apathy can further evolve because you don't add new and exciting products or because your site and its content are stale and outdated. Customers are left with a feeling that you don't care about your business.

✦ **Lack of site awareness:** Your site isn't demanding the attention of your customers. In most instances, this problem is tied directly to an absence of marketing, advertising, or direct communication with customers. In turn, they've forgotten that you're out there.

✦ **The lure of competitors:** Deep discounts, blowout advertising campaigns, and promises of extra perks and rewards make competitors look good. Often, those techniques are just good enough to steal away even the most loyal customers.

✦ **Evolving needs:** Sometimes, customers simply outgrow the need for your product or service, or they no longer have a compelling reason to use it. If you specialize in maternity wear, for example, you will lose that customer in a few months.

✦ **Lost contact information:** Often, you can't reach online customers because their contact information has changed, especially e-mail addresses. Or maybe your site's search engine rankings drop and customers can't find *you* any more. For one reason or another, your relationship with an online customer can quickly become an elusive one.

✦ **A rebel attitude:** Some customers strongly believe that variety is the spice of life. They're loyal to no one, and their buying behaviors are erratic at best.

Signs that a customer might jump ship

Don't wait until a customer leaves to finally take notice. By paying attention earlier, you can anticipate trouble brewing in the distance. Here are some warning signs that a customer is getting ready to leave:

✔ **A drop in orders:** A sure sign of customer dissatisfaction is a sudden or steady decline in orders.

✔ **An increase in returns:** Cross-reference customer order histories with return rates. A high number of returns or exchanges can shed light on unhappy customers.

✔ **A spike in complaints:** An increase in service calls, in e-mails, or in the use of online real-time support can indicate a growing problem.

✔ **Unresolved complaints:** Similarly, customers who have outstanding or unresolved concerns are likely to start shopping with competitors soon.

✔ **An increase in online chatter:** Monitor blogs, community forums, and social networking sites (such as Facebook or Twitter) to find discussions about your online business. An increase in negative mentions or in complaints on social media is easy to spot and especially worrisome. If a customer has a valid complaint, others usually spread quickly alongside it.

✔ **A drop in response rates:** If your purchasing incentives sent by e-mail or direct mail have gone unnoticed, you have a problem. A steady decline in the response rate to these types of offers usually means that customers are shopping elsewhere or are frustrated because the offers don't address their needs.

✔ **Bounced e-mail:** This situation is a sure sign that you're losing a customer. Even if an undeliverable e-mail is just a mistake (a customer changes an e-mail address or forgets to update an account), you're losing touch with her and she doesn't even have the opportunity to respond to you.

✔ **Opting out of e-mails:** Customers who take their names off your mailing list are sending you a clear message. Respect their wishes, but use the opportunity to ask why they're no longer interested in receiving offers from you.

Instituting countermeasures

The reasons that some customers leave are often beyond your control. However, you can counter those situations.

If your site is small, you probably have a tough time competing purely on price with larger sites. Your best strategy is to ensure that you offer some other equally powerful value point, such as one of these examples:

✦ **Exceptional customer service:** Finding online stores that exceed expectations remains a rarity. Filling that gap in your product space can offset even a price differential that you face with competitors.

✦ **Specialized expertise:** If you address a niche, you can easily retain customers because of your narrowly focused expertise. See Book X to find out how to become a niche business.

✦ **Free support:** Offering free customer support or anytime support (availability 24/7) is a way to set yourself apart. Especially for an online business selling technical or web-based services, where the current trend is to require payment for some levels of technical support, providing free technical assistance can be a good competitive advantage.

✦ **Payment plan alternative:** Besides price, customers want two things when it comes to making online purchases — flexibility and security. They often look for ways to stretch their budget, and they want secure options for purchasing goods and services online. If you offer a creative payment plan (such as spreading out payments or allowing full payment later) or provide payment alternatives, customers are more likely to buy from you.

Several service providers make it easy and affordable to add payment plan alternatives to your site. These providers include Bill Me Later (www.billmelater.com) and eLayaway (www.elayaway.com). Your e-commerce software or shopping cart solution may also offer alternative payment tools for your site.

Customers whose need for your product has changed will stop buying. That can't be helped. You can turn around even this situation, however. One strategy is to expand your product line to address your customers' *next* set of needs. If you sell clothes to expectant mothers, for example, you can add items especially for babies (and perhaps, later, children). You can also become a go-to source on a broader topic by introducing content on your site or distributing an online newsletter that offers tips and advice on motherhood — not just maternity. Your goal is to stay connected to your customers. That way, when their needs change again, you're more apt to be the one they go back to. They're also more likely to refer you to other people who also need your service.

To entice fickle customers, you can set up an aggressive marketing campaign and stellar (deep discount) incentives.

Asking for reasons why customers leave

You might be wondering how you can *know* the reason why a customer left. You simply have to ask. Whether you hire a professional or take on the task yourself, you can get the scoop from a former customer in several ways:

✦ **E-mail survey:** An e-mail message targeting former customers can be a quick way to deliver a brief survey. Keep your survey limited to three to five questions. Start by asking for the last time the customer remembers purchasing from you (because he might not realize that he's considered a lost customer). Then start determining the possible reasons for the absence.

Always include a toll-free phone number and a link to your online customer service page. You can even use a Chat Now button on your support page that allows instant online access to customer service. Encourage customers to share with you the details of their shopping experiences. An open invitation to complain can garner much more information than a brief survey.

✦ **Direct mail:** Mailing former customers a more extensive survey is a legitimate way to uncover the details of why they left. You can also use direct mail to invite customers to call and talk to a customer service manager about their experiences with you. In both cases, getting a response requires offering some type of incentive (such as a gift card) in exchange for their time.

✦ **Call:** In Internet-based companies, picking up the phone to contact customers is often a forgotten option. Although some former customers might not appreciate the intrusion, you might find that feeling is the exception and not the rule.

✦ **Focus groups:** Gathering a small group of former customers and questioning them in depth can be revealing. Knowing how to extract the answers you're looking for takes experience, so we advise hiring a professional marketing firm for this endeavor.

Offering Customers Incentives to Return

Whatever the reason for your customers' departure, your objective is to win them back. Enticing customers to return means showing them that you've changed. You listened to their critiques and paid attention to what went wrong, and, most importantly, you're ready to make amends.

Many marketing experts use the *lifetime value (LTV)* concept to quantify what a customer represents to your company. You may also see this concept referred to as the *customer lifetime value (CLTV)*. Basically, to calculate a customer's relative value, you determine how much money the customer spent with you over a certain period and then factor in expenses and other considerations.

Unfortunately, we could fill an entire book explaining lifetime value. Instead, you need to understand why it's worthwhile to invest in winning back your customers, regardless of the dollar value of that effort. Winning back customers is worthwhile for these reasons:

✦ **Cost:** If it costs you $100 to get back a former customer, it would cost at least $500 to win a brand-new customer.

✦ **Profit:** Existing customers often account for more than three-fourths of a site's revenues.

✦ **Familiarity:** Educating former customers on the benefits of your site takes less time. They're already familiar with your business, your products, and your service.

✦ **Upselling:** After you win back a customer, you're more likely to increase the average value of his or her purchase or to upsell to another level of product or service. On the other hand, it takes more time to achieve the same result with a new customer.

✦ **Referrals:** When you regain the value of a customer, you also net the value of all other customers that this one refers to you.

✦ **Brand strength:** Loyal customers increase the strength and value of your overall brand.

To find out how to calculate a customer's LTV, check out the Customer Lifetime Value Calculator from Harvard Business School Publishing. In addition to detailed information about CLTV, they have an online tool you can use, as shown in Figure 4-1. To check out the tool, visit `hbsp.harvard.edu/multimedia/flashtools/cltv/`.

A tailor-made offer

Inviting a lost customer to do business with you again involves far more than simply offering an apology for messing up the first time. More often than not, you just have to connect with your customer's needs again. What better way to do that than to present a personalized offer?

Being able to make this type of offer assumes that you have a database of good historical data that details the customer's preferences. (If you've built that database, this task isn't difficult.)

Most e-commerce shopping cart software now includes database functions for storing and acting on customer data. You can extend that capability by importing the data into a more powerful database (or customizing your own). Better yet, your e-commerce platform may also integrate with a third-party customer relationship management (CRM) program that your business can use to manage the customer experience, such as Salesforce (`www.salesforce.com`) or SugarCRM (`www.sugarcrm.com`).

Figure 4-1:
Calculate the lifetime value for your customers with this CLTV tool.

To customize an offer, start by looking at your customer's buying history. Review the products or services the customer bought most recently and frequently. If the data is available, you also want to find out which offers he or she responded to most often. Some examples are a percentage-off coupon code, an offer to buy one and get one free, a limited-time offer, the option to purchase on a deferred-payment plan, and the opportunity for free shipping. When you have this information, you're ready to create an offer tailored to the consumer's preferences!

For the best results, create the offer *after* you survey to determine the customer's reason for leaving. This way, the enticing offer you construct appeals to the person's present interests or needs and isn't based solely on old (and changed or outdated) buying habits.

A targeted offer

Customizing an offer for every departed customer might appear excessive. However, you can create ready-made targeted offers, such as these examples:

+ **Deep discounts:** An offer of a deep discount on the next purchase gives your customer a chance to experience the product or service again. You can include a coupon code to buy one item and get one for free or half the price.

✦ **A reasonable discount on the next purchase:** Consider a 10 to 15 percent discount on the next purchase, depending on the price point of the product or service you sell.

✦ **A gift card or free gift:** Offer cash up front with no strings attached — a $10 gift card, for example. Or send a small product as a gift to show a customer that you're serious about winning him or her back.

✦ **Invitation to participate in an event:** For example, if you offer customers a special podcast or an informational webinar related to your site or product, they might just buy something from you.

Enticing Customers to Stay

Figuring out why customers no longer purchase from your site is only half the battle of winning them back. To win the war, you have to take care of returning customers and ensure that they don't leave again. That's harder than it sounds because, after you have customers back "in your pocket," you can easily take them for granted. This section helps you figure out what you can do for customers who have a renewed faith in your brand.

If you offer a sensational deal to only *new* customers, your loyal customers may feel left out and underappreciated.

Giving them blow-your-socks-off service!

You can bet that if you finally win back a customer, you had better not disappoint him or her. The first area you're graded in is customer service. No longer can you squeak by and maintain the status quo. After wooing a lost customer, you have to step up your game.

Status quo service involves doing what is already *expected* of you, such as in these examples:

✦ Provide a quality product (or service).

✦ Give the basic information that's necessary to make a purchasing decision.

✦ Be available for questions or support.

✦ Make the ordering process simple and efficient.

✦ Deliver the product as promised.

✦ Make post-purchase support readily available.

✦ Clearly post customer policies on your site.

✦ Honor your policies and terms of agreements.

That's the *minimum* service commitment required from you. It keeps your customers satisfied but doesn't make them feel special. Fantastic, blow-your-socks-off service keeps your customers loyal. This type of service might include these activities:

✦ Anticipate customer needs by using shopping cart and database functionality.

✦ Communicate regularly with customers to keep them informed about related topics and up-to-date on the latest trends.

✦ Ask for customer feedback, and then respond to it.

✦ Provide easy-to-find links on every page to access online customer service.

✦ Offer real-time support (live customer service over the Internet) and other traditional options (such as toll-free numbers and e-mail).

✦ Allow customers to choose the type of information or promotions they want to receive based on their interests or needs.

✦ Follow up purchases with personalized thank-you notes.

✦ Offer worthwhile incentives to buy more.

✦ Make it easy to change orders or agreements.

✦ Be flexible so you can address the changing needs of your customers.

Keep customers engaged and build continued brand loyalty with social media. Use sites such as LinkedIn, Twitter, Facebook, and even YouTube to post information about products, special discounts, surveys, and contests.

Rewarding loyalty

Customers appreciate being rewarded for their loyalty. You can reward customers with these special benefits:

✦ **Personalized coupons:** Offer discounts on products targeted to customers' specific interests (based on past buying habits).

Send personalized e-greeting cards to your customers on their birthdays, for example. Including a coupon code for a special offer targeted to your customer is an effective way to reward loyalty.

✦ **Freebies:** Occasionally give a free upselling product or other perk to reward loyal buying behavior.

✦ **Inside information:** Give existing customers special access to sales or new products *before* new customers receive it.

✦ **Buyer's club:** Customers get a special offer, a gift, or money back every time they reach a certain purchasing level at your site.

✦ **Frequent shopper:** No matter how much or how little the amount you choose, customers appreciate some type of monetary reward for buying regularly from you.

✦ **Special events:** Invite loyal customers to special online or offline marketing events (for example, cooking classes, forums with experts or celebrity guests, and training webinars).

Don't let a lack of funds stop you from rewarding customers. Get creative. For example, if you can't afford to give a free gift to a hundred customers, two customers might be a manageable number of recipients. When customers spend a certain amount of money each month, enter their names in a drawing and select two customers to receive gifts. Make a big deal out of the drawing by sending an e-mail to everyone on your customer list and posting the winners' names on your website.

You really have no limit on the type of reward program you can offer customers. The only downside is that the program can become difficult to manage, especially as your business grows. That's the time to enlist the help of a professional.

Luckily for you, many skilled and reputable companies specialize in the development and management of customer loyalty programs. Look into these companies:

✦ **Belly:** `www.getbelly.com`

✦ **NextBee:** `www.nextbee.com`

✦ **Online-Rewards:** `www.online-rewards.com`

✦ **RepeatRewards:** `www.repeatrewards.com`

Saying "Thank You"

One of the most overlooked customer rewards is the simple expression of thanks. As the owner of an online business, you can show appreciation to your customers in many ways:

✦ **Post-order landing pages.** After your customer completes an order, send an entirely new page (or *landing* page) created specifically to say "thank you" for the order. Surprisingly, many sites still overlook this opportunity.

✦ **Send automated thank-you notes.** Use an autoresponder program to automatically send a thank-you e-mail to your customer immediately following each purchase.

The option to send automated e-mail messages (and order confirmations) is already built into many shopping cart and e-commerce software programs.

+ **Send thank-you notes in shipments.** Customers appreciate opening their shipments and finding thank-you notes right on top.

+ **Post-order e-mail.** After an order is scheduled to be delivered or a ship date is confirmed, send an e-mail expressing thanks. Sending the thank-you note after the order has arrived is also a good time to ask for feedback on your customer's shopping experience.

+ **Send personalized cards.** Just because you run a website doesn't mean that you can't communicate the old-fashioned way. Send loyal customers a thank-you card by way of the U.S. Postal Service to seal your relationship.

+ **Give social shout-outs.** Increasingly, your customers are spending more time on social media sites, and they love to hear from and be recognized by their favorite brands. Find your best customers on Twitter, Facebook, Instagram, and other social networking sites, and give a shout-out, or a public thank you for their loyalty. At the very least, be sure to respond to your customers when they give your business a favorable shout-out on social media.

+ **Make phone calls.** Let your customer service department (even if it's just you!) make a few calls rather than just receive them. Phoning customers to say thanks provides the opportunity to make a direct connection with your customer.

Any time a thank-you is issued, offer an incentive. You make the customer feel special while inviting the person to do business with you again.

Chapter 5: Revisiting Marketing Strategies

In This Chapter

✔ Reviewing your company's past year

✔ Involving everyone in your marketing strategy

✔ Analyzing your mistakes openly

✔ Learning from past failures and successes

✔ Growing your marketing efforts in the right areas

✔ Tailoring your efforts to fit your company

✔ Working with partners on new campaigns

*W*hoever said that nothing lasts forever was definitely thinking of the Internet. Strategies, trends, and perspectives change at lightning speed, as more and more people use the web in different ways and companies respond to meet those ever-changing needs. In the beginning, the marketing strategy was all about grabbing attention for a site. Then the strategy moved from attention to conversion, as the all-important order volume dictated the online focus of a business. Now your strategy to get customers should contain a more comprehensive approach, the same that is required of any business, online or offline! Your strategy requires a mixture of providing quality content, ample variety, competitive prices, mobile-based interactions — as well as plenty of opportunity for customer engagement via social media.

Bottom line? As these expectations shift, you must update your marketing strategy. What worked well a few years ago might not work now. Examine your successes and failures and compare them with your overall industry and then with all web businesses to form an idea of what to do next. If you stay ahead of the curve, you stand a much better chance of adapting to changes in the Internet business and surviving while others march on, unchanged, and watch their businesses fade or close.

In this chapter, you find out how to make a tough assessment of your business by looking at past advertising efforts, gathering their strategic points and lessons, and matching your future plans with the marketing strategies you need to get there by creating new plans (or *campaigns*). We show you how to look at both successes and failures because both elements contribute to a healthy future. Finally, we focus on the issues that will affect you the most and suggest ways you can tailor a custom solution.

Reviewing the Progress Report: Tracking the Deluge of Data

Year-end reviews are standard practice in any business. As an online business, you typically have access to a large amount of data that tells a detailed story about your business — and you don't have to wait until the end of the year to review it. When tracking the progress of your business, we recommend making use of the most telling data that's at your fingertips every day — from website analytics of your traffic and SEO efforts to reports of goal conversions (sales) and social mentions — so that you can tweak campaigns and make adjustments across your business as needed, throughout the year.

That's not to say that the tried-and-true annual review isn't also needed. Looking at data in a single view across a 12-month period sometimes make it easier to spot trends, or changes in the business. These changes are not always as obvious when looking at only a week's or a month's worth of information, where an unexpected change can appear as just a small blip These summaries, or examinations of what has happened in the past, help us understand what's coming next.

Public companies provide a comprehensive review of the year by issuing annual reports, as they prepare their financial statements and make comments about looking forward to the opportunities and challenges ahead. Your year-end review should take a similar approach. As part of your annual review process, also look at yearly industry reviews, trend reports, and projections for the year ahead. In addition, other organizations (including competitors) release public reports and analyses that you can read and compare to your own results. To find such reports, check out some of the following sources:

✦ Government websites, such as the Small Business Administration (www.sba.gov)

✦ Industry associations, such as the National Retail Federation (www.nrf.com)

✦ National membership-based organizations, such as the U.S. Chamber of Commerce (www.uschamber.com)

✦ Industry analysts or researchers, such as Gartner (www.gartner.com) or Forrester Research (www.forrester.com)

✦ Companies or organizations that collect data from their large customer base and then create best-practices guides, such as MailChimp (www.mailchimp.com), Hubspot (www.hubspot.com), and Eloqua (www.eloqua.com)

No matter what size company you're running, seeing a report of the past year always helps you judge how you're doing. You can easily become so caught up in the day-to-day operations of your company — adding to your catalog, fulfilling orders, and answering questions — that you might not want to stop. We recommend looking at this type of annual assessment, as well as weekly and monthly progress reports, so that you can see in detail where you've been and ensure that you're headed in the right direction.

Don't feel that you have to wait for January 1 to assess your company. Choose a date that's close to a 12-month mark that doesn't interfere with any heavy workload for your company. For example, if you're an online retailer of gifts, don't do this examination in October or November while you're trying to capture your holiday market; try January or February, when you're recovering from the holiday rush.

Getting the right reports

As an online business owner, you probably generate mounds and mounds of data. Over the course of 12 months, you probably generate enough invoices, plans, receipts, marketing campaigns, and other sales figures to make your head swim. When you do your yearly review, you might not know where to start. Here are some common report types you should look at:

✦ **Financial:** Any business generates some form of cash flow and has a balance sheet. You definitely want to construct some form of profit-and-loss (P&L) statement to see whether you're making money, breaking even, or losing money. (Figure 5-1 shows an example of a P&L statement.) You want to see how much of your revenue is eaten up by costs and whether certain costs are growing faster than others.

Figure 5-1:
Add up your revenue and expenses to figure out your profit or loss.

✦ **Customer:** If you're not keeping track of your customers, in some form or another, you really need to start. You have to see whether your customer database is growing, and in what demographics. Maybe you're noticing numerous repeat buyers or one-time-only buyers, or maybe sales in certain product categories are picking up compared to others. You're looking for a healthy increase in the quantity and quality of customers.

Automation tools, called customer relationship management (CRM) software, make it easy to keep up with current and prospective customers. Even as a small online business, you can use CRM tools to track your customers and their interactions with your site, associate leads or customers with specific marketing campaigns, and generally keep watch over specific customer data. Try web-based CRM software, such as Salesforce. com (`www.salesforce.com`) or SugarCRM (`www.sugarcrm.com`) for less than $500 annually (per user); you can usually try before you buy with a limited-time trial.

✦ **Inventory:** Determine how quickly you're sending merchandise out the door. We don't just mean packing and shipping. If you weren't buying new inventory, how long would it take to sell out? Are you holding on to products forever, or turning over inventory often? You want to ensure that you have enough inventory to last until the next order comes in but not so much that you can't get rid of it without selling at a huge discount or making a generous donation to charity.

✦ **Marketing:** In the world of online marketing, many reports and data points are available to review. Get started by checking conversion rates of landing pages (or key entrance pages for your site) and conversion goals and traffic as part of your website's analytics. What about the e-mails you sent throughout the year? Look at reports that show the number of opens and shares of e-mails sent, and the click-through rate (CTR) of various e-mail campaigns. Run reports that show which subject lines of your e-mails were most effective. Look at the social media and marketing campaigns you launched in the past year. How well did your Google AdWords perform? What offers got the most engagement? Who did you reach? How many people visited your site? Even more importantly, how many customers ordered something, and how many of them returned? How much did you spend to acquire your customers?

Although you can compute all sorts of ratios, your report has to be able to answer this question: "Did I make more in profit or awareness than I spent on marketing?" That's the bottom line for a small online business: If you're spending $50,000 to make $10,000 extra in profit, that's not the way to survive. Although you can spend some money to build brand awareness, most of the time you need to spend that money to generate orders and profit. Large, established brands may have big budgets and can afford to spend money on campaigns that promote brand awareness but may not lead to direct sales. A lean online business doesn't always have that luxury, so you must invest in marketing programs that help drive sales.

Sharing your progress report with your team

When you review all the numbers and campaigns for your business, you must make sure that your whole team understands the situation. If you're running a business by yourself, this issue isn't critical. If you have employees, independent contractors, family members, or friends helping out, spend a little time going over the basics with them.

We're not saying that you should rent a private bungalow for a three-day retreat to assess your business. (Nothing's wrong with that strategy, though. We hear that Maui is nice.) Allocate some time during the workday for a meeting. You can take everyone out for dinner or have a weekend barbecue at your house.

The point is to cover your company's highlights, its highs and lows of the past year, its successes, its challenges ahead, and the direction it's heading. Ask for feedback or for employees to share their success stories and memories of the past year.

Getting your team involved ensures that

+ Everyone has a clear understanding of your company's progress.

+ Employees feel some company ownership because you share the situation and ask for their help and opinions.

+ You get a sense of whether your employees agree with your assessment and rally behind the cause or just nod and stay silent.

+ You gain a new perspective on the health of your company, from the stories and experiences of your employees.

You should never allow one of these gatherings to turn into a cold, finger-pointing assessment of where the company went wrong. It's not about blame — you're assessing the situation and agreeing on a plan to move forward. If the situation starts turning negative, move the conversation to another topic and focus on the company's successes and future plans.

Figuring Out What Worked and What Didn't

You can plan and research and make a great effort to present your company and your products to your customer base, and sometimes it just doesn't work. (Few people get everything right on their first try — that's why you must continuously test, test, test.) You can invest in a product line that turns cold the moment you try to sell it, and your marketing message can miss your audience completely or even attract the wrong crowd.

Mistakes happen — it's what you do about them that makes the difference. You can easily hide from missteps, blame them on something or someone else, and ignore their results. That strategy, however, is probably the worst thing you can do. You should instead look closely at every mistake and treat it as a learning exercise. Although the exercise might be expensive, if you analyze it correctly, it can make money for you down the road because you won't make that mistake again. Some people call this process the most valuable education you can give yourself.

One way to know whether or not something is working in your company is to *benchmark* it, or compare your company's results to that of other companies. These benchmark reports can also be found as part of best-practices research, as we mentioned a few pages back.

Analyzing a failure

Admitting that you made a mistake is difficult. Spending time and effort picking apart your campaign and determining the root cause of the failure might be even more difficult. Some business owners respond to mistakes by simply avoiding those areas altogether and shifting their focus elsewhere. They often believe that if they attempt to enter a new market and the campaign fails, it must not be right for them after all, so they should shift gears and try something else.

When you make a mistake in a campaign — and spend no time trying to learn why — the mistake contains no value and no lesson learned. It can even be detrimental to the future of your business. After all, you spent some time planning this effort, so the key is to find out the difference between your planned expectations and the reality of the situation.

When you discover this disconnect in your analysis, you can update your plans and benefit from the mistake. Here are some issues that might come up:

✦ **Bad implementation:** Your marketing message wasn't formatted correctly or contained the wrong price, link, or information. You can learn from this type of mistake immediately and then implement careful screening to avoid it the next time you put together marketing materials.

Always include yourself in any marketing lists that are sent out, whether it's a direct-mail, telemarketing, or e-mail effort. Simply insert your address, phone number, or e-mail address so that you can judge any messages resulting from your marketing campaign. If you're relying on outside parties to handle your marketing, make sure that they're doing their jobs.

✦ **Wrong price:** Your initial research into price points neglected to include a competitor who was underpricing you. Your special price wasn't competitive for your customers when they added such extra costs as shipping and handling.

✦ **Wrong audience:** You thought that certain customers would love a new product but it didn't appeal to them. You got your customers interested, but the call to action to purchase something wasn't compelling enough or easy to find.

When you evaluate a campaign, look for issues that would turn you off if you were a customer. Start at the beginning and pretend that you know nothing about your business, to see whether the campaign makes sense to you. Determine whether you're expecting customers to make the mental leap to a certain page when you're not drawing a clear connection.

Bring in other employees, or even friends and family members, to walk through the same campaign and express their opinions. Sometimes, a fresh perspective is all you need to determine a potential weakness.

The key is to find the weakness or drawback in your plan without placing blame. Treat this process as a learning exercise for you and your employees so that your next effort is that much stronger. Don't dwell on a mistake, except to make sure that you don't make exactly the same mistake again.

Examining a success

Although the reason that a marketing campaign was successful might seem obvious to you, it's worth exploring which elements brought you that success. That way, you can apply those valuable lessons to the other parts of your business and future campaigns. As the saying goes, "Learn from the best!" Why shouldn't you learn from yourself when you do something right?

Some people are afraid of overanalyzing something that made money because they fear that they will disrupt some magical chain of events that made it possible. The reason that you look a little harder is so that you can make it happen again. Although every success is important to building your company, long-term success comes when you can repeat a valuable campaign and make it successful again.

Sometimes, the answer to the success of a campaign becomes apparent afterward, such as in these examples:

✦ You chose a new product line to promote, and the products became red-hot right around the time of your campaign. Your success came not from the technique but from having the right product.

✦ Your promotion found the right price point to induce lots of purchases. You tested a lower price point and saw a wide adoption rate. Your success came from choosing a level that guaranteed you some profit while increasing the volume of products sold.

Book XI Chapter 5

Revisiting Marketing Strategies

At other times, determining the success of a promotion requires additional investigation. Businesses commonly send out follow-up surveys to select groups of customers who took advantage of particular marketing campaigns. This type of survey should contain questions that pinpoint the buyer's motivation, such as

✦ "What encouraged you to make this purchase today?"

✦ "What were the top two or three reasons for buying something?"

✦ "How important were price, selection, presentation, and message to your decision to buy?"

✦ "What aspects of the offer were the most appealing?"

You should also leave at least one or two nonpurchase questions, where you're looking more for customers' general comments rather than offer-related answers. Your goal is to find out which parts of your marketing message worked and which parts can be improved. Sometimes, the answer lies in a combination of the right product, price, message, and audience.

Be sure to keep track of the positive feedback you receive after a marketing effort. Whenever you find a message or an offer that encourages people to leave positive comments after the fact, you discover something that connects directly with your customers, to the point that they spend extra time telling you how good it is.

Customer success stories and positive feedback also make excellent content for future promotions. Whenever customers give you rave reviews, thank them for their comments and ask permission to reprint their quotes on your website. Most people love receiving the extra attention and seeing their names in print. If some of your customers ask that you use only their initials or first names, you should accede to their request.

Changing Plans for a Growing Company

Former IBM chairperson Louis V. Gerstner, Jr. had a favorite small-business comment: "I've never met a small company that didn't want to become a big company one of these days." Most business owners nod and smile when they hear this bit of wisdom. The goal of starting your own business is usually to have the business grow to the point that you can quit your other job, hire people to maintain the day-to-day aspects of your business, and have the time and resources available to pursue your own dreams, whether those involve traveling, resting, or starting more businesses.

As your company grows, you realize that the same processes you used when your company was small don't truly apply to a bigger business. You can't run your expenses by using pen and paper any more, and you need to consult or hire a CPA or an accountant — or maybe even a chief financial officer

(CFO) — to coordinate your finances and file all the appropriate paperwork. Your inventory systems have to become more formal because pen and paper and mentally keeping track of your products don't apply to a 20,000-square-foot warehouse full of products that are selling at hundreds of orders per day.

The same concept applies to your marketing strategies. At first, your goal is probably to raise brand awareness of your company, find some initial cash flow to sustain your business, and gain more customers and market share. After you start seeing sustained results — after you're achieving a certain level of sales and revenue without massive or unprofitable sales — you have to start shifting your marketing strategy to that of a mature company.

Focusing on specific elements of your strategy

One of the first shifts in marketing strategy should occur when you start concentrating on one part of your business rather than on the entire company. An individual product line might be worthy of having its own marketing efforts, or each product line might bring in a piece of your overall sales.

Shift your marketing focus to center on a particular unit of your company. This way, your message can be concentrated on a single product line rather than on the expectation that customers will check out all the products your company offers. Choose a target sales level based on past sales of that one unit, and don't assume that you will attract any extra traffic to the rest of your site.

Even though you're more focused in your campaign, bringing in customers eventually lifts the other areas of your business, as some of these people become repeat customers in multiple areas. Don't rely on getting this business to make the campaign successful. Consider it the icing on the cake.

At this point, you're no longer selling your company, necessarily. You're selling the product and providing a reason to buy it immediately. You can use several strategies to prompt an immediate buying decision, including:

✦ Offering specials for a limited time only

✦ Making the special available to only a select group, such as repeat customers

✦ Giving a deep discount to buy immediately

✦ Offering an immediate reward to buy now, such as free shipping, a certain dollar amount off the total order, or a free item with purchase

Testing your ideas

Opportunity comes when you least expect it, and that statement definitely rings true when you operate your online business. You never know when you're going to get the opportunity to load up on a new product line, to offer a deep discount on some reliable bestsellers, or even to branch out into something only partially related to your current business. After all, as you gain a loyal set of customers, you have the chance to capture more of their dollars by providing similar goods that appeal to them.

When you see the opportunity to either bolster your current product areas or branch out into new, uncharted waters, you should consider doing some test-marketing campaigns to see how your customers will respond. In some cases, if the new product area is wildly different from your current brand, create a new subsidiary or partner company and build up that new brand name.

Choose a subset of your customer base, or partner with another company to market to its users. Then create a campaign that focuses on this new product line and reinforce the connection between the new product area and your existing brand. If you're creating a new brand, make some sort of connection that lets people know that your business is recommending, but not necessarily carrying, this brand.

For example, if your business is a leading supplier of video games for the Xbox One game system, you might have the opportunity to carry a variety of toys related to both video games and superheroes. You could create a new company named Master Toy Supplier and create a specialized campaign that says, "Hey, gamers! We've created a special deal just for you at Master Toy Supplier."

Test marketing has several benefits, beyond the obvious one of determining whether anyone wants to pay money for your product. You can form an idea of people's interest and response rates, and find out whether your product brings any good or bad reactions from your customer set. This new product area might be well served by specialized competitors, and the best price in the world won't diminish your customers' loyalty to their suppliers. You benefit much more by finding out this information from a test-marketing campaign than by investing heavily and hoping that the product will sell down the road.

Automating your campaign

Business owners measure the success or failure of their first marketing campaigns by keeping track of orders by using pen and paper or a Microsoft Excel spreadsheet. As the size of your business and marketing campaigns grows, you have to make sure that everything is recorded properly so that you can go back and analyze the data in whatever way you need.

This process becomes especially important when you start having multiple campaigns running at one time. Suppose that you're using e-mail marketing to promote a few product lines that you're carrying and you're using direct mail or telemarketing to continue to build brand awareness and add to your customer database. With both these campaigns running, you want to know exactly which source is delivering that new customer to your website so that you can determine separately the profitability and success of each campaign. This process is often handled using *UTM (Urchin Tracking Module)* parameters. UTM is simply the process of adding special tags to a site's URL to track the source of traffic.

Here's how UTM works:

1. You assign each campaign a specific code or keyword (the UTM parameters).

2. When you build your e-mails, you assign a link that includes the code or keyword to the product you're selling.

3. When a potential customer clicks the link, it goes directly to the product page on your website.

4. Your e-mail marketing program then counts how many times the keyword shows up in the links that people use to access your website and matches that number against the orders placed on your website. That way, the program can determine important measurements, such as the *click-through rate*, or the percentage of people who saw the ad and clicked it to go to your website.

 Google URL Builder is a free tool that lets you create custom links with UTM parameters for tracking all types of campaigns, including mobile and e-mail. Use it by visiting http://support.google.com/analytics/answer/1033867?hl=en&ref_topic=1032998.

To learn more about e-mail marketing and automation tools, you can find a host of information and resources at the Be Relevant! Email Marketing Blog (www.b2bemailmarketing.com). Also check out *Marketing Automation For Dummies,* by Mathew Sweezey.

After you start automating your campaigns and relying on individual, targeted codes for each campaign, you can follow your prospects throughout your site to see how your campaigns are working together. You can follow, for example, how a customer who clicked in response to Campaign A might have checked out three or four more web pages on your site and responded to Campaign B for something completely different. This data becomes quite useful as you plan future campaigns and figure out which campaigns you can combine.

In e-mail marketing, this testing technique is often referred to as A/B testing or split testing. Usually, you divide your target email customer list into two groups and send both groups an e-mail that is the same, except for one item, such as the subject line. Or perhaps group A gets an e-mail that uses photos while group B's e-mail doesn't have photos. (You can also test for multiple differences, called multivariate testing, but that's more complex. We prefer to keep it simple!) To demonstrate this concept, Anne Holland, an experienced marketing researcher, helped create the WhichTestWon.com site (www.whichtestwon.com). The site gives you a weekly test (shown in Figure 5-2) using real examples, and let's you try to determine which of the two test e-mails or landing pages for a campaign generated the most response. Not only is this a good way to test your gut about what works, but you also capture real ideas that can be used in your own campaigns!

Figure 5-2: Can you choose which website converts more buyers?

E-mail marketing software and automation tools are available starting at $20 per month, although MailChimp offers a free basic version. Check out the following tools to make testing easier and help increase your online marketing efficiency:

✦ Constant Contact (www.constantcontact.com)

✦ Eloqua (www.eloqua.com)

✦ Hubspot (www.hubspot.com)

✦ MailChimp (www.mailchimp.com)

✦ Marketo (www.marketo.com)

When you rely on these automated tools, you gain many benefits, too:

✦ Your employees can spend more time on other parts of the business rather than generate e-mails and count results.

✦ The automated tools handle the mundane tasks of resending e-mails when an error occurs and collecting e-mail verification receipts from customers who open your e-mail.

✦ These tools usually provide built-in reporting capabilities so that you can view results without you or an employee having to summarize the data and calculate results.

You're in the business of selling something, not generating marketing campaigns. Although these issues are important to your business, your time is better spent building your business rather than on handling the details of a marketing campaign. Outsource these tasks so you can focus on others.

Finding Your Place in the Market

You can quite easily sit in a room with fellow business colleagues and say, "Hey, let's do what Google does!" or "Let's take the same approach to this problem as Microsoft does" or "What would Zappos do in a situation like this?" Some of the business concepts now practiced by the largest companies are sound, and others simply do not apply to the area you occupy. Although you can easily latch on to a good idea or latest trend, it's more important to understand why that trend is useful, to see whether you can apply it to your company.

Your business has to offer something unique to distinguish it from your competition. If you practice the same techniques, marketing messages, and focus as everybody else, your message begins to blend with everyone else's. After you become part of the crowd, determine what motivates your potential customers to shop with you rather than with someone else.

Focusing on your strengths

In the area of competition, you shouldn't follow other companies' techniques that highlight your weaknesses. If you provide a high level of service and charge a premium price for your products, following the techniques of Walmart is counterproductive to your business. Its effort to provide the masses with merchandise that matches its slogan, "Always Low Prices — Always," doesn't help you if you lower prices only occasionally to compete with Walmart during a sale.

Therefore, to adapt your campaigns, focus on competitors that share a common strength. If you're a high-service company, perhaps you should study a company such as Nordstrom or Coldwater Creek to see how their marketing messages are reinforcing the service levels they provide.

When you look at competitors, keep the size of your campaign in perspective. Because Nordstrom can appeal to millions of customers in its database, certain campaigns might be profitable because they need only a small percentage of customers to respond. In your case, you might need campaigns that appeal to a larger set to break even.

Emphasizing quality, not quantity

As you're planning new marketing campaigns and your budget becomes an issue, you have to start asking yourself about the best way to move your message through all the "noise." You might tend toward trying to reach the largest audience possible and to hammering out the message, in the hope that enough people respond to each effort to be profitable.

As your business and customer set grow, your goal should be to achieve quality, not merely quantity. Suppose that you're paying for a display or banner ad that receives 50,000 impressions from 50,000 distinct users. If the ad contains an offer so focused that it creates an impulse for a response right away, it's the right technique.

If your ad requires multiple impressions to wear away at your potential customers' screening process and convince them gradually to try you out, you should invest in multiple impressions among a smaller, focused group of participants. Rather than pay for 50,000 random banner-ad impressions, you might pay for 5 targeted placements inside a newsletter that goes to 10,000 enthusiastic group members in your product area. Or, you might use *retargeting,* which lets you show specific ads to specific people. Retargeting is a method of tracking visitors to your website who do not *convert* (they do not click an offer or make a purchase) and then following them as they visit other websites or social media networks (such as Facebook) and showing them a particular display ad. You follow customers around the Internet with ads, reminding them that they were interested in your site at one point and giving them a specific offer to get them to finally convert. We discuss retargeting and other online advertising strategies in Book VI, Chapter 3.

Some research shows that customers need to hear something a minimum of five times before they remember it. Radio and TV ads continually repeat phone numbers, for example, so that you call in and order.

Increasing your profit, not buzz

In their quest to gain attention, companies routinely shift their marketing strategies by creating advertising campaigns designed to be slick, funny, or appealing. Some large companies can afford this approach to preserve their brand awareness or announce new initiatives. Most companies, however, need a measurable result from their marketing — typically, an increase in orders, customers, or profit.

When you plan a new marketing campaign, always try to include something to differentiate yourself. Make sure that you're also persuading customers to take some sort of action. Ad campaigns to generate buzz, or a coolness factor, tend to cool off over time and provide no lasting benefit — or increased revenue, which is necessary for the next effort.

Not every campaign you create has to be solely about orders. Maybe you're launching a new weekly newsletter for your business, and the purpose of your marketing campaign is to increase the number of subscribers. Although you don't enjoy an immediate bump in orders, a newsletter can bring loyalty and repeat customers and pay off over time.

Borrowing Strategies from Others

Your company is typically not the only player in your market that's having an effect. Therefore, to see where you're going in your industry, you must learn from the fellow companies in your industry. After all, you can't compete if you don't know what the other players are doing. Your customers will compare you to the competition, so know where you stand and update your plans accordingly.

Stealing a page from your competitor's playbook

Evaluate your competitors and understand how their marketing strategies are reaching consumers and affecting their buying decisions. Start by identifying the largest companies in your area that directly compete with you for customers, and then move on to companies that indirectly compete with you.

Always be informed of your competitors' new promotions by signing up for their newsletters and promotions. Use a free e-mail account from Gmail or Yahoo! so that your competitor doesn't see your company's website on its e-mail list.

As you scope out your market, start developing a sense of the overall feel that your competitors present as their marketing message, and look at the ways they use to communicate that message. Then ask yourself these questions to compare their strategies with yours in these areas:

✦ **Appeal of the campaign:** What's eye-catching, unique, or appealing about their messages? Are they more current or relevant than you?

✦ **Product selection:** Do your competitors carry a bigger or wider selection than you, or do they focus on one niche?

✦ **Price and promotion:** Where do your competitors' prices fall in comparison with yours? Do they rely on pricing promotions to lure the initial sale?

✦ **Customer policies:** What kind of return, payment, and shipping policies do they have? Are they more flexible or generous than yours?

✦ **Additional services:** What bonuses do other companies offer their customers? Do they provide free delivery, gift wrapping, bonus items, or customization, for example? Do they offer something that you don't, or can't, provide?

✦ **Tactics:** Are other companies sticking to the same marketing mediums as you are, whether it's print (direct mail or coupons), TV or radio, outdoor billboards, or Internet marketing? Have they found some new, clever way to distribute their marketing?

When you evaluate your competitors, you begin to learn more about your own company and where you can play up your strengths and take advantage of any perceived weaknesses you find in your competitors. Making this type of evaluation regularly is a healthy strategy because your competitors are also evaluating you and changing their strategies. Make an honest evaluation so that you know where you stand — and not where you *think* you stand.

Updating your strategy for survival

Adding a marketing message to stay competitive is different than updating your campaign to compete more effectively. If your customers see a new technology or offering as essential to doing business, you need to add the same element to effectively compete, not just stand out.

When real-time credit card processing on websites was unveiled, it was a cool bonus for customers who could pay instantly after ordering a product rather than fill out a form online and wait for the e-commerce owner to process the credit card at a later date. Now, if an online retailer doesn't process the customer's credit card instantly, its customers see the business as behind the times and inefficient and leave for another online retailer that has real-time processing. Therefore, borrowing this technique becomes essential for survival.

This concept also applies to marketing strategies. If your customer base is mostly concerned with features, hammering a message about price makes you seem out of touch. Conversely, if you're selling a product that people view as a commodity, you have to either make some alteration and focus on the difference or focus on the lower price you can provide.

Here are some ways you can differentiate yourself through marketing:

✦ **Combine products and services.** Maybe you can extend a product you're offering by adding a service that no one else does. Perhaps you can customize a clothing item you're selling to match each customer's wishes. This way, you make the product and your business more valuable to the customer.

✦ **Package different items.** Rather than be a retailer of goods, be a solution provider. Combine different products that fill a similar need into an all-in-one solution for your customers. They will pay for the convenience of putting everything in one basket and reward your business for supplying their needs.

✦ **Extend an offer.** If you can extend a promise to your customers, use it as your message when you market yourself. Domino's became known as the pizza place where your order is delivered in 30 minutes or less or your pizza is free.

✦ **Conquer a niche.** Maybe an area of the market isn't being properly served. Even if your business goal is to serve more than one niche, conquering an area gives you a hook for doing business. A customer might say, "Oh, yeah, that's the place that handles the small-business market well. Hmm, maybe I should think of it for my business." (We discuss niche markets in more depth in Book X, Chapter 1.)

✦ **Provide a personal touch.** Sometimes, the little things make a big difference. If you do something unique that benefits your customers, they remember you for it. For example, an antiques seller includes a little homemade gift with every order she sells online. Some of her customers become more excited now when they order because they can't wait to see their cool gift.

Partnering with other companies

As your business grows, you should always consider an opportunity to partner with other companies in your industry (or compatible with your industry). We're not saying, however, to go out and ask your direct competitor to engage in a joint advertising campaign. Consider creating partnerships with companies that reach the same audience as you, to leverage each other's positions and gain (you hope) more customers and orders in the process.

Here's an example of how this strategy works. The target audience of Redbox, the company that rents $1 videos out of video-vending machines, often shops at Walgreens drugstores. As it happens, Redbox vending machines are often located outside this national drugstore chain. For those reasons, Redbox began partnering with Walgreens to offer special incentives for customers renting movies on certain nights. For example, Walgreens may offer customers who purchase popcorn and a two-liter soft drink on a Wednesday night a code for a free Redbox rental for that same night. Redbox has also offered a free movie rental to Walgreens customers who check in at the drugstore using Foursquare (a social media application that lets users show friends where they are at any given time by publicly checking in online). In these examples, both companies promote these special offers on each of their websites, through e-mails to their customers, and through text messages on mobile phones. These types of deals are good business for both Redbox and Walgreens because they encourage customers to shop at Walgreens if they happen to be picking up a Redbox movie — or to pick up a movie if they're already shopping at Walgreens!

Start by evaluating your own network. Perhaps you work frequently with a certain vendor and see that you're both reaching the same market, but in different ways. Be sure to do your research before proposing any deals: You don't want to do business with any company that might negatively affect your image or pick a partner that your employees or customers don't support.

Be sure to consult your customers, business colleagues, or employees. If there's a natural fit, where you both bring something valuable to the other party, you can create a successful partnership.

Just make sure that both companies benefit and share the costs. The last thing you want is to do all the work and have your partner walk away with all the new business.

When you network with other companies, see how you can adapt their strengths or innovations to your own organization. Sometimes, the result of making an effective alliance is gaining a valuable education for yourself.

Chapter 6: Hiring Experts to Get Business Rolling Again

In This Chapter

✔ **Knowing when to seek a consultant to guide you**

✔ **Finding an advisor who knows your business**

✔ **Choosing the right professional to work with you**

✔ **Creating binding contracts to define the rules of engagement**

✔ **Approaching change with realistic requests and firm goals**

Several early e-commerce pioneers founded in the mid- to late 1990s — Amazon, Zappos, and eBay — are online powerhouses still going strong today. However, not everyone on the Net found that same success. Many recognizable online brands folded, and plenty of unknown online businesses, like their offline peers, simply couldn't make it. Other businesses managed to stay around but continue to struggle.

Is your site one of the smaller online businesses that has been around a while but has never taken off? If so, you might need a new strategy and a little kick in the pants! Or perhaps your site is among the well-established and formerly lucrative e-commerce sites whose sales have recently stalled. You're a good candidate for bringing in expert advice and revamping your game plan. In this chapter, we explain how and when to bring in professional advisors, set new goals, and make a new plan.

Bringing In the Pros

Most online business owners are used to taking risks and calling the shots — alone. That's why the hardest part of being an online entrepreneur is realizing that you don't have all the answers. The second most difficult part is to understand when to turn for help, when you finally admit that you need it!

If you're unsure whether your site warrants outside help, trust us: Ailing businesses leave plenty of clues to that answer. If any of the following problems sound familiar to you, you might need some outside help:

✦ **Declining sales:** A steady drop in online orders is a sure sign that something is wrong. The number of products or services you offer doesn't matter — if overall sales decrease month after month, you're losing precious dollars.

A sharp and immediate decline in online orders is treated differently from sales that drop steadily over a long period. If you suddenly lose a disproportionate number of sales, first check out these issues before you start panicking:

- Your site lost its search engine rankings.

- Your site or server is temporarily down.

- You had a security breach.

✦ **Stagnant sales:** If your online orders aren't growing as your business matures, you have a problem. You might see an occasional spike in sales on a new product or from new customers. Stagnant sales mean that you're losing loyal customers, however, which means that you're either not attracting new visitors to the site or not adding enough products to account for attrition. No matter the reason, it's money out of your pocket!

✦ **Recent management or partnership changes:** Dissolving a relationship with a business partner or experiencing a high level of management or employee turnover is often a sign of more serious issues lurking in the background. Making bad decisions, experiencing limited or no growth, and tolerating a hostile work environment are issues that can scare away business partners and employees. Your business is in need of a fresh perspective.

✦ **Difficulty in attracting new visitors:** Don't blame the search engines! Websites with strong search engine rankings can have trouble increasing their numbers of visitors. The same percentage of visitors consistently hovers over your site. Why? Lots of possible reasons can explain why your site isn't attracting more eyeballs — or the *right* eyeballs. The bottom line is that if your site isn't gaining exposure, it's time for you to find out why.

✦ **Fewer visitors to your site:** Even worse than being unable to attract new visitors is watching your numbers decline — steeply or not. If the drop is consistent and it isn't occurring over a holiday weekend or as part of a seasonal slump, it's time to stop the bleeding.

✦ **Drop in search engine rankings:** You used to be in the top ten returned searches in Google for your main product category, but now you aren't even in the first ten pages of returned search results. This drop doesn't mean you're operating your business poorly or your product quality has declined, but it does indicate that you haven't kept up with the changing rules for search engine optimization or made the most of search engine marketing (SEM) to keep your site visible. In return, your sales may very likely suffer if you don't get help.

✦ **Increased customer complaints:** If your customers take the time to complain, consider yourself lucky. Not all customers are kind enough to tell you about it — they simply go somewhere else to shop! An increasing number of complaints is one of the best indicators that something is wrong with your site, your product or service, or your customer service.

✦ **Increased negative chatter:** Another side to customer complaints is negative *chatter,* or word of mouth. Unlike the customers who take the time to let *you* know they're unhappy, an equally vocal group of customers prefer to let everyone else in the universe know you haven't met their needs! These customers write negative reviews online, and chatter about their bad experience on social networking sites, such as Twitter, Facebook, and even YouTube.

✦ **Added competition:** Your site likely has plenty of competition online — and offline. Even if you don't think that you're taking a direct hit from competitors, they're probably targeting your customer base with competing products and services.

✦ **Profit void:** Depending on how well you maintain your accounting procedures, you might not immediately realize that profitability is an issue. As you watch sales come in and pay your expenses, everything seems okay. Of course, as a more established online business, you analyze the numbers closely (we hope!) to allow the real story to surface. When the amount of money you clear begins to decrease (or isn't increasing), you have to find out why and correct it.

These red flags are the most common signs that your business is in need of a tune-up. Of course, sometimes a flag is just the tip of the iceberg. You might be experiencing several problems simultaneously, some more critical than others.

Looking at the age of your business

Making the decision to enlist professional help depends on how long your business has been around, what's appropriate for that stage in its life span, and the types of problems or changes occurring. A start-up company (in its first year or two) is in the early phase of establishing *baselines*, or the indicators that show what's normal for the site. In other words, you begin to see patterns emerge in sales trends and traffic patterns during this stage of your business. You also experience the ups and downs that come along with a brand-new endeavor. Minor problems are to be expected and may not require extensive outside help.

If your online business has been around for three years or longer, you should have a definite feel for what's a minor bump in the road and what will stop you in your tracks. As your online business evolves, you will move through different stages of business. Figure 6-1 shows how the Fairfax County (Virginia) Office of Business defines the four stages of a business life cycle and what challenges you might face during each stage of the cycle. You can check out all four stages at www.fairfaxcounty.gov/dpsm/osb/four_phases.htm. The mature business stage, for businesses that have withstood the test of time, still face common challenges.

Book XI
Chapter 6

Hiring Experts
to Get Business
Rolling Again

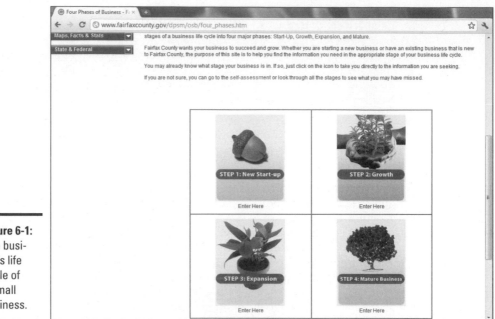

Figure 6-1:
The business life cycle of a small business.

By the time you have been in business online for three to five years, your baseline numbers are established because you have a consistent track record in maintaining profitability, making sales, keeping visitor logs, and tracking other customer- or product-related trends and data. For example, if you sell trampolines over the Internet, you know to expect a dip in orders during the winter months. If you see significant dips in the warmer months across consecutive summers, though, that's not a good situation — and you need help.

If you have a mature site that has been doing business online for longer than five years, you're probably even more tuned in to subtle indicators. Slight variations in profitability, a loss of visitors to specific pages on your site, or an inability to increase sales during a typically good time of year for your product line immediately causes concern. Your instinct tells you that these problems aren't going away.

In today's world of automation software and other data-tracking technology, you have no excuse for not knowing detailed information about your business or customer trends, regardless of the age of your business! *Business intelligence,* or BI, is basically the process of using or gathering data to improve performance. We mentioned KPIs, or key performance indicators, in Chapter 1. KPIs and other business metrics are part of the available business intelligence you can use to make good decisions based on facts, instead of ones based on your gut feelings about your business.

Looking at the severity of the problem and attempts to solve it

The truth is that you're not going to call for help at the first sign that your site is starting to tumble. And you don't have to. Instead, consider how bad the problem is before you panic. One summer of decreasing trampoline sales might be a fluke. A consecutive or long-term drop in orders during the peak selling season, however, can cause outright worry. Most importantly, do you understand what part of the customer cycle is at the root of the problem? As we discuss in Chapter 1 of this minibook, the problem is likely associated with one of these three areas: customer acquisition, point of conversion, or customer retention.

Consider which actions you have taken to correct the problem. What have you done differently to correct a negative trend? Have you consulted peers, customers, or trusted personal advisors about the problem?

Only when you have exhausted all potential solutions — and free resources — is it time to pay for an outside advisor.

Looking at your skill level

Sometimes, regardless of what the problem is, finding an answer is simply outside your skill level or experience level. The Internet evolves rapidly, as do the rules of the game for e-commerce. And, as an online business owner, you're already wearing many hats. Because you can't be expected to keep up with every area of e-commerce (or every general small-business issue), your site can benefit from bringing in a security expert, a search engine optimization specialist, a tax advisor, or any other professional who specializes in a particular field and knows it inside out.

Looking at the timing

A critical part of determining the severity of a problem on your site is deciding to what degree time factors into resolving the issue. If you have a bit of a cash flow cushion, you might be able to work on the problem for a few months. Then again, you might have a rapidly depleting bank account or seasonal deadlines; a competitor might be launching a site soon; or other time-sensitive factors might demand that you find help immediately. Timing is everything, as they say!

If you aren't sure whether a steady decline in sales is affecting your competitors or is specific to your site, check with a reputable member-based association, trade journal, or research firm that tracks the sales cycles and trends affecting your industry. Access best-practices research and other benchmark reports that help you compare your business results to that of your peers. You might discover that the problem is industry-wide. In addition, web-based tools are available for monitoring competitor traffic, social media influence, pricing, and the amount spend on marketing and advertising.

Matching the Right Advisors to Your Business Needs

Half the battle of fixing a problem with your site is realizing that it has a serious problem and needs help. Before you can tackle the other half of the problem — solving it — you have to find the right person to assist you.

First, take a look at the types of help available to you. Here are your options, depending on the severity of your problem, the amount of resources you have to spend, and your comfort level in seeking outside consultation:

✦ **Trusted advisors:** You can usually find two types of trusted advisors:

- *The people closest to you whom you already turn to regularly for help:* They might be family members, college roommates, or former coworkers.

- *A structured set of advisors:* If you've been in business for a while, you probably have in place a board of directors or an informal panel of business professionals who offer you advice occasionally. Or perhaps you belong to, and network with, a group of industry professionals, and you serve as resources for one another.

✦ **Free resources:** These nonprofit organizations, government-sponsored entities, and membership-based associations typically offer counseling and business advice at no charge (or for a nominal fee or donation). These groups often consist of retired executives or employed professionals who enjoy mentoring and advising others.

The Service Corps of Retired Executives (SCORE), shown in Figure 6-2, is one of many organizations that offer free resources to small businesses at all stages, from start-up to mature businesses. SCORE offers online training and guidance from its membership of retired professionals. Be sure to check out its mentoring section, which is designed to give you immediate and personal support. You can visit SCORE at www.score.org.

Figure 6-2:
Get help from the SCORE business toolbox.

✦ **Professional consultants:** The defining characteristic in this category of resources is that you pay money for the services you receive. Additionally, these people have specific expertise in the area in which you need assistance. You also have a formal relationship with a paid consultant because you sign a contract for services. Professionals can be independent consultants, or you can hire a larger consulting firm or associate firm.

Use the stable of resources you probably already cultivated in the course of running your business. If a trusted advisor has expertise in your area of need, go to that person for help. If your problem is more complicated or you don't know anyone in that field, tap in to other free resources. Exhaust your free resources before shelling out money for professionals.

Choosing the Right Consultant

After you decide that you need help, you have to choose a specific consultant who best suits you and the needs of your site. Finding the right consultant is tricky because in most cases, you're forming a long-term, intimate relationship with the person.

You're putting your trust in this person to help guide the future of your business, and that process gets personal. At times, you might feel uncomfortable because the consultant questions your management style, the direction of your online business, and even your routine daily tasks. The person's honesty and your willingness to listen are critical, however, to turning your site around. Trust and experience are not only important but also crucial to finding a good match between your consultant's style and personality and your style and personality.

To ultimately achieve a good relationship, carefully consider these issues when you're hiring an outside consultant:

✦ **Expertise:** Knowing that you have to match a consultant's area of expertise to your problem is a no-brainer. Regardless of whether you need someone who specializes in search engine optimization, Internet security, or long-range business planning, however, verify that the person has the educational and professional credentials to back up the claims about their expertise. That evidence can include formal education, on-the-job training, professional certifications from accredited affiliations, and any other applicable and verifiable background information.

✦ **Experience:** The consultant should share with you any accomplishments and successes with other projects or clients. Request detailed specifics on the consultant's experience with other clients and the results he or she achieved.

Don't ask for only finished results. Discuss the processes and methods used to reach those goals. By listening carefully, you discover a great deal about the consultant's approach to solving problems, in addition to confirming whether he or she met the intended goals.

✦ **References:** Never accept a consultant's word and stop there. Do a little digging. Ask for references, and call them. Talk about what that client liked and disliked about the relationship with the consultant. If you can, contact one of the consultant's previous clients whose name wasn't offered as a reference.

Be fair to the consultant, too. Ask which projects didn't go well and why. Find out which client relationships didn't last. Trust us: Disastrous projects aren't always the consultant's fault. Sometimes, a client isn't willing to listen or to make recommended changes. In that case, success is hard to come by with any consultant!

✦ **Philosophy:** Discuss the consultant's belief about what makes a project work and what doesn't. Find out exactly what she deems a successful client relationship and what she needs from you to accomplish that goal. Then decide whether you can agree to those terms.

✦ **Working style:** Uncovering a consultant's working style involves understanding his approach to problem solving. Does he require full 24/7 access to you, your employees, and the online business? Or does he use more of a hands-off style and want to deal directly with you? Will he take a while to analyze your situation from a distance? Or does he prefer to jump right in and get his hands dirty from the start? You need to decide whether you can live with, and agree to, the consultant's approach in helping resolve your problem.

Check out these resources to find the right match for you:

✦ **Institute of Management Consultants USA:** Search the member directory for a consultant, including those with certified credentials and professional status, in one of its nationwide chapters. Consultants specialize in a variety of fields, including finance, technology, marketing, logistics, manufacturing, and human resources. Visit them at `www.imcusa.org`.

Before making your final hiring decision, verify whether your consultant is a member of a professional association for consultants, or if he or she has any applicable certifications.

✦ **PATCA:** The Professional and Technical Consultants Association features professionals in over 200 areas of expertise. You can search the site's database of consultants or post a project online at `www.patca.org`.

✦ **Guru.com:** Hire an independent consultant on a project-by-project basis using this global Internet site for freelancers (`www.guru.com`). Check the Business Consultants category for a complete list of available professionals and specialty areas.

✦ **Organization of Search Engine Optimization Professionals:** Locate a search engine optimization consultant or an Internet marketing consultant from this organization's consultant directory. The directory lists consultants from both inside and outside the United States, and you can use the site's RFP Generator tool to create a Request for Proposal at www.seopros.org/RFP-Generator.

Defining the Relationship

When you settle on a professional consultant, you can establish the rules of the game. Remember to fine-tune the working relationship in the form of a contractual agreement. Make sure that your contract covers these items:

✦ **The scope of the project:** Agree on clear goals and the expected outcome. Determine whether the consultant will identify the specific problem, solve the problem, or both. Then decide on a start and finish date for the project (within reason, of course).

✦ **The price:** When you hire outside help, expect the person to be upfront and clear about fees. Understanding the cost of the project is a big part of making your final decision to hire. If the fee is based on an hourly rate, don't be afraid to ask for the estimated number of hours to complete the job. Or you might prefer to negotiate a flat rate that covers everything, regardless of the number of hours it takes to complete.

Keep on your toes to avoid being surprised by a huge bill. Check to see whether travel expenses or other incidentals are covered in the hourly rate or the flat-fee amount. You also need to find out how and when the consultant bills you. Do you pay half up front, or is the total amount spread out over several months? When does the consultant invoice you, and when does he expect payment?

✦ **The process:** Understand what the consultant expects from you, and which information he needs for you to provide to get the job done. Find out whether he expects to have access to your financial information, your Internet passwords, and your customers. Another gotcha can be the tools or services the consultant expects you to use as part of the process. If you are required to buy or subscribe to outside services or tools, both the success of the process and the cost to you are affected. Now is the time to ask about and understand the consultant's specific methodologies for meeting the goals you've set.

✦ **Working parameters:** You need to understand the consultant's time availability and how much is allotted to your project. Find out how often he provides a status report, whether you need to set up space for he inside your office for a long-term project (or whether he works only off-site), and how you can reach him after hours in case of an emergency. Be specific so that both you and the consultant understand the expectations.

**Book XI
Chapter 6**

**Hiring Experts
to Get Business
Rolling Again**

Ensure that your consultant operates as a true independent contractor (under the terms established by the IRS) and not as an employee. Otherwise, you can be fined and have to pay back employment taxes.

✦ **A confidentiality and nondisclosure agreement:** Nondisclosure agreements are a standard but necessary practice. In the simplest of terms, a nondisclosure agreement tells the consultant what topics about your company he can and cannot discuss outside the organization. The goal of these documents is simple: Prevent the consultant from sharing your private matters with customers, competitors, or any other source that might benefit from the information — or cause you to suffer because it was made public.

✦ **A written contract:** Spell out the agreed-on terms in a written contract signed by you and the consultant. Then put the contract in a safe place!

✦ **An escape clause:** Provide an option for getting out of an agreement if the relationship doesn't work. Find out the penalty for using the escape clause. Terminating a contract early usually involves a charge. Alternatively, check the conditions that allow a consultant to bail. He might leave you with no recourse for recouping your money!

Always take out your magnifying glass and read the fine print.

If the contractor you hire doesn't have a formal agreement for you to sign, insist on a contract. You can find online templates at BizTree (`www.biztree.com`) and generate your own legal agreement for a contract-for-hire work.

Overcoming Great Expectations and Getting Results

If you poll small-business owners, most would probably say that the majority of their experiences with consultants were positive but that more than a few didn't work out well. The relationship might have been frustrating for both the company's owner and the consultant because of a simple misunderstanding — or great expectations. *Great expectations* happen when the owner, or the consultant, or both are unrealistic about the results that can be achieved. You can avoid unrealistic ideals about the consulting process and still achieve tangible results with these techniques:

✦ **Set specific, achievable goals.** Identify the most critical problem and agree on which goals must be met to correct it. Avoid taking on more than three or four major goals during a given period.

✦ **Break down each goal into action items.** By dividing each goal into a list of action items or a to-do list, you understand better what you need to do to meet the goal. These items should be specific actions that can be completed by a specific time.

✦ **Assign responsibility.** Designating who is responsible for each action in a goal prevents confusion and frustration. If you don't assign responsibility, you can easily assume that someone else will take care of the item, and it never gets completed.

✦ **Determine a timeline.** After digesting what's needed to turn your site around, you and your consultant must agree on a reasonable time frame for accomplishing each goal.

✦ **Know the cost.** The best-laid plans quickly go astray if you don't know and agree to the costs of implementing them!

REMEMBER

You hired a consultant because you have a problem. Maybe you messed up along the way and something needs to be corrected. Or perhaps you didn't fully understand how to grow your online business to the next level. Either way, the issue has taken quite a while to develop. It takes more than a day or two, therefore, to undo the damage or to correct your path toward success.

When you bring in a consultant or advisor to help your business, make a commitment to the following ten phrases, which can help you avoid being disappointed by great expectations:

✦ Agree on the problem.

✦ Set reasonable goals of what is required to correct the problem.

✦ Be realistic about the amount of time, effort, and money required to fix the problem.

✦ Remain honest and open, and respectful of the process.

✦ Accept responsibility for the past.

✦ Commit to doing what it takes to change your future.

✦ Remember that the decisions you make are not personal; they're about doing good business.

✦ Know that the result is for your benefit.

✦ Be patient, but also be determined and unrelenting.

✦ Keep in mind that change can be difficult, but making improvements to your site is worthwhile in the end.

Book XI
Chapter 6

Hiring Experts to Get Business Rolling Again

Chapter 7: Transitioning a Small Site into Big Business

In This Chapter

✔ **Mapping out your growth options**

✔ **Investing in the next level of technology**

✔ **Figuring out what to do after you hit the big time**

✔ **Creating your final strategy**

Truthfully, plenty of entrepreneurs are satisfied with their online businesses staying small. For the rest of us, growth is the carrot that's continually being dangled in front of us. In this chapter, we share the strategies and resources that allow you (and your site) to finally take a bite out of that carrot.

Seeking Out the Next Level of Your Business

Entrepreneurs can tell you that the process of growing your business almost always starts out the same way — by planning for it.

Before transitioning your online business to the next level, you have to identify exactly *what* that next level is. You have to put all your options under a microscope and decide which one makes the most sense to pursue. What are your choices? Well, each of the most common paths to growth has its advantages and disadvantages.

Expanding the business

An obvious choice is to add products or services to your existing site. The purpose is to use variety to attract a wider customer base while bringing in larger revenues. This strategy is certainly the one that many entrepreneurs implement regularly, whether they realize it or not. After you consciously identify it as your preferred growth strategy, you can become more aggressive and targeted with your actions.

Here are the pros of expanding your business:

✦ You retain full control of the business, just like always.

✦ You can explore different areas, which can be fun for an entrepreneur.

The cons of expanding your business are that they

✦ Can take more time to show results

✦ Might require a large investment in back-end systems to support added inventory or a product base

We discuss ways to expand your product base in Chapter 3 of this minibook.

Acquiring other sites

Buying existing sites is another fairly typical development strategy. You can easily start by making a list of competitors' sites that might be worth purchasing. Also look at sites that complement your current business. These noncompeting sites offer products or services that are different yet still a good fit.

Of course, the larger or more established a site, the higher its asking price. Sometimes, a better strategy is to identify up-and-coming sites or sites that (like yours) have also remained small.

The pros of acquiring other sites are that they

✦ Provide a quick way to expand or diversify

✦ Introduce your current site to a wider customer base

The cons of acquiring other sites are that they

✦ Usually require substantial out-of-pocket cash

✦ Sometimes aren't for sale, so it takes time to convince their owners to negotiate a price

Becoming an affiliate or a partner

Maybe you're not ready to purchase another company outright. A better solution might be to expand through partnering opportunities or affiliate programs. For example, you might partner with a national membership-based organization as the sole provider of a particular service or product.

Expanding your business through partnership agreements is a good idea. You're typically unrestricted in the number of partners you have, and you retain control — and can cancel an agreement if the partnership doesn't work.

In a similar arrangement, starting your own affiliate program becomes a viable option. Unlike in a partnership, you're developing a specific program that another site can replicate in exchange for a commission.

Although an affiliate program is often associated with e-books and other content products, it's a viable delivery method for almost any product or service. You even see traditional e-commerce stores offering a flat percentage of revenues to affiliate sites that sell their products by using links. Or you might see payroll services companies that create affiliate opportunities. In that case, the affiliate earns a flat dollar amount for every customer referral that comes through the site.

To make affiliate programs attractive (and worthwhile) for others to participate in, you should have a viable product to promote and pay a decent commission.

The pros of going the affiliate or partner route are that they

✦ Are relatively easy to set up

✦ Are inexpensive to develop

✦ Are compatible with almost any type of business (whether it's product-, content-, or service-oriented)

✦ Can produce a quick return on sales

Here are the cons of going the affiliate or partner route:

✦ Brand control becomes an issue (primarily with affiliates), as you lend your name for others to use.

✦ Administrative duties increase (monitoring affiliate sales, cutting checks, and distributing 1099 forms, for example).

✦ You're essentially marketing two companies now (your original concept and your affiliate or partner program).

In Book IV, Chapter 2, we discuss signing up for affiliate programs.

Going international

Expanding your operations outside your home country is a proposition that's both exciting and scary. This strategy becomes easier when you have, or a partner has, experience in working outside the United States. However, the return on the investment can be lucrative. Products can become oversaturated in the ever-competitive American market. Yet overseas, the product might be a relatively new and sought-after item with few — if any — distributors.

The pros of taking your business internationally are that they can

✦ Have more opportunity for growth and increased sales in foreign countries

✦ Achieve global name recognition

Here are the cons of taking your business internationally:

✦ Language barriers can complicate the process.

✦ Selling the product might require setting up foreign distributors and manufacturing plants.

✦ Laws and regulations vary by country, which adds another layer of compliance.

Bringing in financial partners

Recruiting a financial partner might be a desirable option for your site. If you do it correctly, you end up with needed money for growth and a business partner who has expertise that you might not possess. Finding a financial partner is a little different from simply going out and finding money to support your expansion because you're taking on an actual partner in this scenario.

Unlike a bank or another lender, a *financial partner* is a person who has a say-so in your business. She participates in both operational and financial decisions. You can consider angel investors, depending on the arrangement, and venture capitalists as examples of investment partners (see Book I, Chapter 4). More than likely, your financial partner will end up being a former coworker, a business associate, or a friend or family member.

The pros of finding a financial partner are that the person

✦ Provides needed capital to upgrade and expand your site

✦ Introduces fresh, alternative ideas from an experienced financial partner

Here are the cons of including a financial partner:

✦ You sacrifice some control (and ownership) of your business.

✦ The situation can become ugly if you find out that you don't share a united vision for growth.

✦ Your partner might bail out at an inopportune time.

A newer alternative to bringing in financial partners is to get a peer-to-peer loan or investment by using websites such as Prosper (`www.prosper.com`), or Lending Club (`www.lendingclub.com`). Recent changes in finance laws have allowed smaller companies to *crowdsource,* or raise funds from lots of small investors, rather than seek out a small amount of large investors. Check out sites such as Grow Venture Community (`www.growvc.com`) or MicroVentures (`www.microventures.com`) for more information.

Going public

The good old days are connected with a bit of nostalgia. You might remember the heyday of the dot-com era, when companies went public with shares breaking Wall Street records. Well, going public remains a viable option for your Internet business, even if it takes more work (and a good battle against skepticism). Companies such as Google, Twitter, and LinkedIn certainly have proven that the dot-com magic is still viable.

Here's the catch: You have to follow the same game plan as any other company that wants to go public, which includes these tasks:

✦ Create a sustainable business concept that's capable of keeping share-holders happy over the long haul. Your financial statements must be in tip-top shape, and you must have a critical strategy in place to support sustained growth.

✦ Take a closer look at your employees, vendor partnerships, and customers, and then begin investing in some heavy hitters (if you haven't already).

✦ Attract executives who are knowledgeable about the process of going public, and who have substantial experience with recognizable companies. You also need to partner with, or sell to, big-name vendors and customers. The more attention your company gets, the higher your public stock will be.

The pros of going public with your company are that you

✦ Increase its net worth (you hope)

✦ Jump into the big leagues

The cons of going public with your company are that

✦ The process is complicated, time consuming, and expensive.

✦ You get no guarantees.

✦ A *venture capitalist* (a firm or person that prepares your company to go public) might ask you step down as CEO or president if your skills aren't a match for taking your company public.

You usually don't decide to go public overnight. If you're on this path, you will experience some lower-level rounds of fundraising first. During that time, you typically work with angel investors and work your way up to venture capitalists.

Listing your site for sale online

You can advertise that your business is for sale or search for a prospective buyer on these websites:

✔ **BizBuySell:** `www.bizbuysell.com/sell`

✔ **BizByOwner:** `www.bizbyowner.com/Public/SellABusiness.aspx`

✔ **BizQuest:** `www.bizquest.com`

✔ **BusinessBroker:** `www.businessbroker.net/services/sell-your-business.aspx`

✔ **BusinessMart:** `www.businessmart.com/`

✔ **Entrepreneur:** `www.entrepreneur.com/classifieds/index.html`

✔ **MergerPlace:** `www.mergerplace.com/business-seller/list-business-for-sale`

Passing on your company and retiring

For some owners, passing the company on to a family member might qualify as following an exit strategy rather than making plans for growth. We disagree. In this particular strategy, you're in essence growing your heir, who in turn grows the business. The first step is to decide whether you have a next-generation family member interested in taking over your business. Then you have to take an honest and objective approach to deciding whether that person has the necessary skills or talents. At this point, it's like hiring an employee whom you plan to groom for a management position. Obviously, it's not always easy to be objective.

The upside is that you might find an untapped resource who has a terrific energy level and pushes you.

The pros of handing off your business to someone else are that

✦ You continue to have a lifeline to the business, even after you step away from it.

✦ The person brings a fresh perspective that can accelerate your site's growth.

✦ Your business stays within your family.

The cons of handing off your business to someone else are that

✦ "Grooming" an heir can take several years.

✦ You might hurt your relationship or cause increased tension in the family.

✦ The business stays within the family. (Yes, this one is also a pro —family has a tendency to have both positive and negative aspects in running a business.)

Selling your site

Selling your site is considered an exit strategy. Yet, selling your site is sometimes the only way to grow it.

You might be tired, tapped out of money, and looking for a way out. Maybe you recognize that your site has fantastic potential and you lack the experience and knowledge to make it happen. You might also have a limited window of opportunity, or you simply might not have the resources to expand your site within that optimal time frame.

Keep in mind that developing a plan to identify a buyer is quite different from someone unexpectedly calling you with an offer. If selling is your strategy, preparing your business can take as long as six months to a year. If you have a smaller site, or have been lax in sticking to a management regimen, you need a few months just to clean up your organizational act.

Depending on your asking price and the current market, finding the right buyer can take another year (or longer). This time frame is where you see the difference between selling as an exit plan and selling as a growth strategy. When expansion by selling is your goal, finding the right buyer match is critical. A professional broker can help you identify key characteristics.

In general, you want to look for someone who has these characteristics:

✦ A shared vision for your site

✦ Experience in taking a business beyond the start-up phase or past the early-growth years

✦ Peers in the industry who can substantiate her reputation and skills

✦ Verifiable liquid assets and net worth to invest in the business beyond the purchase price

You can locate a reputable business broker through BizBuySell (`www.bizbuysell.com`). The site has a free, searchable database that's broken out by state, as shown in Figure 7-1.

You don't have to work with a professional to sell your site. However, a broker often has extensive contacts of potential buyers and can speed up the selling process. Regardless, selling your site might be the ideal opportunity for you.

**Book XI
Chapter 7**

**Transitioning a
Small Site into Big
Business**

Figure 7-1:
Find a business broker.

Following are the pros of selling your company outright:

✦ You receive a potentially large chunk of change for all your hard work.

✦ The burden of growth is removed.

✦ You can try something else.

Here are the cons of selling your company outright:

✦ If you stay with the company, you lose control.

✦ If you leave outright, you have to start a new business from scratch, find a job, or retire.

✦ You have no guarantee that the buyer will succeed in growing the site.

✦ Because payment terms might be spread out, realizing the full sale price can take a while.

✦ The buyer may require you to sign a noncompete clause, which means you cannot compete with the buyer by starting another business in the same industry for many years. Given that your experience is heavily tied to the company you just sold, this could limit your opportunities in the future.

✦ The business could go under before you collect all your money, leaving the site wiped out and you fighting in court for restitution.

What to do before your site goes on the market

Although the decision to sell might come easily to you, preparing your site for that transaction doesn't happen overnight. Check out this to-do list before you hang a For Sale sign on your business:

✔ Put your financial house in order with a set of audited financial statements.

✔ Meet with your accountant to discuss tax strategies for a sale.

✔ Have a professional valuation conducted to determine a feasible asking price.

✔ Contract with a business broker who has experience in selling Internet companies.

✔ Review all vendor agreements, equipment leases, and miscellaneous contracts, and then take a thorough inventory.

✔ Make sure that written policies and procedures are in place and are being strictly followed.

✔ Update all back-end functions (as long as doing so doesn't require a significant cash investment).

✔ Work on increasing the number of visitors to your site and the average length of time they spend there.

✔ Hire an expert in search engine optimization to improve your position at search engine sites.

✔ Step up your PR activities to get attention. (Unlike in the area of marketing, PR gives you more exposure for the money.)

Selling your domain

An alternative to selling your entire business is to sell only its URL. A popular domain name can fetch a pretty penny, which can help you expand your site.

Suppose that you have a limited amount of money to invest in any type of tools for growth. However, a key asset is your domain name. You can, in theory, sell the domain — to provide a needed influx of capital — and retain, as a condition of the sale, the rights to all content and services. That way, you move the content to another domain and use the money from the sale to build up the new site.

This strategy is particularly feasible if you already own a domain for a smaller site that has a similar theme or customer demographic. Of course, unless you have another domain name in your back pocket, starting over might be difficult.

The pros of putting your domain name up for sale follow:

✦ The process is fast and can have a high monetary return.

✦ You retain ownership of your content, products, or services.

✦ You gain capital to reinvest in a new site.

Here are the cons of putting your domain name up for sale:

✦ The purchaser of your domain can develop a competing site that uses your old URL.

✦ The purchaser can use your domain name for a less-reputable type of site or as a gateway to a scam site.

✦ You lose traffic, search engine rankings, and ratings for your previous site.

Dealing with Accidental Success

Ahh, sweet success. Admittedly, the term *accidental success* is a bit humorous. Ask any rock star or well-known actor about an overnight boost of fame. The honest ones don't hesitate to explain that years of hard work preceded their "accidental" good fortune.

The same concept holds true for any online business owner. Imagine finding yourself in the throes of a major public relations blitz, with skyrocketing sales following close behind. The reality is that you might be unprepared to handle the level of business that this scenario brings. But we guarantee you that your success is no accident.

How do you prepare for an onslaught of hard-won business? After all, if your site is merely mentioned on a TV talk show or featured in a short segment on one of the news channels, your URL can be rocketed into the glare of the spotlight (in an extremely good way). Before you know it, you would have back orders and your site would be bogged down from the jump in visitors. You wouldn't be able to get UPS to pull into your driveway fast enough. Lest this blitz of good fortune turn into your sudden demise, you had better be ready.

The following list describes both immediate and short-term actions you should take when opportunity comes knocking at your domain:

✦ **Identify your pressure points.** Determine where the biggest demand for your time or resources is coming from. You might be beseeched by the media for interview requests and can't make it to the phone. More than likely, your production and distribution cycles have kinks, and you have to get (or keep) products stocked at the higher demand levels. Also, your customer service functions must handle the incoming request load. Maybe your biggest problem is figuring out how to pack and ship this steep increase in orders. After you identify your most immediate (and demanding) source of frustration, you can begin developing a solution.

✦ **Hire temporary help.** When your manpower runs out of "man," you have to call in the cavalry. Going from a solo operation to one with a dozen employees, however, is daunting. Screening and hiring people and putting benefits in place take time. The solution is to hire temporary workers to provide an immediate boost to your productivity levels, without the hassle. Use a professional staffing agency to quickly add qualified and prescreened workers. An added benefit to this approach is that you can pull back on staffing levels if demand slows down.

✦ **Outsource certain tasks.** After a sudden influx of orders, the most economical solution (for both the short and long terms) is to outsource some of your functions. As the owner of a small site, you're probably used to processing each order and then packaging and shipping the product yourself. Factor in a 50 percent to 75 percent increase in orders, and you can no longer physically keep up the pace. Combat the problem by finding a local call center that can take over functions related to customer service. Or try contracting with a distribution center to warehouse your products and handle order-packing and order-shipping functions. See Book IV, Chapter 7 to find an in-house or a third-party solution to your packaging and shipping dilemmas.

✦ **Adjust the back end.** Another victim of your site's growing pains is the back-end function. From your shopping cart program to inventory control, the programs that were once suited for a start-up site can quickly become antiquated. To survive an unexpected sales rush, work with your vendors to make minimal improvements to your existing support systems. Then schedule time to research advanced products and features that can be better scaled to your new sales levels. We discuss all your back-end solutions in Book IV, Chapter 7.

✦ **Seek funding.** The changes you have to make to your business require money. Even if you decide not to invest in new equipment or tools, you need money to handle inventory spikes and hire staff. One of the best things you can do is take a trip to your bank — or other lender. As long as your credit score is reasonable and your relationship with the bank is good, establishing a line of credit is an easy way to gain access to cash. A *line of credit* is basically a loan with a preestablished limit. Rather than take out the full amount at one time, you can withdraw money in smaller amounts only when you need it.

✦ **Talk, talk, talk.** Now, more than ever, you need to communicate with vendors, distributors, employees, and customers. Take time out for daily or weekly 10-minute staff meetings. Take the opportunity to share operational changes and find out about problems that might otherwise fly under the radar in your stepped-up pace of activities. Let customers know about back orders, shipping delays, and any other minor problems that are surfacing. The worst thing about overnight success is that if you don't address concerns effectively, you lose the customers who came to you during this crunch time of good fortune.

Take notes when you're talking to customers, especially when they have a positive comment or a success story concerning your product. Turn these stories into case studies or testimonials that you post on your website, and use them as offline marketing materials, too.

✦ **Spend wisely.** We hope that your burst of success is proportionate to the rising number in your bank account. With years of hard work behind you, you might be tempted to splurge. Instead, think of this influx of funds as investment capital and put it back into your company as much as possible.

Meet with your accountant to review or update your financial strategy. A substantial increase in revenues, and subsequent expenditures, brings along plenty of tax implications. Ask your accountant to discuss your options to maximize the use of your money.

✦ **Take it to the next level.** With momentum on your side, consider leveraging it a little further. With increased recognition and revenues, you have a good shot at negotiating partnering opportunities, developing another line of products or services, and riding out a wave of expanded publicity. Use your moment in the spotlight to further establish your site's brand and position it for the future.

Purposefully Making the Next Move

Whether your site is growing because of fate or strategy, your next move should be well thought out. Follow these strategies:

✦ **Assemble an advisory board.** You might already have a formal board of directors that you assembled immediately after you incorporated. In that case, consider the value of expanding your board and adding individuals with specific expertise. If you're not comfortable bringing on directors, assemble a somewhat less formal *advisory board.* This group of professionals from your network meets regularly to review your business goals and provide guidance. Similar to when you have a board of directors, look for people with experience who complement your strengths and weaknesses.

✦ **Update planning tools.** Growth means digging into that old business plan and marketing plan. You know which ones we mean — the ones you threw together half a decade ago because everyone said that you had to have them. Those people were right: You need both documents, even though they're long overdue for an update. Use the old plans as a foundation to reassess your current goals and strategies.

✦ **Focus on long-term financial planning.** In addition to working more closely with your accountant, seek input from a financial planner or a CPA who specializes in your industry. You're no longer simply moving from one tax year to the next. As both your company revenue and personal income increase, you want to make calculated decisions about your money.

✦ **Stay current.** It's all about the research. Growing companies tend to put up walls around themselves. By not paying attention to what's happening in the world around them, they are quickly outpaced by more innovative businesses. The best way to ward off this curse is to become a vigilant researcher:

- Watch for developing trends.

- Read business and trade publications.

- Talk with peers in your industry.

- Attend trade shows.

- Skim the Internet for information that might affect your site.

- Keep an eye on your competitors.

✦ **Find a mentor.** You might not want to invite your closest competitor to have coffee with you, and getting the CEO of Google on board might be a little farfetched. You can, however, look for sites that embody your philosophies and implement similar growth strategies. Approach the founder or president by e-mail, and see whether she's open to answering some questions. (Be honest about why you're contacting her.) Striking up an online mentorship is easier than you might think.

✦ **Participate in industry activism.** As a small-business owner, you have to focus primarily on your site. Your number-one priority is figuring out how to make your site work, which can be isolating at times. As you expand, you're in the position to broaden your horizon. Make a point of joining national industry associations or professional organizations in your local community. Get involved with issues that affect your business and your peers' businesses. Table 7-1 highlights a few of the national member-based organizations that cater to Internet professionals and small-business owners.

Table 7-1	Associations for Online Business Professionals	
Organization	*URL*	*Annual Membership Fee*
Direct Marketing Association	www.thedma.org	$1,500
eMarketing Association	www.emarketingassociation.com	$175
National Federation of Independent Businesses	www.nfib.com	$195
Search Engine Marketing Professional Organization	www.sempo.org	$125
Shop	www.shop.org	$2,750

Becoming active in your professional community and your industry associations is also a proven and powerful networking tool.

Index

I

About the Authors

Shannon Belew has been championing the benefits of online marketing for more years than she cares to admit. A passionate advocate for small businesses and start-up entrepreneurs, she loves using social media to spread the word about how to use online marketing to grow your business. She has owned several online businesses and currently leads the online marketing efforts for a global telecommunications company. A freelance writer, Shannon has written for many online websites, magazines, and newspapers; and has written several books about online marketing, e-commerce, and social media, including her most recent book, *The Art of Social Selling, Finding and Engaging Customers on Twitter, Facebook, LinkedIn, and Other Social Networks*. Shannon is a frequent guest speaker on webinars, Google Hangouts, radio shows, and other events, discussing topics such as social selling, online marketing, and social media marketing. As a former marketing and PR consultant, she has helped clients share their stories in such venues as *Inc. Magazine* and CNN. Never one to sit still for too long, Shannon most recently has brought all her years of experience together and is sharing it with others on her website, OnlineMarketingToGo.com, where you can keep up with the latest online trends and tips to keep your business growing. She also hopes you'll help her keep the conversation about online marketing going by following her on Twitter @ShannonBelew.

Joel Elad has authored or coauthored seven leading books in the fields of e-commerce, social media, and technology, including *LinkedIn For Dummies*, *Facebook Advertising For Dummies*, and *Starting an iPhone Application Business For Dummies*. He is the head of Real Method Consulting, where he provides consulting and advice for e-commerce companies and entrepreneurs. He sells online as a PowerSeller on eBay and runs several websites, including JoelElad.com, which focuses on his books and upcoming educational products. Through institutions such as the University of California, Irvine, the University of San Diego, and the Learning Annex, he has trained thousands of people on e-commerce and how to start a small business. He's an Educational Specialist trained by eBay and a contributor to *Entrepreneur* magazine, AuctionBytes, and SmartBiz.com.

Dedication

Shannon: It is with much love that I dedicate this book to my best friend and husband, Tom, and to my children, who are filled with an entrepreneurial spirit of their own and are starting the amazing process of spreading their own wings in this crazy, exciting world: my son, Holden, and my daughter,

Wiley. Thanks to each of you for helping me stay motivated to always do my best! As promised, I dedicate this book also to the next generation of entrepreneurs, including a special group of boys who have become an extended part of our family — Cole, Leo, Ben, Matt, Andrew, Michael, Chris, Daniel, Austin, and Gaurav — and who fill our house every summer with energy, humor, and excitement.

Joel: This book is dedicated to the hardest-working man I will ever have the privilege of knowing — my father. Thank you for showing me the value of planning, discipline, and love. You will always be my inspiration.

Authors' Acknowledgments

Shannon: My sincere thanks to the entire team at Wiley Publishing for making this book a reality, including Kyle Looper, Jim Kelly, and my coauthor, Joel Elad. Special thanks goes out to another Wiley team member, Susan Pink, for all her gentle encouragement and direction to keep me on track, and for the many entertaining nuggets of e-mail conversation that help make the writing process all that much more fun. It's truly a privilege to work with this entire team. Thanks also to all those who choose to read this book and who aspire to become entrepreneurs. Your entrepreneurial spirit and dream for a brighter future makes this world go round, and your enthusiasm and energy for new endeavors continue to inspire me.

Joel: My biggest round of thanks has to go to the team at Wiley Publishing for their constant and amazing support of this title: Kyle Looper, Rebecca (Senninger) Whitney, my coauthor Shannon Belew, James Kelly, and definitely Susan Pink, whose patience and guidance helped make this book, in all its editions, possible. Thanks to my friends and contacts, including Anthony and Yvonne Choi, Lynn Dralle, James Ninness, Shannon Forrey, Cindy Sorley, and Greg Goldstein, for the contacts, information, and support I needed along the way to fill in the gaps. Finally, I have to give a special acknowledgment to my usual coconspirator, Michael Bellomo, who put me on the path of being an author and keeps me going with a bizarre sense of humor mixed with a powerful dose of inspiration.

Publisher's Acknowledgments

Acquisitions Editor: Kyle Looper

Project Editor: Susan Pink

Copy Editor: Susan Pink

Technical Editor: James Kelly

Editorial Assistant: Claire Johnson

Sr. Editorial Assistant: Cherie Case

Project Coordinator: Emily Benford

Project Manager: Mary Corder

Cover Image: © John Lund/Marc Romanelli/ Jupiter Images